**W9-CMR-459**

SINCE U.S. AND CANADIAN MEAT CUTS ARE NOT ALWAYS IDENTICAL, REFER TO THESE CHARTS FOR EQUIVALENTS.

KNOW YOUR BEEF CUTS

AMERICAN CUTS	CANADIAN CUTS
CHUCK	**CHUCK**
Eye Roast Boneless	—
Shoulder Steak	Shoulder Steak
Blade Steak	Blade Steak
Arm Pot Roast	Shoulder Pot Roast
BRISKET	**BRISKET AND SHANK**
Point Half Brisket	Brisket Point
Flat Half Brisket	Flat and Rolled Brisket
Shank Crosscut	Shank Steak
RIB	**RIB**
Rib Steak	Prime Rib Steak
Rib Roast	Prime Rib Roast
Rib Eye Steak	Rib Steak Boneless
Rib Steak Boneless	Rib Eye Steak
Rib Eye Roast	Rib Eye Roast
	Rolled Rib Roast
SHORT PLATE AND FLANK	**PLATE AND FLANK**
Plate Skirt Steak	—
—	Short Ribs
Flank Steak	Flank Steak
SHORT LOIN AND SIRLOIN	**LOIN AND SIRLOIN**
Top Loin Steak	Wing Steak
Tenderloin	Tenderloin
T-Bone Steak	T-Bone Steak
Porterhouse Steak	Porterhouse Steak
Pinbone Sirloin Steak	Pinbone Sirloin Steak
Sirloin Steak Boneless	Sirloin Steak Boneless
Tip Roast	—
Flat Bone Sirloin Steak	Flat Bone Sirloin Steak
Wedge Bone Sirloin Steak	Wedge Bone Sirloin Steak
ROUND	**HIP**
—	Sirloin Tip Roast and Steak
Round Steak	Round Steak
Rump Roast	Rump Roast
Top Round Steak	Inside Round Steak
Eye of Round Roast	Eye of Round Roast
Heel of Round Roast	Heel of Round Roast
Bottom Round Roast	Outside Round Roast and Steak

KNOW YOUR VEAL CUTS

AMERICAN CUTS	CANADIAN CUTS
SHOULDER AND SHANK	**SHOULDER AND SHANK**
Arm Steak	Shoulder Steak
Arm Roast	Shoulder Roast
Shoulder Roast Boneless	Shoulder Roast Boneless
Blade Roast	Blade Roast
Blade Steak	Blade Steak
Shank	Shank
RIB, LOIN AND BREAST	**RIB, LOIN AND BREAST**
Rib Chop	Rib Chop
Breast	Breast
Loin Roast	Loin Roast
Loin Chop	Loin Chop
—	Rack of Veal or Crown Roast
SIRLOIN AND ROUND (LEG)	**SIRLOIN AND LEG**
Cubed Steak	Cubed Steak
Sirloin Steak	Sirloin Steak
—	Top Sirloin
—	Tenderloin
Cutlets	Cutlets
Round Steak	Round Steak
Rump Roast	Rump Roast
Round Roast	Round Roast

KNOW YOUR LAMB CUTS

AMERICAN CUTS	CANADIAN CUTS
SHOULDER AND FORE SHANK	**SHOULDER AND FORE SHANK**
Blade Chop	Blade Chop
Shoulder Roast	Shoulder Roast
Arm Chop	Arm Chop
Blade Chop Boneless	Blade Chop Boneless
Shoulder Square Cut Whole	Shoulder Square Cut Whole
Fore Shank	Fore Shank
RIB AND LOIN	**RIB AND LOIN**
Rib Chops	Rib Chops
Rib Roast	Rib Roast
Loin Chop	Loin Chop
Double Loin Roast	Double Loin Roast
Double Loin Chop	Double Loin Chop
	Crown Roast
BREAST	**BREAST**
Breast	Breast
Spareribs	Spareribs
Rolled Breast	Rolled Breast
Riblets	Riblets
SIRLOIN, LEG AND HIND SHANK	**SIRLOIN, LEG AND HIND SHANK**
Leg Shank Half	Leg Shank Half
Frenched Leg	Frenched Leg
Leg Sirloin Half	Leg Sirloin Half
Leg Whole French Style	Leg Whole French Style
Leg American Style	Leg American Style
Sirloin Roast	Sirloin Roast
Sirloin Chop	Sirloin Chop
Hind Shank	Hind Shank

KNOW YOUR PORK CUTS

AMERICAN CUTS	CANADIAN CUTS
BOSTON SHOULDER	**SHOULDER BUTT**
Blade Roast	Shoulder Butt Roast
Blade Steak	Shoulder Butt Steak
Blade Roast Boneless	Shoulder Butt Roast Boneless
PICNIC SHOULDER	**PICNIC SHOULDER**
Arm Picnic (fresh)	Picnic Shoulder Roast
Arm Picnic (smoked)	Smoked Picnic Shoulder Roast
Arm Steak	Picnic Shoulder Chop
Arm Roast	
LOIN	**LOIN**
Blade Chop	—
Rib Chop	Rib End Chop
Butterfly Chop	Butterfly Chop
Blade Roast	Rib End Roast
Double Loin Roast Boneless	Double Boneless Loin Roast
Back Ribs	Back Ribs
Center Loin Roast	Center Cut Roast
Loin Chop	Center Cut Chop
Top Loin Chop	
Tenderloin Whole	Tenderloin
Sirloin Roast	Tenderloin End Roast
Sirloin Roast	Tenderloin End Chop
Top Loin Chop	
SPARE RIB AND BACON	**BELLY**
Slab Bacon	Slab Bacon
Spareribs	Side Ribs
Salt Pork	
LEG (HAM)	**LEG**
Leg Rump Portion (smoked)	Ham Butt End Roast
Leg Shank Portion (smoked)	Ham Shank End Roast
Ham Center Slice	Ham Center Slice or Steak
Leg Boneless (fresh)	Leg (fresh ham) Roast Boneless

KITCHEN
SECRETS

READER'S DIGEST

KITCHEN

SECRETS

Tips, Tricks, Techniques & Recipes

Reader's
Digest

The Reader's Digest Association (Canada) Ltd., Montreal

KITCHEN SECRETS

CANADIAN STAFF

Project Editor
Anita Winterberg

Art Director
John McGuffie

Designer
Manon Gauthier

Copy Editor
Gilles Humbert

Production Manager
Holger Lorenzen

Production Coordinator
Susan Wong

U.S. STAFF

Project Editor
Judith Cressy

Project Art Editor
Nancy Mace

Art Production Associate
Wendy Wong

Address any comments about *Kitchen Secrets* to:
Editor, Books and Home Entertainment, c/o Customer Service,
215 Redfern Avenue, Westmount, Quebec H3Z 2V9

For information on this and other Reader's Digest products or to request a
catalogue, please call our 24-hour Customer Service hotline at 1-800-465-0780.
You can also visit us on the World Wide Web at http://www.readersdigest.ca

CONTRIBUTORS

Text Development and Copyediting
K&N Bookworks Inc.

Writers
Holly Garrison
Jeanne Voltz

Photographer
Martin Jacobs

Food Stylist
Polly Talbott

Assistant Food Stylist
Carrie Orthner

Prop Stylist
Debrah E. Donahue

Recipe Developers
Jo Ann Brett
Sandra Gluck
Helen Taylor Jones
Karen Pickus

Recipe Testers
Georgia Downard
Susan Shapiro Jaslove
Jeanne Lesem
Leslie Glover Pendleton
Miriam Rubin
Sabrina Buck Shear

Illustrator
Lionel Kalish

Indexer
Sydney Wolfe Cohen

CONSULTANTS

Chief Consultant
Jean Anderson

Nutrition Analyst
Barbara Deskins, Ph.D., R.D.

Barbecuing
Ben Barker

Meat and Poultry
Merle Ellis

Italian Food
Mary Ann Esposito

Seafood
Nancy Harmon Jenkins

Baking
Nick Malgieri

Entertaining and Catering
Sara Moulton

French Food
Jacques Pépin

Drinks
Gary Regan

Cooking Equipment
Mardee Haidin Regan

Canadian Cataloguing in Publication Data

Main entry under title:
    Kitchen Secrets

Includes index.

ISBN 0-88850-607-4

1. Cookery. I. Reader's Digest Association (Canada).

TX652.K4683 1997a   641.5   C97-901016-0

TABLE OF CONTENTS

About This Book

Every cook comes up against questions in the kitchen from time to time. What should you do if a recipe calls for buttermilk and there's none to be had? Why does a soufflé recipe work perfectly for you one time and fail the next? Wouldn't it be great to have a cookbook that provides the answers to your questions right on the page with the recipe? Kitchen Secrets *is that book.*

On these pages we've covered the recipes, techniques, and ingredients that are at the heart of North American cooking—a blend of traditional and new ideas. With each recipe we've tried to address the many questions that both novice and experienced cooks are apt to have, whether they're about working with dough, keeping a quiche from curdling, or making a more flavorful chicken broth. Our answers appear as hundreds of hints, tips, and secrets that range from step-by-step sequences and easy-reference charts to suggestions for lowering cholesterol, substituting ingredients, choosing the right equipment, getting the best flavor—everything you need to know for dependable results. All of the hints and tips are cross-indexed in the back of the book.

We think you will find Kitchen Secrets *fun to browse through and easy to use. We hope you will enjoy every recipe you make from these pages.*

STOCKING THE KITCHEN

*Y*ou don't need a huge kitchen or a battery of equipment to cook well, but there are certain tools, appliances, and food staples that are indispensable. Of course, everyone's idea of what is indispensable differs.

GETTING STARTED

There are endless choices when it comes to pots, pans, and kitchen tools and gadgets, but how many of them do you actually need?

Each time you think of buying something new for the kitchen, ask yourself a few important questions. What kind of cooking do you actually do, how often do you cook, how many people do you cook for, and how much space have you got?

Everyone's wish list will vary. As a general guide, we've sorted the items on our list into 3 categories—in order of importance—for everyday cooking.

SMALL APPLIANCES

Grandma got along perfectly well without most appliances, but why should you? These days, a food processor is considered mandatory by most cooks. Other appliances are merely helpful to have.

It's worthwhile buying good quality appliances; cheap ones

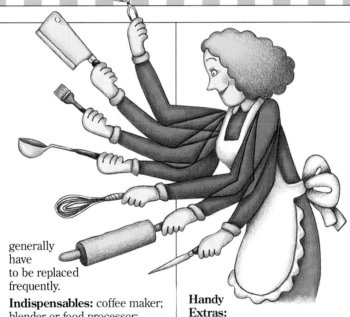

generally have to be replaced frequently.

Indispensables: coffee maker; blender or food processor; handheld mixer (with 2 sets of beaters, if available); toaster (with slots wide enough to accommodate bagel halves and extra-thick bread slices).

Useful Tools: citrus juicer; coffee grinder; blender or food processor (whichever one you don't already have); electric skillet; knife sharpener; microwave oven; slow cooker; waffle iron.

Handy Extras: bread machine; deep-fat fryer; electric can opener; espresso/cappuccino machine; immersion blender; juice extractor; mini food processor; pasta machine; stand mixer (with an extra set of beaters, if available); toaster oven.

POTS AND PANS

Good pots and pans can last for generations and make cooking a pleasure. It's helpful to know the characteristics of the various cooking materials.

Aluminum: Aluminum alloy is considered second only to copper as a heat conductor. However, aluminum can react adversely with acidic foods, giving them an off taste and darkening the pan.

Anodized aluminum cookware, which has a fused-on coating, reduces the degree of reaction, resists sticking, and makes the cookware stronger and easier to care for. Good aluminum cookware should be thick yet light. It is an excellent choice for both stovetop cooking and baking.

Cast iron: Iron heats slowly, evenly, and retains heat, making it a good choice for frying, baking, and slow cooking. The disadvantages are that iron is slightly porous and can absorb flavors and can react with some acidic ingredients. It also rusts. These problems are eliminated with enameled ware.

Plain cast iron must be seasoned before it is used and

NONSTICK COATINGS

Methods for applying nonstick coatings keep getting better and better. When the coating is used on reactive metals, such as aluminum, it makes them not only nonstick but also nonreactive.

Coated aluminum cookware is very affordable. Coated stainless-steel cookware is sandwiched with aluminum to boost heat conduction. These pans are more costly than aluminum, but the bonding process produces a pan that will last for many years without denting, scratching, chipping, or losing its nonstick qualities.

ABOUT SLOW COOKERS

A slow cooker is a very handy appliance to own. It is designed to cook at low heat—for hours on end if necessary—while you are busy doing something else. Even on their lowest setting, however, slow cookers raise food temperature to over 165°F and maintain that heat so that bacteria cannot grow.

Manufacturers always include instructions for converting regular recipes to slow cooking.

reseasoned occasionally to prevent food from sticking.

Clad metals: These pots are made of several metals fused together for their superior properties. For example, copper for quick and even heat conduction combined with stainless steel for durability and easy care.

Copper: Although pricey, copper pots are the best heat conductors. Copper cookware is traditionally lined with tin, nickel, or stainless steel to prevent the toxic interaction of copper with some foods.

The best copper cookware is thick and heavy. To keep copper shiny, clean the outside with a commercial copper cleaner or a paste made of vinegar and salt; rinse and polish with a soft cloth.

Earthenware, stoneware, clay bakers: These materials retain heat well but are poor heat conductors. Most will crack if used for stovetop cooking or if exposed to dramatic temperature change. Recommended usage is for baking only. Follow the manufacturer's instructions.

Enameled metal: Enameled cast iron and steel cookware combines good looks with durability and is available in all price ranges. Much enameled cookware can go from stovetop to table. However, enamel chips fairly easily, so it must be handled with reasonable care.

Glass, ceramic, and porcelain: These products are easy to care for but are not good heat conductors. They are best suited for baking. Space-age ceramics, now used for a variety of baking dishes, can move straight from the freezer to the oven or microwave.

Rolled steel: This is an excellent heat conductor. It's a good material for cookware that is used over high heat, such as omelet pans and woks. However, rolled steel rusts and food sticks to it easily. It should be cared for like cast iron.

Stainless steel: Although a durable metal, stainless steel is a poor heat conductor. It is often combined with at least one other metal—usually copper or aluminum—with better heating properties.

THE BEST YOU CAN AFFORD

Flimsy cookware warps, dents, and develops hot spots. It's best to start off with one or two really good pots and pans and fill in with less expensive ones that will be replaced later on.

Even on a very restricted budget, however, it's possible to buy decent pots and pans. For every type of cookware on the market, there's generally a

range of prices. Buy the best you can afford.

SHOPPING FOR POTS

Visit a store that carries a large selection of cookware in all price ranges. Pick up pots and pans to see how they feel. (How heavy will the roasting pan be when it contains a 20-pound turkey?) Lids should fit snugly. Read warranties and guarantees as well as directions for use and care.

GET A HANDLE ON IT

Not all handles on pots and pans are created equal. To be truly useful, handles should be insulated; ovenproof up to 350°F or 400°F; broilerproof in some cases. Look for handles that are riveted or screwed solidly to the pan, easy to grab, and comfortable in the hand.

Indispensables: 10-inch skillet; 6- or 7-inch skillet; two 3-quart saucepans with tight-fitting lids; 1-quart saucepan with a tight-fitting lid; 4- to 6-quart Dutch oven or heavy kettle; 4-gallon stockpot/pasta pot; baking/roasting pan, 13" x 9" x 2"; loaf pan, 9" x 5" x 3" or 8½" x 4½" x 2¾".

Useful Tools: 12-inch skillet; 2-quart saucepan; covered roasting pan as large as your oven will accommodate; double boiler. A metal double boiler is more durable than glass, but glass offers the advantage of allowing you to see what's going on inside.

Handy Extras: 10-inch sauté pan; 1½-quart saucepan; fish poacher; pasta kettle with perforated lift-out liner; popcorn popper; pressure cooker; grill pan; wok.

BOWLS, BAKEWARE, AND CASSEROLES

Indispensables: 2 shiny aluminum baking sheets, 17 by 14 inches; 1- and 3-quart casseroles, microwave safe, with lids; extra-large bowl for rinsing greens, tossing stuffing, mixing dough; 1½-, 2-, and 3-quart glass baking dishes; jelly-roll pan, 15½ by 10½ inches; nested set of mixing bowls, preferably stainless steel or glass; two 6-cup muffin pans; 8- or 9-inch pie plate; two 8- or 9-inch layer cake pans; two 10- by 13-inch wire cooling racks.

Useful Tools: 18- by 12-inch wire cooling rack; 1½-, 2-, and 3-inch biscuit cutters; 9-inch bundt pan; cookie cutters; 6

ramekins or custard cups; 6- and 8-cup soufflé dishes; 9- or 10-inch springform pan; two 8- or 9-inch square pans; 10-inch tube pan; 4- and 6-cup ring molds.

Handy Extras: baking stone or tile; charlotte mold; cornbread pan; French bread pans; 10-inch tart pan with removable bottom; miniature-muffin pan; pastry board; 10- or 12-inch pizza pan; popover pan.

SWITCHEROO

It's always best to use the size pan called for in a cake recipe, but in a pinch the following are some acceptable substitutions:

If the recipe calls for 2 (9-inch) round pans, substitute: 1 (13" x 9" x 2") pan or 1 (15½" x 10½" x 1") jelly-roll pan or 2 (8" x 8" x 2") pans or 1 (9-inch) tube pan or 2 (6-cup) muffin pans.

If the recipe calls for 2 (8-inch) round pans, substitute: 1 (9" x 9" x 2") pan or 2 (6-cup) muffin pans.

If the recipe calls for 1 (9-inch) tube pan, substitute: 2 (9" x 5" x 3") loaf pans.

KNIFE NOTES

One of the most important kitchen tools is the knife. A whole set can cost a lot, but only one or two good ones are needed to start out—an 8- to 10-inch chef's knife and a smaller paring or utility knife.

Good knives were once made only of carbon steel. Carbon steel blades sharpen to a razorlike edge, but they need to be sharpened frequently. They also stain and rust easily and can impart a metallic taste when used to cut acidic foods. The best knives these days are mechanically forged or stamped from high-carbon stainless steel.

Good knives are joined to their handle with a full tang. This means that the tang, or shank end of the blade, extends through the handle and is held in place with rivets.

A knife is a personal tool and should be handled before you decide to purchase it. It should be heavy for its size, well balanced, and should feel comfortable in your hand.

A SHARP BLADE

A knife sharpener is a good investment—it's the dull knife that's apt to give you a bad cut. The best sharpeners are electric with three slots: one for grinding, a second for sharpening, and a third for keeping the blade "tuned up." Less expensive manual sharpeners work in a similar manner but are not as effective. Traditional sharpening steels work beautifully, but take some practice.

CARE NOTES

Take care of your knives and they will last for years. Use the back, not the blade, to scrape food off the cutting board. Wash knives by hand in hot water; dry immediately and store in a knife block or on a magnetic bar.

KNIVES AND OTHER CUTLERY

Indispensables: 8- to 10-inch chef's knife; all-purpose kitchen scissors with one serrated blade; knife storage block or magnetic bar; 2- to 4-inch paring knife; 9- to 10-inch serrated bread knife; 5½- to 6-inch utility knife.

Useful Tools: carving knife and fork; paring knife with an angled tip; poultry shears; second paring knife; 8- to 10-inch slicing knife; 6- to 8-inch utility knife.

Handy Extras: Chinese cleaver; frozen food knife; grapefruit knife; meat cleaver.

MEASURING EQUIPMENT

Indispensables: dry-measure nesting cups; set of measuring spoons; 1-, 2-, and 4-cup spouted glass measures.

Useful Tools: second set of dry-measure cups and measuring spoons; 8-cup spouted

glass measure (can double as a mixing bowl); whiskey jigger.

Handy Extras: kitchen scale: Electronic scales are not only reasonably priced but are very accurate. Spring scales, the least expensive, lose accuracy over time. Beam-balance

scales, used for precise measurements, are expensive and rarely necessary for everyday cooking. Measure beaker: Its tapered design ensures accurate measurement of small amounts of both liquid and dry ingredients.

ACCESSORIES

Indispensables: bulb baster; mesh or perforated colander (stainless steel is more durable than plastic); expandable steamer; wood or synthetic cutting board; 6- and 8-inch fine sieves; 10-inch sieve that can double as a flour sifter and small colander; 4-sided grater; freezer/refrigerator thermometer; large slotted spoon; long-handled ladle; long-handled spoon; meat thermometer or instant-read thermometer; oven thermometer; pancake turner; pastry blender; pepper mill; potato masher; rolling pin; 2 rubber spatulas; 18-inch metal ruler; salad spinner; timer; tongs (scissors and self-locking tweezer type); 2-prong roast or carving fork; whisks (balloon, sauce, and flat); 3 wooden spoons.

Useful Tools: bamboo steamer; candy/sugar thermometer; deep-fat thermometer; food mill; funnels (large, medium, and small); gelatin molds (large, medium, and small); grill thermometer; meat pounder; meat tenderizer; mesh skimmer; pizza wheel (can double as a pastry cutter); potato ricer; second timer; second colander; second cutting board; six 8-inch skewers; 3-prong kitchen fork.

Handy Extras: flame moderator; gravy separator; mandoline (for shredding, slicing, and crinkle cutting vegetables); tasting spoon.

GADGETS

Indispensables: bottle opener; can opener; cheese grater (rotary); citrus juicer; citrus zester; corkscrew; egg slicer; garlic press; poultry trussing pins; vegetable parer (swivel blade).

Useful Tools: apple corer; cake tester/toothpicks; cheese plane; citrus reamer; melon baller; ice cream scoop; icing spatula; nutcracker; 2 pastry brushes; sandwich spreader; spaghetti lifter; tweezers.

Handy Extras: cherry pitter; corn stripper; nutmeg grater; strawberry huller.

MICROWAVE COOKWARE

Cooking in a microwave oven requires special equipment, usually made of glass or plastic. However, not all glass and

plastic is microwave safe.

To test glass, fill a 1-cup glass measure with water and set it in the dish you want to test. Place it in the oven and microwave at 100 percent power for 1 minute. The water should be hot, but if the dish is also hot, it's not microwave safe.

Certain plastics are not appropriate for microwaves; these include polystyrene containers. Plastic wrap and paper toweling should be labeled microwave safe.

MICROWAVE NOTES

Make sure that the microwave cookware you choose is the right size for your microwave oven. Ovens range in size from about .5 to 1.6 cubic feet. The larger the oven, the greater its wattage; the greater its wattage, the faster it cooks.

An oven with a 1.2 cubic-foot capacity and 900 watts will handle a large bowl with ease. Microwave ovens need a lot of counter space, so you might want to consider an under-the-counter or over-the-stove unit.

CONTAINERS AND PAPER PRODUCTS

Indispensables: airtight spice jars; airtight canisters (for flour, sugar, cereal, coffee, crackers); aluminum foil (reg-

Although synthetic cutting boards are convenient because they can be washed in the dishwasher, maple cutting boards are actually regarded as more hygienic. That's because bacteria that will live on a synthetic surface cannot survive on maple.

Whether you choose a synthetic or maple board, it's very important to keep the board absolutely clean. Wash the board with soap and hot water, rinse, and let it air dry each time you use it.

To sterilize a board—which should be done after using it for cutting raw or cooked meat, poultry, or fish—soak wooden boards for 2 minutes in a weak solution of 3 tablespoons of bleach per 1 gallon of water. Rinse well and air dry. The same procedure is recommended for wooden spoons and butcher block counters.

To sterilize a synthetic board, soak it for 5 to 10 minutes in a solution of 1 tablespoon of bleach per 1 gallon of water. Rinse and air dry.

ular and heavy-duty); cotton kitchen towels; freezer wrap; oven mitts/pot holders (make sure they are thick or insulated); plastic storage bags; plastic wrap; paper toweling; sponges, brushes, scrubbers;

storage containers (plastic and glass in a variety of sizes); wax paper.

Useful Tools: apron; bread box; cake plate with cover; cork-top glass canisters (for pasta and dry beans); baking parchment.

Handy Extras: cheesecloth; doilies; muffin-pan liners (foil or paper); plastic freezer containers (in 1/2-pint, 1-pint, and 1-quart sizes).

STAPLES FOR COOKING

It's a good idea to keep staple ingredients within arm's reach both for everyday use and for cooking emergencies. Staples include a variety of dry goods, canned and bottled goods, and frozen foods.

BAKING SUPPLIES

Indispensables: baking powder; baking soda; cornstarch; cornmeal; extracts (vanilla and almond); flour; evaporated and condensed milk; honey; molasses; sugar (granulated, confectioners', light and dark brown); vegetable oil and solid shortening; dry yeast.

Useful: cake and cookie decorations; chocolate products; grated coconut; corn syrup (light and dark).

CONDIMENTS

Indispensables: ketchup; mayonnaise; mustard; salad dressing; soy sauce; steak sauce; vinegars (cider, white, balsamic, red and white wine); Worcestershire sauce.

Useful: capers; chutney; hot pepper sauce; prepared horseradish; sesame oil.

FREEZER STAPLES

Indispensables: fruit juice concentrates; piecrusts; stocks and broths; tomato sauce; vegetables (carrots, spinach, whole-kernel corn, and peas, for example).

Useful: bread dough; pesto; phyllo dough; puff pastry; pizza dough.

GRAINS, PASTA, AND BREAD PRODUCTS

Indispensables: bread crumbs; cornmeal; crackers; pasta (strands and soup shapes); rice (white, brown, arborio); oatmeal; stuffing mix.

Useful: barley; couscous; grits; kasha; tortillas; wild rice.

THE CUPBOARD SHELF

Indispensables: bouillon cubes or granules; broth; canned fruit and applesauce; canned beans; cocoa; coffee; soups; dried fruit; dried mushrooms; dried peas and beans; gelatin; nuts; olive oil; olives; peanut butter; pie fillings; preserves; salt (table and Kosher); tea (regular and herb); tomato juice; tomato paste (cans or tubes); tomato purée; tomatoes (whole, chopped, and crushed); tuna.

Useful: anchovies/anchovy paste; artichoke hearts; bamboo shoots; capers; chilies; clam juice; clams; pimientos and/or roasted red peppers.

THE SPICE SHELF

Store herbs and spices tightly capped in a dark, cool cupboard. Since they should be replaced when they lose potency (every year or so), mark the jar with the date when it is opened.

Indispensables: basil; bay leaves; black pepper (ground and peppercorns); cinnamon (ground and stick); chervil; dill; oregano; red pepper (ground and flakes); rosemary; sage; sesame seeds; tarragon; thyme.

Useful: caraway seeds; cardamom; celery seeds; cloves (ground and whole); curry powder; ground cumin; ground mace; marjoram; mustard (powder and seeds); nutmeg (ground and whole); paprika; poultry seasoning; saffron threads; savory; white pepper (ground and peppercorns); spice blends (regular and low sodium).

DRINKS AND APPETIZERS

HOT COFFEES

*T*he *coffeehouse reigns supreme in Europe, and a stellar menu of coffees keeps customers coming back for more. We offer two perennial favorites, Italian Caffè Latte and coffee-based Viennese Hot Chocolate.*

A COFFEE PRIMER

Espresso: A strong dark coffee that Italians not only sip from tiny cups but also use as the basis for other drinks. Espresso requires a special coffee—dark roasted and finely ground. It is brewed in a machine that forces boiling water through the grounds. There are simple espresso brewers for home use and several excellent instant espressos as well.

Caffè Latte: Italy's breakfast drink of choice combines a shot of espresso with plenty of hot milk. Italians don't froth the milk—we've taken license here. We've also used skim milk to trim the fat. Tip: The lower in fat the milk, the airier the froth (fat greases and breaks the bubbles).

Cappuccino: A "coffee-er" caffè latte, topped by a froth of hot milk and a dusting of cinnamon. The traditional coffee/milk ratio in cappuccino ranges from 40/60 to 50/50.

Viennese Hot Chocolate: Sweet and seductive, this winter warmer teams milk, cocoa, and coffee. In Austria it's served *mit schlag*—"with whipped cream."

CUSTOMIZED CAFFÈ

For stronger flavor, use 1½ times the amount of espresso whether you are brewing your own or using instant espresso.

To steam by microwave, pour milk into a 1-quart glass measure and heat, uncovered, at medium (70 percent power), just until bubbles form around the edge—about 2 minutes.

Make your own variations by trying flavored coffees or by spicing things up with freshly grated nutmeg, ground cinnamon, or green cardamom pods. (Arabs stuff the spouts of their coffeepots with cardamom pods and trickle the coffee through them.)

COCOA NOTES

To make cocoa powder, manufacturers extract most of the cocoa butter from chocolate and then grind the remaining solids. Dutch-process cocoa is treated with alkali to make it less acidic. It's darker, richer, and dissolves a little more easily than regular cocoa. Use either type for Viennese Hot Chocolate—but never a sweetened cocoa mix.

To ensure that your cocoa is smooth, mix the powdered cocoa with the other dry ingredients first, pressing out all lumps. Blend in a little of the liquid—about ½ cup—before adding the balance.

WORK SAVER
Stovetop Steamer

This handy cappuccino steamer consists of a closed container for water and a steaming spout that protrudes from the top. Set the container over high heat and when steam begins piping through it, stick the end of the spout into a cup of hot milk. The steam will churn the milk into froth. Many housewares stores and kitchen shops carry these little "frothers."

Caffè Latte

1½ cups skim or low-fat milk
⅔ cup freshly brewed espresso
Optional garnishes:
ground cinnamon
sweetened cocoa powder

1 In a small saucepan, heat milk over low heat just until tiny bubbles begin to form around the edge of the pan—10 to 15 minutes; do not boil. If a skin forms on the surface of the milk, remove it with a spoon and discard.

2 Divide espresso between two 8-ounce cups, then pour ⅓ cup hot milk into each.

3 Using an electric mixer or wire whisk, beat the remaining hot milk until frothy, then spoon into cups; dust with cinnamon or cocoa, if desired. Makes 2 servings.

1 Serving: Calories 66; Total Fat 0 g; Saturated Fat 0 g; Protein 6 g; Carbohydrates 9 g; Fiber 0 g; Sodium 96 mg; Cholesterol 3 mg

prep time-15 minutes • cooking time-15 minutes

Viennese Hot Chocolate

⅓ cup unsweetened cocoa powder (not a mix)
⅓ cup sugar
2½ cups milk
1½ cups freshly brewed strong coffee or espresso

1 In a medium-size saucepan, combine cocoa and sugar, pressing out lumps. Blend in enough milk to moisten dry ingredients—about ½ cup—then whisk in the coffee and remaining 2 cups milk.

2 Set over moderately low heat and cook, stirring occasionally, until mixture steams but does not boil—8 to 10 minutes. Pour into mugs and serve. Makes 4 servings.

1 Serving: Calories 176; Total Fat 6 g; Saturated Fat 4 g; Protein 6 g; Carbohydrates 28 g; Fiber 2 g; Sodium 79 mg; Cholesterol 21 mg

prep time-5 minutes
cooking time-8 to 10 minutes

Caffè Latte, left, and Viennese Hot Chocolate, right, make a breakfast or coffee break really special. Serve with rolls or crumbly cookies.

ICED DRINKS

If you've had trouble getting your iced tea to the perfect strength, follow our brewing tips. Our Lemon Squash recipe is a variation on classic lemonade, made with carbonated water.

CHOOSING A TEA

For the best iced tea, choose a fermented black tea from India or Sri Lanka. These include Darjeeling, Assam, Earl Grey (a bergamot-scented blend), English Breakfast (a mix of India and Sri Lankan teas), and other breakfast teas. Chinese green teas are not full bodied enough to serve on the rocks. However, many of the caffeine-free herbal teas on the market are delicious on ice.

FOR THE BEST BREW

Tea should be brewed only in a glass, porcelain, or enameled pot or pitcher; metal will give the tea a metallic taste.

To avoid bitter tea, remove the tea bags after only 3 to 5 minutes of brewing time. Never squeeze the bags into the tea.

To keep iced tea from becoming watery as the ice cubes melt, start with a strong brew. As a rule of thumb, double the amount of tea or tea bags you would use for hot tea.

You can also avoid watery tea by brewing an extra pot of tea and making iced-tea cubes.

CHASE THE CLOUDS AWAY

If you do not plan to use the tea right away, let the tea cool to room temperature, cover, and store in the refrigerator. Tea will become cloudy if it is put in the refrigerator while it is still hot. If tea does become cloudy, no problem. Stir in a little boiling water, and the tea will clear up.

FRESH FLAVORS

For a little variety, try a squeeze of fresh lime or orange in your tea instead of lemon. If you prefer mint-flavored tea, consider one of the fruity varieties—pineapple, ginger, and apple mints make interesting additions.

LEMONS FOR LEMONADE

In general there are about 5 medium-size lemons per pound. For 1 cup of juice you will need to squeeze 4 to 5 large lemons.

To get the most juice out of a lemon, be sure to buy lemons that are heavy for their size.

Before squeezing lemons, bring them to room temperature or briefly microwave them at high (100 percent power) about 30 seconds; then roll the fruit around the counter, pressing firmly with your palm. This will break up the pulp and release the juice.

QUICK TIPS

You can prepare your own lemonade mix. To make enough for a dozen servings, combine 2 cups of lemon juice, 1/2 cup of sugar, and 1 cup of Sugar Syrup, right. Store in a covered jar in the refrigerator. When you are ready to use it, shake the mixture well, pour 1/4 cup into a glass, then add water and ice.

For jiffy lemonade, use frozen lemon juice that has thawed, not lemonade concentrate, which can be very sweet.

MADE WITH ZEST

Citrus zest is the thin layer of colored, aromatic, and slightly oily outer rind. The white part underneath is the pith, which is bitter. You can remove the zest with a special tool called a zester or with a common swivel-bladed vegetable parer. Always wash lemons before removing the zest whether for use as a garnish or to flavor a drink or food.

SUGAR SYRUP

Sugar Syrup is ideal for sweetening chilled tea because the sugar is already dissolved.

In a small saucepan, **combine** 2 cups sugar and 2 1/2 cups water. **Set** over moderate heat and **cook**, **stirring** frequently, until mixture boils and sugar dissolves completely. **Remove** Sugar Syrup from heat, **cover** for 1 or 2 minutes to let the steam dissolve any unmelted crystals on the sides of the pan.

Pour into a 1-quart jar, cover tightly, and **store** in the refrigerator. **Use** to sweeten iced tea and other cold drinks. Makes 3 cups.

HOW TO ZEST

Using a swivel-bladed vegetable parer or sharp knife, cut a shallow 1/2-inch-wide swath of zest. For a long spiral of zest, turn the lemon in your hand, continuing to cut in a sideways direction.

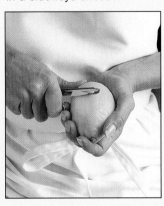

CRANBERRY ICED TEA

Prepare as directed at right through Step 2, **doubling** the amount of tea. **Strain** out tea leaves, then **mix** in 2 cups cranberry juice cocktail and Sugar Syrup to taste. **Garnish** with fresh or frozen whole cranberries, raspberries, strawberries, or slices of lime. Makes 4 servings.

For a special touch, **make** a double recipe of Cranberry Iced Tea. **Place** 1 or 2 cranberries in each square of an ice-cube tray and **fill** with tea. **Freeze** and **serve** with the tea.

LEMON SQUASH VARIATIONS

Lime Squash: Prepare as at right. **Substitute** lime zest and lime juice for the lemon and **sweeten** with 1 cup Sugar Syrup or to taste. **Garnish** with lime slices and fresh strawberries. Makes 4 servings.

Triple Citrus Squash: Prepare as at right. **Use** two 3-inch strips each of grapefruit, lemon, and orange zest and **add** 1/3 cup each of grapefruit, orange, and lemon juice instead of all lemon zest and juice. **Sweeten** with 1/3 cup Sugar Syrup or to taste. **Garnish** if desired with a slice of each fruit. Makes 4 servings.

Perfect Iced Tea

> 1 **quart cold water**
> 2 **tablespoons tea leaves or 6 regular-size tea bags**
> **Sugar Syrup to taste**
> **Optional garnishes:**
> **lemon wedges**
> **fresh mint leaves**

1 In a large saucepan or teakettle, bring 2 cups of the cold water to a full rolling boil over high heat.

2 Place tea in a teapot that has been rinsed out with boiling water. Slowly pour the 2 cups of boiling water into the teapot, cover, and steep tea 3 to 5 minutes.

3 Stir tea once, strain tea leaves or remove tea bags. Add the remaining 2 cups of cold water and sweeten to taste with Sugar Syrup.

4 To serve, pour into 4 tall ice-filled glasses and garnish as desired. Makes 4 servings.

1 Serving: Calories 4; Total Fat 0 g; Saturated Fat 0 g; Protein 0 g; Carbohydrates 1 g; Fiber 0 g; Sodium 11 mg; Cholesterol 0 mg

prep time-15 minutes
steeping time-3 to 5 minutes

Lemon Squash

> **Four 3-inch strips lemon zest, cut into thin slices**
> 1 **cup fresh lemon juice**
> 1/2 **cup Sugar Syrup**
> 3 **cups chilled club soda, seltzer, or water**
> **Optional garnishes:**
> **lemon slices**
> **fresh mint leaves**

1 Place lemon zest in a 2-quart pitcher. Add lemon juice and Sugar Syrup to taste and stir well.

2 To serve, stir in club soda and pour into 4 tall ice-filled glasses, straining out lemon zest. Garnish as desired. Makes 4 servings.

1 Serving: Calories 209; Total Fat 0 g; Saturated Fat 0 g; Protein 0 g; Carbohydrates 55 g; Fiber 0 g; Sodium 38 mg; Cholesterol 0 mg

prep time-15 minutes
chilling time-2 to 3 hours

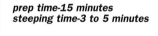

FILLED TORTILLAS

Many Tex-Mex favorites begin with tortillas. It's no longer necessary to make your own tortillas, but working with purchased varieties requires a certain savvy too.

CHOOSING THE RIGHT TORTILLA

There are two types of tortilla and Tex-Mex cooks know that their uses differ.

Flour tortillas: Made of wheat flour, these flat, round breads measure 8 to 10 inches across and are as thin as crêpes. Baked but not browned, they are soft, pliable, and perfect for burritos (tortillas twirled around spicy fillings), chimichangas (plump cheese- or meat-filled half-moon pies), or quesadillas, shown opposite. In Mexico, wheat tortillas are also warmed, piled into baskets, and served like bread.

Corn tortillas: Made of a fine white, yellow, or blue cornmeal, these tortillas owe their nutty flavor to the boiling lye bath the corn is given before it is dried and ground. The purpose of the bath is to puff the kernels and loosen their skins. Corn tortillas are coarser than flour tortillas, stiffer, and smaller too, averaging only 6 inches in diameter. Use them for tacos, enchiladas, and tostados (crisply fried tortilla wedges).

TORTILLAS TO GO

Most supermarkets now routinely stock packaged "fresh" flour and corn tortillas. Look for them in refrigerator sections. Corn tortillas are also available by the can in the Tex-Mex section.

COLD STORAGE

Store "fresh" tortillas as the manufacturer directs. Or layer them between squares of wax paper, wrap them in plastic wrap, pop them into a self-sealing plastic bag, and freeze. Frozen tortillas will keep for 6 months.

FROZEN ASSETS

To thaw tortillas, spread them out on the counter. Brush off any ice crystals. If allowed to melt on the tortillas, the ice will cause soggy spots.

CUT THE FAT

Quesadillas are traditionally fried in deep fat. The surefire way to cut fat is to bake them (as directed in our recipe) instead of frying. A single quesadilla can sponge up as much as 1 tablespoon of fat. That equals 120 extra calories and 14 extra grams of fat.

FAT-FREE YOGURT CHEESE

You can trim a lot of fat from quesadillas or tacos by topping them with homemade yogurt cheese instead of sour cream. To make yogurt cheese, line a large fine-meshed sieve with coffee filters. Pour in 1 quart of well-drained plain, nonfat yogurt, and slash the yogurt criss-cross fashion with a knife. Place the sieve over a large bowl, cover, and refrigerate 24 hours. Drain off all liquid, spoon the yogurt cheese into a 1-pint jar, cover, and store in the refrigerator. Use within 8 to 10 days. Whisk well before using. Makes 1¾ cups. A tablespoon of yogurt cheese contains no fat, no cholesterol, and a mere 11 calories.

QUICK TORTILLA TIPS

Before grating cheese in a food processor, set the cheese in the freezer for 20 minutes. The harder the cheese, the neater the shreds.

To soften tortillas that are too dry and brittle to roll, bundle in aluminum foil and warm in a 350°F oven for 10 minutes. Or bundle in paper toweling and microwave at 50 percent power for 15 to 20 seconds.

To keep filling from oozing out of quesadillas or tacos,

MINI TACOS

Use two tortillas only and **cut** each in half. **Bundle** tortilla halves in foil and **set** in a 425°F oven just until hot but not crisp—about 5 minutes. Meanwhile, **combine** ¼ cup each salsa and shredded Monterey Jack (plain or peppery), 2 thinly sliced scallions, and 2 ounces finely chopped chorizo. **Spread** salsa mixture on hot tortilla halves, **dividing** amount evenly. **Roll** up jelly-roll style and **bake**, uncovered, on an ungreased baking sheet until crisped—about 10 minutes. **Top** with sour cream or yogurt cheese, left, and **serve**. Makes 4 servings.

---

start with the tortilla lying flat. Arrange all the ingredients to one side of center on the tortilla, then fold over and press the edges all around.

To keep quesadillas from opening as they bake, it helps to moisten the edges slightly before pressing closed and wrapping with foil.

For jiffy nachos, sprinkle Red Pepper and Cheese Quesadillas ingredients over tostados or packaged tortilla chips and microwave, uncovered, at 50 percent power for 1 to 1½ minutes.

BITE-SIZE NIBBLES

For cocktail tacos, cut tortillas into 2-inch rounds with a cookie cutter. Then fill, fold in half, seal, and bake 3 minutes.

1 Lay a tortilla flat. Fill it with all the quesadilla ingredients (except sour cream) in a small mound just to one side of center.

2 Moisten edges of tortilla, fold in half, and press the edges closed.

3 Place each quesadilla on the bottom edge of a 12-inch piece of aluminum foil. Fold right and left sides of foil over the quesadilla; then, starting at the bottom, fold over to encase.

Red Pepper and Cheese Quesadillas

Four **8-inch flour tortillas**
1 **cup (4 ounces) coarsely shredded Monterey Jack cheese or Monterey Jack with hot peppers**
1 **large sweet red pepper, cored, seeded, and cut into 1/4-inch strips**
1/4 **cup cooked fresh or thawed frozen corn kernels**
3 **scallions with tops, thinly sliced**
1/4 **cup chopped fresh coriander (cilantro)**
1/2 **cup prepared mild or medium-hot salsa**
Optional garnishes:
      reduced-fat sour cream
      yogurt cheese

1 Preheat the oven to 425°F. Top each tortilla with cheese, red pepper, corn, scallions, coriander, and salsa, dividing evenly. Fold tortillas in half, moisten, and press edges closed.

2 Wrap in foil, as shown at left. Place on a baking sheet and bake until cheese melts—about 7 minutes. Remove from oven, unwrap, and top with a little sour cream or yogurt cheese, if desired. Makes 4 servings.

1 Serving: Calories 266; Total Fat 13 g; Saturated Fat 7 g; Protein 11 g; Carbohydrates 27 g; Fiber 2 g; Sodium 446 mg; Cholesterol 31 mg

prep time-12 minutes
cooking time-7 minutes

CRUDITÉS AND DIPS

*F*resh, crunchy vegetables are more popular now than ever before. Keep them on hand for everyday snacks or serve them at a special party with an array of delicious dips.

DECORATIVE CUTTING

Cutting vegetables into decorative shapes is easier than you may think. The steps for making five showy finger foods appear at right. Use them as a garnish on individual serving plates or to trim platters of plain-cut crudités or other cocktail nibbles.

EASY STEPS

When shopping for vegetables for crudités, look for fresh, young, unblemished produce.

Use a small, sharp paring knife to cut the vegetables into bite-size pieces.

If you are preparing for a party, cut the vegetables the day before and keep them refrigerated in ice water.

BLANCHING FOR BRIGHTNESS

Many people prefer the flavor and texture of vegetables that have been blanched for 1 to 2 minutes in boiling water.

When lifted out of the water, the vegetables are immediately plunged into ice water, to stop the cooking process.

CHOOSING BY COLOR

If you are planning to include big bowls of crunchy vegetables at your next get-together, you might want to think about your color scheme when you make the shopping list.

Bowls of red, yellow, and orange vegetables have a sunny, festive look (carrots, summer squash, radishes, three colors of bell pepper, cherry tomatoes, and wax beans). Platters of green and white vegetables give a table a cool and elegant look (scallions, asparagus, mushrooms, endive, broccoli, cucumbers, cauliflower, green beans, zucchini, white radishes, snow peas, and green beans).

SALSA TIPS

When making salsa, wait until near serving time

COOK'S SECRETS

Sara Moulton,
Executive Chef,
Gourmet
Magazine

"If you don't have time to make your own pastry for little party hors d'oeuvres, you can 'fake it' by using thin-sliced, firm-textured commercial bread. Roll the bread piecrust thin with a rolling pin and brush it with melted butter. Cut into 1½- to 2-inch rounds or squares and fill, fold, and bake just as you would bite-size pastry turnovers. Or make jiffy tartlet shells by pressing the rounds into mini muffin cups and baking at 350°F until crisp—5 to 10 minutes. Fill with salsa, guacamole, shrimp or crab salad, or any favorite spread."

before adding the coriander (cilantro). It will lose its savor during the hour of chilling.

Salsa ingredients should be chopped fine enough to scoop up with chips.

GREEN GODDESS TIPS

To halve and pit an avocado, use a short, sharp knife to cut through the skin and flesh to the pit. Swivel the knife blade around the pit, scoring the avocado into two halves.

To separate the halves, grasp one half in each hand and twist in opposite directions. Cup the half with the pit in the palm of your hand and firmly but carefully stick the blade of a chef's knife into the meatiest part of the pit. Lift the knife, twisting gently, and the pit will come out.

To keep avocado from browning, sprinkle lemon juice over the avocado slices and toss gently after chopping so that all surfaces are coated.

GARLIC SPREAD TIPS

When buying garlic, choose the firmest, heaviest heads you can find. Heads of garlic tinged with purple are the most pungent.

Elephant garlic, now available in many supermarkets, is mild and sweet, and the cloves are huge. One large clove of elephant garlic equals 8 to 10 medium-size cloves of regular garlic.

To dress up a garlic spread, pipe the spread onto 1½- to 2-inch rounds of melba toast using a pastry bag fitted with a large star tip.

TIPS FOR ALL DIPS

Dips should be made thick enough to cling to vegetables without dripping.

To turn a dip into a spread, reduce the amount of liquid, adding only enough for a good spreading consistency.

Serve in small colorful bowls. For a festive presentation, serve in cored and seeded peppers or in hollowed-out red and green cabbages.

Choice Cuts

Select a knife that has a short, firm, and very sharp blade. Keep a bowl of ice water handy while you work. Place each cut vegetable in the water when complete. Ice water will set the cuts and allow vegetable "flowers" to open.

Scallion Daisies

1 Trim scallion ¼ inch from root. Trim off leaves just where they begin to spread.

2 Insert knife at mid-shaft, 2 inches from root end, and slice. Rotate scallion and repeat at ⅛-inch intervals. Place in ice water to open the "petals."

Carrot Curls

1 Using a swivel-bladed vegetable parer, peel strips the length of carrot.

2 Curl each strip around your finger. Remove and secure with toothpick. Chill in ice water. Remove toothpicks before serving.

Pepper Fans

1 Cut peppers into quarters, then halve quarters crosswise. Flatten each piece and make evenly spaced cuts to within ⅜ inch of bottom. Place in ice water to open.

Radish Coin Jacks

1 Slice radish crosswise into ⅛-inch coin slices. Make a cut from the center of each coin slice to the outer edge.

2 Bend 2 coin slices slightly to open the cuts. Slide the cuts into each other so that the coins interlock at right angles.

Radish Chrysanthemums

1 Choose as round a radish as possible. Using a sharp paring knife, trim off the leaves and tip.

2 Make very thin parallel cuts in radish, as close together as possible and to within ⅛ inch of the stem.

3 Turn the radish 90 degrees and make an equal number of parallel cuts perpendicular to the first. Soak in ice water for several hours to open fully.

4 Insert one end of a toothpick into the bottom of a radish chrysanthemum. Insert opposite end into the top of a scallion daisy to form flower stem.

Roasted Garlic Spread (Skordalia)

- **14** unpeeled cloves garlic
- **5** slices firm-textured white bread, preferably stale
- **1½** cups mashed potatoes
- **½** cup shelled walnuts
- **¼** cup fresh lemon juice
- **¾** teaspoon salt
- **¾** teaspoon black pepper
- **⅔** cup olive oil

Optional garnishes:
  parsley sprigs
  lemon zest

1 Preheat the oven to 350°F. Bundle garlic in aluminum foil. Place in a small baking dish with ½ inch water and bake until garlic is tender—about 45 minutes.

2 Meanwhile, place bread in a large, shallow baking dish, cover with water, and soak 5 to 10 minutes.

3 Squeeze bread dry and place in a food processor. When garlic is cool enough to handle, squeeze to extract flesh, then place in the food processor. Add potatoes, walnuts, lemon juice, salt, and pepper, and pulse just enough to combine. With the motor running, drizzle in olive oil and continue processing until smooth.

4 Spoon into a serving bowl and garnish as desired. Serve with mini pita rounds, split in half and toasted, or with assorted crudités or chips. Makes about 3 cups.

1 Tablespoon: Calories 51; Total Fat 4 g; Saturated Fat 1 g; Protein 1 g; Carbohydrates 4 g; Fiber 0 g; Sodium 71 mg; Cholesterol 0 mg

prep time–50 minutes
baking time–45 minutes

Ripe Tomato Salsa

- **3** medium-size ripe tomatoes, cored, seeded, and chopped
- **3** small scallions, trimmed and coarsely chopped
- **1** medium-size jalapeño pepper, cored seeded, and finely chopped
- **1** clove garlic, finely chopped
- **¾** teaspoon salt
- **⅓** cup coarsely chopped fresh coriander (cilantro)

Optional garnish:
  coriander sprigs

1 Toss all ingredients except chopped coriander in a large bowl until well combined. Set aside for 1 hour to let flavors mellow.

2 Just before serving, mix in chopped coriander. Transfer to a serving bowl and garnish with coriander sprigs. Makes 3½ cups.

1 Tablespoon: Calories 4; Total Fat 0 g; Saturated Fat 0 g; Protein 0 g; Carbohydrates 1 g; Fiber 0 g; Sodium 36 mg; Cholesterol 0 mg

prep time–30 minutes
standing time–60 minutes

Green Goddess Dip

1 cup sour cream
1 cup mayonnaise (use low-fat or nonfat, if desired)
1 small ripe avocado, peeled, pitted, and chunked
2 large scallions, trimmed and chunked
1/3 cup fresh parsley
2 tablespoons lemon juice
2 teaspoons anchovy paste
1 peeled garlic clove
1 teaspoon dried tarragon, crumbled
1/2 teaspoon black pepper
1/4 teaspoon salt

Optional garnishes:
   avocado slices
   parsley sprigs

1 Working in batches if necessary, purée all ingredients (except garnishes) in a blender at high speed or in a food processor until smooth, scraping down container sides as needed.

2 Transfer to a small bowl, smooth plastic wrap flat on surface of dip, and refrigerate 2 to 3 hours. If mixture seems thick, mix in a little additional mayonnaise. Also, taste and adjust seasonings as needed.

3 To serve, spoon into a serving bowl. Garnish, if desired, with slices of avocado or parsley sprigs. Serve with assorted chips or crackers. Makes about 3 cups.

1 Tablespoon: Calories 67; Total Fat 7 g; Saturated Fat 2 g; Protein 1 g; Carbohydrates 1 g; Fiber 0 g; Sodium 64 mg; Cholesterol 7 mg

prep time-30 minutes
chilling time-2 to 3 hours

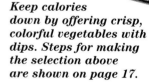

Keep calories down by offering crisp, colorful vegetables with dips. Steps for making the selection above are shown on page 17.

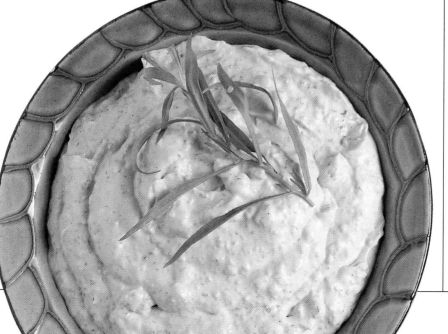

PEKING RAVIOLI

Chinese dumplings, or "Peking ravioli," are paper-thin squares of dough wrapped around spicy fillings. Steamed and dipped in sauce, they're fat free and guaranteed to please.

ABOUT CHINESE DUMPLINGS

True Chinese dumpling dough is made at home from a mixture of flour, salt, and water rolled paper thin. You can get the same results by buying packaged Chinese wonton (dumpling) wrappers. Packages of 3 1/4-inch square wrappers are available in the refrigerated or produce sections of most supermarkets.

Brands vary in quality, so if you have a choice, you may want to try different ones to see which you like best. In general, the thinner the wrappers the better.

Unused squares from a package of wonton wrappers can be frozen for future use. Layer between squares of wax paper, wrap carefully in plastic wrap, then in aluminum foil. They will keep 6 months in the freezer.

HANDLING THE DOUGH

It's easy to get the hang of folding dumplings, so urge your children or grandchildren to join in. Children love to help mold the little crescents around the stuffing. The steps are shown at right.

Once stuffed, dumpling wrappers become sticky as they absorb moisture from the filling. As dumplings are completed, place them on a floured surface but don't cover them with a cloth.

CHINESE INGREDIENTS

Many of the foods integral to Chinese cooking are available nationwide in supermarkets. We offer substitutes for some of those ingredients in our recipe, but for an authentic flavor, you might want to give the originals a try.

Chinese black mushrooms are only available dry. They come in small packages and can be bought in specialty grocery shops. Properly wrapped, the unused portions of the packages will last virtually forever. Once they have been soaked in water for half an hour, black mushrooms have a pleasant chewy texture and a smoky-woodsy taste. If you can't find them, dried European mushrooms can be substituted.

Oriental sesame oil is pressed from roasted sesame seeds. It is used as a flavoring rather than as a fat and adds a lovely nutty flavor to food. If you don't wish to use it, simply leave it out of the recipe.

COOKING AHEAD

You can prepare dumplings well ahead of the day you plan to serve them. Fill, fold, and pleat the dumplings, then freeze them in a single layer (not touching each other) on a plate. When frozen, seal the dumplings in an airtight plastic bag or container. When ready to use, place the still-frozen dumplings on the steamer rack and cook as directed, allowing an extra 10 minutes' cooking time. Do not let them thaw before cooking.

IMPROVISED STEAMERS

You don't need a Chinese steamer to steam Chinese dumplings. An ordinary stainless steel, expandable steamer basket will work fine if it is opened flat in a Dutch oven with a tight-fitting lid.

VEGETABLE DUMPLINGS

Prepare as directed at right through Step 2 but **omit** the shrimp; **set** mixture aside. In a large nonstick skillet, **stir-fry** 6 ounces trimmed and coarsely chopped shiitake mushrooms, 1 chopped leek, and 1 chopped sweet red pepper in 1 tablespoon peanut or vegetable oil. **Cook** over moderate heat about 7 minutes, or until tender. **Combine** with reserved black mushroom mixture, then **fill**, **fold**, and **steam** dumplings as directed in Steps 3, 4, and 5. Makes 32 dumplings.

In a pinch you might also use a round cake rack. Keep the rack above the steaming water by making a trivet of 3 juice glasses in the pan and placing the rack on top.

WORK SAVER

Bamboo Steamer

The traditional Chinese steamer is a model of efficiency. The basic steamer is a round wooden box with a tight-fitting domed lid and an open-weave bottom of bamboo slats. When ready for use, the steamer is placed above a little water in a wok or other pot. The boxes are used singly or stacked several layers high—the steam travels up through them so that the food in all the boxes—dumplings, vegetables, fish—can be steamed at the same time.

1 Place 1 wonton skin on a flat surface; mound filling in the center.

2 Fold dough diagonally over filling; moisten edges to seal. Using fingertips, press around filling to remove any air pockets.

3 Begin pleating and crimping edges of dough into a rough half-moon shape; place dumplings on wax paper or a flour-dusted baking sheet. Continue with remaining filling and skins. Refrigerate dumplings until needed.

Pleated Shrimp Dumplings

- **6** dried Chinese black mushrooms or dried European mushrooms
- **8** ounces shrimp, shelled, deveined, and minced
- **2** scallions with tops, thinly sliced
- **1** clove garlic, minced
- **1** tablespoon minced ginger
- **1/2** teaspoon salt
- **1/4** cup finely chopped, canned water chestnuts
- **3** tablespoons soy sauce
- **1** tablespoon dry sherry
- **1** teaspoon dark Oriental sesame oil (optional)
- **2** teaspoons cornstarch
- **32** wonton skins
- **4** teaspoons molasses
- **2** teaspoons dark brown sugar
- **1** tablespoon lime juice

1 In a small bowl, cover mushrooms with boiling water and let stand until soft—about 20 minutes. Drain, stem, and finely chop the mushrooms and transfer to a medium-size bowl.

2 Mix in shrimp, scallions, garlic, ginger, salt, water chestnuts, 1 tablespoon soy sauce, sherry, sesame oil (optional), and cornstarch.

3 Spoon a teaspoon of the mixture onto each wonton skin. Follow directions at left to fold and pleat.

4 Working in batches if necessary, arrange the dumplings on a lightly oiled steamer rack and lower into a pan of simmering water, making sure bottom of rack does not touch water. Cover and steam just until filling is firm and shrimp are cooked through—5 to 7 minutes.

5 In a small bowl, whisk together the remaining 2 tablespoons soy sauce, molasses, brown sugar, and lime juice and serve as a dipping sauce for the dumplings. Makes 32 dumplings.

1 Dumpling: Calories 38; Total Fat 0 g; Saturated Fat 0 g; Protein 2 g; Carbohydrates 7 g; Fiber 0 g; Sodium 188 mg; Cholesterol 11 mg

prep time-25 minutes • cooking time-7 minutes

STUFFED SHELLS

S tuffed mussels and other mollusks make an elegant appetizer and are an excellent choice for a party buffet. Though they are easy and inexpensive to make, stuffed mussels look impressive.

ON THE MARKET

Mussels can be anywhere from 1½ inches to nearly 4 inches long. The little ones are the sweetest and most tender; the larger have a richer, meatier flavor. Both are delicious. For Stuffed Mussels, look for mussels that are between 2 and 3 inches long.

SAFETY FIRST

Mussels have a very short shelf life. They must be alive when you cook them.

If possible, only buy mussels on the day you will use them. If you must store them overnight, mound them in a large bowl and cover loosely with several layers of paper toweling or newspaper.

TESTS FOR FRESHNESS

One of the best tests for freshness is your nose. Fresh mussels smell like the ocean. Shellfish that has gone bad lets itself be known.

Reject any mussels with broken shells, and be sure they are tightly closed when you buy them. If mussels have

opened slightly when you go to cook them, place them in the freezer for 1 to 2 minutes. Any mussel that stays open should be discarded.

When they are steamed, any mussels that don't open should also be discarded.

CLEANING TIPS

Many of the mussels on the market today are farm raised. They lack the briny tang of their ocean kin but they are far easier to clean.

Scrub or scrape barnacles and seaweed from the shells using a stiff brush or a knife under cold running water.

To remove the brown "beard" that protrudes from the shells, give the beard a strong, steady pull, and if it resists, use pliers for a firmer tug.

ANOTHER OPENING

The easiest way to open mussels is by steam. To steam mussels on top of the stove, place them in a large pot containing 1 inch of simmering water or broth. Cover and steam just until the mussels open—about 4 to 5 minutes. Using kitchen tongs, transfer the mussels to a bowl.

To open by microwave, arrange 6 to 8 chilled mussels in a ring, hinged side out, in a glass pie plate. Microwave, uncovered, at full power 1 to 2 minutes, removing mussels the second they open. Bed at once in crushed ice.

To pry open a mussel, insert a paring knife between the top and bottom shells at the back of the mussel, next to the hinge. Gently work the knife around to the front, twisting the blade slightly as you go.

Whenever mussels are going to be cooked further, as in Stuffed Mussels, be careful not to oversteam them because they will become tough and rubbery.

SAVE THE BROTH

The broth left in the steaming pot is well worth saving for use in soups or paella-type dishes. It can be frozen for later use. Strain the broth into a bowl through a fine sieve.

SCALLOP SHELLS

Scallops are nearly always sold without their shells. That is because the adductor muscle—the part of the scallop that you eat—has to be separated quickly from the stomach, which starts to deteriorate as soon as the scallop leaves the water.

STUFFED SCALLOP SHELLS

Prepare as directed at right, substituting 12 ounces of coarsely chopped sea scallops for the mussels.

For the stuffing, **sauté** the onion and garlic in olive oil, as directed in Step 3. **Add** and **cook** the spinach, then **mix** in the cooked rice, dill, and salt but **omit** the pine nuts and currants. **Stir** the scallops into the spinach-rice mixture and **moisten** with ½ cup broth. **Spoon** into 4 scallop shells or individual gratin dishes. **Cover** with foil and **bake** just until scallops are cooked through—about 10 minutes. Makes 4 servings.

If you want to serve scallops in their shells, buy a package of scallop shells. They come 6 to 8 in a package and in a range of sizes. Buy the smallest shells available.

NO TIPPING

To keep scallops from tipping while they bake, bed them in a pan of rock salt or nestle them in muffin-pan cups.

COOKING AHEAD

Stuffed mussels and scallops may be kept refrigerated, loosely covered, for up to 24 hours before baking. When ready to bake, let them return to room temperature and then proceed as directed in the recipe and serve immediately.

Baked Stuffed Mussels

32 large mussels, scrubbed and bearded
1/3 cup water
1 tablespoon olive oil
1/4 cup finely chopped yellow onion
2 cloves garlic, minced
1 package (10 ounces) frozen chopped spinach, thawed and squeezed dry
1/3 cup cooked white rice
1/4 cup snipped fresh dill or 1 teaspoon dried dill
2 tablespoons pine nuts
3 tablespoons dried currants or dark seedless raisins
1/4 teaspoon salt

1 Preheat the oven to 400°F. In a deep skillet, bring mussels and water to a boil over high heat. Reduce heat to moderate, cover, and cook just until mussels open—about 5 minutes.

2 Using tongs or a slotted spoon, lift mussels to a large bowl, discarding any that did not open. Strain broth and reserve. When mussels are cool enough to handle, shuck, reserving the shells. Coarsely chop the mussels.

3 In a medium-size nonstick skillet over moderate heat, heat oil 1 minute. Add onion and garlic and sauté, stirring often, until soft—about 5 minutes. Add spinach and 1 tablespoon of the reserved broth and cook, stirring frequently, 4 minutes more. Remove from heat and mix in rice, dill, pine nuts, currants, salt, chopped mussels, and remaining reserved broth.

4 Spoon the mixture into the reserved mussel shells. Press gently in place, but don't pack firmly.

Arrange the stuffed shells in 2 jelly-roll pans, cover with aluminum foil, and bake until hot—about 5 minutes. Makes 4 servings.

1 Serving: Calories 180; Total Fat 9 g; Saturated Fat 1 g; Protein 11 g; Carbohydrates 18 g; Fiber 3 g; Sodium 349 mg; Cholesterol 16 mg

prep time-20 minutes
cooking time-20 minutes

Our Baked Stuffed Mussels and Stuffed Scallop Shells are presented on a bed of rock salt, above. Rock salt is also useful for keeping round-bottomed sea shells steady while they are baking.

PHYLLO PASTRIES

These classic Greek appetizers are made with phyllo pastry. Far easier to work with than it looks, phyllo bakes into layers so crisp, so fragile that they shatter at the touch of a fork.

ABOUT PHYLLO

Phyllo pastry consists of tissue-thin sheets of dough. It can be bought frozen; each 16- to 17½-ounce package contains 24 sheets of about 11 by 15 inches, rolled in an airtight wrapper. That's enough for sixty 2½-inch triangles.

Thaw phyllo as directed—some manufacturers recommend thawing it at room temperature; others in the refrigerator. Once thawed, an unopened package of phyllo can be safely refrigerated for about 1 week.

Never refreeze phyllo that has thawed. The sheets will dry and cling to one another.

WORKING WITH PHYLLO

Follow the directions on the package. Work quickly and confidently since phyllo dries rapidly when exposed to air.

Keep the phyllo in its wrapper until ready for use. Unroll the stack on a dry, flat surface. If you're only using half the package, carefully reroll the balance, wrap snugly in plastic wrap, and refrigerate.

To keep phyllo from drying as you work with it, smooth a sheet of plastic wrap over the stack and cover with a damp towel. Remove the phyllo sheets one by one, recovering the stack each time.

To prevent the completed triangles from drying before you bake them, cover with plastic wrap, then a damp towel.

BUTTER OR OIL

A recipe may call for as few as 3 or as many as 17 layers of phyllo, with a light brushing of melted butter or olive oil on each sheet. The oil allows the sheets to separate and crisp individually as they bake. Butter is used for both sweet and savory phyllo dishes; olive oil for savory dishes. Both add calories, but olive oil at least has zero cholesterol.

CUTTING THE FAT

The most effective way to cut fat is to spray the phyllo sheets with butter-flavored or olive-oil-flavored nonstick vegetable cooking spray instead of spreading with butter.

CHOOSING A CHEESE

The cheese traditionally used for flavoring spinach stuffing is feta, a salty, crumbly, white Greek cheese made from sheep and/or goat milk.

Feta comes to market in brine. Rinse it well in cool water before using.

Whenever possible, taste feta before you buy it. It varies greatly in flavor and saltiness.

COOKING AHEAD

Phyllo triangles can be made up to 24 hours before they are baked. Arrange them in a single layer (not touching each other) on a plastic-wrap-lined baking sheet, cover with plastic wrap, then damp paper toweling, and refrigerate.

Unbaked triangles freeze well. Prepare as recipe directs, but do not brush the completed triangles with melted butter. Place in a single layer on a baking sheet and set in a 0°F freezer. When frozen, pop the triangles in a plastic freezer bag. Store in freezer. Use within 3 months.

To bake, arrange the still-frozen triangles on a lightly greased or parchment-lined baking sheet and brush with melted butter. Bake as directed in Step 5, but allow an extra 10 minutes of cooking. Do not thaw the triangles before you bake them—they will become soggy if you do.

GOAT CHEESE STRUDEL

- 10½ ounces goat cheese, crumbled
- 1 egg, lightly beaten
- 1 clove garlic, minced
- ½ teaspoon salt
- ½ teaspoon black pepper
- ½ teaspoon dried thyme, crumbled
- 10 sheets phyllo pastry
- 4 tablespoons melted butter or olive oil

1 Preheat the oven to 350°F. In a medium-size bowl, combine cheese, egg, garlic, salt, pepper, and thyme.

2 Place 1 sheet of phyllo on a clean, damp cloth, and brush lightly with butter. Top with a second phyllo sheet, brush with butter. Repeat 8 more times.

3 Spoon cheese mixture across short end of stacked sheets, leaving 1½- to 2-inch margins. Fold side margins over filling, then roll up jelly-roll fashion, ending with the seam on the bottom.

4 Place strudel on a parchment-lined baking sheet, brush top with remaining melted butter, and bake until lightly browned—about 25 minutes. Slice and serve hot. Makes 8 servings.

CUT, STUFF, FOLD

1 Using a sharp knife and a ruler if you like, cut the stack of 3 butter-brushed phyllo sheets lengthwise into six 1³/₄-inch-wide strips.

2 Cut the sheets in half vertically so that there are 12 half strips. Place ¹/₂ teaspoon of spinach filling at the end of each strip.

3 Fold the end of each strip diagonally over filling to form a triangle. Continue folding diagonally along entire strip, alternating directions (like folding a flag), and ending with a triangle.

Spinach-Feta Triangles

- **1 small yellow onion, finely chopped**
- **4 tablespoons plus 2 teaspoons melted butter or margarine**
- **1 package (10 ounces) frozen chopped spinach, thawed and squeezed dry**
- **1 tablespoon snipped fresh dill or ¹/₄ teaspoon dried dill**
- **¹/₂ cup (2 ounces) crumbled feta cheese**
- **1 egg, lightly beaten**
- **6 sheets frozen phyllo pastry (from a 17¹/₂-ounce package), thawed by package directions**

1 Preheat the oven to 350°F. In a 10-inch skillet over moderate heat, sauté onion in the 2 teaspoons melted butter until translucent—3 to 5 minutes. Add spinach and cook 2 minutes more. Mix in dill. Transfer to a large bowl, mix in cheese, then egg.

2 Lay 1 sheet phyllo pastry on a work surface and brush lightly with some of the remaining melted butter. Top with second phyllo sheet, brush with butter, then top with third sheet, and again brush.

3 Cut, fill, and fold the phyllo sheets as directed in box at left. When each triangle is complete, brush with butter. (If you plan to freeze the triangles at this point, omit the last brushing with butter.)

4 Repeat, using remaining phyllo sheets, butter, and spinach filling to make another 12 triangles.

5 Place triangles on a parchment-lined baking sheet and bake until golden brown—about 25 minutes. Makes 24 triangles.

1 Triangle: Calories 54; Total Fat 4 g; Saturated Fat 2 g; Protein 2 g; Carbohydrates 3 g; Fiber 0 g; Sodium 114 mg; Cholesterol 18 mg

prep time-15 minutes • assembly time-30 minutes cooking time-32 minutes

ANTIPASTO

Marinated vegetables are a delicious appetizer any time of year, but are especially good in summer when you can enjoy vegetables from your garden or buy them fresh at a farm stand.

ROASTING NOTES

Drizzling roasting vegetables with oil helps to keep them moist. A little salt in the roasting mixture draws out the juices and intensifies the flavors. When they are done, roasted vegetables should be limp, but they should still have a bit of crunch. Enjoy them warm or at room temperature, but not refrigerator cold. If possible, marinate roasted vegetables in their dressing for at least 3 hours before you serve them so that the flavors have time to mingle and mellow.

VEGETABLE ROUNDS

If you prefer to roast and serve vegetables that are cut in perfect rounds, slice eggplant, zucchini, plum tomatoes, and red potatoes crosswise into 1/4- to 3/8-inch rounds. Arrange the slices on a lightly oiled baking sheet, brush with oil (preferably a good, fruity olive oil), and bake, uncovered, in a preheated 400°F oven for 10 to 15 minutes. The roasted vegetables should be fork-tender and lightly browned.

COOKING AHEAD

You can roast vegetables the day before you intend to serve them. Cool them thoroughly, cover with plastic wrap, and refrigerate. Be sure to let the vegetables come to room temperature before serving; if they're straight from the fridge they'll seem flavorless.

PEELED PEPPERS

If you want to peel sweet peppers, the quickest way is to roast them. Arrange the peppers on a broiler pan or heavy-duty baking sheet. Set the pan 2 to 3 inches from a preheated broiler and broil 8 to 10 minutes, turning the peppers every few minutes so their skins blacken evenly. Transfer the peppers to a large heat-proof bowl, cover with plastic wrap, and cool until easy to handle—about 10 minutes. The skins will loosen and slip right off the peppers.

Once you've peeled the peppers, halve them lengthwise, remove the cores and seeds, and slice as you wish. The peppers are ready to be eaten or to use in any recipe calling for roasted peppers.

PRETTY PLATTERS

Although marinated roasted vegetables can be slipped into salads or served as an accompaniment to meat, fish, or fowl, they are at their colorful best on an antipasto platter. Go for high drama by contrasting the colors, shapes, and textures of the different vegetables. Arrange them in straight or diagonal stripes on a rectangular tray or in concentric circles on a round one.

CLEANING MUSHROOMS

To clean mushrooms, either rub them with a soft cloth or paper toweling or rinse them under cool running water, then dry on paper toweling.

To stem, cup a mushroom, cap side down, in your palm. Grasp the stem close to the cap and give a gentle twist.

PREPARING NUTS FOR THE STUFFING

To toast pecans or hazelnuts, spread them in an ungreased baking pan and roast, uncovered, at 300°F for 30 to 35 minutes, stirring often.

The quickest way to chop nuts is to pulse them briefly in a food processor. If you have only a few nuts to chop, you might want to do it by hand. Place the nuts in the center of a chopping board. Then, anchoring a chef's knife to the board by pressing your palm down on the top (blunt side) of the blade, move the knife back and forth across the nuts in a gentle rocking motion until the chop is as coarse or as fine as you want. For our mushroom puffs, it should be fairly fine.

HOT STUFFED MUSHROOM PUFFS

Think about roasting the mushroom caps for this recipe while you roast the other vegetables for marinating. You can oven toast the nuts for the stuffing, as directed at left, or skillet toast them. Chop the nuts, then put them in a dry skillet and shake over moderate heat until richly golden—3 to 4 minutes.

Stem 2 pounds button mushrooms and **wipe** clean. **Chop** stems and **set** aside. **Roast** mushroom caps as directed for potatoes in Step 1 of Roasted Marinated Vegetables at right.

Meanwhile, in a 10-inch nonstick skillet, **heat** 1 tablespoon olive oil over moderate heat, **add** 1/2 cup finely chopped red onion and 1 minced clove garlic, and **sauté** for 2 minutes.

Stir in the chopped mushroom stems and **cook** until most of the liquid has evaporated—about 5 minutes more. **Mix** in 1/4 cup finely chopped toasted pecans or hazelnuts, 2 tablespoons each grated Parmesan cheese and chopped parsley, and 1/4 teaspoon each salt and pepper. **Cool** 2 or 3 minutes, then **fold** in 1 beaten egg white.

Spoon mixture into mushroom caps and **bake**, uncovered, at 450°F until puffed and lightly browned—10 to 12 minutes. Makes 6 servings.

Roasted Marinated Vegetables

- 1 pound small new potatoes, quartered
- 3 tablespoons olive oil
- 1 tablespoon chopped fresh rosemary or 1 teaspoon dried rosemary, crumbled
- 1 teaspoon salt
- 1 large sweet red pepper, cored, seeded, and cut into strips 1-inch wide
- 1 large sweet green pepper, cored, seeded, and cut into strips 1-inch wide
- 1 medium-size zucchini, cut into 1-inch slices
- 1 medium-size yellow squash, cut into 1-inch slices
- 2 small red onions, cut into slim wedges
- 8 ounces button mushrooms, stemmed and wiped clean
- 2 cloves garlic, minced

For the marinade:
- 3 tablespoons balsamic vinegar, white wine vinegar, or fresh lemon juice
- 1 tablespoon olive oil
- 1 tablespoon chopped parsley
- 2 teaspoons chopped fresh thyme or 1/4 teaspoon dried thyme, crumbled
- 2 teaspoons Dijon mustard
- 1 small clove garlic, minced
- 1 teaspoon finely grated lemon zest (optional)
- 1/2 teaspoon salt
- 1/4 teaspoon black pepper

1 Preheat the oven to 450°F. In a large shallow pan, toss potatoes with oil, rosemary, and salt. Bake, uncovered, for 15 minutes.

2 Stir in sweet peppers, zucchini, yellow squash, onions, mushrooms, and garlic. Bake, uncovered, stirring frequently, until vegetables are lightly browned and tender—35 to 45 minutes.

3 To prepare the marinade: In a small bowl, whisk together vinegar, oil, parsley, thyme, mustard, garlic, lemon zest (optional), salt, and black pepper until smooth. Pour marinade over vegetables in roasting pan and stir gently but thoroughly to coat. Cool to room temperature. Makes 6 servings.

1 Serving: Calories 178; Total Fat 10 g; Saturated Fat 1 g; Protein 4 g; Carbohydrates 22 g; Fiber 3 g; Sodium 583 mg; Cholesterol 0 mg

prep time-35 minutes
cooking time-60 minutes

Our Roasted Marinated Vegetables and Hot Stuffed Mushroom Puffs, here combined with olives and mozzarella cheese, make a colorful antipasto platter. Roasting vegetables not only softens them but also intensifies their flavor and color.

PUFF PASTRY

*W*orking with puff pastry is a snap now that the dough is available frozen in the supermarket. Roll some out and try our crowd-pleasing Cheese Twists and Niçoise-Stuffed Patty Shells.

ABOUT PUFF PASTRY

Puff pastry is one of the most magical of foods. Rolled out it resembles ordinary piecrust. But put it into a hot oven and it puffs to 6 to 8 times its original size in crisp, lighter-than-air layers. Puff pastry is what chefs use for Napoleons and other fancy French desserts. It's the wrapper that envelops Beef Wellington. And it can be baked into a variety of appetizers like the ones here.

SHORTCUTTING A CLASSIC

Making puff pastry from scratch can, literally, take all day. But no longer is there any need to make it from scratch unless you enjoy the process. Frozen puff pastry can be found in supermarkets in 14- to 17¼-ounce packages. It's available both in bricks of dough and in pre-rolled sheets (two 9½" x 9¼" x ⅛" sheets per package).

Note: Our recipes call for pre-rolled sheets, but you may substitute fresh or frozen puff pastry dough that you roll by hand to the desired size.

For good flavor, buy only puff pastry brands made with real butter. Heed the expiration date on the package; puff pastry becomes stale if improperly stored. Under ideal conditions (0°F), it will keep for 1 year in the freezer.

To thaw, follow package directions. This usually means setting the frozen pastry, still in its original package, in the refrigerator overnight.

PUFF PASTRY TIPS

The cardinal rule for working with puff pastry is to keep the dough cool. If you don't, the butter in the dough will soften, making the pastry unmanageable. Always roll puff pastry in batches, a small amount at a time. Wrap the balance in plastic wrap and refrigerate until ready for use.

Once you have rolled, cut, and shaped puff pastry, arrange on an ungreased baking sheet, cover with wax paper, and chill for at least 40 minutes. This allows the dough to relax, so that it will not shrink or rise unevenly in the oven.

THE CUTTING EDGE

Use a very sharp, thin-bladed knife or pastry wheel to cut rolled puff pastry. Heating the knife or pastry wheel will also ensure good, clean cuts. To keep cuts arrow straight, use a metal-edged ruler.

FOR EVEN RISING

Avoid working with puff pastry on a rainy or humid day. Always apply even pressure on your rolling pin when rolling puff pastry. To roll it into a square, give it a quarter turn each time you roll. To roll it into a circle, give an eighth turn. This same technique works with all doughs.

Don't use rerolled pastry

scraps for patty shells. Cut them from the first rolling. Save and reroll the scraps for cheese twists or other tidbits where being a little lopsided doesn't matter. Or sprinkle the scraps with cinnamon sugar and bake them as a treat for the kids.

Preheat the oven thoroughly—15 to 20 minutes—before baking puff pastry.

COOKING AHEAD

If you want to make twists or patty shells well before you plan to bake them, roll, cut, and shape as directed.

Arrange the shells, not touching, in a single layer on a wax-paper-lined baking sheet and

(continued on page 30)

KITCHEN CHEMISTRY

Puff pastry looks like ordinary dough when it goes in the oven. Why does it rise to stratospheric heights and separate into hundreds of flaky layers when it bakes? The pastry begins as humble flour-and-water dough that is rolled out and wrapped around a large square of butter. Then it is rolled out again, folded triple, and rolled again. The process is repeated 6 times, with the dough's being chilled in the refrigerator for at least half an hour in between each rolling. The repeated triple folding and rolling traps air in the dough and spreads butter between literally hundreds of layers (or folds) of dough. The repeated handling also activates the gluten in the flour, which gives dough its elasticity. Putting the dough in the refrigerator at intervals allows the gluten to rest, so that it doesn't overdevelop and make the dough tough. When placed in a hot oven, the layers of butter melt, separating and crisping the hundreds of layers of dough, and the gluten's elasticity allows it to puff.

Twist Variations

Chili Garlic Twists: Prepare as directed at right, **substituting** for the Parmesan mixture 1 tablespoon chili powder mixed with 1 tablespoon very finely minced garlic. Makes 15 twists.

Curry Twists: Prepare as directed, right, **substituting** for the Parmesan mixture 1 to 2 tablespoons curry powder mixed with 1/2 teaspoon salt. Makes 15 twists.

How to Twist a Cheese Twist

Twist the chilled pastry strips while holding both ends. Lay each strip on the baking sheet, pressing both ends down firmly to anchor them.

Our patty shells, shown here with Parmesan Twists, are filled with a variation of the Niçoise salad made famous in the South of France.

Parmesan Twists

- **1/2 cup grated Parmesan cheese**
- **1/4 teaspoon cayenne**
- **1   sheet (9¹/₂" x 9¹/₄" x ¹/₈") frozen puff pastry, thawed**
- **1   egg yolk blended with 1 tablespoon water (egg wash)**

1 Preheat the oven to 400°F. In a small bowl, combine grated Parmesan and cayenne; set aside.

2 Place pastry on a work surface. Brush lightly with egg wash, then sprinkle with Parmesan mixture and press gently into pastry.

3 With a sharp knife, cut pastry lengthwise into 15 strips, slide onto an ungreased baking sheet, and refrigerate 5 minutes.

4 Using both hands, twist strips; refrigerate 5 minutes more.

5 Transfer to the oven and bake until nicely browned—about 12 to 15 minutes. Makes 15 twists.

1 Twist: Calories 110; Total Fat 8 g; Saturated Fat 2 g; Protein 3 g; Carbohydrates 8 g; Fiber 0 g; Sodium 104 mg; Cholesterol 17 mg

prep time-20 minutes
resting time-10 minutes
cooking time-15 minutes

Niçoise-Stuffed Patty Shells

2 medium-size tomatoes, seeded, and finely chopped

1/2 cup chopped and pitted black olives

2 cloves garlic, minced

4 anchovy fillets, rinsed and finely chopped

1/2 teaspoon dried thyme, crumbled

1 sheet (9½" x 9¼" x ⅛") frozen puff pastry, thawed

1 Preheat the oven to 400°F. In a medium-size bowl, combine all ingredients except puff pastry.

2 Place pastry on a work surface and roll into a rectangle 11 inches long, 10 inches wide, and ⅛-inch thick. Using a 1¾-inch cookie cutter, cut into 30 rounds. Arrange on a parchment-lined baking sheet, spacing about 1½ inches apart, and refrigerate about 10 minutes.

3 Transfer baking sheet to the oven and bake until patty shells are puffed and lightly browned— about 10 minutes.

4 Using the rounded end of a wooden spoon, make a depression in the center of each patty shell, then drop about ½ teaspoon of the tomato mixture into each. Serve at once. Makes 30 mini patty shells.

1 Filled Shell: Calories 29; Total Fat 2 g; Saturated Fat 0 g; Protein 0 g; Carbohydrates 2 g; Fiber 0 g; Sodium 24 mg; Cholesterol 0 mg

prep time-15 minutes • assembly time-10 minutes cooking time-10 minutes

---

(continued from page 28)
set in the freezer. As soon as they freeze, transfer to an airtight plastic container. Use within 3 months.

When ready to bake, do not thaw the cheese twists or patty shells; the puff pastry will become limp if it is thawed. Arrange twists or shells, still frozen, on an ungreased baking sheet and bake as directed, increasing the time slightly if needed.

PATTY SHELL TIPS

To give your patty shells a professional finish, brush the tops (but not the sides) with a simple egg glaze made by

---

COOK'S SECRETS

Sara Moulton, *Executive Chef, Gourmet Magazine*

"Any recipe with Niçoise in its name is sure to include black olives, preferably the tiny olives from Nice in southern France. The fastest way to pit olives? Lay them on a cutting board, whack with the broad side of a chef's knife, and lift out the pits."

beating 1 egg with 1 tablespoon cold water. Take care that the glaze does not dribble down and glue the patty shells to the baking sheet.

The sooner you can fill and serve patty shells the better they will be. If you can't serve them right away, layer the cooled shells between pieces of wax paper and store in an airtight container.

FOR CRISP SHELLS

To reheat and crisp patty shells, preheat the oven to 425°F. Arrange shells on an ungreased baking sheet, set on the middle oven rack, and turn the oven off. Let the patty shells stand in the oven 5 minutes. Then remove. Never fill patty shells until you are ready to serve them.

ALL-PURPOSE PUFF PASTRY SHELLS

For larger patty shells that can be used for main dishes or desserts, look for brick-frozen puff pastry; thaw according to package directions. You'll also need two round cutters, one 3 inches in diameter and the other 2 inches in diameter.

Roll pastry into a 9- by 14-inch rectangle, ¼-inch thick. Using the 3-inch cutter, cut 12 rounds in the pastry. Then, using the smaller cutter, cut centers in 6 of the rounds, to make rings.

Arrange the rounds upside down (this ensures more even rising) on a baking sheet lined with baking parchment. Brush with egg glaze (see Patty Shell Tips).

Brush the tops of the rings with egg glaze and set upside down on the pastry rounds. Brush the rims—but not the sides—of the rings with glaze.

Also place the smaller rounds (the centers of the rings) upside down on the baking sheet and brush the tops with glaze. These will serve as lids. Let patty shells and lids stand at room temperature 30 minutes.

Meanwhile, preheat the oven to 400°F. Bake the shells and lids in the lower third of the oven until puffed and golden—about 20 minutes.

Remove from the oven and if there are doughy parts on the bottom of the shells, gently pull out and discard.

Fill the patty shells while hot with creamed or curried meat, fish, or poultry. Or, to serve for dessert, cool to room temperature and fill with ice cream, custard, and/or sliced sweetened peaches, strawberries, or other fruit. Makes 6 patty shells and 6 lids.

HEARTY SOUPS AND STEWS

BEEF STOCK

Once you've tried our homemade stock, you'll never want to revert to the canned or bouillon-cube variety. Make a big batch and freeze the rest.

FOR THE BEST TASTE

Use mature vegetables; they add more flavor to a stock than young ones. Leave the skins on the onions and carrots; they add color and flavor.

Avoid lamb or ham bones; their flavor is too distinct for a general purpose stock. Freeze them for specific stocks.

Go easy on the salt and pepper. The flavors will concentrate as the stock simmers.

BONES FOR FLAVOR AND BODY

Full-flavored meat stocks (or broths) are made with a balanced mix of meat and bones. Dark meat—and the meat that clings to the bones themselves—have the most flavor.

Marrow bones (shins or shanks) add body and flavor because they contain not only the buttery marrow but also sinew, which converts to gelatin. Too many shanks will make a stock congeal. Crack the bones before roasting.

FOR CLEAR STOCK

Avoid adding potatoes and other starchy vegetables; they will make the stock cloudy.

Trim obvious fat and greasy skin from meat before adding it to the stockpot.

Never allow the stock to boil; keep it at a steady simmer. Boiling will break up any fat and make the broth cloudy. To prevent the stock from boiling, keep the lid slightly ajar.

As stock heats, a foamy scum forms on the surface. Skim off the foam with a mesh skimmer during the first 1/2 hour of cooking. Then wipe the inside of the pot clean, down to the level of liquid.

When the stock is done, strain it into a bowl through a fine-meshed strainer or through two layers of wet cheesecloth.

Let the stock cool thoroughly before refrigerating.

FOR A RICHER STOCK

Place strained broth in a large, clean saucepan and simmer—do not boil—uncovered 30 to 45 minutes to reduce slightly and concentrate the flavors.

BROWNED BEEF STOCK

4 pounds beef shin bones	2 stalks celery with leaves, cut into 2-inch chunks
2 large yellow onions, cut into slim wedges	
3 medium-size carrots, scrubbed and cut into 2-inch chunks	4 quarts water
	4 cloves garlic, bruised
	6 sprigs parsley
1 medium-size white turnip, scrubbed and quartered	8 black peppercorns
	2 sprigs fresh thyme or 1/2 teaspoon dried thyme, crumbled
1 parsnip, scrubbed and cut into 2-inch chunks	

1 Preheat the oven to 450°F. Place the beef bones in a large shallow pan and roast, turning occasionally, until they begin to brown—about 30 minutes. Stir in the onions, carrots, turnip, parsnip, and celery and roast for another 30 minutes or until the bones are well browned.

2 With a slotted spoon, transfer browned bones and vegetables to an 8-quart stockpot and add 3 1/2 quarts of the water and all remaining ingredients. Drain excess fat from the roasting pan. Pour the remaining 2 cups of water into the roasting pan, stirring to loosen the browned bits.

3 Add to the bones and vegetables in the stockpot and bring to a boil over high heat, skimming off any foam. Reduce the heat to moderately low and simmer, uncovered, for about 3 hours, skimming occasionally if necessary.

4 Strain the broth, discarding beef bones and vegetables. Set aside to cool. When broth has cooled, cover and refrigerate until cold. Spoon or scrape any fat from the surface. Use refrigerated stock within 3 days or freeze and use within 3 months. Makes 2 quarts.

CANNED BROTH TIPS

It's easy to perk up the flavor of canned beef broth. Pour a 14-ounce can of broth into a large saucepan. Add about 1/4 cup of chopped onion, 1/4 cup of chopped carrot, 2 tablespoons of chopped celery, and 2 sprigs of parsley. Simmer the broth over medium heat, stirring occasionally, for about 1/2 hour. Strain and use as you would fresh stock.

COOKING AHEAD

For convenience, freeze stock in 1/2-pint freezer containers, leaving 1/2-inch head room. Snap on the lids, label, date, and set in a 0°F freezer. The frozen stock will keep fresh tasting about 3 months and will be ready to thaw whenever you need to add a little of it to a recipe.

If you have the space, freeze bones and leftover meat, and toss them in the pot when you're ready to make a stock—no need to thaw.

Bacon, Lettuce, and Tomato Soup

- 4 slices bacon
- 2 medium-size carrots, peeled and chopped
- 1 large yellow onion, chopped
- 1 stalk celery, chopped
- 1 large clove garlic, minced
- 1 can (28 ounces) whole, tomatoes with their juice
- 3 cups Browned Beef Stock or canned reduced-sodium beef broth
- 2 tablespoons chopped fresh basil or 2 teaspoons dried
- One 1- by ½-inch strip orange zest
- 1 teaspoon salt
- ½ teaspoon sugar
- ¼ teaspoon black pepper
- 4 cups shredded romaine lettuce

1 With sharp kitchen scissors and with bacon slices stacked, cut bacon crosswise into ¼-inch strips.

2 In a 4-quart saucepan over moderately high heat, cook bacon until crisp—about 4 to 5 minutes. Transfer bacon to paper toweling to drain.

3 Add carrots, onion, celery, and garlic to bacon drippings in pan. Sauté over moderate heat until tender—7 to 8 minutes. Stir in tomatoes and their juice, stock, basil, zest, salt, sugar, and pepper. Bring to a boil, reduce heat to moderately low, and simmer, covered, 25 to 30 minutes. Set aside to cool.

4 Working in batches, purée the mixture in a blender at high speed or in a food processor until smooth—about 1 minute. Return soup to the saucepan and cook over moderate heat until heated through—about 5 minutes. Stir in shredded lettuce and cook until wilted—about 1 minute more. Ladle soup into bowls and garnish with reserved bacon. Makes 6 servings.

1 Serving: Calories 137; Total Fat 7 g; Saturated Fat 2 g; Protein 8 g; Carbohydrates 12 g; Fiber 3 g; Sodium 808 mg; Cholesterol 11 mg

prep time-20 minutes
cooking time-40 minutes

BEEF STEW

Could there be a more satisfying dish on a chilly night than a bowl of beef stew with a spicy biscuit topping? The secrets to great taste in a stew are slow, even cooking and the right cuts of beef.

CHILI BISCUIT TOPPING

2 cups all-purpose flour	1/3 cup vegetable shortening
3 teaspoons baking powder	2 tablespoons butter or margarine
2 teaspoons chili powder	1 cup coarsely shredded sharp Cheddar cheese
1/2 teaspoon baking soda	3/4 cup buttermilk
1/2 teaspoon salt	

1 In a large bowl, combine flour, baking powder, chili powder, baking soda, and salt. Using a pastry blender, cut in the shortening and butter until mixture resembles coarse crumbs. Fork in the cheese, then the buttermilk, and continue mixing with a fork until a soft dough forms. On a lightly floured surface, pat dough into a circle 3/4-inch thick, then cut into 6 rounds with a floured 3-inch biscuit cutter.

2 Space biscuits evenly on top of actively bubbling stew, return to the oven, and bake, uncovered, until the biscuits are golden brown—about 12 to 15 minutes.

ABOUT BEEF STEW

A good stew takes a little time but doesn't require a lot of expertise. If you can, prepare beef stew at least a few hours before you plan to serve it. The flavor improves when the stew has had time to sit.

BEEF FOR STEW

The best cuts for stew are some of the most flavorful but also the toughest cuts of beef since they come from muscular parts of the body. The sinew converts to gelatin with slow, moist cooking. Choose short ribs—cut from the tips of ribs near the foreshank— or chuck pot roast—cut from the shoulder.

FOR PERFECT BROWNING

Browning the meat enhances its flavor and the overall flavor of the stew. It also helps to seal juices in the meat.

Use a heavy Dutch oven for even distribution of heat.

Pat meat dry with paper toweling before browning it. Wet meat will not brown properly.

DREDGING

Not all stew recipes call for dredging the meat in flour. However, a thin coating of flour on the meat helps to thicken a stew. Browning the flour on the meat takes away the raw flour taste.

The easiest way to dredge small pieces of meat evenly is to put the meat in a plastic bag along with 1/4 cup of flour and shake the bag. You'll be able to see when the meat is fully coated. When you remove the meat from the bag, tap each piece lightly to remove excess flour.

DEGREASING A STEW

The surefire way to remove fat from a stew is to let the stew cool to room temperature and then refrigerate. Fat will solidify on the surface of the stew and can easily be lifted off with a spatula or serving spoon.

SERVE IT UP

A hearty stew should be served with some kind of starch that lets you enjoy every last spoonful.

Hot baking powder biscuits are sensational with stew. As a new twist on an old favorite, try our Chili Biscuit Topping.

Or mix up a batch of Dropped Dumplings (page 41) and simmer them in the stew.

Boiled new potatoes, either cooked in the broth or cooked separately and served on the side, are a traditional accompaniment to stew.

For a change of pace, serve stew the French way—over a mound of mashed potatoes.

Stew is also delicious served on a bed of fluffy rice or flat egg noodles.

SKIM THE FAT

If you don't have time to chill a stew or stock before skimming off the fat, try this quick and easy method.

Half fill a heavy plastic bag with ice cubes, seal, and set in the freezer. When the stew has cooled, drag the bag across the surface and then lift it out. The fat will harden on the ice-cold bag. Rinse and repeat until all the fat has been removed.

Beef Short Rib Stew with Chili Biscuit Topping

- **3** pounds lean beef short ribs
- **1/4** cup unsifted all-purpose flour
- **3** tablespoons vegetable oil
- **4** medium-size carrots, peeled and cut into 1/2-inch rounds
- **1** large yellow onion, chopped
- **1** clove garlic, minced
- **4** cups Browned Beef Stock or canned reduced-sodium broth
- **1** can (16 ounces) Italian plum tomatoes with their juice
- **1/2** teaspoon salt
- **1/2** teaspoon dried thyme, crumbled
- **1/4** teaspoon black pepper
- **1** cup pearl onions
- **Chili Biscuit Topping (left)**
- **1/4** cup chopped parsley

1 Preheat the oven to 350°F. In a large self-sealing plastic bag, dredge beef ribs in batches in the flour. Set aside.

2 In a 6-quart Dutch oven, heat 1 tablespoon of the oil over moderately high heat 1 minute. Add carrots, onion, and garlic and sauté until onion is limp—about 5 minutes. Transfer vegetables to a small bowl and reserve.

3 Heat the remaining 2 tablespoons of oil in the Dutch oven over moderately high heat 2 minutes, add dredged ribs (in batches if necessary), and sauté, turning frequently, until nicely browned—about 5 minutes.

4 Add stock, tomatoes and their juice, salt, thyme, and pepper. Bring to a boil over high heat, cover, transfer to the oven, and bake until meat is almost tender—1½ to 2 hours.

5 Stir in the reserved vegetables and pearl onions, recover, and bake until meat is fork-tender—30 to 40 minutes. Prepare Chili Biscuit Topping.

6 Remove stew from oven and increase the oven temperature to 450°F. Skim fat from stew.

7 Top stew with Chili Biscuit Topping and bake as directed at left. Sprinkle stew and biscuit topping with parsley and serve. Makes 6 servings.

1 Serving: Calories 720; Total Fat 40 g; Saturated Fat 15 g; Protein 32 g; Carbohydrates 59 g; Fiber 5 g; Sodium 1195 mg; Cholesterol 93 mg

prep time-35 minutes
cooking time-3 hours

ONION SOUP

The only work involved in making onion soup is slicing the onions and grating the cheese. We offer two delicious versions here: one a time-honored classic; the other a new twist that blends the flavors of eight kinds of onions.

FOR THE BEST FLAVOR

The onions of choice are yellow onions, which have a full, strong flavor that holds up well to cooking in broth.

One secret for great taste in onion soup is slow cooking. If you have the time, let the onions sauté slowly, then let them simmer slowly in the soup broth.

Add extra flavor and color to the soup by caramelizing the onions. First, sauté the onions over low heat until they are soft. Then increase the heat to moderate and add 1/2 teaspoon of sugar. Cook, stirring occasionally, for 10 to 15 minutes until the onions turn a rich golden brown. You will not taste the sugar in the soup; it simply helps the onions to brown.

SLICING ONIONS

Slice onions with a sharp stainless steel knife (onion juice will turn carbon steel knife blades black), a slaw cutter, or with the slicing blade in a food processor.

If you are prone to onion tears, slicing onions in the food processor helps, since the lid stays on while the onions are being sliced.

There really is no foolproof way to prevent tears. It helps to slice with a very sharp knife since it is less apt to spritz juice. Work at a comfortable arm's length. And if all else fails, try slicing onions under running water; it rinses the juices downward instead of letting them spurt upward.

SUBSTITUTE BROTH

You can make onion soup with a rich chicken broth instead of beef broth as they do in Burgundy, France. Use the chicken broth by itself or add a little dry white wine.

TOPPING AND SERVING

Onion soup is often baked in individual bowls, but you can also bake the soup and bring it to the table in a single oven-proof tureen. For the crust in a 3-quart tureen, cut 12 to 16 slices of French bread, place them on the soup, letting the pieces overlap slightly. Then top with grated cheese.

When cutting puff pastry tops for individual bowls of soup, be sure to cut each top a little larger than the opening so that it can be crimped to the rim. Otherwise, it will float on top of the soup. For more about puff pastry, see page 28.

WASHING LEEKS

Sandy soil invariably lurks inside the leaves of leeks. To wash it away, slice the leek to within an inch of the root. Spread the leaves apart, and rinse thoroughly in cold water.

Eight Onion Flavors

Chives have a fragrant and mildly garlicky flavor. Use tops only, as fresh as possible.
Garlic has the most pungent flavor of all the onions. Buy plump, firm, heavy bulbs tinged with purple.
Leeks have a mild and elegant flavor. Use the bulb and soft, lower part of leaves, as fresh as possible.
Pearl onions and the slightly larger (and easier to peel) silverskins are pungent minis.

Red onions are the Italian cook's favorite. They have a sweet, strong flavor and can be enjoyed raw in salads.
Scallions, or green onions, are sweet and sharp. Use both the tops and bulb—fresh from the garden if possible.
Shallots have a complex flavor milder than garlic and sweeter than onion. Buy firm bulbs.
Yellow onions are juicy and the strongest flavored of all the dry onions.

WORK SAVER
Rotary Grater

If grating cheese is an unpleasant chore, try a rotary grater. A small bin on top holds the cheese, keeping your knuckles and fingertips safe as the cheese grates on a cylinder that turns with a handle. Choose from three cylinders: one that grates fine, one medium, and one that makes thin sheets or slices. The parts can be disassembled, making them easy to clean.

EIGHT-ONION SOUP WITH A PUFF PASTRY HAT

Prepare soup as directed through Step 1 at right, reducing the sugar to 1 tablespoon and adding 2 thinly sliced washed leeks, 2 thinly sliced shallots, 5 crushed cloves garlic, 20 peeled pearl onions, and 1 thinly sliced red onion.

1 Cook, uncovered, over moderately high heat for 15 minutes. Reduce the heat to moderately low and cook, stirring occasionally, until onions are golden—about 15 minutes more.

2 Add 8 thinly sliced scallions and 7 cups beef stock and simmer, uncovered, for 1 hour. Meanwhile, on a lightly floured work surface, spread two 9½" x 9¼" x ⅛" sheets frozen puff pastry that have been thawed in the refrigerator, and cut into 8 rounds slightly larger than diameter of soup bowls.

3 Divide soup among 8 ovenproof soup bowls or ramekins and sprinkle each portion with 1 tablespoon freshly snipped chives.

4 Fit pastry on top of the soup bowls, crimping edges to seal, and bake, uncovered, until puffed and golden—about 20 minutes. Makes 8 servings.

Eight-Onion Soup with a Puff Pastry Hat, left, and Classic Onion Soup

Classic Onion Soup

- 2   **tablespoons butter or margarine**
- 5   **medium-size yellow onions, thinly sliced**
- 2   **tablespoons sugar**
- 3½   **cups Browned Beef Stock or canned reduced-sodium beef broth**
- 5   **cups water**
- ¼   **cup brandy (optional)**
- ½   **teaspoon salt**
- ½   **teaspoon black pepper**
- Four   **½-inch-thick slices French bread, toasted**
- 4   **tablespoons (2 ounces) grated Gruyère cheese**

1 Preheat the oven to 400°F. In a 5-quart Dutch oven over moderately high heat, melt the butter. Add onions and sugar and sauté over high heat until onions are lightly golden—about 10 minutes. Reduce the heat to moderately low and sauté 10 more minutes, stirring occasionally.

2 Add stock and water and bring to a boil over high heat. Reduce the heat to moderately low and simmer, uncovered, for 20 minutes. Add brandy (optional), salt, and pepper and return to a boil over high heat.

3 Ladle soup into four 8-ounce ovenproof ramekins or soup bowls and place on a heavy-duty baking sheet or ovenproof metal tray. Top each portion with toasted French bread and sprinkle with 1 tablespoon cheese.

4 Bake, uncovered, until grated cheese is melted—about 5 minutes. Makes 4 servings.

1 Serving: Calories 316; Total Fat 12 g; Saturated Fat 7 g; Protein 11 g; Carbohydrates 45 g; Fiber 3g; Sodium 619 mg; Cholesterol 39 mg

prep time-20 minutes
cooking time-55 minutes

CHICKEN STOCK

Fresh chicken stock is the basis for the two lemon-scented chicken soups shown here. One of the soups is made with a clear broth; the other with a broth that is thickened with egg.

TASTE AND COLOR

Bones and meat from leftover cooked chicken are fine in a stock but will not give as much flavor as fresh chicken.

Disjoint the chicken before putting it in the pot, and cut large pieces into two or three smaller ones so that the bone marrow can enrich the stock.

If you make stock using a whole chicken, select as old a hen as you can find. The older the bird, the better the flavor.

For a more intense color and flavor, brown the vegetables in the oven at the same time that you brown the chicken parts.

COOKING AHEAD

Use a large plastic freezer container with a tight-fitting lid to create a chicken-for-stock cache in the freezer. Bag chicken parts and trimmings as you collect them and add them to the container. When you have collected 4 pounds' worth of chicken parts, it's time to make stock.

GOOD CLEAR BROTH

To ensure clear stock, remove the gray scum—residue from blood vessels and bone surfaces—that initially rises to the surface. During the first half hour of cooking, skim the surface of the stock several times with a mesh skimmer.

Keep the pot only partially covered while the stock simmers and never let it boil.

Strain the stock carefully through wet cheesecloth when it's done.

DEGREASING

Cool the fresh broth thoroughly after it has been strained, and then refrigerate. When the fat solidifies on the surface, lift it off with a serving spoon or spatula.

CONVENIENT CUBES

Many recipes require just a small amount of chicken broth. Freeze fresh broth or the remains of a partially used can of broth in ice cube trays. Store the broth cubes in a heavy plastic bag. Whenever you need a small amount of broth, thaw a couple of cubes.

CANNED BROTHS

Choose a low-sodium variety of canned broth. It's not only healthier for you, but it will also make your soup or casserole tastier and less salty.

To intensify the flavor of a broth, add 1 chicken bouillon cube for each quart of liquid.

To degrease canned broth, chill the can for an hour or so before using, so that the fat solidifies on the surface.

GREEK EGG AND LEMON SOUP

In a 4-quart saucepan, **sauté** 1 finely chopped yellow onion in 1 tablespoon olive oil over moderate heat 3 to 4 minutes. **Add** 2 quarts chicken stock and **simmer**, covered, over moderate heat 20 minutes. **Cool** slightly, then **whisk** 1 cup stock into 2 well-beaten eggs along with 1/3 cup fresh lemon juice and 1 1/2 teaspoons salt. **Stir** back into soup and bring just to serving temperature; do not boil or soup may curdle. **Mix** in 1/4 cup snipped fresh dill. **Serve** garnished with dill sprigs or lemon slices. Makes 6 servings.

HOW TO ADD EGG TO HOT STOCK

Eggs added too quickly to a hot soup will curdle instead of thickening the broth. To avoid curdling, the eggs must first be tempered by mixing in a little warm broth, then the egg mixture may be safely stirred into the soup.

RICH CHICKEN STOCK

- 4 pounds chicken wings, necks, backs
- 4 quarts water
- 2 medium-size yellow onions, quartered
- 3 stalks celery with leaves, cut into 2-inch chunks
- 2 medium-size carrots, scrubbed and cut into 2-inch chunks
- 4 cloves garlic, minced
- 10 sprigs parsley
- 4 sprigs fresh thyme or 1 teaspoon dried thyme
- 2 whole bay leaves
- 12 black peppercorns
- 4 whole cloves

1 Preheat the oven to 450°F. Arrange chicken pieces in a large shallow pan and roast, turning occasionally, until browned—40 to 45 minutes.

2 With a slotted spoon, transfer chicken parts to an 8-quart stockpot. Add 3½ quarts of the water and all remaining ingredients. Pour the remaining 2 cups of water into the roasting pan, stirring to loosen the browned bits.

3 Transfer to the stockpot and bring to a boil over high heat, skimming off any foam. Reduce the heat to moderately low and simmer, uncovered, for about 2 hours, skimming the surface occasionally if necessary.

4 Strain the broth, discarding bones, vegetables, and bay leaves. When broth has cooled, cover and refrigerate until cold. Spoon or scrape fat from the surface. Use refrigerated stock within 3 days or freeze and use within 3 months. Makes 2 quarts.

Chicken Soup with Rice, Mint, and Lemon

- 2 quarts Rich Chicken Stock or canned reduced-sodium chicken broth
- 1 whole chicken breast
- 1 large yellow onion, coarsely chopped
- Four 2- by ½-inch strips lemon zest
- 3 sprigs fresh mint
- 2 sprigs parsley
- 1 sprig fresh thyme or ¼ teaspoon dried thyme, crumbled
- 1 clove garlic, minced
- 4 black peppercorns, crushed
- 1 cup cooked long-grain rice
- 1 to 2 teaspoons lemon juice
- 1 teaspoon salt
- ¼ cup chopped fresh mint
- Optional garnishes:
  lemon slices
  mint sprigs

1 In a 4-quart saucepan over high heat, bring stock, chicken breast, onion, zest, mint, parsley, thyme, garlic, and peppercorns to a boil. Reduce the heat to low and simmer, covered, until chicken is tender—30 to 35 minutes.

2 With a slotted spoon, transfer chicken breast to a cutting board to cool. Strain soup into a large heatproof bowl, discarding all solids.

3 Return soup to the pan, set over high heat, and boil, uncovered, until the soup has reduced slightly— about 10 minutes.

4 Meanwhile, shred the chicken. Add to soup along with rice, lemon juice, salt, and chopped mint. Heat

about 2 minutes more, ladle into soup bowls, and garnish with lemon slices and mint if desired. Makes 4 servings.

1 Serving: Calories 237; Total Fat 4 g; Saturated Fat 1 g; Protein 21 g; Carbohydrates 29 g; Fiber 1 g; Sodium 641 mg; Cholesterol 60 mg

prep time-20 minutes
cooking time-50 minutes

DUMPLINGS

Dumplings are a satisfying addition to many soups and stews. Here's how to make them so they melt in your mouth.

TENDER DUMPLINGS

To ensure a light texture, follow the recipe and measure carefully. A little too much flour or liquid will result in tough or heavy dumplings.

Combine the ingredients only until they just hold together. Don't overmix the dough.

The broth should be kept at a tremble—just below boiling—while the dumplings cook. Never boil the dumplings.

If the broth needs last-minute thickening, remove the dumplings before stirring in a little cornstarch or flour paste.

ARE THEY DONE YET?

The only foolproof way to tell when dumplings are done is to break one open. Dumplings are ready to eat when they are cooked through, with no doughy part remaining inside.

The stiffer the dough, the longer the cooking time. The hotter the cooking liquid, the shorter the cooking time.

TASTIER DUMPLINGS

To punch up the flavor of dumplings, mix a little seasoning into the dry ingredients. Try one of the following: minced fresh chives, parsley,

sage, thyme, dill, or rosemary; caraway seeds; minced yellow onion; grated Cheddar or Parmesan cheese; crumbled bacon; or a touch of saffron, curry powder, chili powder, or cayenne pepper.

DUMPLING SHORTCUT

In a hurry? Make quick dumplings from canned refrigerated biscuits. Just separate the biscuits and place on top of a simmering stew, cover, and cook about 15 minutes.

CHOOSING A CHICKEN

Old-fashioned chicken and dumplings was made with a hen whose laying days were over but whose flavor was at its fullest. Stewing hens are hard to find today, so for an updated chicken and dumplings, choose a meaty 5- to 6-pound roaster.

COOK'S SECRETS

Jean Anderson,
Award-Winning Cookbook Author

"You need a light touch for light dumplings: A heavy hand guarantees heavy ones. When mixing up a batch, sift the flour before you measure it, then sift it again with the baking powder and salt. Also, be sure your shortening is ice cold so that it remains solid after cutting in. It's these little 'chips' of shortening that give dumplings their flaky consistency. When cooking dumplings, space them evenly on the stew, leaving an inch or more between them. They spread as they cook and will become a solid mass unless steam can circulate around them."

ROLLED DUMPLINGS

Dumplings come in many different varieties. A favorite in some households is the flat, noodlelike rolled dumpling.

- 1/3 cup vegetable shortening
- 1 1/3 cups very hot water
- 1 egg, lightly beaten
- 1 teaspoon salt
- 3 1/4 cups all-purpose flour

1 In a large bowl, melt shortening in the water. Let cool until warm. Mix in egg and salt. Sift 3 cups flour into egg mixture, then stir until just mixed.

2 Dust a pastry board with some remaining flour. Knead dough lightly for 1 to 2 minutes. Flour a rolling pin and roll dough 1/8-inch thick. Cut into 2-inch squares.

3 Slide dumplings into simmering stock, cover, and cook 10 minutes.

KITCHEN CHEMISTRY

The secret to light dumplings is steam, which fluffs dumplings by expanding the starch granules in the flour. If you lift the lid and let the steam out of the pot while the dumplings cook, they will fall. So remember, no peeking.

WORK SAVER
Skimmer

The long-handled flat mesh strainer known as a skimmer is a handy tool for cooking dumplings. Use it for scooping dumplings out of simmering broth without shattering their fragile surfaces. When working with any soup broth, use the skimmer for keeping the surface clear of fat and cooking scum.

DROPPED DUMPLINGS

- 1½ cups sifted all-purpose flour
- 3 teaspoons baking powder
- ½ teaspoon salt
- ¼ cup vegetable shortening
- ½ to ⅔ cup ice water

1 Combine flour, baking powder, and salt in a bowl. Cut in shortening until crumbly. Using a fork, mix in just enough water to make a soft, biscuitlike dough. Do not overmix or dumplings will be tough.

2 Drop dumplings by the rounded tablespoon onto gently bubbling stew, spacing as evenly as possible. Cover and simmer. Cook 15 minutes without lifting the lid. Dumplings should be cooked through with no doughy part inside.

Chicken and Dumplings

- One 5-pound chicken
- 8 cups fresh or low-sodium canned chicken broth
- 3 cups chopped celery
- 3 cups chopped yellow onions
- 1 cup peeled carrots, thinly sliced
- 1 teaspoon celery seed
- ½ teaspoon salt
- 1½ teaspoons poultry seasoning
- ½ teaspoon ground white pepper
- ⅛ teaspoon saffron threads, crushed
- 1 cup whole milk
- ½ cup sifted all-purpose flour
- 1 recipe Dropped Dumplings
- 2 tablespoons minced parsley

1 Wash chicken and remove giblets. Put chicken and giblets in a large stockpot. Add broth and 2 cups each of celery and onions. Bring to a boil over high heat, cover, and reduce the heat to moderately low. Let simmer 45 minutes or until chicken is tender. Remove chicken and set aside on a plate. When cool enough to handle, remove meat from bones, discarding skin. Cut meat into bite-size pieces.

2 Strain the broth, skimming fat and discarding vegetables and giblets. Pour 6 cups broth into the pot. Add remaining celery and onions, carrots, celery seed, salt, poultry seasoning, white pepper, and saffron. Bring to a full boil.

3 Cover, reduce the heat, and cook 30 minutes or until vegetables are tender. Taste for seasoning.

4 In a bowl, whisk together milk and flour. Add to stock, bring to a boil, and cook, stirring, 3 to 5 minutes until thickened. Return chicken to pot.

5 Meanwhile, prepare dumplings. Drop them by the spoonful into simmering stock. Cook as directed.

6 Serve in large bowls and garnish with minced parsley. Makes 6 generous servings.

1 Serving: Calories 672; Total Fat 25 g; Saturated Fat 7 g; Protein 66 g; Carbohydrates 42 g; Fiber 3 g; Sodium 1355 mg; Cholesterol 170 mg

prep time-35 minutes • cooking time-1½ hours

GUMBO

Gumbo is derived from an Angolan word for okra—one of the ingredients that most gumbos have in common.

ABOUT GUMBO

Call it a soup or call it a stew, gumbo is part of the repertoire of Creole and Cajun cuisine native to Louisiana. A flavorful gumbo can be made with whatever land or seafood is tasty and in season.

THICKENING WITH OKRA

What makes gumbo distinct from all other soups and stews is the peculiarly thick quality of the broth. In large part the thickness comes from the juice and pulp of chopped or sliced okra. In some recipes the ratio is 1 quart of okra to 2 quarts of broth.

For an old-fashioned gumbo base guaranteed to thicken just about anything, traditionalist cooks start a gumbo by sautéing plenty of sliced onions in a Dutch oven. Then they add chopped okra and cook it, stirring for 40 to 50 minutes, until the okra becomes "ropy," or reduced to a sticky pulp. It is then ready to be mixed with broth and other gumbo ingredients.

You can also freeze the okra base at this point. Let it cool thoroughly, then spoon into cup or quart containers, cover, and freeze. When you're ready to make a pot of gumbo, thaw some base and stir it in.

FILÉ ALERT

Until recently, Creole cooks also thickened their gumbos by swirling in a spoonful or two of moistened filé powder before serving. Although it is a good thickener, filé—the powdered, aromatic leaves of the sassafras tree—is now believed to be a carcinogen and should not be used.

Okra, however, is an equally powerful thickener, and cooks who pride themselves on their gumbos never use filé powder *and* okra in the same recipe. They choose one.

BUYING OKRA

For many people north, east, and west of the deep South, okra is a vegetable rarely encountered outside of a bowl of gumbo. Okra's green pods have a delicate flavor somewhere between that of eggplant and asparagus. Inside are edible seeds surrounded by a clear, gluey juice that is okra's magical ingredient for thickening gumbo.

Buy okra that is firm and bright green with no yellow spots. Look for pods that are between 2 and 4 inches long: Larger pods are apt to be woody and juiceless.

Frozen okra is available everywhere. It is fine to use for making gumbo if fresh okra is not available.

GUMBO Z'HERBES

There are as many versions of Gumbo z'Herbes as there are people who make it. The second part of the name (pronounced *zairb*) comes from the French *des herbes*, meaning "from herbs" or greens.

Gumbo z'Herbes is a dish that is more likely to be served in someone's home than in a restaurant. Our version, which is traditional, includes both beef brisket and ham. However, some cooks make Gumbo z'Herbes as a vegetarian Lenten dish and with as many as 13 different greens to represent those present at the Last Supper (or so it is said). Other cooks prepare it as a delicious spring tonic and include 7 kinds of greens for good luck.

However much the lists of called-for greens may vary from one version of the recipe to another, cabbage, spinach, and watercress are virtually always present.

HOW TO SEED A PEPPER ZIP QUICK

Lay the pepper on its side and, using a sharp utility knife, slice off a small portion of the bottom. Stand the pepper upright and slice down. Repeat 3 times, turning the pepper a quarter turn each time. You'll be left with 4 large clean slices of pepper—the seeds will remain attached to the core.

SERVING IDEAS

Gumbo is generally served in soup bowls over a small mound of boiled rice and with a green salad and crusty bread on the side.

WORK SAVER

Tasting Spoon

A tasting spoon is designed to let you sample hot soup. It has a medium-size bowl for stirring at one end and a small bowl for tasting at the other. The two bowls are connected by a channel in the handle. To taste, dip up a small amount of broth with the stirring end, tilt the handle so the soup runs into the small bowl (cooling as it goes), and taste. Tasting spoons are available in wood and porcelain.

Gumbo z'Herbes

- 1/4 cup olive oil
- 1 pound beef brisket or chuck steak, cut into 1/2-inch chunks
- 6 ounces baked ham, cut into 1/2-inch chunks
- 1 large yellow onion, finely chopped
- 6 scallions, including tops, thinly sliced
- 1 large sweet red pepper, cored, seeded, and diced
- 3 tablespoons all-purpose flour
- 1 cup thinly sliced fresh okra or 1/2 package (10 ounces) frozen
- 4 cups Rich Chicken Stock or canned reduced-sodium chicken broth
- 8 ounces cabbage, cored

and cut into 1/2-inch chunks
- 4 cups thinly sliced mustard greens
- 3 cups thinly sliced turnip greens
- 1/2 teaspoon salt
- 1/4 teaspoon black pepper
- 1 whole bay leaf
- 1/2 teaspoon each dried thyme and marjoram, crumbled
- 4 allspice berries
- 2 whole cloves
- 1/8 teaspoon cayenne
- 6 cups trimmed, washed, and coarsely chopped spinach
- 1 bunch watercress, tough stems removed and leaves coarsely chopped

1 In an 8-quart Dutch oven over moderate heat, heat the oil about 2 minutes. Add brisket and ham and cook, stirring frequently, until lightly browned—about 5 minutes. Transfer to a bowl and set aside.

2 Add onion and scallions and cook, stirring frequently, until softened—about 5 minutes. Add sweet red pepper and cook, stirring frequently, until crisp-tender—about 4 minutes. Stir in flour until well coated. Add okra and cook, stirring constantly, until well combined. Gradually add stock, stirring until well combined.

3 Add cabbage, mustard greens, turnip greens, salt, black pepper, bay leaf, thyme, marjoram, allspice, cloves, cayenne, and reserved meats. Bring to a boil, reduce the heat to moderately low, cover, and simmer, stirring occasionally, until the gumbo is thickened and the beef is tender—about 1½ hours.

4 Add spinach and watercress, cover, and cook until tender—about 15 minutes more. Remove and discard bay leaf. Makes 4 servings.

1 Serving: Calories 627; Total Fat 42 g; Saturated Fat 13 g; Protein 40 g; Carbohydrates 27 g; Fiber 8 g; Sodium 1285 mg; Cholesterol 114 mg

prep time-25 minutes
cooking time-2 hours

VEGETABLE BROTH

Broths prepared from vegetables cost almost nothing to make, take a fraction of the time of meat stocks, and provide a healthy and flavorsome base for soups and stews.

FOR THE BEST FLAVOR

Roast the vegetables at a fairly high temperature before they go into the pot. This will enrich their flavor and color.

If you don't want to take the time to roast the vegetables before you simmer them, you can brown them in a little oil in a skillet on top of the stove in minutes.

When the vegetables have finished roasting or sautéing, scrape the brown bits from the bottom of the pan and add them to the pot with the vegetables and water.

Use cold water to start the broth; it will draw out the flavorful juices of vegetables as it heats up.

Simmer the broth until the vegetables have given up all of their color and flavor. About 1 hour should be enough. Many vegetables become bitter if cooked too long.

Strain the broth immediately when it has finished simmering. Discard the broth vegetables and start with fresh vegetables for the soup.

For a richer flavor, boil the

strained vegetable broth, uncovered, 15 to 20 minutes to reduce slightly.

WHAT TO USE

A trio of vegetables—onions, celery, and carrots—is basic to all broths and stocks, vegetarian or otherwise. After the basic three, the combinations are up to you.

Vary your vegetable stocks to suit whatever kind of soup or stew you plan to make with them: light-bodied stocks for summer soups; richer, darker stocks for hearty stews.

Strong-flavored vegetables such as asparagus and Brussels sprouts will overpower a general purpose broth. Use them only in broth for soups containing asparagus or Brussels sprouts.

VEGETABLES FOR BROTH

Vegetable broths are ideal for using up all the odds and ends of vegetables that don't get used in main dishes. The trimmings and parings can be frozen until you are ready to use them. It is essential to remember to wash the vegetables well in cool water before trimming and peeling them.

Asparagus	Use only in broths for asparagus soups.
Beets	Avoid using the root part in stocks unless you are making borscht. Beet greens can be used. They add body and pungency.
Broccoli and cauliflower	Avoid using in stocks, or add only at end of cooking time.
Cabbage	Good flavor if used sparingly.
Carrots	Add sweetness to a broth. Use all orange part of carrot, including peelings. Avoid using carrot tops.
Celery and celery root	Add body and flavor. Use outer celery ribs and leaves.
Corn	Adds sweet flavor but the starch in the kernels will make a stock cloudy.
Dried peas and beans	Avoid using in stocks.
Garlic	Becomes surprisingly mellow in a stock. Adds richness. Crush to intensify flavor.
Green beans	Use all parts, including trimmed ends.
Leeks	Clean well. Use leaves as well as white parts.
Mushrooms	Add richness to stock, especially if sautéed first. Use stems and trimmings.
Onions	Basic to all stocks. Add a pleasant sweetness. Use generously.
Parsnips	Add a subtle bite and sweetness. Use sparingly.
Peas	Impart a surprisingly strong flavor in broths. Better to use snow pea pods.
Potatoes	Add sweetness to stock. Use well-cleaned skins. Starchy part of potato has good flavor but will make a broth cloudy.
Spinach	Only add at end of cooking time.
Summer squash	Adds pleasant, light flavor. Use all parts including skins and seeds.
Tomatoes	Add acidity and color to stock. Use all parts of ripe tomatoes.
Turnips	Add sweet flavor if used sparingly.
Winter squash	Adds sweetness to stock.

Barley-Mushroom Ragout

- ½ ounce dried porcini mushrooms
- 1 cup boiling water
- 4 teaspoons olive oil
- 1 large yellow onion, finely chopped
- 4 cloves garlic, minced
- 1 tablespoon minced fresh ginger
- 1 carrot, peeled, quartered, and thinly sliced
- 1 sweet red pepper, cored, seeded, and chopped
- 6 ounces shiitake mushrooms, stemmed, wiped clean, and thinly sliced
- 6 ounces button mushrooms, stemmed, wiped clean, and thinly sliced
- ½ cup chopped canned tomatoes
- ⅓ cup medium pearl barley
- 1 cup Vegetable Broth or canned reduced-sodium vegetable broth
- ½ teaspoon salt
- ¼ teaspoon dried rosemary, crumbled

1 Place dried porcini mushrooms in a small bowl and pour in boiling water. Let stand until softened—about 40 minutes. Drain mushrooms, reserving liquid, and coarsely chop. Strain liquid and set aside.

2 Meanwhile, in a heavy saucepan over moderate heat, heat oil 1 minute. Add onion, garlic, and ginger and cook, stirring frequently, about 7 minutes. Stir in carrot and red pepper and cook, stirring occasionally, until tender—about 5 minutes.

3 Add the reserved mushrooms, 2 tablespoons of mushroom liquid, and shiitake and button mushrooms, and cook, stirring frequently, until tender—about 5 minutes. Stir in tomatoes and barley.

4 Add the remaining mushroom liquid, broth, salt, and rosemary and bring to a boil. Reduce the heat to moderately low, cover, and simmer until barley is tender—about 45 minutes. Makes 4 servings.

1 Serving: Calories 195; Total Fat 6 g; Saturated Fat 1 g; Protein 7 g; Carbohydrates 32 g; Fiber 6 g; Sodium 525 mg; Cholesterol 0 mg

prep time-20 minutes • cooking time-80 minutes

Vegetable Broth

- 2 tablespoons olive oil
- 3 large carrots
- 2 medium-size parsnips, peeled
- 2 medium-size leeks, halved lengthwise
- 2 stalks celery with leaves, halved
- 1 large yellow onion, peeled and halved
- 4 unpeeled cloves garlic
- 3 plum tomatoes, halved
- 6 sprigs parsley
- 3 unpeeled slices fresh ginger, each about the size of a quarter
- 7 cups water
- ¾ teaspoon dried rosemary, crumbled
- 1 teaspoon salt

1 Preheat the oven to 400°F. Pour olive oil into a 13" x 9" x 2" roasting pan. Add carrots, parsnips, leeks, celery, onion, and garlic and stir to coat. Roast, uncovered, until vegetables are lightly colored—about 30 minutes.

2 Transfer vegetables to a 5-quart Dutch oven or stockpot, add tomatoes, parsley, ginger, and water. Bring to a boil over high heat and stir in rosemary and salt. Reduce the heat to moderately low and simmer, partially covered, until vegetables are very tender and broth is richly flavored—about 1 hour.

3 Strain, discarding vegetables. Taste for salt and adjust as needed. Makes 5½ cups.

VEGETABLE SOUP

Make it one day, serve it the next; a good, dense, vegetable soup is even better when the flavors have had time to mingle and mellow.

EASY STEPS

Vegetable soups are among the easiest soups to make. You can stop anywhere during the cooking process and complete the recipe later. You can chop all the vegetables before starting to cook or you can prepare them as you go along, chopping some while the others are already softening in the soup pot.

FOR THE BEST FLAVOR

Vegetable soups are best made with the freshest possible produce. Vary the ingredients according to what is in season. Canned tomatoes are the soup staple, but if homegrown, sun-ripened tomatoes are available, by all means use them instead.

FOR EXTRA FLAVOR

One of the very best flavorings for a vegetable soup is Parmesan cheese. When buying Parmesan, choose a piece with the rind attached. The rind will help the cheese stay fresh longer. Grate fresh Parmesan onto steaming bowls of soup. Better yet, save the rind after most of the

cheese has been used, wrap, and store in the freezer. When you make a soup, add the rind and let it simmer along with the vegetables. Remove the rind before serving soup.

A TASTE OF SUMMER

Add an extra measure of summertime flavor to a vegetable soup by serving it the way the French do. Swirl a spoonful of *pistou* (that's French for basil pesto) into each bowl of hot soup at serving time.

HERBS FOR SOUPS

Herbs can be used in soups generously when they are fresh, but should be used sparingly when they are dried. This is because the leaves are largely water when they are fresh, and the flavor becomes more concentrated

as the leaves dry. For soups use basil, parsley, marjoram, oregano, rosemary, thyme, and bay leaf. The flavor of herbs should never dominate.

BOUQUET GARNI

Many recipes call for a bouquet garni, a little bouquet of herbs. The benefit of the bouquet garni is that herbs will not fall apart in the soup, and they are easily removed.

To make a bouquet garni of fresh herbs, gather 2 sprigs of parsley, a bay leaf, and 2 sprigs of thyme into a bouquet and tie the stems with a piece of white cooking twine.

To make a bouquet garni of dried herbs, cut a 3-inch square of cheesecloth, place the dried herbs in the center of the square, pull up the 4 corners, and tie the bundle with a piece of cooking twine.

VEGETABLES ONLY

Vegetable soups can be made with beef, chicken, or vegetable broths. For a cholesterol-free Tuscan Vegetable Soup, replace the bacon with 2 tablespoons of olive oil.

Minestrone-type soups like this one, which are flavored with cabbage and a complement of other vegetables, can be made successfully with water instead of stock.

SERVING VARIATIONS

In Tuscany, toasted bread is a usual part of a vegetable soup. In other regions of Italy, rice or pasta is added instead. If you prefer pasta, add it for the last 15 minutes of cooking time. If white rice is more to your taste, cook it separately in broth and serve with soup.

ROOT VEGETABLE SOUP

Prepare Tuscan Vegetable Soup as directed in Step 1 at right, **adding** along with the carrots 2 medium-size parsnips, 2 medium-size turnips, and 2 medium-size beets, each **peeled** and **cut** into 1/2-inch dice. Proceed as directed **omitting** cannellini, cabbage, spinach, and bread and **substituting** 3/4 teaspoon crumbled dried marjoram leaves and 1/2 teaspoon black pepper for the sage and thyme. **Simmer**, covered, over moderately low heat until vegetables are tender—40 to 50 minutes. **Serve** with or without toasted Italian bread. Makes 4 servings.

SERVING LEFTOVERS

If you want to revive some leftover vegetable soup, serve it the way the Italians do. Boil some rice until just done. Spoon 1/2 cup of rice into each bowl. Ladle leftover soup over the rice and let it sit until it reaches room temperature. Serve topped with slivers of fresh basil and a grating of Parmesan cheese.

COOKING AHEAD

If you don't plan to serve vegetable soup right away, let it cool, then refrigerate. It will keep for up to 5 days. Or freeze the soup in quart or single-serving containers and keep up to 3 months.

Tuscan Vegetable Soup

- 1 tablespoon olive oil
- 4 ounces thick-sliced bacon, cut into 1/2-inch dice
- 1 large red onion, diced
- 5 cloves garlic, minced
- 2 large carrots, peeled, halved lengthwise, and thinly sliced
- 1 can (28 ounces) tomatoes, drained and chopped
- 5 cups Vegetable Broth or reduced-sodium canned broth
- 1 pound new potatoes, peeled and cut into 1/2-inch dice
- 2 1/2 cups drained, cooked, dried cannellini beans (page 48) or one 19-ounce can cannellini beans, drained and rinsed
- 3/4 teaspoon salt
- 1/2 teaspoon dried sage, crumbled
- 1/2 teaspoon dried thyme, crumbled
- 4 cups shredded Savoy cabbage
- 4 cups tightly packed trimmed, rinsed, and torn spinach
- 3 slices Italian bread, toasted and torn into 1-inch chunks

1 In a 5-quart Dutch oven over moderate heat, heat oil 1 minute. Add bacon and cook, stirring frequently, until lightly crisp—4 to 6 minutes. Remove all but 2 tablespoons of bacon drippings from the pan, add onion and garlic, and cook, stirring occasionally, until soft—about 5 minutes. Add carrots and cook, stirring frequently, until soft—about 5 minutes.

2 Add tomatoes, broth, potatoes, beans, salt, sage, and thyme and bring to a boil over high heat. Reduce the heat to moderately low, cover, and simmer until the potatoes are firm-tender—about 12 to 15 minutes.

3 Add cabbage, cover, and cook until tender—12 minutes. Add spinach and bread and cook, uncovered, until the spinach wilts—about 1 minute longer. Makes 6 servings.

1 Serving: Calories 386; Total Fat 11 g; Saturated Fat 4 g; Protein 16 g; Carbohydrates 58 g; Fiber 11 g; Sodium 824 mg; Cholesterol 18 mg

*prep time-35 minutes
cooking time-45 minutes*

Tuscan Vegetable Soup, below left, is traditionally served with crusty bread. Root Vegetable Soup, below, gets its ruddy color from beets and carrots.

BEAN SOUPS

*B*ean soups invite improvisation. Turning our Black-eyed Pea Soup into the Black Bean classic entails only a few quick changes.

ALL ABOUT BEANS

Archaeologists have found evidence that beans were cultivated some 11,000 years ago, which means they were cultivated before grains. Dried beans are inexpensive, fat-free, low-sodium power-houses of energy. They are rich in iron, potassium, and phosphorus and fair sources of protein.

SORTING THINGS OUT

No matter how carefully they are processed, dried beans nearly always contain some pebbles and little pellets of mud. No problem. Simply dump the beans into a large fine sieve, set it under cold running water, and discard all bits of gravel and shriveled or broken beans. Clumps of mud will dissolve and wash away.

GETTING SOAKED

Soaking dried beans softens them, reduces their gassiness, and trims cooking time about an hour. There are three ways to do it. Weigh the pros and cons before deciding which is best for you.

Overnight Soak: Place 1 pound of beans in a large bowl, add 1 quart of cold water, and let stand 12 hours or overnight. Pros: No tending needed. Cons: It takes all day or night.

Quick Method: Place 1 pound of beans in a large heavy pot, add enough water to cover by 1 inch, set uncovered over high heat, and bring to a boil. Boil, uncovered, for 2 minutes, remove from the heat, cover, and cool to room temperature. Pros: This shortcuts soaking time by 10 1/2 hours. Cons: You must keep one eye on the beans, another on the clock.

Microwave Method: Place 1 pound of beans in a 3-quart casserole, add 3 cups of cold water, cover, and microwave 12 minutes at full power, stirring once at half time. Cool, covered, for 40 minutes, stirring once or twice. Pros: Half an hour faster than the quick method. Cons: Microwaving firms the beans—bad for soups, good for salads.

SAVE THE WATER?

Should you use the bean soaking water when cooking the beans? It depends. Adding it to the pot will make the beans gassier. (The more changes of fresh water, the less gassy the beans.)

If you pour the soaking water down the drain, how-ever, soluble vitamins and minerals go with it.

BLACK BEAN SOUP

Prepare Step 1 of Black-eyed Pea Soup as directed at right, **substituting** black beans for black-eyed peas, and **drain**. **Omit** Steps 2 and 3. **Increase** bacon to 8 slices and **proceed** as directed in Steps 4 and 5. In Step 6, **use** 8 cups water for cooking the beans and **cook** 45 minutes instead of 30. **Omit** Step 7. **Mix** 1/2 teaspoon hot red pepper sauce into soup; **remove** and discard bay leaves. **Purée** 1 cup soup mixture in a blender at high speed or in a food processor; **return** to pan and **mix** in the reserved bacon along with 1/4 cup chopped fresh coriander (cilantro) and 2 tablespoons lemon juice. **Ladle** into soup bowls and **garnish**, if desired, with sour cream or yogurt, sieved hard-cooked eggs, or chopped coriander. Makes 8 servings.

KITCHEN MATH

Dried peas and beans swell quite a bit when they cook. Softer, starchier beans swell more than firm ones.

1 pound dried small beans = 2 cups uncooked = 5 1/2 – 6 cups cooked (black-eyed peas, navy beans, kidney beans)

1 pound dried large beans = 2 1/2 cups uncooked = 6 – 7 1/2 cups cooked (chickpeas, great northern beans, Fordhook lima beans, marrowfat beans)

2 cups drained, cooked dried beans = 2 cups rinsed, drained canned beans

---

WORK SAVER

A Sieve for Eggs

To make hard-cooked eggs fine enough to sprinkle over Black Bean Soup, push the yolks and cut-up whites separately through a small fine sieve with the back of a spoon. For a coarser chop, use an egg slicer. Slice the egg one way, turn it 90 degrees in the slicer, and slice once again.

Black-eyed Pea Soup

- 1 pound dried black-eyed peas, sorted and rinsed
- 8 cups water
- 1½ teaspoons salt
- 6 thick slices bacon
- 2 large yellow onions, coarsely chopped
- 2 stalks celery, coarsely chopped
- 2 medium-size carrots, peeled and chopped
- 2 garlic cloves, minced
- 2 whole bay leaves
- 1 teaspoon dried thyme, crumbled
- 5 cups Rich Chicken Stock or canned reduced-sodium chicken broth
- 2 cups chopped, trimmed collards, mustard, kale, or turnip greens, rinsed
- 3 tablespoons lemon juice
- ½ teaspoon hot red pepper sauce

1 Place peas in a 5-quart Dutch oven, add cold water to cover, and bring to a boil over high heat; cook for 2 minutes. Remove peas from the heat and let stand, covered, for 1 hour.

2 Drain peas and rinse; return to the Dutch oven and add water and salt. Bring to a boil over high heat, reduce the heat to moderately low, and simmer, covered, for 30 minutes. Drain peas, reserving 1 cup liquid.

3 Purée 1 cup peas in a blender at high speed or in a food processor, adding 1 to 2 tablespoons of the reserved cooking liquid, if necessary.

4 With sharp kitchen scissors and with bacon slices stacked, cut bacon crosswise into ½-inch strips.

(This step is easiest if the bacon is placed in the freezer for ½ hour before cutting.) Add bacon to Dutch oven and cook over moderately high heat, stirring occasionally, until crisp—5 to 8 minutes. With a slotted spoon, transfer bacon to paper toweling to drain.

5 In bacon drippings, sauté onions, celery, carrots, garlic, bay leaves, and thyme over moderate heat, stirring occasionally, until vegetables soften—8 to 10 minutes.

6 Add reserved cooking liquid, stock, peas, and pea purée and bring to a boil. Reduce the heat to moderately low and simmer, covered, for 30 minutes.

7 Stir in greens, return to a simmer, and cook, covered, until greens wilt—about 15 minutes. Mix in lemon juice, red pepper sauce, and reserved bacon and bring just to serving temperature.

8 Remove and discard bay leaves, ladle into soup bowls, and serve. Makes 8 servings.

1 Serving: Calories 189; Total Fat 8 g; Saturated Fat 3 g; Protein 10 g; Carbohydrates 21 g; Fiber 5 g; Sodium 702 mg; Cholesterol 18 mg

prep time-1 hour • standing time-1 hour cooking time-1 hour 45 minutes

PURÉED SOUPS

Butter-smooth on the tongue, our cool, puréed squash soups are low in fat. Use the basic techniques to create any puréed vegetable soups you fancy.

CREAMY BUT CREAMLESS

Puréeing cooked vegetables both thickens and "creams" cold soups. There's no need to up the fat, calorie, or cholesterol counts by adding cream—or even milk.

FAT SLASHERS

Though our cold squash soups are naturally low in fat, you can reduce the fat further

still. First, halve the amount of olive oil used to sauté the onion. Second, skim all fat from the chicken stock before adding it to the soup. And instead of browning the croutons in butter and olive oil in a skillet, spray them with butter- or olive-oil-flavored nonstick vegetable spray, spread on a baking sheet, and toast

in a 350°F oven—10 to 12 minutes should do it. Or omit the croutons or other rich toppings and replace them with dollops of low-fat yogurt.

BIGGER FLAVOR

Cold numbs the palate, so any soup that is to be served cold needs extra seasoning. This usually means twice the amount of fresh herbs and perhaps 1½ times the amount of dried. Cooking the vegetables in a rich chicken or vegetable broth instead of water heightens the flavor too.

THICK AND THIN

If your soup is too thick, thin with a little chicken stock before chilling. If it's too thin, boil, covered, over moderate heat until it's as thick as you want. Tip: Soup will reduce and thicken faster if you boil it in a large heavy skillet.

SEED REMOVAL

If your squash are large, their seeds are probably bitter and should be discarded. Use a melon baller to remove them. Halve the squash lengthwise, then run the melon baller down the seeds, scooping them out.

ROSEMARY-SCENTED YELLOW SQUASH SOUP WITH PARSLEY PESTO

Prepare and **chill** as directed at right, **substituting** yellow squash for zucchini and ¼ cup chopped fresh rosemary (or 1 teaspoon crumbled dried rosemary) for dill. **Omit** croutons. While soup chills, **prepare** Parsley Pesto: In a blender at high speed or in a food processor, finely **chop** 1 cup parsley leaves, 1 trimmed and chunked scallion, and 1 tablespoon fresh rosemary with 2 teaspoons lemon juice and ⅛ teaspoon salt. With motor running, **add** 2 tablespoons softened butter and 2 tablespoons olive oil and **purée** until smooth. To serve, **ladle** soup into bowls and **top** with small dollops of pesto. Makes 6 servings.

PICK OF THE CROP

Yellow squash and zucchini are only two summer vegetables that make wonderful puréed soups. Here are some other good choices. Try them with our suggested flavorings or experiment with additions and seasonings of your own.

Vegetable	Good Additions	Seasonings
Asparagus	Butter-browned leeks, shallots, or scallions	Fresh dill or chervil; freshly grated nutmeg
Beets	Cooked apples, carrots, and/or onions; red wine or orange juice	Fresh dill or parsley; allspice, cinnamon
Broccoli, Cauliflower	Sautéed leeks, scallions, shallots, or garlic	Fresh dill or rosemary; freshly grated nutmeg
Carrots	Butter-browned apples and onions; roasted sweet red or yellow peppers	Fresh chervil, dill, rosemary, tarragon, or thyme; grated orange zest
Green peas	Butter-browned leeks, shallots, or scallions; steamed sorrel or lettuce	Fresh mint or rosemary; grated orange zest
Sweet red peppers	Roasted onions and garlic; orange and/or lemon juice	Fresh basil, marjoram, rosemary, sage, or thyme; hot red pepper
Tomatoes	Sautéed onions, leeks, or garlic; sautéed sweet red pepper; orange juice	Fresh basil, marjoram, oregano, rosemary, or thyme

CROUTON HOW-TO

1 Cut ½-inch-thick slices of bread and trim off the crusts. Using a sharp utility knife, cut the slices of bread into ½-inch cubes.

2 Melt butter over moderate heat in a large skillet. Stir in olive oil and heat until bubbly. Add bread cubes in a single layer.

3 As croutons brown, turn with tongs. When browned on all sides, remove to a plate covered with paper toweling and drain. Use warm or at room temperature.

Cold Zucchini Soup

3	tablespoons olive oil
1	large yellow onion, chopped
8	medium-size zucchini, chopped
¼	cup snipped fresh dill or 1 teaspoon dried dill
3	cups Rich Chicken Stock or canned low-sodium chicken broth

¼	teaspoon salt
⅛ to ¼	teaspoon black pepper

Croutons:

2	tablespoons butter or margarine
2	teaspoons olive oil
2	slices firm-textured bread

1 In a large saucepan, over moderate heat, heat oil 1 minute. Add onion and sauté, stirring occasionally, until limp—about 5 minutes.

2 Add zucchini, dill, and stock, and bring to a boil. Reduce the heat to low and simmer, uncovered, until zucchini is tender—8 to 10 minutes; remove from the heat and cool slightly.

3 Working in batches, purée the zucchini mixture in a blender at high speed or in a food processor. Mix in salt and pepper.

4 Pour into a large bowl, cover, and refrigerate up to 3 hours. Meanwhile, prepare croutons as directed at left.

5 To serve, ladle thoroughly chilled soup into 6 soup plates and top with croutons. Makes 6 servings.

1 Serving: Calories 188; Total Fat 14 g; Saturated Fat 4 g; Protein 6 g; Carbohydrates 13 g; Fiber 3g; Sodium 232 mg; Cholesterol 11 mg

prep time-30 minutes • cooking time-20 minutes chilling time-2 to 3 hours

NEW VICHYSSOISE

True vichyssoise, a creamy cold leek and potato soup, was created nearly eighty years ago by chef Louis Diat at New York City's Ritz-Carlton Hotel. Our lower fat sweet potato-carrot version uses buttermilk and makes the cream optional.

YAMS VS. SWEET POTATOES

What we call yams are really sweet potatoes. True yams, starchy tropical tubers, have white flesh and are not sweet.

Sweet potatoes are oval or elongated with tapered ends. For top quality, choose sweet potatoes with slightly rough skins free of nicks, bruises, or blemishes. Unwashed sweet potatoes—with the soil still on them—will last the longest. Store in an open basket or bin in a cool, dark, dry spot.

NUTRITIONAL NOTE

All sweet potatoes brim with beta-carotene, which our bodies convert to vitamin A. The deeper orange a sweet potato's flesh, the greater its vitamin A potential. Since our vichyssoise is made with carrots as well as sweet potatoes, it's a beta-carotene bonanza.

ABOUT BUTTERMILK

Originally a by-product of butter churning, buttermilk is now mass produced. Like its predecessor, however, it is low

in fat and full of sharp flavor. In our vichyssoise, its sharpness balances the sweetness of carrots and potatoes.

Lacking buttermilk, use whole milk, half-and-half, or evaporated milk (regular or skim), substituting measure for measure. Note: These substitutions will increase the fat, calories, and cholesterol.

PREVENT CURDLING

All milk-vegetable mixtures are prone to curdling, especially those made with sharply acid buttermilk. Prevent the problem by adding buttermilk only after the soup has finished cooking and has been puréed. The puréeing helps to cool the soup in a hurry.

EASY WINTER SQUASH SOUP

For a change, substitute 1 thawed 10-ounce package of frozen puréed winter squash for the 2 sweet potatoes and proceed as the recipe directs.

GOOD HOT OR COLD

Our puréed soups are equally good hot. Just make sure they never boil—or even simmer—once the milk is added, because they may curdle.

BLEND OR PROCESS?

You can use either a blender or a food processor to purée a

TO THE RESCUE

If, despite all precautions, your soup should curdle, churn it in a blender at high speed or in a food processor until smooth. Or force it through a sieve lined with several layers of damp cheesecloth; it's tedious but effective.

soup, though the blender is easier. It's best to purée the soup in batches, only half filling the blender cup each time.

SOUP PAINTING

Dress up a soup with heavy cream or a mixture of 2 tablespoons of yogurt and 2 tablespoons of low-fat milk.

For a flower, drizzle cream in a spiral. Draw the tip of a knife outward through the spiral in 5 places, and then, alternately, inward.

For a central star, put a drop of cream in the center, draw the knife outward from it in 5 places. Surround with hearts as described below left.

To make hearts, drip cream in evenly sized dots in concentric circles and draw a knife through them.

For a comet, put a large drop of cream in the center. With a twist of the wrist, draw a knife outward from it in 5 places.

Sweet Potato and Carrot Vichyssoise

3 **tablespoons butter or margarine**

2 **small leeks, halved lengthwise, thoroughly washed and sliced**

1/2 **teaspoon ground nutmeg**

2 **medium-size sweet potatoes, peeled and cut into 2-inch chunks**

2 **medium-size carrots, peeled and cut into 2-inch chunks**

4 **cups Rich Chicken Stock or canned low-sodium chicken broth (about)**

1 1/2 **cups buttermilk (about)**

Salt and freshly ground black pepper to taste (optional)

1 **cup heavy cream**

2 **tablespoons snipped chives**

1 In a medium-size saucepan, over moderate heat, melt butter. Add leeks and nutmeg and sauté, stirring occasionally, until tender—about 5 minutes.

2 Add sweet potatoes, carrots, and stock and bring to a boil over high heat. Reduce the heat to low and simmer, uncovered, until the sweet potatoes and carrots are tender—15 to 20 minutes. Remove from the heat and cool 10 minutes.

3 Working in batches, purée the mixture in a blender at high speed or in a food processor. Stir in buttermilk, salt, and pepper (optional). If soup seems too thick, thin with a little additional stock or buttermilk.

4 Transfer to a large bowl, cover, and refrigerate 2 to 3 hours. When ready to serve, spoon into serving bowls. For a fancy presentation, paint the surface with cream as described at left. Sprinkle with chives, if desired. Makes 6 servings.

1 Serving: Calories 197; Total Fat 8 g; Saturated Fat 4 g; Protein 7 g; Carbohydrates 26 g; Fiber 4 g; Sodium 194 mg; Cholesterol 18 mg

prep time-30 minutes
cooking time-28 minutes
chilling time-2 to 3 hours

FISH SOUPS

A fragrant fish broth makes the difference between so-so soups and superb ones like our Algarve Pork and Clam Cataplana. Best of all, making fresh fish broth is easier than you might think.

COOK'S SECRETS

Jeanne Voltz
Award-Winning Cooking Author

"What kind of wine to add to a fish broth? Pass up the chardonnay. It is relatively expensive and its touch of bitterness can overpower a mild-mannered broth. Go for a sauvignon blanc or pinot blanc or an inexpensive bottle labeled 'white table wine.'"

FISH BROTH

2 tablespoons olive oil	2½ pounds heads and bones from flounder, cut up, gills removed, and well washed
1 medium-size yellow onion, halved and thinly sliced	
1 medium-size leek, halved lengthwise, and thinly sliced	½ cup dry white wine
	6 cups cold water
1 clove garlic, crushed	6 parsley sprigs (preferably Italian flat leaf)
1 stalk celery, thinly sliced	½ teaspoon dried thyme, crumbled
2 medium-size carrots, thinly sliced	½ teaspoon salt

1 In a 5-quart Dutch oven, over moderate heat, heat oil. Add onion, leek, and garlic and cook, stirring frequently, until softened—about 7 minutes. Add celery and carrots and cook, stirring frequently, until carrots are soft—about 6 minutes.

2 Add fish pieces, stirring to coat. Add wine and cook 2 minutes to evaporate slightly. Add water and bring to a boil over high heat, skimming any foam that rises to the surface. Reduce the heat to moderately low, add parsley, thyme, and salt, partially cover, and simmer, until broth is richly flavored—about 40 minutes.

3 Strain broth, skimming fat and discarding bones and vegetables. Makes 6 cups.

WHAT'S IN A NAME?

The Algarve is a province in southern Portugal and a cataplana is the pot Portuguese cooks use to make this stellar soup. A cataplana looks like a giant copper clam shell hinged at the back. The soup goes in the bottom, the top is clamped down, and it is set over a brisk fire. Many kitchen shops sell cataplanas but they are pricey. Luckily, a Dutch oven with a snug lid works just as well.

FINE KETTLE OF FISH

Not every fish makes good broth. Oily fish—bluefish, salmon, swordfish, trout, and others—are too strong for broth, which should scent but never overpower a soup.

Good choices: flounder, cod, haddock, halibut, and sea bass. Use the head, bones, and trimmings, not the whole fish.

CLARITY COUNTS

Wash all fish parts before they go into the stockpot. Also cut out and discard the gills.

Start the fish bones and trimmings in cold water and bring very slowly to the boil, skimming off the gray foam that floats to the surface.

Simmer—never boil—the broth. Boiling will muddy it.

Strain the broth into a large heatproof bowl through a large fine sieve lined with several thicknesses of damp cheesecloth. When all the broth has dripped through, carefully bundle up the solids in the cheesecloth—without squeezing—and discard.

PARTIALLY COVERED

Many recipes—our Fish Broth included—call for the pot to be partially covered. A tightly covered kettle will be constantly diluted as steam beads on the bottom of the lid and drips back into the broth.

FROZEN ASSETS

Once the broth has been strained, cool to room temperature and ladle into ½-pint or 1-pint freezer containers, leaving a ½-inch space at the top so the broth can expand as it freezes. Snap on the lids, label, date, and store in a 0°F freezer up to 6 months.

IN A PINCH

You can buy frozen fish stock in 8-ounce containers in many fish markets and fancy food shops. Stored at 0°F, it will keep 6 months.

Fish bouillon cubes can be reconstituted into an acceptable broth. They will keep for about a year.

You can make another jiffy broth by combining equal parts of bottled clam juice and cold water.

Algarve Pork and Clam Cataplana

- 2 tablespoons olive oil
- 1 large yellow onion, finely chopped
- 4 cloves garlic, minced
- 2 large sweet green peppers, cored, seeded, and diced
- 4 ounces linguiça or chorizo sausage, halved lengthwise and thinly sliced
- 3 ounces prosciutto, chopped
- 1 can (28 ounces) tomatoes, drained and chopped
- 1 cup Fish Broth or 1/2 cup each bottled clam juice and water
- 1 cup minced parsley (preferably Italian flat leaf)
- 1/2 teaspoon hot red pepper sauce
- 2 dozen littleneck clams in the shell, well scrubbed

1 In a 5-quart Dutch oven with a tight-fitting lid, over moderate heat, heat oil 1 minute. Add onion and garlic and cook, stirring frequently, until softened—about 6 minutes.

2 Add peppers and cook, stirring frequently, until softened—about 5 minutes. Add linguiça and prosciutto and cook, stirring often, until some of the fat cooks out—about 4 minutes.

3 Stir in tomatoes, broth, parsley, and red pepper sauce and bring to a boil over high heat. Add clams, reduce the heat to moderate, cover, and cook just until clams open—about 10 minutes. Discard any clams that do not open. Makes 4 servings.

1 Serving: Calories 362; Total Fat 23 g; Saturated Fat 6 g; Protein 22 g; Carbohydrates 19 g; Fiber 4 g; Sodium 1012 mg; Cholesterol 57 mg

prep time-20 minutes
cooking time-26 minutes

CREAMY BISQUES

A bisque, according to definition, is a thick and creamy soup often made of shellfish but sometimes made of puréed vegetables. Our Crab and Sweet Pepper Bisque fits all the requirements and then some.

MELLOW FLAVOR

We mellow the vegetables for our bisques by a technique known as sweating. The purpose is to concentrate flavors in the vegetables by forcing out their juices. You can sweat vegetables slowly in a covered pan. Our lid-off method is much quicker.

REDUCING FAT

No ingredient is more essential to bisque than cream. In more carefree days, it was heavy cream all the way. With 36 percent milk fat, that's 6 grams per tablespoon, equal to 1/2 tablespoon of butter.

To trim the fat we've substituted part half-and-half (10 to 18 percent milk fat, or about 2 grams per tablespoon). Forget about lowering the counts further by replacing all of the cream with milk; the bisque will curdle. Tip: The lower the milk-fat content, the greater the risk of curdling.

OTHER CREAMS

For an interesting change of taste, replace 1/2 cup of the

heavy cream with either crème fraîche or Devon cream. Specialty markets sell these ever-so-slightly-sour, spoon-up-thick creams.

PICKING OVER CRAB

The top choice for crab bisque is lump or backfin crab—snowy nuggets from East Coast blue crabs. Cooked and ready to use, lump crab is expensive. It usually comes in 14- to 16-ounce tins and should be carefully picked over for shell and cartilage.

Flaked crab—bits from the body and claws—is less expensive. However, it is brownish in color, stringy, and requires a lot of picking over and cleaning. It too usually comes packed in 14- to 16-ounce tins.

Imitation crabmeat is made

from cheap white-fleshed fish paste that has been extruded and colored to resemble crab. It lacks the flavor, texture, and delicacy of fresh crab.

DOUBLE-DUTY FLOUR

Flour is added to bisque to thicken it, but flour also stabilizes the mixture and helps to prevent curdling. Believe it or not, sweet red peppers have the strength to curdle half-and-half. Blending flour into the cooked red pepper and pimiento neutralizes them and ensures a smooth bisque.

GENTLE HEAT

Bisques require moderately low heat for several reasons. First, the flavors must have a chance to marry. Second, the bisque must reduce slightly so that it will thicken and its flavor will heighten. Finally, if the bisque is allowed to come to a boil, it will curdle.

SMOOTHING THINGS OUT

For a smooth-as-silk bisque, purée the mix at the end of Step 3, allowing the bisque to cool for 10 minutes first. Use a blender at high speed or a food processor and work in batches, no more than 1/2 fill-

ing the blender cup or 1/3 filling the processor work bowl.

OTHER FISH TO TRY

Our bisque variation calls for cooked shrimp, but you'll find cooked lobster meat equally delicious. You might also try flaked, cooked salmon, flounder, hake, or haddock.

CHILLING OUT

Our bisques are as good cold as they are hot. To quick chill, pour into a large shallow bowl and set in a larger bowl filled with ice. Stir often and the bisque should be cold enough to serve in 20 minutes.

An easier but longer method is to pour the hot bisque into a large shallow bowl, cool 15 minutes, then cover and refrigerate several hours.

SWEET PEPPER SHRIMP BISQUE

Prepare as directed at right but in Step 4 **substitute** 8 ounces peeled, deveined, and halved medium-size raw shrimp for the crab and **simmer** for 5 minutes. Makes 4 servings.

WORK SAVER

Flame Moderator

If your stovetop burner won't hold a gentle heat, slide a flame moderator between the pan and burner. These hollow metal insulators can be bought at any housewares store. By spreading burner heat slowly and evenly, they eliminate hot spots and keep liquids below the boil.

Crab and Sweet Pepper Bisque

1 tablespoon butter or margarine
2 large stalks celery, finely chopped
1 large sweet red pepper, cored, seeded, and finely chopped
2 tablespoons chopped pimiento
1½ tablespoons all-purpose flour
1 bottle (8 ounces) clam juice
¼ cup dry sherry
1 cup heavy cream
1 cup half-and-half
¼ teaspoon salt
¼ teaspoon black pepper
6 ounces lump crabmeat, well picked over (or canned or imitation crabmeat)

1 In a medium-size saucepan, over moderate heat, heat butter. Add celery and sauté for 5 minutes. Add red pepper and pimiento and cook until pepper is softened—about 10 minutes more.

2 Blend in flour, then gradually whisk in clam juice, stirring constantly, until smooth. Add sherry and cook, stirring, 2 to 3 minutes.

3 Add heavy cream, half-and-half, salt, and black pepper, reduce the heat to moderately low, and cook, uncovered, for 30 minutes. Do not overheat or soup may curdle.

4 Add crab and simmer another 2 minutes. Makes 4 servings.

1 Serving: Calories 411; Total Fat 33 g; Saturated Fat 20 g; Protein 13 g; Carbohydrates 16 g; Fiber 1 g; Sodium 619 mg; Cholesterol 142 mg

prep time-10 minutes
cooking time-50 minutes

CHOWDERS

*C*howders—milk-based fish and vegetable soups—originally came to Canada's eastern shore with the French settlers. "Chowder" derives from "chaudière," the French cauldron once used to make these husky soups.

CHOOSING THE FISH

In the 16th and 17th centuries, French fishermen crossed the Atlantic to Newfoundland in search of cod. In their sole cooking utensil, a chaudière, they would prepare a fish-and-biscuit stew with the catch of the day, a process they called "making a chaudière."

Many cooks favor haddock for their chowders. A full-flavored, lean white fish, haddock will not cook to cottony shreds. Other good choices are cod, or even dried salt cod (a Portuguese influence), which must first be freshened by soaking in several changes of water.

Halibut (first choice for chowder in the Pacific Northwest),

blackfish, rockfish, salmon, tuna, swordfish, and mako shark are also good choices. For shellfish try clams, of course, but also mussels, oysters, scallops, shrimp, lobster, and crab.

GROUPER ALERT

Long a favorite chowder fish in the Caribbean and the U.S. Gulf states, grouper should be avoided today. It is one of the warm water fish most apt to be riddled with ciguatoxin, a parasite-produced toxin that causes serious food poisoning. Cooking, freezing, and canning do not destroy it.

ONE POTATO, TWO

Not all potatoes are suitable for chowder. Use Maine, eastern, or all-purpose potatoes, which are firm yet starchy enough to thicken the chowder. Cooked new potatoes are too gluey to make good chowder and "bakers" will cook down to mush.

LOSING THE FAT

Unlike bisques, which brim with cream, chowders are made with milk. Still, there are ways to prune their fat content a little if not a lot.

Substitute chopped lean bacon or Canadian bacon for salt pork and sauté in a nonstick skillet well coated with vegetable cooking spray.

Replace half of the milk with evaporated skim milk.

CURDLEPROOF CHOWDER

The lower in fat the milk, the more chance there is of curdling. But there are lean ways to keep chowder curd free.

Instead of blending the flour into the sautéed onion (see Step 2 of our Cape Ann Haddock Chowder), combine it with the milk to make a kind of slurry.

Very slowly whisk the milk-flour slurry into the hot ingredients in the pan and continue whisking until the chowder thickens lightly. Keep the heat

under the chowder low or moderately low and never let the chowder boil after the milk is added. Serve the chowder as soon as it's done.

POINT COUNTERPOINT

Silky chowders beg for something crunchy as an accompaniment. Common crackers, big, old-fashioned water biscuits are marvelous crumbled into chowder. Soda or oyster crackers are also good.

As for breads, the best choices for chowder are French or Italian breads. Slice them thin, toast until crisp, and eat like crackers. Or tear them apart and drop pieces in the chowder. If you are lucky enough to find *pão*, a sturdy Portuguese country bread, by all means buy it. It's perfect plain and perfect toasted.

Buttered bread crumbs are another good choice. Two chowders on page 60 are baked with fresh crumbs.

(continued on page 60)

CHOWDER BASICS

All good chowders—clam, fish, corn—begin with salt pork or bacon, onion, and milk. Potatoes also go into fish and shellfish chowders. Use this elementary formula plus the method set forth in our haddock chowder at right to improvise a variety of chowders. The proportions are for 4 servings.

Chopped Salt Pork or Bacon:	1/4 cup
Chopped Onion:	1 cup
Milk (milk/fish broth or milk/clam juice):	2 1/2 cups total liquid
Chopped Potato:	1 large
Shellfish, Fish, or Corn:	8 to 12 ounces

Experiment with fish and/or vegetable combos; play around with the seasonings. Add diced carrots to a fish chowder; diced sweet green or red pepper (and maybe a bit of jalapeño) to a corn chowder. All chowders benefit from minced parsley; chopped fresh coriander (cilantro) adds a Mexican accent to corn chowder.

Cape Ann Haddock Chowder

- 1 ounce salt pork, finely chopped (1/4 cup)
- 1 large yellow onion, coarsely chopped
- 1 1/2 tablespoons all-purpose flour
- 1 bottle (8 ounces) clam juice
- 1 1/2 cups milk
- 1/2 teaspoon black pepper
- 1/4 teaspoon salt
- 1 large all-purpose potato, peeled and chopped
- 12 ounces skinned and boned haddock, cut into 1 1/2-inch chunks

1 In a large saucepan over high heat, cook salt pork for 2 minutes, stirring occasionally. Add onion and continue cooking until softened—about 2 minutes more.

2 Blend in flour, then gradually pour in clam juice, whisking to combine. Add milk, pepper, salt, and potato and bring to a simmer.

Reduce the heat to moderately low and simmer, uncovered, until potato is tender and soup is nicely thickened—15 to 20 minutes.

3 Add haddock and cook just until fish almost flakes at the touch of a fork—about 5 minutes more. Makes 4 servings.

1 Serving: Calories 246; Total Fat 5 g; Saturated Fat 2 g; Protein 23 g; Carbohydrates 26 g; Fiber 2 g; Sodium 503 mg; Cholesterol 68 mg

prep time-15 mininutes
cooking time-30 minutes

SALMON CHOWDER

Prepare Tuna Chowder as directed at right, **substituting** 1 can (7½ ounces) boned and skinned salmon for tuna. **Omit** red pepper, tomatoes, and thyme and **sauté** diced pimiento along with green pepper. Makes 4 servings.

YANKEE SCALLOP CHOWDER

Prepare as directed at right, **substituting** 8 ounces sea scallops, rinsed and halved crosswise, for the haddock. Makes 4 servings.

(continued from page 58)

ABOUT CRUMBING BREAD

Some chowders call for buttery crumb toppings, which are infinitely superior if you make them fresh. Using a food processor, you can crumb the bread and toss it with butter, garlic, and parsley in a single operation.

The same technique works almost as well in a blender. If you have neither blender nor food processor, crush the garlic, melt the butter, and combine the two. Hand chop the parsley. Crumb the bread by rubbing it over the second coarsest side of a four-sided grater (you'll have better luck with unsliced bread). Measure out 2 cups of crumbs and toss with garlic butter and parsley.

Tuna Chowder with Buttery Crumb Topping

    2 tablespoons butter or margarine
    2 medium-size yellow onions, finely chopped
    1 large sweet red pepper, cored, seeded,
       and finely chopped
    1 large sweet green pepper, cored, seeded,
       and finely chopped
    1 cup chopped canned tomatoes
    2 bottles (8 ounces each) clam juice
  ¼ cup chopped pimiento
    1 large all-purpose potato, peeled and diced
  ½ teaspoon salt
  ¼ teaspoon black pepper
  ½ teaspoon dried thyme, crumbled
    1 can (6½ ounces) water-packed chunk-
       light tuna, drained and flaked

1 In a 2-quart saucepan over moderate heat, melt butter. Add onions and sauté until limp—about 2 minutes. Add red and green peppers and sauté 2 minutes more. Add tomatoes, clam juice, pimiento, potato, salt, black pepper, and thyme.

2 Bring to a boil, reduce the heat to moderately low, and simmer, uncovered, until potato is tender—about 30 minutes.

3 Mix in tuna and heat 1 minute more. Ladle into 4 bowls and top with Buttery Crumb Topping. Makes 4 servings.

> **Per Serving: Calories 349; Total Fat 10 g; Saturated Fat 6 g; Protein 18 g; Carbohydrates 48 g; Fiber 4 g; Sodium 1212 mg; Cholesterol 38 mg**

prep time-20 minutes
cooking time-37 minutes

NO MORE TEARS

All chowders contain a good measure of chopped onion. Here are a few tips for keeping their sulfurous fumes from making you cry. For more onion tips, see page 36.

Pour a little white vinegar on your chopping board before chopping onions. It'll absorb the fumes. For double protection, burn a candle as you work. The flame will neutralize the fumes.

Or try chopping grandma's way—with a slice of bread between your lips.

BUTTERY CRUMB TOPPING

    1 large clove garlic
    4 slices white
       bread, torn into
       small pieces
    1 tablespoon but-
       ter or margarine,
       softened and cut
       into small pieces
    1 tablespoon
       chopped parsley

1 Preheat the oven to 350°F. Drop garlic into a blender or the feed tube of a spinning food processor. Add bread, butter, and parsley. Process until uniformly fine.

2 Spread in a thin layer on an ungreased baking sheet and bake, uncovered, turning every 5 minutes with a spatula until golden brown—15 to 20 minutes. Set aside while you prepare the chowder.

KITCHEN MATH

1 slice firm-textured white bread=

½ cup soft bread crumbs

1 slice crisp dry bread =

⅓ cup dry bread crumbs

If you make too many bread crumbs, put the excess in a container with a tight-fitting lid and freeze. Scoop out as many as you want as you need them. They thaw almost instantly.

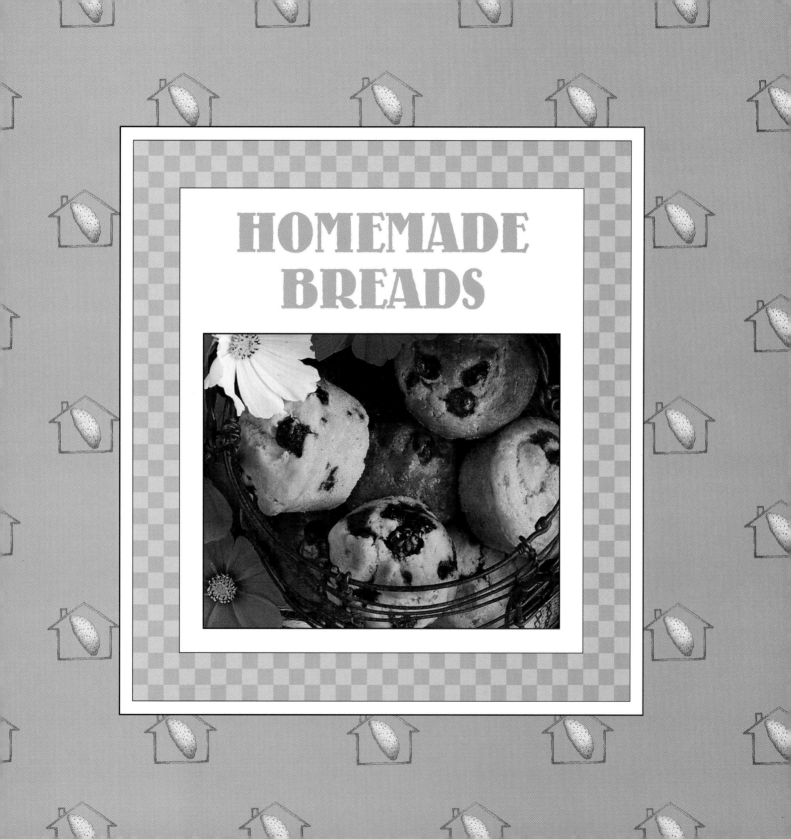

HOMEMADE BREADS

DROP BISCUITS

*G*olden-brown biscuits on the table can make even the most humble meal special. Perfect biscuits are easy to make. The secret is in the mixing.

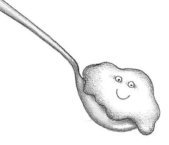

DROP BISCUITS

Drop biscuit dough is too soft to be rolled and cut. Instead, the dough is pushed off a spoon onto the baking sheet, producing a free-form biscuit that is tender, flavorful, quick to make, and best when served straight from the oven.

STRONG REACTIONS

Buttermilk provides the acid necessary for baking soda to release carbon dioxide, which is what makes biscuits rise. The difference between baking soda and baking powder is that baking powder is manufactured with the acid blended in; it will react when mixed with any liquid. The action starts the instant the dry and wet ingredients come together. That means biscuits must be baked as soon as the dough is mixed.

TESTS OF TIME

Baking powder and baking soda do not last forever. Replace baking powder about once a year and baking soda once every 2 years or if it gets lumpy or discolors.

To test for freshness, mix baking powder with a little warm water; baking soda with a little vinegar. If they bubble furiously, they are fresh.

SUBSTITUTE BUTTERMILK

In a pinch, you can make your own version of buttermilk by stirring 1 tablespoon of white vinegar or fresh strained lemon juice into 1 cup of whole milk; set aside for about 10 minutes until thickened.

TENDER BISCUITS

Give the oven at least 15 minutes to preheat before baking.

Measure the ingredients accurately. Use a whisk or your fingers to mix the dry ingredients until well blended. Sifting is not necessary.

When cutting in the fat, mix only until the mixture resembles coarse crumbs.

Use a fork to blend in the liquid just until the mixture forms a very soft dough. Resist the temptation to keep mixing. Avoid kneading the dough too hard or too long or you will toughen the biscuits.

Bake only until the biscuits are golden brown. They should have doubled in height. Serve immediately. If biscuits are to be frozen, cool first on a wire rack.

FROZEN ASSETS

Place cooled biscuits on a baking sheet and cover lightly with plastic wrap. Set in the freezer just until firm. Pop the biscuits into a self-sealing plastic bag, pressing out as much air as possible. Label and freeze for up to 3 months.

To reheat, remove as many biscuits as needed. Wrap in aluminum foil and set in a 350°F oven until hot—about 15 minutes.

FLAVOR BOOSTERS

Hot biscuits are delicious plain, but for change, add one of these to the dry ingredients: 1 to 2 tablespoons of snipped fresh or freeze-dried chives or chopped fresh parsley; 1½ teaspoons of dried (or 1½ tablespoons of fresh) dill, crumbled rosemary, sage, or thyme; 3 tablespoons of finely chopped ham or bacon.

TO THE RESCUE

If you have followed the recipe correctly but your biscuits still aren't up to snuff, here are a few problem solvers.

Dry biscuits may be overbaked; bake only until golden brown. Reduce baking time slightly; check oven temperature with an oven thermometer.

Tough biscuits are usually the result of overmixing the moist ingredients with the dry or of kneading too hard and too long.

Heavy and squat biscuits result when the dough is undermixed or underkneaded so that the leavening is not thoroughly distributed. Yellowish spots that appear on the crust are another tipoff that the dough was underworked.

Leaden biscuits can result from using over-the-hill baking powder or soda. Be sure to check freshness dates before you begin.

WORK SAVER

Pastry Blender

A pastry blender does a quick and efficient job of cutting fat into dry ingredients. Choose one that is sturdy, with a handle that feels good in your hand. The cutting edges of the U-shaped wires or thin blades should be slightly sharp.

Buttermilk Spoon-Drop Biscuits

- **2** cups unsifted all-purpose flour
- **3** teaspoons baking powder
- **1** teaspoon sugar
- **1/2** teaspoon baking soda
- **1/2** teaspoon salt
- **1/4** cup (1/2 stick) butter, cut up
- **2** tablespoons vegetable shortening
- **1** cup buttermilk

1 Preheat the oven to 450°F. In a large bowl, combine flour, baking powder, sugar, baking soda, and salt. Using a pastry blender, cut in the butter and shortening until mixture resembles coarse crumbs.

2 Add buttermilk and stir lightly with a fork just until a soft dough forms.

3 Turn dough onto a lightly floured work surface and knead gently 6 to 8 times.

4 Drop dough by heaping tablespoonfuls 1 inch apart on ungreased baking sheets and bake until golden—12 to 15 minutes. Serve immediately. Makes 16 biscuits.

1 Biscuit: Calories 104; Total Fat 5 g; Saturated Fat 2 g; Protein 2 g; Carbohydrates 13 g; Fiber 1 g; Sodium 214 mg; Cholesterol 8 mg

prep time-10 minutes
cooking time-12 to 15 minutes

Our biscuits are delicious plain, but are equally good mixed with some of the flavor boosters listed at left. Above, plain, cheese, bacon, and chive-flavored Buttermilk Spoon-Drop Biscuits.

PARMESAN DROP BISCUITS

Prepare dough as at left, **adding** 1/2 to 2/3 cup freshly grated Parmesan cheese to the dry ingredients in Step 1. Makes 16 biscuits.

CREAM SCONES

Simply put, scones are the Scottish cousins of North American rolled and cut biscuits. The Scots take theirs with tea. On this side of the Atlantic, we like them for breakfast.

SWEET BISCUITS

Scones and cut biscuits are much alike; the technique for making them is identical. The differences are that scones are usually sweeter, enriched with eggs or cream, and larger than standard biscuits.

Compare our Cream Scone recipe with an equivalent cut biscuit dough: 2 cups of flour, 1 tablespoon of baking powder, 1/2 teaspoon of salt, 1/4 cup of chilled shortening, and 3/4 cup of milk, producing about 1 1/2 dozen biscuits.

ROLLING AND CUTTING

See Tender Biscuits on page 62 for hints about mixing and kneading dough.

Roll out the dough with a rolling pin or pat it down lightly and evenly with your hands. If the dough is uneven, the scones will be lopsided. Measure the thickness with a ruler to be certain.

To cut scones, use a 3-inch round cutter. A clean empty tuna can will serve the purpose in a pinch.

When you gather the scraps

after cutting, roll them out without rekneading them; rekneading will produce tough scones.

Use a wide spatula to transfer the cut scones to the baking sheet. For soft-sided scones, place them close together on the baking sheet. For firm-sided scones, space them at least 1 1/2 inches apart.

SOMETHING EXTRA

Raisins and dried currants are both traditional additions to scones. Add about 1/3 cup per 2 cups of flour to the dry ingredients at the same time as adding the egg mixture.

GRIDDLE SCONES

Another traditional way to cook scone dough is as a single large griddle scone (or what the Scots call a girdle

scone) cut into wedges.

When the dough is mixed, divide it in half, then knead each half lightly on a floured board. Roll or pat into 2 flat rounds, 1/4- to 1/2-inch thick. Cut each round into 6 wedges and place half of the wedges on an ungreased griddle over medium heat. (Don't raise the heat or the scone will scorch before it has time to cook through.)

Cook until lightly browned on one side—about 5 minutes—then turn and brown the flip side. Repeat with the remaining 6 wedges. Serve hot with butter and jam.

Revive cooled scones by splitting them in half and toasting in a toaster oven or broiler.

SHORTCAKES

Scones make perfect fruit shortcakes. Prepare and bake as directed. Split the scones while still warm; fill and top with strawberries, blueberries, peaches, or other ripe fruit with their juices and sweetened whipped cream.

ACCOMPANIMENTS FOR SCONES

At tea time in Scotland and England, the time-honored companions for scones are fruit preserves and clotted cream (whipped cream cheese and unsweetened whipped cream are acceptable substitutes). Each piece of scone is spread with preserves and cream just before it's popped into the mouth.

SPREADABLES

Honey and fruit butters are excellent spreads for scones. Whip about 1/3 cup of honey

CUTTING SCONES

1 Roll or pat the dough to an even 1/2-inch thickness. Dip the edges of a 3-inch cutter into flour to prevent sticking.

2 Firmly push the cutter into the dough and lift it straight up. Twisting the cutter makes lopsided scones. Cut scones as close together as possible to eliminate most scraps.

or fruit preserves into 1/2 cup (1 stick) of softened butter or margarine. Spoon into a small bowl and chill to firm slightly before serving.

A HINT OF HONEY

The kind of honey you use in Honey-Oatmeal Scones and other recipes can affect flavors in an interesting way. In general, light-colored honeys are milder than dark-colored honeys. Mild honeys include clover, alfalfa, and orange blossom. For a bolder flavor, try buckwheat, sourwood, or wildflower honey.

CHEDDAR SCONES

Prepare as directed at right, **forking** in 1/2 cup shredded Cheddar cheese after **cutting** in the butter. Makes 8 scones.

HONEY-OATMEAL SCONES

Prepare as directed at right, **reducing** flour to 1 1/2 cups, **adding** 1/2 cup quick-cooking oats to flour, **omitting** sugar, **reducing** eggs to 1, and **adding** 2 tablespoons honey to egg/cream mixture in Step 2. **Roll** dough to a 3/4-inch thickness. **Bake** until golden—10 to 15 minutes. Makes 5 scones.

The coffee-break selection at right includes an oven-baked Cheddar Scone and a stovetop-baked griddle scone wedge.

Cream Scones

- 2 **cups unsifted all-purpose flour**
- 1 **tablespoon sugar**
- 3 **teaspoons baking powder**
- 1/2 **teaspoon salt**
- 1/4 **cup (1/2 stick) butter, cut up**
- 2 **eggs**
- 1/3 **cup heavy cream (about)**

1 Preheat the oven to 425°F. In a large bowl, combine flour, sugar, baking powder, and salt. Using a pastry blender, cut in butter until mixture resembles coarse crumbs; set aside.

2 In a medium-size bowl, beat eggs and cream with a fork until well blended. Stir egg mixture lightly into dry ingredients (adding an additional 1 to 2 tablespoons cream, if necessary, to make a soft but manageable dough).

3 Turn dough onto a lightly floured work surface and knead gently 5 to 6 times.

4 Roll dough to a 1/2-inch thickness. Cut into rounds with a floured 3-inch biscuit cutter, rerolling (but not rekneading) scraps as necessary.

5 Arrange scones 2 inches apart on an ungreased baking sheet and bake until golden—10 to 15 minutes. Serve hot. Makes 8 scones.

**1 Scone: Calories 224;
Total Fat 11 g; Saturated Fat 6 g;
Protein 5 g; Carbohydrates 26 g;
Fiber 1 g; Sodium 337 mg;
Cholesterol 82 mg**

*prep time-20 minutes
cooking time-10 to 15 minutes*

GRIDDLE CAKES

Griddle cake and waffle batters are so simple to make and so superior to mixes, it's a wonder why anyone would take the shortcut on a regular basis.

BATTER UP

Whether you call them griddle cakes, flapjacks, or pancakes, you'll want a light hand when you make them. Mix the batter only briefly. It should not be smooth. Tip: For the best results, cover the bowl and let the batter rest in the refrigerator for 1/2 hour or more before cooking.

For soufflé-light griddle cakes, separate the eggs and beat the whites until stiff. Add the yolks to the dry ingredients with the milk and fold the egg whites in at the end. If you use beaten egg whites in your batter, cook the griddle cakes immediately after mixing; don't rest the batter in the refrigerator.

Griddle cake batters must be thick enough to hold their shape in a skillet. Thin batter will thicken if left to stand for 20 minutes or so. Thick batter can be thinned with water or milk, but add it gradually, whisking gently as you do so.

GRIDDLES AND PANS

Use a heavy, well-seasoned skillet or griddle. A nonstick finish virtually eliminates sticking problems. If the pan

needs to be oiled, do so sparingly, removing excess with a piece of paper toweling, or use vegetable cooking spray.

Set the pan over moderately high heat. It is important that it be hot enough for the cakes to start cooking immediately when the batter is poured into the pan. If the skillet is too hot, they will brown too quickly, before the inside has a chance to cook. When perfectly heated, a drop of water will dance across the skillet.

TINY BUBBLES

As the griddle cakes bake, bubbles form on the surface. The moment they start to break (1 to 2 minutes depending on thickness), use a pancake turner to lift one edge and peek underneath. If it is golden brown, flip the cake

and cook until the second side is browned, which takes about half as long as the first side.

Serve griddle cakes immediately. Covering them or keeping them in a warm oven will only result in soggy cakes.

WAFFLE TIPS

Griddle cake batter can be turned into waffle batter by adding more fat (2 extra tablespoons for every 2 cups of flour). The extra fat is necessary to prevent the waffles from sticking to the hot iron. The batter must be thin enough to spread evenly over the surface of the heated iron. The exact amount may take some experimentation. Better to pour out a bit too little batter than too much.

Wrap and freeze leftover waffles. Reheat at 350°F in a toaster oven for 5 minutes or pop them into a toaster.

TEMPTING TOPPINGS

Maple syrup is the traditional favorite for griddle cakes. Its flavor is best when it's heated before serving and less is used because warm syrup spreads more easily than cold.

Cut back on the amount of butter you use by stirring it into the hot syrup. Figure on about 2 teaspoons of butter for each cup of syrup.

For other great griddle cake breakfast toppings try: berries or chopped fruit with their juice; fruit preserves thinned with fruit juice and heated; applesauce with a sprinkling of cinnamon powder; sour cream mixed with brown sugar and minced crystallized ginger.

If you enjoy griddle cakes for supper, try topping them with creamed or curried chicken or shrimp, lobster Newburg, or creamed chipped beef.

LOW-FAT CAKES

To reduce fat and cholesterol in pancakes and waffles, make the batter substituting 1 whole egg and 2 egg whites for each 2 eggs.

COOKING AHEAD

Stir up your own griddle cake mix by blending the dry ingredients and storing them in the refrigerator in a tightly covered container. Bring to room temperature before adding the fat and liquid.

Griddle cake and waffle batters can be covered and refrigerated overnight. However, the resulting griddle cakes and waffles will not be as light as they should be because the baking powder will have lost much of its oomph overnight.

WORK SAVER
Wire Whisk

A wire whisk with a sturdy handle is the ideal tool for mixing griddle cake and waffle batters. It combines wet and dry ingredients efficiently, and with little resistance, thereby making the threat of overmixing far less than with a spoon.

Silver Dollar Griddle Cakes

2 cups unsifted all-purpose flour
2 tablespoons sugar
4 teaspoons baking powder
1 teaspoon salt
2 eggs
1½ cups milk
¼ cup vegetable oil, melted butter or margarine

1 In a large bowl, whisk together flour, sugar, baking powder, and salt; set aside.

2 In a medium-size bowl, beat eggs lightly. Whisk in milk and oil.

3 Gradually pour milk mixture into dry ingredients, whisking continually, just until dry ingredients are moistened and only a few small lumps remain.

4 Lightly grease a griddle or large skillet with oil and heat over moderately high heat until a drop of cold water will dance across the griddle—1 to 2 minutes.

5 For each silver dollar griddle cake, pour 1 level tablespoonful batter onto the hot griddle or, if larger griddle cakes are desired, use ¼ cup batter.

6 Cook until bubbles form on the surface and the underside is golden brown—2 to 3 minutes. Turn and brown flip side. Makes thirty-six 3-inch griddle cakes or twelve 4-inch griddle cakes.

Per Three 3-Inch Cakes:
Calories 156; Total Fat 7 g;
Saturated Fat 2 g; Protein 4 g;
Carbohydrates 20 g; Fiber 1 g;
Sodium 355 mg; Cholesterol 40 mg

prep time-30 minutes
cooking time-20 minutes

RICE GRIDDLE CAKES

Prepare as directed at left, **adding** ½ cup cooked white, brown, or wild rice to the dry ingredients. Makes thirty-six 3-inch griddle cakes or twelve 4-inch griddle cakes.

WAFFLES

Prepare as directed at left, **adding** an additional 2 tablespoons vegetable oil, melted butter or margarine for a total of 6 tablespoons. **Pour** batter into preheated waffle iron and **cook** according to manufacturer's directions until steaming stops and waffle is golden—about 4 minutes. Makes four 8-inch waffles.

PERFECT MUFFINS

Though quick and easy, muffins have a reputation for being difficult to make. If you follow our lead, your muffins will be perfect every time.

MUFFIN TECHNIQUE

Muffin batters go together quickly. If you have children at home, they will love to have a hand in the process.

It's the way muffins are mixed that makes them tender or tough, fine-crumbed or coarse. There's no need to sift the dry ingredients together. The best way to combine them is with a wire whisk. You'll aerate the dry ingredients as you mix them, which makes for lighter muffins.

It's important that the liquid and dry ingredients be mixed only enough to moisten—no more. Nothing toughens a muffin faster than overmixing. If you mix muffin batter too long or too hard, you develop the gluten (protein) in the flour. Overactivated gluten makes the texture leathery. It is also what sends tunnels through the muffins.

KEEPING FRUIT ALOFT

To keep fruit and nuts from sinking to the bottom of muffins, dredge them lightly in flour and wait until the batter is nearly mixed before folding them in.

Juicy fruits such as blueberries can turn the dredging flour into paste. To solve the problem in our recipe, we've folded the blueberries in along with the softly beaten egg white.

ARE THEY DONE YET?

Stick a toothpick in the center of a muffin in the middle of the muffin pan. If it comes out clean, the muffins are done. Or press the center of a muffin lightly with your finger. If it is springy and shows no fingermark, it's done.

Cool muffins briefly in their pan before turning it upside down to remove the muffins.

BERRY TIPS

Wash and stem berries before using, and be sure to pat them dry on paper toweling. Water on the berries can cause soggy spots in the muffins.

If fresh blueberries are not available, use dry-pack frozen berries, but don't thaw them first. If they are thawed, they will lose their shape and will color the muffin batter purple.

BLUEBERRY BREAD

To make bread from muffin batter, pour the batter into a well-greased 9" x 5" x 3" loaf pan. Bake at 350°F or until a cake tester inserted in the center comes out clean— about 40 to 45 minutes. Cool 10 minutes in the pan on a wire rack, turn out onto the rack, and cool right side up.

Whenever you adapt a muffin recipe for bread or make a quick bread into muffins, be sure to adjust the oven temperature: 400°F for muffins; 350°F for breads.

KITCHEN CHEMISTRY

We use brown sugar to enrich the flavor of our muffins. Brown sugar (honey and molasses too) provides extra acid in a recipe—in our recipe it is heightened by the acidity of buttermilk. The reaction of the two acids with the two alkalis—baking powder and soda— gives the muffins extra "lift" as they bake.

COOKING AHEAD

Shortcut prep time by making your own muffin mix. Whisk together 8 1/2 cups all-purpose flour, 1/2 cup sugar, 1/4 cup baking powder, and 4 teaspoons salt. Refrigerate airtight for up to 3 weeks.

For 15 muffins: Use 2 1/3 cups of mix (brought to room temperature), 1 cup of milk, 1/4 cup of vegetable oil, and 1 egg. Combine and bake.

TASTY CHANGES

Replace the blueberries with 1 cup of any of the following: diced pitted dates, raisins, chopped pecans or walnuts. Or add 1/2 cup crisp crumbled bacon, substituting 2 tablespoons of bacon drippings for 2 tablespoons of oil.

KITCHEN MATH

1 pint supermarket blueberries =

2 cups; 1 1/4 to 1 7/8 cups after stemming, washing, sorting

1 pint piled-high farmer's market blueberries =

2 1/2 cups; 2 1/4 to 2 1/3 cups after stemming, washing, sorting

WORK SAVER

Ice Cream Scoop

To ensure that your muffins are uniform in size, use an ice cream scoop with a spring release to drop the batter into the muffin cups. The cups must be greased or lined with paper liners. For best results, never fill a cup more than 3/4 full.

Cranberry Muffins

Prepare as directed at right, **substituting** 1 cup washed fresh or (un-thawed) frozen cranberries for blueberries. **Increase** sugar to 2/3 cup. **Substitute** orange zest for lemon zest and **omit** the pepper. Makes 12 muffins.

Cranberry-Cheddar Muffins

Prepare as directed for Cranberry Muffins, above, **omitting** orange zest, **stirring** 1/2 cup shredded Cheddar cheese into the dry ingredients, and **adding** 1/8 teaspoon ground cayenne to the dry ingredients. Makes 12 muffins.

Best Blueberry Muffins

2 **cups unsifted all-purpose flour**
1/2 **cup firmly packed light brown sugar**
2 1/2 **teaspoons baking powder**
1/2 **teaspoon baking soda**
1/2 **teaspoon salt**
1/4 **teaspoon ground allspice**
1/8 **teaspoon black pepper**
1 1/4 **cups buttermilk**
1/4 **cup (1/2 stick) butter, melted**
1 **egg, separated**
1 **teaspoon grated lemon zest**
1 **cup washed and stemmed fresh blueberries or solidly frozen blueberries**

1 Preheat the oven to 400°F. Line with paper liners or grease twelve 2½-inch muffin cups.

2 In a large bowl, whisk together flour, sugar, baking powder, baking soda, salt, allspice, and pepper until well combined.

3 In a small bowl, whisk together buttermilk, melted butter, egg yolk, and lemon zest. In a separate bowl, beat egg white until soft peaks form.

4 Make a well in the center of the dry ingredients and stir in the liquid ingredients until they are just combined. Do not overmix. Fold in the beaten egg white and blueberries.

5 Spoon into prepared cups, filling each ¾ full. Bake until a toothpick inserted in the center of a muffin comes out clean—about 20 minutes. Cool on a rack for 10 minutes, loosen around the edges, and turn out on the rack. Makes 12 muffins.

1 Muffin: Calories 156; Total Fat 5 g; Saturated Fat 3 g; Protein 4 g; Carbohydrates 25 g; Fiber 1 g; Sodium 279 mg; Cholesterol 29 mg

prep time-17 minutes • cooking time-20 minutes

Our recipes include Blueberry, Cranberry, and Cranberry-Cheddar muffins, right.

FRUIT BREADS

Quick breads include fruit and nut loaves such as our Banana-Apricot Bread as well as vegetable variations like zucchini and carrot. All are easy to put together and take just an hour to bake.

FOR TENDER LOAVES

Most quick-bread batters begin with creaming butter and sugar, adding eggs, and beating the mixture until it is light. This is the one instance in quick-bread making where a little overbeating is better than underbeating. When adding the dry ingredients, beat only until incorporated into the creamed mixture and not a second longer.

As soon as the batter is mixed, pour it into the baking pan and put it in the hot oven as quickly as possible. If you let the batter sit, the carbon dioxide released by the baking powder and soda will dissipate before it has chance to make the bread rise.

The batter should be at room temperature when the loaf is put in the oven. If it is cold, the loaf may brown before the center is cooked.

Adjust the oven rack so that the pan sits squarely in the middle of the oven, allowing the heat to circulate evenly all around it. The bread is done when the top is golden brown and a toothpick inserted in the center comes out clean.

COMMON CRACKS

Don't worry if a crack forms down the center of a loaf while it bakes. Baking powder and soda breads often crack, particularly if they are heavy with nuts and moist fruits.

EASY RELEASE

Prepare the pan properly and you'll have no problem removing the loaf when it's done. Grease the pan lightly but thoroughly, making sure you get into the corners. Then dust the pan lightly with flour, covering all surfaces evenly. Remove the excess flour by turning the pan upside down and giving it a sharp rap.

Cool the bread in the pan for at least 10 minutes before turning it out on a rack. The steam that accumulates around the bread as it cools helps release it from the pan.

COOKING AHEAD

The moisture in fruit breads makes them good keepers; flavor and texture improve when a loaf has had time to rest. When cooled, wrap a loaf securely in foil or plastic wrap. It will keep well in the refrigerator for several days and freeze well for up to 1 month. To thaw, unwrap and let the loaf sit at room temperature for about 1½ hours.

You can warm up or refresh a loaf by wrapping it in a moist towel, placing it on a steamer rack over a little water in a covered pan, and steaming for about 10 minutes.

PICK A LOAF PAN

Metal and glass pans conduct heat differently. Recipes usually specify which type to use. If you use glass when a metal pan is specified, lower the oven temperature 25°F to prevent overbaking. If you use metal when a glass pan is specified, raise the heat 25°F.

For golden-brown breads, use dark metal pans. For paler loaves, choose shiny pans. If breads tend to brown too quickly in your oven, use a shiny pan and put it on a baking sheet in the oven.

CLEAN CUTS

Fruit and nut loaves should be sliced thin, no more than about ¼-inch thick. Loaves will slice more easily if they are first cooled, wrapped, and refrigerated for a day.

For perfect slices, use a long sharp knife, wiping the blade clean between cuts. Use a light sawing motion to prevent slices from breaking.

To slice bread containing lots of nuts, use a length of dental floss pulled taut.

CRUNCHY TOPS

Add a little extra crunch to a loaf by sprinkling one of the following on the top just before baking: sesame seeds, wheat germ, poppy seeds, or finely chopped nuts.

ZUCCHINI NOTES

Zucchini is mild enough to suit both sweet and savory quick breads. It makes a particularly good addition to cornbread, for instance, where it adds moisture.

To shred zucchini, use the mid-size blade on a standard 4-sided grater. When adding the grated zucchini to the batter, fold it in gently to avoid bruising, which will make the batter wetter than it should be.

KITCHEN MATH

It's best to bake bread in the exact pan size called for in a recipe. For an evenly shaped loaf, never fill the pan more than ¾ full. There are two standard-size rectangular loaf pans, one only slightly smaller than the other, but their volumes differ widely.

9" x 5" x 3" pan = maximum volume 8 cups
8½" x 4½" x 2¾" pan = maximum volume 6 cups

Banana-Apricot Bread

- 1/2 **cup unblanched whole almonds**
- 1 3/4 **cups unsifted all-purpose flour**
- 1 1/2 **teaspoons baking powder**
- 1/2 **teaspoon baking soda**
- 1/2 **teaspoon salt**
- 1/2 **cup (1 stick) butter, at room temperature**
- 1/3 **cup firmly packed light brown sugar**
- 1/2 **cup granulated sugar**
- 2 **eggs**
- 1 **cup mashed bananas**
- 1/3 **cup buttermilk**
- 1/4 **teaspoon almond extract**
- 1 **cup coarsely chopped dried apricots**
- 2 **tablespoons finely chopped crystallized ginger**

Our trio of fruit and vegetable breads include Banana-Apricot, top right, Zucchini, foreground, and Carrot, top left.

1 Preheat the oven to 350°F. Grease a 9" x 5" x 3" loaf pan; dust with flour.

2 Place almonds in a pie pan and toast, uncovered, in the oven until lightly browned—about 7 minutes. Cool, coarsely chop, and set aside.

3 In a large bowl, stir together flour, baking powder, baking soda, and salt and set aside.

4 In the bowl of an electric mixer, cream butter at moderate speed until soft. Gradually add the 2 sugars, beating well after each addition. Add eggs, 1 at a time, again beating well after each addition. Mix in flour mixture, a little at a time, beating after each addition only enough to incorporate. Batter should not be smooth.

5 In a small bowl, combine bananas, buttermilk, and almond extract. Mix into batter, then fold in apricots, ginger, and reserved almonds.

6 Scrape into the prepared pan and bake on the middle oven rack until a toothpick inserted in the center comes out clean—50 to 55 minutes.

7 Cool in the pan on a rack for 10 minutes, loosen around the edge, and turn out on the rack. Cool before slicing. Makes 1 loaf, about 12 slices.

1 Slice: Calories 331; Total Fat 15 g; Saturated Fat 7 g; Protein 6 g; Carbohydrates 47 g; Fiber 3 g; Sodium 171 mg; Cholesterol 68 mg

prep time-22 minutes • cooking time-62 minutes

ZUCCHINI BREAD

Prepare as directed at left, **substituting** 1 cup chopped pecans for almonds. **Add** 1 teaspoon ground cinnamon to the dry ingredients. **Use** 3/4 cup granulated sugar only, **substitute** 1 1/2 cups shredded zucchini for bananas, and **omit** apricots and crystallized ginger. **Increase** baking time to 1 hour. Makes 1 loaf.

CARROT BREAD

Prepare as directed at left, **omitting** almonds and baking soda and **increasing** baking powder to 2 1/2 teaspoons; also **mix** 1/4 teaspoon each ground cardamom, ginger, and allspice into dry ingredients. **Use** 2/3 cup granulated sugar only, **substitute** 1 1/2 cups shredded peeled carrots for bananas and 1/2 cup orange juice for buttermilk. **Omit** almond extract, apricots, and crystallized ginger. **Increase** baking time to 1 hour. Makes 1 loaf.

BANANA-NUT LOAF

Prepare as directed at left, **adding** 1/2 teaspoon ground cinnamon and 1/4 teaspoon ground allspice to the dry ingredients. **Substitute** chopped walnuts for almonds and golden seedless raisins for apricots; **omit** crystallized ginger. Makes 1 loaf.

CORNBREAD

To turn out a golden loaf of old-fashioned cornbread, you need a heavy ovenproof skillet, a light touch, and just the right proportion of stone-ground cornmeal and flour.

COLORFUL CORNMEAL

North America's native people not only gave us corn but also taught us how to make cornbread. Cornmeal is an ingredient in many other traditional specialties, such as hush puppies, spoon bread, batter bread, johnnycakes, and corn muffins.

Depending on the region, cornbread can be sweet, salty, or something in between. Cornmeal is available in white, yellow, and blue. The various colors of cornmeal can be used interchangeably, since they have virtually the same flavor, however, bear in mind that blue cornmeal is more crumbly and difficult to work with, and may make some dishes look unusual.

THE RIGHT MIX

Most cornbeads follow the muffin method of mixing: Dry ingredients are combined, then the liquids, and the two are stirred together only long enough to moisten. Overmixing guarantees tough bread.

FOR CRISP CRUSTS

For crisp-crusted cornbread, place the fat in the skillet (purists insist on bacon drippings) and set it in the oven to heat as the oven preheats. Batter should sizzle when it's poured into the skillet, a practice that harks back to the old days when it was "baked" over an open fire. Don't be tempted to save time by skipping this crucial step.

When cornbread is done, it's crisp and golden on top and a toothpick inserted in the center comes out clean.

PICKLED PEPPERS

Jalapeño pepper contributes a little fire to our Santa Fe Cornbread. We've used a pickled pepper, which is a little hotter than the fresh. If you prefer milder stuff, a fresh jalapeño pepper can always be substituted. For hotter flavor, use a more incendiary chile. Keep in mind that the flavor will become less fierce as it bakes in the bread.

TOO HOT TO HANDLE

It's the seeds and veins that contain most of a pepper's heat, which is why so many recipes call for them to be seeded. Wear rubber gloves when you clean and chop hot peppers and be sure to wash your hands well afterward. Volatile pepper oils really sting if you get any in your eyes. If you should get some in your eyes, rinse repeatedly with clear cold water.

SHOPPING FOR CORNMEAL

Old-fashioned stone-ground cornmeal is preferable to commercially milled cornmeal, which is ground to a powder between heavy steel rollers.

When cornmeal is stone ground, it retains some of the kernel's hull and germ. It's more nutritious and definitely more flavorful than powdered cornmeal, with the slightly gritty texture that is so important to cornbread lovers.

Because the corn oil in the germ is perishable, stone-ground cornmeal should be refrigerated or used within a month or so if stored at room temperature. Commercially milled cornmeal is shelf stable for about 3 months.

A NEW HERB IN TOWN

Fresh coriander, also known as cilantro, is growing in popularity. The herb—which is part of the parsley family and resembles Italian parsley—is used extensively both in Mexican and Asian cooking. It has a pungent flavor that may take some getting used to, but once the love affair with cilantro begins it never dies.

In spring, grow cilantro in a flowerpot or plant it directly in the garden. Enjoy it fresh throughout the summer. Bring the plant indoors when the weather cools for an extended supply of this delicious herb in autumn.

Store cilantro the same way as parsley—in a plastic bag in the crisper section of the refrigerator or, like a bouquet, with the stems in water, covered with a plastic bag.

FLAVOR BOOSTERS

Plain cornbread cries out for something to be added to the batter—try 1/2 cup of any of the following: crisp crumbled bacon; bits of ham; cooked carrots or zucchini; minced hard sausage; shredded Cheddar, Gruyère, or Monterey Jack cheese; cream-style corn.

WORK SAVER
Corn-Stick Mold

For a little change of pace, bake your batter in a corn-stick mold. Made of cast iron, like the skillet in our recipe, the mold is first greased and then heated good and hot before the batter is spooned in—filling the individual molds no more than 3/4 full. The sticks need only bake at 400°F for 20 minutes. When they are turned out of the mold, they resemble puffy, golden ears of corn.

Santa Fe Cornbread

- 5 tablespoons olive oil or bacon drippings
- 2 scallions, thinly sliced
- 2 cloves garlic, minced
- 1 small sweet red pepper, cored, seeded, and chopped
- 1/2 cup minced fresh coriander (cilantro)
- 1 pickled jalapeño pepper, cored, seeded, and minced
- 1 1/3 cups stone-ground yellow cornmeal
- 3/4 cup unsifted all-purpose flour
- 2 tablespoons sugar
- 3 teaspoons baking powder
- 1 teaspoon salt
- 1/2 teaspoon baking soda
- 1 1/4 cups buttermilk
- 2 eggs

1 Preheat the oven to 450°F. Brush a 10-inch cast-iron or ovenproof nonstick skillet with oil and set aside.

2 In a small skillet over moderate heat, heat 1 tablespoon of the oil 1 minute, add scallions and garlic and sauté, stirring frequently, until soft—about 2 minutes. Add red pepper and sauté, stirring frequently, until soft—about 4 minutes. Stir in coriander, jalapeño pepper, and the remaining 4 tablespoons oil and set aside.

3 Place the cast-iron skillet in the oven. Meanwhile, in a large bowl, stir together cornmeal, flour, sugar, baking powder, salt, and baking soda. In a small bowl, whisk together buttermilk and eggs. Stir onion-pepper mixture into buttermilk mixture.

4 Make a well in the center of the dry ingredients, pour in the liquid ingredients, and stir until just combined. Do not overmix.

5 Pour into the hot skillet, smoothing the top. Bake until a toothpick inserted in the center comes out clean—about 20 minutes. Cut into wedges; serve hot. Makes 8 servings.

1 Serving: Calories 242; Total Fat 11 g; Saturated Fat 2 g; Protein 6 g; Carbohydrates 31 g; Fiber 2 g; Sodium 593 mg; Cholesterol 55 mg

prep time-30 minutes • cooking time-23 minutes

CORNBREAD VARIATIONS

Corn Muffins: Prepare as directed at left, but preheat the oven to 400°F and **reduce** olive oil or bacon drippings to 4 tablespoons. **Omit** scallions, garlic, sweet red pepper, coriander, and jalapeño pepper. **Reduce** the salt to 3/4 teaspoon. **Scrape** a generous 1/4 cup of batter into each of twelve 2 1/2-inch muffin cups lined with paper liners or, if you prefer, well-greased muffin cups. **Bake** until lightly browned and springy to the touch—17 to 20 minutes. **Cool** 10 minutes in the pan, then **remove**. Makes 12 muffins.

Peppercorn Cornbread: Prepare as directed at left, **omitting** scallions, garlic, and jalapeño pepper. **Add** 1/2 teaspoon coarsely ground or crushed black peppercorns and 1/2 teaspoon rubbed sage or crumbled dried thyme. Makes 8 servings.

DINNER ROLLS

Once the technique is mastered for making Parker House Rolls, the door is open for creating all sorts of variations.

ABOUT YEAST

Yeast appears dry when shaken from its packet but it is actually a one-cell plant. Given moisture, food, oxygen, and warmth, yeast grows, emitting carbon dioxide, which makes dough rise.

What yeast feeds on is the starch in the flour. In our Parker House Roll recipe, sugar and potato provide extra food. The result is rolls that are tender, feather light, and pleasantly sweet.

There are two basic types of yeast. Fresh, or compressed, yeast is sold in cakes. Active dry yeast is granulated and comes in foil packets.

Most recipes call for active dry yeast. It has a longer shelf life and is more readily available than compressed, though either type of yeast can be used. Always check the freshness date on the package.

Yeast must be dissolved in water before it is mixed with other ingredients. The temperature of the water is critical—105°F to 115°F for dry yeast; no more than 95°F for compressed yeast. Too cool and the water will not activate the yeast; too hot and it will kill it. Use a thermometer to be sure.

KNEADING

For yeast breads and rolls, gluten in the flour has to be developed in order for the bread to rise. Kneading is the hand action used to stretch gluten strands. The strands create a network of cells that trap and hold the carbon dioxide released by the yeast. When the kneading is completed, the dough should be springy, smooth, and warm.

If you have an electric mixer with a dough hook or paddle attachment, it will do the work for you, but it's not nearly as satisfying—or as much fun— as kneading by hand.

CLEAN CUTS

When the recipe directs you to divide the dough in half after kneading, use a sharp knife to cut it cleanly. Pulling the dough apart will thin and break the strands of gluten that you have worked to form.

KNEADING AND RESTING DOUGH

1 When the ingredients are mixed, gather the dough into a ball on a lightly floured work surface. The dough will be shaggy; sprinkle with a little flour. Flatten the ball slightly and fold it toward you.

2 Using the heels of your hands, push the dough away with a downward motion and give the dough a quarter turn. Continue kneading for 5 to 10 minutes until the dough is smooth, satiny, and elastic.

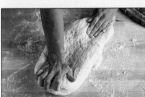

3 When the dough is well kneaded, shape it into a ball, then place it in a large well-buttered bowl and turn to grease all over. Cover with a cloth and set aside to rise.

4 Allow the dough to rise until it doubles in bulk. The amount of time this step takes will vary. For white flour dough in a moderately warm room, 50 to 60 minutes should do it.

5 When the dough has doubled in bulk, punch it down. Then transfer the dough to a lightly floured work surface. At this point, the dough will be kneaded again, shaped into rolls or loaves, and set aside to rise a second time.

PROPER RISING

Once the dough is kneaded, it is set aside to rise. Butter the surface of the dough by turning it over in a large buttered bowl. This keeps the dough from sticking to the bowl as it rises and keeps the surface of the dough from drying.

Most bread recipes require dough to rise once in the bowl and again after being shaped. As bread rises, the gluten strands stretch, becoming

(continued on page 76)

Parker House Rolls

- 2 tablespoons sugar
- 1/2 cup lukewarm (105°F to 115°F) water
- 2 packets (1/4 ounce each) active dry yeast
- 1 cup milk
- 1 cup water
- 2 teaspoons salt
- 1/2 cup (1 stick) plus 3 tablespoons butter, melted
- 1 large all-purpose potato, peeled, diced, boiled, and riced
- 6 1/2 to 7 cups unsifted all-purpose flour
- 1 egg, lightly beaten

1 In a small bowl, combine sugar, water, and yeast. Stir to dissolve and set aside until bubbly—about 10 minutes.

2 In a small saucepan over moderately high heat, bring milk and water to a boil. Transfer to a large bowl. With a wooden spoon or in an electric mixer with paddle attached, add salt and 3 tablespoons of the melted butter and cool 10 minutes. At moderate speed, mix in potato, 2 cups of the flour, and egg, beating for 1 minute after each addition.

3 Add yeast mixture and beat 1 minute more. If using an electric mixer, replace paddle with dough hook. Add 4 1/2 cups of the remaining flour and beat 3 to 5 minutes, adding 1/4 to 1/2 cup flour, if necessary, to make a soft, manageable dough.

4 Shape dough into a ball, place in a well-buttered 5-quart bowl, and turn to grease all over. Cover with a cloth and let rise in a warm, draft-free place until doubled in bulk—about 50 minutes.

5 Punch dough down, transfer to a lightly floured work surface, and divide into 4 equal portions. Working with 1 portion at a time, roll dough into an 8- by 10-inch rectangle 1/4-inch thick. Cut into 12 rounds with a floured 2 1/2-inch biscuit cutter; reroll scraps and cut 4 more circles.

6 Brush each circle with melted butter; then, using a ruler or the blunt side of a knife, crease each circle along the diameter and fold, stretching the top half so it covers the bottom half. Pinch edges to seal. Repeat with the remaining 3 portions of dough.

7 Arrange rolls on lightly greased baking sheets and brush tops with the remaining melted butter. Cover with a cloth and let rise 30 minutes. Preheat the oven to 350°F.

8 Bake rolls until golden brown—about 30 minutes. Serve warm or transfer to a rack to cool. Makes 64 rolls.

1 Roll: Calories 136; Total Fat 5 g; Saturated Fat 3 g; Protein 3 g; Carbohydrates 20 g; Fiber 1 g; Sodium 140 mg; Cholesterol 18 mg

prep time-30 minutes • rising time-80 minutes baking time-30 minutes

One dough recipe makes our Parker House Rolls, Fantans, and Cloverleaf Rolls, shown at right.

(continued from page 74)

thinner; thus the texture grows finer each time the dough rises.

Dough is at its best rising at 80°F to 85°F. The bowl should be kept out of drafts and covered with a cloth or a piece of plastic wrap coated with vegetable spray.

If the room temperature is cool, set the bowl of dough on a rack over a pan of steaming water or set the bowl in an unlit oven over a pan of steaming water. If the dough rises too quickly, move it to a cooler location.

If necessary, the process can be interrupted by placing the dough in the refrigerator. It will continue to rise but at a snail's pace, until you return it to room temperature.

Let the dough rise until it is doubled in bulk; the time this takes will vary according to the recipe and room temperature. It will take about half as long for the second rising as it did for the first.

Tip: To test whether dough has doubled in bulk, quickly press the tips of two fingers about 1/2 inch into the dough. If the dents stay, the dough has risen sufficiently.

Make a fist and push straight down into the center of the risen dough. This rids the dough of excess carbon dioxide and redistributes the rest. Pull the edges of the dough into the center and turn it over. At this point, the dough is ready to be shaped.

AVOIDING PROBLEMS

Beware of adding too much flour when kneading dough. The more flour that's added,

the drier the bread will be.

If the dough rises quickly and then stops before it's fully risen, you might have forgotten to add salt to the dough. Salt regulates the yeast.

If the bread doesn't rise high and light, you might have used water that was too hot when dissolving the yeast. Or the dough might not have been kneaded long enough.

If your bread has large holes, you might have overkneaded the dough—not likely if you knead by hand but very possible if you use an electric mixer to knead. Or the dough

might have been given too much time to rise, trapping gases inside. Or it might have risen too quickly.

If the baked bread is too dense, it probably was not given enough time to rise properly and double in bulk.

If a loaf baked without a bread pan spreads too much, the dough was probably too soft.

If a loaf is soggy when you slice it, it probably remained in the pan too long after baking. Some breads must be removed from their pans immediately after baking. Follow recipe directions.

PARKER HOUSE ROLL VARIATIONS

(See page 75 for basic recipe)

Fantans: Prepare as directed through Step 5, **cutting** out 25 rounds with a 2-inch biscuit cutter. **Stack** 5 rounds, **brushing** butter between the layers, and **stand** stacks on end in buttered muffin cups. **Brush** tops with butter. **Repeat** with remaining 3 portions of dough. **Cover** with a cloth and **let rise** 30 minutes. **Bake** as directed. Makes 20 rolls.

Cloverleafs: Prepare as directed through Step 4. **Punch** dough down, **transfer** to a lightly floured work surface, then **pinch off** 72 bits of dough and **roll** into 1-inch balls. **Place** in lightly greased muffin cups, 3 balls per cup. **Brush** tops with melted butter, **cover** with a cloth, and **let rise** for 30 minutes. **Bake** as directed. Makes 24 rolls.

Sticky Buns: Prepare as directed through Step 4. **Punch** dough down, **transfer** to a lightly floured work surface, and **divide** in half. **Roll** each into a 15- by 12-inch rectangle 1/4-inch thick. In a small bowl, **mix** together 1/2 cup each light brown sugar and light corn syrup, 2 teaspoons cinnamon, and 1 cup (2 sticks) softened butter. **Spread** half on each dough rectangle, leaving 1/2-inch margins, then **scatter** each with 1 cup chopped pecans. Beginning with the long side, **roll up** each rectangle jelly-roll fashion and place seam side down. With a sharp knife **cut** each roll into fifteen 1-inch slices. **Arrange** slices, not touching, in a lightly greased 15- by 10-inch jelly-roll pan. **Cover** with a cloth and let rise 20 minutes. **Bake** as directed but **increase** baking time to 40 minutes. **Brush** sticky buns with a little melted butter and **bake** 5 minutes more. Makes 30 buns.

CLOVERLEAFS

1 After it rises, transfer the dough to a floured work surface. Pinch off 72 bits and roll into 1-inch balls.

2 Place 3 balls in each greased muffin cup for each cloverleaf. Cover and let rise.

MAKING FANTANS

1 Roll dough, then cut rounds with a 2-inch cutter. Butter and stack, allowing 5 rounds per roll.

2 Stand the fantans on end in buttered muffin cups. Cover and let rise.

1 Roll out half of the dough at one time, spread with filling, and scatter nuts evenly on top. Roll lengthwise, jelly-roll fashion.

2 Seal and place seam side down. Cut rolls into 1-inch-thick slices. Arrange on baking sheet. Cover with a cloth and let rise.

Sticky Buns, right, start with the same dough as Parker House Rolls, but when they emerge from the oven, they're bubbling over with buttery cinnamon syrup.

SOURDOUGH BREAD

Sourdough breads and rolls have a distinct and tangy flavor. They require a sourdough starter, a fermented leavening, that you can make yourself.

WHAT IS SOURDOUGH?

Sourdough is a yeast starter that bakers were using long before the days of commercial yeast. A starter is a mixture of flour, water, and sugar which, when left in a warm place, attracts airborne yeast.

In traditional sourdough baking, the starter is left to sit until it is foamy—an indication that the yeast has fermented. The process takes days—or as long as 2 weeks—depending on temperature, humidity, and how much yeast is in the air. By the time it is ready to be used, the starter has developed a distinct sour flavor, which it imparts to the bread; hence the name.

Part of the starter is used for making a batch of bread right off, and the rest is saved and "fed" with flour, water, and sugar to keep it alive until the next batch of bread is baked. Although making starter is a lengthy process, it has to be done only once.

A FRESH START

Sourdough bread is made the traditional way by bakers around the country. Others simplify the process to guarantee dependable rising. Our version is a simplified one. We make the starter with a commercial yeast instead of airborne spores. It takes only about a day to develop.

Once the starter has been worked into the dough, the dough's handling is the same as for other yeast breads.

PERFECT BROWNING

To get a good, crunchy crust on bread such as sourdough, you need to give it a little steam. Use an atomizer spray

WHOLE-WHEAT SOURDOUGH

Prepare as directed at right, **substituting** 2 cups unsifted whole-wheat flour for 2 cups of the bread flour. Makes 2 loaves, about 10 slices each.

ONION SOURDOUGH BREAD

Prepare plain or Whole-Wheat Sourdough Bread as directed. During the first rising, **sauté** 1 pound thinly sliced yellow onions (about 3 medium-size) in 1 tablespoon butter in a heavy skillet over low heat 8 to 10 minutes until limp but not brown. **Cool** and **sprinkle** on loaves before final rising. **Bake** as directed. Makes 2 loaves, about 10 slices each.

HOW TO SLASH A LOAF

When dough has risen for the second time, use a sharp utility knife to slash the top with diagonal or cross-hatched strokes about 1/2-inch deep. After baking, the slashes dress up the loaf and add a little crunch.

bottle to spritz a light mist over the loaves just before they are put in the oven. Then spritz the hot oven 3 times during the first 10 minutes of baking.

For chewy crusts, bake the bread at slightly lower temperatures than directed. For thinner, crisper crusts, bake at slightly higher temperatures than directed.

For proper browning, bread needs plenty of room for air to circulate in the oven. In a regular-size oven, bake no more than 2 pans of bread at one time, switching them from side to side and front to back once during baking.

CHOOSING A FLOUR

"Hard" and "soft" flours are millers' terms. They refer to the hardness of the variety of wheat from which the flour was milled. The harder the wheat, the more gluten it contains and the chewier the bread made from it will be. Wheat and rye are the only grains that contain gluten.

The main types of wheat flours used in baking include bread flour, all-purpose flour, and whole-wheat flour. Bread flour is milled from hard wheat and requires the most kneading. It is the top choice for many kinds of breads. All-purpose flour is a blend of hard and soft flours and, as its name implies, is excellent for all general baking purposes, including many bread recipes. Whole-wheat flour contains the least amount of gluten of the three.

Our Onion Sourdough Bread variation is baked with a topping of sautéed onions.

2 For the Dough: Place Starter in a large bowl. With a wooden spoon or in an electric mixer with the paddle attached, mix in water, sugar, salt, and 2½ cups of the flour. Beat the dough at moderate speed until smooth—about 15 seconds.

3 If using an electric mixer, remove paddle and insert dough hook. Add 3 tablespoons of the melted butter and 2½ cups of the remaining flour, ½ cup at a time. Continue beating about 10 minutes, adding an extra ½ to 1 cup flour, if necessary, to make a smooth and elastic dough. (If mixing by hand, you will probably have to knead in the last of the flour.)

4 Shape dough into a ball, place in a well-buttered 5-quart bowl, and turn to grease all over. Cover with a cloth and let rise in a warm, draft-free place until doubled in bulk—1 to 1½ hours. Punch dough down, recover, and let rise 1½ hours more.

5 Punch dough down, turn onto a lightly floured work surface, and knead lightly until smooth—2 to 3 minutes. Divide dough in half and roll each into a ball. Place balls in lightly greased 8-inch round layer cake or springform pans, cover with a cloth, and let rise until doubled in bulk—45 minutes to 1 hour. Preheat the oven to 350°F.

6 Brush risen loaves with the remaining 1 tablespoon melted butter; then with a sharp knife, make a diagonal slash in the top of each.

7 Bake until the loaves are richly golden and sound hollow when tapped—45 to 50 minutes. Transfer at once to racks to cool. Makes 2 loaves, about 10 slices each.

1 Slice: Calories 94; Total Fat 7 g; Saturated Fat 4 g; Protein 1 g; Carbohydrates 7 g; Fiber 0 g; Sodium 321 mg; Cholesterol 19 mg

starter time-12 hours • prep time-45 minutes
rising time-3¼ to 4 hours • cooking time-45 to 50 minutes

Sourdough Bread

Starter:
- 2 cups lukewarm water (105°F to 115°F)
- 1 packet (¼ ounce) active dry yeast
- 1½ cups bread flour

Dough:
- 1½ cups Starter
- 1 cup water
- 2 tablespoons sugar
- 1 tablespoon salt
- 5 to 6 cups unsifted bread flour
- 4 tablespoons (½ stick) butter, melted

1 For the Starter: In a medium-size glass or ceramic bowl, whisk together water, yeast, and bread flour. Cover loosely with wax paper and set in a warm, draft-free place for 12 hours or overnight.

Spice Breads

Transforming basic yeast dough into sweet and spicy breads and rolls is just a matter of adding good things like dried fruits, nuts, and cinnamon swirls.

PRACTICE MAKES PERFECT

After you gain confidence in your yeast-dough-making skills, you'll want to expand your repertoire. The next step is sweet breads and rolls that are wonderful to serve for breakfast or a coffee break.

HOW TO SHAPE A LOAF

For all breads baked in standard bread pans: Pat or roll the dough into about a 9- by 15-inch rectangle. Starting with a short side, roll the dough up tight, pressing down on it to push out air and seal it after each roll.

After the final roll, seal the ends by pressing down on them with the sides of your hands; fold the ends under the bread, making sure that the loaf is the same length as the pan. Place the shaped loaf, seam side down, in a greased loaf pan.

The shaped dough should touch all sides of the pan. This ensures that it will be supported as it rises and bakes.

For rolled loaves, such as our Cinnamon Raisin Swirl, be sure the seam is well sealed after rolling in the filling and before placing the loaf in a pan to rise a second time. If the seam comes undone, pinch it closed before baking.

PICK A PAN

Most baking experts agree that uncoated aluminum pans produce the most evenly browned and uniform results. Dark metal and glass loaf pans absorb more heat and make very dark crusts.

CHOOSING A FRUIT

Thompson seedless and muscat are the grape varieties commonly used for raisins. Both dark seedless raisins and golden sultanas begin as Thompson seedless grapes. The color difference is due to their drying and processing techniques. Dark raisins are sun dried; light raisins are

COOK'S SECRETS

Nick Malgieri
Director of Baking Program, Peter Kump's New York Cooking School

"When rolling fillings into dough, jelly-roll fashion, make sure the dough is evenly thick. Roll firmly, but not too tight, which can create thin spots and cause the filling to pop through the dough while it bakes.

"A dough scraper and a pancake turner are both useful for scraping up dough when it sticks to a work surface."

mechanically dried and have had sulfur dioxide added to preserve their sunny color.

Muscat raisins have the most intense sweet flavor. They also have seeds. When tiny zante grapes are dried, they become currants, smaller and tarter than raisins.

SOAKING RAISINS

Soaking raisins (and other dried fruits) in hot water for 15 to 30 minutes before baking ensures that they will remain moist. Plumping also helps to prevent fruit from sinking to the bottom of the loaf. Drain well before using.

CHOICE NUTS

The best nuts for baking include pecans, almonds, hazelnuts, pine nuts, peanuts, pistachios, walnuts, and macadamia nuts.

Currant-Hazelnut Bread

Prepare as directed at right through Step 3. In Step 4, **knead** 1 cup drained, soaked dried currants and 1/2 cup chopped, toasted hazelnuts into dough instead of raisins. In the filling (Step 5), **substitute** 1 teaspoon each ground coriander and ground ginger for cinnamon. **Shape** loaves, **let rise**, and **bake** as directed. Instead of icing cooled loaves, **dust** with 1/4 cup sifted confectioners sugar. Makes 2 loaves.

Hot Cross Buns

Prepare as at right through Step 3. **Punch** dough down, **transfer** to a lightly floured work surface, and **knead** gently for 2 minutes. **Divide** dough into 12 equal portions (for large buns) or 24 (for small buns). **Knead** each portion into a ball. **Arrange** on 1 or 2 greased baking sheets. With sharp scissors or knife, **cut** an "X" in the top of each bun. **Bake** in a 375°F oven until golden brown—12 to 15 minutes. **Prepare** icing as directed in Step 9, **pour** into a self-sealing plastic bag, **snip** a 1/8-inch hole in one bottom corner, and **pipe** icing into a cross on top of each bun. Makes 12 large or 24 small buns.

Cinnamon-Raisin Swirl

- 6 teaspoons sugar
- 1 cup lukewarm (105°F to 115°F) whole or 2% milk
- 2 packets (1/4 ounce each) active dry yeast
- 2 1/4 cups lukewarm (105°F to 115°F) water
- 5 tablespoons butter or margarine, melted
- 2 teaspoons salt
- 6 to 6 1/2 cups unsifted all-purpose flour
- 1 cup dark seedless raisins, soaked

Cinnamon Swirl Filling:
- 3 tablespoons butter or margarine, melted
- 1/2 cup sugar
- 1 tablespoon ground cinnamon

Icing:
- 2 cups sifted confectioners sugar
- 2 tablespoons water

1 In a large bowl, combine 1 teaspoon sugar with milk and yeast and stir to dissolve. Set aside until bubbly—5 to 10 minutes. In a medium-size bowl, combine 1 1/4 cups water, 4 tablespoons butter, salt, and the remaining 5 teaspoons sugar. Stir into yeast mixture.

2 With a wooden spoon or in an electric mixer with the dough hook attached, beat in flour, 1 cup at a time, until a soft dough forms. Continue to beat at moderate speed until dough is elastic—7 to 8 minutes (or knead on a floured work surface 8 to 10 minutes).

3 Pour the final 1 tablespoon butter into a 5-quart bowl, shape dough into a ball, place in bowl, and turn to grease. Cover with a cloth and set aside to rise in a warm, draft-free place until doubled in bulk—about 1 hour.

4 Lightly butter two 9" x 5" x 3" loaf pans. Punch dough down, transfer to a lightly floured work surface, and knead gently for 2 minutes. Divide dough in half and let rest, covered, 5 to 10 minutes. Working with 1 portion at a time, roll into a 9- by 15-inch rectangle. Sprinkle 1/2 of the raisins over each portion of dough and gently knead until evenly distributed. Cover and let rest 10 minutes.

5 For the Filling: In a small bowl, combine 2 tablespoons butter, sugar, and cinnamon. Again roll each portion of dough into a 9- by 15-inch rectangle; spread each with 1/2 cinnamon filling. Beginning with a short side, roll up jelly-roll fashion. Place loaves, seam side down, in prepared pans, cover, and set aside to rise for 1 hour. Preheat the oven to 400°F.

6 Brush loaves with the remaining 1 tablespoon butter and bake until bread is brown and sounds hollow when tapped—35 to 40 minutes. Cool in pans on a rack for 10 minutes, loosen around the edges, and turn out.

7 For the Icing: In a small bowl, combine confectioners sugar with water, stirring until smooth. Brush over cooled loaves. Makes 2 loaves, about 16 slices each.

1 Slice: Calories 180; Total Fat 4 g; Saturated Fat 3 g; Protein 3 g; Carbohydrates 32 g; Fiber 1 g; Sodium 179 mg; Cholesterol 12 mg

prep time-30 to 35 minutes
rising time-2 hours total
baking time-35 to 40 minutes

OATMEAL BREAD

Rolled oats are the basis for a crunchy, nutty bread that is as good for sandwiches as it is for toasting.

OATS FOR FLOUR

Since oatmeal does not contain gluten, it is too soft to use on its own in bread recipes. It must be combined with wheat flour—the two pair up beautifully. Oatmeal can be used to replace up to 1/3 of the all-purpose flour in bread, muffin, and cookie recipes, adding fiber, texture, and flavor.

WHICH OATS TO CHOOSE?

When the inedible hull is removed from an oat, what is left is the groat, or kernel.

Old-fashioned, or rolled, oats are oat kernels that have been toasted, steamed, and rolled flat into flakes.

Quick-cooking oatmeal is made from kernels that have been cut into 2 or 3 pieces before steaming and rolling to shorten cooking time.

Instant oatmeal is made from finely cut oat kernels that are twice steamed and rolled extra thin to eliminate the need for cooking.

Rolled oats and quick-cooking oats can be used interchangeably. Instant oatmeal is not suitable for baking.

Steel-cut oats, or Scotch

COOK'S SECRETS

Nick Malgieri
Director of Baking Program, Peter Kump's New York Cooking School

"Eventually you will learn what is meant by 'soft, manageable dough.' Meanwhile, if you have doubts when kneading dough, lightly flour a work surface and place the dough on it. With floured hands, fold the dough over on itself several times. It should just hold together without losing its shape. Also, the dough will be only slightly elastic and will feel light for its size."

oats, are coarsely cut oat kernels. They require a much longer cooking time than rolled oats and should be used only when specifically called for in a recipe.

For best results, cook oatmeal before mixing it into a bread dough. Because it has had plenty of time to absorb liquid, cooked oatmeal results in a lighter, finer textured bread.

BREAD GLAZES

You can change the texture, sheen, and color of a crust by brushing on a glaze just before baking.

For a dark and very shiny crust, brush on whole egg or egg yolk that has been lightly beaten (or lightly beaten with 1 tablespoon of water per egg). For more shine than color, brush on beaten egg white.

For a crisp crust, brush with a little water.

For browned but soft crusts, brush on melted butter. For a soft crust without the extra browning, brush on melted butter immediately after taking the loaf from the oven.

COOKING AHEAD

When you're making bread dough, make an extra batch and freeze it for future use.

After kneading the dough, shape it into a disk. Place in a self-sealing plastic bag and freeze for up to 1 month. When you're ready to bake,

OATMEAL-MOLASSES BREAD

Prepare as directed at right, **substituting** 1/4 cup molasses for 4 teaspoons brown sugar. **Use** the fifth teaspoon sugar with yeast mixture. Also **increase** the all-purpose flour by 1/4 cup, if necessary. Makes 1 loaf.

MULTIBRAN BREAD

Prepare as directed at right, **adding** 1/4 cup wheat or rice bran (or mixture of both) and 1/4 cup toasted wheat germ with the whole-wheat flour. **Decrease** the amount of all-purpose flour to between 2 and 2 1/2 cups. Makes 1 loaf.

thaw the dough in the bag in the refrigerator or on the countertop. Thawing in the refrigerator takes 8 to 16 hours; on the countertop, 4 to 9 hours.

WORK SAVER
Bread Knife

If you are going to invest time in learning to bake a great loaf of bread, it's worth investing in a great bread knife too. Buy a knife of good quality steel with a long serrated blade. The serrations allow you to saw easily through both thick and crisp crusts and both chewy and soft-textured loaves without ripping them. A good serrated blade can be sharpened by running the flat side of the cutting edge along a sharpening steel. Be sure to wait until fresh bread has cooled thoroughly before it is cut. And to make even slices, turn a loaf on its side before cutting.

Oatmeal Bread

1¼ **cups milk**
¼ **cup (½ stick) butter or margarine plus 1 tablespoon, melted**
1 **cup plus 2 tablespoons quick-cooking oats**
5 **teaspoons light brown sugar**
¼ **cup lukewarm (105°F to 115°F) water**
2 **packets (¼ ounce each) active dry yeast**
1 **egg, beaten**
2 **teaspoons salt**
1 **cup unsifted whole-wheat flour**
2½ **to 3 cups unsifted all-purpose flour**
Glaze:
1 **egg beaten with 1 tablespoon water**

1 In a small saucepan over moderate heat, heat milk and ¼ cup butter until steaming. Add the 1 cup oats and stir until evenly moistened—about 1 minute. Remove from the heat and cool to room temperature—25 to 30 minutes.

2 In a large bowl, combine 1 teaspoon of the brown sugar, water, and yeast and stir to dissolve. Set aside until bubbly—about 10 minutes. With a wooden spoon or in an electric mixer with the dough hook attached, beat in the cooled oatmeal mixture, the remaining 4 teaspoons brown sugar, egg, salt, whole-wheat flour, and 2½ cups all-purpose flour. Continue beating at moderate speed, adding the remaining ¼ to ½ cup all-purpose flour, if necessary, to form a soft but manageable dough—7 to 8 minutes. (Or knead on a lightly floured work surface for 8 to 10 minutes.)

3 Shape dough into a ball, place in a well-buttered 5-quart bowl, and turn to grease all over. Cover with a cloth and let rise in a warm, draft-free place until doubled in bulk—about 1 hour.

4 Lightly grease a 9" x 5" x 3" loaf pan. Sprinkle bottom and sides with 1 tablespoon of the remaining oats. Punch dough down, transfer to a lightly floured work surface, and knead gently for 2 minutes (dough will be soft). Shape into a loaf, place in prepared pan, cover, and let rise until doubled in bulk—1 to 1½ hours. Preheat the oven to 375°F.

5 Lightly brush top of loaf with glaze and sprinkle with the final 1 tablespoon oats. Bake until golden brown and bread sounds hollow when tapped—40 to 45 minutes. Cool in the pan on a rack for 10 minutes, loosen around the edge, and turn out on the rack. Cool before slicing. Makes 1 loaf, about 16 slices.

1 Slice: Calories 177; Total Fat 6 g; Saturated Fat 3 g; Protein 6 g; Carbohydrates 26 g; Fiber 2 g; Sodium 322 mg; Cholesterol 39 mg

prep time-20 to 35 minutes • rising time-2 to 2½ hours baking time-40 to 45 minutes

MULTIGRAIN BREADS

*A*dding whole-wheat and rye flours as well as stone-ground cornmeal and other whole grains to a basic white-bread recipe adds flavor, texture, and health benefits too.

BUYING AND STORING WHOLE GRAINS

Look for whole grains and special flours at health-food stores. Locate a store that has a high turnover so that the products you buy are as fresh as possible.

Unless you plan to do a lot of bread baking on a regular basis, buy whole-grain flours in relatively small amounts. They are far more perishable than bleached white flours, which have had the germ of the grain removed in order to give them longer shelf life. The germ is full of vitamin-rich oil, which turns rancid if left to sit too long. Sniff the flour and you'll know at once if it has turned.

If you must keep whole grains at room temperature, use them within 2 weeks. If possible, store grains—well sealed—in the refrigerator where they will keep for several months.

Make sure that refrigerated grains and flours are allowed to come to room temperature before they are mixed into bread dough. If they are cold, they can slow down or stop the action of the yeast, and bread will not rise properly.

KNEADING HEAVY DOUGHS

Expect a workout when you knead dough made with whole grains; it will be heavier and stronger than dough made with refined flours.

In the first stages of kneading, break your rhythmic

(continued on page 86)

A MULTIGRAIN GLOSSARY

Bran is the protective covering of a kernel of grain. It is present in whole wheat, stone-ground corn, steel-cut oats, and other minimally processed grains. You can buy packaged oat and wheat bran. Added to a recipe, it contributes valuable fiber and a nutty flavor.

Buckwheat is not a true grain. Whole buckwheat groats are added to recipes for crunch and nutty flavor. They are also ground into a heavy flour that is most often used in batter breads.

Corn is the largest grain. Watch its ratio to wheat flour in a multigrain recipe because it softens gluten. Choose coarsely ground cornmeal that contains the germ—the flavor holds up well in a multigrain bread.

Cracked wheat is also known as bulgur. It is coarsely cut unprocessed wheat kernels that add nutritional value and a healthy crunch to a recipe.

Gluten flour is wheat flour with the starch removed. Its extremely high gluten content adds strength to multigrain breads made with nongluten flours.

Graham flour is another name for whole-wheat flour.

Rye is the only grain other than wheat that contains gluten. However, it contains so little gluten that in order to rise properly, it must be mixed with wheat flour, as it is in rye and pumpernickel breads.

Wheat kernels are composed of bran, germ, and endosperm. They are used in multigrain recipes since their gluten gives strength to dough. In white flours the nutritious bran and germ have been removed.

Whole-wheat flour is ground whole kernels of wheat. It has far more flavor, fiber, and texture than white flour. However, the iron, niacin, and B vitamin content of the two is approximately the same because white flour is enriched.

Wheat germ is the oily embryo of the wheat kernel. It is rich in vitamins, iron, phosphorus, and potassium. Mix it into dough for extra nutritional value.

Wheat berries are highly nutritious wheat kernels with just the hulls removed. They contribute a sweet crunchiness to bread, but they must be soaked until soft before they are mixed into the dough.

Multigrain Bread

- **2** teaspoons sugar
- **1/2** cup lukewarm (105°F to 115°F) water
- **2** packets (1/4 ounce each) active dry yeast
- **1 1/4** to 1 1/2 cups unsifted all-purpose flour
- **1** cup unsifted whole-wheat flour
- **1** cup unsifted rye flour
- **1/3** cup sifted stone-ground yellow or white cornmeal
- **1/4** cup wheat bran
- **1/4** cup wheat germ, plain, toasted, or honey crunch
- **1** cup buttermilk
- **3** tablespoons butter, melted
- **1 1/2** teaspoons salt

1 In a large bowl, combine sugar, water, and yeast and stir to dissolve. Set aside until bubbly—about 10 minutes.

2 In another bowl, combine 1 1/4 cups all-purpose flour, whole-wheat and rye flours, cornmeal, wheat bran, and wheat germ.

3 In a small saucepan over low heat, heat buttermilk, butter, and salt until lukewarm.

4 Stir buttermilk mixture into yeast mixture. With a wooden spoon or in an electric mixer with the dough hook attached, mix in flour mixture 1 cup at a time. Beat at moderate speed, adding the remaining 1/4 cup all-purpose flour, if necessary, to make a soft, manageable dough. Continue beating until smooth and elastic—7 to 8 minutes (or knead on a lightly floured work surface for 8 to 10 minutes).

5 Shape dough into a ball, place in a well-buttered 5-quart bowl, and turn to grease all over. Cover with a cloth and let rise in a warm, draft-free place until doubled in bulk—1 1/2 to 2 hours.

6 Lightly grease a 9" x 5" x 3" loaf pan. Punch dough down, transfer to a lightly floured work surface, and knead gently for 2 minutes. Shape into a loaf, place in prepared pan, cover, and let rise until doubled in bulk—about 1 hour. Preheat the oven to 375°F.

7 Bake until bread sounds hollow when tapped—40 to 45 minutes. Cool in the pan on a rack for 10 minutes, loosen around the edge, and turn out on the rack. Cool before slicing. Makes 1 loaf, about 16 slices.

1 Slice: Calories 139; Total Fat 4 g; Saturated Fat 2 g; Protein 4 g; Carbohydrates 23 g; Fiber 3 g; Sodium 314 mg; Cholesterol 8 mg

prep time–about 15 minutes
rising time–2 1/2 to 3 hours
baking time–40 to 45 minutes

Multigrain Bread makes great sandwiches. Here it is stacked with ham, onion, cheese, lettuce, tomato, mustard, and mayonnaise.

(continued from page 84)

push and pull on the dough occasionally by lifting the dough high and slapping it back down on the work surface. For some whole-wheat doughs, you may want to knead the dough for as long as 20 minutes.

The heaviness of the flour also affects the time it takes for the dough to rise; some will take twice as long as white flour doughs. In some instances, 3 rounds of rising will be required to produce a tender-textured loaf: 2 before the dough is shaped and 1 afterward.

MUST-HAVES FOR MIXING

Multigrain doughs are not the recipes for flimsy equipment. Choose a sturdy spoon for mixing the dough. If you use wooden spoons for baking, keep them separate from the ones you use for general cooking. Wooden spoons absorb flavors and will transfer them to the dough.

Choose a mixing bowl that will not easily slide on the counter. Bowls should be wide with gently sloping sides. A damp towel or dishcloth placed beneath the bowl will help keep it from slipping.

OLD SWEETIE

Molasses, an old-fashioned ingredient, adds its own distinctive flavor, as well as sweetness, to bread.

Molasses is made by boiling the juices extracted from sugarcane. Light molasses, from the first boiling, has a milder flavor than dark molasses, which comes

from the second. Blackstrap molasses is from the third boiling. It's thick, bitter, and best avoided for baking.

FLAVORFUL SEEDS

Many bread recipes call for a little extra flavoring with seeds. Toasting seeds releases their natural oils and brings out their most intense flavor. Cumin, coriander, mustard, sesame, and poppy seeds, for example, benefit enormously from a few moments in a dry skillet over moderate heat. Stir constantly and remove from the heat the moment the seeds begin to release their fragrance.

WHEAT-BERRY TIPS

Soaking alone will not soften wheat berries—whole-wheat kernels with the hull removed. About 8 hours before you plan to use them, pour boiling water over the berries in a bowl—1½ cups of water for each ½ cup of berries—and let them soak in a cool spot. Drain and pat dry on paper toweling.

COLD STORAGE

If your bread is to be kept for more than a day, wrap it tightly and freeze. It will keep well for up to 1 month.

UNINVITED GUESTS

Tiny bugs that make their home in flour and grain are a fact of life. The less refined the flour, the more appealing it is to unwanted kitchen guests. Two surefire ways to eliminate bug problems are to keep all flour refrigerated or frozen or to store in ½-gallon preserving jars with the lids screwed down tight.

WHEAT-BERRY BREAD

Prepare as directed on previous page, **omitting** wheat bran and germ and **adding** ½ cup drained, soaked wheat berries to the flour mixture in Step 2. Makes 1 loaf, about 16 slices.

RYE BREAD

Prepare as directed on previous page, **reducing** whole-wheat flour to ½ cup and **increasing** the rye flour to 1½ cups. **Add** 2 tablespoons toasted caraway seeds to the flour mixture in Step 2. Makes 1 loaf, about 16 slices.

SHAPING DOUGH

For long loaves, roll dough with your palms to form a baton slightly shorter than the pan (French bread pan shown above) or baking sheet. Let it rise, covered with a cloth.

Most bread recipes can double as rolls. A recipe for 1 loaf of bread can be expected to make 2 batches of 9 rolls in an 8-inch round or square pan. Bake only about 20 to 30 minutes.

For an oval loaf, form the dough into a ball. Flatten slightly and elongate with your hands by pulling gently from either side. Smooth out finger marks, slash top, and let rise, covered, on greased baking sheet.

For braided breads, divide dough into 3 equal parts. Roll 3 batons, as above. Place on greased baking sheet. Pinch ends together and braid. Pinch opposite ends and tuck under. Let rise, covered, on the baking sheet.

PLENTY OF PASTA

Pasta Basics

Pasta has become one of our favorite foods, served hot or cold, dressed up for company, or simply prepared for a quick family meal.

THE SECRETS OF PERFECT PASTA

It's easy to make a bowl of pasta—so why doesn't it always come out just right? Here are the tricks to cooking pasta to perfection.

Use a pot large enough to hold at least 4 quarts of water for every pound of pasta. (Figure on 3 to 4 ounces per person.) Bring the water to a rolling boil before adding the

pasta and bring it back to a boil once the pasta is stirred in. Cooking pasta in plenty of boiling water ensures that it cooks evenly and prevents it from sticking together.

A little salt in the cooking water brings out pasta's best flavor. Add it when the water first comes to a boil. Some

cookbooks suggest pouring oil in the water to prevent pasta from sticking together. But adding oil is generally frowned on by pasta lovers because it coats the surface of the pasta, affecting its ability to absorb sauce.

Pasta should be cooked until it's firm-tender, or, as the Italians say, *al dente*, meaning firm to the tooth. The suggested cooking times on packaged pasta vary. When you find a brand whose cooking times suit you, follow its instructions to the letter. Until then, test for doneness by tasting a strand of pasta at brief intervals toward the end of the cooking time.

Turn off the heat and drain pasta immediately when it tests just slightly underdone. (It will continue to cook on its own as long as it is hot.)

Place a colander in the bowl that will be used for tossing the pasta with the sauce. Pour in the steaming pasta, then lift the colander to drain the pasta and empty the bowl of water. Add the pasta; the hot bowl will keep it hot.

If you're serving the pasta hot, don't rinse it after draining. The sticky starch on its sur-

face helps sauce to cling. If you're serving the pasta cold and are not dressing it right away, rinse it after draining. Rinsing will prevent the pasta from sticking as it cools.

Toss pasta gently with its sauce immediately after draining. Pasta best absorbs flavors and liquid when it's hot.

MATCHING SHAPES AND SAUCE

There are no hard and fast rules when it comes to matching pasta with a sauce, but some combinations work better than others.

Thin strands: Fine pastas, like **capellini** (angel hair) and **spaghettini,** are best served with lightweight sauces, such as those with broth bases, garlic and oil sauces, or a light tomato purée. Chunky or creamy sauces will overwhelm them.

Flat strands: Thin flat pasta, such as **linguine,** is often paired with white clam sauce and other seafood sauces where there are both broth and chopped ingredients. It is thin enough to absorb the liquid quickly, but substantial enough to support the chopped clams.

Ribbons: Narrow ribbon pastas, such as **fettuccine,** are a good choice for cheese and creamy sauces because their flat surfaces can be coated with clinging sauce. Wider ribbon pastas, such as **pappardelle,** are generally paired with thick stew-type sauces containing larger pieces of meat.

Corkscrews: **Fusilli** is another good choice for cream sauces and tomato sauces containing bits of meat and vegetables. The twists in fusilli trap and hold the sauce.

Little shapes: Chunky formed pasta that holds its shape well—**bow ties, seashells, orecchetti** (little ears), and short **fusilli**—are good choices with chunky sauces, such as those with lots of cut vegetables in broth.

Tubes: Tubular pastas, such as **ziti** and **rigatoni,** are frequent choices for use in casseroles since they can be coated inside and out with sauces and cheese.

All-around favorites: Two of the most versatile pastas are **penne** (hollow quills) and **spaghetti**. Both are as appropriate for use with meat sauces as they are with purées. **Bucatini**, a sturdy hollow spaghetti, makes a good replacement for spaghetti when paired with sauces full of chopped meats and vegetables.

Grated cheese and sauces (such as pestos) that contain cheese will coat pasta thinly and evenly if tossed in when the pasta is piping hot.

In general you'll need less sauce if the pasta is good and hot when the sauce is mixed in. It should never be swimming in sauce.

MAKE YOUR OWN

There are two very good reasons to make your own pasta: The fresh flavor and delicate texture are incomparable.

There are two basic recipes for egg pasta. One, which includes our pasta recipe on page 91, combines flour, salt, eggs, oil, and water. The other is mixed up solely from eggs and flour (2 large eggs to about 1½ cups of flour). Both are made in the same way; choosing one is simply a matter of preference.

THE RIGHT FLOUR

Some commercial pasta is made with semolina flour milled from hard durum wheat. Home pasta makers may find semolina dough too difficult to manipulate.

Good choices for home use include bread flour, which produces a firm yet pliable dough, and all-purpose unbleached white flour. Bleached all-purpose flour makes too soft a dough for pasta. Pasta dough should be firm but pliable.

PROCESSOR DOUGH

It's easy to mix up pasta dough in a food processor fitted with a plastic dough blade or a metal chopping blade. For 1 pound of pasta, process 2¼ cups of unsifted all-purpose flour with 2 eggs, ¼ cup of water, 1 tablespoon of olive oil, and 1 teaspoon of salt until the dough rides up in the center—20 to 30 seconds.

On a lightly floured work surface, knead the dough into a smooth ball. Cover with a large bowl or plastic wrap and let stand for 30 minutes.

Mary Ann Esposito
Television host of Ciao Italia

"To give strength to the dough without making it dry or difficult to manage, I substitute ¼ to ½ cup of semolina flour for some of the all-purpose flour in pasta-dough recipes. In a recipe that calls for 2¼ cups of flour, I use 2 cups of all-purpose flour and ¼ cup of semolina flour."

FLAVORED PASTAS

For spinach pasta, prepare in a food processor as directed at left, adding one 10-ounce package of frozen spinach that has been thawed, squeezed dry, and puréed. Reduce the water to 1 to 2 tablespoons. (Start with 1 tablespoon, then add more, if needed, to form a workable dough.)

For tomato pasta, prepare in a food processor as directed at left, adding ⅓ cup of oil-packed dried tomatoes that have been drained, patted dry, and puréed. Reduce the water to 1 to 2 tablespoons. (Start with 1 tablespoon, then add more, if needed, to form a workable dough.)

KNEAD AND CUT WITH A PASTA MACHINE

It's quick and easy to cut pasta with a pasta machine. The most common type is hand cranked; it both kneads and cuts the dough. Kneading

MIXING AND KNEADING PASTA DOUGH BY HAND

1 Dump the flour in a mound on a roomy work surface. Make a well in the center. Mix the wet ingredients together and slowly pour them into the well; sprinkle with salt.

2 Carefully push the flour from around the edge into the well, stirring with your fingers to form a batter. Continue adding flour to the well until the mixture becomes a soft dough.

3 Knead the dough with the heel of your hand for at least 5 minutes until it is smooth and elastic.

4 Cover the dough with an inverted bowl or plastic wrap and let it rest for 1 hour before rolling.

is completed by passing the dough several times through the machine's rollers. The machine then rolls out the

dough in stages until it is thin enough to cut. Finally, it can cut the dough into shapes from fettuccine and lasagne noodles to ravioli.

ROLLING AND CUTTING BY HAND

To roll and cut fettuccine, use a long narrow (1- to 1½-inch diameter) rolling pin and give yourself a large lightly floured surface to work on. Roll out the dough as thin as possible—about 1/16 inch. A pound of pasta should yield about a 20- by 14-inch rectangle. Trim the edges with a sharp knife and a ruler, if necessary. Lightly dust the top of the dough with flour so that it will not stick when folded.

Fold the rolled-out dough in half lengthwise, then once again, ending with a 5- by 14-inch rectangle. Slice the dough crosswise into strips 1/4-inch wide; unfold the strips and lay them flat on a cloth. Allow to dry for 1 to 2 hours.

DRYING PASTA

Fresh loose pasta needs to air dry before it is cooked. Without this step, it becomes gluey

in the boiling water and will cook unevenly because it cooks too quickly.

TO COOK FRESH PASTA

Boil the pasta, uncovered, in a large pot of lightly salted water. Fresh pasta cooks very quickly, so beware. Thin pastas might be done by the time they float to the surface. Other loose varieties will cook in 1 to 2 minutes; ravioli in about 6 minutes.

TO STORE FRESH PASTA

Homemade pasta can be refrigerated or frozen but it needs to be dried beforehand so that it won't stick together.

Arrange small cut pasta, uncovered, in a single layer on a work surface and let it stand for several hours until it feels dry to the touch but not brittle.

If you have made fettuccine or another long-strand style of pasta, try the following: When the cut dough has dried

SPINACH-STUFFED SHELLS

For the Shells: Prepare filling as directed in Step 2 at right, **adding** one 10-ounce package thawed and squeezed-dry frozen chopped spinach to the skillet along with the garlic. **Using** a pastry bag without a tip, **pipe** filling into 24 large cooked pasta shells. **Arrange** in a lightly greased 13" x 9" x 2" baking pan, **top** with sauce, **cover**, and **bake** in a preheated 350°F oven until bubbly—about 25 minutes. Makes 6 servings. **Note:** This filling may be used to stuff ravioli.

GROUND TURKEY-STUFFED SHELLS

Prepare filling as directed above, but **increase** garlic to 4 cloves and **add** 8 ounces ground turkey to the skillet along with the spinach; **cook** and **stir** until no longer pink—5 to 8 minutes. **Mix** in 1/4 cup dried currants, then **pipe** into 32 large cooked pasta shells. **Cover** with sauce and **bake** as directed. Makes 8 servings.

slightly but is still pliable, loosely wrap several strands at a time around your hand, then slide them off to form a "nest." Repeat with the remaining pasta. Let the nests air dry.

Place the cut pasta pieces or nests in plastic bags or freezer containers and seal airtight. Refrigerate for up to 1 week; freeze for up to 1 month. Thaw pasta in its bag.

MAKING RAVIOLI
Divide the dough into 2 equal portions. Work with 1 portion at a time, keeping the rest covered with a cloth or plastic wrap. Roll the dough on a lightly floured work surface into a 9- by 12-inch rectangle about 1/16-inch thick.

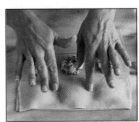

1 With a sharp knife or pastry wheel, cut the dough crosswise into 4 strips 3 inches wide and 9 inches long.

2 Drop 3 mounds of filling on each of 2 pasta strips, spacing about 1 inch apart and leaving 1/2-inch margins.

3 With a pastry brush, brush margins around each mound of filling with water. Cover with remaining strips.

4 Firmly press the dough along the margins and around each mound to seal the strips firmly.

5 Slice each strip crosswise into 3 ravioli. Repeat with remaining portion of dough. You will have 12 ravioli.

Cheese-Stuffed Ravioli

Pasta Dough:
- 2 cups unsifted all purpose flour
- 1/2 teaspoon salt
- 2 large eggs
- 2 teaspoons olive oil
- 2 tablespoons water

Filling:
- 2 teaspoons olive oil
- 1 ounce Canadian bacon or prosciutto, coarsely chopped
- 3 cloves garlic, minced
- 1 cup part-skim ricotta cheese
- 1/2 cup grated Parmesan cheese
- 1 egg yolk
- 1/2 cup minced fresh basil
- 1/2 teaspoon salt
- 1/4 teaspoon black pepper

Sauce:
- 2 teaspoons olive oil
- 1 small yellow onion, chopped
- 2 cloves garlic, minced
- 1 can (28 ounces) Italian plum tomatoes, chopped with their juice
- 1/2 teaspoon salt

1 Prepare Pasta Dough as shown on page 89. Cover dough with a cloth or plastic wrap and let stand 1 hour. Meanwhile, prepare the Filling. In a large nonstick skillet over moderate heat, heat oil 1 minute. Add bacon and garlic and cook until garlic is soft—about 2 minutes. Transfer to a bowl and cool to room temperature. Blend in ricotta, Parmesan, egg yolk, basil, salt, and pepper; set aside.

2 Divide dough into 2 equal portions. Working with 1 portion at a time and keeping the rest covered, roll dough and fill ravioli as shown at left.

3 For the Sauce: In a large non-stick skillet over moderate heat, heat oil 1 minute. Add onion and sauté, stirring occasionally, until soft—about 5 minutes. Add garlic and cook 2 minutes more. Add tomatoes and their juice and salt, bring to a boil over moderately high heat, adjust heat so mixture bubbles gently, and cook, uncovered, stirring often, until sauce thickens slightly—about 10 minutes.

4 Meanwhile, in a large pot of boiling water, cook ravioli until firm-tender—about 6 minutes. Drain well, divide among 4 heated serving plates, and top with sauce. Serve with freshly grated Parmesan. Makes 4 servings.

1 Serving: Calories 546; Total Fat 21 g; Saturated Fat 8 g; Protein 26 g; Carbohydrates 63 g; Fiber 4 g; Sodium 1568 mg; Cholesterol 192 mg

prep time-1 hour • cooking time-22 minutes

MEAT SAUCES

$\mathcal{M}$any of us learned to love spaghetti and meat sauce long before we knew there was any other kind of pasta. We offer it two ways.

MEAT SAUCE NOTES

You can use flavorful meat sauce on top of a bowl of spaghetti, stirred into a casserole, or layered into a lasagne.

We make our meat sauce with a combination of ground beef and Italian sausage, but there are other ways to make it too. Another favorite sauce combines ground veal, pork, and beef. For a slightly different texture, replace the ground meat with lean beef cut into 1/2-inch cubes. Or do the same with cubed lamb.

Instead of browning the ground or cubed meat with onion and garlic only, use the classic trio, a combination of chopped onion, carrot, and celery. The most famous meat sauce with this base is Bolognese. Its flavor gets extra distinction when the browned meat is simmered in milk and seasoned with a little nutmeg before the tomatoes are added.

Spark up the flavor of a meat sauce by adding and sautéing thin slices of sweet red or green pepper just after the meat is browned.

Or add sliced sautéed mushrooms or soaked and chopped

dried mushrooms to the sauce for the last 1/2 hour of cooking.

LOWERING THE FAT

To lower the fat content of our toppings, substitute turkey or chicken sausage for pork sausage. You will knock off about 63 calories and 7 grams of fat from each serving.

For meatballs, instead of browning in oil, brown them in a shallow pan in a preheated 325°F oven for 12 minutes, turning occasionally.

NO WASTED PASTE

The flavor of tomato paste can overwhelm a sauce. It should always be used sparingly, but that means there will be a lot left over. One way to avoid waste is to buy tomato paste in a tube so you can squeeze out the amount you want and refrigerate the rest.

HOW TO CHOP BASIL

Stack 5 or 6 leaves of about the same size on top of one another. Roll up tightly from a long side and slice crosswise into thin shreds.

If you buy canned tomato paste, freeze the leftovers: Spoon level tablespoonfuls of tomato paste onto wax paper or aluminum foil. Freeze until the paste is solid. Peel the paste from the paper or foil and store in a freezer container. It will keep well for up to 6 months.

FROZEN MEATBALLS

Meatballs and their sauce can be made ahead, cooled, and frozen separately in sealed containers. To serve, thaw overnight in the refrigerator. Add the meatballs to the sauce and cook just until heated through.

MAMA'S SPAGHETTI AND MEATBALLS

Prepare sauce as directed at right, but **omit** ground beef and sausages. While sauce cooks, **make** the meatballs. In a large bowl, **mix** 1 1/2 pounds lean ground beef, 1 cup fresh bread crumbs, 1 finely chopped medium-size yellow onion, 1/3 cup finely chopped parsley, 1/4 cup cold water, 2 minced garlic cloves, 1 lightly beaten egg, 1 tablespoon Worcestershire sauce, 1 teaspoon salt, and 1/4 teaspoon black pepper. **Shape** into thirty-two 1 1/2-inch balls. In a large nonstick skillet over moderately high heat, **brown** meatballs in batches in a little vegetable oil, **allowing** about 10 minutes per batch and **adding** a little extra oil, if needed. **Add** meatballs to sauce and **simmer**, **stirring** occasionally, about 10 minutes. **Ladle** over hot pasta and serve. Makes 6 servings.

WORK SAVER
Pasta Lifter

To serve pasta, you can use a pair of large forks, kitchen tongs, or a pasta lifter. This handy tool looks like a large spoon or paddle with prongs around the edge. The prongs make it easy to hold on to wiggly noodles as you transfer them and easy to release them on the plate.

Spaghetti and Meat Sauce

2 tablespoons olive oil
2 large yellow onions, chopped
2 cloves garlic, finely chopped
1/2 pound lean ground beef
1/2 pound sweet or hot Italian-style sausages, removed from casings
1 can (28 ounces) Italian plum tomatoes, chopped with their juice
1/2 cup dry red wine
1/2 cup water
1/4 cup tomato paste
2 tablespoons chopped fresh basil or 2 teaspoons dried basil, crumbled
1 tablespoon chopped fresh oregano or 1 teaspoon dried oregano, crumbled
1 tablespoon chopped fresh thyme or 1 teaspoon dried thyme, crumbled
1 whole bay leaf
1 1/2 teaspoons salt
1 teaspoon sugar
1/4 teaspoon black pepper
1 1/2 pounds spaghetti, cooked and drained

1 In a large nonstick saucepan over moderate heat, heat oil 1 minute. Add onions and sauté, stirring occasionally—about 5 minutes. Add garlic and sauté, stirring occasionally, until onion and garlic are soft—2 to 3 minutes more.

2 Add ground beef and sausages and sauté, breaking up clumps of meat, until no longer pink—8 to 10 minutes.

3 Stir in tomatoes, wine, water, tomato paste, basil, oregano, thyme, bay leaf, salt, sugar, and pepper. Bring to a boil over high heat, reduce the heat to low, and simmer, uncovered, stirring occasionally, until sauce thickens—about 60 minutes. Discard the bay leaf.

4 Ladle over hot spaghetti and serve. Pass a bowl of freshly grated Parmesan. Makes 6 servings.

1 Serving: Calories 701; Total Fat 17 g; Saturated Fat 5 g; Protein 29 g; Carbohydrates 105 g; Fiber 7 g; Sodium 1095 mg; Cholesterol 40 mg

prep time-20 minutes
cooking time-1 hour 20 minutes

TOMATO SAUCES

Tomatoes are the basis for a wide range of quick and inexpensive sauces. Our trio of sauces is a sampler of styles: spicy, rustic, and smooth.

FRESH FLAVOR

Time was when popular wisdom dictated that tomato sauce had to simmer all day in order to be good. Now the opposite is true—the fresher the flavor, the better we like it.

Many tomato sauces can be prepared in as little as 45 minutes—the time it takes to mellow the flavors and reduce and thicken the sauce.

To ensure the freshest flavor, keep the lid off the pan while cooking the sauce. Covering the sauce gives it a tired, steamed taste and prevents it from reducing quickly.

Fresh herbs make a big difference in flavor, but beware that both parsley and basil lose their pungency if simmered too long. Stir them in only when the sauce is nearly done.

CHOOSING A TOMATO

Plum tomatoes are the best choice for sauce making. This is because they have fewer seeds, contain less water, and, consequently, have denser flesh for their weight than other tomatoes. Canned plum tomatoes range widely in flavor and quality. Purists insist that for true Italian flavor, only

San Marzano plum tomatoes should be used. A label will indicate if a brand uses San Marzano tomatoes.

CANNED VS. FRESH

Good quality canned tomatoes make excellent sauce all year-round. The only time to choose fresh over canned is when there are sun-ripened tomatoes at hand.

If it's that time of year, nothing quite compares with sauce made from just-picked tomatoes and basil. Make up a big batch and freeze it so that you can enjoy a taste of summer all winter long.

If you grow your own tomatoes, San Marzano tomato seeds and plants are available in this country, and there are many other flavorful plum tomato varieties as well. If you

have a bumper crop of tomatoes other than plums, by all means use them for sauce. If they are particularly juicy, the sauce will take a little extra time to thicken.

SERVED WITH STYLE

Virtually all tomato sauces begin with tomatoes that have been peeled and seeded. But after that starting point, sauce styles differ widely.

Rustic, or chunky, sauces are particularly good when they're made with coarsely chopped garden-fresh tomatoes that are cooked quickly with garlic and herbs. Serve with spaghetti or a chunky pasta, such as penne. Rustic tomato sauces also make a wonderful base for baked fish or shrimp.

Puréed sauces are thick and smooth, and they meld the flavors of the tomatoes with the other ingredients. The puréeing is usually done after the tomatoes, onions, and other ingredients have cooked together for at least 20 minutes and have had time to soften. The sauce is then returned to the pan to thicken and heat through.

Puréed sauces can be used on virtually any kind of pasta. They also make a delicious sauce for meat loaf.

Tomato-cream sauce dresses up a purée with extra richness. Simply stir a little heavy cream into a tomato purée during the last 1 minute of cooking. Tomato-cream sauces are usually served on stuffed pastas, such as tortellini or ravioli.

Tomato-vegetable sauces are a little darker and richer than other tomato sauces.

TO PEEL AND SEED A TOMATO

1 Score the bottom of a tomato with an *X*. Drop into boiling water for 30 seconds. Lift out with a skimmer or slotted spoon.

2 Plunge tomatoes briefly into ice water and remove. The skin will peel off easily.

3 Cut tomatoes in half crosswise. Gently squeeze each half to expel the seeds.

Start by sautéing chopped onions, carrots, celery, and garlic if you wish. Then add the tomatoes and herbs. Serve either puréed or rustic style.

Spaghetti All' Amatriciana

In a large saucepan over low heat, **sauté** 3/4 pound diced lean Canadian bacon or prosciutto and 3 chopped medium-size yellow onions in 1 tablespoon olive oil, **stirring** occasionally, until bacon is golden—about 15 minutes. **Add** chopped tomatoes, 1/2 teaspoon salt, black pepper, and red pepper flakes and **simmer** as directed. **Ladle** over hot spaghetti and **serve**. Makes 6 servings.

Spaghetti Puttanesca

In a large saucepan over moderately low heat, **heat** 2 tablespoons olive oil. **Add** 2 cloves minced garlic and **sauté**, **stirring** occasionally, until soft—about 2 minutes. **Add** tomatoes, 1 cup halved pitted large black Greek olives, 1/4 cup drained capers, 8 coarsely chopped anchovies, and 1/8 to 1/4 teaspoon crushed red pepper flakes and **simmer** as directed. **Ladle** over hot spaghetti and serve. Makes 6 servings.

Spaghetti Arrabiata

3	pounds peeled fresh or canned Italian plum tomatoes, drained and chopped
1/4	cup olive oil
1	teaspoon salt
1/4 to 1/2	teaspoon black pepper
1/8 to 1/4	teaspoon red pepper flakes
1 1/2	pounds spaghetti, cooked and drained
2/3	cup chopped fresh basil or Italian parsley

1 In a large saucepan over moderate heat, bring tomatoes, oil, salt, and black pepper to a boil. Reduce the heat to low and simmer, uncovered, for 25 minutes.

2 Working in batches, purée sauce in a blender at high speed or in a food processor until smooth, scraping down container sides as needed. Return to the pan, add red pepper flakes, and simmer, uncovered, over moderately high heat, for 15 minutes; stir often.

3 Ladle over hot spaghetti, sprinkle with chopped basil, and serve. Makes 6 servings.

> **1 Serving: Calories 421; Total Fat 11 g; Saturated Fat 2 g; Protein 12 g; Carbohydrates 170 g; Fiber 5 g; Sodium 377 mg; Cholesterol 0 mg**

prep time-30 minutes • cooking time-45 minutes

CREAMY SAUCES

When you're in the mood for a pasta indulgence, nothing quite fills the bill like fettuccine with a creamy sauce flavored with a full-bodied cheese.

A CLASSIC DISH

In this country, Fettuccine all' Alfredo is almost as famous as spaghetti and meatballs. There was indeed an Alfredo who made the dish famous at his restaurant in Rome, but cream sauces have always been part of Italian cuisine. This one is known regionally as *fettuccine alla panna*, which simply means with cream.

THE PERFECT NOODLE

Fettuccine (and its cousin tagliatelle) is the perfect pasta for cream sauces. The long flat sides of the noodles carry the sauce beautifully. But fettuccine is also good with other types of toppings. We include a noncreamy prima-vera sauce here (the name means springtime and indicates that a recipe brims with fresh young vegetables). The ribbonlike noodles are substantial enough to support a chunky vegetable topping.

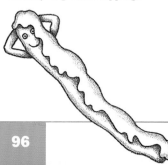

CREAM OF THE CROP

In the days when no one worried about cholesterol, Alfredo sauce was made solely with heavy cream. We use a combination of light and heavy creams to lessen the butterfat content. However, our Light Alfredo sauce, though richly flavored, contains no cream at all. It's based on milk and evaporated milk and is thickened with a little cornstarch.

PUT THE LIGHT ON

To cut down on calories, fat, and cholesterol, use our Light Alfredo sauce in place of cream sauces in other favorite pasta recipes. Try it in place of the cream sauce in the well-known dish called Straw and Hay, in which yellow and green fettuccine noodles are tossed with mushrooms, peas, and thinly sliced prosciutto.

Other combos that work well with creamy or light creamy sauces include ham and asparagus, and spinach and mushroom. Shrimp, scallops, and salmon are also delicious in cream sauces. Fish and shellfish, however, should not be mixed with Parmesan cheese because it overpowers their flavors. Point up their

sauces with garlic and tomato, saffron infused in a little warm water, or snipped fresh dill.

THE RIGHT CHEESE

Fettuccine all' Alfredo's rich flavor relies heavily on the quality and bite of the cheese that's mixed into it. It's worth shopping for a good one.

For low-fat recipes, such as our Light Alfredo, it's even more important to use strong-flavored cheese for big flavor.

CHEESES FOR GRATING

Pasta lovers know that choosing a good grating cheese is just as important as choosing the right sauce. Best flavor bets for hard grating cheeses include:

Aged Asiago: A rich, salty, mild to sharp cow's milk cheese.

Parmesan: A mellow, grainy, and straw-colored cow's milk cheese. Parmesan varies in quality. Parmigiano Reggiano is considered to be the best of the Parmesans. Look for the name stamped on the rind.

Pecorino Romano: A cow-, goat-, or sheep-milk cheese similar to Parmesan, but slightly sharper and more acidic. Peccorino Romano (or simply Romano) is sometimes blended with Parmesan to give it more pungency.

Ricotta Salata: A pungent cured sheep-milk cheese that is very sharp and crumbly.

Sapsago: A granular cheese that's made with sour skim milk, then flavored and colored with sweet green clover.

WORK SAVER
Nutmeg Grater and Grinder

The powdered nutmeg in a jar on your spice rack might be convenient, but when you use fresh nutmeg for the first time, you won't believe the difference. You can grate nutmeg on the smallest holes of a 4-sided grater or on a small, inexpensive steel nutmeg grater, right. If you use nutmeg often, you might want to try a nutmeg grinder, above.

The grinder works like a peppermill, allowing you to dust a sauce, stew, or custard with the aromatic spice. Whole nutmegs keep their flavor indefinitely while ground nutmeg quickly loses its punch.

Light Alfredo

Prepare as directed at right, **reducing** butter to 2 tablespoons and blending 1 tablespoon cornstarch into cooked shallots. **Substitute** 1 cup each milk and evaporated skim milk for the 2 creams and **add** 1/4 teaspoon black pepper along with the Parmesan. Makes 4 servings.

Fettuccine Gorgonzola

Prepare as directed at right, **reducing** grated Parmesan to 1/3 cup and **adding** 3/4 cup crumbled Gorgonzola cheese. Makes 4 servings.

Fettuccine Primavera

Prepare as directed at right, **substituting** 2 large minced cloves garlic for the shallots and **sauté** until soft—2 to 3 minutes. **Omit** cream, salt, nutmeg, and Parmesan. Instead, **add** 6 cups julienned vegetables (sweet red or yellow peppers, zucchini, yellow squash, red onion, snow peas, carrots) and **sauté** until crisp-tender—6 to 7 minutes. **Sprinkle** with 1/4 cup finely chopped fresh basil and 1/4 teaspoon black pepper. **Toss** with the fettuccine and **serve**. Makes 4 servings.

Creamy Fettuccine Alfredo

- **3 tablespoons butter or margarine**
- **1/3 cup minced shallots**
- **1 1/4 cups heavy cream**
- **1 cup light cream**
- **1/2 teaspoon salt**
- **Pinch ground nutmeg**
- **3/4 cup grated Parmesan cheese**
- **1 pound fettuccine, cooked and drained**

1 In a medium-size saucepan over moderate heat, melt butter. Add shallots and sauté until soft—3 to 4 minutes. Stir in heavy cream, light cream, salt, and nutmeg and bring to a boil over high heat, stirring constantly. Reduce the heat to moderately low and simmer, uncovered, until sauce thickens—4 to 5 minutes. Stir in Parmesan.

2 Transfer fettuccine to a heated serving bowl, pour sauce over all, and toss well. Makes 4 servings.

1 Serving: Calories 868; Total Fat 60 g; Saturated Fat 34 g; Protein 22 g; Carbohydrates 61 g; Fiber 2 g; Sodium 1236 mg; Cholesterol 286 mg

prep time-15 to 20 minutes
cooking time-about 12 to 15 minutes

CHEESE SAUCES

Four great cheeses go into our two great recipes: one Italian, the other a twist on a perennial favorite. The sauces are creamy and a snap to make.

ABOUT CHEESE SAUCES

Pasta with four cheeses is a relatively new addition to Italian cuisine, and it's made in many varieties. Italy's fine selection of cheeses invites experimentation with different combinations—usually a mix of hard, semifirm, and soft cheeses.

Cheese melts and blends relatively quickly if it is grated, shredded, or crumbled before it is mixed into the sauce. Use the coarsest side of a 4-sided grater to shred cheeses. All cheeses grate, shred, and crumble more easily when they are refrigerator cold. However, their flavors will not be at their best at that temperature. If possible, let the grated or shredded cheeses soften to room temperature before melting.

SHOPPING FOR CHEESE

The flavor of the dish depends almost entirely on the quality of the cheeses in it. Using the best quality Parmesan makes a noticeable difference in a sauce, but it's expensive, so buy only as much as you

need. Price alone never guarantees the quality of cheese. Where it was made, its age, and how it's been stored all come into play.

In most cheese shops you can ask to sample a smidgen before you buy. Your nose and taste buds should be the ultimate determining factor.

THE BIG FOUR MELTING CHEESES

Fontina: This is a semifirm but creamy cow's milk cheese strewn with tiny holes. Real Italian fontina (look for varieties with a light-brown rind) has a mild, nutty flavor that gets richer, not stronger, as it ages. Fontina melts beautifully and is often used in cheese sauces. Shred fontina on a 4-sided grater.

Mozzarella: This is the cheese that's shredded and liberally scattered over pizza.

Its best use is as a melting cheese and it is appreciated as much for its chewy texture as for its mild flavor. If possible buy fresh mozzarella, because some commercial varieties "string" when melted. Since it is soft, fresh mozzarella is more easily shredded with a knife than with a grater.

Parmesan and Romano: These hard cheeses—the favorites for grating over pasta—also melt superbly. For this dish they must be freshly grated; packaged pregrated varieties cannot be substituted. Grate either by hand or in a food processor.

Provolone: This pale yellow, semifirm cow's milk cheese from southern Italy has a mild, slightly smoky flavor. It becomes harder and sharper in flavor as it ages, but young cheese (aged for 2 to 3 months and the most readily available) is best for melting.

Alternative cheeses: Another version of this dish combines 4 ounces each of shredded fontina, mascarpone (an Italian cream cheese) cut into small pieces, grated Parmesan, and 2 ounces of crumbled Gorgonzola (a creamy Italian blue cheese that is often used on pasta).

If finding imported fontina or

provolone cheese for our recipe presents a problem, you will get excellent results (though a different flavor) with Swiss cheese and Gouda as substitutes.

STORING CHEESE

As a general rule, it's best to buy cheese in small quantities and use as soon as possible.

If tightly wrapped in plastic wrap and refrigerated, semifirm cheeses keep well for 2 or 3 weeks while hard cheeses, like Parmesan and Romano, keep for months.

FREEZE CHEESE?

Hard cheese, such as Parmesan and aged provolone, can be frozen—wrapped in plastic wrap and overwrapped with aluminum foil—for up to 6 months without noticeable change. But semifirm cheeses, such as fontina and mozzarella, become rubbery and watery if frozen.

CUT SOME FAT

To trim the fat from our Four-Cheese Sauce, use a nonstick saucepan and cut the butter down to 2 tablespoons. Substitute 1 cup of whole milk or evaporated skim milk for the light cream and use reduced-fat mozzarella cheese.

KITCHEN CHEMISTRY

For the smoothest, creamiest consistency, cook cheese sauce over low heat and stir almost constantly while the cheese is melting. High heat causes the protein in cheese to become stringy and tough and the cheese itself to clump. Aged natural cheese blends more easily into sauces than cheese that hasn't been aged. That's because the protein is tenderized somewhat during the aging process. Processed cheese also blends more easily than unaged natural cheese because of the emulsifying agents it contains.

Baked Macaroni in Four-Cheese Sauce

Prepare cheese sauce as directed at right, but **use** 2 cups each light cream and milk and **add** 1/4 teaspoon dry mustard. Also **substitute** elbow macaroni for penne. **Combine** macaroni and cheese sauce in a buttered 3-quart casserole. **Mix** 1/2 cup grated Parmesan cheese and 1/4 cup each fresh white bread crumbs and minced Italian parsley and **scatter** on top. **Bake**, uncovered, at 350°F until bubbly—20 to 25 minutes. To brown, **slide** under the broiler for about 30 seconds. Makes 6 servings.

Penne with Four Cheeses

- 3 **tablespoons butter or margarine**
- 2 **cloves garlic, minced**
- 2 **tablespoons all-purpose flour**
- 1 **cup light cream**
- 1 **cup milk**
- 1 **cup shredded fontina cheese**
- 1 **cup shredded provolone cheese**
- 1/2 **cup shredded mozzarella cheese**
- 1/2 **cup grated Parmesan cheese**
- 1/2 **teaspoon salt**
- 1/4 **teaspoon black pepper**
- 1 **pound penne, cooked and drained**
- 1/4 **cup minced Italian parsley**

1 In a large nonstick saucepan over moderate heat, melt butter. Add garlic and cook until soft—about 2 minutes. Blend in flour and cook until bubbly—about 1 minute. Remove from heat and gradually whisk in cream and milk. Return to moderate heat and cook, stirring often, until sauce boils and thickens—3 to 5 minutes.

2 Add cheeses, salt, and pepper and cook, stirring constantly, until cheeses melt and sauce is smooth—1 to 2 minutes.

3 Transfer penne to a heated serving bowl, add cheese sauce, and stir well to mix. Sprinkle with parsley and serve. Makes 4 servings.

1 Serving: Calories 956; Total Fat 48 g; Saturated Fat 29 g; Protein 42 g; Carbohydrates 89 g; Fiber 4 g; Sodium 1226 mg; Cholesterol 143 mg

prep time-30 minutes • cooking time-10 minutes

Oil and Garlic Sauces

*G*arlic and oil are the basis for many pasta sauces that can be put together in the time it takes to boil the pasta water.

EASY SAUCES

For some pasta lovers there is no more heavenly way to serve it than tossed with olive oil flavored with a little sautéed garlic and parsley. Olive oil has the capacity to pick up the flavors of other ingredients instantly and spread them to the last bit of pasta in the bottom of the bowl.

There are many ingredients that combine beautifully with oil and garlic. Try chopped sun-ripened tomatoes and basil; roasted vegetables with red pepper flakes; chopped cooked broccoli, fresh tomatoes, and sliced black olives; tuna and tomatoes; scallops and chopped red pepper; shrimp and chives.

If you need more liquid in an oil and garlic sauce, extend it with a little broth, wine, or pasta-cooking water.

ABOUT OLIVE OIL

For sauces based on oil, good quality olive oil is crucial.

Extra-virgin oil is the unqualified best. It comes from the first pressing of olives and is greenish in color. Because it is relatively expensive this fruity oil is usually reserved for use in salad dressings and sauces.

Virgin oil is from the second pressing of olives. It has more acidity and less finesse than extra-virgin oil and is used for general purpose cooking.

Products labeled pure olive oil or simply olive oil have been highly processed. These oils generally have little flavor.

GARLIC NOTES

Garlic requires gentle handling when it is sautéed. It will burn and become bitter quickly if the heat is too high.

If you like the flavor but not

How to Peel a Garlic Clove

Place a garlic clove on a work surface. Cover it with the flat side of a chef's knife blade and press down on it hard with your fist. The clove will pop out of its skin.

the bite of garlic in a sauce, try roasting it first. Separate the cloves of a head of garlic. Place them, unpeeled, on a baking sheet and roast in a 350°F oven for 20 to 30 minutes. Roasted garlic is so mellow you'll find that you need to add 2 or 3 times more to recipes as you would raw.

CLAM SAUCE TIPS

White clam sauce is easy to make and can quickly be turned into a red sauce with

Linguine with Red Clam Sauce

Prepare as directed through Step 1 at right, but **omit** vermouth and **add** one 28-ounce can Italian plum tomatoes, drained and chopped, 1 teaspoon crumbled dried basil, 1/4 teaspoon crumbled dried thyme, and 1/2 teaspoon sugar; also reduce salt to 1/4 teaspoon. **Simmer**, uncovered, over moderately low heat, **stirring** occasionally to break up tomatoes, until sauce thickens—15 to 20 minutes. **Proceed** as directed in Steps 2 and 3. Makes 4 servings.

the addition of canned tomatoes. Although most pasta sauces can wait for the pasta, that's not so with clam sauce since reheating the sauce can toughen the clams. Prepare the sauce while the pasta is boiling so that the moment the pasta is drained, the sauce can be tossed in.

WORK SAVER
Mini Food Processor

For anyone who makes pasta often, one of the greatest tools to have on hand is a mini food processor. It's the perfect tool for chopping or mincing small amounts of parsley, garlic, and other ingredients that go into a recipe or are used as a garnish. The work bowls of these mini tools hold about a cup, and they're easier to take apart and wash than the full-size models.

HOW TO CLEAN AND OPEN CLAMS

To clean clams: Scrub the clams under cool running water. Place in a large bowl and cover with cold salted water. Sprinkle the water with cornmeal and set in a cool place for several hours. When the clams ingest the cornmeal they expel grit and sand. Discard any that remain open when tapped with a finger.

To open clams by steaming: Place the clams in a large pot with a tight-fitting lid. Pour in 1 cup of water, cover, and bring to a boil over moderate heat. Steam until clams open—5 to 10 minutes. Using kitchen tongs, remove clams as they open. Discard any that do not open. Set clams aside in a bowl until cool. Remove clam meat, reserving the liquid. Chop the clam meat and set aside. Pour the liquid through a fine sieve to remove any grit. Use the clam meat and liquid as directed in the recipe.

Linguine with White Clam Sauce

- 1/4 **cup olive oil**
- 1 **large yellow onion, chopped**
- 3 **cloves garlic, minced**
- 1/3 **cup dry vermouth**
- 1/2 **teaspoon salt**
- 1/8 to 1/4 **teaspoon crushed red pepper flakes**
- 2 **cans (6 1/2 ounces each) minced clams, with their liquid, or the chopped meat and liquid from 2 dozen littleneck clams (see box, left)**
- 1/4 **cup minced Italian parsley**
- 1 **pound linguine, cooked and drained**

1 In a large skillet over moderate heat, heat oil 1 minute. Add onion and garlic and sauté until soft— about 5 minutes. Add vermouth, salt, and red pepper flakes and simmer, uncovered, for 3 minutes.

2 Stir in clams and their liquid and cook 1 minute more. Stir in parsley.

3 Transfer linguine to a large heated serving bowl, pour sauce over all, and toss well. Makes 4 servings.

1 Serving: Calories 596; Total Fat 16 g; Saturated Fat 2 g; Protein 26 g; Carbohydrates 81 g; Fiber 7 g; Sodium 460 mg; Cholesterol 33 mg

prep time-about 25 minutes
cooking time-10 minutes

PESTO SAUCE

Not all pesto sauces are made of basil; they don't even have to be green. Our pesto sampler includes mushroom, parsley, and onion variations.

ABOUT PESTO

In Italian, *pestare* means "to pound," the traditional technique for making this versatile uncooked pasta sauce. Although some cooks still use a mortar and pestle to pound together the ingredients for pesto, these days it is more often made in a blender or a food processor, which makes short shrift of a tedious job.

AN ALL-PURPOSE SAUCE

Pesto is delicious on both hot and cold pastas. Try it also as a sauce for gnocchi (Italian dumplings) and rice dishes.

Stir a spoonful into hot vegetable soup.

Toss a little in with steamed vegetables or add a forkful to a baked potato.

Dab a little on a pizza or focaccia before baking.

Make a mint and basil pesto as an accompaniment to lamb.

Stuff cherry tomatoes with basil pesto for a sensational holiday-time hors d'oeuvre. In fact, pestos in general combine nicely with cheese, cold shrimp, olives, and other hors d'oeuvres.

BASIL TIPS

In Italy, the flavor of small-leaf bush basil is preferred for pesto. In this country, large-leaf varieties are more commonly available. If there is a choice or if you grow your own, try a small-leaf basil.

When buying basil, choose bunches that have lively looking leaves with no black spots. When basil leaves are stored wet or in too cold a refrigerator, they quickly become limp and turn black.

Don't wash basil until you are ready to use it. It can be stored for about a day in the refrigerator in a plastic bag. Or store it with the stems in water with a plastic bag popped over the leaves.

When preparing basil for pesto, be sure to remove all of the tough stems. Pesto purists go so far as to remove the central veins from each leaf of large-leaf basil.

EASY SUBSTITUTIONS

You can substitute any flavorful green for basil. Try fresh spinach, arugula, or parsley or a combination of any two. Flavor them with a teaspoon or so of chopped fresh tarragon or sage, if you like.

Walnuts or almonds can be used in place of pine nuts.

Shallots or the white portions of scallions can be substituted for, or used along with, garlic.

To cut down on a little cholesterol, replace the butter with a little extra oil.

The flavor of a good olive oil is critical in pesto. Corn and other vegetable oils do not make good substitutes.

ADDED TEXTURE

For extra texture, grate the cheese by hand and fold it into the processed pesto sauce by hand with a rubber spatula. If you plan to freeze pesto, leave out the cheese. When you thaw the frozen pesto, grate the cheese and stir it in then.

PESTO ON ICE

Pesto can be refrigerated for about a week. Spoon it into a small jar; pour a thin layer of olive oil on top and cover tightly. If the top surface darkens in color, simply stir it in before mixing with the pasta.

Freeze pesto for about 1 month in a tightly sealed plastic bag. Or freeze it in ice-cube trays covered with plastic wrap: Use it a cube at a time as you need it.

MIXING PESTO

The combination of ingredients in pesto makes a very sticky paste. There must be enough oil in the mix to make it creamy.

To ensure spreadability, mix in the pesto while the pasta is very hot. Add the pesto in stages, tossing thoroughly to mix. If it is very sticky, add a spoonful of hot pasta water to thin.

MUSHROOM PESTO

In a large skillet over moderately high heat, **sauté** 10 ounces thinly sliced mushrooms and 1 minced clove garlic in 2 tablespoons butter until golden—2 to 3 minutes. **Transfer** to a blender or food processor, **add** 2 tablespoons each softened butter and snipped chives or scallion tops, 1/2 cup grated Parmesan, 3/4 teaspoon salt, and 1/4 teaspoon black pepper and **purée** until smooth. Makes 3/4 cup, enough for 4 servings.

Roasted Onion-Garlic Pesto

In a 13" x 9" x 2" roasting pan, **toss** 4 peeled and quartered medium-size yellow onions with 12 peeled cloves garlic, 1 tablespoon olive oil, 1/2 teaspoon crumbled dried thyme, 3/4 teaspoon salt, and 1/4 teaspoon black pepper. **Roast**, uncovered, in a preheated 350°F oven until golden—about 1 hour. **Cool** until easy to handle, coarsely **chop**, then **toss** with 1 pound cooked, drained spaghetti along with 1 cup ricotta cheese and 1/4 cup grated Parmesan. Makes 1 cup, enough for 4 servings.

Parsley-Gorgonzola Pesto

Pulse 4 cups firmly packed Italian parsley and 1 peeled clove garlic in a blender or food processor 6 to 8 times until coarsely chopped. With the motor running, **drizzle** in 1/4 cup olive oil in a slow, steady stream. **Add** 4 ounces Gorgonzola, the grated zest of 1 lemon, 1 teaspoon salt, and 1/2 teaspoon black pepper and **purée**, **scraping** down the sides of the container as needed, until smooth—about 2 minutes. Makes 1 cup, enough for 4 servings.

Classic Pesto

6 1/2   **cups (about 2 bunches) firmly packed fresh basil**
2   **cloves garlic, peeled**
1/4   **cup extra-virgin olive oil**
2   **tablespoons butter or margarine, softened**
1/2   **cup grated Parmesan cheese**
3/4   **cup pine nuts**
1/2   **teaspoon grated lemon zest**
1   **teaspoon salt**
1/4   **teaspoon black pepper**

1 Purée basil and garlic in a blender at high speed or in a food processor for 2 minutes, scraping down the sides of the container as necessary. With the motor running, drizzle in oil in a slow, steady stream.

2 Add butter, Parmesan, pine nuts, lemon zest, salt and pepper, and purée, scraping down the sides of the container 2 or 3 times, until mixture forms a paste—about 3 minutes. Add 1 to 2 tablespoons water if mixture seems too stiff. Makes 1 1/2 cups, enough for 4 servings.

1 Tablespoon: Calories 47; Total Fat 5 g; Saturated Fat 1 g; Protein 2 g; Carbohydrates 1 g; Fiber 0 g; Sodium 83 mg; Cholesterol 3 mg

prep time-23 minutes

STUFFED CRÊPES

*I*n Italy, crêpes are called crespelle, and they're used in a wide range of recipes. Here we roll them for cannelloni. Crêpes are as easy to make as pancakes and can be made days ahead of serving.

BAKED AND STUFFED

In most areas of Italy, cannelloni are made with large pasta tubes or rolled squares of dough. Crêpes are a delicious alternative. Once they are stuffed, cannelloni are baked, usually topped with either a creamy white sauce or a meaty tomato sauce.

CRÊPE TIPS

When the batter is prepared and the pan is hot, crêpes take only a minute to make. However, it's crucial to let the batter rest in the refrigerator for 1/2 hour or up to 2 hours before you start. That gives the flour time to absorb liquid and expand, which ensures that the batter will spread thinly and without holes.

When you pour crêpe batter into a hot skillet, tilt the skillet quickly to spread the batter. Cook until the crêpe slides when the pan is tilted. Tip: Use a coffee measure to scoop and pour out the perfect amount of batter for a 6-inch skillet.

To flip a crêpe, use a small spatula or simply grab the edge of the crêpe with your fingers and flip it by hand.

The side of the crêpe that's cooked first is usually better looking; use it for the outside of a rolled crêpe.

Master the knack of making crêpes and you can use them in many dishes. Wrap them around creamy seafood fillings, vegetables in cheese sauce, curries, or even chilis.

COOKING AHEAD

Crêpes keep beautifully, making it easy to prepare a dish partially in advance. Cooled crêpes can be stacked separated with wax paper, covered with plastic wrap, and refrigerated for a day or two. Or seal them tightly in plastic wrap and freeze.

ABOUT CAPONATA

Our cannelloni variation is flavored with caponata. This cooked Sicilian "salsa" is made with flavorful ingredients, including eggplant, capers, celery, tomato sauce, onions, and olives and is generally used as a condiment. Commercially made caponata is available in small jars.

Jacques Pépin
Cookbook author and host of
Today's Gourmet

"Professional crêpe makers use special pans and can juggle 3 or 4 crêpes at once. For making crêpes at home, I recommend using a heavy, nonstick 6-inch skillet and advise making only 1 crêpe at a time. The secret of thin crêpes is to spread a minimum of batter as quickly as possible in the pan."

CAPONATA CANNELLONI

Prepare crêpes as directed at right. **Omit** mushrooms, flour, and broth from filling. Instead, **add** one 14 1/2-ounce can no-salt-added stewed tomatoes, chopped with their juice, two 5-ounce cans caponata, and 1/2 cup chopped parsley when chicken is no longer pink. **Cook** 5 to 10 minutes, **stirring** often, until mixture thickens slightly. **Fill**, **roll**, and **arrange** crêpes in pan as directed. **Omit** cheese sauce; **top** instead with 1 1/2 cups of your favorite tomato sauce and bake, uncovered, until bubbly—about 20 minutes. Makes 4 servings.

TO COOK AND ROLL A CRÊPE

1 Oil a 6-inch skillet and heat over moderate heat. When hot, pour 2 tablespoons of batter into the center and swirl the skillet to spread batter evenly.

2 Cook until lightly browned—about 30 seconds. With a small spatula, turn the crêpe and cook the flip side 10 seconds. Slide out of the pan onto a plate. Repeat to make 12 crêpes.

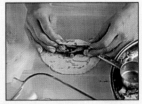

3 Place 1 crêpe on a work surface; spoon a scant 1/4 cup of filling to one side of center. Roll crêpe around filling. Fill and roll remaining 11 crêpes. Place them, seam side down, in a greased 9-by 13-inch baking pan.

Chicken and Mushroom Cannelloni

Crêpe Batter:

- 1/2 cup unsifted all-purpose flour
- 1/4 teaspoon salt
- 3/4 cup low-fat (1%) milk
- 2 eggs
- 2 tablespoons plus 2 teaspoons olive oil

Filling:

- 1 tablespoon olive oil
- 1 medium-size yellow onion, finely chopped
- 8 ounces assorted mushrooms (button and shiitake), stemmed, wiped clean, and thinly sliced
- 12 ounces skinless, boneless chicken thighs, cut into 1/2-inch chunks
- 2 tablespoons all-purpose flour
- 1 cup canned low-sodium chicken broth
- 1/2 teaspoon salt
- 1/4 teaspoon dried rosemary, crumbled
- 1/8 teaspoon black pepper

Cheese Sauce:

- 1 1/3 cups low-fat (1%) milk
- 2 tablespoons all-purpose flour
- 1/4 teaspoon salt
- 1/4 teaspoon black pepper
- 1/2 cup grated Parmesan cheese

Asparagus is a perfect complement to Chicken and Mushroom Cannelloni.

1 For the Crêpe Batter: In a small bowl, stir together flour and salt. In a 2-cup measure, combine milk, eggs, and 2 tablespoons of the oil. Gradually add liquid ingredients to flour mixture, whisking until smooth. Cover and refrigerate at least 30 minutes. Strain through a fine sieve.

2 Brush a 6-inch nonstick skillet with a little of the remaining oil and place over moderate heat. Cook 12 crêpes as shown at left.

3 For the Filling: In a large nonstick skillet over moderate heat, heat oil 1 minute. Add onion and sauté until soft—3 to 5 minutes. Add mushrooms and cook, stirring occasionally, until tender—about 5 minutes. Add chicken and cook until no longer pink—about 5 minutes. Sprinkle flour over chicken and stir to coat. Gradually add broth, salt, rosemary, and pepper and cook, stirring frequently, until sauce thickens slightly and chicken is cooked through—about 5 minutes.

4 For the Cheese Sauce: In a saucepan, whisk milk into flour. Add salt and pepper and set over moderate heat, whisking constantly, until sauce is bubbly and as thick as heavy cream—about 4 minutes. Stir in 1/4 cup Parmesan.

5 Preheat the oven to 400°F. Fill and roll crêpes as shown in box at left. Spoon cheese sauce over filled crêpes, sprinkle with the remaining Parmesan, and bake, uncovered, until bubbling and lightly browned—about 25 minutes. Makes 4 servings.

1 Serving: Calories 478; Total Fat 24 g; Saturated Fat 7 g; Protein 34 g; Carbohydrates 30 g; Fiber 2 g; Sodium 956 mg; Cholesterol 192 mg

*prep time-33 minutes
cooking time-1 hour*

LAYERED PASTA

*I*n today's lighter lasagnes, vegetables, turkey, or chicken replace ground beef and are every bit as flavorful.

A FLEXIBLE FEAST

The great thing about lasagne—aside from its irresistible taste—is its flexibility. You can stick to making classic lasagne recipes or adapt a recipe to whatever ingredients you have on hand, including leftovers. You can bake it and serve it immediately, assemble it one day and bake it the next, or warm and serve it the day after it's baked. It's the perfect pot-luck dish since it travels well in its pan.

THE MAKINGS OF LASAGNE

In making vegetable lasagne, almost any cooked vegetable or vegetable mixture can be used. The vegetables should be slightly underdone, because they will cook a second time when the lasagne bakes.

Too much liquid in a lasagne guarantees soggy, leaden results. To make a lasagne as light as it can be, all vegetables must be well drained before they are layered in.

Be sure that excess water has been pressed out of steamed or boiled leafy greens. Mushrooms should be cooked until they have exuded all of their liquid and it has evaporated; yellow squash and zucchini should be grilled or sautéed until crisp. Puréed winter squash should be set aside to drain in a fine sieve.

The standard cheeses for lasagne are mozzarella, ricotta, and Parmesan. You can use low-fat cheeses or change the flavor of a lasagne by trying some new varieties.

Use Monterey Jack or smoked mozzarella instead of regular. Substitute aged provolone or Asiago for the grated Parmesan. Spice up mild ricotta by crumbling in a little tangy white goat cheese or even goat cheese with herbs. Or replace the ricotta with farmer's cheese, which bakes beautifully.

If you want a meaty lasagne, you can use lean ground beef, lamb, or pork, sliced chicken, ground or sliced turkey, loose sausage, pork or turkey sausage, or, better yet, a combination of two or three.

PERFECT NOODLES

Cooking lasagne noodles is simple, but it presents a number of dilemmas. What kind of noodles should you use? How do you prevent them from becoming soggy? How do you keep noodles from sticking together? A few noodle pointers follow.

WHAT NOODLES TO CHOOSE?

There is indeed a lot of choice. Many pasta lovers enjoy making their own fresh noodles—either by hand or with a pasta machine—since they can be rolled wonderfully thin. Packaged varieties come flat, ridged, and with or without ruffled edges. If a recipe doesn't specify which type, it's your choice; but choose the thinnest noodles you can find. Thick noodles become wet and doughy as they cook.

NOODLE FLAVORS

Both green spinach noodles and yellow egg noodles are traditional in lasagne. The spinach noodles give the dish a little extra flavor.

Building a lasagne with alternating layers of green and yellow noodles is also traditional. Keep in mind, however, that spinach noodles cook a little quicker than egg noodles. (Whole-wheat noodles cook a little slower.)

WHAT ABOUT NO-COOK NOODLES?

It's true, there are now lasagne noodles that don't have to be boiled, and many pasta lovers swear by them.

(continued on page 108)

HOW TO LAYER LASAGNE

1 Pour ½ cup tomato sauce in the pan. Arrange noodles on top with the edges slightly overlapping.

2 Cover the noodles evenly with ¾ cup tomato sauce, then sprinkle with ¼ cup grated Parmesan and dot with 1 cup ricotta.

3 Arrange slices of cooked eggplant on top. Repeat the process twice, beginning with noodles. Replace the eggplant with zucchini in the second round and with peppers in the third.

Vegetable Lasagne

Sauce:

- **2 cans (28 ounces each) Italian plum tomatoes**
- **1 medium-size yellow onion, finely chopped**
- **4 cloves garlic, minced**
- **1/2 teaspoon dried thyme, crumbled**
- **1/4 cup chopped fresh basil**
- **1 1/2 teaspoons salt**
- **1/2 teaspoon black pepper**
- **2 tablespoons flour mixed with 1/4 cup cold water**

Filling:

- **1 medium-size eggplant, peeled and cut lengthwise into 1/2-inch slices**
- **2 1/2 tablespoons olive oil**
- **2 small zucchini, peeled and cut lengthwise into 1/2-inch slices**
- **2 small sweet green peppers, cored, seeded, and cut into 1/2-inch strips**
- **2 small sweet red peppers, cored, seeded, and cut into 1/2-inch strips**
- **1 cup grated Parmesan cheese**
- **1 cup shredded mozzarella cheese**
- **1 pound lasagne noodles, cooked until almost tender and drained**
- **3 cups low-fat ricotta cheese**

1 For the Sauce: In a 5-quart Dutch oven over moderately high heat, bring tomatoes and their juice, onion, garlic, thyme, basil, salt, and black pepper to a boil. Reduce the heat to moderately low and simmer, uncovered, stirring occasionally to break up tomatoes, for 15 minutes. Slowly whisk in flour-water paste and simmer, stirring constantly, until sauce thickens—about 2 minutes. Meanwhile, preheat the broiler.

2 For the Filling: Brush both sides of eggplant slices using 1 tablespoon oil, place in a single layer in a 15½" x 10" x 1" pan, set in the broiler 5 to 6 inches from the heat, and broil 5 minutes on each side. Oil zucchini slices using another 1 tablespoon oil and broil for 3 minutes each side. Toss peppers with the remaining ½ tablespoon oil and broil 7 minutes; toss well and broil 7 minutes more.

3 Reduce the oven temperature to 350°F. Blend the Parmesan and mozzarella and reserve.

4 Cover the bottom of an ungreased 13" x 9" x 2" baking dish with ½ cup tomato sauce. Lay 4 lasagne noodles over sauce with edges overlapping. Now layer the lasagne, distributing each ingredient evenly: ¾ cup tomato sauce, ½ cup Parmesan mixture, 1 cup ricotta, all eggplant slices, ¾ cup tomato sauce, and 4 lasagne noodles. Repeat layering twice, using zucchini in place of eggplant in the second layer and the pepper mixture in the third. Top with a layer of noodles, then the remaining sauce and Parmesan mixture.

5 Cover with foil, shiny side down, set on a baking sheet and bake until bubbly—45 to 55 minutes. Let stand 10 minutes before serving. Makes 6 servings.

1 Serving: Calories 750; Total Fat 27 g; Saturated Fat 12 g; Protein 40 g; Carbohydrates 91 g; Fiber 10 g; Sodium 1703 mg; Cholesterol 62 mg

prep time-1 hour • cooking time-1 hour 27 minutes to 1 hour 37 minutes

(continued from page 106)

They cost a little more than regular noodles but they are good and thin, and they eliminate the possibility of overcooked pasta in a lasagne.

Most no-cook noodles require a brief soaking in warm water to become pliable, and care must be taken that they remain well covered with sauce while the lasagne bakes.

HOW TO AVOID SOGGY NOODLES

Because lasagne noodles are cooked twice, they can easily become too soft. If you use regular packaged noodles, don't wander away from the stove when you put them on to boil. The noodles should be removed from the heat and drained just before they reach the firm-tender stage.

STICKY PROBLEMS

Lasagne noodles present more sticking problems than other pastas. Since they are long and wide, they're apt to get stuck together in the pot. And since they have to be set aside while a lasagne is assembled, they stick to whatever surface they're on while they cool.

Adding a tablespoon or so of oil to the cooking water should be avoided for most pasta varieties. However, it can be the right thing to do when cooking lasagne noodles. The oil will help to keep them from sticking together as they cook.

The alternative is to cook the noodles in batches, a few at a time, removing them with tongs or a skimmer.

When it comes to eliminating sticking during assembly, some cookbooks recommend rinsing the noodles in cold water after they are drained. But rinsing causes lasagne to become watery and to fall apart when cut.

That's because rinsing away the starch eliminates its ability to absorb moisture during baking and "glue" the lasagne together. Also, if the noodles are not properly dried after rinsing, the excess water is absorbed and added to the liquid in the baking pan.

If you want to rinse the noodles after cooking, be sure to blot up every drop of moisture with a cotton towel.

Even better, however, is to simply drain the noodles and immediately lay them flat on cotton towels: The moisture on their steaming surfaces will evaporate quickly and the starch will be retained. Then assemble the lasagne quickly before the noodles have chance to stick.

COOKING AHEAD

Lasagne is the perfect party dish since it can be assembled 3 to 5 hours ahead of baking time and held in the refrigerator. (If you bake the dish straight from the refrigerator, add 10 or 15 minutes' cooking time.) You might also want to assemble and bake 2 pans of lasagne at once, freezing one for later use.

FROZEN ASSETS

If you plan to freeze lasagne after baking, line the pan with enough heavy-duty aluminum foil to come up and over the sides and cover the lasagne. Bake as directed and cool completely on a wire rack.

"Here are 3 tips for better lasagne. Watery lasagne is usually the result of noodles that were boiled too long or rinsed after cooking.

"To avoid lasagne that is dry on the outside, make sure it is uniformly covered with sauce all the way to the edges and that it is covered with foil for the first 20 minutes of baking.

"For easy slicing, let the dish stand on a rack for 20 minutes after baking so that any liquid can be reabsorbed into the ingredients."

Then cover securely with the foil liner and freeze. Once frozen, the foil-covered lasagne can be lifted out of the pan, overwrapped in foil, and returned to the freezer. Bake within 3 months.

To reheat, return the frozen lasagne to the original baking pan and thaw for about a day in the refrigerator. Undo the wrapping, but cover the lasagne loosely with foil. Bake at 325°F for about 30 minutes or until heated through.

SLICE AND SERVE

Use a sharp or serrated knife to cut the lasagne into rectangles. Lift out one corner piece first, and the others will come out easily. A pancake turner makes a good lasagne server.

TURKEY LASAGNE

Prepare tomato sauce as directed in Step 1 on page 107 and **set aside**. **Cook** and **drain** 8 curly edged lasagne noodles by package directions and **set aside**. In a large heavy skillet over high heat, **sauté** 1 cup chopped yellow onion and 4 minced garlic cloves in 1 tablespoon butter until golden— about 3 minutes. **Add** 1 pound ground turkey and **cook, stirring** occasionally until no longer pink—about 10 minutes. **Transfer** to a large bowl. In the same skillet, **melt** 2 tablespoons butter over high heat. **Add** 10 ounces coarsely chopped mushrooms and **cook** until light brown—about 5 minutes. **Add** to turkey mixture along with 4 cups of the tomato sauce. **Cover** the bottom of an ungreased 13" x 9" x 2" baking dish with 1/2 cup of the remaining tomato sauce. **Top** with 4 lasagne noodles, overlapping edges, 3 cups turkey mixture, and 1/4 cup grated Parmesan. **Repeat** the layers, beginning with the lasagne noodles, then **scatter** 1 cup shredded mozzarella on top. **Bake** as directed in Step 5. Makes 6 servings.

RICE, GRAINS AND BEANS

A SIDE OF GRITS

In the American South, a spoonful of grits always accompanies ham and eggs for breakfast. But grits can be enjoyed as a dish at lunch and dinner too.

A GRITS HISTORY

North America's native people showed early settlers how to preserve corn by drying it and removing the hull. Grits is made from hulled and milled dried corn or from hominy—field corn kernels that are puffed and hulled in a lye bath.

WHICH GRITS?

Grits comes three ways: regular, quick cooking, and instant. Regular grits can be coarsely stone ground or commercially milled. Of the three types, it takes the longest time to cook—up to 40 minutes for stone ground—so quick-cooking grits is the more common choice these days.

The instant variety of grits is precooked, and although fine on its own, it does not work well in recipes.

SMOOTH MOVES

When cooked in water, broth, or milk, grits becomes thick and smooth. To guarantee smoothness, add grits slowly and steadily to the cooking liquid. If you are using the regular or stone-ground variety, you'll find that the slower you cook it the creamier it becomes. Commercially milled grits will always produce a smoother dish than stone-ground grits.

SERVED IN STYLE

For breakfast, served with milk and brown sugar, grits is a great alternative to hot oatmeal. Served hot from the saucepan, like our Cheesy Grits, it makes a delicious side dish. It can also be mixed with beaten egg and baked as a soufflé, poured into a baking dish and baked in the oven with cheese, or molded and fried like fritters.

When cooked grits is turned into a shallow pan and cooled, it becomes firm enough to cut into squares like polenta. Fry the squares in butter or oil, then top with stew or pasta or serve as a side dish to ham and eggs. An alternative style for fried grits in many households is to pour the hot grits into a drinking tumbler. When cooled, it's unmolded and the cylinder of grits is then sliced into rounds and fried.

SIMPLE STIR-INS

For a little extra flavor stir one of the following into a simmering pot of grits: a splash of hot red pepper sauce; sautéed garlic; crisp cooked bacon bits or coarsely chopped ham; chopped, fried onions; or sweet or hot peppers.

EASY CLEANUP

If you have one, use a non-stick saucepan to cook grits. If you use a regular pan set it aside to cool after ladling out the grits. When cool, grits residue will pull away from the sides of the pan.

HOW TO MAKE PEPPER-BAKED GRITS

1 Cut the cooled and solidified grits into twenty-four 1 1/2- to 2-inch squares.

2 Arrange squares of grits in a greased baking dish and top with chopped red peppers and mozzarella and Parmesan cheeses.

3 Repeat with 2 more layers of grits and topping, placing squares over the spaces in the previous layer. Bake about 20 minutes, until the cheeses have melted and browned.

Cheesy Grits

PEPPER-BAKED GRITS

Prepare as directed at right, **substituting** 1/2 cup grated Parmesan for Cheddar, **increasing** salt to 3/4 teaspoon, and **omitting** the added butter. **Melt** 1 tablespoon butter or margarine in a small skillet over moderate heat. **Add** 7 to 8 finely chopped small scallions and **sauté** for 4 to 5 minutes. **Stir** scallions into grits, **pour** into greased 2-quart shallow baking dish, and **cool** for 30 minutes. Meanwhile, **drain** one 7-ounce jar roasted red peppers, **chop,** and **set aside**.

Preheat the oven to 425°F. **Invert** cooled grits onto a cutting board and **cut** into twenty-four 1½- to 2-inch squares. **Arrange** 8 squares about 1 inch apart in a well-greased 8" x 8" x 2" baking dish, **top** with 1/3 of the chopped peppers, 1/2 cup shredded mozzarella, and 2 tablespoons grated Parmesan. **Repeat** layers twice, placing squares over the spaces in the previous layers. Bake, uncovered, until lightly browned—20 to 25 minutes. Makes 4 servings.

- **3** **cups water**
- **1** **to 2 cloves garlic, minced**
- **1** **cup quick-cooking grits**
- **1/2** **teaspoon salt**
- **1 1/4** **cups shredded Cheddar cheese or 3/4 cup chèvre**
- **2** **tablespoons butter or margarine**
- **1/4** **to 1/2 teaspoon ground white pepper**

1 In a large saucepan over high heat, bring water and garlic to a boil. Gradually mix in grits and salt, stirring constantly.

2 Reduce the heat to moderately low and cook, covered, stirring frequently until thickened—5 to 7 minutes.

3 Remove from the heat; add Cheddar, butter, and pepper, stirring constantly until cheese is melted and smooth. Makes 4 servings.

> **1 Serving: Calories 372; Total Fat 20 g; Saturated Fat 12 g; Protein 14 g; Carbohydrates 34 g; Fiber 5 g; Sodium 581 mg; Cholesterol 59 mg**
>
> *prep time-5 minutes*
> *cooking time-10 to 12 minutes*

CRUNCHY GRAINS

Homemade granola is a near-perfect snack. It's crunchy, delicious, and good for you. Our recipes include an especially healthful low-fat variation.

GRANOLA NOTES

Granola started out as a breakfast cereal but it has evolved into a snack that's eaten by the handful or baked into bars. There are excellent commercial granolas available but they're expensive, and making your own is easy.

Use a pan large enough to hold the granola in a thin layer so that the oats toast evenly in the oven.

If you use a dark pan, granola will bake to a darker color. If your granola tends to get too dark before it's thoroughly toasted, lower the oven temperature to 275°F and bake it a little longer than directed in the recipe. Or simply line a dark pan with aluminum foil before pouring in the granola.

Any dried fruit can be substi-tuted for cherries or raisins. Try dried blueberries, cur-rants, or cranberries.

Large dried fruits, such as apples, apricots, dates, figs, peaches, pineapples, and prunes, can be used but first cut them into small pieces.

Add dried fruits to the mix after baking. They'll become hard pellets if they're baked in the oven.

NOT JUST FOR SNACKING

There are many ways to enjoy granola. Make a healthy sun-dae in a parfait glass with lay-ers of granola and frozen yogurt. Top with a fruit purée.

Sprinkle unbaked granola (minus the dried fruit) on the crumble toppings of fruit pies and cobblers before baking.

Crush and use it like graham cracker crumbs to make crusts for cheesecake and pie.

Stir 1/2 cup or so into a basic drop-cookie, muffin, or quick-bread batter.

FAT FACTS

Although it's very nutritious, granola is not low in fat. That's because nuts and whole grains contain fat.

The fat in nuts and whole grains is mostly in the form of polyunsaturated and monoun-saturated oils, the so-called good fats that don't cause cho-lesterol buildup and may actu-ally be beneficial to the cardiovascular system. The exception is coconut, which is loaded with saturated fat.

NATURE'S LITTLE POWERHOUSE

The tiny germ in each grain of wheat provides hearty helpings of three B vitamins plus iron, magnesium, phos-phorus, zinc, vitamin E, and dietary fiber.

Toasted wheat germ, which has a slightly sweet and nutty flavor, can be found in jars in the cereal section of most supermarkets. Natural, untoasted wheat germ is avail-able in health-food stores.

When you buy wheat germ, keep in mind that it is rich in oil, which will become rancid. Wheat germ must be stored in the refrigerator from the moment the jar is opened.

How to Toast Granola

1 When the liquid and dry ingredients have been mixed, spoon the granola in an even layer in an oiled jelly-roll pan.

2 Bake the granola at 300°F, stirring every 15 minutes, until golden brown and crunchy— about 1 hour. When cooled, stir in the dried cherries and raisins.

WORK SAVER

Storage Containers

Whole grains need to be stored properly to keep them safe from moisture and bugs. Fortunately, there are any number of con-tainer types available that do the job well. Many are also attractive enough to keep on the counter as canisters. Look for heavy glass or plastic storage jars with lids that securely clamp down, screw on, or fit like a plug. A rubber or cork gasket around the opening of a jar offers extra pro-tection against moisture.

Homemade Granola

Low-Fat Granola

Prepare as directed at right, **substituting** 1 cup wheat germ for almonds and **increasing** apple juice concentrate to 1/2 cup and honey to 1/4 cup. **Omit** water, butter, and vegetable oil. Makes 5 to 6 cups.

Trail Mix

Prepare granola as directed at right. In a large bowl, **toss** together 2 cups granola, 2 cups mini pretzel ring twists, 2 cups crunchy corn cereal, 1/2 cup each dried cranberries, reduced-fat chocolate chips, reduced-fat honey-roasted peanuts, and toasted pumpkin or sunflower seeds. Makes 8 cups.

- **4** cups old-fashioned rolled oats
- **1** cup natural wheat and barley cereal
- **1** cup sliced unblanched almonds
- **1/2** cup firmly packed light brown sugar
- **1** teaspoon salt
- **1** teaspoon ground cinnamon
- **1/4** cup frozen apple juice concentrate, thawed
- **1/4** cup water
- **2** tablespoons butter, melted
- **2** tablespoons vegetable oil
- **2** tablespoons honey
- **1** teaspoon vanilla
- Grated zest of 1 orange
- **1** cup dried pitted cherries
- **1** cup light seedless raisins

1 Preheat the oven to 300°F. Lightly coat a 15" x 10" x 1" jelly-roll pan with vegetable spray and set aside.

2 In a large bowl, combine oats, cereal, almonds, sugar, salt, and cinnamon; set aside.

3 In a small bowl, whisk together apple juice concentrate, water, butter, oil, honey, vanilla, and orange zest. Pour over oats mixture, tossing until well combined. Spread the mixture evenly in prepared pan.

4 Bake, stirring every 15 minutes, until golden and slightly crunchy—about 1 hour.

5 Remove the pan to a rack to cool completely—about 1 hour. When cooled, stir in cherries and raisins. Store in an airtight container. Makes 7 cups.

1 Cup: Calories 595; Total Fat 18 g; Saturated Fat 4 g; Protein 14 g; Carbohydrates 110 g; Fiber 10 g; Sodium 460 mg; Cholesterol 9 mg

prep time-20 minutes • cooking time-1 hour

A Bowl of Chili

Chili was concocted back in the early 1800s. The original chili, known as a bowl of red, was beanless and tomatoless. Chili has come a long way since then.

THE PERFECT DISH

Although every chili aficionado may claim that their recipe is *the one*, the fact is there is no single way—and there are no rules—of making chili. Whatever way you like it is the right way.

Chili styles range from mild to incendiary, depending on the number of chile peppers and amount of chili powder used. We've included a spicy Two-Alarm Chili as well as a hotter Four-Alarm version.

Although chili is traditionally based on chopped meat and chile peppers, these days vegetarian chili—which is based on beans and has far less fat—is just as popular. We introduce both styles with our beanless Bowl of Red and our meatless Vegetarian Chili.

CHILI NOTES

Beans for chili are more or less interchangeable. Our recipes call for red kidney beans, but you can also use pink kidney beans, pinto beans, or even black beans. To save time, use well-rinsed canned beans.

Chili improves with age; if possible, make it a day before you plan to serve it. Some chili buffs say that 3 or 4 days is even better. Cool the chili for at least 30 minutes, then cover and refrigerate. If you have room in the refrigerator, leave the chili right in its pan. Reheat gently, stirring frequently until heated through.

HOW TO CUSTOMIZE CANNED CHILI

If the chili isn't hot enough, add more cayenne to taste. For extra flavor, stir in crushed cumin seeds.

To enrich canned chili, add about 1/4 cup of beer per can of chili and simmer until the alcohol has evaporated.

To stretch chili, spoon it over hot rice or add a can of drained, rinsed kidney beans or frozen home-cooked beans.

Bowl of Red

Substitute 3 pounds finely diced beef round or chuck for ground beef and **brown** well in 3 tablespoons vegetable oil in a Dutch oven over moderately high heat; **remove** to paper toweling to drain. In drippings, **sauté** the onions and garlic as directed; **omit** green peppers. Also **omit** tomatoes, beer, jalapeño, tomato paste, and kidney beans. **Return** beef to the Dutch oven, **add** chili powder, cumin, oregano, coriander, 1/2 teaspoon each salt and hot red pepper sauce, and three 14 1/2-ounce cans beef broth. **Simmer**, uncovered, over low heat until beef is tender and broth slightly thickened—1 to 1 1/2 hours. Makes 4 to 6 servings.

COOK'S SECRETS

Merle Ellis
Expert butcher and cookbook author

"Old-timers say the best meat for chili is from an old, lean longhorn bull, but these are hard to come by. Ground beef can be used to make excellent chili but I also like to use beef shank cut into 1/4-inch cubes. Shank meat is flavorful but tough, so if you use it, you'll have to simmer the chili longer than if you used ground beef, about an hour longer or even a little more."

KNOW YOUR CHILES

Chiles are spicy flavor enhancers but they're also extremely good for you. Capsaicin—the main chemical responsible for a chile's heat—is an anticoagulant that guards against heart attack and strokes. Moreover, peppers in general contain bioflavonoids, plant pigments that may prevent cancer. Some of the most popular chiles appear below.

1. Anaheim: Very commonly used. Red or green slender pod; 6 to 7 inches long. Range from mild to tepid.

2. Ancho: Dried poblano chiles; generally red, with wrinkled skin; 3 to 4 inches long. Mild to moderately hot.

3. Jalapeño: Usually sold green but sometimes red. Also available canned; 2-inch-long tapered pod. Moderately hot.

4. Poblano: Green ancho chiles, similar in size to a bell pepper. Mild.

5. Serrano: Used fresh in salsas. Red or dark green; 1 to 2 inches long. Very hot.

FOUR-ALARM CHILI

Prepare as directed at right, **adding** 6 to 7 tablespoons chili powder and 2 tablespoons chopped jalapeño peppers. If additional heat is still desired, **add** ground black pepper or cayenne, crushed red pepper flakes, or hot red pepper sauce to taste. Makes 8 servings.

VEGETARIAN CHILI

Prepare as directed at right, using a 6- to 7-quart Dutch oven and **omitting** beef. **Substitute** 1 tablespoon olive oil for the vegetable oil and 1 large sweet red pepper for 1 of the green peppers. At end of Step 2, **add** 2 small peeled and diced carrots and cook, covered, for 2 minutes. In Step 3, **add** an additional can of tomatoes, 2 tablespoons tomato paste, and one 10-ounce package thawed frozen baby lima beans. Also **substitute** one 14¹/₂-ounce can vegetable broth for beer. **Simmer**, partially covered, 10 to 15 minutes. **Stir** in one 10-ounce package thawed frozen corn kernels and **add** one 16-ounce can drained and rinsed black beans. **Return** to a boil, then **simmer**, uncovered, for 10 minutes. Makes 8 servings.

Two-Alarm Chili

- 2 tablespoons vegetable oil
- 2 pounds lean ground beef chuck or round
- 2 large yellow onions, chopped
- 2 large sweet green peppers, cored, seeded, and chopped
- 3 cloves garlic, minced
- 1 can (28 ounces) whole plum tomatoes, coarsely chopped with their juice
- 1 can (12 ounces) beer
- 1 medium-size jalapeño pepper, cored, seeded, and finely chopped
- 1 tablespoon tomato paste
- 4 to 5 tablespoons chili powder
- 1 tablespoon ground cumin
- 1¹/₂ teaspoons salt
- 1 teaspoon dried oregano, crumbled, or 1 tablespoon chopped fresh oregano
- 1 teaspoon ground coriander
- 2 cups cooked, drained, and rinsed canned red kidney beans

1 In a 5-quart Dutch oven over moderately high heat, heat oil 1 minute. Add beef and sauté, breaking up chunks of meat with a wooden spoon, until browned—5 to 7 minutes. Drain off all but 1 tablespoon of fat.

2 Reduce the heat to moderate, add onions, green peppers, and garlic, and cook, stirring occasionally, until soft—about 8 minutes.

3 Add tomatoes, beer, jalapeño, tomato paste, chili powder, cumin, salt, oregano, and coriander. Bring to a boil over high heat. Reduce the heat to low and simmer, uncovered, stirring occasionally, until thickened—about 25 minutes. If chili becomes too thick, thin with a little water.

4 Stir in beans and cook 5 minutes more. Makes 8 servings.

1 Serving: Calories 348; Total Fat 15 g; Saturated Fat 6 g; Protein 28 g; Carbohydrates 24 g; Fiber 7 g; Sodium 710 mg; Cholesterol 73 mg

prep time-30 minutes
cooking time-44 to 46 minutes

Bean Casseroles

*O*ur bean casserole combines the tastes and textures of three kinds of beans. Although baked in the traditional way, it's not the least bit sweet.

BEAN KNOW-HOW

Buy beans from a store where the turnover is quick. Dry beans dry out even more as they age on the shelf and take a long time to cook. Old beans look dull and faded.

Buy beans as you need them. Keep them in a cool, dry cupboard. Loose beans should be transferred to a jar or other airtight container.

When ready to use, pick over the beans, pulling out pebbles or beans that are shriveled. Rinse by placing in a large bowl and filling it with cold water. Skim off anything that floats to the surface; drain in a colander and rinse under cold running water. Then soak the beans: Place them in a large bowl and cover—by about 2 inches—with cold water. For alternative soaking methods, see page 48.

To determine if beans have soaked long enough, cut one in half and look at the center. If the core is a lighter color, the beans need more soaking.

COOKING BEANS

When dried beans are boiled, foam rises to the surface during the first few minutes.

Skim the foam off with a large spoon and discard.

Wait until the end of cooking time, when the beans are tender, before adding acidic ingredients such as tomatoes. Acids prevent beans from softening properly while they cook and slow down the cooking process.

ARE THEY DONE YET?

To test for doneness, Grandma used to blow on a spoonful of beans. If the skins billowed, they were ready. Here's a more foolproof test: Taste a bean. When done, it will be firm-tender and will not taste of raw starch. If the beans are to be added to a recipe and cooked further, take them from the heat 20 to 30 minutes before they are done.

COOKING AHEAD

When the beans are done, let them cool in their liquid, then drain in a colander. If you want, save and freeze the liquid and use it in minestrone or other bean-based soups.

Cooked beans with their liquid keep for several days in the refrigerator stored in a tightly covered container.

CASSOULET NOTES

Cassoulet is a French country version of baked beans. It's a true casserole, filled with meats as well as beans. Guaranteed to satisfy the heartiest appetite, cassoulet is the perfect dish for a winter supper or party buffet.

In its traditional form, cassoulet can take several days to make. It's cooked off and on as the various meats are added in stages and rested in between. Our cassoulet is a quick version. The chicken requires marinating overnight, but the rest can be prepped, assembled, and baked in just a couple of hours.

WORK SAVERS
Pressure Cooker

Cooking beans in a pressure cooker generally takes only between 25 and 35 minutes. However, care must be taken that foam or bean skins do not clog the vent. Read the appliance manual and follow directions exactly.

BEAN COOKING TIMES

Cooking times vary for different varieties of beans. The following times are for soaked dried beans.

Adzuki beans 30 to 45 minutes	**Cranberry beans** 1 to 1½ hours	**Lima beans** (large) 1 to 1½ hours (baby) 1 hour
Black beans 1½ hours	**Fava beans** 1 to 2 hours	
Black-eyed peas 30 minutes to 1 hour	**Great northerns** 1 hour	**Mung beans** 45 minutes to 1 hour
Chickpeas 1 to 1½ hours	**Kidney, navy, pea, or pinto beans** 1½ to 2 hours	**Soybeans** 3 to 4 hours

Cooked beans are ready for use hot or cold. Cooled beans can be refrigerated in a covered container for 4 or 5 days.

QUICK CASSOULET

Prepare as directed at right, but in Step 1 **use** one type of bean only—2½ cups dried navy *or* lima beans. **Combine** 1 tablespoon olive oil, 1 crushed clove garlic, and ½ teaspoon crumbled dried thyme and **rub** over 4 skinless chicken thighs; **cover** and **marinate** overnight in the refrigerator.

The next day, **brown** chicken thighs and 8 ounces sliced kielbasa along with bacon; **drain** on paper toweling. In pan drippings, **sauté** 1 cup diced carrot along with onion and garlic in Step 3. **Add** chicken and kielbasa along with other ingredients in Step 3 and **continue** as directed through Step 4. **Stir** 2 large peeled, cored, and diced ripe tomatoes into bean mixture, **scatter** crumb topping evenly over surface, and **bake**, uncovered, as directed in Step 5. Makes 6 servings.

Mixed-Bean Casserole with Crumb Topping

1 **cup dried navy or pea beans,** sorted and rinsed
1 **cup dried baby lima beans,** sorted and rinsed
½ **cup dried red kidney or pinto beans, sorted and rinsed**
6 **strips bacon, cut crosswise into ½-inch-wide strips**
1 **large yellow onion, coarsely chopped**
3 **cloves garlic, minced**
2 **tablespoons dark brown sugar or maple syrup**
1 **teaspoon dry mustard**
1 **whole bay leaf**
½ **teaspoon dried thyme, crumbled**
½ **teaspoon dried marjoram, crumbled**
1 **teaspoon salt**
¼ **teaspoon black pepper**

Topping:
2 **cups soft white bread crumbs**
¼ **cup minced parsley**
¼ **cup melted butter or margarine**
1 **clove garlic, minced**

1 Serving: Calories 533; Total Fat 19 g; Saturated Fat 9 g; Protein 26 g; Carbohydrates 17 g; Fiber 18 g; Sodium 825 mg; Cholesterol 38 mg

prep time-25 minutes plus beans' soaking time cooking time-4 to 4½ hours

1 Soak the three dried beans overnight in 1½ quarts water. Drain, reserving soaking liquid and adding enough cold water to total 1½ quarts.

2 Preheat the oven to 350°F. In a 6-quart Dutch oven over moderate heat, cook bacon until crisp—about 5 minutes; transfer to paper toweling to drain.

3 To pan drippings, add onion and garlic and sauté over moderate heat until soft—about 5 minutes. Add  reserved beans and bacon, brown sugar, mustard, bay leaf, thyme, marjoram, salt, pepper, and reserved soaking liquid.

4 Bake, covered, for 3½ to 4 hours, stirring 3 or 4 times during cooking. Add boiling water if level of liquid drops below surface of beans. Remove and discard bay leaf.

5 For Crumb Topping: In a medium-size bowl, stir together crumbs, parsley, butter, and garlic. Sprinkle topping over beans and bake, uncovered, until brown—about 30 minutes. Makes 6 servings.

RICE AND BEANS

Rice can be steamed, baked, or micro-waved to perfection. When combined with beans as in our trio of recipes, it provides high-quality protein.

A GLOBAL DISH

For thousands of years, rice has been a staple food for more than half the world's population. And, throughout the world, rice combined with beans have become popular dishes in their own right. Cuisines everywhere have developed their own regional specialties, such as Louisiana red beans and rice. Traditionally, red beans and rice was made on a Monday to take advantage of the ham bone left over from Sunday's dinner.

NO RINSING

Most rice is enriched with a high-vitamin coating that replaces vitamins and minerals lost in milling. Don't rinse the rice before cooking or you will wash the nutrients away.

PERFECT BOILED RICE

For best results, follow package directions or use this easy method: Combine the rice, water or broth, 1 teaspoon of salt (optional), and 1 tablespoon of butter or margarine (optional) in a heavy 2- to 3-quart saucepan. Heat to boiling, stirring once or twice.

Adjust the heat so the liquid bubbles gently and cover with a tight-fitting lid. Resist the temptation to stir the rice or it will become sticky.

Cook the rice according to the suggested cooking time on the box or as listed below, then fluff with a fork. Fluffing allows steam to escape and helps to keep the grains separate. Rice that isn't fluffed can become gummy.

The exact amount of liquid and cooking time depend on how firm you like your rice. Use more liquid and longer cooking time for soft rice; less liquid and less cooking time for firmer rice.

MICROWAVE RICE

For 3 cups of cooked rice, combine 1 cup of uncooked rice and 2 cups of hot liquid ($2^1/_4$ cups for brown rice) in a $2^1/_2$-quart casserole. Cook, covered, on high (100 percent power) 4 to 6 minutes until small bubbles form around the edge.

Stir, recover, and microwave on medium (50 percent power), allowing 8 minutes for long-grain white rice, 10 for parboiled, and 28 to 30 for brown. Let stand, covered, 5 minutes, then fluff and serve.

CARIBBEAN BLACK BEANS AND RICE

Prepare as directed at right, **substituting** dried black beans for kidney beans. **Add** 1 large chopped, cored, and seeded sweet red pepper along with onion, green pepper, celery, and garlic. **Proceed** as directed, but **increase** cooking time to between 2 and $2^1/_2$ hours. **Add** $1/_2$ cup minced parsley or $1/_4$ cup minced coriander, and 1 teaspoon finely grated orange zest along with vinegar and salt. **Remove** and **discard** bay leaf. **Increase** rice to 3 cups but do not mix in; also do not bake. Instead, **serve** immediately over rice and **top**, if desired, with sour cream. Makes 6 servings.

NEW MEXICO CHILI RICE AND PINTO BEANS

Prepare as directed at right, **substituting** dried pinto beans for red kidney beans. **Omit** chorizo and **increase** smoked ham to 1 pound (or use 1 pound diced cooked pork shoulder). **Proceed** as directed, **adding** two 4-ounce cans drained, chopped mild green chilies and 1 seeded, cored, and finely chopped jalapeño along with beans, ham, and seasonings. **Cook** as directed for Bayou Red Beans. **Mix** in vinegar and salt. **Remove** and **discard** bay leaf. **Increase** rice to 3 cups but do not mix in; also do not bake. Instead, **serve** immediately over rice. Makes 6 to 8 servings.

OVEN COOKING

Bring the liquid to a boil, then combine the ingredients in a baking dish and stir. Cover tightly and bake at 350°F for 25 to 30 minutes for white rice; 30 to 40 minutes for parboiled; 1 hour for brown rice.

WHAT WENT WRONG?

If the rice is too firm:
It might have been cooked in too little liquid or for too short a time. The pan might have been too large, causing some liquid to evaporate. Or the pan lid might have been loose.

If the rice is too soft:
It might have been cooked for too long or in too much liquid.

If the rice is too sticky:
It might have been cooked in too much liquid, stirred during cooking, or held too long before serving.

STEAMING TIMES (FOR 3 CUPS COOKED RICE)

1 Cup (Uncooked)	Cold Liquid	Minutes to Cook
Long grain	$1^3/_4$ to 2 cups	15 to 20
Medium or short grain	$1^1/_2$ to $1^3/_4$ cups	15 to 20
Parboiled	2 to $2^1/_2$ cups	20 to 25
Brown long grain	$2^1/_4$ to $2^1/_2$ cups	45 to 50

Bayou Red Beans and Rice Casserole

- **2** cups dried red kidney beans, sorted and rinsed
- **1** tablespoon vegetable oil
- **8** ounces chorizo, sliced, or hot Italian sausage, removed from casings and crumbled
- **1** large yellow onion, coarsely chopped
- **1** large sweet green pepper, cored, seeded, and chopped
- **1/2** cup chopped celery
- **2** cloves garlic, minced
- **8** ounces smoked ham, diced
- **4** cups Browned Beef Stock, canned broth, or water
- **2** whole bay leaves
- **1/2** teaspoon dried thyme, crumbled
- **1/2** teaspoon dried marjoram, crumbled
- **1/8** to **1/4** teaspoon cayenne
- **2** cups cooked long-grain rice
- **1** tablespoon red wine vinegar
- **1/2** teaspoon salt or to taste

1 Soak beans overnight in water to cover. Drain beans (if cooking beans in water instead of broth, reserve soaking liquid and add water to total 1 quart liquid); set aside.

2 In a 6-quart Dutch oven over moderate heat, heat oil 1 minute. Add chorizo and sauté until brown—about 5 minutes; transfer to paper toweling to drain. Drain all but 2 tablespoons of pan drippings. Add onion, green pepper, celery, and garlic and sauté until soft—about 5 minutes. Add reserved beans, ham, stock, bay leaves, thyme, marjoram, and cayenne. Bring to a boil over high heat. Reduce the heat to moderately low and simmer, covered, until beans are tender—about 1½ hours. Remove and discard bay leaves. Preheat the oven to 350°F.

3 Drain beans, reserving 1 cup liquid. Put beans and liquid into a lightly greased 3-quart casserole; stir in chorizo, rice, vinegar, and salt to taste.

4 Bake, covered, until hot—about 40 minutes. Serve with hot red pepper sauce. Makes 6 servings.

1 Serving: Calories 558; Total Fat 19 g; Saturated Fat 6 g; Protein 32 g; Carbohydrates 67 g; Fiber 8 g; Sodium 1044 mg; Cholesterol 54 mg

prep time-25 minutes plus beans' soaking time cooking time-2½ hours

LENTIL SALAD

Peas and beans, including lentils, split peas, and chickpeas, are as good served warm in salads as they are piping hot in soups and casseroles.

ALL DRESSED UP

Dried peas and beans make healthy and delicious salads. Use a single variety in a salad, combine several varieties, or mix them with cooked rice, couscous, buckwheat, or small pasta for added texture, flavor, and color.

For best results, dress peas and beans while they're still hot—that's when they absorb flavors best. Toss them gently so you don't mush the beans.

Lentils are a great salad staple; they cook quickly and their flavor combines well with other salad ingredients. Dress them with oil and vinegar or fresh lemon juice and mix them with fresh or roasted sweet peppers, minced garlic or chives, chopped fresh dill and/or mint, or chopped nuts and seedless raisins.

A SEED OF MANY COLORS

Lentils come in several colors and varieties, which require different cooking times. **Brown or yellow lentils,** the most common varieties, have the most intense flavor and must be cooked the longest. Brown and yellow lentils are recommended for salads because they retain their shape during cooking.

Tiny green French lentils are prized for their delicate peppery flavor. They cook a little more quickly than brown lentils. They are also much more expensive.

Red or pink lentils have had the outer skin coat removed, revealing the bright orange inner coat. They are a staple in East Indian, Asian, Middle Eastern, and African cooking. At least one red variety is becoming more widely available in Canada.

NO SOAKING

Split green and yellow peas can almost always be substituted for common lentils. Packaged lentils and split peas require only a light rinse under running water before they are cooked. If soaked, they will become mushy when cooked.

A GREEK SPECIALTY

Yellow pea dip is one of the most popular offerings on the Greek *meze* (appetizer) table. To make it, simmer yellow split peas with a little lemon juice and chopped onion until very soft and almost all of the water has been absorbed. Purée or mash the pea mixture, leaving a few small lumps. Minced red onion, mashed garlic, a splash of fruity olive oil, and salt and pepper to taste are added for pungent flavor.

Cover and refrigerate overnight to give the flavors a chance to mingle. Cubes of bread or wedges of pita are good dippers for this low-fat appetizer.

THICK AND THIN

When lentils and split peas are cooked until very soft, they can be puréed in a blender or food processor and used as a thickener for stews. For each cup of lentils, use 2 1/2 cups of liquid. Simmer, covered, for 45 minutes to 1 hour until very soft. When puréeing, add a little cooking water, if necessary, to give the mixture a thick but spoonable consistency.

CHICKPEA CHECKLIST

In most recipes calling for chickpeas (aka garbanzo beans, ceci beans, or ram's head peas), either canned or dried varieties can be used.

Dried, these large, round, and slightly crunchy peas need a thorough soaking overnight and 1 to 1 1/2 hours of cooking time. Canned, they simply need to be drained and rinsed and they're ready to eat, to purée with olive oil and garlic, or to blend into any recipe.

NUTRITIONAL NOTES

A whole cup of boiled lentils has only 1 gram of fat and no cholesterol. But it delivers a good supply of fiber, iron, phosphorus, potassium, and protein. Split peas and chickpeas have similar nutritional profiles.

CHICKPEA SALAD

Prepare as directed at right, **substituting** 2 cups drained, cooked or canned chickpeas for lentils. **Reduce** red pepper to 1/4 cup and garlic to 1 clove. **Increase** celery to 2 stalks and lemon juice to 3 tablespoons. **Add** salt to taste. Makes 4 servings.

COOKING TIMES

Lentils

Red or pink: 10 to 15 minutes

Green (French): 15 to 20 minutes

Brown or yellow: 20 to 30 minutes

For purées: 40 to 45 minutes

Dried yellow and green split peas

For salad recipes: 10 to 15 minutes

For main-dish recipes: 30 to 40 minutes

For purées: 45 minutes to 1 hour

Dried Chickpeas

1 to 1 1/2 hours (soak overnight)

Warm Lentil and Roasted Pepper Salad

- 3 cups water
- 1 cup brown lentils
- 1 teaspoon salt
- 1/4 cup chopped parsley
- 1/2 cup diced, drained, and rinsed canned roasted sweet red pepper
- 1 medium-size stalk celery, diced
- 1/2 cup diced red onion
- 1 cup diced and seeded plum tomatoes
- 2 cloves garlic, minced
- 2 tablespoons lemon juice
- 2 tablespoons olive oil
- 1/4 teaspoon black pepper

1 In a 3-quart sauce-pan over high heat, bring water, lentils, and 1/2 teaspoon of the salt to a boil. Reduce the heat to moderately low and simmer, covered, until lentils are firm but fully cooked—about 20 to 30 minutes.

2 Meanwhile, mix remaining ingredients, including the remaining 1/2 teaspoon salt, in a large serving bowl.

3 Drain lentils, add to serving bowl, and toss. Serve warm. Makes 4 servings.

1 Serving: Calories 250; Total Fat 8 g; Saturated Fat 1 g; Protein 15 g; Carbohydrates 34 g; Fiber 8 g; Sodium 253 mg; Cholesterol 0 mg

prep time-45 minutes
cooking time-30 to 35 minutes

FLAVORFUL CURRY

We make our curry with a flavorful combination of turkey and wild rice. Curry's zesty mix of spices complements many ingredients.

A MOVABLE FEAST

Curry sounds exotic but it's actually as practical a dish as you can make. The best thing about it (aside from its being delicious, economical, and easy to prepare) is that it is so adaptable. Indian curries run the gamut from potato to lamb, from chicken or chickpea to shrimp. You can adapt the curry-making process to whatever vegetables, meat, poultry, or fish are to your taste.

MAKE IT EASY

In most curry recipes, the larger part of the ingredient list is spices. We've made it easy by seasoning our Turkey and Wild Rice Curry with curry powder—in which many spices have been combined.

You don't have to make curry to use curry powder. Sprinkle a little into bean or rice dishes.

Rub it on a leg of lamb. Use it as a flavoring for vegetables or eggs, in salads dressed with mayonnaise, or in creamy hot or chilled soups.

WHAT MAKES A CURRY A CURRY?

In India, a curry is any dish flavored with a rich blend of spices. Curry powder is rarely used in India; instead, spices are blended differently for individual curries. Blends range from fiery hot, heavily flavored with chilies, to mellow, relying on cinnamon, cardamom, and other aromatic spices.

The liquid in a curry comes from the meat or vegetable juices that are often supplemented with broth, coconut milk, or yogurt added at the end of cooking time. A curry should be juicy but not swimming in liquid. Note: Coconut milk is available canned but make sure you buy the unsweetened low-fat kind.

The featured ingredients in a curry are cut into bite-size pieces before they are cooked. A little meat, chicken, or shellfish can be made to go a long way since they are combined with vegetables.

WHAT KIND OF RICE TO CHOOSE

Our use of wild rice is a delicious departure from tradition. Curry is normally served on a bed of Indian long-grain basmati rice, which has an aromatic scent. Basmati rice is usually washed before it is cooked. This extra step rinses away a little starch, so the rice grains remain separate and don't become sticky as they cook.

As a change, try a North American-grown aromatic rice, such as Texmati or Calmati, or use any other long-grain rice.

Puréed red or yellow lentils are a traditional accompaniment for curry—there are some 60 varieties of lentils in India. You might also try a combination of lentils and rice.

CHICKEN BIRYANI

Prepare as directed at right, **substituting** skinless, boneless chicken for the turkey and basmati rice cooked according to package directions for the wild rice. Makes 4 servings.

SERVED WITH STYLE

Curries are sometimes served accompanied by condiments. Set them out in small bowls so your guests can select their own toppings: sliced scallions, chopped peanuts, chopped crystallized ginger, mango chutney, shredded coconut, raisins, sieved egg yolk, or chopped cucumbers in yogurt.

CURRY FLAVORINGS

Dozens of aromatic flavorings are used in curries; some appear above. They're blended differently in each curry depending on the main ingredient.

1.Cumin Seeds **2.**Turmeric **3.**Mace **4.**Black Peppercorns **5.**Fennel Seeds **6.**Crushed Red Pepper **7.**Coriander **8.**Cinnamon **9.**Nutmeg **10.**Cloves **11.**Tamarind **12.**Cardamom Seeds

Turkey, Vegetable, and Wild Rice Curry

1½ pounds skinned and boned turkey breast
¼ cup all-purpose flour
1½ teaspoons salt
¼ teaspoon black pepper
3 tablespoons vegetable oil
1 large yellow onion, chopped
2 cloves garlic, minced
2 small stalks celery, chopped
1 tablespoon curry powder
1¾ cups Rich Chicken Stock or canned reduced-sodium chicken broth
4 medium-size carrots, peeled and cut crosswise into ½-inch slices
2 cups cauliflower florets (about ½ medium-size cauliflower)
1¾ cups water
1¼ cups wild rice

1 Cut turkey into 1-inch pieces. In a large self-sealing plastic bag, mix flour, ½ teaspoon of the salt, and pepper. Shake turkey, a few pieces at a time, in the flour mixture to dredge.

2 In a large skillet with a tight-fitting lid over moderately high heat, heat oil 1 minute. Sauté turkey in 2 batches until lightly brown—about 5 minutes per batch. Remove turkey to paper toweling to drain.

3 In the drippings, sauté onion, garlic, and celery, stirring occasionally, until soft—about 5 minutes.

4 Add curry powder, stock, carrots, cauliflower, and reserved turkey, reduce the heat to low, and simmer, covered, until cauliflower is just tender—20 to 30 minutes. Note: Flavor will be better if you cool curry, refrigerate overnight, then proceed about 1 hour before serving. The curry needs only to be brought to serving temperature over low heat—about 10 minutes.

5 In a 2-quart saucepan over high heat, bring water to a boil. Add the remaining 1 teaspoon of salt and rice, reduce the heat to moderate, and simmer, covered, until rice is tender—about 45 minutes.

6 Transfer rice to a large heated serving bowl and pour curry over all. Makes 4 servings.

1 Serving: Calories 601; Total Fat 13 g; Saturated Fat 2 g; Protein 57 g; Carbohydrates 67 g; Fiber 8 g; Sodium 976 mg; Cholesterol 128 mg

prep time-30 minutes
cooking time-45 minutes

FLAVORFUL KASHA

Kasha, or buckwheat groats, is full flavored, quick and easy to prepare, and makes a delicious accompaniment to meat, poultry, and game.

A NEW LOOK AT AN OLD-WORLD DISH

In Eastern Europe, kasha is as popular as potatoes are here. But this flavorful, versatile, and nourishing cereal didn't quite make it into our mainstream cuisine until recently, when more of us became health conscious.

So what is kasha? Roasted, hulled, and cracked buckwheat groats (kernels) that are low in calories and high in protein and B vitamins.

Although buckwheat is used as a cereal grain, it's actually a distant relation of rhubarb. It's grown in Asia, Eastern Europe, and parts of Canada and the U.S.

Kasha is sold three ways: coarse, medium, and fine. You'll find it in the rice aisle or in the gourmet section at the supermarket. Or you can buy it loose in health-food stores.

TEXTURE AND FLAVOR

Although plain buckwheat groats are mild flavored, roasted kasha has a bold taste—like dark toast—which lessens as it cooks. Cooked kasha has the consistency of rice. The texture lends itself

particularly well to the addition of chewy or crunchy tidbits, such as the chopped dried tomatoes, raisins, and nuts in our recipes.

KASHA BASICS

Here is the basic method for cooking kasha: In a 2-quart saucepan, bring 2 cups of water and 1 teaspoon of salt (optional) to a boil; stir in the kasha. Cover and simmer for about 12 minutes or until almost all the water has been absorbed and holes appear on the surface. Remove it from the heat and set aside for about 7 minutes or until the water is fully absorbed. Fluff with a fork. Makes 3 1/4 to 3 1/2 cups.

HOW TO USE IT

Kasha is usually paired with ingredients that complement its assertive flavor.

Add a little cooked kasha to stuffings for poultry, chops, cabbage rolls, or sweet peppers. Mix it into meat loaf, croquettes, and burgers (about 1 part kasha to 4 parts meat).

Sprinkle a little onto green salads or blend it half and half into rice or lentil salads. Toss some into stir-fries and pasta dishes for added texture. Use it instead of rice in a pilaf or with a stir-fry. Stir it into stews or soups when they require a little thickening.

MIX UP AN EGG WASH

Before kasha is mixed into a dish, it is often given an egg wash. It gets mixed with beaten egg and then toasted in a skillet. The egg wash coats each grain of kasha, which helps the grains to remain separate when they toast in the pan and when mixed with other ingredients. The technique is used in our Pecan-Studded Kasha.

WARM-UPS

Kasha remains soft when refrigerated, so it's ready to use. To reheat, stir in about 1 tablespoon of water per cup of cooked kasha. Reheat in a saucepan over very low heat or covered in a microwave.

NO DELICATE HERBS

Faint flavorings will be lost in kasha. Season it with pungent herbs and spices that hold their flavor. These include rosemary, sage, thyme, ginger, allspice, and nutmeg.

TOMATO STAPLES

Like all dried fruits, dried tomatoes are somewhat chewy. They also have an intense fla-vor and acidic bite that complement many dishes. They are a good staple to keep on hand in the cupboard.

At one time, what are called sun-dried tomatoes really were dried in the sun to preserve their home-grown goodness. These days, plum tomatoes are mechanically dried and available loose in cellophane packages or packed and jarred in olive oil flavored with herbs.

Cellophane-packed dried tomatoes, if soft enough, can be used as is. Otherwise, they should be rehydrated for a few minutes in boiling water.

Oil-packed dried tomatoes may require a light rinsing or patting dry with paper toweling before use.

SUN-DRIED TOMATO KASHA

Prepare as directed at right, **adding**, in Step 3, 1/3 cup sun-dried tomatoes (not oil-packed) that have been **blanched** for 4 minutes in boiling water, then **drained**, **squeezed** dry, and coarsely **chopped**. **Omit** rosemary and **stir** in 1/2 cup chopped fresh basil along with pecans.

KASHA WITH RAISINS AND NUTS

Prepare as directed at right, **substituting** 1/4 cup toasted pine nuts for pecans and at the same time **adding** 1/3 cup light seedless raisins.

In a bowl, beat a large egg and stir into kasha until thoroughly coated. Pour the mixture into a hot skillet lightly coated with oil and cook, stirring, over moderate heat until just toasted.

Pecan-Studded Kasha

- **1 tablespoon olive oil**
- **2 large yellow onions, cut in ¼-inch dice**
- **3 cloves garlic, finely chopped**
- **½ teaspoon sugar**
- **1 cup coarse or medium kasha**
- **1 large egg, lightly beaten**
- **2 cups boiling Rich Chicken Stock or canned reduced-sodium chicken broth**
- **½ teaspoon dried rosemary, crumbled**
- **½ teaspoon salt**
- **¼ teaspoon black pepper**
- **⅓ cup coarsely chopped pecans**

1 In a large skillet over moderate heat, heat oil 1 minute. Add onions and garlic, sprinkle with sugar, and cook, stirring frequently, until golden brown—about 10 minutes.

2 In a medium-size bowl, stir kasha with the egg until well coated. Add kasha mixture to skillet and cook, stirring constantly, until lightly toasted and grains separate—about 3 minutes.

3 Stir in stock, rosemary, salt, and pepper and bring to a boil over high heat. Reduce the heat to moderately low and cook, covered, until liquid has been absorbed—about 8 minutes. Stir in pecans and serve. Makes 4 servings.

1 Serving: Calories 298; Total Fat 12 g;
Saturated Fat 2 g; Protein 14 g;
Carbohydrates 59 g; Fiber 5 g;
Sodium 334 mg; Cholesterol 58 mg

prep time-15 minutes • cooking time-28 minutes

VERSATILE COUSCOS

There are nearly as many ways to serve couscous as pasta. Topped with an aromatic sauce or stew, couscous is one of the easiest one-dish meals around.

A NATIONAL DISH

Couscous is a staple in North Africa. In Morocco, hot fluffy couscous is the base for pungently spiced stews called *tagines*. It will work just as well with your favorite stews and sauces.

MINIATURE PASTA

Like some pastas, couscous is made from semolina flour. Several varieties of commercially produced couscous are available. In traditional North African households, couscous is still made the ancient way. Flour is combined with salt water and the mixture is pushed through a screen to make tiny pellets, which are spread out to dry in the sun.

BEAT THE CLOCK

The time it takes to make couscous depends on the variety that you buy. Our recipes call for quick-cooking couscous because it takes only minutes to prepare and requires no special equipment. Regular couscous takes about 1 hour.

If you choose regular couscous, you'll need a steamer like the one described below. Or you can improvise by using a colander lined with damp cheesecloth set over a deep pot. The fit must be made snug by wrapping damp cheesecloth around the seam where the two parts join.

ANY TIME OF DAY

Topping couscous with stew is only one way to serve it. The grain's pleasant texture and flavor can be enjoyed at any meal.

For breakfast, as a rib-sticking hot cereal, couscous needs no more than a sprinkling of brown sugar and warm milk. Dried fruits and nuts can be stirred in too.

Any sauce that's good with pasta (especially meaty tomato sauce) is good with couscous too, but don't use too much. Couscous is best when only lightly coated.

Top couscous with bite-size stir-fried vegetables. Use it as a bed for fish that is baked or steamed with vegetables. Or serve it as a side dish with roast chicken or turkey, tossed with chopped nuts and dried fruits, and flavored with broth or apple juice.

A VARIETY OF COUSCOUS SALADS

Arrange strips of roasted vegetables on cooled couscous. Drizzle with balsamic vinegar or lemon juice and a few drops of fruity olive oil.

Create a hearty tossed salad by mixing couscous with finely cut raw vegetables (don't forget diced tomatoes when they're in season) as well as drained and rinsed kidney beans, chickpeas, or black beans. Add a favorite dressing and toss until blended.

Make a Middle Eastern- or Greek-style salad by tossing together couscous, marinated artichoke hearts, pitted black olives, chopped tomatoes, cucumbers, and onions. Lightly mix with lemon juice and extra-virgin olive oil; sprinkle with crumbled feta cheese and minced parsley.

WHAT'S FOR DESSERT?

Mix finely chopped fresh and dried fruits or drained canned fruit with couscous for a healthy and delicious dessert. Serve it warm or cooled with a dollop of vanilla- or lemon-flavored yogurt.

COUSCOUS WITH MOROCCAN APRICOT LAMB

Prepare as directed at right, **substituting** 2 pounds boneless lamb shoulder **cut** into 1-inch chunks for chicken. **Cook** lamb with onion and spices for 30 minutes before adding carrots, then **proceed** as directed. Makes 4 servings.

WORK SAVER

Couscousier

If you want to be authentic in your couscous making, you must use regular couscous and steam it for about 1 hour. A special 2-piece steamer called a couscousier is made just for the purpose. Water, broth, or stew is put in the bottom section. Dried couscous is put in the top section, which has a perforated bottom. The hard pellets of couscous soften and cook while absorbing the flavor of the liquid that cooks below. Couscousiers are expensive but you don't need one if you use quick-cooking couscous.

Couscous with Moroccan Apricot Chicken

- 2 cloves garlic, peeled and blanched 3 minutes
- 1 cup drained and rinsed canned roasted sweet red pepper
- 1 tablespoon no-salt-added tomato paste
- 1/4 teaspoon hot red pepper sauce
- 2 tablespoons olive oil
- 1 broiler-fryer (about 3 pounds), cut up for frying and skin removed
- 1 large yellow onion, cut into 1-inch chunks
- 1 1/2 teaspoons sweet Hungarian paprika
- 1 1/4 teaspoons ground ginger
- 1 teaspoon ground coriander
- 3/4 teaspoon salt
- 1/2 teaspoon black pepper
- 2 large carrots, peeled, halved lengthwise, and cut into 2-inch chunks
- 2 1/2 cups Rich Chicken Stock or canned reduced-sodium chicken broth
- 1 small zucchini, halved lengthwise and cut into 2-inch chunks
- 1 small yellow squash, halved lengthwise and cut into 2-inch chunks
- 1/2 cup dried apricots, quartered
- 1 cup quick-cooking couscous
- 1/2 cup chopped fresh coriander (cilantro)

1 In a blender at high speed or in a food processor, purée garlic, red pepper, tomato paste, and red pepper sauce until smooth; set aside.

2 In a large heavy skillet or Dutch oven over moderately high heat, heat oil 1 minute. Add chicken and brown in batches, allowing 3 minutes per side. Remove with tongs and set aside. Reduce the heat to moderate, add onion, and stir-fry until limp and golden—about 5 minutes.

3 Stir in paprika, ginger, coriander, salt, and black pepper. Add carrots, stirring to coat. Add stock and bring to a boil over high heat. Reduce the heat to moderately low, return chicken to pan, and cook, covered, until carrots are crisp-tender—about 15 minutes.

4 Add zucchini, yellow squash, and apricots and cook, covered, until chicken is just done and squash is crisp-tender—about 10 minutes more.

5 Stir in couscous and coriander and cook 2 minutes more. Remove from the heat and let stand, covered, until couscous is tender—about 5 minutes. Transfer to a heated serving platter and serve with reserved sauce on the side. Makes 4 servings.

1 Serving:
Calories 615;
Total Fat 13 g;
Saturated Fat 3g;
Protein 62 g;
Carbohydrates 61g;
Fiber 8 g;
Sodium 1078 mg;
Cholesterol 147 mg

*prep time-
30 minutes
cooking time-
40 minutes*

EASY PILAFS

If you can make pilaf—seasoned rice or grains—you can make many dishes. Add a few fancy ingredients and it's party food. Stir in last night's leftovers, and dinner is on the table.

A GRAIN OF THOUGHT

It's easy to forget that anything but white rice can be used for pilaf, but other grains—brown rice, bulgur (cracked wheat berries), barley, and wild rice, for example—make wonderful pilafs. Grains cooked by this method have infinitely more character than those simmered in water, and take only a few minutes longer.

PLAIN OR FANCY

Pilaf can be anything you want it to be: Vary the liquids, the grains, the seasonings, and other additions. Here are a few possibilities:

Replace the cooking water with chicken, beef, or vegetable broth. Tomato juice, orange juice, or wine can also be substituted for 1/4 to 1/3 of the water or broth.

Stir steamed or roasted vegetables, cooked meat, chicken, shrimp, mussels, or clams into the cooked pilaf. Vegetables such as seeded and chopped tomatoes and sweet peppers are classic additions. So are toasted nuts—pine nuts, pistachios, or pecans.

During the last few minutes of cooking, small pieces of semisoft cheese, such as feta or fontina, can be stirred into pilaf. Grated Parmesan or Romano cheese can be stirred into or sprinkled over pilaf at serving time.

SKILLET TALK

A deep heavy skillet or a wide-bottom saucepan with a tight-fitting lid is a good choice for pilaf. If the pan is too light-weight or the cover doesn't fit, the liquid will cook away before the grain has a chance to absorb it.

THE RIGHT OIL

The choice of oil is important in pilaf. Virgin olive oil and vegetable oil are best since they can be heated to a high temperature without smoking. More intensely flavored oils—sesame, walnut, hazelnut—are not recommended.

Butter is not the best choice, either. You can use unsalted butter, but be careful that it doesn't burn. For a buttery flavor, use a mixture of half unsalted butter and half oil. Or use clarified butter.

BASIC TWO-STEP PILAF

For the most basic pilaf, you'll need 1 cup of long-grain white rice, 1 tablespoon of olive or vegetable oil, and 2 cups of broth or water.

In a medium-size heavy saucepan, heat the oil until very hot; stir in the rice. Cook and stir over moderately high heat until the oil is absorbed and the rice is translucent—about 5 minutes. (This preliminary step, common to all pilafs, not only enriches the grain but also prevents the kernels from sticking together in the finished dish.)

Add the broth and bring to a boil over high heat. Stir once; lower the heat and cover tightly. Simmer until the broth is absorbed and the rice is tender—15 to 20 minutes. These should happen simultaneously. Makes about 3 cups or 4 to 6 servings.

HOW TO CLARIFY BUTTER

It's the milk solids in butter that cause it to brown and burn. Remove them and you've got a clear, golden oil. To clarify butter, melt it in a small saucepan over very low heat. Let stand, off the heat, until the white milk solids sink to the bottom of the melted butter. Carefully pour off the liquid butter and strain through damp cheese-cloth. Store in the refrigerator in a covered jar.

GRAINS TO CHOOSE AND COOKING TIMES FOR PILAF VARIATIONS

Bulgur: Cooking time 40 minutes. 1 cup requires 2 cups of liquid. 1 cup dried = 3 cups cooked.

Kasha: Cooking time 30 to 35 minutes. 1 cup requires 2 cups of liquid. 1 cup dried = 4 cups cooked.

Long-grain brown rice: Cooking time 50 to 55 minutes. 1 cup requires 3 cups of liquid. 1 cup dried = 3 cups cooked.

Long-grain white rice: Cooking time 20 to 25 minutes. 1 cup requires 2 cups of liquid. 1 cup dried = 3 cups cooked.

Pearl barley: Cooking time 35 to 40 minutes. 1 cup requires 3 cups of liquid. 1 cup dried barley = 2 1/2 cups cooked.

Wild rice: Cooking time 35 to 45 minutes. 1 cup requires 3 cups of liquid. 1 cup dried = 4 cups cooked.

Three-Pepper Pilaf

- **3** tablespoons butter or margarine
- **1** small yellow onion, finely chopped
- **2** cloves garlic, minced
- **1** large sweet red pepper, cored, seeded, and diced
- **1** large sweet green pepper, cored, seeded, and diced
- **1** Italian frying pepper, cored, seeded, and diced
- **1** cup long-grain rice
- **2½** cups Rich Chicken Stock or canned reduced-sodium chicken broth
- **½** teaspoon salt
- **¾** teaspoon dried rosemary, crumbled
- **¼** teaspoon black pepper

1 Preheat the oven to 350°F. In a 5-quart flameproof casserole or Dutch oven over moderate heat, melt 1 tablespoon of the butter. Add onion and garlic and cook, stirring frequently, until soft—about 5 minutes. Add red, green, and Italian peppers and cook, stirring frequently, until tender—about 7 minutes more.

2 Add 1 tablespoon of the remaining butter and melt over moderate heat. Add rice and cook, stirring frequently, until well coated—about 3 minutes. Add stock, salt, rosemary, and black pepper and bring to a boil.

3 Cover, transfer casserole to the preheated oven, and bake until liquid is absorbed and rice is tender—about 20 minutes. Uncover and stir in the remaining tablespoon of butter. Makes 4 servings.

1 Serving: Calories 236; Total Fat 3 g; Saturated Fat 2 g; Protein 5 g; Carbohydrates 46 g; Fiber 3 g; Sodium 324 mg; Cholesterol 14 mg

prep time-16 minutes • cooking time-39 minutes

Brown Rice Pilaf

Proceed as directed at left, **substituting** brown rice for long-grain rice. **Increase** stock to 3 cups and **increase** baking time to 40 minutes. Makes 4 servings.

129

CREAMY RISOTTO

A faultless risotto will bring raves at the table. Serve it as a first course with dinner or as a meal in itself.

RISOTTO NOTES

One bite of rich-tasting risotto and you think you are putting away countless fat calories. But it's actually rice starch that makes each forkful a creamy delight.

Risotto is a specialty of northern Italy, where rice takes precedence over pasta. It's made in a great range of styles from plain (made with just butter, rice, broth, and Parmesan cheese) to versions mixed with vegetables, seafood, smoked meats, poultry, and various cheeses.

The dish is enjoying a surge of popularity in North American restaurants, perhaps because people assume that anything so delicious must be impossible to duplicate at home. But there's no trick involved. Success with risotto is a matter of good ingredients, proper stirring, and careful timing.

SLOW BUT STEADY

In perfect risotto, every grain of rice remains separate and firm-tender, yet the rice is held together by a creamy substance. These characteristics are what make risotto unique among rice dishes.

The steps and details that con-

tribute to a perfect risotto are as follows: Bring the broth to a boil, then reduce the heat and simmer. Meanwhile, heat the butter or oil in a separate saucepan. Add a little chopped onion, if desired, and cook until soft. Then stir in the rice until it's well coated with butter or oil. This step helps ensure that the grains will remain separate throughout the cooking process.

Add the simmering broth to the rice, 1/2 cup at a time, stirring into the rice with a wooden spoon. Add more broth to the rice only after each addition has been completely absorbed. Stir continually while the rice cooks. Toward the end of the cooking time, stir in freshly grated Parmesan—and a little cream, if desired.

When it's done, the rice should

be firm to the bite but not the least bit hard; soft and creamy but not dripping wet. A plain risotto, made as described, takes about 25 to 30 minutes to prepare. A vegetable, seafood, or other risotto will take a little longer.

THE RIGHT RICE

The best rice to use for risotto is Italian arborio rice. Its short fat grains look like tiny footballs and have the capacity to absorb a lot of liquid—and yet retain their shape—while standing up to constant stirring. Long-grain rice will disintegrate in the stirring process. Arborio also has more starch than other rices. The starch becomes creamy as it softens and the rice is stirred.

Until recently, all arborio rice was imported from Italy. Now, however, very good arborio rice is grown in the United States, which has reduced the price considerably.

CHECKLIST FOR PERFECT RISOTTO

Choose your ingredients carefully. Use a homemade broth or stock if possible and a good quality Parmesan. Parmesan is salty: Be sure to taste risotto before adding extra salt.

Don't wash the rice before cooking it. You'll wash away some of the starch that is so important to the dish.

Be careful not to overpower the flavor of risotto with too many onions or herbs.

Add only 1/2 cup of broth at a time. The rice should never be submerged or come to a boil.

Stir the rice over moderate heat. If the temperature is

(continued on page 132)

HOW TO STIR RISOTTO

1 In a saucepan over low heat, melt butter and stir in rice until each grain is well coated.

2 With a wooden spoon, stir the rice, adding hot broth 1/2 cup at a time. Only when each 1/2 cup has been absorbed should more be added. Keep stirring throughout the process.

3 When the risotto is done, it should be moist and creamy but the individual grains distinct and firm-tender to the bite. Stir in the Parmesan cheese and serve immediately.

Asparagus and Cheese Risotto

- **3** tablespoons butter or margarine
- **2** shallots or 1 small yellow onion, finely chopped
- **1¼** cups arborio or short-grain rice
- **⅔** cup dry white wine
- **12** ounces asparagus, trimmed, peeled, and cut into 1-inch lengths
- **½** teaspoon dried marjoram, crumbled
- **3¼** cups Rich Chicken Stock or canned reduced-sodium chicken broth
- Pinch saffron threads, crumbled
- **½** cup grated Parmesan cheese
- **½** teaspoon black pepper

1 In a medium-size heavy saucepan over low heat, melt 1 tablespoon of the butter. Add shallots and cook, stirring occasionally, until very tender—about 7 minutes. Add rice and cook, stirring until well coated—about 1 minute. Add wine and cook, stirring until evaporated—about 4 minutes.

2 Meanwhile, in a large skillet over moderate heat, melt 1 tablespoon of the remaining butter. Add asparagus, sprinkle with marjoram, and cook, stirring frequently, until crisp-tender—about 4 minutes. Set aside.

3 In a medium-size saucepan over low heat, bring stock and saffron to a simmer.

4 Add ½ cup of the stock to rice mixture and cook over moderate heat, stirring constantly, until almost all stock is absorbed—about 3 minutes. Continue adding the remaining stock, ½ cup at a time, stirring after each addition until all stock is absorbed. In about 40 minutes, the rice will be soft and creamy.

5 Stir in reserved asparagus. Remove from the heat and mix in Parmesan, pepper, and the final tablespoon of butter. Makes 4 servings.

1 Serving: Calories 431; Total Fat 13 g; Saturated Fat 8 g; Protein 14 g; Carbohydrates 59 g; Fiber 2 g; Sodium 313 mg; Cholesterol 41 mg

prep time-8 minutes
cooking time-47 minutes

(continued from page 130)

too high, the broth will evaporate before the rice has chance to absorb it. If the temperature is too low, the rice will become soft and the grains will lose their definition.

Taste a few grains of the rice periodically to check for doneness. Blow on the grains before putting them in your mouth—piping hot risotto is a tongue scorcher.

Serve risotto immediately when done. For best results, don't try making it for more than 6 people.

ENTERTAINING NOTES

Wait until your guests arrive before you start to cook risotto. Pacing its preparation is a little easier if you serve it by itself as a first course. In an Italian meal, it's followed by a main course of meat or fish with salad or vegetables but no starch.

A seafood or vegetable risotto makes a great one-dish family supper that needs only a salad on the side.

LEFTOVER RICE

Risotto cannot be reheated but there is a way to use leftovers. The Italians call it *Risotto al Salto*, or leaping risotto. Let the leftover risotto come to room temperature and form it into patties. Place the patties in a hot greased skillet, cover, and cook over medium heat until browned on one side. Flip the patties over, sprinkle with a little Parmesan, and cook until the cheese melts.

DRIED MUSHROOMS

One of the most popular ways to make risotto is with mush-

COOK'S SECRETS

Mary Ann Esposito
Television host of Ciao Italia

"To save time, risotto can be partly made a day ahead. Allow 2/3 of the broth to be absorbed by the rice. Spread the rice on a lightly buttered baking sheet. Cover and refrigerate overnight. Return the rice to a saucepan and warm slowly. Reheat the remaining broth and add slowly to the rice in small amounts, allowing the rice to absorb each addition. The rice should remain firm-tender, but fluid and creamy."

rooms; dried mushrooms add a special woodsy flavor.

Many species of mushrooms that would be hard to come by fresh are available dried. Although small packages of dried mushrooms may seem outlandishly expensive, remember that when you buy fresh mushrooms, you are paying mostly for moisture. The best buys in dried mushrooms are Polish *boletus* (spongetype) mushrooms, which are usually labeled simply "imported mushrooms."

Dried mushrooms must be reconstituted in boiling water for about 20 minutes before use. The water becomes colored and flavored by the mushrooms as they soak, so don't throw it away. Stir it into risotto or freeze it and use for flavoring soups and stews.

WILD MUSHROOM RISOTTO

Soak 1/2 ounce dried Polish mushrooms in 1 cup boiling water 20 minutes. **Remove** mushrooms and **rinse** under running water. **Strain** soaking liquid through a cheesecloth-lined sieve or a coffee filter and reserve. Now **prepare** recipe as directed on page 131, but **reduce** chicken stock to 2¼ cups and **add** mushroom soaking liquid to stock. **Substitute** 8 ounces trimmed and thinly sliced mushrooms sautéed in 1 tablespoon butter for 7 minutes for the asparagus (**add** the reconstituted dried mushrooms to the sliced mushrooms halfway through sautéing). **Continue** as directed in recipe, **stirring** in mushrooms when rice is done. Makes 4 servings.

WINTER SQUASH RISOTTO

Prepare Step 1 as directed in recipe on page 131, **omit** Step 2, then **proceed** as directed in Steps 3 and 4, **adding** one 10-ounce package thawed frozen winter squash purée, 8 crushed Amaretti cookies, and 1/2 teaspoon each salt and rubbed sage to the rice mixture along with the final 1/4 cup stock. **Continue cooking** until soft and creamy. **Remove** from heat, **stir** in Parmesan, pepper, and 1 tablespoon butter and serve. Makes 4 servings.

WINE IN RISOTTO

Risotto recipes frequently call for wine. If you don't want to use it, a flavorful broth can be substituted instead. If you do use wine, it is generally stirred into the rice just before the broth is added. The alcohol evaporates, leaving behind only an essence of flavor.

There are no hard and fast rules about which wine to select for a risotto. Often the same wine that is used to flavor the rice is served along with it. Indeed, risotto is as often made with red wine as with white. Red wine, of course, lends the rice a light purple-brown tone.

Leftover wine can be recorked and used for cooking within a few weeks.

THREADS OF GOLD

Many risotto recipes, including our Asparagus and Cheese Risotto, call for saffron, the threadlike stigmas from a type of purple crocus (*Crocus sativus*). Saffron is the most expensive spice in the world. That is because it takes more than 14,000 stigmas to make 1 ounce. Fortunately, a little goes a long way in flavoring a rice dish. The spice is sold in tiny vials or cellophane packages that should be kept tightly closed in a cool, dark place and used within 6 months. The threads should be crushed or crumbled just before using.

Powdered saffron, which loses its strength quickly and can be easily adulterated in manufacture, is not recommended.

FRESH VEGETABLES

VEGETABLE BASICS

The best way to preserve a vegetable's goodness is to cook it quickly; in other words, steam, boil, or microwave. Our listings give all the basics.

WHAT YOU NEED TO KNOW

Buy perishable vegetables no more than 2 days before serving. Store loosely bagged in plastic in the refrigerator crisper. Tuck a sheet or two of paper toweling in with leafy greens. The toweling will absorb extra moisture and extend the greens' shelf life. Potatoes, onions, and winter squash need to be stored in a cool, dark, dry spot.

Boiling: To preserve nutrients, cook vegetables whole or in large chunks, unpeeled, using only enough water to keep them from scorching. Start timing the cooking only after the water returns to a boil. When done, drain the vegetables in a colander. To get rid of excess moisture, return them to the pan and shake them briefly over moderate heat before seasoning.

Steaming: Not all vegetables steam well, but those that do all steam by the same method. Use a steamer basket over—never touching—1/2 inch of boiling water in a tightly covered pot. Don't crowd the vegetables or the steam won't circulate evenly. Note: To avoid getting burned when you open the pot, use the lid to deflect the steam away from you.

Microwaving: Our microwave times are for 700- to 800-watt ovens. Choose vegetables of uniform size or cut them into uniform pieces. The fresher they are the faster they cook.

Use shallow, round, microwave-safe casseroles. Vegetables microwave more evenly when arranged in a ring than when piled or lined up in rows. Arrange the vegetables spoke style, with the thickest portions facing outward. Turn or stir the vegetables once or twice during cooking, so that they cook more evenly.

Microwave no more than 4 servings of a vegetable at a time. Larger amounts may cook no faster than boiled or steamed vegetables.

If you cover the vegetables, use a casserole lid or plastic wrap with one corner turned back to allow steam to escape. Always microwave vegetables on high (100 percent power) and be sure to let them stand for several minutes when they come from the oven to complete the cooking.

ASPARAGUS

Allow 6 to 10 per person. Snap off woody ends; peel the lower section of thick asparagus stalks with a vegetable parer. Peeling the stalks evens the thickness so that the ends and tips are done at the same time.

Boil, covered, in a large skillet with salted water to cover, 4 to 5 minutes. Asparagus should be laid flat in the skillet, tips pointing the same direction.

Steam tips 5 to 7 minutes; spears 8 to 10.

Microwave: Arrange 12 to 14 spears spoke style in a shallow round dish. Cover and microwave 5 to 7 minutes; let stand 3 minutes.

Season with nutmeg, grated Parmesan, hollandaise, browned butter, or vinaigrette. If you use lemon juice, add it at the last minute; otherwise, the asparagus will turn olive green.

BEANS

Allow 1/4 pound of green or wax beans per person. Snap off the tips, leave the beans whole, cut them into 1 1/2- to 2-inch lengths, or "French" them by slivering lengthwise.

Boil, covered, in salted water 5 to 10 minutes, depending on how the beans are cut.

Steam snapped beans 10 to 15 minutes; whole beans 15 to 20.

Microwave: Arrange 1 pound of beans in a shallow 2-quart casserole. Add 1/2 cup of water, cover, and microwave 10 to 15 minutes; let stand 3 minutes.

Season with dill, chervil, garlic, tarragon, grated Parmesan, vinaigrette, or hollandaise.

BEETS

Allow 2 to 3 small to medium-size beets per person. Trim off all but 1 inch of the stems; leave the roots intact; scrub gently but do not peel.

Boil, covered, in salted water 40 to 60 minutes, depending on size and age of the beets.

Steam: Not recommended.

Microwave: Arrange six 2-inch beets in a shallow 2-quart casserole, add 1/4 cup of water, cover, and microwave 16 to 20 minutes; let stand 3 minutes.

Season with caraway, cranberries, dill, fresh ginger, horseradish, lemon, vinegar, red wine, sour cream, or yogurt.

(continued on page 136)

WORK SAVER

Steamer Basket

An expandable stainless-steel steamer is just the thing for vegetables: It's inexpensive, easy to use, and can be opened to fit just about any size pot. A plastic version of the steamer is made for microwave use. If you do a lot of steaming, you might want to invest in an electric steamer with a built-in timer.

How to Skin and Shred Beets

When you buy fresh beets, trim off the leaves as soon as possible: They leach moisture from the root. To prevent beets from bleeding color and losing vitamins while they cook, scrub them gently, but don't peel. Leave 1 inch of stems when you trim off the leaves; don't trim off the root.

To avoid staining your hands when peeling cooked beets: Slip the beet skins off under cool running water.

For a shredded beet dish such as the recipe at right, cool beets slightly for easy handling. Then shred beets on the second coarsest side of a flat or a 4-sided grater, being careful to keep fingers out of the way.

Shredded Beets and Red Cabbage with Cranberries

2	tablespoons olive oil
1½	cups coarsely shredded red cabbage
1½	cups peeled, coarsely shredded cooked fresh or canned whole baby beets
⅓	cup fresh or canned whole berry cranberry sauce
1	tablespoon balsamic vinegar
1	teaspoon salt
¼	teaspoon black pepper
⅛	teaspoon ground allspice
⅛	teaspoon ground cloves

1 In a 10-inch skillet or Dutch oven over moderate heat, heat oil 1 minute. Add cabbage and sauté, stirring occasionally, 5 minutes.

2 Stir in beets, cranberry sauce, vinegar, salt, pepper, allspice, and cloves. Cook, covered, until tender— 10 minutes. Makes 4 servings.

1 Serving: Calories 129; Total Fat 7 g; Saturated Fat 1 g; Protein 1 g; Carbohydrates 17 g; Fiber 2 g; Sodium 785 mg; Cholesterol 0 mg

prep time-20 minutes • cooking time-16 minutes

(continued from page 134)

BROCCOLI

Allow 4 to 6 ounces per person. Trim off woody ends, leaving stalks with 2-inch stems. Or separate into florets.

Boil: Not recommended. Better to steam or microwave.

Steam stalks 13 to 18 minutes; florets 8 to 10.

Microwave: Arrange 1 pound of florets spoke style in a baking dish. Add 1/4 cup of water, cover, and microwave 8 to 10 minutes; let stand 2 minutes.

Season with garlic, marjoram, oregano, buttered bread crumbs, hollandaise, grated Parmesan, or vinaigrette.

BRUSSELS SPROUTS

Allow 3 to 4 ounces per person. Discard the outer leaves; trim the stems flush with the bottom and make an X-shaped cut in the bottom of each.

Boil, covered, in salted water 10 to 15 minutes.

Steam 15 to 20 minutes.

Microwave: Arrange 1 pound of sprouts in a single layer in a 1 1/2-quart baking dish, add 3 tablespoons of water, cover, and microwave 6 to 8 minutes; let stand 3 minutes.

Season with chestnuts, dill, mustard, white sauce, buttered bread crumbs, grated Parmesan, or cheese sauce.

CABBAGE

Buy compact heavy heads. Allow 4 ounces per person. Discard the coarse outer leaves; quarter the cabbage and remove the core. Leave as quarters, halve lengthwise to form eighths, and cut into chunks, slice, or shred.

Boil: Not recommended. Better to steam or microwave.

Steam eighths or quarters 15 to 18 minutes; chunks 12 to 15; sliced cabbage 8 to 10.

Microwave: Arrange slim wedges 1 layer deep in a 3-quart casserole, overlapping them slightly. Add 1/4 cup of water, cover, and microwave 10 to 12 minutes; let stand 3 minutes. Or microwave 6 cups sliced or shredded cabbage the same way 7 to 10 minutes; let stand 3 minutes.

Season with caraway, chestnuts, dill, vinegar, or buttered bread crumbs. For red cabbage only: cranberry juice or sauce, red wine, or red wine vinegar. For green cabbage only: white sauce, cheese sauce, mustard, or curry powder.

CARROTS AND PARSNIPS

Allow 1 to 2 per person. Remove the tops and root ends.

Boil whole carrots or parsnips, covered, in salted water 15 to 20 minutes. For carrots that are thinly sliced or julienned, boil 5 to 10 minutes

Steam 25 to 35 minutes.

Microwave: Cut 1 pound of trimmed, peeled carrots or parsnips into 2-inch chunks. Arrange in a 2-quart casserole, add 3 tablespoons of water, cover, and microwave, giving the carrots 8 to 10 minutes,

the parsnips 7 to 9 minutes; let stand 3 minutes.

Season with dill, chervil, fresh ginger, lemon, orange, mint, nutmeg, parsley, or tarragon.

CAULIFLOWER

One medium-size head (2 pounds) serves 4 to 6. Remove the leaves and trim the stem level with the base. Leave whole or divide into florets with 1-inch stems.

Boil whole cauliflower, covered, in 2 to 3 inches of salted water 15 to 20 minutes. Add 3 to 4 lemon slices to keep the cauliflower white. Loose florets should be steamed or microwaved.

Steam whole cauliflower 25 to 30 minutes; florets 10 to 12.

Microwave: For a whole cauliflower, hollow out as much of the core as possible. Microwave in a covered 2-quart casserole with 2 tablespoons of water 12 to 15 minutes; let stand 3 minutes. For florets: Place 4 cups of florets in a covered casserole with 1/4 cup of water. Microwave 8 to 10 minutes; let stand 3 minutes.

Season with browned butter, curry powder, buttered bread crumbs, grated Parmesan, or cheese or mustard sauce.

CORN ON THE COB

Allow 1 to 2 ears per person. When ready to cook—not before—husk, desilk, and break off stems and tips.

Boil, covered, in a kettle of unsalted water 6 to 9 minutes.

Steam: Not recommended. Better to boil or microwave.

Microwave: Lay 4 unhusked ears flat on the oven floor, spacing evenly and alternating

---

HOW TO STRIP KERNELS

Stand an ear of corn on a work surface. Using a sharp knife, cut straight down along the cob, freeing several rows of kernels at a time.

---

the direction of the tips. Microwave, uncovered, 6 to 8 minutes; let stand 3 minutes.

Season with melted butter, lime juice and crushed red pepper flakes, fresh coriander (cilantro), or rosemary.

GREENS

(spinach, beet, mustard, and turnip greens; collards; kale)

Allow 1/2 pound per person. Discard stems and blemished

(continued on page 138)

Fresh Creamed Corn

When corn is at its peak, take advantage of its natural sweet flavor to make your own cream-style corn.

1 Allowing about 1 ear of corn per serving, slice fresh kernels off the cob (see opposite). Place in the bowl of a food processor fitted with a steel blade. Pulse 5 to 6 times until finely chopped and slightly creamy.

2 In a heavy saucepan over moderate heat, cook with a little butter until very tender and all the raw taste is gone. Season to taste with salt and pepper. For extra creaminess, stir in a little cream during the last minute or two of cooking.

Green Bean Succotash

Prepare as directed at right, **substituting** 2 cups trimmed green beans for lima beans and 2 tablespoons fresh chopped thyme or 1/2 teaspoon crumbled dried thyme for chives. Makes 4 servings.

Succotash

- **2 cups fresh or frozen baby lima beans**
- **2 cups fresh or frozen corn kernels**
- **1 cup half-and-half**
- **2 tablespoons butter, margarine, olive oil, or bacon drippings**
- **3/4 teaspoon salt**
- **3 tablespoons chopped fresh chives or 2 teaspoons freeze-dried chives**
- **1/4 teaspoon black pepper**

1 In a large saucepan over high heat, bring lima beans, corn, half-and-half, butter, and salt to a boil.

2 Reduce the heat to moderate, cover, and cook until tender—10 to 12 minutes. Remove from the heat and stir in chives and pepper. Makes 4 servings.

1 Serving: Calories 302; Total Fat 14 g; Saturated Fat 8 g; Protein 10 g; Carbohydrates 38 g; Fiber 0 g; Sodium 642 mg; Cholesterol 38 mg

prep time-30 minutes
cooking time-10 to 12 minutes

(continued from page 136)

leaves; rinse in several changes of cold water; drain well.

Boil: Not recommended. Better to steam.

Steam in a large pan; no rack is needed. The rinse water on the leaves is enough to cook spinach and other fragile greens. Longer-cooking kale and collards need 1 to 2 cups of water. Cover and steam over moderate heat until greens wilt: 3 to 5 minutes for spinach and fragile greens; 10 to 15 minutes for turnip or mustard greens; 15 to 20 minutes for kale and collards. Note: Add more water as needed for longer-cooking greens.

Microwave: Not practical; too large a casserole needed.

Season with bacon drippings, browned butter, olive oil and vinegar or lemon juice, garlic, onion, nutmeg, or rosemary.

LIMA BEANS

Allow 1/2 pound per person. Shell just before cooking.

Boil, covered, in unsalted water 10 to 15 minutes.

Steam 15 to 25 minutes.

Microwave: Place 2 cups of shelled beans in a 2-quart casserole. Add 1/2 cup of water, cover, and microwave 10 to 15 minutes; let stand 3 minutes.

Season with bacon drippings, sour cream, nutmeg, parsley, thyme, white sauce, cheese sauce, or toasted pecans.

ONIONS

Allow 3 to 5 small white or silverskin onions per person.

Boil unpeeled onions, covered, in a large pan of salted water 10 to 15 minutes, then remove the skins.

Steam: Not recommended. Better to boil or microwave.

Microwave: Peel 1 pound of onions and arrange in a 1 1/2-quart casserole. Add 2 tablespoons of broth, water, or wine, cover, and microwave 7 to 10 minutes; let stand 3 minutes.

Season with cream, mace, marjoram, nutmeg, rosemary, sage, tarragon, thyme, white sauce, or cheese sauce.

GREEN PEAS

Allow 1/2 pound per person. Shell when ready to cook.

Boil in 1 to 2 inches unsalted water, giving small peas 3 to 4 minutes, large ones 5 to 8.

Steam 9 to 12 minutes.

Microwave: Place 2 1/2 cups of shelled peas in a 1 1/2-quart casserole, add 2 tablespoons of water, cover, and microwave 5 to 7 minutes; no standing time is needed.

Season with chervil, mint, orange zest, rosemary, tarragon, shallots, or white sauce.

POTATOES

(red, white, all-purpose, new)

Allow 1 medium-size or 2 to 3 small potatoes per person. Scrub but do not peel or cut up. Remove the eyes and any green patches. Pierce each potato with a fork to prevent bursting.

Boil, covered, in a large pan of salted water 20 to 30 minutes until fork-tender.

Steam: Not recommended.

Microwave: Not recommended.

SNOW PEAS

(and sugar snap peas)

Allow 4 ounces per person.

Pull off the string along the pod seam, then rinse and cook. Snow peas and sugar snaps are eaten pods and all.

Boil, covered, in unsalted water 1 to 3 minutes. Plunge into ice water to set the color and crunch; drain, then warm quickly in butter.

Steam 5 to 7 minutes.

Microwave: Arrange 1 pound of pea pods in a 2-quart casserole; add no water. Cover and microwave 4 to 5 minutes; let stand 2 minutes.

Season with cream, fresh ginger, mint, orange zest, roasted sesame oil, scallions, soy sauce, or teriyaki sauce.

SUMMER SQUASH

(yellow, zucchini, pattypan)

Allow 1 small squash per person. Scrub gently but do not peel. Cut the zucchini and yellow squash into 1- to 2-inch rounds; pattypan into bite-size pieces. Note: Baby squash can be cooked whole.

Boil: Not recommended. Better to steam or microwave.

Steam 10 to 15 minutes.

Microwave: Arrange 4 cups of thinly sliced yellow squash or zucchini or 4 cups of cubed pattypan in a 2-quart casserole. Add 2 tablespoons of water, cover, and microwave 6 to 8 minutes; let stand 2 minutes.

Season with basil, chives, dill, garlic, oregano, tarragon, thyme, grated Parmesan, buttered bread crumbs, or cream.

TURNIPS

Allow 2 small or 1 medium-size white turnip per person or 1/2 cup (about 4 ounces) of cubed turnip. Remove the tops and root ends; scrub

---

HOW TO FRENCH BEANS

Trim beans to equal lengths. Line up several beans at a time. Using a sharp chef's knife, **cut** the beans from end to end in 1/8-inch slices.

PEAS WITH ORANGE AND MINT

Prepare as directed at right, **omitting** onions, **substituting** 2 tablespoons chopped fresh mint or 1 teaspoon mint flakes for rosemary, and **adding** 2 teaspoons grated orange zest. Makes 4 servings.

---

small turnips but do not peel; leave whole.

Boil whole, covered, in salted water 20 to 30 minutes.

Steam 1/2-inch cubes 10 to 12 minutes.

Microwave: Place 3 1/2 cups of cubed turnip in a 1 1/2-quart casserole, add 1/4 cup of water, and microwave, covered, 7 to 9 minutes; let stand 3 minutes.

Season with white sauce, cheese sauce, yogurt, mace, nutmeg, orange zest, or thyme.

How to Peel Small Onions

The easiest way to peel small onions is to **blanch** them with their skins on for 1 to 2 minutes in boiling water. **Drop** in cold water just so they are not too hot to handle, then **slip** off the skins.

To Shell Peas

Squeeze the pod gently until it opens along the seam. **Push** the peas out with your thumb.

Green Peas and Onions

- **1** cup water
- **1½** cups small onions, peeled, or ½ package (16 ounces) frozen small whole onions
- **1** teaspoon salt
- **2** cups fresh or frozen green peas
- **2** tablespoons butter or margarine
- **1** tablespoon coarsely chopped fresh rosemary or ½ teaspoon dried rosemary, crumbled
- **¼** teaspoon black pepper

1 In a large saucepan over high heat, bring water to a boil. Add onions and salt and return to a boil. Reduce the heat to moderate and cook, covered, 8 minutes.

2 Add peas, return to a boil and cook, covered, 7 to 9 minutes more.

3 Meanwhile, in a small saucepan over low heat, melt butter. Add rosemary and steep 2 to 3 minutes.

4 Drain peas and onions, add butter and pepper, and toss lightly to mix. Makes 4 servings.

1 Serving: Calories 116; Total Fat 6 g; Saturated Fat 4 g; Protein 4 g; Carbohydrates 12 g; Fiber 4 g; Sodium 265 mg; Cholesterol 16 mg

prep time-20 minutes
cooking time-20 minutes

GLAZED VEGETABLES

Vegetables get a special boost when combined with a glaze that adds flavor and color in a matter of minutes.

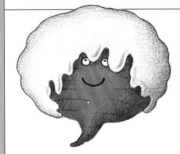

GLAZING BASICS

No vegetables take to glazing better than tubers, roots, and sturdy members of the cabbage family. The vegetables should be cooked just until firm-tender. If too soft, they will disintegrate when they are stirred with a glaze.

Glazes should be cooked until thick enough to stick to a vegetable—about the consistency of honey. Coat vegetables just before they are served so that they emerge jewel bright.

A PERFECT FORMULA

The most successful glazes are a balance of sweet and sour tastes. The sweet ingredient might be caramelized granulated sugar, brown or maple sugar, honey, corn syrup, molasses, jelly, or marmalade. On the sour side, citrus juices in general—and orange and lemon juices in particular—are the first choice. Also try apple cider or cranberry juice, flavored vinegars, wines, and spirits.

Cranberry sauce does double duty as a glaze by providing both sweet and sour tastes and a rosy blush.

MIX AND MATCH

As a rule, naturally sweet vegetables, including carrots and beets, need tart glazes. Bland vegetables, such as potatoes, require glazes with a lot of character. Pungent vegetables, like those in the cabbage family, do better with delicate glazes. But there are exceptions: Gingery glazes do wonders for parsnips, even though they have plenty of bite.

INSTANT SPARKLE

To glaze beets, carrots, winter squash, or parsnips zip-quick, add a couple of tablespoons of marmalade or fruit jelly to the pan along with some butter

To the Rescue

If a glaze is **too thick** to coat a vegetable evenly, thin with a little citrus juice, vinegar, water, or broth. **Too thin and runny,** boil, uncovered, over high heat, stirring often, until the consistency of honey. **Too dark,** replace 2 to 3 tablespoons of glaze with light corn syrup or honey. **Too pale,** blend in a little dark corn syrup, dark brown sugar, or gravy browner. Then cook and stir to the proper consistency. **Drab,** stir in 1 to 2 teaspoons of red currant jelly. **Granular,** put it through a fine sieve lined with several thicknesses of damp cheesecloth.

and turn the vegetable in the mix until it glistens.

FLAVOR BOOSTERS

A teaspoon of freshly chopped dill, marjoram, or thyme (or a pinch of dried) enhances most glazes. For a clear glaze, strain out the herb before you add the vegetable.

A tablespoon of wine, vermouth, or liqueur also punches up the flavor of a glaze. Boil until only the essence remains.

TO BUTTER OR NOT?

Butter enriches the glaze and makes it silky smooth, no question. If you're trying to trim fat, calories, and cholesterol, use only half the amount called for or omit it altogether.

GLAZED CARROTS

Prepare as directed at right for Cranberry Beets, **substituting** 1 pound peeled, chunked, boiled large carrots for beets. To glaze, **cook** and **stir** 3 tablespoons each ginger marmalade (or lime marmalade), butter, and lemon juice, 1/2 teaspoon salt, and 1/4 teaspoon pepper in a medium-size skillet over moderate heat 1 to 2 minutes until marmalade melts and mixture is syrupy. **Add** carrots and **turn** just enough to coat. Note: Parsnips are also excellent prepared this way. Makes 4 servings.

HERB-GLAZED ONIONS

Prepare as directed at right for Glazed Onions, **substituting** dry white vermouth or cognac for water and **adding** 1 tablespoon minced fresh thyme or rosemary. Makes 4 servings.

SAVORY GLAZES

Another way to glaze vegetables is with a savory glaze—beef or chicken stock boiled down until syrupy.

The stock can be flavored with a shot of Madeira, port, or sherry, with a bouquet garni or just a sprig of parsley, rosemary, or thyme. To finish the glaze, swirl in a tablespoon or two of butter, which pulls all the flavors together.

Glazed Onions

- **1** quart water
- **1½** pounds small white onions in their skins
- **3** tablespoons butter or margarine
- **¼** cup firmly packed light brown sugar
- **2** tablespoons water
- **½** teaspoon salt
- **¼** teaspoon black pepper

1 In a 2-quart stockpot over moderate heat, bring 1 quart water to a boil. Add onions and cook until crisp-tender—9 to 10 minutes. Drain in a colander and plunge into cold water. Trim off root ends and gently slip off skins.

2 In a large heavy skillet over moderate heat, heat butter, sugar, water, salt, and pepper. Cook, stirring, until syrupy—3 to 4 minutes. Add onions and cook until glazed—4 to 5 minutes. Makes 4 servings.

> **1 Serving: Calories 175; Total Fat 9 g; Saturated Fat 5 g; Protein 2 g; Carbohydrates 24 g; Fiber 3 g; Sodium 363 mg; Cholesterol 23 mg**
>
> *prep time-20 minutes*
> *cooking time-20 minutes*

Glazed Beets

- **¾** cup orange marmalade
- **2** tablespoons lemon juice
- **½** teaspoon grated orange zest
- **18** small beets (about 1½ in diameter), boiled and peeled

1 In a large skillet over moderate heat, cook and stir marmalade, lemon juice, and orange zest until marmalade melts and mixture is syrupy—about 3 minutes.

2 Add beets and turn in syrup mixture until glazed and heated through—5 to 6 minutes. Makes 4 servings.

> **1 Serving: Calories 219; Total Fat 0 g; Saturated Fat 0 g; Protein 3 g; Carbohydrates 56 g; Fiber 3 g; Sodium 154 mg; Cholesterol 0 mg**
>
> *prep time-10 minutes • cooking time-1 hour*

BAKED VEGETABLES

Potatoes, sweet potatoes, and winter squash all respond beautifully to baking. But beets, carrots, and even asparagus are good bakers too.

BAKING BASICS

Baked and roasted vegetables have a depth of flavor that boiled and steamed vegetables can never match. Once baked, vegetables need only a little seasoning and a quick turn in melted butter or oil, lemon juice, or balsamic vinegar. Or top them with freshly grated Parmesan cheese.

WHICH SQUASH?

Acorn, buttercup, butternut, and golden nugget squashes—universal favorites because of their nut-sweet flesh—are small enough to halve and bake. Their hollows, moreover, hold seasonings nicely. Giant Hubbard and banana squashes are difficult to split and cut. Many grocers now sell them by the piece.

Allow 1/2 a small squash per person or 6 ounces of chunked large squash. Preheat the oven to 350°F. Brush squash halves or toss chunks with melted butter or vegetable oil and sprinkle with salt and pepper.

Arrange squash, hollow or cut sides up, in an ungreased shallow roasting pan and bake, uncovered, 30 to 60 minutes until fork tender.

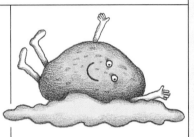

PERFECT BAKED POTATOES

Choose russets (Idahos or Burbanks). They are high in starch and low in moisture, so they bake up dry and fluffy.

Pierce each potato in two or three places with a fork. This allows steam to escape and keeps the potatoes from bursting as they bake.

Avoid oiling potatoes unless you want the skins to be soft. Wrapping bakers in aluminum foil will result in limp skins and soggy flesh.

Preheat the oven (about 20 minutes); place the potatoes on the middle rack so that hot air can circulate evenly. At 425°F, a medium-size potato will be done in 3/4 to 1 hour. Potatoes can be baked from 325°F to 425°F, but for a crisp-skinned potato with easily fluffed flesh, 425°F is the right heat.

To test for doneness, pierce a potato with a fork; the fork should go in easily.

Note: Sweet potatoes can be baked exactly the same way but fare better at 350°F than at higher temperatures.

DOUBLE BAKED

To stuff baked potatoes, bake as described above. When just done, remove the potatoes from the oven and split them in half lengthwise.

Scoop out the insides and mix it with your choice of cheese, salsa, sautéed mushrooms, or sour cream and spoon the mix back into the skins. Sprinkle with grated cheese, place the halves on a baking sheet, and bake at 400°F until bubbly.

OTHER LOVELY BAKERS

Potatoes and squash are not the only vegetables fit for the oven. The vegetables below are all delicious when baked.

Asparagus: Arrange trimmed, peeled or unpeeled asparagus in a shallow baking dish, drizzle with melted butter or olive oil, and shake pan to coat each spear. Bake, uncovered, 10 to 12 minutes at 425°F until lightly brown.

Beets: Arrange scrubbed, unpeeled, small whole beets in a shallow baking dish, add 1 tablespoon vegetable oil, and turn beets in oil to coat. Bake, uncovered, 40 minutes at 375°F, turning occasionally. Raise heat to 425°F and bake for another 15 to 20 minutes until tender.

Carrots: Turn whole or chunked peeled or unpeeled medium-size carrots in 1 tablespoon oil or melted butter in a shallow baking dish. Bake, uncovered, 30 minutes at 375°F, turning occasionally. Raise heat to 425°F and bake 20 minutes more until tender.

Onions: Peel silverskin onions, turn in oil in a shallow baking dish, and bake, uncovered, 30 to 35 minutes at 350°F until tender and brown. Note: Large onions can be peeled, halved, and placed cut side up in a baking dish. Brush with oil and bake, uncovered, 1 to 1½ hours at 350°F until soft and brown.

Parsnips: Turn whole or chunked peeled medium-size parsnips in 1 tablespoon oil or melted butter in a shallow baking pan and bake as directed for carrots (see above).

Potatoes (redskin or new): Scrub but do not peel; turn small whole potatoes in a little oil in a shallow baking dish and bake, uncovered, 1 to 1½ hours at 350°F, turning occasionally, until tender and richly browned. For extra flavor, tuck in a couple of rosemary or thyme sprigs and a clove or two of garlic.

Summer squash (pattypan, yellow, zucchini): Scrub, cut yellow squash and zucchini in 1- to 2-inch chunks, pattypan in wedges, and bake, uncovered, 45 minutes at 450°F until fork-tender and nicely browned.

Turnips: Peel and quarter medium-size white turnips, then bake as directed for carrots (see above).

How to Tackle a Winter Squash

The easiest, safest way to split a winter squash is with a large sharp chef's knife and a rubber mallet.

1 Snap off the stem. Work the blade of a chef's knife gently into the midline of the squash so that it runs the length of the squash. Then using a rubber mallet, gently pound the top of the blade near the handle, driving the knife into the squash until it splits in half. Alternatively, the blade of a knife can be rocked back and forth on the squash until the squash splits.

2 Scoop out and discard all seeds, strings, and fiber in the squash. Leave small squash as halves or cut each half lengthwise to form quarters; do not peel. Cut large squash into serving-size pieces and peel or not, as desired, using a vegetable parer or paring knife. If you've bought a Hubbard or banana squash by the piece, it can be baked as is, then portioned.

Baked Acorn Squash

- **2 medium-size acorn squash**
- **¼ cup (½ stick) butter or margarine**
- **2 tablespoons brown sugar or maple syrup**

1 Preheat the oven to 350°F. Halve squash lengthwise, scoop out seeds with a spoon, and if halves wobble when placed cut side up in a shallow roasting pan, level as needed by cutting small slivers off the bottoms.

2 Place squash halves cut side up in roasting pan, dot evenly with butter, and sprinkle with brown sugar.

3 Bake, uncovered, until fork-tender—about 45 minutes. Makes 4 servings.

1 Serving: Calories 196; Total Fat 12 g; Saturated Fat 7 g; Protein 2 g; Carbohydrates 24 g; Fiber 6 g; Sodium 125 mg; Cholesterol 31 mg

prep time-15 minutes • cooking time-45 minutes

STUFFED AND BAKED

When they're stuffed with juicy and flavorful fillings, baked vegetables become a meal in themselves.

THE RIGHT SHAPE

Look for globe-shaped vegetables for stuffing. Tomatoes should be ripe but firm. Large, mild Spanish or sweet onions, such as Vidalia and Walla Walla, are good choices.

FIRST STEPS

Parboiling reduces the time required for baking firm vegetables such as peppers and onions. Drop the vegetable into a pot of boiling water and simmer until tender. (About 5 minutes for a hollow pepper, about 20 for a whole onion.) Then stuff as directed.

Another way to trim the cooking time of stuffed vegetables is to add about 1 cup of water or broth to the baking pan. The water allows the vegetables to steam while they bake and keeps them from drying as they cook. This is especially important with rice, bread, or other dry stuffing.

NO TIPPING

To keep vegetables from tipping as they bake: Use a baking dish that is just large enough for the vegetables to sit snugly so that they hold each other up. Or set each vegetable in a muffin-pan cup that has been lightly greased. Note: Empty cups should be filled with water during baking to prevent buckling.

Tomatoes are particularly prone to tipping. In Greece, where stuffed vegetables are served regularly, cooks get around the problem by turning tomatoes upside down and cutting the cap from the bottom.

If a pepper doesn't stand up well, hollow it out on its side, as shown in our recipe.

VARIED FILLINGS

Depending on the size of the vegetable, you'll need between 1/3 and 3/4 cup of filling for each. If you use a rice or grain mixture for stuffing, it should be cooked until nearly done—about 15 minutes for a 20-minute rice—with broth and other ingredients first. Don't stuff the vegetable completely full, because the rice will need space to expand as it finishes cooking. Then bake at 350°F for 35 or 40 minutes.

Traditional flavorings for rice stuffings include parsley or mint, chopped tomatoes and tomato juice, minced onion, chopped pepper, golden raisins, cinnamon, olive oil, chopped pine nuts and ground beef or lamb.

HOW TO HOLLOW AN ONION

Cut a 1/2-inch slice from the top of an onion; parboil the onion 20 to 25 minutes. With a spoon or other tool (see below), scoop out the center, leaving a 1/2-inch-thick shell.

SPINACH-STUFFED TOMATOES

Prepare as directed at right through Step 1, **substituting** 6 medium-size very firm but ripe tomatoes for sweet peppers; **scoop** out centers, but do not reserve. Do not blanch tomatoes, but do **drain** upside down while you prepare filling. **Sauté** 1 chopped large yellow onion in 1 tablespoon olive oil in a large heavy skillet over moderate heat 3 minutes, **stirring** occasionally. **Add** 2 minced cloves garlic and sauté 2 minutes more. **Mix** in 2 thawed 10-ounce packages frozen creamed spinach, 1/4 cup grated Parmesan, 2 teaspoons lemon juice, and 1/4 teaspoon each ground nutmeg, salt, and pepper; **heat** just until bubbly. **Spoon** mixture into tomatoes. Quickly **mix** 1/4 cup soft white bread crumbs, 2 tablespoons grated Parmesan, and 1 tablespoon melted butter and spoon 1 tablespoon on each tomato. **Bake** as directed in Step 4. **Omit** Step 5. Makes 6 servings.

WORK SAVER

Butter Curler, Melon Baller, Grapefruit Knife

The most useful implements for digging out the insides of vegetables were really made for other jobs. Try a French butter curler—a hook-shaped tool with a jagged edge—a melon baller, or a serrated grapefruit knife.

Tex-Mex Stuffed Peppers

- **4** medium-size sweet green, red, and/or yellow peppers
- **4** slices lean bacon, snipped crosswise into julienne strips
- **1** cup chopped scallions
- **2** cups corn kernels (cooked fresh, canned, or thawed frozen), drained
- **¼** cup chopped pimientos
- **3** tablespoons chopped coriander (cilantro)
- **1** small jalapeño pepper, cored, seeded, and chopped
- **1¼** teaspoons chili powder
- **1¼** teaspoons ground cumin
- **½** teaspoon salt
- **1** cup (about 4 ounces) shredded Monterey Jack cheese with hot peppers
- **¼** cup crushed tortilla chips

1 Preheat the oven to 350°F. Slice ½ inch off 1 side of each pepper. Chop and reserve slices. Scoop seeds and membranes out of peppers, then blanch peppers 5 minutes in lightly salted boiling water. Drain upside down.

2 In a medium-size skillet over moderate heat, cook bacon until crisp—3 to 4 minutes. Transfer to paper toweling to drain. Pour off all but 2 tablespoons bacon drippings from skillet.

3 Sauté reserved chopped pepper in bacon drippings, stirring occasionally, until limp—about 5 minutes. Add scallions and sauté, stirring occasionally, for 3 minutes. Add corn, pimientos, coriander, jalapeño, chili powder, cumin, and salt and cook and stir 3 minutes more. Remove from heat and stir in reserved bacon and ¾ of the Monterey Jack.

4 Fill peppers with corn mixture, dividing total amount evenly. Stand in an ungreased 1- to 1½-quart baking dish and bake, uncovered, until filling is heated through—about 30 minutes.

5 Toss crushed tortilla chips with the remaining Monterey Jack, spoon 1 tablespoon on top of each stuffed pepper, and bake, uncovered, just until cheese melts—about 5 minutes. Makes 4 servings.

1 Serving: Calories 406; Total Fat 27 g; Saturated Fat 12 g; Protein 17 g; Carbohydrates 29 g; Fiber 5 g; Sodium 835 mg; Cholesterol 49 mg

prep time-20 minutes
cooking time-60 minutes

VEGETABLE PURÉE

To purée a vegetable is to mash it to a smooth consistency. Virtually any vegetable that can be cooked until soft can be made into a purée.

DIFFERENT STROKES

You can purée vegetables by forcing them through a food mill, hand mashing with an old-fashioned potato masher, or by zapping them quickly in a food processor or blender. Forcing vegetables through a food mill gives the finest texture.

PURPOSEFUL PURÉES

The starchiness of a vegetable determines the thickness of the purée. Carrots, potatoes, winter squash, peas, and cooked dried beans, for example, produce thick purées; green beans, broccoli, and asparagus thin ones.

Purées made with starchy vegetables make the best side dishes served along with roasts and other meats, poultry, and fish. They can also be stirred into soups, stews, and gravies to thicken and flavor them.

Thinner vegetable purées, enhanced with herbs, fruit juices, and flavored vinegars instead of butter, can be used as low-fat sauces and flavorings for meats, fish, and pasta.

PURE COMFORT

Nearly everyone's favorite purée is mashed potatoes. The best potatoes for purées are russets (Idahos and Burbanks). All-purpose Maine or eastern potatoes also mash well.

Potatoes should never be whipped in a food processor; its high-speed blade breaks down the starch and the potatoes become gluey. Use a hand masher for smooth to comfortingly lumpy mashed potatoes; a hand-held electric mixer for smooth whipped potatoes.

FOR EXTRA FLAVOR

Herbs and spices add flavor to purées, but use a light hand when you sprinkle them in. The flavor of the vegetable should dominate, not the seasoning. When in doubt, a pinch of freshly grated nutmeg always works.

To trim fat, purée vegetables with milk, sour cream, reduced-fat sour cream, or yogurt instead of butter.

FROZEN ASSETS

Purées can be refrigerated for up to 4 days and frozen for 1 month in tightly covered containers. Add a small amount of liquid and reheat in a heavy saucepan, stirring constantly, over very low heat or use a double boiler.

PERFECT PURÉES
(Makes 2 servings)

Asparagus: 2½ cups cooked fresh or frozen asparagus. Purée with browned butter, 1 pinch mace, salt and pepper to taste.

Broccoli/cauliflower: 2 cups cooked fresh or frozen broccoli or cauliflower florets. Purée with ½ teaspoon salt, ¼ teaspoon marjoram, savory, sage, or rosemary plus 1½ tablespoons butter.

Brussels sprouts: 2 cups cooked fresh or frozen Brussels sprouts. Purée with 1 medium sautéed onion, 2 tablespoons butter, ½ cup yogurt, 1 pinch nutmeg, salt and pepper to taste.

Green beans: 2½ cups cooked fresh or frozen green beans. Purée with 4 scallions (white part only), 3 tablespoons snipped fresh dill, 1½ tablespoons butter, ¼ cup chicken or beef broth, 2 tablespoons heavy cream, salt and pepper to taste.

Lima beans/green peas: 2 cups cooked fresh or frozen baby lima beans or green peas. Purée with ¼ teaspoon each salt, thyme, marjoram, or oregano plus 2 tablespoons butter.

Mushrooms: 1½ pounds thinly sliced trimmed raw mushrooms. Sauté with 2 chopped large shallots or scallions in 3 tablespoons butter in a large heavy skillet over moderately low heat until limp and all juices evaporate. Purée with 2 to 3 tablespoons cream; season to taste with salt and pepper. Mix in 1 tablespoon minced parsley and 1 teaspoon paprika.

Parsnips: 2¾ cups cooked fresh or frozen parsnips. Purée with ¾ teaspoon minced fresh ginger, 2 tablespoons sour cream or low-fat sour cream, salt and pepper to taste.

Spinach/kale/collards/mustard greens: 2½ cups well-drained fresh or frozen cooked greens. Purée with ½ teaspoon salt, ¼ teaspoon oregano or marjoram, 1 pinch ground nutmeg plus 2 tablespoons butter.

Winter squash: 2½ cups cooked and mashed butternut or Hubbard squash. Purée with 2 tablespoons butter, 2 teaspoons brown sugar, ½ teaspoon salt, ¼ teaspoon ground ginger plus a little scalded cream or heated orange juice.

WORK SAVER
Food Mill

A food processor may be faster, but a food mill is a great tool to have on hand. It's cheaper than a food processor and is easily taken apart for thorough cleaning. It also comes in handy for many jobs. Use it for ricing potatoes, for making jelly and applesauce, for turning cooked rice into a thickener for soups, or for making homemade baby food.

Bavarian Carrot Purée

Puréed Carrots and Potatoes

Prepare as directed at right, **reducing** the number of carrots to 3 and **adding** one 8-ounce peeled and thinly sliced Idaho potato. Makes 4 servings.

Best Ever Mashers

Prepare as directed at right, **substituting** 2 pounds Idaho potatoes, **peeled** and cut into eighths, for the carrots. **Boil** in lightly salted water in a large covered saucepan over moderate heat for 20 to 30 minutes until very tender. **Drain** well, reserving 1/2 cup cooking water. **Mash** with a potato masher until smooth, **adding** butter and reserved cooking water, and **substituting** 1/3 cup hot milk or cream for the stock as you mash. **Season** to taste with salt and pepper. Makes 4 servings.

Garlic Mashed Potatoes

Prepare as directed in Best Ever Mashers above, **cooking** 8 peeled and halved cloves of garlic along with the potatoes. **Mash** and **season** as directed. Makes 4 servings.

- 6 **large carrots, peeled and thinly sliced**
- 1/2 **teaspoon salt**
- 1/2 **teaspoon dried thyme, crumbled**
- 1/4 **teaspoon black pepper**
- 1 **cup water**
- 1 **cup Browned Beef Stock or canned beef broth**
- 2 **tablespoons butter or margarine**

1 In a medium-size saucepan over moderate heat, bring carrots, salt, thyme, pepper, and water to a boil. Reduce the heat to moderately low and simmer, covered, stirring occasionally, until carrots are tender—about 25 minutes. Drain.

2 Meanwhile, in a medium-size saucepan, boil stock, uncovered, until it reduces to 1/3 cup—5 to 6 minutes. Transfer carrots and stock to a food processor and process until smooth—about 1 minute. Add butter and pulse until just melted. Makes 4 servings.

1 Serving: Calories 109; Total Fat 6 g; Saturated Fat 4 g; Protein 2 g; Carbohydrates 13 g; Fiber 3 g; Sodium 540 mg; Cholesterol 16 mg

prep time-10 minutes • cooking time-32 minutes

STIR-FRIED VEGETABLES

The secrets to successful stir-frying lie in cutting the ingredients to a similar small size and shape and adding them to the pan in the right order.

A MEAL IN MINUTES

Stir-frying is done quickly and in only a small amount of oil. It virtually guarantees a fresh-tasting dish served on a bed of steaming rice or other grains.

The process is so quick because the ingredients are cut into small uniform shapes. The cooking is done over intense heat while the cook stirs or, more accurately, tosses the ingredients. The object is for all the pieces to come into contact with the hottest part of the pan, but never long enough to stick.

GETTING STARTED

You don't need a lot of fancy equipment for stir-frying. For preparation, have on hand a good sharp paring knife and a chef's knife for trimming and slicing vegetables and other ingredients. For cooking, you'll need 2 long-handled utensils for tossing the ingredients as they cook. They should have a broad flat working end that can lift and turn a lot of sliced ingredients at one time. There are special Chinese shovel-style steel utensils for the purpose but an inexpensive pair of wooden or metal spatulas will perform the job just fine.

Whatever utensils you choose, they should be made of metal or wood, not plastic, which might melt if it comes in contact with the hot pan.

PICK A PAN

A heavy nonstick skillet 12 to 14 inches in diameter works perfectly for stir-frying and is the pan best suited for North American range tops.

If you work on a gas range, you can use a wok instead, if you prefer. The deep curved sides of a wok make it particularly easy to scoop and toss the ingredients. For the best heat coverage, remove the burner guard, replacing it with the circular steel collar that comes with a wok.

THE RIGHT MIX

Take your pick of oils for stir-frying; corn, peanut, and vegetable oil are all fine.

Our recipes call for vegetables only, but you can combine vegetables with sliced poultry, meat, or seafood if you wish. (See Mandarin Chicken Stir-fry, page 271.)

Vegetables should be cut into uniform sizes, whether diced, sliced diagonally, or cut into matchstick pieces. Matching shapes are as important to how a stir-fry dish looks as they are to the cooking.

Different vegetables require different cooking times. It's easiest to use combinations of vegetables that cook at similar speeds, such as in our Spring Vegetable Stir-fry.

If you want to combine a variety of both quick-cooking and slow-cooking vegetables in a stir-fry, add them to the pan in the following order: First: carrots, cauliflower, onions, peppers, turnips. Second: asparagus, broccoli, green beans, sugar snap and snow peas, sweet peppers, winter squash. Third: celery, mushrooms, peas, scallions, summer squash. Fourth: fresh herbs.

CONVENIENCE CUTS

You can also buy vegetables precut for stir-frying. They save time, but they cost more than fresh and do not offer quite as much nutritional value.

GINGER CUTS

Ginger is so pungent you need use only a little. Cut off a length of the root. Trim the skin with a paring knife. Slice across the fibrous grain to make rounds. Chop with a chef's knife using a rocking motion.

MATCHSTICK CUTS

1 To cut round vegetables such as carrots into matchstick or julienne slices: Cut into 1½- to 2-inch sections. Stand the sections on end and cut downward into even slices between ⅛- and ¼-inch thick.

2 Stack several slices and cut lengthwise into even strips between ⅛- and ¼-inch thick.

1 Heat oil in a large heavy skillet. If you wish to flavor oil with garlic, cook minced garlic over low heat and then remove garlic from pan.

2 Turn heat to high and when oil is hot, begin adding vegetables. Firm-walled vegetables, such as sweet peppers and onions, should be added to the pan first.

3 Use wood or metal utensils to scoop and toss the ingredients so that all vegetables come in contact with the pan bottom. Continue until ingredients are softened and lightly browned.

Spring Vegetable Stir-fry

1 tablespoon olive oil	**6** ounces snow peas or sugar snap peas, strings removed
3 cloves garlic, finely chopped	**3** scallions, white and tender green parts, cut into 2-inch lengths
1 tablespoon chopped fresh ginger	
2 large sweet red peppers, cored, seeded, and cut into 3" x 1/2" strips	**1/2** teaspoon dried marjoram or oregano, crumbled
12 ounces thin asparagus, trimmed, peeled, and cut into 2-inch lengths	**1/2** teaspoon salt
	1/4 teaspoon black pepper

1 In a large nonstick skillet over low heat, heat oil 1 minute. Add garlic and ginger and cook, stirring frequently, until tender—about 4 minutes.

2 Add red peppers, raise the heat to high, and cook, stirring frequently, until crisp-tender—about 2 minutes. Add asparagus, snow peas, scallions, marjoram, salt, and black pepper and cook, stirring frequently, until crisp-tender—about 6 minutes. Makes 4 servings.

1 Serving: Calories 86; Total Fat 4 g; Saturated Fat 1 g; Protein 4 g; Carbohydrates 12 g; Fiber 4 g; Sodium 273 mg; Cholesterol 0 mg

prep time-30 minutes • cooking time-20 minutes

Deep-fried Vegetables

When deep-frying is done correctly, very little fat remains on the food, which is hot and crispy on the outside and soft and savory within.

GARLIC POTATO CHIPS

Slice peeled potatoes into rounds 1/8-inch thick. Before you fry the potatoes, **melt** 2 tablespoons butter with 1 tablespoon olive oil in a very small pan over low heat. **Add** 3 minced cloves garlic and let steep off the heat while you fry the chips. **Deep-fry** chips in batches in 375°F oil until crisp and golden—3 to 5 minutes. **Drain** on paper toweling. **Strain** garlic from butter mixture, then **drizzle** over chips. Makes 4 servings.

SWEET POTATO CHIPS

Peel and slice 1 pound firm sweet potatoes 1/8-inch thick. **Deep-fry** as directed for Garlic Potato Chips. Note: **Choose** a dry sunny day for making sweet potato chips; in rainy or humid weather, they will go limp. Makes 4 servings.

FRESH VEGETABLES

FRYING BASICS

Almost any vegetable can be deep-fried. The only requirement is that it be cut thin enough to cook through by the time the outside browns.

The quality and temperature of the oil and careful timing are the keys to successful frying. You'll need a deep-fat thermometer to determine the temperature of the oil or an electric deep fryer with thermostat heat control.

PERFECT FRIES

If the oil isn't hot enough to seal the surface of vegetables instantly, the oil will be absorbed and you'll have greasy vegetables. The cooking oil must reach a temperature of 375°F before the sliced vegetables are added, and the temperature must be maintained during frying.

One of the best ways to keep the temperature of the oil constant is to add food gradually. The temperature should not drop below 360°F while the food is being added. Tip: Use a pan that is deeper than it is wide. Less heat escapes from the surface so it holds the temperature better.

Scoop vegetables out of the oil the instant their surfaces are crisp and golden brown. A deep-fry basket with a long handle makes lifting easy. Otherwise, use a large skimmer.

BROWNING NOTES

If the oil is too hot, vegetables will brown on the outside before they have chance to cook on the inside.

The oil temperature should not rise above 390°F. At much over 400°F, oils reach their smoking points and begin to break down, ruining the flavor.

TIPS FOR DRAINING FRIED FOODS

Fried vegetables must be properly drained on paper toweling as soon as they are removed from the hot oil.

To avoid wasting paper toweling, place 1 or 2 sheets on top of several layers of newspaper, replacing the toweling when necessary.

CHOOSING AND CARING FOR OIL

Vegetable oil and shortening are both suitable for deep-frying. They can be used for more than one deep-frying session, but the smoking temperature becomes lower with each round. When the fat smokes at 390°F or below, it should be discarded.

Oil that will be reused should be strained through a sieve or a colander that has been lined with a double thickness of cheesecloth. This removes bits of debris that will burn the next time the oil is heated.

THE BEST POTATOES FOR DEEP-FRYING

Baking potatoes such as Idahos or Burbanks are the best for deep-frying because their starchy texture does not readily absorb oil. Choose potatoes that are about 4 inches long for french fries.

POTATO PREP

For french fries or potato chips, peel the potatoes and cut them into the desired lengths or rounds. As they're cut, drop the slices into a bowl of ice water. The water removes surface starch, thus keeping them from sticking together as they fry. Ice water also prevents potatoes from darkening. Just before you're ready to fry them, lift the slices from the water. Pat them completely dry on paper toweling so they won't spatter when they hit the fat.

BATTER-FRYING

Vegetables that cook quickly—zucchini and onion rings, for example—can be batter-fried in a flour-and-water batter. Parboil harder vegetables—such as carrots—to make them suitable for batter-frying.

To make sure that batter sticks properly, vegetables must first be dredged in flour. Shake off the excess, then dip them into the batter, letting the excess drain off before the cut vegetables are added to the fryer.

FOR FRENCH FRIES AND POTATO CHIPS

1 Cut potatoes into ½-inch strips for fries or ¼-inch strips for shoestring potatoes. Or use a slicing blade to cut thin rounds for potato chips. Place in ice water.

2 Heat oil to 375°F in a deep kettle or an electric deep-fryer. Put a single layer of potato strips in the fryer basket and submerge in the hot oil.

3 When potatoes are crisp and golden, lift them out of the oil. Drain and immediately pat dry on paper toweling placed on several thicknesses of newspaper.

BATTER-FRIED ZUCCHINI STRIPS

Prepare as directed at right, **substituting** 1 pound 2" x ¼" x ¼" strips firm, bright green zucchini for potatoes. **Prepare** a batter by whisking together ½ cup each all-purpose flour and cold water or stale beer. **Dredge** zucchini strips in flour, **shaking** off excess, then **toss** in the batter, **separating** any strips that cling together. **Deep-fry** and **drain** as directed. Instead of salting zucchini, **sprinkle** with balsamic vinegar. Note: Vidalia onion rings may be batter fried exactly the same way. Makes 4 servings.

Shoestring Potatoes

Vegetable oil for deep-fat frying (about 2 quarts)
1 pound Idaho potatoes, peeled and cut into 2" x ¼" x ¼" strips
½ teaspoon salt

1 Pour oil into a deep-fat fryer or large saucepan to a depth of 3 inches. Insert a deep-fat thermometer and heat oil to 375°F. Add potatoes in batches, frying each until golden brown and crisp—about 5 minutes. Let oil return to 375°F before adding each new batch of potatoes.

2 With a slotted spoon or skimmer, transfer to paper toweling to drain. Sprinkle potatoes with salt and serve. Makes 4 servings.

**1 Serving: Calories 130; Total Fat 6 g;
Saturated Fat 1 g; Protein 2 g; Carbohydrates 18 g;
Fiber 1 g; Sodium 271 mg;
Cholesterol 0 mg**

prep time-8 minutes
cooking time-15 minutes

VEGETABLE GRATINS

A gratin makes it easy to put food on the table in no time at all. Many of the ingredients are already cooked when the dish is assembled.

WHAT'S IN A NAME?

In France, a gratin is the friction patch on the side of a box of matches. The same word is used to name a style of casserole, referring to the crusty surface that forms on the sides and top as it bakes.

PICK A TOPPING

A gratin can be prepared many ways. It might or might not be topped with grated cheese or buttered bread crumbs. The vegetables can be ensconced in a custardy base like a crustless quiche (such as our Gratin of Green Beans) or embedded in a seasoned white sauce. Or they can be baked without a sauce as in our Gratin of Mushrooms. The various toppings and sauces are what form the crusty gratin surface.

PRECOOKING NOTES

Precooking vegetables for a gratin accentuates and preserves flavors, textures, and colors. It also ensures that baking time for the assembled dish will be brief.

For eggplant, sweet peppers, and summer squash, a preliminary browning in a hot broiler does double duty: It evaporates excess moisture, guaranteeing that the finished gratin won't be watery, and by caramelizing the cut surfaces, it also enriches the flavor.

PRIME CANDIDATES

Apply the techniques used in our gratins of mushrooms and green beans to other vegetables. Be sure to choose vegetables that are firm enough not to lose their shape when shredded or thinly sliced; also those that won't exude a lot of excess water. Prime candidates include: artichoke hearts, asparagus, broccoli, carrots, cauliflower, celery and celery root, endive, parsnips, potatoes, rutabagas, summer squash, and turnips. Leftover meat, fish, and poultry can quickly and easily be recycled in gratins, with or without vegetables.

WHAT'S ON TOP?

Gratin toppings should be long on crunch and flavor. Sprinkle them with buttered bread crumbs or use finely chopped nuts for a change of pace. Parmesan, Cheddar, and Gruyère cheese all melt well and brown even better.

MUSHROOM BASICS

Mushrooms are among the most popular vegetables for gratins. When you buy them, make sure they are firm and blemish free with no sign of slipperiness or shriveling.

It's best to store mushrooms just as they are when purchased, with a little soil still clinging to the stems. Simply wrap them loosely in paper toweling and refrigerate in an aerated plastic bag for no more than 3 or 4 days. Leave packaged mushrooms in their tray, but discard the plastic wrap and cover with paper toweling instead.

Most mushrooms need nothing more than a quick wipe with damp paper toweling. If they need washing, rinse briefly under cool water and pat dry on paper toweling. You'll rinse away flavor if you soak mushrooms.

HOW MANY TO BUY?

Mushroom yields vary depending on the variety and whether or not the stem is used. When mushrooms are served as a vegetable, figure on 1/2 to 3/4 pound per person if both caps and stems are eaten and 1 pound if only the caps are used. Since they are about 90 percent water, fresh mushrooms may shrink as much as 40 percent during cooking. As a rule of thumb, 1 pound of chopped or sliced raw mushrooms equals 5 to 6 cups loosely packed.

WORK SAVER

Gratin Dishes

Any shallow glass, ceramic, or enameled baking dish will do for baking a gratin. But for an authentic country French look, a brown-glazed earthenware *tian* or gratin dish is just the thing. These handsome baking dishes are usually oval or round and come in a variety of sizes. They conduct heat more slowly than metal, which allows the flavors of vegetables, sauces, and cheese to blend. And of course they can be used for baking any kind of casserole, gratin or otherwise.

Gratin of Mushrooms

4 tablespoons butter or margarine
1 medium-size white onion, diced
3 cloves garlic, minced
2 large shallots, chopped
1 pound cultivated mushrooms, trimmed and thinly sliced
8 ounces portobello or other fresh wild mushrooms, trimmed and thinly sliced
1 teaspoon salt
1/4 teaspoon black pepper
1/2 cup fine dry bread crumbs
1/4 cup grated Parmesan cheese
1/4 cup chopped parsley

1 Preheat the oven to 400°F. In a 10-inch skillet over low heat, melt 1 tablespoon of the butter. Add onion, 2 teaspoons of the garlic, and shallots and sauté until lightly browned—about 5 minutes. Remove to a small bowl and set aside.

2 Sauté mushrooms in 2 tablespoons of the butter, in 2 batches if necessary, until juices cook out and evaporate—about 5 minutes. Add salt, pepper, and reserved onion mixture and spoon into an ungreased 10-inch oval gratin dish or a 10" x 6" baking dish.

3 Melt the remaining 1 tablespoon butter in a small skillet. Add to bread crumbs along with Parmesan, the remaining 1 teaspoon garlic, and parsley and toss well to mix.

4 Scatter bread crumb mixture evenly over mushrooms and bake, uncovered, for 30 minutes. Makes 4 servings.

1 Serving: Calories 165; Total Fat 10 g; Saturated Fat 6 g; Protein 6 g; Carbohydrates 16 g; Fiber 2 g; Sodium 567 mg; Cholesterol 23 mg

prep time-40 minutes • cooking time-30 minutes

GRATIN OF GREEN BEANS

Prepare as directed above, **substituting** for the mushrooms 1 pound trimmed, frenched green beans that have been blanched for 1 minute in boiling salted water. **Omit** garlic, onion, and shallots. **Whisk** together 1 cup heavy cream, 1 egg, 1/4 teaspoon salt, and 1/8 teaspoon pepper and pour over beans. **Prepare** bread crumb mixture as directed in Step 4, **substituting** grated Gruyère cheese for Parmesan and **omitting** garlic. **Top** beans with crumb mixture and bake, uncovered, until lightly browned—30 to 40 minutes. Makes 4 servings.

SCALLOPED VEGETABLES

Vegetables baked in a creamy sauce with a topping of crumbs are a perfect accompaniment to roasted meats. Our tips will keep your sauces curdle free.

SCALLOPING NOTES

Vegetables can be scalloped in various kinds of sauces or broths but most often it's a milk, cream, or white sauce that is used.

Essentially, scalloping is the baked version of creamed vegetables. Instead of mixing cream or white sauce (see page 364) with sliced vegetables and heating the mix in a saucepan, the vegetables are layered in a casserole, covered with sauce, topped with bread or cracker crumbs, and heated through in the oven.

TOP CHOICES

The best vegetables for scalloping are those that retain their shape and texture when they're sliced, chopped, or shredded, and baked. Potatoes, cabbage, carrots, turnips, parsnips, cauliflower, corn, and whole small onions all scallop well.

Potatoes tend to be everyone's favorite. Choose waxy, all-purpose potatoes rather than

starchy bakers, which will fall apart during cooking.

Flavor scalloped potatoes with onions, peppers, or pimiento, as in our recipe, or layer and bake the potatoes along with slices of ham for a one-dish meal.

Paired with a green salad and crusty bread, scalloped corn also makes a terrific supper dish. Try serving this dish with roast turkey—it makes a delicious accompaniment.

NO CURDLING

To avoid problems with curdled milk when baking scalloped vegetables, check the following: The oven temperature should be no higher than 375°F to 400°F, and the vegetables shouldn't bake too long. We parboil the potatoes in our recipe so that they need no more than 30 to 35 minutes in the oven.

Make sure there is no excess moisture on the potato slices when you layer them into the baking dish. Pat them dry with paper toweling if necessary. If you're using acidic ingredients such as onion, parsley, and pimiento in the dish, follow our steps for binding the sliced potatoes with a flour-thickened sauce instead of merely covering them with milk or cream.

A TOUCH OF GARLIC

When just a hint of flavor is needed, rub the inside of the baking dish with a cut clove of garlic. Allow enough time for the garlic juice to dry before buttering the dish.

COOKING AHEAD

Scalloped vegetables can be prepared up to the point of sprinkling the dish with bread crumbs hours before serving. Allow the sauce to cool. Then to prevent a skin from forming on the sauce, cover the dish with plastic wrap, pressing it directly onto the surface, and refrigerate.

One half hour before baking, transfer the dish from the refrigerator to the kitchen counter and let stand. Remove the plastic wrap, sprinkle with crumbs, and bake as directed.

Scalloped corn can be baked a day ahead, refrigerated, and reheated for about 20 minutes in a 350°F oven. Scalloped potatoes and cauliflower do not reheat very well.

SCALLOPED CAULIFLOWER WITH ONIONS

Prepare as directed at right, **substituting** 4 1/2 cups moderately thinly sliced cauliflower florets for potatoes (you'll need about 1 1/2 pounds cauliflower). **Boil** cauliflower with onions as directed in Step 2, but **decrease** salt to 1 teaspoon; **drain** well. **Prepare** sauce as directed in Step 3, then **stir in** 1/2 cup grated Parmesan. **Proceed** as directed, **omitting** pimientos in Step 4. Makes 4 to 6 servings.

CORN PUDDING

Prepare as directed at right, **omitting** Step 2. **Make** sauce as directed in Step 3, but **reduce** butter and flour to 1 1/2 tablespoons each and half-and-half and milk to 1/2 cup each. Do not add any flour to half-and-half; also increase salt to 3/4 teaspoon. **Whisk** a little hot sauce into 1 lightly beaten egg, **stir** back into pan, then **mix** in 2 cups drained, cooked or canned corn kernels, one 8 1/2-ounce can cream-style corn, 1 tablespoon prepared yellow mustard, and the 1/4 cup parsley; **omit** pimientos. **Turn** into prepared baking dish, **top** with buttered crumbs, and **bake** as directed. Makes 4 to 6 servings.

Scalloped Potatoes with Pimientos

1 Preheat the oven to 400°F. Lightly butter a 1½-quart shallow baking dish and set aside.

2 In a large heavy saucepan over high heat, bring 1 inch of water to a boil. Add potatoes, onions, and 2 teaspoons of the salt, return to a boil, reduce the heat to moderate, and boil, covered, 5 minutes. Drain and reserve.

3 In a medium-size saucepan, blend 3 tablespoons of the butter with flour, the remaining ½ teaspoon salt, and pepper. Set over moderate heat, and, when bubbly, gradually whisk in half-and-half mixture, then milk, and cook, whisking constantly, until thickened and smooth—5 to 8 minutes.

4 Layer ⅓ of the potato mixture into the prepared baking dish, sprinkle with ½ the pimientos and parsley, and top with ⅓ of the sauce. Repeat layers, then top with remaining potato mixture and sauce.

5 In a small bowl, toss crumbs well with remaining butter and scatter evenly on top of casserole.

6 Bake, uncovered, until browned and bubbling—30 to 35 minutes. Makes 6 servings.

1 Serving: Calories 306;
Total Fat 17 g; Saturated Fat 10 g;
Protein 7 g; Carbohydrates 34 g;
Fiber 3 g; Sodium 778 mg;
Cholesterol 48 mg

prep time-30 minutes
cooking time-about 1 hour

1½ **pounds all-purpose potatoes, peeled and thinly sliced**
2 **large yellow onions, thinly sliced**
2½ **teaspoons salt**
⅓ **cup melted butter or margarine**
2 **tablespoons flour**
¼ **teaspoon black pepper**

1 **cup half-and-half blended with 1 tablespoon flour**
1 **cup milk**
1 **jar (4 ounces) pimientos, drained, chopped, and patted dry on paper toweling**
¼ **cup chopped parsley**
½ **cup dry bread or cracker crumbs**

VEGETABLE TARTS

Crisp-crusted vegetable tarts are perfect for lunch or a hot first course, and they're as easy as pie to make.

TARTS ANYTIME

Tarts are not just for dessert. Baked with vegetables and cheese, these savory pies are impressive to look at but simple to prepare, and they're delicious anytime.

There are many ways to make a tart. Depending on the type of dough you use and how you shape it, a tart can resemble anything from an eggless quiche to a vegetable pizza.

THE LOWER CRUST

For our Tomato-Onion-Parmesan Tart, we've used plain pie crust dough, which is among the easiest doughs to make. Once the dough has rested, it simply needs to be rolled evenly into a circle and sprinkled with the cheese and vegetable toppings. If you prefer, you can crimp or flute the dough around the edge.

For a butterless crust, make tarts with a plain bread dough, as we do for our pizzas on page 354.

Another traditional crust for both savory and dessert tarts is puff pastry. It can either be rolled into a large rectangle or shaped into pretty pies, as shown at right. See page 28 for complete details on how to buy and work with frozen puff pastry.

TOP THIS

The best known tart of all is the classic onion tart. Its puff pastry or bread dough base is sprinkled with grated Parmesan cheese, smothered with sliced sautéed onions, and then topped with anchovies and chopped black olives. Ingredients can either be scattered or artfully arranged on top of the dough.

As alternative toppings, try Parmesan, mozzarella, Gruyère, or soft white goat cheese with any or several of the following: crushed garlic, chopped basil, parboiled broccoli florets or asparagus tips, sliced oil-packed dried tomatoes, roasted sweet red peppers, roasted zucchini slices.

FOR A CRISP CRUST

When tarts come out of the oven, the bottom of the crust

GORGONZOLA-ARUGULA TART

Prepare as directed at right, **substituting** 2 cups arugula for basil, 3 ounces crumbled Gorgonzola for grated Parmesan, and 1/2 cup thinly sliced roasted red peppers (see page 26) for cherry tomatoes. **Omit** the onion. Makes 6 servings.

HOW TO MAKE A TART

To make a flat-crusted tart with pie dough:

1 Place dough on a lightly floured work surface and roll out into a 10-inch circle. Place on a baking sheet. Prick dough all over with a fork, leaving a 1-inch margin around edge.

2 Set baking sheet and dough in the freezer for about 20 minutes. Remove and top dough with your choice of cheese and vegetables. Bake at 500°F for 20 to 25 minutes.

To make a formed tart with puff pastry dough:

1 Roll frozen puff pastry dough to 1/8 inch. Cut a 9-inch circle and place on baking sheet. Cut leaves and attach around edge using a mixture of 1 egg yolk and 2 tablespoons water as glue.

2 Brush leaves with egg mix. Prick dough and pre-bake at 400°F about 10 minutes to seal. Top with cheese and vegetables, cover leaf edge loosely with foil, and bake 10 to 15 minutes more.

should be crisp and brown. Be sure the oven is thoroughly preheated—about 20 minutes—when the tart goes in. Place it in the center of the middle rack. Using a light coating of vegetable spray on the baking sheet will prevent the tart from sticking and make it easier to serve.

Tomato-Onion-Parmesan Tart

Crust:
- 1 cup unsifted all-purpose flour
- 1/8 teaspoon salt
- 1/2 cup (1 stick) cold butter, cut up
- 1/4 cup ice water

Topping:
- 1 tablespoon olive oil
- 1 small red onion, cut into 1/4-inch slices
- 1 cup thinly sliced fresh basil
- 1/2 cup grated Parmesan cheese
- 3/4 cup halved yellow cherry tomatoes
- 3/4 cup halved red cherry tomatoes

1 For the Crust: Pulse flour, salt, and butter in a food processor until mixture resembles coarse meal. Add water slowly through the feed tube and pulse just until dough holds together. Remove and shape into a ball. Flatten the ball slightly, wrap in plastic wrap, and refrigerate 1 hour.

2 Preheat the oven to 500°F. Remove dough from refrigerator and place on a lightly floured work surface. Using a floured rolling pin, roll dough into a 10-inch circle and ease onto a baking sheet. Set in freezer for 20 minutes (this relaxes the dough and helps keep it from shrinking as it bakes).

3 For the Topping: Drizzle oil over dough circle leaving 1/2-inch margins all around. Distribute onion evenly on top, then sliced basil, and sprinkle with 1/2 the Parmesan. Arrange yellow and red tomatoes on top and sprinkle with remaining Parmesan.

4 Bake until bubbling and lightly browned—about 25 minutes. Makes 6 servings.

1 Serving: Calories 220; Total Fat 13 g; Saturated Fat 7 g; Protein 7 g; Carbohydrates 20 g; Fiber 2 g; Sodium 284 mg; Cholesterol 27 mg

prep time-20 minutes
resting time-1 hour 20 minutes
cooking time-30 minutes

Our Tomato-Onion-Parmesan Tart appears in the foreground. In the background, a Gorgonzola-Arugula Tart with a puff pastry crust.

CASSEROLES

Making casseroles of layered vegetables is easy. It's a particularly handy style of cooking in summer when fresh eggplants and tomatoes are plentiful.

CASEROLE NOTES

Most vegetables can easily be browned or partially cooked, sliced, and layered in an oiled casserole along with sauce, and perhaps some meat, herbs, and a topping of white sauce, grated cheese, or buttered bread crumbs. The possibilities are endless.

Moussaka, for example, is best known as an eggplant dish, but in Greece, where the dish originated, the ingredients sometimes vary. It can be made with sliced and browned zucchini, cucumbers, or potatoes or sliced boiled artichoke hearts. The sauce can be meatless, and the topping can be mixed up from beaten eggs and yogurt or left off altogether in favor of a simple gratinlike sprinkling of grated cheese or buttered bread crumbs. Mix and match the parts anyway you like.

HOW TO PICK AN EGGPLANT

For our recipes, at right and on page 160, we've chosen the deep purple Western eggplant, which is the most familiar variety in this country—as well as the least expensive.

Choose eggplants that are heavy for their size. The skin should be smooth and glossy with no shriveling or bruising. The skin can be left on for most recipes.

Purple Western eggplants usually weigh between 1 and 5 pounds. If there's a choice, select smaller size eggplants; they have smoother flesh, more tender skin, and smaller, less bitter seeds than large ones. Refrigerate for no more than 3 or 4 days.

EGGPLANT PREP

Eggplant soaks up oil like a sponge. It also contains excess water and may be slightly bitter.

New strains of eggplant have been developed that are far less bitter than in the past. They can be sliced and used as is if desired. Otherwise, get rid of bitterness and excess water by the following method.

Slice the eggplant and sprinkle both sides of each slice lightly with salt. Lay the slices between several layers of paper toweling and top with a baking sheet weighted down with several plates or cans of food for about 30 minutes. Compressing the slices this

PICK OF THE CROP

Eggplant is low in calories and fat free. Its mild flavor allows it to blend well with other ingredients. It's grown throughout the world in many varieties. The four below can be found in supermarkets and green markets.

1. White Mediterranean eggplants have firmer flesh and tougher skins than Western eggplants. They should be peeled before use in most recipes. **2.** Japanese eggplants are long and slender. They are milder than Western eggplants and have sweeter flesh and more tender skins. **3.** Deep purple, pear-shaped Western eggplants are the most familiar to North American cooks. They are perfect for use in casseroles like Moussaka. **4.** Baby eggplants are available in both purple and white varieties. They're sweet and tender and are good choices for stuffing and pickling.

way helps to make them less porous. Wipe the slices free of salt when done.

Note: The same technique can be used to remove excess moisture from zucchini before using it in a casserole. Or use it to remove the bitterness from cucumbers that have grown too large.

If you are making ratatouille or a spaghetti sauce that calls for chopped eggplant, cut it in a dice, then toss it with salt. Arrange the chopped eggplant

between layers of paper toweling and weight it as above.

GOOD LOOKS

When cooking eggplant, be sure the baking pan or saucepan you use is not aluminum. Eggplant flesh will discolor in an aluminum pan.

BROWNING TIPS

Eggplant slices can be browned in the broiler as

(continued on page 160)

Moussaka

- **1** can (28 ounces) peeled, reduced-sodium whole tomatoes, drained and coarsely chopped
- **1** large yellow onion, finely chopped
- **2** cloves garlic, minced
- **1/2** teaspoon dried thyme, crumbled
- **1/2** teaspoon dried oregano, crumbled
- **1 1/2** teaspoons salt
- **1/2** teaspoon black pepper
- **1** pound ground lean lamb shoulder
- **1/2** teaspoon ground cinnamon
- **1** large eggplant, cut into 1/2-inch rounds
- **6** tablespoons olive oil
- **2** tablespoons unsalted butter
- **2** tablespoons flour
- **1** cup milk
- **1** egg, lightly beaten

1 In a 5-quart saucepan over moderately high heat, bring tomatoes, onion, garlic, thyme, oregano, 1 teaspoon of the salt, and pepper to a boil. Reduce the heat to moderately low and simmer, uncovered, stirring occasionally, for 20 minutes.

2 Meanwhile, in a large skillet over moderate heat, sauté lamb in its own fat until brown—about 20 minutes. Stir lamb into tomato sauce, add cinnamon, and set aside.

3 Preheat the broiler. Brush both sides of eggplant generously with oil, place on baking sheet in a single layer, and broil about 4 inches from the heat, in batches if necessary, for 5 minutes on each side. Set aside.

4 Preheat the oven to 350°F. Arrange 1 layer of eggplant in an ungreased 8" x 8" x 2" baking dish and top with 1 1/4 cups meat sauce. Repeat layers twice.

5 In a medium-size saucepan over moderate heat, melt butter. Blend in flour and remaining 1/2 teaspoon salt. Gradually whisk in milk to make a white sauce and cook, whisking constantly, until thickened—3 to 5 minutes. Whisk 2 tablespoons white sauce into egg, stir back into pan, and whisk until smooth.

6 Pour white sauce over moussaka and bake, uncovered, until bubbling and lightly browned—about 40 minutes. Let stand 10 minutes before serving. Makes 4 servings.

1 Serving: Calories 619; Total Fat 43 g; Saturated Fat 11 g; Protein 28 g; Carbohydrates 34 g; Fiber 9 g; Sodium 941 mg; Cholesterol 136 mg

prep time-45 minutes
cooking time-45 minutes

How to Salt and Drain Eggplant

1 At least ½ hour before cooking, cut eggplant into ½-inch slices. Sprinkle lightly with salt on either side.

2 Arrange slices between several layers of paper toweling, then weight with a baking sheet or plates.

How to Broil Eggplant Slices

Brush or spray slices with oil and place on broiler pan or baking sheet. Broil about 4 inches away from heat until brown, then turn and brown flip side.

(continued from page 158)

described in our recipe or browned in the oven or skillet.

To brown in the oven, preheat the oven to 400°F. Pour just enough olive oil into a jelly-roll pan to lightly coat the bottom. Place the pan in the oven to heat the oil. When hot, add the slices in one layer and bake, turning once, to brown lightly on both sides.

You can brown eggplant in a skillet without a lot of fat. Lightly spray nonstick vegetable spray on both sides of each slice. Heat a heavy skillet until very hot. Brown the slices on both sides.

To keep slices from cooling while the next batch browns, arrange on a baking sheet lined with paper toweling and place in a 250°F oven.

SLICE OF LIFE

When flavored with a little garlic, or topped with grated Parmesan cheese, browned eggplant slices can be used by themselves as a vegetable, layered into sandwiches with tomatoes and mozzarella, or used as a topper for burgers.

HEALTHY CHOICES

You can make Moussaka much leaner by substituting ground turkey for lamb, using olive oil-flavored vegetable spray instead of oil for browning, and substituting low-fat milk for

whole. For Eggplant Parmesan, use low-fat mozzarella instead of regular.

COOKING AHEAD

Both Moussaka and Eggplant Parmesan are good party dishes and can be assembled a day ahead. Cover tightly and refrigerate. Let the casserole stand at room temperature about 30 minutes before baking. Also, if needed, increase the baking time slightly.

EGGPLANT HARVEST

If you've got a bumper crop of eggplants, there are many ways to use them. Add them diced to a chunky-style pasta sauce. Or broil slices until brown, cut them into strips, and toss with pasta, then top with fresh tomato sauce.

For a delicious garlicky eggplant dip, trim the stem from an eggplant and slice it in half lengthwise. Score the flesh, salt, and set aside to sweat for ½ hour. Then wipe off excess salt, spray the flesh with vegetable oil, and roast, flesh side up, on a baking sheet in a 400°F oven for 30 minutes. Add 3 garlic cloves in their skins to the baking sheet and roast for another 15 minutes. When cooled, scrape the eggplant from its skin. Purée the flesh along with peeled garlic

Eggplant Parmesan

Prepare sauce as directed in Step 1 on page 159. **Omit** Step 2. In Step 3, **broil** 2 eggplants as directed but reduce olive oil to 2 tablespoons. **Reduce** the oven temperature to 350°F. **Mix** 1 cup fine soft or dry bread crumbs with 2 tablespoons melted butter, ½ cup grated Parmesan, and 2 tablespoons minced parsley. **Pour** ¼ cup tomato sauce into an ungreased 13" x 9" x 2" baking dish. **Top** with ⅓ of the eggplant, ½ cup of the bread crumb mixture, 1 scant cup sauce, and 1 cup shredded mozzarella. **Repeat** layers twice. **Cover** with foil, shiny side down, and **bake** for ½ hour. **Let stand** 10 minutes before serving. Makes 6 servings.

cloves, 2 tablespoons of lemon juice, 3 tablespoons of olive oil, 2 tablespoons of sesame paste (tahini), ¼ cup of parsley, and a little salt and freshly ground black pepper. Chill, covered, for 1 hour before serving.

KITCHEN CHEMISTRY

The calorie count of a cup of eggplant can go from about 25 to 700 in only a minute when it's deep-fried. Why does it absorb so much oil? Eggplant's large cells are full of air. When the vegetable is sliced and exposed to heat, air rushes out of the cells, allowing cooking oil to fill the void. By the time an eggplant dish has cooked and begun to cool, the cells collapse again, leaving a pool of oil. Better to broil or otherwise cook eggplant using a vegetable spray or just a thin brushing of olive oil.

SALADS AND DRESSINGS

FRUIT SALADS

A harmonious blend of fruits makes a pleasing salad presentation. Follow our hints for cutting fruit and keeping it from discoloring.

PEAK PICKS

Choose fruit at the peak of readiness and in prime condition. Be careful not to use too many different types of fruit in a salad or the individual flavors and textures will be lost on the palate.

Wait until just before serving to wash and trim fruit. Most need no more than a brief rinse in cool water. For best flavor, bring fruit to room temperature before eating.

TO PREVENT DARKENING

Prevent crisp fruits such as apples and pears from darkening after they are peeled by giving them a quick dip or toss with acidulated water. Mix 1/2 cup of white wine, 3 tablespoons of lemon juice, or 2 tablespoons of vinegar to 1 quart of water.

Soft fruits, including apricots, bananas, peaches, and nectarines, also discolor. Brush or toss them with lemon or lime juice mixed with a little sugar.

FRUIT AFFINITIES

Cheese: The general rule is delicate cheese with delicate fruit and more flavorful cheese with flavorful fruit. For example, Camembert with grapes, Cheddar with apples.

Vanilla extract: A few drops enhance the natural sweetness of most fruits, meaning you can use less sugar.

Herbs: Mint is good, but try basil with strawberries, coriander (cilantro) with peaches, apricots, and citrus fruits, and rosemary with citrus fruits.

Cream and yogurt: Plain or whipped cream, sour cream, and yogurt are delicious with berries and stone fruits.

Liqueurs: A few drops of fruit liqueurs perk up the flavors of berries and citrus fruits.

TOOLS OF THE TRADE

For cutting and peeling small fruits, use a 3-inch paring knife. Vegetable parers do a good job of peeling apples, pears, and other hard fruits.

KITCHEN MATH

1 lemon = 2 to 4 tablespoons of juice

1 lime = about 2 tablespoons of juice

1 medium-size orange = 1/3 to 1/2 cup of juice

HOW TO TACKLE A TROPICAL FRUIT

It's easy to peel a peach or nectarine by dropping it into boiling water for a few seconds, just as you do when peeling a tomato (see page 94). To prepare other fruits, try the following:

Kiwi: Slice 1/4 inch off one end. Run a spoon around opening. Gently peel skin away from flesh.

Star Fruit: Trim away top edge of star ridges and slice fruit crosswise.

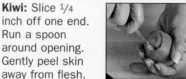

Mango: Cut thick slice from either side of pit. Score flesh into cubes or slice and remove from skin.

Papaya: Peel with a vegetable parer or knife. Cut in half lengthwise. Scoop out seeds and cube or use flesh as desired.

Melon: Cut melon into wedges. Use a boning knife or vegetable parer to cut flesh from rind. Or cut flesh into shapes while attached to rind.

Pineapple: Using a very sharp knife, cut pineapple skin under the eyes in a spiral fashion. Peel off skin. Cut fruit crosswise into rounds or slice flesh downward around the core.

Berries in Low-Fat Snow

Prepare as directed at right, **substituting** 2/3 cup reduced-fat sour cream for sour cream, 1/4 cup low-fat vanilla-flavored yogurt for heavy cream, and 1 tablespoon apricot nectar and 1/4 teaspoon ground nutmeg for orange-flavored liqueur.

Tropical Fruits and Sesame Cream

Whisk together 1 tablespoon toasted sesame seeds, 1/2 cup sour cream, 1/4 cup orange juice, 2 tablespoons white wine vinegar, 5 teaspoons dark sesame oil, 2 tablespoons honey, and 1/2 teaspoon grated orange zest. **Serve** over wedges of cantaloupe or honeydew melon, sliced kiwi, pineapple, mango, and papaya or any fruit combination. Makes 3/4 to 1 cup dressing, enough to dress 4 servings.

Stone Fruits with Spicy Vinaigrette

Whisk together 3 tablespoons balsamic vinegar, 3 tablespoons sherry wine vinegar, 2 tablespoons walnut oil, 1/2 teaspoon black pepper, and 1/2 teaspoon sugar. **Serve** over sliced nectarines, peaches, and/or plums. Makes 1/2 cup dressing, enough to dress 4 servings.

Bowl of Berries in Snow

- 2/3 **cup sour cream**
- 1/4 **cup heavy cream**
- 3 **tablespoons maple syrup**
- 1 **tablespoon orange-flavored liqueur**
- 2 **teaspoons vanilla extract**
- 1 **cup whole blackberries**
- 1 **cup whole blueberries**
- 1 **cup whole raspberries**
- 2 **cups strawberries, hulled and sliced**

1. In a small bowl, stir together sour cream, heavy cream, maple syrup, liqueur, and vanilla extract; refrigerate, covered, until ready to serve.

2. Just before serving, rinse the berries (except the sliced strawberries) and pat dry on paper toweling.

3. Place in a large bowl, pour dressing over, toss to mix, and serve. Makes 4 servings.

1 Serving: Calories 266; Total Fat 14 g; Saturated Fat 9 g; Protein 3 g; Carbohydrates 32 g; Fiber 5 g; Sodium 31 mg; Cholesterol 38 mg

prep time-15 to 20 minutes

MOLDED SALADS

There is no more dramatic way to serve a salad than molded into a shimmering aspic. It's easy with proper molding and layering.

ASPECTS OF ASPIC

Aspics—savory jellies—begin with gelatin, an animal protein that's packaged in powdered form. When heated in water or other liquids, it forms a sticky solution that gels when chilled. A tablespoon (1 package) of powdered gelatin will set about 2 cups of liquid containing 1¹/₂ cups of fruit or vegetables.

PERFECT LAYERS

If layers of gelatin are not set properly, they may come apart when unmolded. Before a new layer is added, the previous layer should set just until tacky (not firm). The gelatin being added must be cold and slightly thickened so it does not melt the previous layer.

GET READY, GET SET

Most gelatins set firmly after 3 or 4 hours in the refrigerator. To be on the safe side, allow 6 to 8 hours or overnight.

Gelatins that thicken gradually in the refrigerator are sturdier than quick-set gelatins. However, if you need to hasten the gelling process, set the bowl of gelatin in a larger bowl full of ice cubes and stir until the gelatin thickens.

PREPARING THE MOLD

To ensure that unmolding is successful, take a moment to prepare the mold. Rinse the mold with cold water or, better yet, give it a light coating of vegetable oil. Use nonstick vegetable spray, or oil spread with paper toweling.

GELLING PROBLEMS

If you have ever had problems getting a fruit salad to gel, it might have included pineapple, figs, kiwi, or papaya. These fruits contain enzymes that break down gelatin, which is a protein. With the exception of kiwi, the pared, cut-up flesh of these fruits can be boiled for 5 minutes, which will deactivate the enzyme. But you may still need to add 1¹/₂ times the normal amount of powdered gelatin to make the salad set up properly.

HOW TO UNMOLD A SALAD

Before unmolding gelled salads or desserts, be sure they are solidly set, not sticky.

1 Dip a knife in water and run it around the edge of the mold. Moisten the serving platter and the top layer of the gelatin with your fingertips.

2 Dip the mold up to the rim in warm (not hot) water about 10 seconds. Gently shake the mold to loosen. Place platter on top of the mold and invert.

3 Lift the mold to release the gelled salad. Tilt the platter gently to center the salad.

LAYERED TERRINE

Prepare as directed at right through Step 4, **substituting** ¹/₂ cup chopped fresh coriander (cilantro) for basil. **Pour** ¹/₂ the mixture into a large bowl and refrigerate until slightly thickened—45 to 60 minutes. **Fold** in ¹/₂ cup thawed frozen corn kernels and ¹/₄ cup finely chopped sweet green pepper. **Prepare** Steps 5 through 9 as directed. **Pour** remaining tomato mixture into another large bowl and **refrigerate, stirring** occasionally, until slightly thickened—30 to 45 minutes. **Fold** another ¹/₂ cup thawed frozen corn kernels and ¹/₄ cup finely chopped sweet green pepper into the thickened tomato mixture, **pour** on top of the cream layer in the loaf pan, and **chill** as directed in Step 10. **Unmold** and **serve**. Makes 8 servings.

RIBBON MOLD VARIATIONS

For the recipe at right:

Tomato Layers: Substitute one of the following combinations for the celery, carrot, and scallion: ¹/₂ cup chopped celery, ¹/₂ cup each chopped sweet orange and yellow pepper. Or ¹/₂ cup chopped scallions, ¹/₂ cup diced avocado, ¹/₂ cup chopped jicama.

Cream Layer: Add any of the following to the cream layer at the end of Step 8: 1 cup peeled, seeded, chopped cucumber, ¹/₄ cup chopped red onion, or ¹/₄ cup finely chopped fresh dill.

Red and White Ribbon Mold

Tomato Layers:

4½ cups tomato or 100 percent vegetable juice or 3½ cups plus 1 cup Vegetable Broth

1 stalk celery, thinly sliced

1 carrot, peeled and thinly sliced

1 scallion, chopped

½ cup chopped fresh basil or 3 tablespoons dried basil, crumbled

½ teaspoon whole black peppercorns

2 envelopes unflavored gelatin

2 tablespoons balsamic vinegar

½ to ¾ teaspoon hot red pepper sauce

Cream Layer:

½ cup Vegetable Broth

1 envelope unflavored gelatin

½ cup milk

2 cloves garlic, minced

1 package (8 ounces) cream cheese or 1 cup sour cream

¼ teaspoon hot red pepper sauce

1 For the Tomato Layers: In a medium-size saucepan over high heat, bring 2¼ cups of the tomato juice, celery, carrot, scallion, basil, and peppercorns to a boil; reduce the heat to low and simmer, covered, 8 to 10 minutes.

2 Meanwhile, pour remaining 2¼ cups tomato juice into a large bowl, sprinkle with gelatin, and let stand 1 to 2 minutes to soften.

3 Place a sieve lined with a double thickness of cheesecloth over the bowl of softened gelatin. Pour in hot juice mixture, pressing out as much juice as possible.

4 Stir mixture frequently until gelatin dissolves—3 to 5 minutes. Stir in vinegar and red pepper sauce.

5 Pour ½ the gelatin mixture into an ungreased 9" x 5" x 3" loaf pan or individual molds and set in the refrigerator, uncovered, until mixture is firm but not set—45 to 60 minutes.

6 Meanwhile, for the Cream Layer: Pour Vegetable Broth into a saucepan and sprinkle in gelatin. Let stand 2 minutes to soften.

7 Add milk and garlic, set over low heat, and stir often until gelatin dissolves—3 to 5 minutes.

8 Place cream cheese and red pepper sauce in a blender and pour in gelatin mixture through a fine sieve. Blend at high speed until smooth—about 30 seconds. Pour mixture into a large bowl and refrigerate, uncovered, stirring occasionally, until slightly thickened—20 to 30 minutes.

9 Slowly pour thickened cream mixture over the chilled tomato mixture in the loaf pan and refrigerate, uncovered, until firm but not set—30 to 40 minutes.

10 When cream mixture is firm but still tacky, slowly pour remaining tomato mixture on top and refrigerate, uncovered, until fully set—at least 3 to 4 hours. Unmold as described in box at left. Makes 8 servings.

1 Serving: Calories 151; Total Fat 11 g; Saturated Fat 7 g; Protein 6 g; Carbohydrates 9 g; Fiber 1 g; Sodium 619 mg; Cholesterol 33 mg

prep time-30 minutes
cooking time-15 minutes
chilling time-5½ hours

TOSSED SALADS

The healthiest salads begin with the best greens. Our chart tells you how to make your salads healthier than ever.

PICKING LETTUCE

It's easy to find lettuce in colors from bright green to red and in textures that range from butter soft to crunchy. Use a mixture of fresh young leaves for the most attractive salads.

WASH, DRY, AND CRISP

Most greens are best refrigerated in the crisper, then washed and dried just before using. However, if you like to have salad greens washed and ready when you need them, try the following:

Trim away the roots and undesirable leaves. Place the lettuce in a large bowl and rinse with plenty of cold water. Lift the greens from the water so that any bits of grit are left in the bowl and transfer them to a colander. Shake and turn the greens occasionally until they have stopped dripping.

Wrap loosely in several layers of paper toweling or a cotton kitchen towel. Place in an aerated plastic bag and store in the crisper.

Don't cut or tear stored lettuce leaves until you're ready to use them. Tearing lettuce causes it to release an enzyme that destroys vitamin C.

ALL BEEFED UP

Most tossed green salads can be turned into main dishes by adding cooked and thinly sliced meat, poultry, seafood, or hard-cooked eggs.

In some cases, you may want to dress the meat and seafood ahead of time so that flavors can mingle. At serving time, arrange the dressed ingredients on individual serving plates of mixed greens.

CAESAR SALAD NOTES

Traditionally, raw egg has been indispensable in a Caesar salad dressing, but today it's risky. Although the incidence of salmonella bacteria in eggs is only about 10 percent of the total egg supply, most cooks prefer not to use raw eggs and risk food poisoning.

In some recipes, hard-cooked egg yolks beaten in oil are used to replace raw eggs. In our version of the salad, commercial mayonnaise is used as the replacement. (Mayonnaise contains eggs but the processing makes it safe.) Bottled Caesar dressings do not contain raw egg.

In any Caesar salad dressing, you can always substitute 1 teaspoon of anchovy paste for 3 anchovy fillets.

GRAND SLAM GREENS

All leafy greens are good for you, but some are better than others. In fact, the more research into nutrition continues, the more important leafy vegetables appear to be.

Arugula, also known as rocket, has a pungent peppery flavor and generally requires a lot of rinsing to get rid of sand. Arugula has more vitamin C than other lettuces and also brims with calcium. Like cabbage, arugula is a crucifer (meaning it has cross-shaped flowers). Cruciferous vegetables contain indoles, which are cancer-fighting compounds.

Beet greens and other dark leafy vegetables, including turnip, dandelion, and mustard greens, can be used in salads when they are young and tender. These vegetables are full of beta-carotene (a precursor of vitamin A) and vitamin C, both of which fight some forms of cancer. Turnip greens are also a fair source of calcium.

Kale has a chewy, ruffled leaf with a light cabbagy flavor. Like other members of the cabbage family, it is a crucifer and a cancer fighter. It is a source of vitamin C as well as beta-carotene, which may help to guard against heart disease and certain forms of cancer.

Parsley is too good to be wasted as an uneaten garnish. It is full of vitamin C and beta-carotene (see beet greens, above). Its spicy bite adds interest to salads and dressings.

Spinach, like arugula (above), often needs a lot of rinsing before use, but it's worth the effort. Spinach is a stellar source of beta-carotene as well as vitamin A, folacin (a B vitamin), and potassium.

Watercress is pungent, peppery, and deserves to be used often as a salad green. Like arugula (see above), it is a crucifer and believed to combat certain forms of cancer. It also provides vitamin C and calcium.

WORK SAVER
Salad Spinner

These handy devices dry greens in a jiffy. The greens are placed in an inner basket. The basket is spun by means of a hand crank or a pull string. The baskets are easily taken apart to drain out the rinse water and to clean. Both crank and string-type spinners work well, but the string types are prone to tangling problems.

Slender Goddess Salad

Prepare as directed at right, but do not brush bread with olive oil; **toast** it, then **rub** with garlic. For the dressing, **substitute** 3 tablespoons plain nonfat yogurt and 1 tablespoon reduced-fat sour cream for olive oil, and 3 tablespoons fat-free mayonnaise for regular. **Reduce** lemon juice to 1 tablespoon. **Add** 2 thinly sliced scallions and 1/2 teaspoon dried tarragon. Makes 4 servings.

Wilted Spinach Salad with Sesame Dressing

Prepare Step 1 as directed at right. In a skillet over moderately low heat, **cook** 3 ounces finely slivered prosciutto until crisp—about 5 minutes; **drain** on paper toweling. **Measure** drippings and **add** dark sesame oil as needed to make 1/4 cup. **Return** drippings to skillet, set over moderately high heat, add 2 tablespoons plus 1 teaspoon red wine vinegar, 2 teaspoons sugar, and 1/2 teaspoon salt, and cook 2 minutes. In a serving bowl, **toss** 10 ounces washed and torn spinach, 8 ounces thinly sliced mushrooms, croutons, and prosciutto. **Pour** hot dressing over all and **toss** well. Makes 4 servings.

Updated Caesar Salad

- **3 cloves garlic, peeled and halved**
- **Four 1/2-inch-thick slices Italian or French bread**
- **5 tablespoons olive oil**
- **3 tablespoons mayonnaise**
- **3 tablespoons lemon juice**
- **6 anchovies, mashed, or 2 teaspoons anchovy paste**
- **1/4 teaspoon salt**
- **1/4 teaspoon black pepper**
- **1 medium-size head romaine lettuce, torn into bite-size pieces**
- **1/4 cup grated Parmesan cheese**

1 Preheat the oven to 400°F. Using 2 cloves of the garlic, rub the slices of bread on both sides. Brush with 2 tablespoons of the oil and cut into 1/2-inch dice. Spread on an ungreased baking sheet and bake, uncovered, tossing occasionally, until golden brown and crisp—about 10 minutes.

2 Meanwhile, rub a large chilled bowl with remaining garlic. Add mayonnaise, lemon juice, anchovies, salt, pepper, and remaining 3 tablespoons oil and whisk until creamy. Add romaine, Parmesan, and croutons and toss until well coated. Divide evenly among 4 chilled plates. Makes 4 servings.

1 Serving: Calories 356; Total Fat 29 g; Saturated Fat 5 g; Protein 8 g; Carbohydrates 18 g; Fiber 2 g; Sodium 586 mg; Cholesterol 15 mg

prep time-15 minutes • cooking time-10 minutes

TANGY CABBAGE SLAWS

S hredded cabbage stands up bravely to piquant warm or cold dressings without giving up a bit of its familiar crunchy texture and lively flavor.

WHAT'S IN A NAME?

In Dutch, *kool sla* (our coleslaw) means cabbage salad. Although a slaw can be made from other vegetables—parsnip slaw is particularly good—cabbage has remained the most popular.

GOOD EATING

Cabbage is nutritionally excellent. A cup of cooked green cabbage contains almost 100 percent of the recommended nutrient intake of vitamin C, and for red cabbage, the amount is 100 percent. It is also a great supplier of fiber, is believed to fight cancer, and helps to boost the immune system.

TRIMMING THE FAT

Cabbage itself has no cholesterol, but the dressings mixed with it usually do. Warm slaws, for instance, are often made with bacon and bacon fat. You can modify standard recipes by substituting Canadian bacon or turkey bacon. Or leave out the meats altogether and make a tangy warm dressing with corn or other vegetable oil instead.

To reduce the fat in chilled mayonnaise-dressed slaws, use a low-fat mayonnaise, a low-fat mayonnaise blended with plain yogurt and a little cider vinegar, or a creamy yogurt dressing. Make it by blending 1/3 cup of plain nonfat yogurt, 2 tablespoons of chopped parsley, 2 tablespoons of olive oil, 1 tablespoon of Dijon mustard, and 2 teaspoons of lime juice.

CRISP AND COOL

For chilled slaws, you'll get the crispest results if you shred the cabbage, then

HOW TO SHRED CARROTS

Use the medium blade on a 4-sided grater. Hold the carrot firmly with the knuckles away from the grater blades.

immerse it in ice water for an hour. Drain it, blot it very dry on kitchen towels, then refrigerate until ready to use.

PICKING CABBAGE

The three popular cabbages—green, red, and crinkly leafed Savoy—can all be used for slaw. They are available year-round, although Savoy can sometimes be hard to find in the dead of winter.

Choose compact heavy heads. Figure on about 1/3 pound per person—1 pound yields about 4 cups of shredded cabbage.

Store cabbage, loosely wrapped in the crisper, for no more than 2 weeks.

SAUERKRAUT TIPS

Our slaw variation is made with cabbage and prepared sauerkraut, which is available two ways. Precooked sauerkraut comes canned or packed in plastic bags. Taste the kraut before using it, and if it is too salty or sour, soak it in cold water for 15 to 30 minutes, then drain well before using.

TO CORE AND SLICE CABBAGE

T o shred cabbage, use the widest blades of a 4-sided grater or the medium (3 mm) slicing disk of a food processor or do the following:

1 With a long chef's knife, cut the cabbage head in half through the stem, then halve again and slice out the core.

2 With the cut side down, slice the quarters crosswise into thin strips, which will separate into shreds. The shreds can be chopped further for a finer cut.

Some specialty stores and delicatessens carry fresh sauerkraut, which has been pickled but not cooked. Drain it and place in a nonreactive saucepan with just enough water or chicken broth to cover. Simmer, covered, until it's tender—30 to 40 minutes.

Sweet and Sour Cabbage and Carrot Slaw

- 8 cups shredded cabbage (about 1 small green cabbage)
- 2 carrots, peeled and grated
- 1 sweet red pepper, cored, seeded, and finely chopped
- 1/3 cup corn oil
- 1 medium-size red onion, finely chopped
- 2 tablespoons dark brown sugar
- 1/3 cup cider vinegar
- 1 tablespoon sweet pickle relish
- 1 teaspoon Dijon mustard
- 1 teaspoon salt
- 1/4 teaspoon black pepper

1 Place cabbage, carrots, and sweet red pepper in a large heatproof serving bowl.

2 In a large skillet over moderately high heat, heat oil 1 minute.

3 Add onion and sauté 2 to 3 minutes. Stir in sugar and sauté 2 minutes more. Stir in vinegar, pickle relish, mustard, salt, and black pepper.

4 Pour hot dressing over cabbage mixture and toss to mix well. Serve at room temperature. Makes 8 servings.

1 Serving: Calories 208; Total Fat 17 g; Saturated Fat 6 g; Protein 6 g; Carbohydrates 10 g; Fiber 2 g; Sodium 573 mg; Cholesterol 20 mg

prep time-45 minutes
cooking time-10 minutes

Hot Cabbage and Sauerkraut Slaw

Prepare as directed in Step 1 above, **using** 2 cups each shredded green and red cabbage and **omitting** carrots and sweet red pepper. **Omit** Steps 2 and 3. In a large skillet over moderate heat, **heat** 2 cups sauerkraut, 1 tablespoon Dijon mustard, 2 cups mayonnaise-type salad dressing, 1/4 cup sugar, 1 tablespoon celery seeds, and 1/4 teaspoon each salt and black pepper, **stirring** frequently, about 10 minutes; do not allow to boil. **Pour** over cabbage and **toss** well to mix. Makes 6 to 8 servings.

POTATO SALADS

Tossing white or sweet potatoes with warm vinegar dressing makes an interesting change from the more familiar mayonnaise-dressed potato salads.

WHAT IS WAXY?

Most potato salads call for waxy boiling potatoes. The term describes white potatoes that have less starch than baking potatoes and, consequently, a firmer texture after cooking. Because waxy potatoes hold their shape, they make a better looking salad. Round red potatoes, new potatoes, and California long whites are ideal for salad.

VINEGAR AS A PRESERVATIVE

A potato salad like ours, made with a vinegar dressing, is a good take-along food since it is egg and mayonnaise free, and the vinegar acts as a preservative. However, no perishable food should be allowed to linger at room temperature for more than 2 hours, and less time in hot weather.

At picnics and cookouts, serve the salad in small quantities, keeping the remainder chilled in a cooler until needed for second—or third—helpings.

HINTS FOR PERFECT POTATO SALAD

Choose potatoes that are about the same size or cut

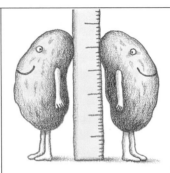

them into same-size chunks so that they cook in the same amount of time.

If you want to slice the potatoes first to save on cooking time, cut them into 1/4-inch slices and drop into cold water to prevent the slices from turning brown. But don't let the slices sit for more than 1/2 hour before cooking.

Sliced potatoes need to simmer for only about 5 minutes: Test with a fork for doneness. Drain the slices, then let stand, covered, in the pan for another 3 mintues before cooling, slightly, and dressing.

If you want potatoes to stay white, don't cut them with a carbon steel knife or cook them in an aluminum or iron pan. Chemicals in potatoes react with those metals and will turn the flesh dark.

To preserve nutrients and

keep the potatoes firm, cook them in their skins, then peel and slice as soon as they are cool enough to handle.
Note: Leave red potatoes unpeeled to heighten the color of the salad.

Dress potatoes while they are still warm. They will absorb the dressing and its flavors much more readily than cooled or cold potatoes.

If the potatoes are cold, warm them in a microwave oven at 50 percent power for 4 to 5 minutes before dressing.

Toss the ingredients gently to keep the potatoes from breaking any more than necessary. Use wooden salad servers or your hands to do the job.

SWEET POTATO TIPS

Boil sweet potatoes with a watchful eye: They fall apart easily when overcooked. Cook them in their skins, if possible. Drop into boiling water, cover, and boil slowly. A whole potato takes 45 to 50 minutes and large chunks about 30 to 35 minutes. They are done the moment the tines of a fork penetrate to the center without much resistance.

MORE MAYONNAISE-FREE POTATO SALADS

Warm potato salad with French dressing: For every 3 pounds of cooked and sliced potatoes, combine 3/4 cup of olive oil, 1/4 cup of tarragon vinegar, 1/2 teaspoon of salt, 1/2 teaspoon of prepared mustard, 1/8 teaspoon of freshly ground black pepper, 3/4 teaspoon of fresh minced thyme or 1/4 teaspoon of crumbled dry thyme.

Shake the ingredients well in a

covered jar or blend them with a whisk. Then pour into a small saucepan and heat over moderate heat until just warmed through. Pour over sliced cooked potatoes. Toss with capers and chopped parsley if desired.

Greek potato salad: For every 3 pounds of cooked and sliced potatoes, combine 3/4 cup of olive oil, 1/3 cup of lemon juice, 1 tablespoon of minced onion, 3 tablespoons of minced parsley, and 3 sliced hard-cooked eggs (optional). Mix with the potatoes while still warm.

KITCHEN CHEMISTRY

Why are new potatoes the best boilers and salad makers? New (or very young) potatoes are harder and contain far more moisture than they do when they are older. Consequently, they don't absorb much cooking water or excessive dressing and don't get as soggy in the salad bowl.

KITCHEN MATH

Figure on 1/2 pound of potatoes for a single serving.

California long whites:
3 to 5 per pound

New potatoes:
6 to 12 per pound

Round red potatoes:
4 to 8 per pound

Sweet potatoes:
1 to 4 per pound

Hot German Potato Salad

- **4** thick slices bacon, diced
- **1/2** cup finely chopped yellow onion
- **1** tablespoon flour
- **1/2** cup Browned Beef Stock or canned reduced-sodium beef broth
- **1/2** cup cider vinegar
- **2** tablespoons sugar
- **1** teaspoon salt
- **1/4** teaspoon black pepper
- **3** pounds small red- or white-skinned new potatoes, boiled, peeled, and cut into 1/4-inch-thick slices
- **1** cup sliced scallions
- **1/4** cup minced parsley

1 In a medium-size skillet over moderately low heat, cook bacon until crisp—about 5 minutes. Transfer to paper toweling to drain.

2 Add onion to bacon drippings and sauté until soft—about 5 minutes. Blend in flour, remove from the heat, and gradually stir in stock, vinegar, sugar, salt, and pepper. Return to the heat and cook, stirring, until mixture boils. Cook 1 minute more, reduce the heat to low, and keep dressing warm.

3 Place potatoes in a heatproof serving bowl, add scallions, parsley, and reserved bacon, pour dressing over all, and toss gently to mix. Makes 6 servings.

1 Serving: Calories 307;
Total Fat 13 g;
Saturated Fat 5 g;
Protein 12 g;
Carbohydrates 37 g;
Fiber 3 g; Sodium 778 mg;
Cholesterol 24 mg

prep time-30 minutes
cooking time-about 45 minutes

SWEET POTATO AND GREEN APPLE SALAD

Prepare as directed above, **substituting** firm-cooked diced sweet potatoes for new potatoes, **omitting** sugar, and **adding** 1 diced, cored, unpeeled tart green apple (Granny Smith). Makes 6 servings.

RICE AND PASTA SALADS

*B*oth rice and pasta salads pair up naturally with roasted or steamed vegetables. Our recipes provide one of each, plus a variety of tasty vinaigrettes.

RICE FOR SALAD

Rice prepared for salad should be firm textured and fluffy, not sticky. Choose long-grain rice for best results. Cook in plenty of boiling salted water until just tender. As soon as the rice is drained, dress and season it: the oil in the dressing will help to keep the grains of rice separate.

PASTA FOR SALAD

Pasta for salad should be cooked just until it's firm-tender. Drain it and dress it while it's still warm. If you must let the pasta cool before dressing it, rinse it well after cooking to remove the starch, which will cause it to stick together as it cools.

Although any pasta shape can be used for salad, consider how it will be served. Long pasta strands are fine for sit-down meals. Short pastas are better shapes for the buffet table, picnics, and other meals where diners have to hold their plates in their laps.

SEASONING SALAD

Chilling dulls flavors significantly, which means that you should be more liberal when adding salt, herbs, and spices to any recipe that will be served cold. As a rule of thumb, use about 1/4 to 1/3 more dried or fresh herbs than normal if the dish is to be served warm.

SALAD BOWLS

Salads made with small pasta shapes or rice can be served in hollowed-out vegetables or fruits. Try papayas, avocados, tomatoes, sweet red or yellow peppers, parboiled zucchini, or large mushroom caps.

COOK'S SECRETS

Sara Moulton,
Executive Chef,
Gourmet
Magazine

"Always be sure to season rice and pasta salads while they are still warm. If you wait until they cool, you will be putting the flavor on the food, not in it."

COOKING AHEAD

Pasta salads can be made a day ahead and are even better when the ingredients have had a few hours to mingle. Cover tightly and refrigerate until about an hour before serving.

Rice salads tend to get soggy if made too far ahead. Mix rice with its dressing the day the salad is to be served.

To get a head start, cook the rice and refrigerate. When ready to assemble, reheat the rice covered, in the microwave. Lightly sprinkle the rice with water. Then, per 1 cup of rice, microwave at 100 percent power for 1 to 1 1/2 minutes, stirring at halftime.

ONE-DISH MEALS

Try any of the following combinations for a delicious light lunch or supper:

Rice or Pasta Niçoise: Toss with tuna, cooked sliced green beans, chopped tomato, black olives, chopped red onion, olive oil, and lemon juice.

Greek Shrimp Salad: Toss pasta or rice with boiled shrimp, crumbled feta cheese, snipped fresh dill, olive oil, and lemon juice.

Turkey Salad: Toss pasta or rice with cooked sliced turkey, chopped pine nuts, golden raisins, diced celery, and curry-flavored yogurt dressing. Blend 3 tablespoons of plain yogurt, 2 tablespoons of parsley, 1 tablespoon of olive oil, 2 teaspoons of curry powder, and 1 teaspoon of lemon juice.

Summer Chicken Salad: Toss pasta or rice with cooked sliced chicken breasts, chopped basil, tomatoes, and garlic. Dress with vinaigrette.

Quick Salad: Toss rice or pasta with canned, drained chickpeas, kidney beans, and artichoke hearts. Mix with capers, chopped pimientos, olives, and chopped scallions. Dress with vinaigrette.

Any of the vinaigrettes listed below can be used on rice or pasta salads.

VINAIGRETTES

Whisk together 1/4 cup olive oil, 4 teaspoons vinegar, and 1/2 teaspoon salt. Makes 1/4 cup.

Mustard Vinaigrette: **Prepare** Vinaigrette, **adding** 1 teaspoon Dijon mustard.

Herbed Vinaigrette: **Prepare** Vinaigrette, **adding** 1 tablespoon finely chopped tarragon, basil, chives, or parsley.

Garlic Vinaigrette: **Prepare** Vinaigrette, **adding** 1 clove blanched and chopped garlic or 1 tablespoon finely minced shallots or scallions.

Fusilli with Roasted Peppers

8 ounces fusilli

1 medium-size sweet red pepper, roasted and cut into 1/4-inch strips

1 medium-size sweet yellow pepper, roasted and cut into 1/4-inch strips

2 tablespoons olive oil

2 tablespoons red wine vinegar

1/2 teaspoon salt

1/4 teaspoon black pepper

2 tablespoons minced parsley

2 tablespoons minced fresh basil

2 tablespoons drained capers

2 cloves garlic, minced

1/2 cup diced red onion

1 cup chopped, cored, peeled tomatoes

1 Cook fusilli according to package instructions until still a bit firm. Drain and place in a large serving bowl.

2 Add remaining ingredients and toss to mix well. Let stand at room temperature 30 minutes before serving. Makes 4 servings.

1 Serving: Calories 308; Total Fat 9 g; Saturated Fat 1 g; Protein 10 g; Carbohydrates 48 g; Fiber 4 g; Sodium 278 mg; Cholesterol 17 mg

prep time-50 minutes
cooking time-30 minutes

SUMMER RICE SALAD

Prepare as directed at left, **substituting** 2 cups firm-cooked rice for fusilli, lemon juice for vinegar, 1/2 cup thinly sliced scallions for red onion, and 1 tablespoon chopped fresh tarragon for basil. **Add** 3/4 cup thinly sliced cooked carrots and 3/4 cup halved, blanched, trimmed snow peas. Makes 4 servings.

SANDWICH SALADS

Make salad sandwich stuffers the traditional way, with real mayonnaise or with other lighter dressings.

LIGHT AND LIGHTER

Real mayonnaise contains 11 grams of fat per tablespoon, but there are reduced-fat versions. These range downward from 5 grams per tablespoon to mayonnaiselike dressings that contain no fat at all. Flavor and smoothness vary from brand to brand.

Tip: Blending regular mayonnaise with no-fat mayonnaise dressing reduces calories yet provides enough traditional flavor to satisfy most mayonnaise lovers. You can also spark up the flavor of a low-fat mayonnaise by mixing in a generous spoonful of mustard, ketchup, tomato salsa, Worcestershire sauce, or pickle relish.

Some suggestions follow:
Ham salad: Mix together 1 cup of minced ham, 1/4 cup of mayonnaise or low-fat mayonnaise, 2 tablespoons of sweet pickle relish, 2 teaspoons of prepared mustard, and 1 teaspoon of drained prepared horseradish.

Egg salad: Gently blend 4 chopped hard-cooked eggs, 1/4 cup of chopped green olives, and 1/4 cup of mayonnaise or low-fat mayonnaise.

Chicken or turkey salad: Stir together 1 cup of finely chopped cooked chicken or turkey, 1/4 cup of mayonnaise or low-fat mayonnaise, 1/4 cup of minced celery, and 1 tablespoon of chili sauce.

SALAD DRESSINGS

Any meat, fish, or shellfish salad that is traditionally made with mayonnaise can also be made without.

Vinaigrettes, either plain or made "creamy" by mixing with plain yogurt, are fine, but use them sparingly so they don't drip. Try balsamic or cider vinegar in the vinaigrette for chicken and turkey salads, lemon juice for tuna, salmon, shrimp, and lobster salads.

LETTUCE LINERS

Iceberg lettuce may be the familiar standby in salad sandwiches or salad plates but there are many greens that offer real flavor as well as crunch. Try arugula, endive, radicchio, romaine, and watercress.

BREAD NOTES

To prevent salads from squeezing out of sandwiches, use soft breads and rolls. It also helps to use a pita pocket or hot dog-type roll that is not open on all sides. Line the bread or roll with lettuce to keep it from absorbing too much moisture.

MINCING LESSONS

For a perfectly textured salad, additions such as onions and celery should be chopped fine.

1 Cut an onion in half lengthwise, lay one half on its flat side, and cut lengthwise into thin slices.

1 Trim the leaves and root end from a celery stalk and cut lengthwise in thin parallel strips.

2 Turn the stack of slices 90 degrees and make equally spaced cuts perpendicular to the first.

2 Turn the strips 90 degrees and cut perpendicular to the first, in as fine a dice as desired.

Shrimp Salad

Prepare as directed at right, **substituting** diced cooked shrimp for lobster and 2 tablespoons chopped fresh tarragon for parsley. Makes 4 servings.

Crab Salad

Prepare as directed at right, **substituting** lump crabmeat for lobster. **Add** 1/4 cup diced sweet red pepper. **Omit** rolls, butter, and romaine; instead, **serve** salad on seeded, peeled, lengthwise quarters of papaya and **sprinkle** with chopped parsley. Makes 4 servings.

Tuna Salad

Prepare as directed at right, **using** only 2 tablespoons chopped celery. **Increase** mayonnaise by 1 tablespoon. **Substitute** 1 tablespoon chopped fresh dill for parsley and **add** 3 tablespoons each finely chopped red onion and sweet pickle, and 1 tablespoon capers. **Substitute** two 6 1/2-ounce cans drained solid white tuna for lobster. Makes 4 servings.

Lobster Salad Roll

- 1/4 **cup finely chopped celery**
- 2 **tablespoons lemon juice**
- 1/4 **cup mayonnaise**
- 1/4 **cup finely chopped parsley**

Pinch cayenne

- 1/4 **teaspoon salt**
- 1 **pound cooked lobster meat, cut into 1/2-inch cubes (about 6 lobster tails or four 1 1/4-pound lobsters)**
- 4 **teaspoons unsalted butter or margarine, softened**
- 4 **soft rolls, split and toasted**
- 4 **romaine leaves, cut to fit rolls**

1 In a medium-size bowl, mix celery, lemon juice, mayonnaise, parsley, cayenne, and salt. Add lobster and toss to mix well.

2 Spread 1 teaspoon butter on each roll bottom, divide lobster salad equally among them, top with romaine, and cover with the top halves of rolls. Makes 4 servings.

1 Serving: Calories 379; Total Fat 18 g; Saturated Fat 5 g; Protein 28 g; Carbohydrates 26 g; Fiber 2 g; Sodium 905 mg; Cholesterol 100 mg

prep time-20 minutes

Main Dish Salads

A warm entrée served on a bed of mixed greens offers the same advantages as a one-pot meal. All you need to add is a crusty piece of bread.

WARM, COOL, AND CRISP

Serving warm sliced poultry, meat, or shellfish on a bed of greens is a relatively new way of enjoying a light but flavorful meal. It makes an interesting combination of crisp and chewy textures and warm and cool tastes.

Toss the greens with dressing before adding the topping, as we have done with our Grilled Chicken Salad with Mango. Alternatively, you can use the sauce or juices from the freshly cooked topping to moisten the greens.

Use combinations of greens for extra texture and attractiveness. Vary the dressing to suit the topping. Vinaigrettes are good with most salads. Lemony flavors are a good choice for shellfish, a hint of anchovy is great with tuna, spicy peppers complement pork, blue cheese does the same for steak, and anything from citrus flavors to curry suits chicken and turkey.

TOP OF THE LIST

Warm toppings should be juicy, but not dripping with sauce. First picks for warm salads include grilled chicken breasts, London broil, or fresh tuna; sautéed turkey, duck breasts, or pork medallions; boiled shrimp or steamed mussels in a warm vinaigrette; grilled, sliced mushrooms, eggplant, and peppers.

MANGO NOTES

There are hundreds of different varieties of mangoes. We make our salad with a fresh mango chutney or relish. A ripe mango, which generally weighs 1 to 1½ pounds, should be slightly soft and yielding, with speckled red-yellow-green skin.

HOW TO SLICE AND ARRANGE CHICKEN OR STEAK FOR A SALAD

Mix up a one-dish warm salad meal with slices, matchstick cuts, or cubes of meat or poultry.

Cut a grilled steak in thin slices. Roll up the slices or fan them out on a bed of fresh greens. Or slice the steak while it's raw, stir-fry, and toss while still warm with fresh greens.

Cut a broiled chicken breast into thin slices. Cut into matchstick pieces and arrange on a plate with vegetables while still warm. Or dice and toss with dressed greens, vegetables, or fruit.

KITCHEN CHEMISTRY

Pour two clear liquids—olive oil and vinegar—into a jar, screw on the lid, shake it well, and the liquid turns opaque and creamy. Why is that? The answer is emulsification, which is nature's way of allowing liquids that generally repel one another (such as oil and water or, in this case, vinegar) to join, at least temporarily.

What happens is that when shaken, the oil breaks into minute globules that are then suspended in the other liquid. Since the proportions in salad dressing are usually about 3 parts oil to 1 part vinegar, that means there are an awful lot of suspended globules—and consequently the liquid thickens and appears opaque.

If left to sit long enough, most emulsions will separate into oil and liquid again. Other emulsions include homogenized milk, mayonnaise, and hollandaise sauce.

Grilled Chicken Salad with Mango

2   **whole skinless, boneless chicken breasts (about 1½ pounds)**

2   **tablespoons lime juice**

2   **tablespoons vegetable oil**

2   **teaspoons minced garlic**

½   **cup flaked coconut**

2   **cups shredded romaine**

1   **medium-size mango, peeled, pitted, and cut into ½-inch cubes**

¼   **cup light seedless raisins**

⅓   **cup coarsely chopped toasted cashews**

1   **cup julienned carrots**

2   **tablespoons chopped coriander (cilantro)**

1 Place chicken, 1 tablespoon each of the lime juice and oil, and garlic in a glass bowl and marinate, covered, in the refrigerator for 5 hours.

2 Preheat the oven to 350°F. Spread coconut in an ungreased shallow baking pan and toast, stirring often, until golden brown—about 10 minutes; reserve.

3 Preheat the broiler and broil chicken 4 to 5 inches from the heat until dark brown—about 10 minutes on each side.

4 Meanwhile, in a large bowl, toss together remaining 1 tablespoon lime juice and oil, toasted coconut, romaine, mango, raisins, cashews, carrots, and coriander.

5 Slice broiled chicken into strips about ¼-inch thick.

6 Divide salad equally among 4 individual serving plates, top with chicken slices, and serve immediately. Makes 4 servings.

1 Serving: Calories 412; Total Fat 18 g; Saturated Fat 8 g; Protein 38 g; Carbohydrates 28 g; Fiber 5 g; Sodium 170 mg; Cholesterol 94 mg

prep time-50 minutes
marinating time-5 hours
cooking time-30 minutes

COMPOSED SALADS

For a special presentation, compose a colorful salad on individual plates or a large platter. It's the diner's choice whether to nibble the elements separately or to mix them together.

CELEBRATED SALADS

Our composed salads are two of the best known. Niçoise salad, the great classic from Southern France, usually includes new potatoes, green beans, tomatoes, hard-cooked eggs, anchovies, capers, tiny ripe Niçoise olives and—without exception—tuna, all glistening in vinaigrette dressing. In France, the vegetables in the salad are subject to change depending on seasonal availability. We've taken artistic license and added a few colorful choices of our own.

Cobb salad was created at Hollywood's famous derby-shaped Brown Derby Restaurant in 1936 by restaurant owner Robert Cobb. It always includes cooked chicken or turkey, crumbled bacon, hard-cooked eggs, avocado, and tomato on a bed of lettuce. Crumbled Roquefort cheese is the traditional topping.

Although elegantly composed when served, Cobb salad is so delicious it quickly becomes a colorful tossed salad once diners dig in.

ANYTHING GOES

Our salads combine fish or meat with vegetables. But you can make eye-catching and delicious composed salads simply with vegetables or fruit.

For vegetable salads, some cooked vegetables, such as pea pods, mushrooms, and summer squash, can simply be sliced or chopped and served raw. Others, such as carrots and broccoli, must be parboiled until firm-tender and cooled to room temperature.

To be sure that all parts of a composed salad get their share of dressing, arrange lettuce leaves and other greens on the plate first and sprinkle them with dressing. Then arrange the other ingredients on top and dress them.

THE RIGHT STUFF

Compose a salad from any variety of ingredients you like, but before you head out to shop, give some thought to textures, shapes, colors, and even themes.

Make an all-green salad with a bed of light- and dark-leaf lettuces topped with an arrangement of some of the following: cooked asparagus spears, green beans, zucchini slices, or snow peas. Add a few accents with sliced leek or other white onion, tiny black olives, and add a sprinkling of capers.

For a colorful Tex-Mex salad, on a bed of lettuce arrange: cooked corn kernels; spicy

(continued on page 180)

WORK SAVER
Dressing Shaker

Some of the best kitchen tools are the simplest. A purchased shaker with a tight-fitting lid or a clean jelly or canning jar makes the best dressing shaker. It allows you to shake the dressing with a rocking motion that combines ingredients quickly and thoroughly while letting the dressing thicken.

PRETTY WAYS TO COMPOSE A SALAD

All-Green Salad

Tex-Mex Salad

Tricolor Italian Salad

Fruit Salad

Tuna Niçoise Salad

- 1 large shallot, minced
- 1 tablespoon Dijon mustard
- 1 tablespoon drained capers
- 1 tablespoon red wine vinegar
- 3 tablespoons olive oil
- 1 medium-size head romaine, cut into 2-inch-long pieces
- 2 hard-cooked eggs, peeled and halved lengthwise
- 1/2 cup drained, bottled roasted sweet red peppers, cut into 2- by 1/4-inch strips
- 3 plum tomatoes, cut lengthwise into 8 wedges
- 2 carrots, peeled, parboiled, and thinly sliced
- 1/2 pound green beans, trimmed, blanched, and halved crosswise
- 1 pound small red potatoes, boiled and sliced 1/4-inch thick
- 24 Niçoise olives
- 1 can (6 1/2 ounces) oil-packed tuna, drained

1 Place shallot, mustard, capers, and vinegar in a large bowl and whisk in oil. Pour off 1/2 the dressing and set aside.

2 Add romaine to bowl, toss well, and divide equally among 4 serving plates.

3 Arrange remaining ingredients artfully on the romaine, dividing amounts equally, and spoon reserved dressing over all. Makes 4 servings.

1 Serving: Calories 432; Total Fat 21 g; Saturated Fat 4 g; Protein 24 g; Carbohydrates 40 g; Fiber 8 g; Sodium 728 mg; Cholesterol 123 mg

prep time-1 hour 10 minutes

COBB SALAD

Prepare as directed at left, **omitting** capers, carrots, green beans, potatoes, and tuna. **Add** 1/2 cup crumbled blue cheese, 1 peeled, pitted, and cubed avocado, and 1/2 cup crisp crumbled bacon. Coarsely **chop** hard-cooked eggs, roasted peppers, tomatoes, and olives and **arrange** ingredients over romaine. Makes 4 servings.

(continued from page 178)

grilled chicken slices; sliced avocado; sliced, roasted red pepper; drained and rinsed pinto beans; chopped red tomatoes; slices of Monterey Jack cheese; and a generous spoonful of salsa. Top with chopped onions and coriander. Garnish with a pickled chile pepper.

For a red, white, and green Italian salad, make a bed of arugula and red-and-white radicchio lettuce. Top with a choice of drained and rinsed white cannellini beans; sliced tomatoes; sliced, rolled prosciutto or Italian ham; and marinated artichoke hearts. Top with scallions or crumbled Gorgonzola cheese. Garnish with black olives or anchovies.

For a cooling summer fruit salad, make a green and white bed of endive and watercress or other greens. Arrange slices of honeydew and cantaloupe melons, peaches, mango, and green grapes. Add strips of a delicately flavored cheese, such as fontina. Garnish with raspberries or sliced apricots and slivered almonds. Serve with a creamy yogurt dressing on the side.

SALAD PALETTE

Let a composed salad bring out your creative side. Use ingredients for different effects: Red, orange, and yellow sweet peppers can be sliced thin for colorful accents or diced fine for a confettilike topping. The same is true for hard-cooked eggs, which can be arranged as wedges or pushed through a sieve and crumbled on top. Chop tomatoes in a dice to make a colorful mound or cut into thin wedges and fan them out.

PANZANELLA WITH OLIVES

Prepare as directed at right, **substituting** 1/4 cup balsamic vinegar for red wine vinegar, 1 tablespoon dried oregano for basil, and sourdough bread for Italian bread. **Add** 1/2 cup pitted, halved black Kalamata olives and **reduce** salt to 1/4 teaspoon. Makes 4 servings.

The vibrant array of vegetables and other salad foods at supermarkets these days makes it fun to shop for composed-salad ingredients. Consider some of the following for your color palette:

White: sliced chicken or turkey, drained and rinsed cannellini beans, sliced leek or scallion, white radishes, sliced white mushrooms, cooked cauliflower florets, sliced hearts of palm, sliced cooked potato, endive, small pasta, minced or whole egg white, feta, or white goat cheese.

Yellows and oranges: sweet yellow and orange peppers, sieved egg yolks, drained and rinsed chickpeas, yellow and orange tomatoes, sliced or chopped summer squash, cooked sliced carrots, yellow or red lentils, grated or sliced Cheddar or other yellow cheese, baby corn or whole corn kernels, or wax beans.

Reds: chopped or sliced beets, drained and rinsed kidney beans, chopped or sliced tomatoes, tiny red potatoes, sliced salami or ham, boiled shrimp or lobster, sliced steak, chopped radishes, sliced red cabbage, sweet red pepper, sliced roasted red pepper, chopped red onion, red salsa, red-leaf lettuce, and radicchio.

Green: sliced avocado, cooked green beans, cooked asparagus, chopped or sliced zucchini, tomatillos (green tomatoes), cucumber, green salsa, capers, scallions, chives, cooked broccoli florets, artichoke hearts, snow peas, sugar snaps, or green peas,

Accents: black olives, anchovies, grilled eggplant, caponata, grilled or pickled mushrooms, sliced purple cabbage, or purple basil.

PANZANELLA

Panzanella is a sturdy dish—part salad, part soup—from the Italian countryside. Devised as a way to use up day-old bread and ripe tomatoes, it's flavorful and filling.

For the bread, use chunks of coarse-textured country-style breads, including French or Italian loaves. (Many Italian cooks remove the crust before using it in the salad.)

INGREDIENTS

The bread should be hard, or nearly so, when it is added to the soup. Cut the bread into chunks and leave it to air dry on a rack, turning the pieces occasionally until dry.

Note: If French or Italian bread is unavailable, use firm-textured white bread cut into cubes and toasted.

Make sure the tomatoes are at the very peak of ripeness. Italians favor plum tomatoes because of their meatiness and mellow flavor. But any tomato bursting with flavor will do.

Panzanella Salad

- **2 tablespoons red wine vinegar**
- **3 tablespoons olive oil**
- **1 cup coarsely chopped fresh basil**
- **1/2 teaspoon salt**
- **1/2 teaspoon black pepper**
- **1 small loaf (about 10 ounces) day-old or toasted Italian or French bread, sliced 1/2-inch thick and cubed**
- **8 ripe plum tomatoes, cut into 1/2-inch cubes**
- **1 medium-size red onion, diced**

1 In a large bowl, whisk together vinegar, oil, basil, salt, and pepper.

2 Add bread, tomatoes, and onion and toss until well coated. Makes 4 servings.

1 Serving: Calories 326; Total Fat 13 g; Saturated Fat 2 g; Protein 8 g; Carbohydrates 45 g; Fiber 4 g; Sodium 629 mg; Cholesterol 3 mg

prep time-30 minutes

FROM THE GRILL

GRILLED STEAK

For great flavored steak, choose the cut carefully and give it a dry rub of seasonings before putting it on the grill.

GOOD GRILLERS

The tenderest steaks are cut from the section between the ribs and the hips along the back. Steaks from the short loin, just behind the ribs, include porterhouse, T-bone steaks, the boneless strip loin (or New York steak), and most of the tenderloin. Steaks from the sirloin section, just behind the loin, include top sirloin, sirloin, and the rest of the tenderloin. These steaks can be cooked a number of ways: on the grill, broiled in the oven, or pan-broiled.

Rib steaks (with a bone) and rib-eye or club steaks (without a bone) are tender enough to grill or broil. Of the less expensive cuts, skirt steak is cut from the diaphragm muscle. It's full flavored and tender and can be grilled or pan-broiled.

Flank steak, true London broil, is a flavorful favorite for the grill, but it tends to be tough. It is best to keep flank steak fairly rare since it will toughen if it's overcooked. When you slice it, be sure to cut across its fibrous grain (see How to Slice a Flank Steak, above). Flank steak is not recommended for pan-broiling.

STEAK PREP

The current fat content of beef is about 50 percent less than it was in the early 1980s. This change is largely due to consumer demands for leaner beef. Beef cattle are now being fed less corn and more grass, and meat packers are trimming away more of the visible fat.

The outer layer of fat on most steaks should be trimmed to about 1/8 inch before grilling. Slash the fat at 1- to 1 1/2-inch intervals to prevent the steak from curling as it cooks, and season the meat with a dry rub or herbs, if desired. Refrigerate until 1/2 hour before cooking.

Remove the grill rack and oil or spritz it with nonstick vegetable spray. Set it 4 to 5 inches above the fire for thin cuts such as flank steak; 6 to 7 inches for a thick sirloin.

Light the fire about 45 minutes before cooking so it will have a chance to burn down to glowing coals covered with ash.

Place the steak on the grill. Baste with marinade or barbecue sauce if you like. But first-quality steaks should not be marinated with barbecue sauce; it will mask their flavor.

BASIC STEAK RUB

One way to flavor a steak is with dry seasoning rubbed on before grilling. For a basic mix, blend 1 tablespoon of ground black pepper, 1 tablespoon of kosher salt, 1 tablespoon of parsley flakes, 1 tablespoon of paprika, 1 teaspoon of garlic powder, and 1/2 teaspoon of cayenne. You might add Southwestern, Middle Eastern, or other flavorings to the mix.

Dry rubs can be kept on hand in tightly covered jars. To use fresh herbs, garlic, and other ingredients in a rub, prepare a small amount just before use.

PAN-BROILING STEAKS

If you're cooking indoors, pan-broil steak in a heavy skillet or grill pan (a skillet with grids on the bottom). If juices accumulate, remove them periodically with a bulb baster or spoon.

Heat the pan until a drop of water sizzles on it and spritz the bottom with nonstick veg-

HOW TO SLICE A FLANK STEAK

The grain in flank steak is more obvious than in other steak. To ensure tenderness, cut across the grain, on the diagonal, in thin slices.

etable spray. Add the meat and cook over moderately high heat until the grid marks show, turn, and grill the other side until so marked. Lower the heat slightly and cook until done as desired, 2 or 3 minutes for rare; 5 to 6 minutes for medium; and up to 15 minutes for well done. Increase the time 4 to 5 minutes for 1/2-inch thickness.

SMOKE ON GAS

To give barbecue flavor to food on a propane grill, soak a handful of your favorite hardwood chips in water for 15 minutes. Pour off the water and wrap the damp chips in aluminum foil, leaving one end open.

Wearing fireproof mitts, lay the smoker packet on the grill's heated grids or rocks. Smoky flavor will waft over the food.

Allow 15 to 20 minutes on the fire for the smoke flavor to permeate the meat. After the grill has cooled down, discard the foil smoker packet.

Grilled Porterhouse

Prepare as directed at right, **using** the following marinade: 1/4 cup balsamic vinegar, 2 peeled cloves garlic, 1 cup tightly packed fresh basil, and 1/2 teaspoon each salt and black pepper. **Substitute** 1 (1 1/4-inch-thick, 1-pound 10-ounce) porterhouse steak for flank steak. Makes 4 servings.

Grilled Tenderloin

Prepare as directed at right, **using** the following marinade: 1/4 cup red wine vinegar, 2 peeled whole shallots, 2 tablespoons olive oil, and 1/2 teaspoon each salt and black pepper. **Substitute** 4 (1 1/4-inch-thick, 1/2-pound) tenderloin steaks for flank steak. Makes 4 servings.

Rubbed Sirloin

Substitute this dry rub for the marinade: 2 tablespoons ground cumin **mixed** with 3 minced cloves garlic, 1 teaspoon salt, and 1/2 teaspoon each cayenne and dried oregano. **Rub** on both sides of 4 (1/2-inch-thick, 5-ounce) sirloin steaks and **grill** 4 minutes on each side for medium-rare. Makes 4 servings.

Marinated Flank Steak

- 3/4 **cup pineapple juice**
- 2 **cloves garlic, peeled**
- 1/4 **cup soy sauce**
- One **1 1/2-inch cube ginger, peeled**
- 1 **medium-size jalapeño pepper, halved, cored, and seeded**
- 1/4 **cup honey**
- 2 **tablespoons vegetable oil**
- 1 3/4 **pounds flank steak, well trimmed**

1 Purée all ingredients except steak in a food processor. Pour marinade into a large self-sealing plastic bag, add steak, seal, turn to coat well, and refrigerate 5 hours or overnight.

2 Preheat the grill or broiler. Remove steak from marinade, pat dry on paper toweling, and grill over moderate coals or broil 4 inches from the heat until steak is the way you like it—5 to 6 minutes on each side for medium-rare and 6 to 7 minutes for medium. Flank steak cooked beyond medium will be tough. Let stand 10 minutes, then, starting on the shorter side of the steak, slice on the bias and across the grain as thin as possible. Makes 4 servings.

1 Serving: Calories 363; Total Fat 18 g;
Saturated Fat 7 g; Protein 42 g;
Carbohydrates 6 g; Fiber 0 g;
Sodium 170 mg; Cholesterol 104 mg

prep time-10 minutes
marinating time-5 hours or overnight
cooking time-about 15 minutes
standing time-10 minutes

BURGER CLASSICS

Burgers have always been a favorite grill food, and now turkey burgers share the spotlight with beef. Here we offer delicious recipes for both kinds of burger.

WHICH GROUND BEEF?

Federal government regulations require that all ground beef be labeled as extra lean, lean, medium, or regular.

Extra lean ground beef has a maximum fat content of 10 percent. Lean ground beef has a maximum fat content of 17 per-

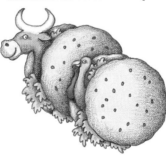

cent. Both make dry, compact burgers. They are best used in recipes in which the ground beef is not precooked and drained of fat before other ingredients are added, such as for cabbage rolls.

Ground beef labeled as medium has a maximum fat content of 23 percent. It is the number-one choice for hamburgers. Three-and-one-half ounces contain 11 grams of fat when broiled to well done.

Ground beef labeled as regular has a maximum fat content of

30 percent. The high fat content means the burgers won't shrink. However, this type of meat is best used in recipes in which the ground beef is cooked and the fat is drained off before other ingredients are added, such as for tacos.

BURGERS OVER FIRE

Shape the meat into neat patties 1-inch thick at the center. Handle them gently or the burgers will be compact and crumbly. Place the meat on a grill rack coated with oil or nonstick vegetable spray and set 6 inches above a hot fire.

For well-done burgers, grill 4 minutes, until browned. Carefully turn and brown the other side, about 3 minutes. Do not press the burgers with a spatula while they cook or they will lose juices and flavor.

When cooking, use a stovetop grilling pan with grids molded into the bottom, if possible. It will prevent burgers from steaming in their own juices.

SAFETY FIRST

The Beef Information Centre recommends that all ground beef be cooked well done. Disease-causing organisms (live *E. coli* bacteria) found in

undercooked ground beef can cause food poisoning.

To make sure burgers are well done, cook until an instant-read meat thermometer inserted in the center registers 160°F to 165°F. Or make a thin cut in the center of a burger. If the burger is well done, the juices will be golden or clear.

TURKEY TOO

For a change of flavor, use ground turkey instead of beef. In Canada, ground turkey does not have to be labeled by type (i.e. lean, medium), so always look for packages that voluntarily carry labels. If a package is labeled as lean, for example, it must not contain more than 17 percent fat—the same as for ground beef.

Bump up the flavor of ground turkey with a tablespoon of Worcestershire sauce. Try adding 2 tablespoons of bottled chili or barbecue sauce to a pound of turkey meat. For a different accent, work 2 tablespoons of Chinese plum sauce and 1 teaspoon of minced fresh gingerroot into the burger and substitute scallions for onion.

TURKEY BURGER

Prepare Classic Burger as directed at right, **substituting** 1 pound ground turkey for ground beef. **Omit** ketchup and mustard and **add** 1/4 cup each finely chopped yellow onion and parsley and 1 minced clove garlic along with salt and pepper. **Grill** 6 to 7 minutes on each side or until well done. Makes 4 servings.

TURKEY BURGER VARIATIONS

To the turkey mix, **add** one of the following: 2 tablespoons chili sauce or barbecue sauce. Or 1 teaspoon Dijon mustard and 1/2 teaspoon each dried thyme and grated lemon zest. Or 2 tablespoons Chinese plum sauce and 1 teaspoon minced fresh ginger. Also **substitute** 1/2 cup finely chopped scallions for yellow onion.

WORK SAVER

Grill Thermometer and Instant-Read Thermometer

Two tools that are indispensable in grilling meats are these thermometers. If you've ever wondered how to tell when the grill surface is the right heat for starting meat, the grill thermometer will tell you. It attaches magnetically to the grill surface. To check for doneness, insert an instant-read thermometer into the flesh of cooking meat or poultry and get a reading immediately.

ROQUEFORT OR BLUE CHEESE BURGERS

Prepare as directed at right, **using** 1½ pounds ground beef. **Divide** into eighths and **shape** into thin patties. In the center of each of 4 patties, **place** 1 tablespoon crumbled Roquefort or blue cheese. **Top** with remaining patties, **pinch** edges to seal completely, and **grill** as directed. Makes 4 servings.

BRIE BURGERS

Prepare Roquefort or Blue Cheese Burgers as directed above, but **sandwich** each 2 thin patties together with 1 (1" x 1" x ¼"-thick) slice chilled ripe Brie instead of crumbled Roquefort. Makes 4 servings.

SURPRISE BURGERS

Prepare Roquefort or Blue Cheese Burgers as directed above, but **sandwich** each 2 thin patties together with 1 tablespoon sautéed diced onion and 1 scant teaspoon each sweet pickle relish and Dijon mustard instead of crumbled Roquefort. Makes 4 servings.

STUFFING A BLUE CHEESE BURGER

1 Top a thin patty with crumbled blue cheese (or another cheese).

2 Place a second thin patty on top and pinch the edges together to seal.

Classic Burger

1　**pound ground beef chuck**
2　**tablespoons ketchup**
2　**teaspoons Dijon mustard**
1　**teaspoon salt**
¼　**teaspoon black pepper**

1 Preheat the grill or broiler. In a large bowl, mix all ingredients until well blended. Form into four 6-inch patties about 1-inch thick.

2 Grill patties over moderately hot coals or broil 4 inches from the heat until well done—6 to 7 minutes on each side. Makes 4 servings.

1 Serving:
Calories 227; Total Fat 14 g; Saturated Fat 5 g; Protein 22 g; Carbohydrates 2 g; Fiber 0 g; Sodium 755 mg; Cholesterol 78 mg

prep time-10 minutes cooking time-about 15 minutes

SHISH KABOBS

It's easy to guarantee success with kabobs if the meat is cooked on its own skewers and vegetables of similar texture are cooked separately on theirs.

THE BEST MEATS FOR KABOBS

Leg of lamb cut in 1- to 1½-inch cubes is tender and full flavored. So are rib-eye or sirloin roasts or steaks. Very tender meat such as tenderloin lacks sufficient character and will only toughen on the grill.

Precut kabob beef sold at many supermarkets is usually top or bottom round or chuck. Though it may seem well priced, it is apt to be tougher than you want.

MAKING A MARINADE

Kabobs are traditionally marinated before cooking. Marinades can also be used to baste the meat as it cooks. They are usually made with an acid base—wine, vinegar, citrus juice—and are often blended with oil and aromatics such as herbs and onions.

Some of the best marinades are the simplest—red wine blended with a little oil and a handful of finely minced Italian parsley, for instance.

A good low-fat marinade can be mixed up from 1 cup of beef broth, 1 tablespoon of red wine vinegar, ½ cup of red wine, 1 minced clove of garlic, and ½ teaspoon of hot red pepper sauce (or more to taste), 1 teaspoon of salt, and ¼ teaspoon or more of freshly ground black pepper.

TIMING IS EVERYTHING

Experts at kabob cooking often thread vegetables on skewers separate from meat and place the vegetables on the grill after the meat has started. It's good practice because vegetables cook faster than meat.

If you want to grill both meat and vegetables on the same skewer, you can equalize the cooking by threading vegetables at the outer ends of the skewers and the meat in the middle. That way the meat can cook over the center of the fire, where the heat is usually the most intense.

BROILING KABOBS

Kabobs are almost as good broiled in the oven as they are grilled. Place them on a rack in a broiler pan or support the skewer ends on the rim of a shallow pan. Brush lightly with a marinade or oil and broil 4 to 5 inches from the heat, turning once or twice to cook evenly, until done as desired. Cubes of beef or lamb cook medium-rare to medium in 10 to 15 minutes.

VEGETABLES FOR KABOBS

Choose firm but mature vegetables for kabobs and cut them in pieces that are large enough to thread without breaking. Peppers should be seeded first, but not tomatoes.

Yellow squash and zucchini should be washed, not peeled, then cut into 1-inch chunks. Skewer them through the skins so their seedy flesh is turned outward.

SKEWER HOW-TO

For well-done meat, leave plenty of space between pieces. For rare meat, close the gaps.

When combining meat and vegetables on a skewer, put the meat in the middle and the vegetables on either side.

KITCHEN CHEMISTRY

Marinades are mainly for flavor, but to some extent they also tenderize. Acids in marinades soften connective tissue. Enzymes in papaya juice also help by breaking down protein. Since raw meat does not readily absorb liquid, however, marinating for a couple of hours will only affect the meat's surface. For the best results, give yourself plenty of time and marinate in a self-sealing plastic bag so that the meat can easily be turned and coated.

WORK SAVER
Skewers

There are many choices for kabob skewers. Inexpensive bamboo skewers need to be soaked in water before use so they do not burn. For metal skewers, look for styles with handles that are easily grabbed and held with a fireproof mitt.

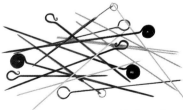

Chicken Kabobs

Prepare as directed at right, but **use** the following marinade: 1/3 cup lemon juice, 2 chopped scallions, 2 tablespoons each soy sauce, Dijon mustard, and olive oil, and 1/4 teaspoon hot red pepper sauce. **Substitute** 1 pound skinless, boneless chicken breasts for beef. **Marinate** at least 4 hours or overnight in the refrigerator. **Grill** over moderate coals or **broil** 4 inches from the heat until no longer pink when cut—8 to 10 minutes. Makes 4 servings.

Scallop Kabobs

Prepare as directed at right, but **use** the following marinade: 1/4 cup soy sauce, 2 chopped scallions, 1/3 cup orange juice, 2 teaspoons grated fresh ginger, 2 tablespoons each olive oil and grated orange zest, and 1 clove minced garlic. **Substitute** 1 pound sea scallops for beef. **Marinate** 30 minutes to 1 hour. **Grill** over moderate coals or **broil** 4 inches from the heat until opaque white when cut—5 to 6 minutes. Makes 4 servings.

Beef or Lamb Shish Kabobs

- 1/4 **cup dry red wine**
- 2 **scallions, chopped**
- 2 **tablespoons balsamic vinegar**
- 1 **tablespoon minced fresh rosemary or 1/2 teaspoon dried rosemary, crumbled**
- 2 **tablespoons olive oil**
- 2 **tablespoons water**
- 2 **cloves garlic, crushed**
- 1/2 **teaspoon salt**
- 1/2 **teaspoon black pepper**
- 1 **pound boneless beef chuck or leg of lamb, cut into 11/4-inch cubes**

1 In a large self-sealing plastic bag, mix together all ingredients except beef. Add beef, seal, turn to coat, and refrigerate at least 4 hours or overnight.

2 Preheat the grill or broiler. Pat beef dry and thread on 4 skewers, spacing evenly.

3 Grill kabobs over moderately hot coals for 10 to 12 minutes for medium-rare to medium, basting frequently with the marinade and turning once. Or broil 4 inches from the heat for 10 to 15 minutes for medium-rare. Makes 4 servings.

1 Serving: Calories 277; Total Fat 17 g; Saturated Fat 5 g; Protein 26 g; Carbohydrates 3 g; Fiber 0 g; Sodium 1085 mg; Cholesterol 82 mg

prep time-1 hour • cooking time-10 minutes

GRILLED CHOPS

*L*amb chops are a great choice for grilling. They're quick, foolproof to cook, and loaded with flavor.

CHOICE CHOPS

Tender lamb chops cut from the loin are the ultimate choice. They are followed closely in tenderness by rib chops.

Shoulder chops, with a round or blade bone, are also delicious and are generally less expensive than loin or rib chops. However, they are also less tender and may need to be marinated, as in our recipe.

CHOP PREP

Trim the outer fat on a chop to about 1/8 inch. The thin layer of fat will moisten the meat as it cooks and can be trimmed off afterward. Rub chops lightly with olive oil and sprinkle with freshly ground black pepper.

THICK OR THIN

For medium-rare 1-inch-thick chops that are nicely browned, place the meat 5 to 6 inches above hot coals covered with gray ash and grill 4 to 5 minutes per side or until the center is pink when slit with a knife. For well-done chops, position the meat 8 inches above a medium fire and grill 6 to 7 minutes on one side and 4 to 5 minutes on the other.

Although 1-inch chops are standard, some markets offer 1/2-inch chops. Estimate their cooking time at about 3 to 4 minutes per side.

Double rib or loin chops for grilling can be custom cut to 2 inches thick. Grill them over coals that are well burned down, turning as needed to brown them nicely: 10 to 12 minutes for rare, 12 to 15 minutes for medium, or 15 to 18 minutes for well done.

YOUR TURN

Frequent turning of chops on the grill prolongs cooking. It's not a good idea for thinner cuts unless they are basted. But do turn thick chops often.

PAN-BROILING CHOPS

Pan-broiling is done in a heavy skillet on top of the stove. It takes about half the time as oven broiling and differs from frying in that it is done over dry heat, with little or no added fat. Pan-broiling is best for meat that is less than 1 inch thick.

EASY MARINATING

The simplest way to marinate meat for any recipe is to put both the meat and the marinade in a heavy self-sealing plastic bag. It makes it easy to move meat around and coat it with marinade, it takes up little space in the refrigerator, and it requires no cleanup.

Heat the skillet and brush the chops with a little oil. Pan-broil 1-inch chops over high heat, cooking halfway through before turning: 8 to 9 minutes for rare, 10 to 12 for medium.

PAN-BROILED CHOPS

Use four 1- to 1 1/2-inch-thick loin or rib chops. In a heavy skillet over moderately high heat, **heat** 1 teaspoon olive oil for 30 to 45 seconds. **Add** chops and brown well on both sides, **turning** once at halftime. **Cook** 8 to 9 minutes total for medium-rare, 10 to 12 minutes for medium, or 12 to 15 minutes for well done. **Remove** chops from the skillet and **keep** warm. To drippings in the skillet, **add** 1/2 cup chicken stock or water and 2 to 3 tablespoons balsamic vinegar. **Cook** for 1 minute over high heat **stirring** to loosen brown bits. **Pour** over lamb chops and serve. Makes 4 servings.

SEASONING VARIATIONS

For grilled chops: Brush chops with bottled barbecue sauce, herb vinaigrette, or Italian dressing. Or throw sprigs of rosemary, thyme, or sage on the coals. Or toss some soaked oak or hickory wood chips on the coals.

For pan-broiled chops: Rub chops with one of the following combinations and set aside 15 to 30 minutes before broiling: garlic, olive oil, and black pepper; garlic and fresh ginger; garlic and soy sauce or balsamic vinegar.

WORK SAVER
Grill Pan

The best pan for pan-broiling is a heavy iron skillet with grids. The grids allow meat to cook at high heat without sticking and elevate it above fatty pan drippings.

Marinated Lamb Chops

3 tablespoons vegetable oil
1 teaspoon grated lemon zest
3 tablespoons lemon juice
2 cloves garlic, minced
1 teaspoon dried rosemary, crumbled
1/2 teaspoon dried thyme, crumbled
1/2 teaspoon salt
1/4 teaspoon black pepper
4 lamb shoulder chops 3/4-inch thick (about 1 1/2 pounds), trimmed of excess fat
1 lemon, cut into 8 wedges

1 In a large self-sealing plastic bag, mix together oil, lemon zest and juice, garlic, rosemary, thyme, salt, and pepper.

2 Add chops, seal, turn to coat well, and refrigerate at least 4 hours or overnight.

3 Preheat the grill. Pat chops dry and place directly over hot coals covered with ash, about 5 to 8 inches from the heat. Grill, turning and basting every 3 minutes with remaining marinade, 12 to 14 minutes. Garnish with lemon wedges. Makes 4 servings.

1 Serving: Calories 261; Total Fat 18 g; Saturated Fat 4 g; Protein 23 g; Carbohydrates 2 g; Fiber 0 g; Sodium 334 mg; Cholesterol 75 mg

prep time-10 minutes • cooking time-12 to 14 minutes

Butterflied Leg of Lamb

A plum marinade makes this dish perfection. The techniques are simple but the results are impressive.

BUTTERFLY NOTES

Grilling is a great way to cook lamb. It brings out the meat's distinctive flavor and also cooks off a lot of excess fat.

When a leg of lamb is butterflied, the bone is removed, then the meat is cut almost in half so that it can be opened flat like a book. Butterflying a leg allows it to cook faster than with the bone in—45 minutes to 1 hour, depending on how well done you like it. Natural irregularities in the thickness make the meat adaptable to serving a crowd since it will have areas that are more rare or well done than others.

Tip: A boned and rolled leg of lamb can also be opened out and grilled flat.

BEST BUYS

Even if you don't plan to serve 8 at one sitting, it's worth buying a whole leg roast—rump and shank—for boning. It's the meatiest and most economical cut. Grilled lamb is so delicious you won't have any problem using up the leftovers.

SIMPLE SEASONINGS

If you want to grill a leg of lamb without a marinade, the meat blends beautifully with the simplest of seasonings. Traditional choices are olive oil, garlic, and a few sprigs of fresh mint or rosemary. Also try lemon juice, curry powder, Dijon-style mustard, or a mix of mustard, soy sauce, and brown sugar.

FOREIGN INTRIGUE

Our recipe calls for an unusual ingredient—pomegranate molasses. If you can't find this Middle Eastern syrup in a specialty shop, mix up a substitute by blending together 3 tablespoons of grenadine and 1 tablespoon of molasses. The mixture makes 1/4 cup.

OUR COMPLEMENTS

The spicy marinade and sauce on our Butterflied Leg of Lamb are reminiscent of Moroccan grilled lamb. Serve the dish with its perfect complement—couscous (see page 126).

For an alternative Middle Eastern flavor, rub the butterflied lamb with lemon juice and ground cumin before grilling. Serve it with a cooling yogurt dill sauce made by combining a cup of plain yogurt with 1 tablespoon of olive oil, 2 teaspoons of minced garlic, 1 chopped cucumber, and 1/4 cup of snipped fresh dill.

WHOLE LEG GRILLING

If you want to cook a whole—not butterflied—leg of lamb on the grill, you will need either a covered grill for slow roasting or a spit rotisserie.

To roast on a spit, do the following: Make 1-inch incisions in the meat and insert thin slices of garlic. Rub the leg of lamb with lemon juice or dry seasonings of your choice. Insert the spit alongside the bone and position the meat 8 or 9 inches above a hot grill. It's wise to put an aluminum drip pan under the meat so that hot fat doesn't drip onto the coals.

Baste the lamb regularly, giving it a quarter turn about every 15 minutes. Figure on at least 1 hour 15 minutes' roasting time for a 5- to 6-pound leg of lamb.

When you insert a meat thermometer, make sure its tip is pointed away from the spit and bone. It should read 140°F to 150°F for rare to medium and 175°F to 180°F for well done. The same process can be used for a rib roast.

How to Carve a Butterflied Leg of Lamb

Carving a butterflied leg of lamb is easy because it has no bone. Cut the meat on the diagonal across the grain. The sliced meat from a large leg will fill a platter.

Ben Barker's Butterflied Leg of Lamb

Marinade:

1½	cups fruity red wine
¼	cup pomegranate molasses
3	tablespoons olive oil
3	cloves garlic, crushed
1½	teaspoons sweet Hungarian paprika
1½	teaspoons ground coriander
1½	teaspoons ground cumin
1	teaspoon salt
½	teaspoon anise seeds, crushed
¼	teaspoon cayenne
¼	teaspoon ground cinnamon
⅛	teaspoon ground cloves
½	cup chopped fresh mint
½	cup chopped fresh coriander (cilantro)

Lamb:

4	pounds boneless leg of lamb
1	teaspoon Kosher salt, or to taste

Plum Sauce:

1	medium-size red onion, finely chopped
2	cloves garlic, finely chopped
⅔	cup fruity red wine
3	tablespoons pomegranate molasses
¼	cup firmly packed light brown sugar
¾	teaspoon ground cumin
¾	teaspoon ground coriander
¾	teaspoon ground ginger
1	teaspoon salt
1½	pounds ripe plums, pitted and cut into ½-inch dice
¼	cup chopped fresh mint
¼	cup chopped fresh coriander (cilantro)

1 For the Marinade: In a large nonreactive bowl, stir together all ingredients.

2 For the Lamb: Add lamb to marinade, turn to coat and refrigerate, covered, between 4 and 24 hours, turning occasionally.

3 For the Plum Sauce: In a medium-size nonreactive saucepan over moderate heat, stir in onion, garlic, wine, molasses, sugar, cumin, coriander, ginger, and salt. Bring to a boil, reduce the heat to moderately low, stir in plums, and simmer, uncovered, until sauce is reduced to 2½ to 3 cups—about 25 minutes. Remove from the heat and add mint and fresh coriander. Cool to room temperature.

4 Prepare the grill by heating hardwood coals to moderately hot at one end. Place lamb on the other end of the rack away from the coals about 8 inches from the heat and grill for 15 minutes.

5 Sprinkle with salt, brush with marinade, cover, and continue grilling, brushing with marinade every 5 minutes until lamb reaches an internal temperature of 140°F to 145°F when tested with an instant-read thermometer—about 30 to 45 minutes more.

6 Let rest 15 to 20 minutes before slicing; meat will continue to cook. Serve with Plum Sauce. Makes 8 servings.

1 Serving: Calories 527; Total Fat 19 g; Saturated Fat 5 g; Protein 48 g; Carbohydrates 32 g; Fiber 2 g; Sodium 929 mg; Cholesterol 145 mg

prep time-30 minutes • cooking time-about 70 minutes

SPARERIBS

Ever since the home barbecue revolution of the 1950s, spareribs have had special status. The crispy finish and wake-up flavor they get at the hands of an artful grill chef are hard to beat.

PICK A RIB

Spareribs are the outer ends of pork ribs, which are sparely covered with meat. A rack of ribs weighs about 3 pounds. If spareribs are to be the main part of a meal, figure on about 3/4 to 1 pound per person.

Back ribs are short sections of ribs, cut somewhat closer to the backbone than spareribs. They're sometimes sold as "baby back ribs."

Country-style ribs are thick and meaty and are cut from the shoulder end of the rib. They are more like pork chops than spareribs. Expect about 3 country-style ribs per pound.

PREP FOR GRILLING

Ribs can be separated and grilled individually, but basting and turning a rack of ribs is easier than working with portion cuts.

Wipe the ribs with paper toweling and trim off any surface fat. For extra tenderness, pull off the parchmentlike filament on the inside of the rack. The ribs can then be rubbed with dry spices or marinated.

SPICY PORK RUB

Mix up a big batch of a dry spice rub, then spoon out just the amount you need when you need it.

Blend together 1/4 cup each of Kosher salt, freshly ground black pepper, sweet paprika, and sugar. Store the mixture in a covered jar. Just before using, mix in 1 tablespoon of grated lemon zest for every 2 tablespoons of the spice mixture.

Or adapt the Basic Steak Rub on page 182 for pork by adding 1 1/2 teaspoons of dried grated orange peel and 1/2 teaspoon of ground ginger.

RIB BASICS

To cut down on grilling time, we poached (parboiled) our ribs ahead of time. Parboiling is frequently called for in recipes for ribs, but if you don't wish to include this step, leave plenty of time for slow cooking over a medium to low fire.

Slow cooking is the secret to tender ribs. Without parboiling, figure on about 1 hour 10 minutes total grilling time for spareribs, and up to 1 1/2 hours for country ribs.

GEORGIA-STYLE SAUCE FOR RIBS

Rib lovers expect a bright and tangy flavor with ribs. The perfect way to get it is to mix up a sweet and sour sauce.

1 1/2 cups ketchup
1 cup cider vinegar
1/3 cup vegetable oil
1/3 cup Worcestershire sauce
1/2 cup firmly packed brown sugar
3 tablespoons prepared yellow mustard
3 cloves garlic, minced
1 lemon, cut in half

Combine all the ingredients in a nonreactive saucepan, squeezing the lemon into the sauce, then adding and stirring in one of the squeezed halves. Heat slowly—about 10 minutes—to blend flavors. Keep warm and brush lightly over the ribs. Remove lemon half, bring the leftover sauce to a boil, and serve with the ribs at the table. Makes about 3 cups.

RIB TICKLERS

To add extra flavor when basting pork or any other grilled meat or poultry, tie a few sprigs of herbs together and use them as the basting brush.

You don't have to baste but if you want to, brush the ribs with a mixture of 1/2 cup of chicken stock, the juice of 1 lemon or lime, and 1 teaspoon of hot red pepper sauce.

If you want to coat the ribs with a tomato-based barbecue sauce while they cook, wait until at least halfway through the cooking; otherwise, the sauce will blacken and burn.

BRUSH AND CUT

Wait until the ribs are cooked about halfway through before brushing on the sauce. It should be thick enough so it doesn't drip. Use it generously.

When the ribs are done, use a sharp heavy knife to cut the rack into 3-rib serving portions.

Tar-Heel Ribs

Poaching Liquid:
- 8 to 10 cups water
- 1 cup cider vinegar
- 1 teaspoon crushed red pepper flakes

Ribs:
- 1 rack (about 3 pounds) pork spareribs
- 2 teaspoons salt

Marinade:
- 2 cups cider vinegar
- 2 tablespoons firmly packed dark brown sugar
- 1 tablespoon molasses
- 1¼ teaspoons crushed red pepper flakes
- ½ teaspoon black pepper
- ½ teaspoon salt

Sauce:
- ¾ cup ketchup
- 3 tablespoons cider vinegar
- 3 tablespoons firmly packed dark brown sugar
- 2 tablespoons bourbon
- 1 tablespoon molasses
- ½ teaspoon mustard seeds

1 For Poaching: In a very large skillet or roasting pan over moderate heat, bring water, vinegar, and red pepper to a boil. Add ribs and simmer, uncovered, until just cooked through—about 30 minutes. Cool in the liquid.

2 For the Marinade: In a large bowl, combine all ingredients. Add ribs, turn to coat, and refrigerate, covered, at least 4 hours or up to 24 hours.

3 Prepare the grill by heating hardwood coals at one end. Place ribs directly over medium coals about 8 inches from the heat.

Cover the grill and vent slightly. Grill until ribs form a crust—about 10 minutes. Sprinkle with the 2 teaspoons of salt.

4 Move ribs so they are not over direct heat, brush with marinade, cover, and continue grilling, brushing every 5 minutes with marinade, until ribs are richly browned, crusty, and very tender—about 30 minutes longer.

5 For the Sauce: In a small saucepan over moderate heat, bring all ingredients to a boil, stirring. Remove from the heat. Serve at room temperature or chilled as a dipping sauce. Makes 4 servings.

1 Serving: Calories 806; Total Fat 49 g; Saturated Fat 18 g; Protein 48 g; Carbohydrates 39 g; Fiber 1 g; Sodium 1237 mg; Cholesterol 194 mg

prep time-20 minutes
cooking time-1 hour 10 minutes

CHICKEN BARBECUE

The aroma of barbecuing chicken is the perfume of summer. There are dozens of ways to enjoy it, including our Texas, Tar-Heel, and Jamaican styles.

CHICKEN PREP

Remove chicken from the refrigerator just before cooking. Pull off any fat and clean the cavity. Don't remove the skin; it keeps the meat moist as it cooks. If you wish, remove the skin after cooking to lower the fat content.

Rub the chicken with a lemon and brush it with a thin film of olive oil. Or try sesame or walnut oil, both of which impart special flavor. Season with salt and pepper and with parsley, rosemary, sage, or tarragon.

IS IT DONE YET?

Outside temperature affects the interior heat of a grill. Chicken parts, quarters, and halves require 45 to 60 mintues on the grill on a balmy day and as much as 1 hour 15 minutes on a cold or windy day.

Test halves and quarters with an instant-read thermometer for doneness—180°F for breast meat; 185°F for dark meat. Or slit a joint or meaty spot with a thin knife. If the

COOK'S SECRETS

Jeanne Voltz,
Cookbook Author and Grill Expert

"Too much charcoal ruins a barbecue, causing flames and burned food. Small chicken legs need a minimum of 30 minutes to cook, large legs 45. So, for a relatively slow fire, put 2 loose layers of charcoal pieces or briquettes on a tiny fire. If more charcoal is needed later, push it in at the edges, otherwise it will shoot soot onto the food."

juices run clear and the flesh shows no signs of pink, the bird is done. If still pinkish, cook a few minutes longer.

WHOLE CHICKENS

Spit roasting over a fire gives chicken crisp skin and great flavor. To prep the chicken,

season it inside and out with salt, pepper, and sauce, if desired. Tie the legs to the tail and wrap cooking twine around the breast to hold the wings in place. Push the spit from the neck through the body and out the tail. Fasten spit forks at the front and back. Engage the spit and turn once to balance.

Push the coals to the back of the grill and set a drip pan below the cooking spot. Lock the spit in place, start the motor, and cook the chicken until the skin blisters and browns lightly. (Raise the spit for a roaster weighing more than 6 pounds so the drip pan is 7 inches from the bird.)

Cook, basting with sauce or equal parts of olive oil and lemon juice every 15 minutes, until a meat thermometer reaches 185°F.

SAUCY STRATEGY

If you like to slather sauce onto chicken while it cooks, the following is a good sauce to choose. It adds punchy flavor but will not cause flare ups.

In a small saucepan, stir together 1/2 cup of chicken stock, 1/4 cup of lemon juice, 1 tablespoon each of olive oil, minced parsley, tarragon, or rosemary, and 1 minced clove of garlic. Add 1/2 teaspoon of salt, 1/4 teaspoon of freshly ground black pepper, and, if wanted, 1/2 teaspoon of hot red pepper sauce. Place the pan of sauce at the edge of the grill so it stays warm and is handy for basting the chicken.

A FINISHING TOUCH

For traditional barbecue flavor, brush this sauce on chicken when it is done. In a small

saucepan over moderate heat, sauté 1/4 cup of finely chopped yellow onion in 1 tablespoon of oil 2 to 3 minutes, add 1/2 cup of bottled barbecue sauce, and 1/4 cup each of lemon juice and chicken stock. Keep hot at the edge of the grill. This is enough for 4 chicken quarters.

JAMAICAN JERK CHICKEN

Prepare as directed at right, but **use** the following sauce: 1/4 cup olive oil, 2 minced cloves garlic, 2 tablespoons each white wine vinegar, lime juice, and grated fresh ginger, 1 tablespoon molasses, 1 teaspoon each hot red pepper sauce, salt, and ground allspice, and 3/4 teaspoon ground cinnamon. **Use** sauce to marinate and baste the chicken. Makes 4 servings.

TAR HEEL BARBECUED CHICKEN

Prepare as directed at right, but **use** the following sauce: 6 tablespoons cider vinegar, 2 tablespoons each vegetable oil and firmly packed light brown sugar, 2 minced cloves garlic, and 1 teaspoon each hot red pepper sauce and salt. **Let** sauce stand at room temperature for several hours before using to marinate the chicken. Makes 4 servings.

Texas-Style Barbecued Chicken

- 2 tablespoons olive oil
- 1 large yellow onion, chopped
- 1 stalk celery, chopped
- 2 cloves garlic, minced
- 1 cup ketchup
- 1/2 cup bourbon
- 1/2 cup Rich Chicken Stock or canned reduced-sodium chicken broth
- 1/4 cup molasses
- 3 tablespoons cider vinegar
- 1 tablespoon prepared yellow mustard
- Zest and juice of 1 lemon (about 2 teaspoons zest, 4 1/2 teaspoons juice)
- 1/4 to 1/2 teaspoon hot red pepper sauce
- 1 broiler-fryer (3 to 3 1/2 pounds), quartered

1 In a medium-size saucepan over moderate heat, heat oil 1 minute. Add onion and celery and sauté, stirring occasionally, until soft—about 5 minutes. Add garlic and sauté 2 minutes more.

2 Add ketchup, bourbon, stock, molasses, vinegar, mustard, lemon zest and juice, and hot red pepper sauce and bring to a boil over high heat. Reduce the heat to low and simmer, uncovered, for 20 minutes; set aside or cool, store in a container with a tight-fitting lid, and refrigerate for up to 3 days.

3 Gently pull the skin back from the chicken to expose the flesh but do not tear or remove it. Place in a large self-sealing plastic bag, add 1/2 the sauce, seal, and refrigerate for at least 4 hours or overnight, turning occasionally. Refrigerate remaining sauce until ready to use.

4 Preheat the grill or broiler. Remove chicken from bag, reserving sauce. Smooth chicken skin back into place and arrange chicken, skin side down, 5 inches above a drip pan over glowing coals. Cover the grill, leaving the vents halfway open (or adjusting for the wind and outdoor temperature. Cook chicken, turning once, until both sides are browned—15 to 20 minutes. Brush chicken generously with sauce and continue grilling and basting, turning once, until the meat near the thigh bone is no longer pink when cut—25 to 30 minutes more. Note: To broil in the oven, place chicken, skin side down, 7 to 9 inches from the heat and broil 10 minutes. Brush with sauce and broil 5 minutes more. Turn chicken and continue broiling and basting about 15 minutes more.

5 Meanwhile, in a small saucepan over low heat, heat the refrigerated sauce from Step 3 until hot and bubbly. Serve as a dipping sauce with the barbecued chicken. Makes 4 servings.

1 Serving: Calories 746; Total Fat 29 g; Saturated Fat 7 g; Protein 44 g; Carbohydrates 52 g; Fiber 2 g; Sodium 929 mg; Cholesterol 141 mg

prep time-1 hour • cooking time-about 1 hour

GRILLED SHRIMP

Quick and delicious scampi can be sautéed on the grill or stove. Sautéing intensifies shrimp's natural succulence and savor as do our two easy grill variations—one Asian, one American.

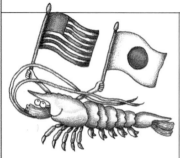

AT THE MARKET

If possible, buy shrimp the day you plan to cook them. Frozen and thawed shrimp come without their heads, fresh shrimp with their heads on. Shells may be gray-green, pinkish, or brown, depending on the variety and where the shrimp were caught.

Shrimp thaw very quickly. If their aroma has turned to the odor of ammonia, ask for a just-thawed bunch.

THE RIGHT SIZE FOR GRILLING

For grilling, buy big shrimp, at least jumbo size. Expect 12 to 15 jumbo shrimp per pound and about 10 colossal.

Smaller shrimp are difficult to handle over fire because they're apt to slip through the rack or the grilling basket, and they're hard to turn with long-handled tongs.

CLEANING SHRIMP

Many recipes call for deveining shrimp. This refers to the large vein or sand track that is located along the back of all shrimp but is particularly visible in large and jumbo shrimp.

It's not always necessary to remove the vein, but if it contains sand it will be gritty. If you can't see the vein, it's clean.

READY TO GRILL

Shell and devein the shrimp if desired. Arrange them in a grilling basket or thread them on skewers and place on the grill 3 to 4 inches above a moderately hot fire.

Brush the shrimp lightly with oil if not marinated, and cook until pink. Turn and grill on the other side. Allow 5 to 7 minutes total cooking time, half on each side. When done, the shrimp will be pink and the flesh opaque white.

To check the shrimp for doneness, taste one. Overcooking toughens shrimp and robs them of flavor.

TO PREPARE SHRIMP

Shrimp can be marinated and grilled with or without their shells.

1 To peel a shrimp, cut the shell along the back with scissors or a sharp knife. Peel off all but the tail shell.

2 To devein, use a short sharp knife to make a shallow cut along the back of each shrimp.

3 Pull out the vein or wash it out under cold running water.

ON THE GRILL

To prevent shrimp from slipping through the rack on a grill, use an oiled grill basket that hinges open and latches shut. The same basket can be used for burgers, buns, and other foods.

As an alternative, thread shrimp on bamboo skewers that have been well soaked in water. Using only 2 shrimp per skewer leaves enough of a handle for turning the shrimp and removing them from the grill.

Jumbo shrimp can be butterflied for the grill. Shell and devein them, leaving the tail intact. Then using a sharp knife, slice them along the back, but not all the way through. Spread them flat.

GRILLED PEPPER SHRIMP

Marinate 1 pound peeled or unpeeled jumbo shrimp in 1/4 cup lemon juice, 1/2 teaspoon salt, and 1 tablespoon cracked black pepper in the refrigerator for 1 hour. **Grill** over moderately hot coals 3 1/2 minutes on each side. Or **broil** 4 inches from the heat of a preheated broiler for 4 to 5 minutes on each side. Makes 4 servings.

GRILLED ASIAN-STYLE SHRIMP

Prepare Grilled Pepper Shrimp as directed above, **omitting** black pepper and **adding** 2 tablespoons dark sesame oil, 1 large minced clove garlic, and 1 tablespoon soy sauce to the marinade. **Grill** or **broil** as directed. Makes 4 servings.

Shrimp Scampi Pan Sauté

- 2 tablespoons unsalted butter or margarine
- 1 pound jumbo shrimp, peeled and deveined
- 2 cloves garlic, minced

- 1/2 teaspoon salt
- 1 teaspoon ground white pepper
- 2 tablespoons chopped parsley
- 3 tablespoons lemon juice

1 Heat a large skillet on a grill rack 4 to 6 inches from the heat or over moderately high heat on the stove. Melt butter in skillet. When foamy, add shrimp and sauté for 2 minutes.

2 Add garlic, salt, pepper, and parsley and cook 1 minute more. Stir in lemon juice.

3 Serve over cooked white rice. Makes 4 servings.

1 Serving: Calories 127; Total Fat 7 g; Saturated Fat 4 g; Protein 15 g; Carbohydrates 2 g; Fiber 0 g; Sodium 423 mg; Cholesterol 150 mg

*prep time-10 minutes
cooking time-3 minutes*

SIZZLING FISH STEAKS

Grilled fish is a fine dish to set before anyone you'd like to treat like royalty. Prepared our way, it comes from the grill succulent and full of flavor.

THE BEST FISH FOR GRILLING

Blackfish, or tautog: firm white flesh; very mild. Buy 1-inch-thick steaks for grilling.

Butterfish: oily fish; sweet flavor. Grill whole (they weigh less than 1/2 pound each).

Mahi-mahi, or dolphinfish: low fat; sweet firm flesh. Grill 1-inch-thick fillets or steaks.

Marlin: meaty, lean, and mild. Grill 1 1/4-inch-thick steaks or cubes for kabobs.

Salmon: pink salmon is the lowest in fat; chinook salmon has the richest flavor. Grill 1-inch-thick fillets or steaks.

Shark: lean to moderately fat; mild flavored. Grill 1-inch-thick or thicker fillets or steaks.

Swordfish: firm, fairly lean, and sweet; stays moist in cooking. Grill 1 1/4-inch-thick steaks or cubes for kabobs.

Tuna: firm, moderately fat; flesh turns gray-brown when cooked. Grill 1 1/4-inch-thick steaks or cubes for kabobs.

BUYING AND STORING FISH

Oily fish are the best fish for grilling. Buy 1/3 to 1/2 pound per person the day you plan to cook it. Remove any heavy wrappings and store the fish, loosely wrapped in wax paper, in the refrigerator meat keeper until it's time to cook.

MARINADES

Marinate the fish, if desired, in 1/4 cup of olive oil, 2 tablespoons of lemon juice, and 1 tablespoon of minced parsley, rosemary, or dill. Or make a marinade of 1/2 cup of bottled Italian dressing thinned with 2 tablespoons of lemon juice or white wine vinegar.

BUTTERS FOR GRILLING

Flavored butters keep fish and other foods moist on the grill.

Mix butter with flavorings. Spoon into ramekins and cover with wax paper. For logs, wait until butter has firmed slightly before forming. Wrap well in wax paper, label, date, and freeze until ready to use.

Put the fish and marinade in a self-sealing plastic bag. Refrigerate for no more than 1/2 hour. Marinating too long will spoil the flavor and texture of fish.

Drain the fish and pour the marinade into a small pan and heat at the side of the grill to brush on the fish while grilling.

STICKY BUSINESS

Fish is delicate. To keep it from sticking to the grill, wrap steaks, fillets, or small whole fish in aluminum foil with holes punched in it.

Or wrap each piece of fish in a lettuce or cabbage leaf. Secure with a poultry trussing pin or a toothpick that has been well soaked in water. Brush the leaf with oil and place on an oiled grill. The leaf is discarded when the fish is served.

Alternatively, spritz the fish and grill with nonstick spray. Or place the fish in a well-oiled hinged grilling basket.

ON THE GRILL

Fish cooks fairly quickly. Depending on thickness, it will need only between 4 and 15 minutes total and will probably have to be turned only once on the grill. Use a wide oiled spatula to turn it. The flesh near the center should almost flake and should be moist when tested with a fork. Serve immediately.

UNDER THE BROILER

To insure even cooking when preparing thick fish steaks indoors, broil the fish quickly to brown the flesh. Then bake at 375°F, basting occasionally, until the flesh turns opaque.

FLAVORED BUTTERS

Horseradish Butter: 1/4 cup butter, 2 tablespoons drained prepared horseradish, 1/8 teaspoon each cayenne and salt

Honey-Mustard Butter: 1/4 cup butter, 4 teaspoons Dijon mustard, 1/2 teaspoon honey

Lemon Butter: 1/4 cup butter, 1/4 teaspoon grated lemon zest, 2 teaspoons lemon juice, 1/8 teaspoon each cayenne and salt

Herb Butter: 1/4 cup butter, up to 3 tablespoons chopped parsley, tarragon, and/or chives, 1/4 teaspoon grated lemon zest, 2 teaspoons lemon juice, 1/8 teaspoon each cayenne and salt

Grilled Tuna with Caper and Olive Butter

Prepare as directed at right, **substituting** tuna steaks for swordfish steaks. For the butter, **omit** anchovies and **add** 1 tablespoon chopped drained capers, 1 tablespoon finely chopped Kalamata olives, and 1/4 teaspoon crushed fennel seeds (optional). Makes 4 servings.

Grilled Salmon with Peach Salsa

Prepare as directed at right, **substituting** salmon steaks for swordfish steaks and **omitting** marinade. Instead, **rub** salmon with 1/2 teaspoon salt, 1/4 teaspoon sugar, and a pinch of ground allspice. **Brush** with 1 tablespoon olive oil and **grill** as directed.

For the Salsa: Mix together 2 diced, peeled, pitted peaches, 3/4 cup thawed frozen corn kernels, 1/2 cup chili sauce, 1/4 cup each finely diced red onion and sweet red pepper, 1/4 cup each chopped fresh mint and coriander (cilantro), 2 tablespoons each honey and lime juice, and 1/2 teaspoon salt. **Spoon** salsa over the cooked fish. Makes 4 servings.

Grilled Swordfish with Anchovy Butter

Swordfish:
- 4 **swordfish steaks (6 ounces each)**
- 1/2 **teaspoon salt**
- 1/2 **teaspoon dried rosemary, crumbled**
- 2 **tablespoons olive oil**

Anchovy Butter:
- 1/4 **cup (1/2 stick) unsalted butter or margarine, softened**
- 4 **anchovy filets, mashed, or 2 teaspoons anchovy paste**
- 1/4 **teaspoon grated lemon zest**
- 2 **teaspoons lemon juice**
- 1/8 **teaspoon cayenne**
- 1/8 **teaspoon salt**

1 For the Swordfish: In a shallow bowl, sprinkle swordfish with salt and rosemary and rub into fish. Sprinkle with oil and turn fish to coat. The fish can be refrigerated, covered, up to 4 hours before grilling.

2 For the Anchovy Butter: In a small bowl or in an electric mixer, combine butter, anchovies, lemon zest and juice, cayenne, and salt. Transfer to a small ramekin and refrigerate, covered, until ready to serve.

3 Preheat the grill or broiler. Generously oil the grill or broiler rack to prevent fish from sticking. Grill over moderately hot coals 8 inches from the heat until just cooked through, 2 to 3 minutes on each side. Or broil 6 inches from the heat of a preheated broiler.

4 Remove with a well-oiled metal spatula and top hot fish with a spoonful of chilled butter. Makes 4 servings.

1 Serving: Calories 310; Total Fat 23 g; Saturated Fat 9 g; Protein 24 g; Carbohydrates 0 g; Fiber 0 g; Sodium 569 mg; Cholesterol 79 mg

prep time-6 minutes • cooking time-4 minutes

VEGETABLES ON THE GRILL

Vegetables benefit almost more than meats from cooking over charcoal. The caramelizing of natural sugars gives old reliables new flavor and style.

GARDEN PICKS

Fleshy vegetables work best on the grill. Try corn on the cob, eggplant, potatoes, summer squashes, and portobello or other large mushroom caps.

PREPPING FOR THE GRILL

Wash vegetables and trim off any blemishes. Don't peel the vegetables unless specified in a recipe. Skin helps them hold their shape and stay moist. Wipe dirt off mushrooms with damp paper toweling.

PRIME CUTS

Cut vegetables in thick slices. Slabs of eggplant, large summer and zucchini squash, and giant sweet Bermuda, Spanish, or Vidalia onions can be turned and basted individually or grouped in a grilling basket and turned all together.

Grill small squash, bell peppers, and unpeeled onions whole. Cut large tomatoes into wedges, small ones in half. Tomato wedges or cherry tomatoes can be cooked on skewers to prevent them from falling through the grill.

When grilling vegetables on skewers, be sure to pair up soft vegetables, such as tomatoes and mushrooms, with other soft vegetables. Cook hard vegetables, such as peppers and onions, together. Alternatively, parboil firm vegetables and then cook them along with softer ones.

CORN ON THE GRILL

Corn is sweeter when it's steamed in its own husks on the grill. To prepare it, follow the steps at right. Corn grilled without its husks or a foil wrap dries out, but it does take on a pleasant roasted flavor. To cook husked corn, place the ears on the grill and brush with barbecue sauce or water every 3 to 5 minutes to prevent burning.

Either way you cook it, grilled corn is terrific served with one of our flavored butters or flavorful dry rubs. The recipes appear on page 202.

(continued on page 202)

TO PREPARE AND GRILL VEGETABLES

Corn in the Husk

1 Peel back husks and pull off silk. Remove excess silk with a vegetable brush.

2 Fold the husks back and secure with string. Soak in water for 1/2 to 11/2 hours.

Corn in Foil

1 Husk the ears, pulling off silk as above. Remove the husks completely.

2 Wrap each ear in aluminum foil. Puncture the foil and place on grill.

Cutting Slices and Slabs

Cut vegetables in slices or strips about 1/2-inch thick. Arrange carefully on grill or set in grill basket.

Small vegetables and small cuts can be grilled on skewers. Cook soft vegetables separately from firm ones.

Marinated Grilled Vegetables

- ³/₄ cup chopped fresh coriander (cilantro)
- ¹/₄ cup white or red wine vinegar
- ¹/₃ cup olive or vegetable oil
- 1¹/₂ teaspoons grated lime zest
- 3 tablespoons lime juice
- ³/₄ teaspoon salt
- ¹/₄ to ¹/₂ teaspoon sugar
- ¹/₄ to ¹/₂ teaspoon hot red pepper sauce
- ¹/₄ teaspoon black pepper
- 1¹/₂ pounds eggplant, zucchini, summer squash, sweet peppers, or portobello mushrooms or a combination, prepared for grilling

1 In a small bowl, whisk together all ingredients except vegetables.

2 Place grill-ready vegetables (except mushrooms) in a self-sealing plastic bag and pour in marinade. Seal and turn to coat vegetables. Refrigerate, turning occasionally, up to 4 hours. Add mushrooms for the last 2 hours.

3 Remove vegetables from the bag and reserve the marinade.

4 Preheat the grill. Oil grill to prevent sticking. Place vegetables directly over medium to medium-hot coals—about 5 inches from the heat—and grill in the order and according to the times listed on page 202, turning and brushing occasionally with marinade. Makes 4 servings, about 1 cup marinade.

1 Tablespoon Marinade: Calories 41; Total Fat 4 g; Saturated Fat 1 g; Protein 0 g; Carbohydrates 1 g; Fiber 0 g; Sodium 100 mg; Cholesterol 0 mg

prep time-30 minutes
marinating time-2 to 4 hours

BASIL-THYME GRILLED VEGETABLES

Prepare as directed at left, **using** the following marinade: ¹/₃ cup olive or vegetable oil, 3 tablespoons lemon juice, 2 tablespoons each chopped fresh basil and thyme or 2 teaspoons crumbled dried basil or thyme, 1¹/₂ teaspoons salt, and ¹/₄ teaspoon black pepper. Makes about 1 cup marinade.

ASIAN GRILLED VEGETABLES

Prepare as directed at left, **substituting** the following basting sauce for marinade: 1 finely minced large shallot, 4¹/₂ teaspoons balsamic vinegar, 2 tablespoons soy sauce, 1¹/₂ teaspoons dark sesame oil, 1 teaspoon Dijon mustard, 1 minced clove garlic, ¹/₄ to ¹/₂ teaspoon sugar, and ¹/₈ to ¹/₄ teaspoon hot red pepper sauce. Do not marinate. Instead, **baste** just before grilling and once at halftime when turning. If using mushrooms, **leave** caps whole. Makes about ¹/₄ cup basting sauce.

(continued from page 200)

NOT SO HOT

When grilling vegetables alone, make the fire small. When grilling them along with meat, make a large fire and place meat in the center and vegetables at the edge.

TO THE GRILL

Arrange the vegetables on a rack set crosswise on the grill to prevent the vegetables from falling onto the coals.

Brush the vegetables with sauce—the same sauce that you use on the meat you are grilling if you wish—or with a simple mixture of 2/3 oil to 1/3 vinegar or lemon juice.

Cook vegetables over moderate heat at the edge of the grill. Turn them with a wide spatula or tongs. Approximate times are:

15 to 20 minutes—thick slices of zucchini or yellow squash, eggplant, whole tomatoes, mixed vegetables on skewers;

20 to 25 minutes—whole zucchini, summer squash, large mushroom caps;

35 to 45 minutes—corn in the husk or husked and wrapped in foil, turned often;

45 to 50 minutes—corn without husk brushed with sauce; whole eggplant for purée; thick onion or potato slices;

Grilled Corn in Husks

4 medium-size ears sweet corn

1 Gently peel husks back to within 2 inches of the base. Remove silk and smooth husks back into place, completely covering kernels. Using kitchen twine, tie husks in several places to secure.

2 Fill a sink or a large sauce pot with ice water and soak corn for 30 minutes to 1 hour. Drain and shake off excess water.

3 Preheat the grill. Generously oil the grill to prevent sticking. Grill directly over medium to medium-hot coals 5 inches from the heat, turning occasionally, until tender—30 to 45 minutes.

4 Remove string and husks and serve with one of the flavored butters at right. Makes 4 servings.

1 Serving (without butter): Calories 83; Total Fat 1 g; Saturated Fat 0 g; Protein 3 g; Carbohydrates 19 g; Fiber 2 g; Sodium 13 mg; Cholesterol 0 mg

prep time-30 minutes • soaking time-30 minutes to 1 hour cooking time-30 to 45 minutes

DRY RUBS FOR CORN

Chili-Cumin Rub: In a small bowl, **stir** together 2 1/2 teaspoons each chili powder and ground cumin and 1 teaspoon salt. Makes 2 tablespoons.

Ginger-Curry Rub: In a small bowl, **stir** together 4 teaspoons grated fresh ginger and 1 teaspoon each curry powder and salt. Makes 2 tablespoons.

Mixed-Herb Rub: In a small bowl, **stir** together 1 tablespoon each freshly chopped rosemary, sage, and thyme or 1 1/2 teaspoons each crumbled dried rosemary, sage, and thyme. Makes 3 tablespoons.

1 1/4 to 1 3/4 hours—whole large unpeeled onions, whole baking potatoes or sweet potatoes, turned every 10 minutes to cook evenly.

FLAVOR TRICK

Dip a sprig of fresh herb in the sauce or oil and vinegar or lemon juice mixture and brush it over the vegetables when you turn them. Just before the vegetables are done, drop the herb onto the coals to flavor the vegetables even more. Use basil for the tomatoes or bell peppers, sage for onions, thyme or dill for squashes, and rosemary for almost any vegetable.

CORN IN FOIL

Clean 4 medium-size ears of sweet corn. **Cut** an 18-inch square of heavy-duty foil and **place** corn in center of foil. **Season** with one of the flavored butters or rubs below, if desired. If using a rub, **dot** each ear with 1 tablespoon butter and **sprinkle** with 1 tablespoon water. **Bring** together 2 edges of foil and **fold** to seal, **leaving** space for steam. **Fold** short ends of foil in to seal. **Grill** as directed until tender—about 45 minutes. **Remove** foil and **serve** with flavored butter if not already seasoned. Makes 4 servings.

FLAVORED BUTTERS

Sun-Dried Tomato and Basil Butter: In a medium-size bowl, **mix** together 1/2 cup (1 stick) softened unsalted butter or margarine, 1/4 cup chopped, well-drained, oil-packed sun-dried tomatoes, and 1/3 cup finely chopped fresh basil until well blended. Makes 1/2 cup.

Roasted Pepper and Black Olive Butter: In a medium-size bowl, **mix** together 1/2 cup (1 stick) softened butter or margarine, 1/4 cup each finely chopped roasted red peppers and chopped, pitted black olives, and 1/4 teaspoon black pepper until well blended. Makes 1/2 cup.

Lemon-Chive Butter: In a medium-size bowl, **mix** together 1/2 cup (1 stick) softened butter or margarine, 1/4 cup snipped fresh chives or 4 teaspoons crumbled freeze dried, and 2 teaspoons grated lemon zest until well blended. Makes 1/2 cup.

FRESH FISH AND SHELLFISH

FISH FILLETS

*F*illets of sole or flounder are excellent grilled, broiled, pan-fried, or poached. Our recipes provide tips and variations for all the basic methods.

IS IT SOLE OR FLOUNDER?

Both sole and flounder are lean white-fleshed flatfish whose names are often interchanged. Gray sole, or witch flounder, and Dover sole are shipped from Europe and served in first-class restaurants but are hard to find in fish markets. The soles and flounders below are easier to find.

Butter, petrale, and rex sole are all small Pacific flounders, with petrale generally ranked the best of the three. Lemon sole, or winter flounder, is fished on the east coast. English sole is a small Pacific flounder and sand dab an even smaller one especially popular on the west coast.

HANDLE WITH CARE

Whatever way you cook them, sole and flounder should be handled as little as possible; the meat is fragile. Use a wide spatula—or two if necessary—to turn the fillets or to lift them when done.

Follow the suggested cooking times in our recipes. Don't cook the fillets any longer than necessary; they will be dry and crumbly if you do.

POACHING LUCK

The best skillets for cooking fillets of delicate white fish include enameled cast iron, heavy-gauge aluminum with a nonreactive lining, stainless steel with a heat-conducting core, or a heavy copper skillet lined with tin or stainless steel.

Unclad iron or aluminum skillets are unsuitable because acid in the poaching liquid takes on a metallic taste and also darkens.

POACHING STEPS

To prevent the fish from sticking, spritz the skillet with nonstick vegetable spray or brush it lightly with butter or vegetable oil.

Barely cover the fillet with poaching liquid. Wine, clam broth, fish stock, water with lemon juice, or a combination

of all are good mediums.

Keep the poaching liquid simmering gently, barely trembling. Never let it boil because the vigorous bubbling may break the fish apart.

Cover the skillet so that steam helps to cook the fish.

READY OR NOT

After 3 or 4 minutes of poaching, test the thickest fillet. Push a fork gently into the center. If the flesh is opaque, the fish is done. If it falls apart in flakes, it is overcooked. A sauce will cover up the error.

Preheat the platter for fish in a warm oven, hot water, or the plate-warming or hot-dry cycle of a dishwasher.

Lift the fish to the platter, cover with aluminum foil, and hold in an oven heated to 175°F to 200°F while you stir the sauce. Do not use higher heat or the fish will continue to cook and dry out.

How to Roll a Fish Fillet

Open the fillet flat, skinned side up, and heap with stuffing. Roll up the fillet lengthwise from wide to narrow ends. Secure the roll with a toothpick.

Jacques Pépin
Host of Today's Gourmet

"For roll-ups, or *paupiettes*, roll fillets fleshy side out. The skinned side of the fillet on the inside will contract during cooking and hold the shape of the roll.

"If the skinned side of the fillet is on the outside, the *paupiettes* will unroll during cooking. If rolled correctly, a toothpick will not even be needed to hold it."

FLOUNDER ROLL-UPS WITH LEMON SAUCE

Place fillets flesh side down, **roll up** starting from wider end, and **secure** with a toothpick. **Place** 1 thinly sliced lemon in a shallow buttered casserole. **Arrange** fish rolls on top, seam side down. **Add** 1/2 cup each dry white wine and fish broth, 2 sprigs parsley, 1 sprig thyme or 1/4 teaspoon crumbled dried thyme, 2 tablespoons finely chopped yellow onion, 1/2 teaspoon salt, and 3 black peppercorns. **Cover** loosely with foil and **bake** in a preheated 350°F oven for 20 to 25 minutes. **Transfer** to a heated serving platter. **Prepare** sauce as directed in Step 3, **adding** 1 tablespoon lemon juice and 1/2 teaspoon grated lemon zest. **Pour** sauce over fillets, **garnish** with minced parsley and lemon slices, and **serve**. Makes 4 servings.

Sole Véronique

Prepare as directed at right, **adding** 1/2 teaspoon grated lemon zest to sauce. **Omit** parsley and **top** sauce with 1 cup halved, peeled, seedless green grapes. **Place** in a preheated broiler and **broil** 6 inches from the heat 1 to 2 minutes. Makes 4 servings.

Sautéed Fillets

Lightly **dredge** fillets in 1/4 cup all-purpose flour mixed with 1/8 teaspoon each salt and pepper, **shaking off** excess. **Sauté** in a heavy skillet over moderately high heat in 3 to 4 tablespoons butter or margarine (or mixture of 1/2 butter and 1/2 oil) until lightly browned—about 3 to 4 minutes on each side. **Drain** fish on paper toweling and serve. Makes 4 servings.

Breaded Fillets

Lightly **dredge** fillets in 1/4 cup all-purpose flour mixed with 1/8 teaspoon each salt and pepper and 1 to 2 teaspoons grated Parmesan cheese or 1/2 teaspoon crumbled dried thyme or marjoram. **Shake off** excess. **Dip** in mixture of 1 beaten egg and 2 tablespoons water or milk, then in fine dry bread crumbs or cornmeal. **Sauté** as directed above. Makes 4 servings.

Fillet of Sole with White Wine Sauce

Sole:
- 4 fillets of sole or flounder (about 1 1/2 pounds)
- 1 cup dry white wine
- 1/2 to 1 cup Fish Broth or water
- 2 sprigs parsley
- 1 sprig thyme
- 2 tablespoons minced yellow onion
- 1/2 teaspoon salt
- 3 black peppercorns

Sauce:
- 2 tablespoons butter or margarine
- 2 tablespoons all-purpose flour
- 1/2 cup heavy cream
- 1/2 teaspoon salt
- 1/8 teaspoon ground white pepper
- 2 tablespoons minced parsley

1 For the Sole: Place fillets in a single layer in a heavy 10-inch skillet. Add wine and enough broth (page 54) just to cover fish. Add remaining ingredients and bring to a boil over high heat. Reduce the heat to moderately low and simmer, covered, until fish almost flakes at the touch of a fork—3 to 4 minutes. Transfer to a heated serving platter, reserving poaching liquid. Cover fish with aluminum foil and keep warm.

2 Strain poaching liquid through a fine sieve and add more broth if needed to total 1 cup.

3 For the Sauce: In a medium-size saucepan over moderate heat, melt butter. With a wooden spoon, blend in flour and cook and stir for 3 minutes. Gradually whisk in reserved poaching liquid, cream, salt, and white pepper. Cook, whisking constantly, until thickened and smooth—2 to 3 minutes.

4 Uncover fish and pour off any accumulated liquid. Pour sauce over fish, sprinkle with parsley, and serve. Makes 4 servings.

1 Serving: Calories 386; Total Fat 20 g; Saturated Fat 11 g; Protein 33 g; Carbohydrates 4 g; Fiber 0 g; Sodium 923 mg; Cholesterol 143 mg

prep time-10 minutes • cooking time-10 minutes

PAN-FRIED FISH

*S*mall whole trout served one to a person make a beautiful presentation at the table. They are also one of the quickest, easiest fish to cook to perfection.

AT THE MARKET

Most trout on the market are farm raised in freshwater ponds. Buy fish that are gutted but whole, which allows you to inspect the eyes and skin for freshness. The trout should have a clean smell, bright eyes that are not sunken, and moist—not slimy—skin. Press the flesh with a finger; it should spring back.

OUNCES PER SERVING

Buy an 8- to 10-ounce fish for each person. This includes bone, tail, and head, which will be trimmed off at the table or just before serving. Cooking whole fish with the head on helps to keep it moist.

If possible, buy fish on the day you plan to cook it. Wrap it loosely in parchment or wax paper and keep it in the meat tray of the refrigerator. Cook it within 24 hours.

A LIGHT COAT

A filmy coating of a flour-cornmeal mixture is just right for fish. A heavy coating will make a pasty or soggy crust. Cornmeal adds a crispness that flour cannot provide by itself.

Dip the fish lightly in a mound of flour, cornmeal, and seasonings and shake off the excess.

To be sure the skillet is hot enough, heat the oil or fat until a cube of bread turns golden in 30 seconds. Remove the bread and add the fish, cooking 1 or 2 at a time.

Reheat the fat for the next batch. Hot fat crisps the coating and keeps it from absorbing excess oil.

DOUBLE INSURANCE

Remove the hot fish to a warmed platter lined with paper toweling to absorb surface oil. A country chef's trick is to drain sautéed catfish in a flat pan lined with sliced bread. The bread can then be frozen and recycled into stuffing for baked fish.

HOT STUFF

Pan-fried or deep-fried fish must be very hot to taste its best. When cooking fish in batches, as in our recipe, have the platter warm beforehand.

Heat the platter in a slow oven, in hot water, or in the dishwasher warming cycle. As fish are added to the platter, crimp a sheet of aluminum foil over them to hold in the heat.

HOW TO FLIP A FISH

The easiest way to flip a fish is to turn the head with kitchen tongs while turning the body with a spatula. Alternatively, use 2 spatulas.

When cooking several batches, slip the freshly cooked trout into a slow (175°F to 200°F) oven and bring it out hot and delicious. Serve the fish within 15 minutes or it will dry out and lose its fresh flavor.

If you're planning to fry fish for a crowd, don't try to serve everyone at one time. It's easier, and the fish tastes better, if you cook and serve in shifts.

MORE FISH THIS WAY

Trout are not the only small fish that are ideal for pan-frying whole. Try our recipes with any of the following:

Small freshwater catfish; sunfish, such as bluegills and redbreasts; smelts—tiny whole fish from the Great Lakes; tilapia—a farmed fish.

Small ocean fish, often called panfish in the market, that are good for sautéing and deep-frying include spot (croaker), butterfish, porgy, butterflied bluefish, or small snappers.

HOW TO BONE COOKED TROUT

1 Using a sharp fillet or boning knife, slice just above the fin line along the back.

2 Rotate the fish and slice just above the fin line along the belly.

3 With a thin spatula, gently lift off the top fillet and backbone.

4 Replace the top fillet on the bottom fillet and, if desired, cut off the head and tail.

Pan-fried Trout with Bacon and Sage

- 4 **whole trout (¹/₂ to ³/₄ pound each), dressed**
- ¹/₄ **cup chopped fresh sage or 2 teaspoons dried sage, crumbled**
- 1¹/₂ **teaspoons salt**
- ³/₄ **teaspoon black pepper**
- ¹/₂ **cup all-purpose flour**
- ¹/₄ **cup white or yellow cornmeal**
- 2 **tablespoons bacon or ham drippings**
- 2 **tablespoons vegetable oil**

1 Pat fish dry and sprinkle inside and out with 2 tablespoons of the sage, 1 teaspoon of the salt, and ½ teaspoon of the pepper.

2 On a piece of wax paper, combine flour, cornmeal, and 2 tablespoons of the sage, ¼ teaspoon of the salt, and ¼ teaspoon of the pepper. Coat fish, shake off excess, and set aside.

3 Spray sides of a large skillet with nonstick cooking spray. Over moderately high heat, heat 1 tablespoon each of the bacon drippings and oil 1 minute.

4 Working with 2 fish at a time, sauté for 5 minutes. Using 2 pancake turners, turn fish and sauté until fish almost flake at the touch of a fork—about 5 minutes more.

5 Transfer to a heated serving platter and keep warm while sautéing the remaining fish the same way. Makes 4 servings.

1 Serving: Calories 427; Total Fat 25 g; Saturated Fat 7 g; Protein 36 g; Carbohydrates 11 g; Fiber 1 g; Sodium 545 mg; Cholesterol 107 mg

prep time-45 minutes • cooking time-30 minutes

PROSCIUTTO-WRAPPED TROUT WITH LEMON THYME

Prepare as directed beginning with Step 2 above, **substituting** lemon thyme for sage and **omitting** salt. **Omit** Step 3. Instead, **wrap** 3 paper-thin 6- by 3-inch slices of prosciutto around each fish, **overlapping** so fish is completely encased. **Continue** as directed in Steps 4 and 5, using vegetable oil instead of bacon drippings-oil mixture. Makes 4 servings.

BLACKENED FISH

Ever since the day that Cajun chef Paul Prudhomme discovered his skillet was so hot that redfish blackened before he could turn it—and that it tasted superb—chefs have been following his lead.

SPICY STUFF

Spicy blackened fish, chicken, and steak are now synonymous with Cajun cooking. Although a blend of seasonings flavors blackened fish, the spices should not be incendiary.

The first time you make it, use the lower amounts of pepper suggested in the recipe at right and build up the heat a little the next time you try it.

The seasoning mixture in our recipe includes 3 types of ground peppers as well as dried herbs and onion and garlic powders.

The heat of the peppers penetrates the fish and the rest of the seasoning mix quickly chars, leaving the fish deliciously succulent inside.

THE HEAT

You will have the best luck blackening fish over heat that can be controlled easily. Instant-response gas flame is ideal. With an electric range, move the skillet on and off the burner as needed to cook fast and evenly. An outdoor gas grill works fine, but a charcoal fire doesn't get hot enough.

SMOKE ALARM

Blackening is apt to create smoke, which can set off the smoke alarm. So open the windows and if you have an exhaust fan, turn it on.

BLACK MAGIC

A heavy well-seasoned cast-iron skillet is essential for blackening food since the high heat required will ruin less sturdy pans. Use a wide spatula with a heat-resistant handle for turning the fish and have ready a heavy-duty pot holder for moving the skillet, if and when necessary.

Note: Many shops offer a choice of mitts and pot holders reinforced for high-heat use.

TO SEASON A SKILLET

A new cast-iron skillet has to be seasoned before it can be used. Wash and dry the pan, rub the inside generously with unsalted shortening, and place in a preheated 350°F oven for about 2 hours.

Once seasoned, do not clean the skillet with detergents. Use Kosher salt and a nonabrasive scrubber, then rinse and wipe dry. To avoid rust, place the pan over low heat to dry thoroughly.

Over time, a well-cared-for and seasoned cast-iron skillet ideally will blacken, developing its own nonstick surface.

TO BLACKEN

When you're ready to blacken fish, have your side dishes and the rest of the meal prepared because the fish cooks quickly.

Sprinkle and pat the spice blend on the fish for maximum seasoning. Have the fish ready beside the stove.

Heat the skillet over high heat until white ash begins to appear on the bottom of the skillet—about 10 minutes. The high heat should char the fish immediately, preventing it from sticking. But if your pan is not sufficiently seasoned, brush the hot skillet with a very thin film of peanut oil.

Place the fish in the hot skillet with a wide spatula. Two or 3 pieces can be cooked at once, but don't crowd them or the quick searing effect will be lost. Sear the fish until it is charred dark brown, turn it, and blacken the flip side.

Cooking times vary slightly depending on the thickness of the fish. Thinner fillets may

BLACKENED CURRIED FISH

Prepare as directed at right, **using** the following rub in Step 1: 2 teaspoons curry powder, 1 teaspoon salt, 1 teaspoon ground coriander, 1 teaspoon sugar, and 3/4 teaspoon ground ginger. Makes 4 servings.

JAMAICAN-STYLE BLACKENED SALMON

Prepare as directed at right, **substituting** 4 salmon or tuna steaks for catfish and **using** the following rub in Step 1: 2 teaspoons sugar, 1 teaspoon ground allspice, 1 teaspoon ground ginger, and 1 teaspoon salt. **Serve** with lime wedges. Makes 4 servings.

cook in 3 minutes per side or less. The cooking is so quick that the interior remains moist while the outside blackens.

GONE FISHING

Overfishing of redfish, the original fillet for blackening, drove cooks to other species, and there are many that blacken well.

Choose firm-textured meaty fillets. Eight-ounce skinned boneless catfish fillets will be about an inch thick. Other fish steaks and fillets to try include bass, swordfish, tuna, and salmon.

Blackened Catfish

- **1 teaspoon garlic powder**
- **1 teaspoon onion powder**
- **1 teaspoon salt**
- **1 teaspoon dried thyme, crumbled**
- **1 teaspoon dried oregano, crumbled**
- **1/2 to 1 teaspoon white pepper**
- **1/2 to 1 teaspoon black pepper**
- **1/4 to 1/2 teaspoon cayenne**
- **1/2 teaspoon sugar**
- **1 teaspoon olive oil (optional)**
- **4 skinless, boneless catfish fillets (8 ounces each) or salmon fillets or swordfish steaks**

1 In a small bowl, combine garlic powder, onion powder, salt, thyme, oregano, white pepper, black pepper, cayenne, and sugar. Rub mixture into both sides of fish.

2 Heat a large cast-iron skillet over high heat until white ash begins to form on the bottom—about 10 minutes. If the pan is not well seasoned, brush with oil to keep the fish from sticking.

3 Add fish, in batches if necessary, and cook until blackened—about 4 minutes on each side. Serve immediately. Makes 4 servings.

1 Serving: Calories 228; Total Fat 7 g; Saturated Fat 2 g; Protein 38 g; Carbohydrates 3 g; Fiber 0 g; Sodium 632 mg; Cholesterol 131 mg

prep time-5 minutes
cooking time-8 minutes

BAKED AND STUFFED

*B*aked whole fish filled with a savory stuffing is a surprisingly easy dish for a special occasion. The stuffing helps keep the fish moist and adds seasoning.

BAKE IT EASY

Stuffing a fish only looks difficult. Use our recipes for bass and snapper for stuffing and baking whole bluefish, mackerel, pike, sea bass, tilapia, and tilefish.

PLAN AHEAD

When baking fish, leave the head on. It helps retain juices and keeps the fish moist. If you prefer not to see the head at the dining table, remove it before transferring the fish to a serving platter.

STUFFING A FISH TO ORDER

We've butterflied our fish to make stuffing easy. To do so, split the fish down the center of the back from head to tail. First slide the knife along one side of the backbone, then the other. Carefully lift out the bone and open the fish flat. The stuffing is simply mounded on top of the butterflied fish.

If you've just reeled the fish in, butterfly it with a sharp boning knife. If you buy the fish, have it done at the fish market.

Buy the fish the day you plan to bake it. At some fish markets it may be necessary to order a cleaned whole fish a day or two in advance.

OTHER METHODS OF STUFFING

You can also stuff a fish by one of two other methods. The traditional way is to bone but not butterfly the fish by slicing it open on its side, along the back. Spoon the stuffing loosely into the cavity. You'll need about 2 cups of stuffing for a 4-pound fish. Close the fish cavity with toothpicks or sew it shut with coarse thread.

Place in an oiled or buttered shallow pan. If the fish is lean, brush with oil or melted butter and bake, uncovered, in a preheated 400°F oven. You'll need to bake it for 10 minutes per inch of thickness, so measure the thickest part.

Alternatively, stuff 2 matching fillets of salmon or other large firm-fleshed fish sandwich fashion. Lay 1 piece flat on a buttered baking pan and place the other over the filling.

Fasten the 2 fillets with toothpicks. Brush oil or melted butter on top. Bake, uncovered, at 400°F for 1/2 hour or until the fish almost flakes when touched with a fork.

OR NOT TO STUFF

If you want to bake a whole fish without stuffing it, prepare the fish as recommended for the traditional method of stuffing above. Lightly sprinkle the cavity with salt and pepper and herbs of your choice.

TO SERVE

Divide a butterflied stuffed fish into 2 portions by cutting down the center from head to tail with a sharp knife.

Cut our traditional boned whole stuffed fish and stuffed fillets crosswise.

HERBS TO TASTE

There are any number of herbs that complement fish. Use any of the following to season the stuffing or lightly sprinkle them on top to enhance the fish: basil, chervil, fresh coriander (cilantro), fresh or dried dill, a bit of mint with parsley or dill, fresh or a smidgen of dried sage, or tarragon.

HOW TO STUFF A BUTTERFLIED FISH

Open the fish flat on a baking sheet and heap each side with stuffing. Bake the fish opened flat.

MUSHROOM-RICE-STUFFED SNAPPER

Prepare as directed at right, **substituting** red snapper for striped bass. For the stuffing, **mix** together 2 cups cooked brown rice, 4 ounces sliced mushrooms sautéed in a little butter, 1/4 cup each chopped parsley and scallions, 1/2 teaspoon salt, and 1/4 teaspoon black pepper. Makes 2 servings.

CORNBREAD-BACON-STUFFED POMPANO

Prepare as directed at right, **substituting** pompano for bass, cornbread crumbs for bread crumbs, and crumbled crisp bacon for Parmesan. **Reduce** butter to 1 tablespoon and **omit** thyme and salt. Makes 2 servings.

Baked Striped Bass Stuffed with Herbed Bread Crumbs

Bass:
- 1 striped bass about (1½ pounds), butterflied, boned, and opened flat, with head and tail left on
- 1 tablespoon lemon juice

Stuffing:
- ¼ cup chopped parsley
- ¼ cup grated Parmesan cheese
- 1 cup dry bread crumbs
- 1 teaspoon dried thyme, crumbled
- 4 tablespoons melted unsalted butter or margarine
- ½ teaspoon salt
- ¼ teaspoon black pepper

1 Preheat the oven to 400°F. Spray a 15- by 10-inch jelly-roll pan with nonstick cooking spray.

2 For the Bass: Rub inside of fish with lemon juice. Place fish, skin side down, with the cavity open in the prepared pan.

3 For the Stuffing: In a small bowl, stir together all ingredients. Press bread crumb mixture evenly into open cavity and bake, uncovered, until golden—15 to 20 minutes. Makes 2 servings.

1 Serving: Calories 624; Total Fat 35 g; Saturated Fat 19 g; Protein 38 g; Carbohydrates 39 g; Fiber 3 g; Sodium 1302 mg; Cholesterol 167 mg

prep time-25 minutes
cooking time-15 to 20 minutes

FISH BAKED IN PACKETS

When you cook fish in a packet, you flavor it in one step, cook with little fat, and there are no pans to clean.

COOKING IN PACKETS

This method of cooking is called *en papillote,* meaning "in a paper casing." The fish and seasonings bake in their own juices sealed inside the packet. The technique allows steam to assist in the cooking. The flavors of scallions, garlic, ginger, and other aromatics become pungent and permeate the fish as they steam.

You can use baking parchment or aluminum foil for the packets. They can be assembled and refrigerated a few hours ahead. Remove from the refrigerator 1/2 hour before baking.

GOOD ALTERNATIVES

Halibut cooks up beautifully by this method. Also try blackfish, bluefish, cod or scrod, pompano, salmon, gray sole, shad, tilapia, tilefish, or any firm-fleshed fish that can be cut into chunks or pieces.

OTHER FOODS

Meat and poultry can also be cooked by this healthy method. Try chicken breasts, turkey cutlets, portion-size cuts of veal or pork tenderloin, or sweetbreads.

SEALED AND DELIVERED

To retain juices, the packet must not leak. Follow the directions at right for folding parchment. For airtight foil packs, double fold the foil all around the rim.

To bake, use a shallow baking pan large enough to hold the parcels without overlapping.

To open, cut an *X* on top of the packet with a knife or scissors and peel the paper or foil back. A burst of steam will be released, so keep your fingers out of the way.

If eating directly from the packets is awkward, serve them on heated shallow soup plates, slit the packets on the side, and slip the fish and vegetables into the bowls.

IS IT DONE YET?

Cooking by this method is quick. To check for doneness, unfold a foil packet along the edge. If the fish is not quite done, simply fold the edges

SHRIMP AND VEGETABLES IN PARCHMENT

Prepare as directed at right, **substituting** shelled and deveined jumbo shrimp for halibut. Also **substitute** 4 tablespoons soy sauce for lemon juice, 1 teaspoon grated ginger for shallots, and 1 cup each julienned leeks and zucchini for sweet peppers. **Omit** salt. Makes 4 servings.

SCALLOPS AND VEGETABLES

Prepare as directed for Shrimp and Vegetables in Parchment above, **substituting** bay scallops for shrimp and 2 cups trimmed snow peas for leeks and zucchini. Makes 4 servings.

again and place in the oven for another few minutes. If you are using parchment, poke a hole in it and test the fish with a fork. If the tines go in easily the fish is done.

JUICES OR CREAM

Fish and vegetables steam in their natural juices in our recipes. For added sauce, a tablespoon of cream may be added to each packet. Or sauté the shallots in a teaspoon of the butter, add 1/4 cup of white wine, bring it to a boil, and sprinkle the mixture over the fish and vegetables just before sealing the packets.

HOW TO WRAP A FISH PACKET

1 Place fish and vegetables to one side of center of baking parchment or foil.

2 Fold parchment in half, then roll and press sides to close firmly.

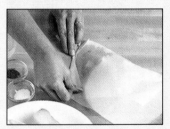

3 Roll and press edges toward the top opening.

4 Complete the closure by rolling and pressing along the top opening.

Halibut and Vegetables Baked in Parchment

- **1 halibut steak (about 1 pound), cut into 4 pieces**
- **1 teaspoon salt**
- **1/2 teaspoon black pepper**
- **4 teaspoons lemon juice**
- **2 shallots, finely chopped**
- **4 tablespoons unsalted butter or margarine, cut into bits**
- **2 medium-size carrots, peeled and julienned**
- **2 sweet peppers, 1 red and 1 green, cored, seeded, and cut into strips 1/4-inch wide**

1 Preheat the oven to 500°F. Place each piece of fish parallel to the narrow side of a 12- by 18-inch piece of parchment paper or foil, about 3 inches from the edge. Top with equal amounts of remaining ingredients.

2 Bring parchment over fish, seal edges tightly, and place on a baking sheet. Bake until parchment puffs out—about 15 minutes.

3 Place each packet on a serving plate, cut an *X* slit on top, and open carefully. Makes 4 servings.

1 Serving: Calories 248; Total Fat 14 g; Saturated Fat 8 g; Protein 23 g; Carbohydrates 8 g; Fiber 2 g; Sodium 604 mg; Cholesterol 164 mg

prep time-30 minutes • cooking time-15 minutes

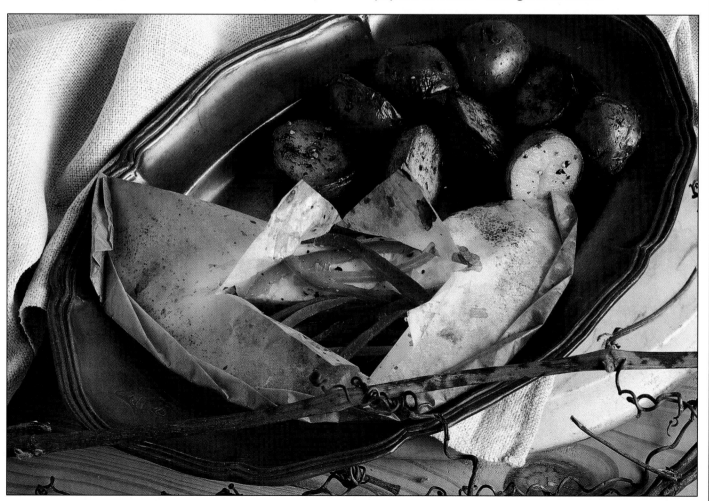

POACHED FISH

Cold poached salmon is a showpiece on a buffet table. Poached salmon fillets, our mini version, are quicker to make and nearly as impressive.

TO YOUR HEALTH

Poached salmon is one of the world's best tasting health foods. The fish oil in fresh salmon brims with Omega-3 fatty acids, which reduce the risk of heart disease by trimming the amount of cholesterol produced in the body.

In addition, poaching requires no fat. You can eliminate the sauce or serve it on the side and offer a squeeze of fresh lemon for waistline watchers.

AT THE MARKET

When choosing salmon for poaching, select fillets that have their skin; they hold up best in the poaching liquid. If the fish scales are still attached, have them cleaned off at the market. Otherwise, they will slough into the poaching liquid.

OTHER SEAFOOD

Other firm-fleshed fish and shellfish that are good for poaching include fresh tuna, swordfish, flounder or sole, shrimp, and scallops. Because flounder and sole fillets are thin, sprinkle them with fresh herbs and roll up or fold lengthwise before poaching.

FINE BONING

Tiny bones in a salmon fillet are easily removed with tweezers. Wash the tool. Run your fingers over the meaty side of a fillet. When you feel a feathery bone, pull it out with the tweezers. The process takes only a few minutes.

THE RIGHT PAN

A 12-inch skillet is best for poaching fillets. The skillet must be nonreactive to prevent any acid or alkali in the poaching liquid from muddying the broth and giving it a metallic taste. Stainless steel, enamel-coated iron, and enamelware are all nonreactive.

DONE TO PERFECTION

The rule of thumb for poaching cut fish is to measure the piece at its thickest point and poach it for 10 minutes per inch. It is a workable formula, but you must still keep an eye on the clock since some fish are denser fleshed than others, and their exact cooking times vary slightly.

SERVING NOTE

To make serving fragile fillets easier, moisten the platter with water or fish broth before adding the fillets.

THE WHOLE THING

Whole small fish can be poached on a rack in a fish poacher. Or wrap the fish in cheesecloth, leaving a couple of extra inches at each end, and tie the ends with string. Use these "handles" for lowering and raising the fish into and out of a simmering broth.

To poach a whole fish that you plan to serve cold, figure on about 3 minutes per pound, and allow the fish to cool in the poaching liquid. If you are serving a whole poached fish hot, cooking time is about 5 minutes per pound.

POACHING LIQUID

The kind of poaching liquid you use should depend on the type of fish being poached. Mild flavored freshwater fish need a well seasoned liquid. Fuller flavored ocean fish require less seasoning.

A poaching liquid can be as simple a solution as lightly salted water (1½ teaspoons of salt to 1 quart of water). Or use a canned or homemade Vegetable Broth (page 45) or Fish Broth (page 54). For best results the liquid should cover the fish by at least 1 inch.

For variety, add the following

HOW TO POACH FISH FILLETS

1 Reduce the heat to moderately low after the liquid boils. Boiling liquid will make fish break apart. Slide a wide spatula lengthwise under the fish and ease it into the simmering liquid.

2 Gently push the fish pieces into place so they don't overlap. If pan is not deep enough to cover the fish with water, cover with a piece of wax paper laid directly on top. Turn once. Cover again with wax paper.

ingredients to the poaching liquid: 1 minced scallion, 2 tablespoons of diced onion, 1 small diced carrot, 1 small diced celery stalk, 3 or 4 strips of lemon zest, 2 or 3 sprigs of parsley or thyme, 3 or 4 black peppercorns, or ½ bay leaf.

Poached Salmon with Egg Sauce

Prepare as directed below, **adding** 1 coarsely chopped hard-cooked egg and ¼ teaspoon hot green pepper sauce to the sauce in Step 3. Makes 4 servings.

Cold Roasted Salmon

Sprinkle salmon fillets with ½ teaspoon salt, **rub** with 1 tablespoon olive oil, and **roast** in a preheated 450°F oven until fish almost flakes at the touch of a fork—about 7 minutes. **Cool** and **refrigerate** as directed in Step 2 below, and **continue** as directed in Steps 3 and 4. Makes 4 servings.

Cold Poached Salmon Fillets

- 2 **cups white wine**
- 2 **cups water**
- ½ **cup snipped fresh dill or 2 teaspoons dried dill, crumbled**
- 1 **whole bay leaf**
- 8 **peppercorns**
- ½ **teaspoon dried thyme, crumbled**
- ½ **teaspoon salt**
- 4 **salmon fillets (6 ounces each)**
- ¼ **cup heavy cream**
- 3 **tablespoons reduced-fat mayonnaise**
- ½ **teaspoon grated lemon zest**
- 2 **tablespoons lemon juice**
- ⅛ **teaspoon ground white pepper**

1 In a large skillet over moderately high heat, bring wine, water, ¼ cup of the dill, bay leaf, peppercorns, thyme, and ¼ teaspoon of the salt to a boil.

Reduce the heat to moderately low, add fish, skin side up, and cover with a piece of wax paper laid on top. Cook, turning fish over at halftime, until fish almost flakes at the touch of a fork—about 7 minutes total.

2 Remove fish from poaching liquid, cool to room temperature, and refrigerate until chilled—about 1 hour.

3 Meanwhile, in a small bowl, whisk together all remaining ingredients, including the remaining ¼ teaspoon of salt and ¼ cup of dill.

4 To serve, remove skin from fish and spoon sauce on top. Makes 4 servings.

1 Serving: Calories 278; Total Fat 14 g; Saturated Fat 5 g; Protein 34 g; Carbohydrates 3 g; Fiber 0 g; Sodium 354 mg; Cholesterol 112 mg

prep time-10 minutes • cooking time-7 minutes

FRESH SCALLOPS

Scallops have universal appeal and cook up quickly. When served over rice, a pound of scallops easily makes four main-dish servings.

SELECT CAREFULLY

Scallops are available in three varieties: sea, bay, and calico. Sea scallops, the largest of the three, may be cut into pieces to substitute for bay scallops, but they are not as tender or sweet. Sea scallops are a good choice for chowders and casseroles, where a full-bodied flavor is desirable.

Bay scallops, about 1/2 inch in diameter, are preferred for many recipes because they have the most delicate flavor.

Look for bay scallops that are beige, not snowy white. White scallops have been soaked in water or phosphate solutions to increase their bulk and extend their shelf life. They will ooze a considerable amount of water as they cook, which must be poured or cooked off.

Calico scallops are the smallest. They are sometimes sold

as bay scallops though they are not as sweet. Because steam is used in opening calico scallops, they come to the market partially cooked, pale white, and opaque around the edges.

OUNCES PER SERVING

Allow 4 to 8 ounces of scallops per person when they are the main dish. When scallops are served in a casserole or in a sauce on top of rice or pasta, 4 ounces are sufficient.

A MEAL IN MINUTES

Scallops are so tender and sweet that they are sometimes eaten raw. They cook in just minutes—3 minutes for bay scallops and 5 to 7 minutes for uncut sea scallops. If overcooked, they will lose their sweetness and turn rubbery.

SKILLET SKILLS

Sautéing is one of the best ways to cook scallops. Dry them carefully with paper toweling before adding them to the pan. Have the butter or oil hot so that when the scallops are added, their surfaces are sealed immediately.

Add scallops to the hot pan 3 or 4 at a time; piling them in

by the handful cools the fat, allowing the scallops to lose their juices before they are sealed. Scallops turn opaque as they cook. When they do, it's the signal to get them out of the pan pronto.

If scallops are to be sautéed and then finished in a sauce, take special care not to overcook them. Remove them from the sauté pan when they are still slightly underdone—after 2 minutes for bay scallops and 3 to 4 minutes for sea scallops.

If the pan drippings are to be used in a sauce, remove the cooked scallops and keep them warm on a plate. Finish the sauce in the pan, return the scallops, and just heat them through before serving.

COOKING VARIETY

Because they keep their shape, scallops are ideal for threading on skewers and grilling as kabobs. Brush them with a mixture of 1 tablespoon of balsamic vinegar or lemon juice whisked together with 3 tablespoons of olive oil, a pinch of salt, 1/4 teaspoon of white pepper, and 1 tablespoon of finely chopped chives or scallions. Cook the kabobs on a preheated grill for 3 to 5 minutes, turning often and brushing with the remaining sauce.

EASY SUBSTITUTES

Scallops' mild flavor makes them an easy substitute for crabmeat or lobster in many recipes. Sprinkle raw scallops into a quiche shell before pouring in the egg mixture. Add cooked scallops to a sauce and roll them up in crêpes or bake them with a little butter and a topping of crumbs for 10 minutes in a 350°F oven.

THREE TYPES OF SCALLOPS

The scallops below show the 3 sizes most commonly found at the market.

Calico Scallops

Bay Scallops

Sea Scallops

Unless you live along the coast, it's unlikely that you will find scallops in their shells at the market. But if you do, they can be opened like other shellfish: by steaming or by inserting a short sharp knife in the hinge and prying open.

Sautéed Bay Scallops with Thyme

¼ cup olive oil
1 pound bay scallops, rinsed and patted very dry
½ cup chopped scallions
1 clove garlic, minced
½ cup dry white wine
1 tablespoon chopped fresh thyme or ½ teaspoon dried thyme, crumbled
½ teaspoon salt
¼ teaspoon black pepper

1 In a large skillet over moderate heat, heat oil for 2 minutes.

2 Add scallops and sauté until they begin to turn opaque—1½ to 2 minutes. Turn and sauté 1½ minutes more. Transfer to a bowl and keep warm.

3 Add scallions and garlic to skillet and sauté just until tender—1 to 2 minutes. Add wine, thyme, salt, and pepper and boil over high heat until liquid is reduced by half.

4 Return scallops to skillet and toss quickly to heat through. Serve immediately. Makes 2 to 4 servings.

One 4-Ounce Serving: Calories 217;
Total Fat 16 g; Saturated Fat 2 g;
Protein 10 g; Carbohydrates 5 g; Fiber 1 g;
Sodium 505 mg; Cholesterol 18 mg

prep time-20 minutes
cooking time-10 minutes

CRABMEAT NORFOLK

Prepare as directed above, **substituting** ⅓ cup butter for olive oil, 2 tablespoons white wine vinegar for wine, 1 pound lump crabmeat for scallops, and ¼ teaspoon cayenne for black pepper. **Increase** scallions to 1 cup and **omit** thyme. Makes 4 servings.

BOILED SHRIMP

Boiled or steamed shrimp is an easy winner for top place on party tables. Set out a bowl of boiled shrimp with sauce for a supper with no complaints.

JUST THE BEGINNING

We offer five sauces for dipping boiled shrimp, which are among the most versatile of foods. Use them on hors d'oeuvre crackers with a bit of dip. Toss them into salads, drop them into a quiche or pasta sauce, or cover them in a lemony marinade and serve them cold.

OUNCES PER SERVING

Four ounces of raw unshelled shrimp are adequate for a first course with hearty food to come. For a shrimp lover's feast, buy at least 1/2 pound per person. Expect about 12 to 15 jumbo, 16 to 20 medium, and 21 to 25 medium-small.

TIMING COUNTS

Overcooked shrimp are briny and tough. Peeled shrimp boil to perfection in just 1 to 2 minutes, unpeeled in about 3 minutes. The moment they turn pink, remove them from the heat, drain, and rinse in cold water to stop the cooking.

ADDING FLAVOR

See page 196 for details on how to clean and devein shrimp. When it comes to boiling or steaming them, some cooks peel the shrimp beforehand so that they can make a stock with the shells. Simmer the shells in water immediately or wrap them tightly in plastic wrap and freeze for up to 1 month. When ready to use the shells, simply simmer them in water or broth for a surprisingly flavorful base for rice dishes, soups, and sauces.

To flavor shrimp, tie herbs, lemon zest, and other flavorings in a cheesecloth bundle, like a bouquet garni, and toss it in the cooking water while the shrimp boil. They'll absorb the flavor but won't get speckled with herbs.

FLAVOR VARIATIONS

For a Spicy Shrimp Boil, prepare the Boiled Shrimp as directed in the recipe, adding 1 quartered celery stalk, 1 tablespoon of white wine vinegar, 1/2 teaspoon of pickling spice, and 1 bay leaf to the cooking water.

For a Lemon Boil, prepare Boiled Shrimp as directed, adding 1 peeled and quartered medium-size yellow onion, 1 quartered lemon, four 1/4-inch-thick slices of fresh ginger, and 2 halved garlic cloves to the cooking water.

GRIBICHE SAUCE

2 **hard-cooked eggs, peeled**	2 **tablespoons finely chopped bread and butter pickles**
1/4 **cup olive oil**	1 **teaspoon Dijon mustard**
2 **tablespoons white wine vinegar**	1 **teaspoon finely chopped chives or parsley**
2 **tablespoons capers, drained**	

1 Finely chop egg whites and set aside. Pulse egg yolks in a food processor until finely chopped. With the processor running, drizzle in 1/2 the oil.

2 Add 1 tablespoon of the vinegar. Again with the processor running, drizzle in remaining oil. (If mixture curdles, beat in 1 to 2 tablespoons boiling water.) Add remaining vinegar and pulse to combine.

3 Pour mixture into a small bowl and stir in chopped whites and all remaining ingredients. Refrigerate, covered, for 2 hours or overnight. Makes 1 cup.

ANDALOUSE SAUCE

1/2 **cup sun-dried tomatoes**	2 **tablespoons chopped pimiento**
2/3 **cup water**	1 **small garlic clove, crushed**
1/2 **cup reduced-fat mayonnaise**	1/8 **teaspoon cayenne**
1/2 **cup reduced-fat sour cream**	

1 In a medium-size bowl, soak tomatoes in water until soft—about 15 minutes. Drain, pat dry, and chop.

2 In the same bowl, combine tomatoes and remaining ingredients. Refrigerate, covered, 2 hours or overnight. Makes 1 1/4 cups.

TARTAR SAUCE

1/2 **cup reduced-fat mayonnaise**	2 **tablespoons lemon juice**
1/2 **cup reduced-fat sour cream**	1 **tablespoon capers, drained**
6 **scallions, finely chopped**	1 **tablespoon minced parsley**
1/4 **cup chopped bread and butter pickles**	1 **tablespoon Dijon mustard**

In a medium-size bowl, combine all ingredients. Refrigerate, covered, 2 hours or overnight. Makes 1 1/4 cups.

ASIAN DIPPING SAUCE

- ¾ cup reduced-sodium soy sauce
- ½ cup sake or dry sherry
- ¼ cup finely chopped scallions
- ¼ cup grated fresh ginger
- 2 teaspoons dark sesame oil
- 2 cloves garlic, minced

In a medium-size bowl, combine all ingredients. Refrigerate, covered, for at least 2 hours or overnight. Makes 1 cup.

GREEN SAUCE

- 1 cup chopped fresh coriander (cilantro)
- ¾ cup chopped parsley
- ⅓ cup chopped scallions
- 2 tablespoons lemon juice
- 1½ tablespoons white wine vinegar
- ¼ to ½ teaspoon hot red pepper sauce
- ¼ to ½ teaspoon salt
- 1 clove garlic, peeled
- ⅓ cup olive oil

1 In a food processor, purée coriander, parsley, scallions, lemon juice, vinegar, red pepper sauce, salt, and garlic.

2 With the processor running, drizzle in oil until smooth and creamy.

3 Transfer to a small bowl and refrigerate, covered, 2 hours or overnight. Makes about 1 cup.

Boiled Shrimp with Five Sauces

- 4 cups water
- 1 tablespoon salt

- 1 pound jumbo unpeeled shrimp

In a large saucepan over high heat, bring water and salt to a boil. Add shrimp, return to a boil, and reduce the heat to low. Simmer, covered, just until shrimp turn pink—about 3 minutes. Drain, peel, and devein, if desired. Makes 4 servings.

1 Serving: Calories 68; Total Fat 1 g; Saturated Fat 0 g; Protein 14 g; Carbohydrates 0 g; Fiber 0 g; Sodium 287 mg; Cholesterol 135 mg

prep time-5 minutes • cooking time-3 minutes

LOBSTER

Though usually reserved for serving on special occasions, lobster is simple to prepare. Our tips cover both boiled and baked-and-stuffed preparations.

SIZING UP

Lobsters weighing 1½ pounds contain about 6 ounces of meat. Served 1 to a person, they are the smallest size to buy for stuffing. Larger lobsters can be split to serve two.

PREFERENCES

Some lobster fanciers swear that the female lobster is sweeter than the male. To tell the difference between male and female lobsters, look at the swimmerets—tiny claws on the underside of the tail. On the female, they are large, soft, and thin; on the male, they are smaller and bonier.

DO I EAT THAT PART?

Once diners have gotten beyond the shell, there are several parts of a lobster that inevitably provoke questions. Coral is the name given to a lobster's ovaries and egg sac in the big cavity above the tail. Easily recognized because of its red color, coral is edible and is prized by diners.

Lobster roe, a rare delicacy, appears as a dark caviarlike mass in the body and upper tail. Serve the roe separately or mix it with tomalley and coral in sauces and stuffings.

Tomalley, the gray-green liver in the hollow of the body cavity, is another delicacy, though many dislike its strong flavor.

The intestinal vein is a soft, beige vein that runs the length of the tail. The vein isn't usually eaten but it won't cause any harm if it is.

The stomach, a papery sac located just behind the eyes, is one part of the lobster that should not be eaten.

FIRST STEPS

Lobsters are highly perishable and must be kept alive until the moment they are cooked. Look for highly active, angry-looking lobsters when you buy one.

If you ever buy a whole cooked lobster, make sure the tail is curled under the body. That is a sign that the lobster was alive when it was steamed or boiled.

COOK'S SECRETS

Nancy Harmon Jenkins
Seafood Expert and Cookbook Author

"If you find killing a lobster for stuffing and baking nerve wracking, here is an easier way. Bring 2 inches of water in a large pot to a boil. Push the lobster down into the steaming water, cover the pot, and let it boil 4 minutes. Remove the lobster, rinse it in cold water to cool it, and proceed with halving and stuffing."

TO BOIL LOBSTERS

Cook no more than 2 at a time. Grab a lobster by the back and plunge it head first into 3 to 4 quarts of boiling sea or salt water (1 tablespoon of salt for each quart of water). Cover, return the water to a boil, and cook 5 or 6 minutes per pound.

Live lobsters are a blue-green color but they turn bright red by the time they are done. You can also tell if a lobster is cooked by pulling one of the antennae off the head. If it pulls easily from the socket, the lobster is done.

SERVING

Diners will need spring-type nutcrackers or lobster crackers to get at the meat in a lobster's claws. Serve lobster hot along with lemon wedges, small bowls of melted butter, or garlic mayonnaise for dipping.

PREPARING A LOBSTER FOR STUFFING

1 To kill the lobster, insert a knife into the crease where the body and tail meet.

2 Place lobster on its back and split down the center.

3 Discard intestines; reserve the tomalley (above).

4 Crack the claws using a nut- or lobster cracker.

STUFFED SHRIMP

Peel, **devein**, and **butterfly** 1 pound (about 12) jumbo shrimp. **Prepare** 1/2 the recipe for stuffing in Step 2 at right, **omitting** tomalley and coral. **Place** shrimp, cut sides up, on a greased baking sheet. **Mound** stuffing on shrimp and **bake**, uncovered, in a preheated 400°F oven until stuffing is browned and shrimp are just done—6 to 10 minutes. Makes 4 servings.

LOBSTER THERMIDOR

Remove meat from tail and claws of 4 cooked 1 1/2- to 2-pound lobsters and **cut** into bite-size pieces. **Reserve** shells. In a medium saucepan over moderate heat, **melt** 2 tablespoons butter. **Whisk** in 2 tablespoons flour until well blended. **Whisk** in 1 1/2 cups milk, 1/4 teaspoon salt, and 1/4 teaspoon cayenne and **simmer**, **stirring**, until thickened and smooth. **Stir** in 3/4 cup shredded sharp white Cheddar cheese and 2 tablespoons grated Parmesan cheese and **cook**, **stirring**, until melted. Mix in lobster meat. **Arrange** shells on a foil-lined broiler pan, **spoon** mixture into shells, and **broil** 6 inches from the heat of a preheated broiler until bubbly—2 to 3 minutes. Makes 4 servings.

Baked Stuffed New England Lobster

- 4 **live lobsters, 1 1/2 pounds each**
- 4 **cups soft bread crumbs**
- 2 **scallions, thinly sliced**
- 1/2 **cup minced parsley**
- 1/4 **cup grated Parmesan cheese**
- 3 **tablespoons lemon juice**
- 1/4 **cup olive oil**
- 1/2 **teaspoon dried rosemary, crumbled**

1 Preheat the oven to 400°F. Place lobster on its stomach and insert a sharp knife in its back where the body and tail meet. Turn lobster over and split it down the center. Remove and discard the stomach and intestine; reserve the tomalley and any coral. Crack the claws.

2 In a medium-size bowl, combine bread crumbs, scallions, parsley, Parmesan, lemon juice, 3 tablespoons of the oil, and rosemary. Stir in reserved tomalley and coral.

3 Arrange lobsters, flesh side up, in a large shallow pan. Brush with remaining tablespoon of oil and mound stuffing in the body cavity. Bake, uncovered, until stuffing is lightly browned and lobsters are done—about 25 minutes. Makes 4 servings.

1 Serving: Calories 330; Total Fat 17 g; Saturated Fat 3 g; Protein 18 g; Carbohydrates 26 g; Fiber 2 g; Sodium 551 mg; Cholesterol 45 mg

prep time-12 minutes
cooking time-25 minutes

221

STEAMED MUSSELS AND CLAMS

M ussels and clams are an inexpensive treat. They steam open in no time and need only a salad and crusty bread to make a meal.

AT THE MARKET

Fresh mussels and hard-shell clams should be alive and tightly closed when you buy them. Gaping indicates that they have been out of the water too long. If just slightly open, tap the shell. If it doesn't close, don't buy it.

Soft-shell clams always gape a little. Test for freshness by touching the necklike siphon. If it pulls in a bit, a clam is okay.

BEST CLAMS FOR STEAMING

Both hard- and soft-shell clams can be steamed open quickly. Hard-shell clams such as littlenecks, small cherrystones, and tiny Pacific Coast Manila clams are enjoyed simply steamed with an aromatic sauce.

Hard-shell quahog clams can also be opened by steaming, but they are too large for eating right from the shell—they have to be chopped first. Quahogs are best used in chowders and casseroles.

Soft-shell clams, known as steamers or long necks, are the clams that are most familiarly served plain with broth and drawn butter (and perhaps some corn on the cob on the side). Soft-shells are rarely used in recipes or for anything other than steaming.

JUST ENOUGH

Mussels and clams are usually sold by the pound. For a main-dish serving, figure on about 1 pound of mussels or soft-shell clams per person and closer to 1½ pounds of littlenecks.

CLEANING THEM

Mussels live in colonies attached to rocks or pilings like barnacles. Therefore, they are rarely full of sand and merely require debearding, scrubbing, and rinsing. See page 22 for details about cleaning them.

Clams, on the other hand, live buried in the sand, so they are apt to be full of grit when you buy them. The grit must be removed before they are cooked and eaten.

To purge clams of their grit, place them in a bucket or a large bowl of cold salted water and sprinkle the water with cornmeal—about ¼ cup per gallon of water. Set aside in the refrigerator or a cool place for at least 2 hours before cooking.

EASY STEAMING

Mussels and hard-shell clams can be steamed simply and deliciously. For every 4 pounds of unshucked mussels or clams, heat about 1 cup of white wine or dry vermouth, 1 cup of chopped onions, the juice of 1 lemon, and ⅓ cup of parsley in a covered, nonaluminum pot. When the mixture comes to a boil, add the mussels or clams and cover. Remove them immediately as they open—about 5 minutes. Serve in their shells in large bowls with some of the cooking liquid.

Steamers can be steamed in a pot in only ½ inch of water—no other ingredients are necessary; their salty tang adds the rest of the flavor. They usually open within 10 minutes. Serve the clams with their broth, strained, in bowls. Melted butter and lemon juice can be served on the side. Note: Discard any mussels and clams that do not open.

COOKING AHEAD

Our sauce and others for shellfish can be made ahead of time and stored in a covered container in the refrigerator for 2 or 3 days, in the freezer

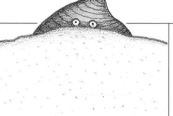

for 3 or 4 weeks. Check seasonings when the sauce is reheated and adjust, if needed. Then add the shellfish and steam 4 or 5 minutes.

Mussels or Clams with Tomatoes and Garlic

- 3 tablespoons olive oil
- 1/2 cup finely chopped yellow onion
- 3 cloves garlic, finely chopped
- 1 can (16 ounces) Italian plum tomatoes, coarsely chopped with their juice
- 1 teaspoon salt
- 1 teaspoon dried basil, crumbled
- 1 teaspoon dried thyme, crumbled
- 1/2 teaspoon sugar
- 1/4 teaspoon black pepper
- 1 tablespoon balsamic vinegar
- 4 pounds mussels or 3 dozen littleneck clams in their shells, prepared for cooking
- 1/4 cup chopped parsley

1 In a 4-quart Dutch oven or heavy kettle over moderate heat, heat oil 1 minute. Add onion and garlic and sauté until soft—about 5 minutes. Stir in tomatoes, salt, basil, thyme, sugar, and pepper. Bring to a boil over high heat, reduce the heat to moderately low, and cook, covered, until sauce thickens—about 30 minutes. Stir in vinegar.

2 Add mussels, increase the heat to moderately high, and cook, covered, until mussels open—about 5 minutes. Discard mussels that have not opened.

3 Sprinkle with parsley and serve with hot crusty bread. Makes 4 servings.

1 Serving: Calories 194; Total Fat 12 g; Saturated Fat 2 g; Protein 11 g; Carbohydrates 12 g; Fiber 2 g; Sodium 936 mg; Cholesterol 21 mg

prep time–15 minutes
cooking time–40 minutes

HOT AND SPICY MUSSELS

Prepare as directed above, **sautéing** 2 cored, seeded, and chopped sweet red peppers and 1/4 to 1/2 teaspoon crushed red pepper flakes along with garlic and onion in Step 1. Makes 4 servings.

BATTER-FRYING

As our tips make clear, the first step toward ensuring crisp, non-greasy deep-fried fish is to keep the fat at a constant high temperature.

TOOLS OF THE TRADE

A heavy-gauge flat-bottom deep kettle or Dutch oven will work just fine for deep-frying fish. It helps to have a fry basket that fits the pot so that all the fish can be lifted out of the hot oil at the same time. You'll need a deep-fat thermometer to ensure heat control.

WHAT ABOUT OIL?

Peanut oil holds its quality well at 375°F, the temperature for frying most seafood. Others suitable for deep-frying fish are canola, corn, safflower, sunflower, and light blended vegetable oils. Many cooks prefer vegetable shortening, claiming it gives deep-fried foods a crispier finish. But, take note, it is high in saturated fats. The oils are not.

Use enough oil to cover the food you are deep-frying and allow it to circulate freely in the bubbling fat—a minimum of 3 inches in medium-size pans. Depending on the size of your fryer, 2 quarts of oil should be sufficient for 4 to 6 servings.

BATTER UP

Most batters can sit for 15 to 30 minutes before being used,

but if you add egg white to a batter it must be used quickly.

TO START

Dip seafood in the batter and drain off any excess. Too much batter makes a pasty coating. If the batter is too heavy, thin it with a few drops of water. Add more flour if it's too thin.

Add food slowly to the hot oil, using tongs or a slotted spoon. Keep the temperature as close to 375°F as possible. Don't let it drop below 365°F: Cooler fat will be absorbed by the batter.

Don't crowd the seafood; freely bubbling oil makes for crisp crust. Stir food gently once or twice with a slotted spoon so that it cooks evenly.

Reheat the fat to 375°F before adding the next batch.

Batter-fried shellfish is done when the coating is lightly golden and the fish feels soft but not spongy when pressed.

BATTER VARIATIONS

Beer Batter: Prepare Basic Batter as directed at right, **omitting** baking powder and **substituting** 1 cup beer or club soda for buttermilk and water. Makes 1½ cups, enough to coat 1½ to 2 pounds of shellfish or fish.

Tempura-Style Batter: Prepare Basic Batter as directed at right, **using** 1¼ cups cake flour or 1 cup all-purpose flour and ¼ cup cornstarch. **Omit** buttermilk and water. Instead, **add** 2 egg whites beaten to a froth and 1 cup ice water all at once and **whisk** until still slightly lumpy. **Use** immediately. Makes 2 cups, enough to coat 2 pounds of shellfish or fish.

DIPPING SAUCE VARIATIONS

Remoulade Sauce: Mix together 1 cup mayonnaise, 1 tablespoon each minced gherkin pickle and parsley, 2 teaspoons anchovy paste, and 1 teaspoon Dijon mustard. Makes 1 cup.

Cocktail Sauce: Mix together 1 cup mayonnaise, ⅓ cup chili sauce, 2 tablespoons chopped gherkin pickle, 1 tablespoon cider vinegar, and 1 teaspoon Worcestershire sauce. Makes 1⅓ cups.

Lemon Caper Sauce: Mix together 1 cup mayonnaise, 3 tablespoons lemon juice, 2 tablespoons each minced capers and parsley, and ½ teaspoon grated lemon zest. Makes 1 cup.

AFTER THE FRY

Lift the shellfish in the frying basket or with a skimmer. Turn it out onto paper toweling that has been laid on top of newspaper or a rack.

Eat immediately or keep warm in a low (200°F) oven until the batch is done. Serve with lemon wedges and set out bowls of our flavorful sauces, above, for dipping.

WORK SAVER

Electric Deep-Fat Fryer

One way to ensure perfect deep-frying is to use an electric deep-fat fryer. The pot's built-in thermostat allows you to keep an eye on fluctuations in the temperature and to make small adjustments, up or down, with no problem. Electric deep-fat fryers are also the safest way to fry, because the fat does not have to come anywhere near an open flame.

Batter-Fried Clams with Tartar Sauce

BATTER-FRIED OYSTERS

Prepare as directed at right, **substituting** 1 pint well-drained shucked oysters for clams. In Step 3, **fry** 5 to 6 at a time until golden—2 to 3 minutes. Makes 4 servings.

BUTTERFLIED SHRIMP

Prepare as directed at right, **substituting** 1 pound peeled, deveined, and butterflied medium or jumbo shrimp for clams. In Step 3, **fry** 5 to 6 at a time until golden —about 3 to 4 minutes. Makes 4 servings.

FISH STICKS

Prepare as directed at right, **substituting** 1 pound boned and skinned firm-fleshed fish for clams. Cut fish into 3- by 1-inch sticks. In Step 3, **fry** 4 sticks at a time until golden—3 to 4 minutes. Makes 4 servings.

Basic Batter:
- 1 cup all-purpose flour
- 1¼ teaspoons baking powder
- 1 teaspoon salt
- 1 cup buttermilk
- ¼ cup cold water

Clams:
- 2 quarts vegetable oil
- 1 pint shucked soft-shell or littleneck clams

Tartar Sauce:
- 1 cup mayonnaise
- ¼ cup minced scallions
- ¼ cup minced gherkin or dill pickle
- 2 tablespoons chopped capers
- 2 tablespoons chopped parsley
- 2 tablespoons cider vinegar
- 1 teaspoon Dijon mustard
- ½ teaspoon sugar

1 For the Batter: Into a medium-size bowl, sift together flour, baking powder, and salt. Whisk in buttermilk and water, cover, and set aside.

2 For the Clams: In a deep-fat fryer or deep heavy skillet over moderately high heat, heat oil to 375°F. Occasionally check oil temperature with a deep-fat thermometer.

3 Pat clams dry on paper toweling, dip in batter, shake off excess, and fry 6 to 8 at a time until golden—1 to 2 minutes. Drain on paper toweling and place, uncovered, in a warm oven while frying remaining clams.

4 For the Tartar Sauce: Combine all ingredients and serve as a dipping sauce with fried clams. Makes 4 servings.

1 Serving: Calories 846; Total Fat 74 g; Saturated Fat 11 g; Protein 21 g; Carbohydrates 27 g; Fiber 1 g; Sodium 1109 mg; Cholesterol 89 mg

prep time-10 minutes
cooking time-30 to 45 minutes

BOUILLABAISSE

*A*uthentic bouillabaisse can be made only in southern France where particular fish are caught. Our version duplicates the soup's aromatic flavors—but with North American fish.

A COASTAL TREAT

Bouillabaisse is a soup rapidly cooked to reduce the stock. The recipe is based on the same combination of vegetables, herbs, and seafood that has been used for centuries by fishermen along the Mediterranean coast.

THE ESSENCE OF A SOUP

Bouillabaisse should be made with a combination of at least 6 fish and/or shellfish, so it's best prepared for a crowd. It's as good served as a refreshing summertime soup—making use of the day's catch—as it is a winter warmer.

One of the most distinctive aspects of bouillabaisse is the rouille—a garlic and pimiento sauce—that is stirred into it just before the soup is eaten. Without the rouille, you will still have a delicious fish soup, but you will miss the essence of bouillabaisse.

A PEPPERY SAUCE

Rouille is orangy-red because it's made with red pepper. Use fresh sweet red pepper or a true pimiento pepper. If no other pepper is available, well-drained canned pimiento is a good substitute.

The rouille can be made the day before and refrigerated. Let it come to room temperature before spooning it into the hot soup.

THE BROTH

For the best flavor, start with a fresh and flavorful fish broth, such as our recipe on page 54. Vegetables simmered in the broth add extra richness.

Choose fully ripened tomatoes, strong-flavored onions, such as large yellow or white onions, plenty of fresh leeks and garlic, and mature carrots.

SHELLFISH IN THE BROTH

Neither mussels, clams, nor shrimp are absolutely essential to a bouillabaisse. You can make the soup without any shellfish at all, but they do make it special.

If you use mussels and clams, scrub the shells well and then steam them open in the soup itself. Serve them with their shells open in the broth.

Be sure to set out some large empty bowls on the table so that diners can discard their clam and mussel shells as they're done with them.

For easier eating, shrimp should be peeled before they are added to the soup.

If you make a broth by simmering the shrimp shells in water, use it to replace some of the clam juice.

For an extra dramatic production, add crabs or crab claws and/or lobster tails to your list of shellfish. Add them to the broth along with the other shellfish.

BOUILLABAISSE RULES

The most important rule for bouillabaisse is: Don't overcook the fish or shellfish. There's no need to. Virtually all the parts of the dish can be prepared ahead up to the point of adding the fish.

The broth should already be full flavored and boiling hot before the fish are added. You can have the shellfish scrubbed, the fish cut into chunks, and the rouille ready and set out on the table ahead of time. So wait until your guests are seated before adding the shellfish, and then the fish, to the pot.

The second rule for bouillabaisse is: Don't worry too much about the selection of fish. Although bouillabaisse is thought of as a company-best dish, it started out as a simple fisherman's soup, and part of its charm is that it's good any way you make it.

Instead of the halibut and scrod in our recipe, use a com-

HOW TO MAKE A ROUILLE

For the best flavor, use a good quality olive oil. For extra garlic flavor, purée the raw garlic separately, then blend it into the cooked puréed vegetables.

1 Simmer all the vegetables together. Then place them in a food processor and purée.

2 Drizzle in the oil slowly with the processor running. The sauce will be thick and red.

bination of any lean and oily fish (chart on page 228). It's not necessary for the fish to be skinned before they are added to the simmering broth.

(continued on page 228)

American Bouillabaisse with Rouille

- 1 **medium-size yellow onion, chopped**
- 2 **medium-size carrots, peeled and thinly sliced**
- 1 **large leek, halved lengthwise, thoroughly washed, and thinly sliced**
- 2 **medium-size tomatoes, cored, seeded, and chopped**
- 2 **large cloves garlic, chopped**
- 1 **cup dry white wine**
- 4 **bottles (8 ounces each) clam juice**
- 6 **cups Fish Broth**
- 2 **pinches saffron threads, crumbled**
- 2 **pounds mussels in the shell**
- 1 **dozen littleneck clams in the shell**
- ½ **pound boneless halibut, cut into 1½-inch pieces**
- ½ **pound boneless scrod, cut into 1½-inch pieces**
- ½ **pound bay scallops**
- ½ **pound large shrimp, peeled and deveined**

(Rouille recipe on page 228)

1 In an 8-quart Dutch oven over moderately high heat, bring all ingredients except fish, shellfish, and rouille to a boil. Reduce the heat to moderately low and simmer, uncovered, for 30 minutes.

2 Strain the broth, discard vegetables, and return broth to the pot. Bring to a full boil.

3 Add clams and mussels, reduce the heat to moderately low, and simmer, covered, until shells open—about 5 minutes. Discard any mussels and clams that do not open. Add fish and simmer, uncovered, 5 minutes more.

4 Divide fish and shellfish among 6 large heated soup bowls, ladle in broth, and top each serving with 2 tablespoons rouille, if desired. Makes 6 servings.

1 Serving: Calories 232; Total Fat 4 g; Saturated Fat 1 g; Protein 33 g; Carbohydrates 3 g; Fiber 0 g; Sodium 798 mg; Cholesterol 115 mg

prep time-20 minutes
cooking time-50 minutes

Rouille

- 1 cup roughly chopped pimientos
- 1 medium-size Idaho potato, peeled and thinly sliced
- 4 cloves garlic
- 1/4 teaspoon dried thyme, crumbled
- 2 cups Fish Broth
- 6 drops hot red pepper sauce
- 1/2 teaspoon salt
- 1/4 cup olive oil

1 In a 2-quart saucepan over high heat, bring pimientos, potato, garlic, thyme, and broth to a boil. Reduce the heat to moderately low and simmer, uncovered, until potato is tender—about 20 minutes. Strain broth, reserving vegetables.

2 In a food processor, purée vegetables and 1/4 cup broth. Add red pepper sauce and salt. With the processor running, drizzle in oil until thick and creamy. Makes 1½ cups.

1 Tablespoon: Calories 40; Total Fat 3 g; Saturated Fat 0 g; Protein 2 g; Carbohydrates 2 g; Fiber 0 g; Sodium 66 mg; Cholesterol 3 mg

prep time-10 minutes • cooking time-20 minutes

FLAVORFUL CHOICES

A half-and-half combination of oily and lean fish balances the flavor and texture of bouillabaisse and other seafood soups and stews, oily fish being stronger flavored. The following are some of the saltwater species that are generally available:

Oily Fish: bluefish, herring, salmon, sturgeon, swordfish, tuna (albacore, bonito), whitefish

Lean Fish: blackfish (tautog), catfish (ocean), cod, dolphinfish (mahi-mahi), hake, halibut, monkfish, orange roughy, perch, sea bass, snapper, tilapia

(continued from page 226)

TO SERVE

Divide the ingredients among large heated serving bowls and ladle in the broth. Spoon the rouille over the fish or put it on the table in bowls so guests can stir it into their soup to taste. Serve with crusty bread or with toasted French bread rounds rubbed with a little garlic.

AFTER THE FEAST

Reheat leftover broth and use it for poaching fish or as cooking liquid for rice. Leftover rouille can be served as a sauce for boiled shrimp or grilled fish.

OTHER FINE KETTLES OF FISH

Nearly every country within the sound of the surf has its own version of bouillabaisse. Here are some of the most famous, which suggest ways that you can vary our bouillabaisse recipe.

Bourride, like bouillabaisse, is a specialty in the South of France. Usually it's made with monkfish and served with aioli, a garlic mayonnaise (page 366). Shrimp in the shell and squid may be used in addition to monkfish, cod, or other fish.

A classic bourride broth contains onion, celery, grated carrot, garlic, leek, tomato, and small whole potatoes. Traditional seasonings are orange and lemon zest and dry vermouth. A pinch of saffron is usually added, as it is in most fish soups from the region.

Bourthetos is a peppery Greek fish muddle, the specialty of the island of Corfu. It may or may not contain tomatoes, but it always begins with olive oil and onions. The fish, freshly caught from sea and stream, usually include carp, cod, mackerel, perch, and trout. They go into the pot with water or fish broth and sometimes a splash of dry white or red wine as well. The classic seasonings are cayenne, paprika, and Italian parsley.

Caldeirada is Portugal's gutsy, garlicky stew, bubbled up from whatever the fishermen netted. The fish are simmered with onion, garlic, sweet green peppers, tomatoes, water, and any dry red or white wine and seasoned with chopped fresh coriander (cilantro).

Kavakia, a Greek bouillabaisse, is named for the large kettle in which it is cooked. A large fish is cut into chunks and stewed with onion, garlic, celery, carrots, and tomato. It's seasoned with lemon juice and bay leaves and brushed with dry white wine.

Zuppa di Pesce is the Italian Riviera's version of seaside soup. The seafood (squid, clams—anything on the dock) is simmered with olive oil, garlic, parsley, tomato, and fennel. Sometimes quartered small artichokes or chunks of cardoon may be added to share the spotlight with the fish.

Zarzuela de Mariscos is Spain's soup of aromatic vegetables, shellfish, and fish. In Spain, it includes Mediterranean fish; in the Caribbean, rock lobster. Onion, garlic, sweet green peppers, and tomato enrich the broth.

Sopa al Cuarto Hora, another Spanish soup whose name means "quarter of an hour" because it takes that long to cook. The flavor makers? Salty Serrano ham, onion, and tomato. These are gently sautéed in a large pot, then fish stock or clam juice and water are added along with cod chunks, shrimp, green peas, and a couple of teaspoons of uncooked rice. It's garnished with minced parsley and finely chopped hard-cooked egg.

BEEF, LAMB, AND PORK

Roast Beef

If you want to serve a great piece of beef, choose a rib roast. It's tasty, supremely tender, a snap to cook, and simple to carve.

A CUT ABOVE

Rib roasts can be bought either with the ribs intact or boned and rolled. Most meat lovers prefer the bone-in roast, which is known as a standing rib roast because it stands on its ribs as it cooks.

If you buy a roast with the ribs intact, have the butcher trim away the cap meat surrounding the eye, remove the backbone (or chine), and clean, or "french," the rib ends.

Other cuts for roasting include top or bottom round, top sirloin, eye round, and chuckeye, but these can't match the rib for succulence.

ROASTING NOTES

To cook a rib roast, set it on its ribs, fat side up, in a shallow roasting pan. Boned and rolled roasts should be set on a rack. Don't add water or cover the roast or the meat will steam as it cooks.

INFORMATION IN AN INSTANT

Use a regular or instant-read meat thermometer when you roast. Thermometers are the only reliable means of gauging when meat is done.

Instant-read thermometers are not meant to stay in the roast during cooking. Instead, from time to time, pull the roast out of the oven and insert the thermometer into the thickest part of the meat, making sure it does not touch the bone. It takes about 15 seconds for the temperature to register. Remove the thermometer after the reading. If left in, the dial cover will melt.

A SHORT REST

When a roast is removed from the oven, it needs to rest for 15 to 20 minutes. This allows the juices time to settle and to be reabsorbed into the meat, which makes it easier to carve.

While the meat rests, it will continue to cook and its internal temperature will rise 5 to 10 degrees.

SLICE AND SERVE

Figure on 2 servings per rib. An alternative way of carving a rib roast is the English style. Turn the roast on its end, anchoring it with a fork on the rib side. Then slice horizontally between the ribs.

Serve with pan-roasted potatoes, mashed potatoes, popovers, or Yorkshire pudding.

YORKSHIRE PUDDING

This traditional English partner for roast beef is made with the same batter as popovers and is cooked in the pan drippings. The secret to a puffy pudding is to be sure the fat is very hot before adding the batter.

Prepare popovers through Step 6 at right. **Pour** 3 tablespoons drippings into a 13- by 9-inch pan or into the roasting pan once the roast has been removed. **Heat** the pan in the oven for 2 minutes. Then **pour** the prepared batter into the pan and **bake** 10 minutes. **Reduce** oven temperature to 450°F and **bake** for another 12 to 15 minutes. Pudding will be puffed and golden. **Cut** into large squares and **serve** with roast.

How to Carve a Rib Roast

Use a long carving knife to make 1/2-inch-thick slices, slicing between the ribs.

Au Jus Gravy

Drain all but 1 tablespoon of clear drippings from the roasting pan. **Add** 2 cups Browned Beef Stock (page 32), hot water, or vegetable cooking water and **heat** over moderate heat, **scraping up** browned bits. **Cook** until slightly reduced—3 to 4 minutes. **Season** with salt and pepper to taste. Makes 2 cups.

Pan Gravy

Pour roast beef drippings into a 1-cup measure to total 1/4 cup (**add** melted butter, if needed, to fill out measurement). **Pour** into a large skillet and **set aside**. **Place** roasting pan over moderate heat, **pour** in 2 cups Browned Beef Stock (page 32) or 1 cup stock and 1 cup water. **Simmer, stirring** to loosen browned bits, for 1 minute.

Place skillet over moderate heat and **heat** pan drippings for 1 minute. **Blend** in 1/4 cup flour and **cook, whisking**, 1 to 2 minutes. Gradually **stir** in stock and **cook, whisking**, until mixture boils and thickens.

Reduce the heat to moderately low and **simmer, stirring** occasionally, 2 to 3 minutes more. **Add** salt and pepper to taste. **Strain** through a sieve, if desired, and **transfer** to a warm gravy boat to serve. Makes 2 cups.

Herbed Roast Beef with Popovers

Roast Beef:
- 1 standing rib roast (about 6 pounds)
- 1 large clove garlic, halved
- 1 teaspoon dried thyme, crumbled
- 1 teaspoon dry mustard
- 1/2 teaspoon dried rosemary, crumbled
- 1/2 teaspoon black pepper

Popovers:
- 1/2 cup sifted all-purpose flour
- 1/2 teaspoon salt
- 1/2 cup milk
- 1/4 cup cold water
- 2 eggs, lightly beaten
- 1 tablespoon melted roast beef drippings

Gravy: (see box at left)

1 For the Roast: Preheat the oven to 450°F. Place roast, fat side up, in a large roasting pan. Rub with garlic. In a small bowl, combine thyme, mustard, rosemary, and pepper; rub over roast.

2 Insert a meat thermometer in center of roast making sure it does not touch bone (or test later with an instant-read thermometer).

3 Roast, uncovered, for 25 minutes. Reduce the heat to 300°F and continue roasting until temperature registers 135°F to 140°F for medium-rare, 150°F to 155°F for medium, or 160°F-165°F for well done. (The internal temperature of the meat will continue to rise when the meat has been taken from the oven.)

4 Remove roast from the oven and let stand for 15 to 20 minutes before carving.

5 For the Popovers: Increase the oven temperature to 500°F. Begin popovers about 30 minutes before beef is done. Combine flour and salt in a small bowl. With an electric mixer or rotary beater, beat in milk a little at a time until smooth. Beat in water and eggs. Cover and set aside in a cool place, but not refrigerated, for about 30 minutes.

6 Beat batter until bubbles appear on the surface—about 1 to 2 minutes.

7 Pour 1/2 teaspoon of the drippings into each of 6 muffin cups and heat in the oven until almost smoking hot—1 to 2 minutes. Pour a scant 1/4 cup of batter into each cup and bake, uncovered, for 8 minutes. Do not open the oven door. Reduce the temperature to 400°F and bake until puffy, brown, and crisp—8 to 10 minutes more. Serve at once with roast and pan gravy. Makes 6 servings.

1 Serving: Calories 598; Total Fat 35 g; Saturated Fat 14 g; Protein 59 g; Carbohydrates 10 g; Fiber 0 g; Sodium 422 mg; Cholesterol 239 mg

prep time-25 minutes • cooking time-about 3 hours

POT ROAST

Few dishes can beat the appetite appeal of a succulent pot roast. The dish makes use of full-flavored but lesser priced cuts of beef.

COOKING UNDER COVER

In moist-heat cooking—or braising in the case of pot roasts—the meat is browned, then cooked slowly with a little liquid along with vegetables until it is fork-tender. The process requires time but not much attention.

THE RIGHT CUT

The best cuts of meat for pot roast are full flavored but somewhat sinewy cuts from the shoulder and hind quarters. These include brisket, shoulder, rump, tip, or bottom round roasts. Long slow cooking tenderizes the meat by converting the sinew to gelatin.

If the meat is not a compact cut, it is tied with string to keep it from falling apart as it cooks. Remove the string before carving.

POT ROAST TIPS

You can begin by dredging the meat in seasoned flour or skip that step, as you choose. Be sure, however, to take the time to brown the meat completely on each side, adjusting the heat as necessary. Don't rush the cooking process, either.

Braising at too high a temperature guarantees tough meat. Keep the liquid just below the boil. Check it periodically to be sure that the bubbles break slowly on the surface as the roast simmers.

Although slow cooking is desirable, overcooking is not and will result in stringy meat. It's done when it can be pierced easily with a fork.

POT LUCK

It's important to use a heavy pot. If it's lightweight, it will be difficult to adjust the heat so that the liquid barely simmers. The cover should fit snugly so that steam does not escape.

COOKING METHODS

The most familiar way to cook a pot roast is on top of the stove. However, you can also cook it in the oven at 350°F for 2 to 2½ hours in an ovenproof casserole with a tight-fitting lid. In an electric skillet, cook at 200°F for 2 to 2½ hours. A pressure cooker can also be used. Cook with ½ to 1 cup of water at 10 pounds pressure for 15 minutes per pound.

ADDING LIQUID

Water is the usual liquid for pot roasts, although there are other possibilities. Consider red wine, tomato juice, beer, or beef or vegetable broth. These liquids are too intensely flavored to use by themselves. A half-and-half mixture with water is about right.

THICKENING WITH VEGETABLES

Instead of using flour to thicken a pot roast gravy, try puréeing some of the soft-cooked vegetables with some of the cooking liquid, stirring them back into the pot.

POT ROAST REVISITED

Pot roast is just as delicious—if not even more so—the second or third day after it is cooked. Store leftovers, covered, in a casserole that can go from the refrigerator to the oven. Reheat just until simmering. Or make one of the following.

Quick Beef Hash: Sauté onions and garlic with diced cooked beef, moisten with broth, and cook in the skillet until crusty.

Chili: Sauté onions, garlic, and sweet peppers. Combine them with canned or fresh chopped tomatoes, kidney beans, chopped cooked beef, and chili powder to season.

HOW TO SLICE A POT ROAST

Transfer the roast to a cutting board. Remove any strings. Carve across the grain in thick slices and arrange on a platter with vegetables.

BURGUNDY POT ROAST

Prepare as directed at right, **substituting** ½ cup burgundy or other dry red wine for cold water in Step 2. In Step 3, **add** 1 teaspoon crumbled dried thyme and 1 whole bay leaf. **Substitute** 20 small peeled whole carrots for chunked carrots and 20 small peeled white onions for quartered onions and **increase** garlic to 6 cloves. **Omit** parsnips and rutabaga and **add** 20 button mushrooms. In Step 5, **add** ½ cup burgundy to beef stock and **simmer** for 5 minutes. **Continue** as directed in Step 6, **removing** the bay leaf before serving. Makes 6 servings.

Pot Roast with Winter Vegetables

2 tablespoons vegetable oil

4 pounds boneless beef roast (rump, chuck, sirloin tip, or bottom round)

3 large yellow onions, 1 chopped and 2 quartered

2 teaspoons salt

1/2 teaspoon black pepper

1/2 cup cold water

1 pound tiny (about 1 inch in diameter) red-skin potatoes, scrubbed

4 medium-size carrots, peeled and cut into 1-inch chunks

2 medium-size parsnips, peeled and quartered lengthwise

1 pound rutabaga, peeled and cut into 1-inch chunks

4 whole cloves garlic, peeled

3 cups Browned Beef Stock or canned reduced-sodium beef broth

1/4 cup unsifted all-purpose flour

1 In a 6-quart Dutch oven over moderately high heat, heat oil for 1 minute. Pat beef dry, add to Dutch oven, and brown well on all sides. Remove beef and set aside.

2 Add chopped onion to Dutch oven and cook, stirring, until golden—about 5 minutes. Return beef and accumulated juices to Dutch oven and sprinkle with 1 teaspoon of the salt and 1/4 teaspoon of the pepper. Add water, reduce the heat to low, and simmer, covered, for 1½ hours.

3 Add potatoes, carrots, parsnips, rutabaga, quartered onions, garlic, ½ cup of the stock, and the remaining 1 teaspoon salt and 1/4 teaspoon pepper. Simmer, covered, until ingredients are tender—45 to 60 minutes.

Both our main recipe and our Burgundy Pot Roast variation, above, require little attention once they're simmering on the stove.

4 Remove meat and vegetables to a heated serving platter, cover, and keep warm. Skim off any fat from drippings. In a small bowl, whisk ½ cup of the remaining stock into flour.

5 Add the remaining 2 cups stock to Dutch oven and cook over moderately high heat, stirring to loosen browned bits, for 2 minutes. Slowly blend in flour mixture and cook, stirring, until mixture boils and thickens. Cook, stirring, about 1 minute more.

6 Carve beef across the grain into thick slices, serve with vegetables, and top with gravy. Makes 6 servings.

1 Serving: Calories 636; Total Fat 19 g; Saturated Fat 7 g; Protein 68 g; Carbohydrates 47 g; Fiber 7 g; Sodium 875 mg; Cholesterol 198 mg

prep time-1 hour • cooking time-about 2½ hours

STEAK WITH A SPICY SAUCE

Beef teriyaki, which is sliced thin and glazed, is a great way to use a tasty but chewy cut of meat like flank steak.

GRILLED AND GLOSSY

Beef teriyaki is a Japanese specialty that has become part of mainstream North American cooking. One recipe goes a long way because the same cooking process, marinade, and glaze can be used with pork, chicken, shrimp, scallops, or fresh cubed tuna. The dish is simple enough to make for an everyday family dinner, but festive enough for a party.

"Teri" means glossy and refers to the shiny glaze that is brushed on the meat just before serving. "Yaki," essentially, means broiled and refers to food that is quickly grilled over coals, grilled under the broiler, or pan-broiled over high heat with little or no fat. Any of the three cooking methods can be used for beef (or other meat or seafood) teriyaki.

THE SAUCE

In our recipe, we've used the same sauce to marinate and glaze the beef. Along with adding flavor, the marinade helps to tenderize the sliced meat. For a chicken or seafood teriyaki, simply dip the ingredients in the sauce before cooking: They will soften too much if left to sit in the marinade.

Teriyaki glazes normally contain a little sugar or, in our recipe, honey, along with soy sauce and other tangy ingredients. The sugar and oil provide the gloss when the mixture is boiled and thickened.

If you are grilling or broiling the meat, the glaze can be brushed on at the end of cooking. If you pan-broil the meat, add the glaze directly to the pan and toss the meat in it.

SERVED IN STYLE

If you're preparing beef or another teriyaki dish for a party, grill or broil and serve it on bamboo skewers. They're disposable and just the right length for finger food. Be sure to soak the skewers in water before use. For extra color, thread 1-inch pieces of scallion between the cubes of meat.

As a dinner dish, serve the skewered or loose cubes of meat along with its sauce on a bed of fluffy white rice.

JAPANESE GARNISHES

The Japanese take great pride in the way their food is presented, often garnishing a dish with leaves or carved vegetables. For a festive touch at a special dinner or buffet, add one of these Japanese garnishes.

1 Cut a cucumber into 2-inch pieces. Insert a small paring knife through the center. With another knife, slice the cucumber diagonally to the depth of the first knife.

2 Turn the cucumber over, using the first knife as a handle. Make another diagonal cut. Remove the knives and pull the pieces apart. This is called a mountain cut.

1 Cut thin slices of carrot into rectangles. Make 2 parallel slits in each so that rectangles open to form *Z*s.

2 Fold one end of the *Z* under to join the opposite end and form a triangle. This is called a pine needle cut.

HOW TO EAT WITH CHOPSTICKS

1 The bottom chopstick stays anchored at the base of the thumb.

2 The top stick is manipulated up and down with thumb and forefinger.

Indonesian Spicy Beef Satay

Prepare as directed at right, **substituting** 3 table-spoons water for vegetable oil and **adding** ½ cup creamy or chunky peanut butter. **Marinate** and **broil** as directed. **Serve** with remaining marinade on the side as a dipping sauce. Makes 4 servings.

Spicy Beef Teriyaki

1½ **pounds flank steak**
¼ **cup tamari soy sauce**
¼ **cup honey**
1½ **teaspoons minced garlic**
1½ **teaspoons minced ginger**
1 **tablespoon vegetable oil**

1 Slice steak on the bias against the grain into slices about 7 inches long, 1½ inches wide, and ½ inch thick.

2 In a large bowl, whisk together remaining ingredients. Place soy mixture and steak in a large self-sealing plastic bag and marinate at room temperature about 1 hour.

3 Preheat the broiler. Thread 3 slices of steak on each of four 12-inch

bamboo skewers that have been soaked in water for 15 minutes.

4 Arrange skewers in a broiler pan and set 4 inches from the heat. Broil 5 minutes on each side, brushing 2 or 3 times with marinade to glaze. Remove from broiler, brush with remaining marinade, and serve immediately. Makes 4 servings.

1 Serving: Calories 312; Total Fat 15 g;
Saturated Fat 6 g; Protein 39 g;
Carbohydrates 5 g; Fiber 0 g;
Sodium 320 mg; Cholesterol 96 mg

prep time-20 minutes
marinating time-about 1 hour
cooking time-10 minutes

MEAT LOAF

For generations, we've had a love affair with meat loaf. Follow our tips for producing a loaf that is light, juicy, and perfectly cooked.

GROUND BEEF BASICS

Ground beef is the foundation for most meat loaves and at a maximum fat content of 17 percent, lean ground beef has the best balance of fat to lean for the dish. Ground beef that is too lean will become overly dry and overly compact as it bakes.

For a more flavorful loaf, combine beef, pork, and veal (about a third of each). Ground turkey or chicken can also be substituted for either pork or veal.

Note: When pork or poultry is added to the mix, it is especially important that the loaf be completely cooked through. This means that an instant-read meat thermometer should register 160°F when inserted into the center of the loaf.

PERFECT MEAT LOAF

Mix the ingredients lightly with your hands. Overmixing compacts the meat, making a heavy loaf.

Make meat loaf in a loaf pan or a ring mold or make it free-form without a mold. Set the free-form loaf in a shallow baking pan. (A free-form loaf has a lot more glazed crust, which many meat loaf lovers enjoy.)

There is no ideal proportion of

liquid to meat; it is simply a matter of taste. For a juicier loaf, increase the amount of chopped onions, celery, green pepper, or other vegetables.

Allow the meat loaf to rest for about 10 minutes before cutting. Use a serrated knife and a slight sawing motion to make neat slices.

EXTENSION COURSE

There are no hard and fast rules for mixing up a meat loaf. If green peppers don't agree with you, leave them out and add more onion, celery, or even grated carrot.

If you like a little inner heat, add some chopped hot pepper. If you don't have any bread crumbs, substitute rolled oats or corn flakes.

CENTERS OF INTEREST

For extra flavor, fill the center of a meat loaf with something interesting. Line the bottom of the loaf pan with half the meat loaf mixture. Lay dill pickles or hard-cooked eggs end to end down the center. Cover with the remaining meat mixture, pat it into shape, then bake as usual. When sliced, each portion will contain a mosaic of pickle or egg.

MAKE AHEAD AND FREEZE

Meat loaf can be mixed, shaped in its pan, and frozen raw. Wrap it tight in aluminum foil and freeze for up to 3 months. Thaw, wrapped, in the refrigerator for 24 hours, then bake as directed.

LEFTOVERS

Cold meat loaf is a terrific dish to have on hand, but don't slice it until you are ready to use it or it will dry out.

Baked meat loaf can be wrapped and frozen for about a month. Thaw it in its wrapping in the refrigerator for 24 hours.

Cut into thin slices for cold sandwich fillings. To make hot sandwiches, cut room-temperature meat loaf into slices. Serve on bread with hot gravy.

GLAZED OVER

Glazing meat loaf toward the end of cooking helps it to stay moist. The glaze forms a glossy crust that holds juices in.

If you like a glaze with meat loaf, there are many possibilities. Try one of our glazes or experiment with a combination of your own. Sweet and sour mixtures such as mustard and brown sugar or mustard and apricot jam are a sure bet.

Spoon on a little extra glaze at the table if desired.

HAM LOAF

Prepare as directed at right, **substituting** 3/4 pound ground ham and 1/2 pound ground pork shoulder for ground beef and 1/2 cup honey mustard for ketchup. **Omit** garlic. Makes 4 servings.

HAM LOAF GLAZES

Cranberry-Ginger Glaze: Combine 1 1/2 cups whole berry cranberry sauce and 1 teaspoon grated ginger and **stir** to mix well. **Brush** on ham loaf instead of honey mustard 15 minutes before loaf is done. Makes 1 1/2 cups.

Orange-Pineapple Glaze: Combine 3/4 cup each orange marmalade and drained crushed pineapple, 1 tablespoon lemon juice, and 1/8 teaspoon hot red pepper sauce. Makes 1 1/2 cups.

Curried Chutney Glaze: In a small saucepan, **bring** 1 1/2 cups chopped chutney and 1 teaspoon curry powder to a boil; **cook, stirring** often, 3 to 5 minutes. Makes 1 1/2 cups.

Maple-Spice Glaze: In a small saucepan, **bring** 1 1/2 cups maple or maple-flavored syrup, 1/2 teaspoon ground allspice, and 1/4 teaspoon ground cloves to a boil; **cook, stirring** often, 3 to 5 minutes. Makes 1 1/2 cups.

MANHATTAN

BLUE PLATE SPECIAL

Blue Plate Special Meat Loaf

2 tablespoons butter or margarine
1 medium-size yellow onion, finely chopped
1/2 medium-size stalk celery, finely chopped
1/4 cup finely chopped sweet green pepper
1 clove garlic, minced
1 egg
1 1/4 pounds ground beef chuck
1/2 cup ketchup
1/3 cup plain dry bread crumbs
1 teaspoon salt
1/2 teaspoon black pepper

1 Preheat the oven to 350°F. In a large skillet over moderate heat, melt butter. Add onion, celery, and green pepper and sauté, stirring occasionally, until almost tender—about 5 minutes. Add garlic and sauté, stirring occasionally, until vegetables are tender but not brown—about 1 minute more; set aside.

2 In a large bowl, beat egg slightly. Add ground beef, 1/4 cup of the ketchup, bread crumbs, salt, black pepper, and sautéed vegetables.

3 Using your hands, mix lightly, turn into an ungreased 8" x 8" x 2" baking dish, and shape into a loaf about 8 inches long by 4 1/4 inches wide.

4 Bake, uncovered, for 45 minutes. Brush top with the remaining 1/4 cup ketchup and bake until an instant-read thermometer inserted into the thickest part of the loaf registers 160°F—about 20 minutes more. Remove pan to a rack for 10 minutes before serving. Makes 4 servings.

1 Serving: Calories 409; Total Fat 23 g; Saturated Fat 10 g; Protein 32 g; Carbohydrates 18 g; Fiber 2 g; Sodium 1110 mg; Cholesterol 170 mg

prep time-30 minutes • cooking time-1 hour 11 minutes

MEAT LOAF GLAZE VARIATIONS

Spicy Tomato Glaze: Combine 1/2 cup ketchup, 1/4 cup molasses, 1/4 cup cider vinegar, 2 tablespoons prepared yellow mustard, and 1 tablespoon Worcestershire sauce and **whisk** together until smooth. **Brush** on meat loaf instead of ketchup 15 minutes before loaf is done. Makes about 1 1/4 cups.

Creamy Mustard Glaze: Combine 1 1/4 cups reduced-fat sour cream, 1/3 cup prepared yellow mustard, and 1 tablespoon firmly packed brown sugar. **Use** with either beef or ham loaf. Makes 1 2/3 cups.

Horseradish Cream Glaze: Combine 1 1/4 cups reduced-fat sour cream and 1/3 cup prepared horseradish. Use with beef or ham loaf. Makes 1 2/3 cups.

MEAT PIES

Empanadas—filled half-moon pies—range from hors d'oeuvre to sandwich size and can be filled with anything from ground beef to sweets.

A PIE BY ANY OTHER NAME

What are called turnovers in Canada are empanadas in Spanish-speaking countries. They are easy to make and children love to have a hand in folding the pastries and crimping the edges.

A simple piecrust dough works perfectly for empanadas. For a fancier presentation, you can also use a flaky pastry such as puff pastry. Information about puff pastry appears on page 28.

The only requirement for filling empanadas is that the mixture be moist enough that it doesn't dry out during baking, but not so moist that it makes the pastry soggy.

Empanadas can be either baked or fried. We've baked ours to save on fat and calories.

PICADILLO

Picadillo is a slightly spicy and richly flavored beef hash. It works perfectly for empanadas and can also be used as a tortilla stuffing for chimichangas or simply as a dip with corn chips. In Cuban households, picadillo is often layered with mashed potatoes, topped with grated cheese, and baked in the oven as a sort of shepherd's pie.

OTHER CHOICES

Use our picadillo stuffing or one that you improvise at home. For instance, mix together diced ham and onion, chopped green olives, and hard-cooked egg, and grated Parmesan cheese. Add a little minced green chili and garlic if you like. Moisten the mixture slightly with olive oil.

As alternatives, make stuffings from leftover meat, cheese and vegetables, garlic sausage, chili, or seasoned chicken.

You can also make sweet empanadas. Stuff them with pie fillings such as pumpkin, apple, or mincemeat or simply with marmalade or jam.

COOKING AHEAD

To freeze unbaked empanadas, prepare them as directed, but don't glaze them. Arrange unbaked empanadas on a baking sheet and set in the freezer until frozen. Place in a self-sealing plastic bag and freeze for up to 2 months. To bake, arrange still frozen on a baking sheet, brush with egg wash, and bake about 30 minutes.

PORK TRIANGLE PIES

Prepare picadillo as directed at right, **substituting** ground pork for beef. **Omit** the jalapeño, pepperoncini, and raisins and **add** 1 medium-size cored, seeded, and chopped sweet red pepper. **Prepare** empanadas as directed but **roll** pastry into a rectangle 1/8-inch thick and **cut** into five 3 1/2-inch squares. **Proceed** as directed, **forming** pastry triangles instead of half moons. Makes 20 triangles.

HOW TO MAKE AN EMPANADA

Start with a basic double-crust pie dough, then roll, fill, fold, and seal as follows:

1 On a lightly floured work surface, knead dough 1 minute. Divide in fourths and shape into rounds. Wrap in wax paper and refrigerate 30 minutes.

2 Roll each round into a circle 1/8-inch thick. Cut into rounds with a 3 1/2-inch cutter. Roll each round again, enlarging into a circle 1/16-inch thick.

3 Spoon 2 teaspoons picadillo on half of each circle. Brush edges with beaten egg, then fold over to form a half moon. Seal by crimping edges with a fork.

4 Prick each pastry with a fork, brush lightly with egg wash, and arrange on a parchment-lined baking sheet. Bake in a 400°F oven for 20 minutes.

Empanadas with Picadillo Stuffing

Picadillo:

- 1 tablespoon olive or vegetable oil
- 1 large yellow onion, chopped
- 1 medium-size sweet green pepper, cored, seeded, and chopped
- 1 small jalapeño pepper, cored, seeded, and finely chopped
- 4 small pepperoncinis or other small very hot chili peppers, cored, seeded, and chopped
- 4 cloves garlic, minced
- 1/2 pound ground lean beef
- 18 pimiento-stuffed olives, chopped
- 1 can (28 ounces) whole peeled tomatoes, chopped with their juice
- 1 teaspoon salt
- 1/2 cup dark seedless raisins or dried currants
- 1 cup canned black beans, drained and rinsed

Empanadas:

- 2 recipes Pastry for a Double-Crust Pie
- 2 eggs, lightly beaten

1 For the Picadillo: In a 4-quart Dutch oven over moderately high heat, heat oil for 1 minute. Add onion, the 3 peppers, and garlic and sauté until onion is soft—about 5 minutes.

2 In a large skillet over moderately high heat, sauté beef, stirring to break up clumps, until browned—about 15 minutes. Drain off fat.

3 Add beef and all the remaining picadillo ingredients to Dutch oven and cook, covered, over low heat for 40 minutes. Meanwhile, prepare empanadas.

4 For the Empanadas: Preheat the oven to 400°F. Prepare Pastry for a Double-Crust Pie (page 307). Roll out and fill as directed at left.

5 Bake until golden—about 20 minutes. Makes 32 empanadas.

1 Empanada: Calories 142; Total Fat 8 g;
Saturated Fat 2 g; Protein 4 g;
Carbohydrates 14 g; Fiber 1 g;
Sodium 228 mg; Cholesterol 14 mg

prep time-30 minutes • cooking time-1 1/4 hours

CALF'S LIVER

O f all the variety meats, calf's liver is the most popular. Keep an eye on the clock when you cook it to preserve its delicate flavor and smooth texture.

AT THE MARKET

Calf's liver, prized for its tenderness and mild nutty flavor, is pricey whether you order it at a restaurant or buy it at the supermarket. Beef liver, which has a stronger flavor and is a little less tender, is far less costly. These days, beef is so young when it comes to market that the difference between the two is less discernible than it used to be.

Be sure you're getting what you're paying for. Calf's liver is pale pink or beige with a pink tinge. Beef liver is dark red.

Allow about 1/3 pound per serving. Since it is highly perishable, fresh liver must be cooked within 24 hours. In some markets, liver is available sliced and frozen.

FOR THE BEST FLAVOR

If people complain about the taste of liver, chances are they've never had it properly cooked. Although it's easy as can be to cook liver perfectly, it's also easy to get it wrong.

Liver is usually sliced before cooking and is best when done only rare to medium-rare. When overcooked, it becomes tough, strong flavored, and strong smelling. When properly cooked, liver is juicy, pink inside, and as flavorful as steak. If it turns gray, it has been cooked too long.

As a rule of thumb, cook thin slices of liver quickly over high heat and thicker slices more slowly over low heat.

Venetian-style calf's liver is always made with thin slices. If you wish to grill liver over coals, use thick slices rubbed with olive oil.

Turn the calf's liver only once while it cooks.

Use tongs, not a fork, which will pierce the meat and release precious juices.

MILK FOR SWEETNESS

Soaking liver several hours in milk sweetens the meat and removes any trace of bitterness that may be present. A milk bath is especially important for stronger flavored beef liver.

FLOUR FOR A CRISP CRUST

Liver does not brown in a hot skillet the way beef does, but dredging it in flour before sautéing gives it a desirable crust. Be sure that the skillet is very hot before adding the liver slices so that the floured coating crisps and adheres firmly.

AND ON THE SIDE

Good quality calf's liver is delicious with only a squeeze of lemon for flavoring, but browned onions or crisp-cooked bacon slices are traditional accompaniments. For a change, you might want to try a mixture of minced garlic and chopped parsley cooked briefly in butter. Spoon a small amount on each slice of liver.

TO PREPARE LIVER

The thin membrane that surrounds liver must be peeled off. It shrinks when cooked and will cause slices to warp or curl.

1 Cut the liver into thin slices. Use the tip of a knife to loosen the membrane and pull it off.

2 Cut away any connective tissue. Cook as directed.

VENETIAN-STYLE LIVER AND ONIONS

Prepare as directed at right, but **slice** liver into 1/4 to 1/2-inch-wide strips and onions into thin rings. **Omit** Steps 2, 3, and 4. Instead, **sauté** onions and 1/4 cup chopped parsley in 1 tablespoon oil over low heat until onions are soft—about 10 minutes. **Add** 2 tablespoons oil, **increase** the heat to moderately high, and **add** liver and 1/2 teaspoon salt. **Cook** 3 minutes, **add** vinegar, and **cook** about 3 minutes more. Makes 4 servings.

TO CARAMELIZE ONIONS

Slice 3 onions. In a skillet over moderate heat, heat 1 tablespoon oil. Add onions and 2 teaspoons sugar. Cook 15 minutes. Add 2 tablespoons balsamic vinegar and 1/4 teaspoon salt. Cook until browned.

Calf's Liver and Caramelized Onions

- 4 slices calf's liver (6 ounces each), trimmed
- 1/2 cup milk
- 3 tablespoons olive oil
- 3 medium-size yellow onions, halved lengthwise and thinly sliced
- 2 teaspoons sugar
- 2 tablespoons balsamic vinegar
- 3/4 teaspoon salt
- 3 tablespoons all-purpose flour

1 Place liver in a medium-size bowl, pour in milk, cover, and refrigerate at least 1 hour or overnight.

2 In a 12-inch nonstick skillet over moderate heat, heat 1 tablespoon of the oil for 1 minute. Add onions, sprinkle with sugar, and cook, stirring frequently, until browned—about 15 minutes. Add vinegar and ¼ teaspoon of the salt and cook until onions are glazed—1 to 2 minutes more. Transfer to a heated plate and keep warm.

3 Blot liver dry on paper toweling. Sprinkle liver with the remaining ½ teaspoon salt and dredge in flour, shaking off excess.

4 In the same skillet over moderately high heat, heat 1 tablespoon of the remaining oil for 1 minute. Sauté liver 1 or 2 slices at a time, adding the remaining oil as needed, allowing 1½ to 3 minutes on each side for medium-rare depending on thickness of liver.

5 Transfer to 4 heated serving plates and top with reserved onions. Serve with mustard and horseradish on the side. Makes 4 servings.

1 Serving: Calories 294; Total Fat 14 g; Saturated Fat 4 g; Protein 25 g; Carbohydrates 16 g; Fiber 2 g; Sodium 460 mg; Cholesterol 611 mg

prep time-12 minutes
cooking time-about 25 minutes

VEAL CUTLETS

Veal cutlets, or scallops, cook up juicy and tender when pounded thin, floured or breaded, and sautéed.

ABOUT VEAL

True veal is the meat from a calf no more than 16 weeks old. It's naturally lean, pale pink, and delicately flavored.

Thin cutlets are among the most popular cuts of veal. Recipes for them are included in nearly every European cuisine. Because veal does not have the fat that beef does, scallops must be cooked quickly to prevent them from toughening and drying out.

The price of veal cutlets seems steep, but there is absolutely no waste and little shrinkage. One pound can easily serve 3, and if richly sauced even 4.

COATING FOR CRISPNESS

Veal scallops are best when given a coating that turns appetizingly brown and crisp in the skillet. In some recipes, such as our Veal Piccata, the coating is simply flour. Others call for an egg and bread crumb coating. The cutlets are given a light dredging in flour (which helps the egg adhere), then they are dipped in beaten egg, and finally in plain or lightly seasoned crumbs.

Breading cutlets is easily done in assembly-line fashion if the flour and bread crumbs are heaped on large individual sheets of wax paper, and the beaten egg is placed between them on a dinner plate.

To prevent the coating from buckling as it cooks, beat a little water in with the egg, and beat only until the yolk and white are just combined. Work quickly to keep the flour from becoming gummy.

If you want the breading to stick to a cutlet, you must air dry the breaded cutlet 10 to 15 minutes before cooking.

When cooking cutlets one at a time, keep the others warm in a 200°F oven.

LIGHT TOPPINGS

Highly seasoned sauces should be avoided. A little freshly squeezed lemon and salt and pepper are all that's necessary.

For something extra, serve a breaded cutlet "garden style" the way Italians do in Milan—topped with a tossed salad and a light vinaigrette.

Or when the cutlets have been removed from the pan, quickly sauté chopped shallots in the drippings, stir in a little white wine, and cook until it reduces slightly. Pour over the cutlets as a sauce.

HOW TO PAN-FRY BREADED CUTLETS

1 Dredge cutlets in flour. Sprinkle with salt and pepper. Dip into egg beaten with a little water and then coat each side with bread crumbs.

2 Heat oil in a skillet until hot. Sauté cutlets one at a time, about 2 minutes per side, turning only once. When crisp and golden brown, transfer to a hot plate.

HOW TO POUND CUTLETS

Veal does not need to be pounded to make it tender, but many recipes call for pounding to make cutlets thinner. To avoid punching holes in the meat, gentle pounding is necessary.

1 Sandwich the cutlets between sheets of plastic wrap or wax paper so that they won't tear or stick.

2 Pound the cutlets gently with a smooth heavy object just until they have reached the desired thickness.

WORK SAVER

Meat Pounder or Cutlet Bat

The easiest and safest way to pound cutlets of veal, chicken, or turkey is with a tool specially made for the job—a heavy disk-type pounder with a vertical handle. Lacking this type of pounder, you can use a rolling pin or the side or bottom of a quart-size bottle. A meat pounder should not be confused with a meat tenderizer, a malletlike utensil that has a jagged pounding surface.

Veal Scaloppine à la Marsala

Prepare as directed in Steps 1 and 2 at right. In Step 3, **pour** off all but 2 teaspoons of drippings. **Add** 8 ounces thinly sliced mushrooms and **sauté** until soft. **Add** 1/4 cup Marsala and boil 1 minute. Add 1/2 cup chicken stock and **cook** 2 minutes. **Omit** the remaining salt, the lemon zest and juice. **Proceed** as directed in Step 4. Makes 4 to 5 servings.

Old World Wiener Schnitzel

Prepare as directed in Step 1 at right, **sprinkling** cutlets with all of the salt. After dredging, **dip** cutlets in 1 egg that has been beaten with 2 teaspoons water. Next, **dip** into 1 cup fine dry bread crumbs. **Use** 1/3 cup unsalted butter instead of 3 tablespoons olive oil to sauté breaded scallops and **cook** until brown and crispy—about 2 minutes on each side. **Transfer** to paper toweling to drain. **Serve** immediately with lemon wedges. Makes 4 to 5 servings.

Veal Piccata

1½ **pounds veal cutlets, pounded thin as for scaloppine**
½ **teaspoon salt**
⅓ **cup unsifted all-purpose flour**
3 **tablespoons olive oil**
1 **cup Rich Chicken Stock or canned reduced-sodium chicken broth**
½ **teaspoon grated lemon zest**
2 **tablespoons lemon juice**
2 **tablespoons butter or margarine, cut up**
2 **tablespoons chopped parsley**

1 Sprinkle veal with ¼ teaspoon of the salt. Dredge in flour, shaking off excess.

2 In a large skillet over moderately high heat, heat ½ the oil for 1 minute. Sauté veal in 2 batches, adding the remaining oil as needed, until golden—1 to 2 minutes on each side. Transfer to a heated serving platter and keep warm.

3 Pour drippings from skillet, add stock, and simmer over moderately high heat for 1 minute, scraping up browned bits. Add lemon zest and juice and the remaining ¼ teaspoon salt and cook until liquid reduces to ¾ cup—about 3 minutes.

4 Remove from the heat, add butter and parsley, and swirl just until butter melts. Spoon sauce over veal and serve. Makes 4 servings.

1 Serving: Calories 337; Total Fat 18 g; Saturated Fat 7 g; Protein 33 g; Carbohydrates 8 g; Fiber 0 g; Sodium 450 mg; Cholesterol 144 mg

prep time-15 minutes • cooking time-10 minutes

LEG OF LAMB

$\mathcal{A}$ perfect blend of delicate texture and unique flavor, with little preparation lamb is a company-pleaser.

AT THE MARKET

A bone-in leg of lamb weighs 5 to 7 pounds and can be roasted whole. Often, however, the leg is cut into sirloin and shank halves. The sirloin contains more meat and costs more per pound than the shank half. You can also buy the leg boned, rolled, and tied.

Because there is no waste, a boned roast costs more than a bone-in roast. A boned and tied leg weighing 2½ pounds will serve 6 people.

Legs can be refrigerated in their packaging for a couple of days. For longer storage, up to 4 days, remove the wrapper and cover loosely with plastic wrap or aluminum foil.

FOR BEST FLAVOR

The distinctive flavor of lamb responds well to certain seasonings. Garlic, oregano, rosemary, mint, thyme, and lemon are the most traditional. The seasonings can be patted on the leg before roasting or inserted into the flesh as shown in the box at right.

FRENCH THE SHANK

The shank bone that protrudes from a leg of lamb is usually cracked and folded. For a fes-

---

COOK'S SECRETS

Merle Ellis
Expert Butcher and Cookbook Author

"A thrifty way to use a whole leg is to have it cut in half. Ask the butcher to remove one steak from the cut end of each half. Freeze half of the roast and the tender leg steaks for other meals. A 1-inch center-cut leg steak feeds 2 or 3 people. Broil 3 to 4 inches from the heat source for about 12 minutes, turning once, for medium-done."

tive presentation, ask the butcher not to crack it. Instead, have him french, or clean, the extended part of the bone. After roasting, the carver uses the bone as a handle to keep the roast steady.

REST TIME

Lamb is usually cooked no more than medium-rare. It will need to rest at least 15 minutes after cooking so that it can reabsorb juices and be easier to carve.

HOW TO INSERT GARLIC AND ROSEMARY

1 Use a sharp knife to make twelve ½-inch-deep cuts in the meaty part of the leg.

2 Insert 1 paper-thin slice of garlic and a little crumbled rosemary in each cut.

HOW TO CARVE A LEG OF LAMB

1 Set roast meaty side up and secure with a carving fork. Cut a wedge-shaped piece from the center of the leg.

2 Holding knife horizontally, carve slices from either side of the wedge. Then turn leg over and make horizontal slices.

SLOW COOKING ROASTING CHART
If you prefer slow roasting, place meat in a 325°F oven.

Cut	Meat Thermometer Reading	Minutes per Pound
Whole leg, bone in (5-7 lbs)	145°F medium-rare 160°F medium	20 25
Boneless rolled whole leg (4-6 lbs)	150°F medium-rare 160°F medium	30 32-34
Leg, shank half, bone in (3-4 lbs)	150°F medium-rare 160°F medium	35-40 40-45
Leg, sirloin half, bone in (3-4 lbs)	150°F medium-rare 160°F medium	30-35 35-40

Herb-Crusted Leg of Lamb

- 2 tablespoons minced parsley
- 1 tablespoon minced fresh rosemary or 1 teaspoon dried rosemary, crumbled
- 1 tablespoon minced fresh thyme or 1 teaspoon dried thyme, crumbled
- 1 tablespoon minced mint or 1 teaspoon mint flakes
- 1 tablespoon olive oil
- 1 tablespoon balsamic vinegar
- 1 tablespoon Dijon mustard
- 1 teaspoon salt
- 1/2 teaspoon black pepper
- 1 whole leg of lamb (about 6 pounds)
- 2 cloves garlic, cut into thin slivers

1 Preheat the oven to 450°F. In a small bowl, combine all ingredients except lamb and garlic.

2 Place lamb, fat side up, on a rack in a shallow roasting pan. With a small sharp knife, cut twelve 1/2-inch-long by 1/2-inch-deep slits, 2 to 3 inches apart, in the top of the lamb. Insert slivers of garlic into each slit, pushing them into the meat.

3 Spread herb mixture evenly over lamb. Insert a meat thermometer into the center of the meat making sure it does not touch bone (or test later with an instant-read thermometer).

4 Roast, uncovered, for 15 minutes. Reduce the heat to 350°F and continue roasting, uncovered, until the temperature registers 145°F for medium-rare or 160°F for medium.

5 Remove from the oven and let stand for 15 to 20 minutes before carving. Makes 8 servings.

1 Serving: Calories 324; Total Fat 14 g; Saturated Fat 5 g; Protein 45 g; Carbohydrates 1 g; Fiber 0 g; Sodium 376 mg; Cholesterol 142 mg

prep time-15 minutes
cooking time-about 1 hour 20 minutes

BRAISED LAMB SHANKS

There's an old saying that the meat is sweetest close to the bone. When you've cooked lamb and veal shanks, you'll have no doubt the saying is true.

SHANK FACTS

Lamb and veal shanks—the bottom portion of the leg—have always been popular in Europe. However, with our broadened interest in international home cooking, these full-flavored sinewy cuts have become much better known.

The techniques for cooking both lamb and veal shanks are identical. They require long, slow cooking in moist heat. Generally, they are braised or stewed in the oven for about 2 hours. Shanks can be cooked with whatever ingredients you like best in a lamb or veal stew, but there are two classic favorites. The country French style is to cook lamb shanks with garlic and white beans that can be either left whole or puréed just before serving.

The most famous Italian shank dish is osso buco, veal shanks stewed with vegetables and served with risotto. Osso buco is subtly flavored, and the bone marrow—scooped out

with a tiny spoon—is one of the highlights. For zest, many cooks serve osso buco with *gremolata*, a pungent garnish of parsley, garlic, and lemon.

AT THE MARKET

Lamb shanks have a large proportion of bone to meat. Each whole shank weighs between 3/4 and 11/4 pounds and is extremely economical.

Ask your butcher to crack the lamb shanks at the center. This will help them to cook more evenly and prevent the meat from riding up on the bone as it cooks.

Veal shanks are meatier and more expensive than lamb shanks. For most recipes, veal foreshanks are fine. For osso buco, choose veal from the hind shank, which has more meat. Ordinarily, veal hind shanks are sold in cross-cut sections. They must be tied around the middle with string to keep them in shape during cooking.

LITTLE LEGS OF LAMB

For dinner for two, roast meaty shanks instead of a leg of lamb. Choose two 3/4-pound shanks. Stud them with garlic slivers. Rub them with olive oil and lemon juice and season with salt and freshly ground black pepper.

Place the shanks on a rack in a roasting pan; cover tightly with foil. Roast in a 325°F oven for 45 minutes, remove the foil, and continue to roast until the meat is fork-tender—30 to 45 minutes.

Osso Buco

Prepare as directed at right, **substituting** 21/2 pounds veal shanks cut into 2-inch lengths for lamb. **Tie** string around each piece to hold the meat in place during cooking. In Step 4, **bake** veal until tender—about 11/2 hours. **Omit** white beans.

Prepare *gremolata* by combining 1/4 cup chopped parsley, 2 cloves blanched chopped garlic, and 2 teaspoons grated lemon zest. **Sprinkle** over veal during last 10 minutes of cooking. **Serve** with rice seasoned with Parmesan cheese. Makes 4 servings.

HOW TO TIE A VEAL SHANK FOR OSSO BUCO

Shanks should be cut into cross sections 11/2 to 2 inches thick. Tie each shank firmly around the middle with twine.

HOW TO PREPARE A LAMB SHANK

1 Buy long sections of meaty shanks for braising. Have the bone cracked at the center.

2 Trim off excess fat and the papery membrane (called the fell).

1 With a sharp paring knife, remove membrane (fell) from lamb shanks and discard. Sprinkle shanks with ½ teaspoon of the salt, and pepper. Dredge in flour, shaking off excess.

2 In a 6-quart Dutch oven over moderate heat, heat oil for 1 minute. Add shanks and cook, in batches if necessary, until browned—about 5 minutes. Remove and set aside.

3 Preheat the oven to 350°F. Add onion and garlic to the Dutch oven and cook, stirring frequently, until soft—about 5 minutes. Add wine, increase the heat to high, and cook for 1 minute, stirring constantly to loosen browned bits. Add tomatoes, stock, orange zest and juice, basil, and the remaining ¼ teaspoon salt and bring to a boil. Add reserved lamb and return to a boil.

4 Transfer the Dutch oven to the middle rack of the oven and bake, covered, for 1 hour. Turn lamb, add beans, and bake, covered, until lamb is tender—about 40 minutes more. Makes 4 servings.

1 Serving: Calories 339; Total Fat 11 g; Saturated Fat 2 g; Protein 25 g; Carbohydrates 32 g; Fiber 6 g; Sodium 655 mg; Cholesterol 56 mg

prep time-30 minutes • cooking time-2 hours

Braised Lamb Shanks with White Beans

4	lamb shanks (about 3 pounds)
³/₄	teaspoon salt
¹/₂	teaspoon black pepper
3	tablespoons all-purpose flour
3	tablespoons olive oil
1	large yellow onion, finely chopped
4	cloves garlic, finely chopped
¹/₂	cup dry white wine
2	cups canned tomatoes, chopped with their juice
²/₃	cup Rich Chicken Stock or canned reduced-sodium chicken broth
3	strips (each 3 inches by ¹/₄ inch) orange zest
¹/₄	cup orange juice
¹/₃	cup chopped fresh basil
2	cups cooked white kidney beans or 2 cans (15 ounces each) white cannellini beans, drained and rinsed

CROWN ROAST

A crown roast, brimming with stuffing, takes a little effort, but is a dazzling tribute at a New Year's day feast or any other celebratory occasion.

A CIRCLE OF RIBS

The meat for this elegant roast must be ordered from the butcher in advance.

To make a crown roast of pork, a butcher uses two center-cut racks of ribs, bending them into a circle—rib bones facing out—and tying them in place with string.

The same is done with racks of lamb, although the cost is considerably higher. Veal and beef are too large to make successful crown roasts.

Have the butcher french the rib tips, or scrape off the meat to expose an inch or more of bone. The cleaned tips make an attractive presentation both for a crown roast and for rib chops. If you intend to use festive paper frills on the rib tips, frenching is necessary. If the frenching isn't done by the butcher, do it yourself, scraping the bones with a sharp knife.

DON'T OVERCOOK

Pork tastes best when it's cooked medium well to well done. That translates as 160°F to 170°F on a meat thermometer, at which point the roast may still be slightly pink at the center.

STUFFING THE CROWN

Bread, sausage, and other stuffings—the same ones you use for turkey—can be loosely packed inside the crown before roasting. Cover the stuffing with aluminum foil. About 45 minutes before the roast is done, remove the foil so that the stuffing has a chance to brown.

If you want to serve a crown roast filled with freshly cooked vegetables—such as peas or mashed potatoes—instead of a stuffing, it should be filled after roasting. To help the crown keep its shape while it roasts, insert a wad of aluminum foil inside the crown. Just before serving, remove the foil and add the vegetables.

SERVED IN STYLE

Applesauce and other cooked-fruit mixtures are always good with pork, served as a side dish or as part of a stuffing.

Pork and poultry have many of the same flavor characteristics. Anything that tastes good with your holiday bird is likely to go well with this roast. Best bets include sweet potatoes and anything seasoned with sage or thyme.

HOW TO CARVE AND SERVE A CROWN ROAST

1 The roast will cut easily between the ribs. Remove it to a cutting board. Remove the string used for tying it.

2 Use a carving fork to steady the roast at one side. Carve downward into 1- or 2-chop portions.

KITCHEN MATH

A crown roast usually weighs 6 to 7 pounds and contains 16 chops. You will need 2 chops for each serving.

HOW TO MAKE PAPER FRILLS

Frills are a festive option. Pop them on the trimmed rib ends just before serving.

1 Cut paper (parchment, freezer wrap, or bond) into 8- by 3-inch pieces; make a loose fold in half lengthwise.

2 Make 3/4-inch cuts from the folded edge, about 1/4 inch apart, down the length of the paper. Wrap the uncut edge around your finger a couple of times (it should be about the same circumference as the ribs) and secure with tape.

3 Reverse the fold and plump out the frills. Fit over the tip of each rib.

1. Preheat the oven to 400°F. Sprinkle roast with 2 tablespoons of the rosemary, salt, and 1 teaspoon of the pepper. Stand roast, rib ends up, on a rack in a large roasting pan. Cover rib ends with foil to prevent burning.

2. Insert a meat thermometer between 2 ribs in the center, making sure it does not touch bone. Roast, uncovered, for 10 minutes. Reduce the oven temperature to 325°F and continue roasting until the thermometer registers 160°F—2½ to 3 hours. Remove roast to a platter and keep warm.

3. Fill crown cavity loosely with Green Peas and Onions (page 139) and keep warm while preparing gravy.

Crown Roast of Pork with Peas and Onions

- **1 (16 rib) crown roast of pork (6 to 7 pounds) Note: Have butcher french the rib tips**
- **3 tablespoons chopped fresh rosemary or 1½ teaspoons dried rosemary, crumbled**
- **2 teaspoons salt**
- **1½ teaspoons black pepper**
- **2 recipes for Green Peas and Onions**
- **2 cups Browned Beef Stock or canned reduced-sodium beef broth (about)**
- **¼ cup unsifted all-purpose flour**

4. Pour drippings from roast into a 1-quart glass measure. Skim fat from drippings into a 1-cup measure to total ¼ cup (add olive or vegetable oil if needed to fill out measurement). Transfer to a medium-size saucepan.

5. Place roasting pan over moderate heat, add 1 cup of the stock, and simmer for 1 minute, scraping up browned bits. Add to drippings in 1-quart measure to total 2 cups (add additional stock if needed to fill out measurement).

6. Place saucepan of reserved fat over moderate heat and heat until bubbly. Blend in flour and cook, whisking constantly, until smooth. Add the remaining 1 tablespoon rosemary and cook, stirring constantly, until mixture thickens and boils—2 to 3 minutes. Gradually add stock mixture and cook, stirring constantly, until thickened and smooth—3 to 5 minutes more. Whisk in the remaining ½ teaspoon pepper and remove to a heated gravy boat. Makes 8 servings.

1 Serving: Calories 659; Total Fat 35 g; Saturated Fat 13 g; Protein 67 g; Carbohydrates 17 g; Fiber 4 g; Sodium 755 mg; Cholesterol 199 mg

prep time-1 hour • cooking time-3 to 3½ hours

249

PORK CHOPS

Pork chops are leaner than they used to be. Slow cooking and added moisture are the secrets to keeping them tender and succulent.

AT THE MARKET

Pork is one of the best buys at the meat market, but there is a range when it comes to the price of pork chops. Top choices for most pork lovers are rib and loin chops, which are tender, flavorful, and the most expensive. Larger blade chops, cut from the shoulder, are less expensive, just as flavorful, but more sinewy.

CHOOSING BY THICKNESS

For flavor and meatiness, choose 1-inch or thicker chops. If you want to stuff them, choose single-rib chops that are at least 1¼ to 1½ inches thick or, for really hearty appetites, double-rib chops that are 1½ to 2 inches thick.

If you want to sauté chops quickly in a skillet, choose chops that are ½-inch thick or less. Any thicker and chops should be braised—cooked slowly in moist heat—in the oven or on top of the stove.

FLAVOR ENHANCERS

For the best results, let the chops sit at room temperature for ½ hour before cooking. Do not trim away all of the fat on the chops. It helps to keep the meat moist as it cooks and adds considerably to its flavor.

Whatever cooking method you choose, chops benefit from a quick browning first. Be sure to pat their surface dry or they will not brown properly. Rub them with salt and black pepper and whatever seasonings you like. Then brown in a hot skillet in just a little oil.

STUFFED CHOPS

Our recipes are for thick stuffed chops. A pocket has to be cut in the chops to hold the stuffing. You can have your butcher do it for you or do it yourself as shown at right. The extra thickness of stuffed chops demands braising in the oven. The braising liquid keeps the chops moist.

STUFFING TIPS

Cut the pockets in the chops ahead of time, if you like. Then wrap them well in plastic wrap and refrigerate until ready to stuff and bake.

Chops should be loosely stuffed. Bake leftover stuffing in a covered baking dish for about 15 minutes or until heated through. However, if the stuffing contains egg, it must be cooked to an internal temperature of 165°F.

Any of the seasoned cornbread, rice, and bread crumb stuffings you enjoy with chicken and turkey will suit pork chops too. The flavors of rosemary, sage, garlic, onions, mushrooms, chiles, and pecans all complement the flavor of pork.

PAN BRAISING

Thinner pork chops can be braised on top of the stove. Brown them and discard the excess fat in the pan. Add ¼ to ⅓ cup of broth or wine to the pan along with the chops. Cover tightly and cook over moderate heat until tender.

For gravy, remove the chops from the pan and add a thin paste of water and flour (about 1 tablespoon of all-purpose flour to ½ cup of water).

Cook on top of the stove, stirring and scraping up the brown bits until thickened. Season with salt and pepper.

BAKED PORK CHOPS WITH PECAN-RICE STUFFING

Prepare as directed through Step 1 at right. In a medium-size bowl, lightly **beat** 1 egg. **Stir** in ¾ cup cooked brown rice, ¼ cup finely chopped pecans, 1 tablespoon chopped rosemary, 1 minced clove garlic, and ¼ teaspoon black pepper. **Spoon** stuffing into chops and **proceed** as directed in Steps 3 and 4. Makes 4 servings.

HOW TO CUT A POCKET AND STUFF A CHOP

1 Insert a knife in the fatty outer edge of chop and slice a pocket in the meaty portion, leaving good margins.

2 Lift chops to open pocket. Spoon in stuffing loosely.

Braised Pork Chops with Thyme and Mushroom Stuffing

4 rib pork chops, cut 1¼ to 1½ inches thick and trimmed of excess fat

2 tablespoons vegetable oil

1 clove garlic, minced

6 ounces medium-size mushrooms, finely chopped

⅓ cup soft bread crumbs

1½ tablespoons chopped fresh thyme or 1 teaspoon dried thyme, crumbled

½ teaspoon salt

¼ teaspoon black pepper

¼ cup boiling Browned Beef Stock or canned reduced-sodium beef broth

1 Preheat the oven to 350°F. Following the directions at left, cut a pocket in each pork chop.

2 In a 12-inch skillet over moderate heat, heat 1 tablespoon of the oil for 1 minute. Add garlic and sauté, stirring constantly, for 1 minute. Add mushrooms and sauté, stirring occasionally, until liquid evaporates—about 5 minutes. Mix in bread crumbs, thyme, and ½ of the salt and pepper. Spoon about ⅓ cup stuffing into each chop.

3 In the same skillet over moderately high heat, heat the remaining oil for 1 minute. Sprinkle chops with the remaining salt and pepper and sauté, turning once at halftime, until lightly browned—5 to 6 minutes. Transfer to an ungreased shallow 12- by 7-inch baking dish. Pour stock over chops.

4 Cover chops with foil and bake until an instant-read thermometer inserted in center of stuffing registers 165°F—about 45 minutes. Makes 4 servings.

1 Serving: Calories 424; Total Fat 22 g; Saturated Fat 7 g; Protein 49 g; Carbohydrates 7 g; Fiber 1 g; Sodium 360 mg; Cholesterol 120 mg

prep time-45 minutes • cooking time-1 hour

BAKED HAM

If the dozens of hams available have made you wonder which is best and why one is more expensive than another, our tips will make the choices clear.

HAM BASICS

For all the differences in size, shape, flavor, and curing methods, every ham on the market has one thing in common: Its meat comes from the hind leg of a hog. Other parts of the hog, shoulder butts, for example, can be cured and cooked by the same methods but are not hams.

CHOOSING A CUT

Whole ham: the entire leg. These are large, weighing between 10 and 24 pounds. Usually a leg is cut into butt and shank halves.

The butt half contains more meat than the shank half and is more expensive. When a ham is sold as a butt or shank "end," it means that the central portion of the leg has been removed.

Semiboneless ham: a butt half ham from which the hip bone is removed. Only the round leg bone remains, making it much easier to carve.

Boneless ham: What is called a boneless ham is actually sectioned pieces of meat from which all of the bones and most of the external fat have been removed.

The meat is rolled or packed into various shapes.

Canned hams: These hams are cured before they are canned. They are cooked in the can before you buy them. They should be kept refrigerated, except for very small ones that are sterilized during processing and are shelf stable. Check the label.

SALTING, SMOKING, AND AGING

Hams are cured by both wet and dry methods. Wet-cured hams are soaked in or injected with brine. Most hams that are commonly available in the meat section of the supermarket are cured this way. Some wet-cured specialty hams are smoked and aged after brining.

In dry curing, fresh ham is rubbed with a seasoned-salt mixture. After the mixture

TWO WAYS TO DECORATE A HAM

1 Remove the rind and skin and trim the fat to ¼ inch. With a sharp knife, score ham in a diamond pattern.

2 Punch a hole in the center of each diamond and insert a clove. Bake as directed.

1 Alternatively, score the browned fat on a smoked ham after baking.

2 Then glaze the ham before bringing it to the table and carving.

has permeated the meat, the ham is washed, dried, smoked, and aged or just dried and aged.

Most specialty hams are dry cured. They are available both raw and cooked.

SPECIALTY HAMS

These are the thoroughbreds of hams. They come from small packinghouses that specialize in their own curing formula for hams from specially fed hogs. They are more costly than mass-produced hams and generally are not available in the supermarket. Purchase them from your butcher or from a specialty market.

Country hams: These hams are dry cured according to age-old recipes and methods, which vary from region to region. Country hams may be precooked or not and may even require scrubbing and soaking before cooking in simmering water until they are finally skinned and baked. Always follow the packer's instructions exactly before preparing a country ham.

Smithfield ham: Smithfield is the official name for country hams that have been specially dry cured by one of several companies in Smithfield, Virginia, in the U.S. These

(continued on page 254)

Baked Ham with Peppery Bourbon-Brown Sugar Glaze

8½ **pounds fully cooked, bone-in shank portion smoked ham**

½ **cup firmly packed light brown sugar**

2 **tablespoons bourbon or beef stock**

1¼ **teaspoons black pepper**

1 Preheat the oven to 325°F. Remove skin, if any, from ham and trim fat to thickness of ¼ inch.

2 Place ham, cut side down, on a rack in a shallow roasting pan. Insert a meat thermometer in center of ham making sure it does not touch bone (or test later with an instant-read thermometer).

3 Bake ham, uncovered, until thermometer registers 130°F to 135°F—about 2 to 2¾ hours. If ham browns too fast, cover loosely with foil. Meanwhile, combine sugar, bourbon, and pepper in a small bowl.

4 Remove ham from the oven and increase oven temperature to 375°F. Using a sharp paring knife, score fat on surface of ham in a diamond pattern. Brush sugar mixture over ham.

5 Return ham to oven and bake, uncovered, until thermometer registers 140°F—15 to 20 minutes. Let stand at least 15 minutes before carving. Makes 16 servings.

1 Serving: Calories 482; Total Fat 13 g; Saturated Fat 4 g; Protein 54 g; Carbohydrates 37 g; Fiber 0 g; Sodium 3107 mg; Cholesterol 117 mg

prep time-1 hour • cooking time-about 2½ hours

GLAZE VARIATIONS

Orange-Brown Sugar Glaze: Prepare as directed above, **substituting** 2 tablespoons orange juice or orange-flavored liqueur for bourbon and 1½ teaspoons grated orange zest for black pepper; also **add** 1 teaspoon Dijon mustard.

Ginger-Brown Sugar Glaze: Prepare as directed above, **substituting** 2 tablespoons lemon juice for bourbon and 1 tablespoon grated fresh ginger for black pepper.

Maple-Brown Sugar Glaze: Prepare as directed above, **substituting** 3 tablespoons maple syrup for bourbon and ¼ teaspoon each ground allspice and cloves for black pepper.

(continued from page 252)

mahogany-colored hams are so rich and dense that they are usually sliced thin and served in small amounts.

Prosciutto: This famous ham from Parma, Italy, is a dry-cured ham that has been aged for 6 months in mountain air. The prolonged curing process dries the meat as it flavors it. Parma ham does not require cooking; it is simply sliced paper thin and used in recipes, as an hors d'oeuvre, or in sandwiches rather than as a dinner ham.

Specialty hams are produced throughout the world. Some of the best known are Bayonne from France, Brandenham from England, and Westphalian from Germany.

There are also wonderful hams from Denmark, Poland, and Portugal. Each has its own distinctive texture, color, and flavor.

HOW MUCH IS ENOUGH?

It is often worthwhile to buy a big ham, certainly a whole half. What is not eaten at the first sitting is not likely to go to waste.

Figure on 2/3 pound per person for a bony ham (such as a shank half), 1/3 to 1/2 pound for all other bone-in hams, and 1/4 to 1/3 pound for boneless hams. Canned hams should be figured on net weight.

COOKED VERSUS READY TO EAT

Most hams have been pre-cooked, so all you need to do is warm them up. Those hams that require cooking are clearly marked "cook before

eating." Fully cooked or ready-to-eat hams develop a richer flavor if they are baked until a meat thermometer registers 130°F. Canned hams fall into this category.

HOW TO BAKE HAMS

If necessary, cut the rind off the ham and trim the fat. Score and decorate the ham if desired. Bake all hams at 325°F. Insert a meat thermometer in the center of the ham, making sure that it does not touch the bone.

Uncooked hams: Place whole hams fat side up on a rack in a shallow roasting pan. (Half hams should be placed cut side down.) Bake, uncovered, until a meat thermometer registers 160°F. Count on 18 to 20 minutes per pound for whole or boneless hams, 22 to 24 minutes per pound for half hams. Let the ham rest for 15 to 20 minutes before carving.

Ready-to-eat hams: Follow the procedure for uncooked hams, but bake only until it reaches a serving temperature of 130°F on a meat thermometer. Whole and boneless hams require 12 to 15 minutes per pound, half hams 18 to 20.

Canned hams: Set on a rack in a shallow roasting pan. Bake, uncovered, for about 20 minutes per pound or until a meat thermometer registers 130°F.

HOW TO SKIN A HAM

1 Anchor ham by bearing down with one hand. Make long downward slices through fat.

2 Rotate the ham slightly, connecting each cut with the previous, until you've trimmed all the way around the ham.

THE END OF THE STORY

There are dozens of ways to use leftover ham, from sandwiches to macaroni with ham and cheese. Cut thick slices and pan-fry them with butter to serve with scrambled eggs for breakfast or brunch. Toss slivers into a green salad or chop it to fill omelets. Stir slices into soups and stews. The smallest scraps can be ground with cream cheese, chopped red pepper, and onion for a sensational cocktail spread or a dip.

HOW TO CARVE AND SERVE A HAM

To carve a shank portion of ham, place it on a cutting board and anchor it with a carving fork.

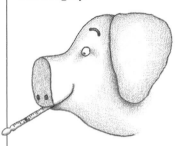

1 Cut a few horizontal slices off one side to give the ham a flat surface. Turn it over to lie on that surface.

2 Starting at shank end, make 1/4-inch parallel slices in the meat, cutting nearly to the bone.

3 Turn the ham on end and slice downward following the bone.

POULTRY FAVORITES

ROAST CHICKEN

There's more than one way to roast a chicken. Our hints and tips show you how to get the best results when stuffing, glazing, and carving.

A FAMILY OF CHICKENS

Rock Cornish hen: a specially bred young chicken, weighing between 1 and 1½ pounds. A small Cornish hen makes 1 serving; a larger one can be split for 2. They are usually roasted, but can be butterflied and broiled.

Broiler-fryer: a chicken about 7 weeks old, weighing 2½ to 4 pounds. Broiler-fryers serve between 2 and 4 people. They can be broiled, fried, roasted, or braised and are a good choice for charcoal grilling and spit roasting.

Roaster: a 3- to 5-month-old chicken, weighing 4 to 6 pounds. Roasters have more flavor than broiler-fryers and more meat per pound. Roasters are also a good choice for cacciatore and other casseroles and stews.

Capon: a young castrated male chicken, weighing about 5 to 8 pounds. Capons are deep breasted and have generous quantities of flavorful white meat. They are the most succulent poultry, but also have the largest percentage of fat. Capons are almost always roasted with stuffing.

AT THE MARKET

A diet of wheat and barley produces chickens with creamy-colored skin. Corn-fed birds produce a yellow-tinged skin. Reject any birds that have dry or purplish skins.

FREEZING AND THAWING

Pay attention to the date on a chicken's packaging. Use or freeze the chicken within 1 or 2 days of the date.

Chicken freezes well for up to 2 months. Discard the packaging and rewrap the chicken with fresh foil before freezing. For longer storage (up to 4 months), overwrap in heavy foil or freezer wrap.

Defrost in the refrigerator. A whole chicken takes 1 to 2 days to thaw. After thawing, cook it within 24 hours.

HOW TO STUFF AND TIE A CHICKEN

Tying or trussing a bird before roasting helps it to keep its shape and stay moist while it's in the oven. Cornish hens and relatively small chickens can be prepared by simply tying the openings closed with a single piece of string, as shown below. Large chickens, capons, and turkeys must be trussed—the opening laced closed with string—before roasting. See directions for how to truss a turkey on page 282.

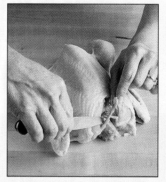

1 For easy carving, remove the wishbone. Using a sharp knife, cut through the flesh along the contours of the bone and lift out.

2 Stuff chicken loosely through the vent and neck cavities. Stuffing expands as it cooks so do not pack it in.

3 Place the chicken on its back with the string underneath its tail. Pull the two ends up and cross them above the tail. Loop the ends over the drumsticks and draw to pull the drumsticks over the vent.

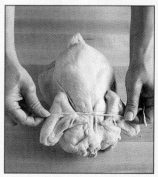

4 Turn the bird over. Draw one string end over the thigh and around the upper wing. Do the same with the other side. Fold up the neck flap and tie the two string ends together firmly over it.

CHICKEN PREP

Remove the giblets and neck from the body: Reserve or freeze for other use if desired. Pull out and discard loose fat. Wipe the chicken with a damp cloth. Freshen the skin by rubbing inside and out with lemon. Season the cavity with salt and pepper.

It's your choice whether to stuff a chicken or not. If you use a standard cornbread or bread crumb stuffing, be sure to spoon it in loosely to give it room to expand as it cooks.

STUFFING FOR FLAVOR

A well-seasoned stuffing adds a lot of flavor to a roast chicken. You can also flavor the meat from the inside without having to make a stuffing.

Depending on what you're serving, tuck a whole lemon, a small orange or onion, or several whole unpeeled garlic cloves inside. If you wish, pierce the lemon or orange skin once or twice with a toothpick. Roast as directed. The fruit, onion, or garlic will steam inside its skin and add its flavor to the meat. Discard the fruit or vegetables after roasting.

Alternatively, tuck fresh thyme, sage, rosemary, or tarragon in the cavity before roasting.

FLAVORING FROM THE OUTSIDE

There are several other options for flavoring a roast chicken. One is to season the chicken under the skin as shown in the box at right. Use butter flavored with herbs, an herbed goat cheese, or simply fresh herbs themselves.

You can also add flavor and a glistening finish to a chicken

HOW TO GLAZE CORNISH HENS OR CHICKEN

Truss hens and set breast side up on a rack in roasting pan. Brush with glaze.

Glaze again during roasting. Hens will be shiny and golden brown when done.

GLAZES FOR CORNISH HENS OR CHICKEN

Apricot-Ginger Glaze: In a small saucepan over moderate heat, **bring** to a boil 1/3 cup Rich Chicken Stock (page 39) or reduced-sodium canned chicken broth, 1/2 cup apricot jam, 1 tablespoon minced fresh ginger, and 1/4 teaspoon black pepper. **Reduce** the heat to low and **cook**, **stirring**, until well blended—about 2 minutes. **Brush** on chicken 2 or 3 times during last 15 to 20 minutes of cooking. Makes about 1 cup.

Oriental Plum Glaze: **Prepare** as directed above, **substituting** 1/2 cup oriental plum sauce or plum preserves for apricot jam and 1/4 cup finely chopped scallions for ginger. **Omit** black pepper but **add** 1 tablespoon cider vinegar. Makes about 1 cup.

Honey-Mustard Glaze with Lemon: **Prepare** as directed for Apricot-Ginger Glaze, **substituting** 2 tablespoons honey for jam, 2 tablespoons Dijon mustard for ginger, and 1/2 teaspoon grated lemon zest for pepper. Makes about 1/3 cup.

by glazing it. Use one of our glazes or devise one of your own to blend with your menu.

Another flavoring technique is to rub seasoning on (or under) the skin before roasting.

Start with a little olive oil, salt, and pepper. Add lemon juice, crushed garlic, and a chopped fresh or crumbled dried herb such as sage, oregano, thyme, or rosemary. Rub the mixture on the chicken and set aside for

about 30 minutes before roasting. Or refrigerate, covered, for up to 24 hours.

JULIA CHILD'S FORMULA FOR PERFECT ROASTING

The old rule of thumb for roast chicken—20 minutes per pound at a constant low temperature—is a ballpark formula at best. It works well for

HOW TO FLAVOR A CHICKEN UNDER THE SKIN

Flavor a chicken by putting herbal butter, plain fresh herbs, or herbed goat cheese under its skin before roasting.

1 Slide your hand under the skin, loosening the membrane on breast, legs, and thighs.

2 Place spoonfuls of butter or cheese at intervals under the skin.

3 Rub butter or cheese to spread it evenly or arrange herbs in place. Smooth skin back and roast as directed.

large roasters and capons, but is less trustworthy for small birds, always the trickiest to roast to perfection.

The problem is that dark meat cooks more slowly than white meat and that small birds with skimpier breasts may emerge from the oven with underdone drumsticks and tough dry breasts.

Julia Child developed a different formula that's foolproof for all chicken including small birds. It is as follows: Roast the chicken for 15 minutes in a preheated 425°F oven. This seals in the juices. Next reduce the temperature to 350°F and roast the bird at that temperature until done. As for timing, figure on 45 minutes plus 7 minutes per pound. A 3-pound broiler-fryer will thus be done in 66 minutes, a 3½ pounder in 69½.

Remove the bird from the oven and let it rest for 20 minutes before carving so that the juices have a chance to settle.

BRINING THE BIRD

Some cooks say that the best way to extract flavor from chickens and turkeys is to brine them. Soak the chicken or turkey in a brine bath of 1½ cups each of Kosher salt and granulated sugar to 1½ gallons of water for 5 hours. Be sure the chicken has not already been injected with brine or it will be too salty.

CRISP AND BROWN

Dry oven heat is what makes skin crisp. You can also prompt crisping by pulling the skin away from the meat but without tearing the membrane that holds the skin to the flesh.

Another trick is to trim excess

ROAST CORNISH GAME HENS

Prepare as directed at right, **substituting** 3 Cornish game hens (1½ pounds each) for chicken and **reducing** roasting time at 350°F to 35 to 45 minutes. Makes 6 servings.

---

skin from the neck and tuck it under the skin covering the breast, thigh, or leg. As the fat melts, it imparts wonderful flavor to the meat while helping the outer skin brown nicely by lifting the skin way from the meat. This method can also be used on turkey.

BUTTER IS BETTER

To promote even crisping and browning, rub the skin with a light coat of soft butter. You can use oil, but butter does a better job. Do not cover or baste. Whether you roast at a high or low heat, the skin should be perfectly browned and crisp by the time the chicken comes from the oven.

DONE TO PERFECTION

You'll know a chicken is done when the legs move easily in their sockets and when the juices, drained from the cavity, are clear yellow, not pink. A thermometer in the breast (not touching bone) should read 160°F, in the thickest part of the thigh 170°F.

With a vertical roaster, right, a chicken takes only about 15 minutes per pound to roast, but the internal temperature must still reach 160°F to 170°F.

HOW TO CARVE A ROAST CHICKEN OR CAPON

1 Remove roasted bird from the oven. Lay breast side up on a carving board. Allow it to rest 20 minutes. Cut trussing string with knife and discard.

2 To remove the leg, using a long flexible knife, cut the skin between the thigh and breast. Bend the leg outward and cut through the joint.

3 To remove the wing, slice downward through the breast toward the wing. Cut through the shoulder joint and remove the wing with the section of breast intact.

4 To carve the breast, hold the carving fork against the breastbone and the carving knife at a slight outward angle. Slice downward, lifting off each slice between fork and knife.

WORK SAVER

Vertical Roaster

Using this stainless-steel device, you can roast a chicken upright in an ordinary oven. Slip the chicken over the roaster, neck end up, set in a roasting pan, and place in a preheated oven. As the steel heats, the chicken cooks from within and the skin browns evenly on all sides. At the same time, the fat drips away from the bird and into the roasting pan.

Best Ever Roast Chicken with Pan Gravy

Chicken:
- **1 roasting chicken (about 5 pounds)**
- **1 teaspoon salt**
- **1/2 teaspoon black pepper**
- **2 tablespoons butter or margarine, melted**

Gravy:
- **2 cups Rich Chicken Stock, Vegetable Broth, or water**
- **3 tablespoons flour**

Salt and black pepper to taste

1 For the Chicken: Preheat the oven to 400°F. Sprinkle chicken inside and out with salt and pepper. Truss chicken and brush with butter. Insert a meat thermometer into the fleshiest part of the thigh making sure it does not touch bone (or test later with an instant-read thermometer).

2 Place chicken, breast side up, on a rack in a shallow roasting pan and roast, uncovered, for 30 minutes.

3 Reduce the temperature to 350°F and continue to roast, basting every 20 minutes with pan drippings, until the thermometer registers 180°F—about 1 hour 15 minutes. Remove chicken from oven and let stand 10 minutes while you make the pan gravy.

4 For the Gravy: Skim fat from roasting pan. Place over moderate heat, pour in 1/2 cup of the stock, and simmer, stirring to loosen browned bits, for 1 minute. Transfer mixture to a skillet.

5 Blend flour with 1/4 cup of the remaining stock and add to the skillet. Set over moderate heat and cook, whisking constantly, until blended. Gradually add the remaining 1 1/4 cups stock and cook, stirring, until mixture boils and thickens slightly—about 3 minutes. Add salt and pepper to taste. Makes 6 servings.

1 Serving: Calories 430; Total Fat 24 g; Saturated Fat 7 g; Protein 49 g; Carbohydrates 0 g; Fiber 0 g; Sodium 503 mg; Cholesterol 158 mg

prep time-10 minutes
cooking time-2 hours

FRIED CHICKEN

There are two ways to fry chicken, with batter or without. Our recipe and variation include both, for great results either way.

FRIED CHICKEN TWO WAYS

Traditionally, fried (or Southern fried) chicken is coated with batter and cooked in deep fat. The crust is thick and the meat is moist.

Our non-batter fried chicken is coated with seasoned flour and pan-fried in shallow fat. The coating is thin and crisp.

A FRESH COAT

Chicken must be coated with flour before it's fried by either method. Flour provides a crisp coating by itself and helps batter to stick.

Dredge the chicken pieces or shake them in a bag containing seasoned flour. Let them dry on a rack for 30 minutes.

White flour can be mixed 3 to 1 with buckwheat, whole-wheat, or rye flours for flavor. For a really light and crispy coating, dip into buttermilk, then into self-rising flour.

The flour is usually seasoned with no more than salt, pepper, and sometimes paprika. For a change of taste, add chili, cumin, or curry powder. Crushed or ground basil, marjoram, oregano, rosemary, tarragon, and thyme are also good complementary flavors.

If you are using a batter, mix it and let it rest for at least 1 hour. If you use the batter too quickly, it will shrink and split in the hot oil.

IN HOT OIL

Vegetable oil, shortening, peanut, corn, and canola oils are all suitable. One of the secrets to nongreasy fried chicken is to keep the temperature of the fat as close to 365°F as possible. Use a deep-fat thermometer to check.

Make sure that all of your equipment is dry before heating the oil. Drips of water can make the oil spatter.

FRIED CHICKEN TIPS

For the best fried chicken: Leave the skin on. Use plenty of hot oil. Don't crowd the pieces in the skillet. Use tongs instead of a fork to turn the pieces so that you don't pierce the skin and lose juices.

Remember that white meat cooks quicker than dark. Remove chicken pieces from the oil as soon as they are done, place them on a baking sheet covered with paper toweling, and keep warm in a very low oven.

HOW TO CUT UP A CHICKEN

If you want to cut up a whole chicken for frying, use a sharp knife and cut on a washable work surface.

1 Place chicken breast side down. To remove wings, cut through the joint that attaches wing to breast.

2 To remove legs, cut through to the thigh joint. Bend leg backward until thigh joint pops. Cut around joint to remove leg.

3 To separate thigh from drumstick, cut through joint, bearing down firmly with the knife.

4 To separate breast from back, set bird on its neck end. Cut diagonally along rib cage to backbone.

5 Place skin side down. Make a cut through the *V* of the wishbone. Bend breast back until keel bone pops.

6 To separate breasts, pull the bone and cartilage from breast. Cut breast in half through the center.

Maryland Fried Chicken with Gravy

Prepare as directed at right, beginning with Step 5. **Reduce** amount of flour to 1/3 cup. In Step 6, **pour** vegetable oil to a depth of 1/4 inch into a large deep skillet and **heat** over moderately high heat until oil is fragrant. **Fry** chicken, a few pieces at a time, until golden—about 5 minutes on each side. **Drain** all but 2 tablespoons of fat from the skillet, **return** chicken to the skillet, **placing** skin side down, and **cook**, partially covered, over low heat for 20 minutes, **turning** occasionally. **Uncover** and **cook** 20 minutes more. **Transfer** chicken to a serving platter and **keep warm**. In the drippings over moderately high heat, **fry** 1 large bunch rinsed and well-dried parsley until **crisp**. **Remove** to paper toweling to drain.

For the Gravy: Blend 2 tablespoons flour with skillet drippings and **stir** constantly until golden—2 to 3 minutes. Gradually **add** 1 cup milk and **cook**, **whisking** constantly, until smooth—3 to 5 minutes. **Season** to taste with salt and pepper. **Serve** with chicken and fried parsley. Makes 6 servings.

Southern Fried Chicken

- **1 broiler-fryer (3 to 3 1/2 pounds), cut up for frying**
- **2 cups buttermilk**
- **2 cups unsifted all-purpose flour**
- **1 1/2 teaspoons baking powder**
- **3 tablespoons paprika**
- **1 teaspoon salt**
- **1/2 teaspoon black pepper**
- **3/4 cup milk**
- **2 eggs**
- **2 tablespoons vegetable oil**
- **Vegetable oil for deep-fat frying**

1 Place chicken and buttermilk in a large self-sealing plastic bag and refrigerate at least 4 hours or overnight.

2 In a small bowl, combine 1 1/2 cups of the flour, baking powder, paprika, 1/2 teaspoon of the salt, and 1/4 teaspoon of the pepper; set aside.

3 In a large bowl, beat milk, eggs, and 2 tablespoons oil. Gradually add flour mixture, whisking just until smooth. Do not overbeat. Let mixture stand at room temperature for 1 hour.

4 Meanwhile, drain chicken and pat dry. Transfer to a rack and air dry for about 20 minutes.

5 Spoon the remaining 1/2 cup flour, 1/2 teaspoon salt, and 1/4 teaspoon pepper into a brown paper bag.

Shake chicken, a few pieces at a time, in the bag. Return to the rack.

6 In a deep-fat fryer or heavy skillet, heat at least 2 inches of oil to 365°F.

7 Dip chicken into batter and turn to coat evenly. Fry a few pieces at a time, turning several times, until golden—18 to 20 minutes. Drain on paper toweling and keep warm. Makes 6 servings.

1 Serving: Calories 437; Total Fat 22 g; Saturated Fat 6 g; Protein 35 g; Carbohydrates 23 g; Fiber 1 g; Sodium 204 mg; Cholesterol 142 mg

prep time-1 hour
cooking time-about 20 minutes per batch

POACHED CHICKEN

A tender chicken breast absorbs the essence of a seasoned poaching liquid, which keeps the meat moist and complements its flavor.

POACHING NOTES

Poaching is done at a slow simmer, which means that only a few bubbles break the surface of the cooking liquid.

Whole chicken is usually poached simply in a kettle of water with a few vegetables. It can be a dish in itself or a means of preparing the meat for another recipe.

Chicken breasts are usually poached in a stock or another flavorful liquid. It is an ideal way to cook skinless, boneless chicken breasts, which easily become dry when cooked by other methods.

Poaching produces a succulent piece of meat with no added fat. The liquid can be reserved and added to a soup or reduced by boiling, strained, and used as a stock. Reducing the liquid intensifies its flavor.

FLAVORING THE BROTH

Our Rich Chicken Stock (page 39) makes an excellent poaching liquid for chicken breasts. Canned broth and broth made from a bouillon cube are also good, but are greatly improved with the addition of a little onion, carrot, celery, and pars-

COOK'S SECRETS

Sara Moulton
Executive Chef Gourmet Magazine

"The easiest way to check for doneness when poaching a whole boneless chicken breast is to separate the halves and take a look inside. If cooking a half breast, make a tiny slit in the thickest part and gently pry it open.

"There should be no sign of the pinkness of raw meat. When pressed, the breast should feel firm but certainly not hard. Total cooking time for a boneless breast half at a slow simmer is 12 to 15 minutes."

ley. Wine, fruit juice, or cider can be substituted for up to $2/3$ of the stock.

Use herbs such as dill, tarragon, rosemary, thyme, or sage to flavor the broth but don't be heavy handed. The flavor of breast meat is easily overpowered by strong herbs.

HOW TO BONE A CHICKEN BREAST

1 Pull the skin off a whole chicken breast and lay the breast on a work surface bone side up. Use the tip of a knife to cut through the membrane covering the breastbone.

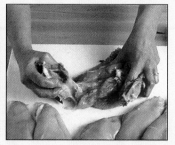

2 Using both hands, bend the halves of the breast backward until the breastbone (or keel bone) pops up. Pull out the breastbone along with the cartilage.

3 Pull the ribs away from the breast meat and trim them free with a sharp knife. Cut out the bones, following their contours with the tip of the knife. Pull out the wishbone.

4 Cut breast in half. Lift up the flap at the wide end of each half and find the tendon. Hold the tendon to scrape off the meat. Tendon will pull away. Trim each half to make a fillet.

TOOLS OF THE TRADE

Choose a wide-bottomed shallow pan for poaching chicken breasts. A wide pan makes it easy to lift or turn the breasts and makes reducing the liquid a relatively quick process. Use a pan with a nonreactive surface if there are acidic ingredients in the poaching liquid.

A skimmer or a large slotted spoon is necessary for lifting the chicken out of the liquid.

THE RIGHT KNIFE

With the right knife, boning a breast takes only about 3 minutes. A very sharp 4-inch utility knife is ideal for the job.

If you prefer, use a boning knife. This specialized knife comes in a variety of weights and lengths. It has a more slender and flexible blade than other knives, which allows it to stay close to the contours of bones as it cuts away the meat.

CHICKEN BREASTS IN BEEF BROTH WITH ORANGE

Prepare as directed at right, **substituting** 2 cups Browned Beef Stock (page 32) for chicken stock and 1 cup orange juice for wine. **Substitute** 2 teaspoons crumbled dried marjoram for parsley and tarragon. **Garnish** with the julienned zest of 1 orange. Makes 4 servings.

CHICKEN BREASTS IN TOMATO JUICE WITH CORN AND ZUCCHINI

Prepare as directed at right, **substituting** 1 1/2 cups tomato juice for stock and wine, 1 cup diced red onion for leek, 1 cup corn kernels for celery, and 1 cup chopped zucchini for carrot. **Add** 2 cloves minced garlic and 1 cored, seeded, and chopped medium-size jalapeño pepper. Just before serving, **add** 2 tablespoons chopped fresh coriander (cilantro) or Italian parsley. Makes 4 servings.

Chicken Breasts Poached in a Savory Sauce

2 **cups dry white wine or 1 cup each apple juice and water**
3 **medium-size stalks celery, chopped**
1 **large leek, thoroughly washed and chopped**
1 **medium-size carrot, chopped**
1 **cup Rich Chicken Stock or canned reduced-sodium chicken broth**
1 **tablespoon chopped parsley**
1 **tablespoon chopped fresh tarragon or 1 teaspoon dried tarragon, crumbled**
4 **skinned and boned chicken breast halves**
1 **tablespoon all-purpose flour**
1 **tablespoon butter or margarine, cut up**
1/2 **teaspoon salt**
1/4 **teaspoon black pepper**

1 In a large skillet over moderately high heat, bring wine, celery, leek, carrot, stock, parsley, and tarragon to a boil. Add chicken, reduce the heat to low, and simmer, covered, for 25 minutes. Remove chicken from skillet, cover with foil, and keep warm.

2 Increase the heat under the skillet to moderate and boil skillet mixture, uncovered, for 5 minutes.

3 Remove 1/4 cup of the skillet mixture to a small bowl. Add flour and whisk until smooth. Stir back into skillet and cook, stirring, until sauce boils and thickens slightly—about 3 minutes.

4 Remove from heat and swirl in butter. Add salt and pepper. Transfer chicken to warmed serving plates and top with sauce. Makes 4 servings.

1 Serving: Calories 346; Total Fat 7 g; Saturated Fat 3 g; Protein 40 g; Carbohydrates 11 g; Fiber 2 g; Sodium 173 mg; Cholesterol 111 mg

prep time-15 minutes • cooking time-36 minutes

STUFFED CHICKEN BREASTS

When boneless chicken breasts, called supremes, are pounded to a uniform thinness, they are just right for stuffing, rolling, and baking.

STUFFING NOTES

As long as the ingredients are not too wet, the choices for chicken breast stuffings are endless. There are vegetable stuffings, such as sautéed mushrooms, cheese stuffings based on ricotta, Swiss, or goat cheese, and traditional bread crumb or cornbread stuffings. And those are just the start.

STEPS FOR STUFFING

Figure on 1 chicken breast half per serving. Buy boneless breasts or bone them yourself as shown on page 262.

Breast halves must be pounded thin before stuffing. This step increases the size of each half, making it far easier to stuff and roll. Boneless breasts are fragile, so pound them gently to prevent the meat from tearing.

To pound chicken breasts, sandwich each half between two sheets of plastic wrap. The plastic sheets should be considerably larger than the meat.

Use a disk-type meat pounder, the side of a rolling pin, or the bottom of a heavy bottle to pound the meat, moving the pounder gradually from one edge to the other.

Turn the chicken over several times and repeat so that both sides are pounded and the meat is an even thickness.

FLAVOR BOOSTERS

After they have been pounded, chicken breasts can be marinated for 30 minutes at room temperature. Since breast meat is already tender, marinating is just for flavor. Don't let the raw meat sit in the marinade for more than 1/2 hour or it will become too soft.

To marinate 4 breast halves, you will need 1/4 cup of olive or vegetable oil mixed with 2 tablespoons of orange, lime, or lemon juice and freshly ground pepper to taste. A crushed clove of garlic and 1/2 teaspoon of dried herbs are optional.

FROZEN ASSETS

Keep a stash of chicken breasts—pounded and ready to stuff—in the freezer for impromptu meals. Separate each piece with a piece of plastic wrap. Wrap in foil and freeze for up to 3 months. Thaw in the refrigerator for several hours. Or unwrap and peel apart, then set aside at room temperature. They'll be ready to stuff and roll in about 30 minutes.

QUICK FIX

If you don't want to stuff the pounded breasts, dust them lightly with flour and sauté them quickly in a little olive oil or butter. The technique and recipes are the same as for veal scallops. See our recipes and serving ideas on page 242.

HOW TO STUFF AND ROLL

It takes only a minute or two to fill, roll, and secure each breast half. Take care not to overfill or to roll too tightly because the chicken breast might split as it cooks.

1 Gently lay out the pounded chicken breast halves with the short side facing you.

2 Spoon stuffing onto the breast. Two to 3 tablespoons of stuffing are enough for each.

3 Starting at the short end, roll the meat gently, keeping the stuffing tucked in.

4 Secure with toothpicks, season with salt and pepper, and arrange in a baking dish.

Boneless Chicken Breasts Stuffed with Goat Cheese and Sage

Prepare as directed at right, **using** 4 boned but unskinned chicken breast halves. Do not pound breasts thin. **Substitute** 2 tablespoons fresh sage or 2 teaspoons crumbled dried sage for prosciutto and **spread** filling under the skin. **Sprinkle** chicken with salt and pepper and **dust** with 1 tablespoon all-purpose flour. In a heavy skillet over low heat, **melt** 1 tablespoon butter. **Add** chicken, skin side down, and **cook**, partially covered, until golden and crisp—about 25 minutes. **Turn** chicken and **cook** 5 to 10 minutes more. Makes 4 servings.

Baked Chicken Breasts Stuffed with Prosciutto and Goat Cheese

- **4 skinned and boned chicken breast halves**
- **1/2 teaspoon salt**
- **1/4 teaspoon black pepper**
- **4 ounces fresh creamy goat cheese**
- **2 ounces prosciutto or ham, coarsely chopped**

1 Preheat the oven to 400°F. Pound chicken between sheets of plastic wrap until ¼-inch thick. Season on both sides with salt and pepper.

2 In a small bowl, blend cheese and prosciutto and spread 3 tablespoons on each breast. Starting at a short end, roll up and secure with toothpicks.

3 Arrange chicken rolls, seam side down, in a buttered 8" x 8" x 2" ovenproof glass baking dish and bake, uncovered, until chicken is cooked through—25 to 30 minutes.

4 Remove toothpicks and slice diagonally at ½-inch intervals. Pour pan juices over chicken and serve immediately. Makes 4 servings.

1 Serving: Calories 303; Total Fat 14 g; Saturated Fat 7 g; Protein 42 g; Carbohydrates 0 g; Fiber 0 g; Sodium 684 mg; Cholesterol 121 mg

prep time-25 minutes • cooking time-30 minutes

CHICKEN CASSEROLES

Our casseroles are made by braising the ingredients, a process like stewing but with less liquid. The flavor of the dishes improves if made a day ahead.

CHICKEN MARENGO

Prepare as directed at right, **using** crumbled dried oregano instead of fresh and **reducing** it to 1 teaspoon; also **add** 1 teaspoon crumbled dried basil. In Step 3, **substitute** 1/2 cup dry white wine for red wine. During the last 10 minutes of cooking, **add** 2 cups quartered mushrooms and 1/2 cup halved, pitted black olives. Makes 4 servings.

WHAT'S IN A NAME?

In Italian, *cacciatore* means hunter's style. It refers to dishes in which the main ingredient is cut up and cooked simply in a pot over a flame with whatever ingredients are available, as a hunter might cook in the forest.

Chicken Marengo is a similar French dish that, according to tradition, was prepared for Napoleon following the Battle of Marengo.

BRAISING BASICS

Braising is an excellent way to prepare chicken because it keeps the meat moist as it cooks. The chicken is first browned quickly to seal in its flavor and then cooked slowly on the stove or in the oven in a tightly covered pan.

In some braised dishes as little as 1/2 cup of liquid is used during cooking. The meat actually steams with the aromatic juices of onions and tomatoes, and broth or wine, all imparting flavor. A whole chicken can be braised the same way as chicken parts. To make the bird as compact as possible, tie it, as if for trussing, before putting it into the pot.

EXCHANGING PARTS

Our two recipes call for a whole cut-up chicken. In these and other dishes, packaged chicken parts can be used instead as long as the total weight is about the same.

TO SKIN OR NOT TO SKIN

Traditionally, the chicken for our two casseroles is braised with the skin on. If you want to cut down on fat and cholesterol by doing without the

skin, there are several options. Remove the skin and fat from the uncooked chicken pieces. Dredge the pieces in seasoned flour, tapping them gently to remove any excess. Then brown the chicken in vegetable oil and proceed as directed.

Alternatively, make the casserole the traditional way a day ahead and refrigerate it overnight. Remove the skin from the cooked pieces before reheating.

DONE TO A TURN

Chicken cooked in moist heat should be fork-tender and just starting to come away from the bone when it's done. Be careful not to overcook, especially the breast.

White meat cooks faster than dark meat. So to avoid overcooking the breast, add it to the pan about 10 minutes after the other pieces or remove it as soon as it's done and keep it warm until the remaining chicken shows no sign of pink in the center.

MORE VARIATIONS

To add color and flavor to either Chicken Cacciatore or Chicken Marengo, try any of the following: Add 1/4 cup of chopped pancetta (Italian bacon) or regular bacon to the pan after removing the chicken. Substitute 2 teaspoons of dried crumbled basil and 1 teaspoon of dried crumbled thyme for the oregano. Add 1 1/2 cups of chopped eggplant along with the green pepper. Substitute 1 cup of small white onions for the yellow onion. Add 1 cored, seeded, and sliced sweet red pepper along with the green pepper.

ANOTHER WAY TO PEEL TOMATOES

Here is a quick way to peel tomatoes. Jab a long-handled fork into the stem end of a tomato. Turn slowly over an open gas flame until the skin splits. Peel away the skin and remove the core with a small sharp knife.

Mary Ann Esposito's Chicken Cacciatore

- 1 broiler-fryer (2 pounds), cut up
- 1 teaspoon salt
- 1/2 teaspoon black pepper
- 3 tablespoons olive oil
- 1 large yellow onion, halved lengthwise and thinly sliced
- 1 large sweet green pepper, cored, seeded, and thinly sliced
- 1 medium-size stalk celery, thinly sliced
- 2 cloves garlic, minced
- 2 tablespoons chopped fresh oregano or 2 teaspoons dried oregano, crumbled
- 2 pounds tomatoes, peeled, cored, seeded, and chopped or 2 cans (28 ounces each) whole canned tomatoes, drained and chopped
- 2 tablespoons tomato paste
- 1/2 cup dry red wine

1 Rub chicken with salt and black pepper. In a large heavy skillet or 5-quart Dutch oven with a tight-fitting lid, heat oil over moderate heat about 2 minutes. Add chicken and cook, turning occasionally, until brown—8 to 10 minutes. Remove chicken and set aside.

2 Add onion and cook until soft—about 5 minutes. Add green pepper and celery and cook, stirring frequently, until tender—about 6 minutes. Stir in garlic and oregano and cook 1 minute more.

3 Return chicken to the pan. Add tomatoes, tomato paste, and wine and cook, covered, over moderately low heat until chicken is tender—35 to 40 minutes.

4 Serve over short pasta such as rigatoni or with cooked rice, orzo, mashed potatoes, or polenta. Makes 4 servings.

1 Serving: Calories 433; Total Fat 25 g; Saturated Fat 5 g; Protein 31 g; Carbohydrates 17 g; Fiber 4 g; Sodium 641 mg; Cholesterol 88 mg

prep time-30 minutes • cooking time-1 hour

COQ AU VIN

By the time the chicken in our two classic recipes is done, it has a rich dark color and hearty flavor, much like that of a meat stew.

CHICK AU VIN

One of the most celebrated chicken recipes in the world is coq au vin, a dish that originated in the Burgundy region of France. Though originally made with a young rooster, most recipes these days call for chicken. Jacques Pépin recommends using a large broiler-fryer rather than a stewing hen because it's lower in fat and cooks faster.

LOWER FAT, HIGH FLAVOR

Traditionally, coq au vin is made with diced bacon or salt pork, which adds flavor but a lot of saturated fat as well.

We've updated our recipe by eliminating the bacon or pork but we've retained the classic flavor and seasoning. We've also added a touch of sugar to the sauce to give it a mellow—not a sweet—flavor.

A FAMILIAR TECHNIQUE

The technique for making a coq au vin is the same as for making a fricassee. It uses a little more liquid than braising and results in a thicker sauce than most stews. The chicken is first browned, which contributes to the meaty taste of the dish, then simmered in liquid, in this case red wine. Just before serving, the cooking liquid is thickened with a cornstarch or flour slurry.

You can also make a delicious and more delicately flavored chicken fricassee using broth or a dry white wine instead of red. To keep the sauce light in color, sauté the chicken pieces to start the dish, but do not let them brown.

COOKING WITH WINE

A red burgundy is the classic wine for cooking a coq au vin, but it's far from the only choice. Any good full-bodied dry red wine can be used.

The wine you use for cooking should be good enough to drink. If it's not tasty in a glass, it won't be tasty in food

TOAST FOR GARNISH

- **4 slices firm white bread**
- **1 teaspoon canola oil**
- **2 tablespoons finely chopped parsley**

1 Preheat the oven to 400°F. Trim crusts and halve each slice of bread diagonally into 2 triangles. If desired, trim each triangle to form a heart.

2 Spread oil on a cookie sheet and press bread into oil so it's moistened on both sides. Bake, uncovered, until brown—8 to 10 minutes.

3 Just before serving, dip one end of each piece of toast into sauce, then into chopped parsley. Garnish each serving with 2 pieces, arranged parsley side up.

either. On the other hand, it's a waste of money to use a great wine for cooking. Ask the wine merchant to help you choose one that is full flavored but not too expensive.

A FLAMING FINISH

For extra flavor, flame the chicken with brandy after it has browned. Warm about 1/4 cup of brandy in a small pan. Remove the coq au vin from the heat. Pour the brandy over the chicken and immediately set it aflame with a long match. Shake the pan until the flames die out.

SPANISH-STYLE CHICKEN IN WINE

Prepare as directed at right, **adding** 6 ounces crumbled sweet pork sausage when heating oil in Step 3. In Step 4, **add** 2 cored, seeded, and diced sweet peppers (1 red, 1 green) along with yellow onion; also **add** 1/4 cup medium-dry sherry along with red wine. **Proceed** as directed through Step 6. Makes 4 servings.

Jacques Pépin's Lower Fat Coq au Vin

Chicken:

- 1 broiler-fryer (3½ to 4 pounds), cut up
- 2 tablespoons olive oil
- ½ teaspoon sugar
- ½ cup water
- 12 small white onions, peeled
- 4 large mushrooms, stemmed and quartered
- 1 medium-size yellow onion, finely chopped
- 3 cloves garlic, finely chopped
- 1¼ cups fruity dry red wine
- ½ teaspoon dried thyme, crumbled
- 2 whole bay leaves
- ¾ teaspoon salt
- ¾ teaspoon black pepper
- 1 teaspoon cornstarch blended with 2 tablespoons dry red wine

Toast Garnish:
(described in box at left)

1 Divide the chicken wings at the joints into 3 pieces. Skin and bone the breasts. Skin the backs, legs, and thighs but do not bone.

2 In a large saucepan over high heat, bring 1 tablespoon of the oil, sugar, and water to a boil. Add white onions and cook until water evaporates and onions start browning—about 4 minutes. Reduce the heat to moderately high and continue cooking until onions are well browned. Add mushrooms and sauté for 1 minute; cover and set aside.

3 In a large skillet over moderately high heat, heat the remaining 1 tablespoon oil for 2 minutes. Add wings and sauté until lightly browned—2 to 3 minutes. Add leg pieces and brown 2 to 3 minutes on each side. Add breasts and back and brown 2 minutes on each side. Remove chicken; set aside.

4 Add yellow onion to the skillet and sauté for 1 minute. Add garlic and sauté about 10 seconds. Add wine, thyme, bay leaves, salt, and pepper and bring to a boil. Return drumsticks, thighs, and wings to the skillet and simmer, covered, 8 minutes. Add breasts and back and simmer 7 minutes more.

5 Add cornstarch mixture to the skillet and stir until juices thicken—about 3 minutes. Add reserved white onions and mushrooms along with their juices and remove from heat. Remove and discard bay leaves.

6 Cut breasts in half and serve 1 piece of breast, 1 drumstick or thigh, 1 piece of wing, and 2 pieces of toast per person. Sprinkle with parsley. Makes 4 servings.

1 Serving: Calories 374; Total Fat 16 g; Saturated Fat 3 g; Protein 34 g; Carbohydrates 23 g; Fiber 2 g; Sodium 674 mg; Cholesterol 92 mg

prep time-22 minutes • cooking time-30 minutes

CHICKEN STIR-FRY

O ur Mandarin Chicken Stir-fry gets its name from the mandarin oranges that are used in the sauce along with tangy ginger and orange juice.

SWEET AND SOUR STIR-FRY

Prepare as directed at right, **substituting** 2 large cored, seeded, and thinly sliced sweet peppers (1 red, 1 green) and 1 cup sliced, trimmed snow peas for broccoli. **Substitute** juice from canned pineapple, listed below, for orange juice. **Omit** grated zest, sesame oil, and red pepper flakes and **add** 2 tablespoons each brown sugar and cider vinegar. Finally, **substitute** 1 can (8 ounces) drained pineapple chunks for mandarin oranges and **add** 1 can (8 ounces) sliced water chestnuts. Makes 4 servings.

STIR-FRY WITH SAUCE

Our two stir-fries are made with chicken that is dipped into a batter before it's cooked. The Mandarin and Sweet and Sour Sauces include sliced fruits as well as vegetables and are thickened with cornstarch just before serving.

You can also make a chicken stir-fry without a batter and without thickening the sauce.

Follow the basic stir-fry tips on page 148, cutting the chicken into matchstick strips and stir-frying them about 3 minutes.

EASY SLICING

Chicken strips cook evenly if they are identically sized. Making even cuts is quick and easy if the chicken is placed in the freezer for an hour or so before it's cut. The chicken should not be frozen, just firm.

CUTTING BOARD SAFETY

Although synthetic cutting boards are convenient to use because they can be cleaned in the dishwasher, they actually are not as safe as hardwood maple cutting boards. The reason is that bacteria die on untreated maple cutting boards but survive on the synthetic variety.

When working with chicken (and meat and fish as well), use a cutting board that can be scrubbed in the sink with soap and hot water after use. Rinse the board well before using again. Any cutting boards that are used for poultry, meat, or fish should also be periodically washed with a 10 percent solution of bleach.

SILKY THICKENER AND BUBBLY BATTER

When cornstarch is mixed with a liquid and stirred into a hot broth, it becomes a clear and silky thickener. It makes a more delicate sauce than flour, but has double flour's thickening power so only half as much is needed.

Cornstarch also makes a crisp and delicate coating for chicken as either a batter, described in our recipes, or dry: It's used in place of flour for extra-crispy fried chicken.

Our cornstarch batter is also made with club soda or beer, either of which gives it a lightness and crispness similar to tempura, Japanese deep-frying.

FRIED FRUIT

The Chinese combine fruit with meat and vegetables in main dish recipes far more than Western cooks. The addition makes for a surprising and delicious contrast of flavors and textures. Citrus fruits, pineapple, mangoes, and peaches are all used in Chinese cooking. Although pineapple caramelizes beautifully, most ripe fruit should be cooked only briefly and stirred gently so that it doesn't fall apart.

OPPOSITES ATTRACT

The joining of opposite flavors—sweet and sour or spicy hot and sour—is important in Chinese cooking. A sweet and sour sauce is generally a thickened sauce, often mixed with the stir-fried poultry, meat, fish, or dumplings at the end of cooking. Sugar and cider or wine vinegar are nearly always components of sweet and sour sauces.

WORK SAVER
Chinese Cleaver

There are three kinds of Chinese cleavers. Heavy cleavers are used for cutting through bones and joints. Lightweight cleavers are for fancy food carving. Medium-weight cleavers, such as the one at right, are used for everything else. A medium-weight cleaver makes quick work of slicing chicken and slicing and mincing all vegetables. Its broad side makes a convenient surface for transporting chopped food to a frying pan or bowl. If you don't have a Chinese cleaver, a sharp utility knife or chef's knife will work for slicing chicken and vegetables. If you do have one, you'll find it as handy for Western cooking as it is for Eastern.

Mandarin Chicken Stir-fry

- ½ cup club soda or beer
- ½ cup cornstarch
- 2 skinned and boned chicken breast halves (6 ounces each), cut across the grain into strips 2 inches long and ¼ inch wide
- 5 tablespoons peanut oil
- ¼ teaspoon crushed red pepper flakes
- 4 cups small broccoli florets
- ½ cup Rich Chicken Stock or canned reduced-sodium chicken broth
- ¼ cup orange juice
- 3 tablespoons soy sauce
- 1 tablespoon minced ginger
- 1 clove garlic, minced
- 1 teaspoon grated tangerine or orange zest
- 1 teaspoon dark sesame oil (optional)
- 1 can (11 ounces) mandarin oranges, drained

1 Pour club soda into a small shallow bowl and place cornstarch in a self-sealing plastic bag. Working in batches, dip chicken strips into soda, then dredge in cornstarch, shaking off excess. Set chicken aside on a rack.

2 Remove 1 teaspoon of the cornstarch from the plastic bag and combine with 1 tablespoon of the soda from the small bowl; set aside.

3 In a deep heavy 12-inch skillet or a wok over high heat, heat 2 tablespoons of the peanut oil until almost smoking. Add ½ the chicken strips and stir-fry until golden—about 3 minutes; remove to paper toweling. Add 2 more tablespoons of the peanut oil to the skillet and stir-fry and drain remaining chicken the same way.

4 Reduce the heat to moderate, add the remaining 1 tablespoon peanut oil, and stir in red pepper flakes. Cook, stirring, for 30 seconds. Add broccoli and stir-fry 2 minutes. Mix in stock, orange juice, soy sauce, ginger, garlic, tangerine zest, and sesame oil and cook, uncovered, until broccoli is crisp-tender—3 to 5 minutes. Add oranges, reserved chicken, and cornstarch mixture. Cook, tossing, until sauce thickens and chicken and oranges are heated through—about 1 minute. Serve over rice. Makes 4 servings.

**1 Serving: Calories 302;
Total Fat 12 g; Saturated Fat 2 g;
Protein 24 g; Carbohydrates 26 g;
Fiber 4 g; Sodium 862 mg;
Cholesterol 51 mg**

*prep time-25 minutes
cooking time-about 20 minutes*

ROAST DUCK

*F*or dark-meat lovers who like a richly flavored bird, duck is a fine choice. But there are rules to be followed for roasting a duck so that it won't be greasy.

FOR STARTERS

The words "duck" and "duckling" are used interchangeably for the bird we eat. But since all commercially raised ducks are young when marketed, they are technically ducklings.

Duck is comprised entirely of dark meat. Although there is a lot of fat under the skin, the flavor is quite special and it's worth the effort to learn to cook the bird properly.

Oven roasting is the traditional way of preparing duck but it also cooks up beautifully by rotisserie or spit-roasting over a grill.

AT THE MARKET

You can order a fresh duckling from your butcher, but frozen ducklings are readily available. When frozen, a duckling requires several days of thawing in the refrigerator before it can be roasted.

Ducklings generally weigh between 3½ and 5½ pounds. However, a 5-pounder will be a 3½-pounder by the time the fat roasts out, so the number of servings per pound of uncooked bird is not great. A 4-pound duckling will feed 4 people, but not generously.

SHEDDING FAT

Fat provides a duckling with much of its flavor, but if enough of it is not melted away while it roasts, the meat will be greasy. Pull out the fat at the vent opening and the neck. Then pierce the skin in many places to help the fat drain off as the duckling roasts.

The fat will smoke during roasting if it's allowed to accumulate. Remove the fat by spooning it from the pan every 15 minutes or so.

HOLD THE STUFFING

It's better not to stuff a duckling with a bread crumb or other absorbent stuffing; it will simply sop up fat and become greasy. Better to cook a dressing separately in a baking dish. Add flavor to the duckling by tucking a lemon, orange, apple, or onion

HOW TO PIERCE THE SKIN OF A DUCK

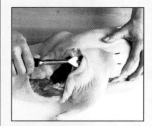

Use a carving fork to pierce the skin. Run the tines just beneath the skin, coming back up through the skin without puncturing the meat.

and herbs into the body cavity before trussing and roasting.

LEFTOVER DUCK

Don't toss out that duck carcass until you've made a broth with it. Duck broth and the leftover meat make a great start for a flavorful gumbo.

GINGER-GLAZED DUCK BREAST

Have your butcher **remove** the breast halves from a 4-pound duck. Or do it yourself, **saving** the rest of the duck for a stock. **Prick** skin several times with a fork and **place** in a large self-sealing plastic bag. In a small bowl, **combine** 1/4 cup soy sauce, 4 teaspoons firmly packed dark brown sugar, 2 minced cloves garlic, and 1 tablespoon minced ginger. **Pour** over the duck, **seal** the bag, and **marinate** in the refrigerator several hours or overnight. **Preheat** the oven to 450°F. **Place** breasts, skin side down, in an ovenproof skillet. **Roast,** uncovered, **pouring off** fat as it accumulates, **allowing** about 35 minutes for medium. **Slice** on the diagonal. Makes 2 servings.

HOW TO CARVE AND SERVE A ROAST DUCKLING

Ducks (and geese) should be carved before they're brought to the table. Cut through the leg joints close to the body and remove legs. Repeat with wings. Then slit the skin along either side of the breastbone.

Slide the knife into the cut on one side of the breastbone and lift off meat in a single piece. Repeat on the other side. Cut the meat into serving pieces and arrange with the legs and wings on platter.

Roast Duckling à l'Orange

- 1 oven-ready duckling (4 pounds)
- 1½ teaspoons salt
- ¾ teaspoon black pepper
- 1 small lemon, pricked well with a fork
- 6 unpeeled cloves garlic
- 2 whole bay leaves
- Zest of 1 orange, finely slivered
- ⅓ cup white wine vinegar
- ¼ cup sugar
- ⅔ cup orange juice
- 1¾ cups Rich Chicken Stock or canned reduced-sodium chicken broth
- 1 teaspoon tomato paste
- ½ cup dry white wine
- 2 teaspoons cornstarch blended with 2 tablespoons cold water

1 Preheat the oven to 450°F. Remove fat from body cavity and discard. Prick skin all over with a fork. Sprinkle cavity with ½ teaspoon of the salt and ¼ teaspoon of the pepper. Insert lemon in cavity along with garlic and bay leaves.

2 Place duck, breast side up, on a rack in a roasting pan. Sprinkle with ½ teaspoon of the remaining salt and ¼ teaspoon of the remaining pepper. Roast, uncovered, 45 minutes, spooning off the fat as it accumulates. Reduce the oven temperature to 350°F and continue roasting until an instant-read thermometer inserted in the meatiest part of the thigh but not touching bone registers 180°F—35 to 45 minutes more.

3 While duck roasts, cook orange zest for 10 minutes in a small saucepan of boiling water; drain and set aside. Meanwhile, in a medium-size saucepan over moderate heat, boil vinegar and sugar without stirring until the color of amber—about 4 minutes. Stir in orange juice, stock, tomato paste, the remaining ½ teaspoon salt, the final ¼ teaspoon pepper, and reserved orange zest; set aside.

4 Pour all fat from the roasting pan. Set pan over moderate heat, pour in wine, and cook for 2 minutes, stirring constantly to loosen browned bits. Add to orange juice mixture and cook, uncovered, until reduced by ⅓—about 10 minutes. Blend in cornstarch mixture and cook, stirring constantly, until mixture bubbles and thickens—about 3 minutes.

5 Transfer duck to a carving board and cut into serving portions, removing the breast from the bone and separating the legs and thighs. Pour the sauce over the duck and serve. Makes 4 servings.

1 Serving: Calories 727; Total Fat 52 g; Saturated Fat 18 g; Protein 36 g; Carbohydrates 23 g; Fiber 0 g; Sodium 963 mg; Cholesterol 159 mg

prep time-15 minutes
cooking time-1 hour 46 minutes

ROAST GOOSE

Roast goose is a traditional favorite for dinner during the holiday season. Pair a goose with the flavors of apples or other fruit for the best flavor.

AT THE MARKET

Most geese weigh between 7 and 12 pounds. They can be ordered fresh from a butcher and they're readily available frozen. A frozen goose requires several days' thawing time in the refrigerator.

Figure on at least 1¼ pounds per serving, but even at that amount don't expect much in the way of leftovers. If there are more than six or eight people sitting down to dinner, serve two small geese rather than one large one.

TO STUFF OR NOT TO STUFF

With roast goose, as with duck, stuffing is an option, not a necessity. Many goose lovers find that stuffing absorbs too much fat as the bird roasts. Yet no one likes to be without a side dish of dressing on a holiday table.

Our three dressing recipes tell you how to stuff a goose, but you can also bake the dressings separately. Prepare your choice of dressing as directed, and instead of spooning it into the cavity of the goose, spoon it into a greased baking dish, cover, and bake. If the dressing contains egg, it is essential that it stay in the oven until it reaches an internal temperature of 165°F. Use an instant-read thermometer in the center of the dressing to be sure.

If no egg was used, the dressing need only remain in the oven until steaming hot—45 minutes to 1 hour should do it.

ROASTING NOTES

An unstuffed goose requires about ½ hour less roasting time than a stuffed goose. Serve the dressing in a warmed bowl or on the platter with the carved goose. Let diners top it with gravy on their plates.

Whether the goose is stuffed or unstuffed when it goes in the oven, it will be done when the temperature registers 180°F to 185°F. Use either a meat thermometer or an instant-read thermometer inserted deep into the thigh muscle, making sure that it does not touch bone.

CUTTING UP

Present the roast goose at table on a decorated platter, but take it back to the kitchen for the easiest carving.

Let the goose rest for 20 minutes after it is taken from the oven. Transfer to a carving board. Remove the legs and wings, then separate the breast meat from the bones. Follow the instructions in the carving box for duckling on page 272.

FRUIT FLAVORS

Fatty birds such as goose and duck are at their best when cooked and/or served with fruit as contrast. Our dressings include apple and dried fruit varieties.

You might also try basting a goose (or duck) with unsweetened cider or orange juice while it roasts. Whole berry cranberry sauce, cranberry-orange relish, tart applesauce, or savory baked apples all make good accompaniments.

A roast goose looks festive brought to the table on a platter surrounded by watercress and bright little crab or lady apples. Or serve it with wedges of orange for squeezing over the sliced meat.

AN ALTERNATIVE COOKING METHOD

If you love the flavor of goose but want to get rid of more fat than the traditional method of roasting described in most recipes allows, steam the goose and then braise it. This method requires more effort but it works.

Place a trussed but unstuffed goose on a rack in a roasting pan with a tight-fitting cover. Add 1 inch of water to the pan, cover, and bring to a boil on top of the stove. Reduce the heat so the water barely bubbles and steam 45 minutes to 1 hour, depending on the size of the bird. Check the pan from time to time and add more water if it threatens to boil dry.

Remove the goose and let it cool slightly. Drain off the fat and put the goose back on the rack. Cover and braise at 325°F for 1 to 1½ hours, basting occasionally. Remove the cover and allow the goose to brown in the oven for about ½ hour.

DRIED FRUIT DRESSING

Prepare Sausage-Apple Dressing as directed at right, **substituting** 2 cups mixed dried fruits that have been plumped in water or brandy for apples.

SAGE, POTATO, AND ONION DRESSING

Boil 2 pounds peeled all-purpose potatoes until tender. **Sauté** 3 chopped large yellow onions in 3 tablespoons vegetable oil until tender. Lightly **mash** potatoes with ⅓ cup milk; **mix** in onions, ¾ teaspoon crumbled dried sage, ¾ teaspoon salt, and ½ teaspoon black pepper. **Spoon** loosely into the body cavity of the goose.

Roast Goose with Sausage-Apple Dressing

- **1** tablespoon olive oil
- **1** tablespoon butter or margarine
- **4** ounces pork sausage, crumbled
- **8** slices firm white bread, lightly toasted and crumbled
- **1** medium-size yellow onion, finely chopped
- **3** cloves garlic, finely chopped
- **2** sweet apples, such as McIntosh, peeled, cored, and cut in 1/2-inch dice
- **1/4** cup chopped parsley
- **1 1/2** teaspoons salt
- **3/4** teaspoon dried sage, crumbled
- **2 1/2** cups Rich Chicken Stock or canned reduced-sodium chicken broth
- **1** goose (7 pounds)
- **1/2** lemon
- **2** tablespoons all-purpose flour
- **1/4** teaspoon black pepper

1 Preheat the oven to 325°F. In a large skillet over moderate heat, heat oil and butter until hot but not smoking. Add sausage and cook until no longer pink—5 minutes. With a slotted spoon, transfer to a large bowl. Add toast.

2 In the skillet drippings, sauté onion and garlic about 5 minutes. Add apples and cook until tender—about 5 minutes. Transfer to bread mixture along with parsley, 3/4 teaspoon of the salt, and sage. Mix in 1/2 cup of the stock.

3 Rub inside of goose with 1/4 teaspoon of the salt. Lightly spoon stuffing into body cavity, pull the tail up over the stuffing, and skewer the opening shut. Tie the legs together with string.

4 Place goose, breast side up, on a rack in a shallow roasting pan. Prick breast skin in several places with a fork. Rub goose with lemon. Roast, uncovered, until an instant-read thermometer inserted in the meatiest part of the thigh but not touching bone registers 180°F—about 3 hours. Spoon off and reserve fat as it accumulates. Remove goose and set aside.

5 Place roasting pan over moderate heat. Pour in remaining 2 cups stock and simmer 2 minutes, stirring to loosen browned bits.

6 Meanwhile, in a medium-size saucepan over moderate heat, heat 2 tablespoons of the reserved fat. Blend in flour and cook, stirring constantly, until lightly browned—about 3 minutes. Gradually add stock from the roasting pan and cook, stirring constantly, until thickened and smooth—3 to 5 minutes. Stir in the remaining 1/2 teaspoon salt and the pepper. Makes 6 servings.

1 Serving: Calories 1003; Total Fat 68 g; Saturated Fat 21 g; Protein 69 g; Carbohydrates 26 g; Fiber 2 g; Sodium 1019 mg; Cholesterol 252 mg

prep time-30 minutes
cooking time-3 1/2 hours

TURKEY BREASTS

*A*vailable whole, boned, bone in, or sliced into cutlets, turkey breast meat makes a great substitute for other cuts of meat or for the entire turkey.

SELECT PARTS

Now that turkey breasts are available fresh and frozen many different ways, the bird can be enjoyed year round.

By roasting just the breast rather than a whole turkey, you can feed a crowd with far less fuss. For the best flavor, select a bone-in breast as described at right.

Turkey breast meat requires frequent basting as it roasts, but you won't have to worry about its drying out while the dark meat finishes cooking—nor will there be family feuds over who gets the white meat.

Whole and half turkey breasts are also available boneless, with or without their skin. If you want to stuff, roll, and roast a boneless breast, buy one with the skin on to help prevent it from drying out while it cooks. Boned breasts need cook for only about 20 minutes per pound.

If you want to use the breast meat for other purposes, such as slicing into cutlets or steaks, buy one with the skin removed. Skinless breast meat has only 1 gram of fat and about 135 calories per 3½-ounce serving.

TURKEY CUTLETS

Turkey cutlets—¼-inch-thick slices from the breast—look a lot like veal cutlets. Virtually anything veal cutlets can do, turkey cutlets can do just as well, for about half the price. Pound them as you would veal, see page 242, or use them as is, breaded or not.

Most turkey cutlets weigh between 4 and 6 ounces, just right for a single serving.

TENDER CARE

Although turkey cutlets can be used in place of veal scallops in most recipes, they cannot be cooked in quite the same way. These tender cuts of turkey breast dry out and toughen quickly in a skillet, so beware. They need about 1½ to 2½ minutes per side and must never be cooked over anything hotter than moderate heat—not even for an initial quick browning.

If you use turkey cutlets in stir-fry recipes, cut the meat into matchstick strips. Add the strips to the mixture at the very end of stir-frying. Then turn the heat down slightly and cook the strips only briefly.

HERBED ROAST TURKEY BREAST

One 5½-pound bone-in turkey breast

1½ teaspoons salt

2 medium-size yellow onions, peeled and quartered

2 medium-size carrots, peeled and quartered

2 medium-size celery stalks, cut into chunks

4 sprigs parsley

1 whole bay leaf

6 tablespoons fresh chopped sage or 2 tablespoons dried sage, crumbled

2 tablespoons fresh chopped thyme or 2 teaspoons dried thyme, crumbled

5 tablespoons butter or margarine (about), melted

½ teaspoon black pepper

4 tablespoons all-purpose flour

3 cups Rich Chicken Stock or canned reduced-sodium chicken broth (about)

1 Preheat the oven to 325°F. Sprinkle turkey with ½ teaspoon of the salt. Mound onions, carrots, celery, parsley, and bay leaf in the center of a large roasting pan.

2 Gently loosen skin from the breast. Sprinkle flesh with ½ the sage and thyme. Carefully reposition skin and arrange breast, skin side up, on vegetables in pan. Brush with 2 tablespoons of the butter, then sprinkle with remaining sage and thyme, ½ teaspoon salt, and ¼ teaspoon pepper. Roast, uncovered, until an instant-read thermometer inserted in the thickest part of the breast but not touching bone registers 180°F—2¼ to 2½ hours.

3 For gravy, skim fat from pan drippings and add enough butter to total ¼ cup. Pour into a small saucepan, blend in flour, and heat and stir 1 minute over moderate heat. Add skimmed pan drippings plus enough Rich Chicken Stock (page 39) to total 3 cups and cook, stirring constantly, until thickened and smooth. Season to taste with remaining salt and pepper. Makes 12 servings.

TO SLICE CUTLETS

You can buy turkey cutlets, but you'll save money by cutting your own.

Hold a turkey breast half carefully with one hand. Using a thin sharp knife, slice the meat lengthwise into ¼-inch- thick cutlets that are as long and broad as possible.

Sautéed Turkey Cutlets

- 4 skinless, boneless turkey cutlets (3 ounces each)
- 1¼ teaspoons salt
- ⅛ teaspoon black pepper
- ⅓ cup unsifted all-purpose flour
- 2 eggs, lightly beaten
- 1 cup fine dry bread crumbs
- 6 tablespoons butter or margarine
- 12 medium-size shallots, chopped
- 1 cup Rich Chicken Stock or canned reduced-sodium chicken broth
- ¼ cup chopped parsley

1 Pound cutlets between 2 pieces of plastic wrap until uniformly thin. Season on both sides with salt and pepper. Dredge in flour, shaking off excess. Dip into eggs, then into crumbs to coat well.

2 In a large skillet over moderate heat, melt 5 tablespoons of the butter and sauté cutlets, in batches if necessary, until golden brown—about 2½ minutes on each side. Shake pan occasionally to allow cutlets to brown evenly. Transfer to paper toweling to drain.

3 In a small saucepan over moderate heat, cook shallots in the remaining 1 tablespoon butter until soft—about 5 minutes. Blend 1 teaspoon of the dredging flour with 2 tablespoons of the stock and stir into shallots. Add remaining stock, bring to a boil, and cook, stirring often, until sauce reduces to about ¾ cup—about 5 minutes. Remove from heat and stir in parsley.

4 Arrange cutlets on individual serving plates and top with sauce. Makes 4 servings.

1 Serving: Calories 294; Total Fat 14 g; Saturated Fat 7 g; Protein 23 g; Carbohydrates 19 g; Fiber 1 g; Sodium 262 mg; Cholesterol 124 mg

prep time-25 minutes
cooking time-20 minutes

SAUTÉED TURKEY CUTLETS IN MUSTARD SAUCE

Pound cutlets as directed in Step 1 at left, **season** with salt and pepper, and **dredge** in flour; **omit** eggs and crumbs. **Brown** as directed, but **use** a skillet well coated with nonstick vegetable spray and **reduce** butter to 2 tablespoons. **Lift** browned cutlets to a heated plate and **keep** warm. **Spoon** ¼ cup dry vermouth and 2 tablespoons Dijon mustard into skillet, then **add** ¾ cup heavy cream and **boil**, uncovered, until slightly thickened—2 to 3 minutes. **Add** ¼ cup half-and-half, **heat**, and **stir** 1 minute (do not boil or mixture may curdle). **Spoon** over cutlets. Makes 4 servings.

CREAMED TURKEY

This homey dish can be made with chicken or seafood as well as with turkey and is still as delicious as it was in grandma's day.

THE SECOND SHOW

Sometimes turkey is even better as leftovers than it is as the main event. When leftover turkey is cut into bite-size pieces, stirred into creamy sauce, and served in crispy toast cups, it's not only delicious, but it's also one of the great comfort foods.

VARIATIONS ON A THEME

This old-fashioned dish goes by many names and under many guises. The basic elements for the sauce are a white sauce and sautéed mushrooms. We've dressed up our version a bit by using dried as well as fresh mushrooms, adding the mushroom-soaking liquid to the sauce instead of broth, and stirring in a scoop of sour cream at the end.

A low-fat sauce can be made by using 1 percent milk instead of whole milk and low-fat sour cream instead of regular.

The basic dish becomes à la king when a little sherry is stirred in, some chopped pimiento is added for color instead of peas, and a beaten egg yolk is used to enrich the sauce at the end of cooking.

For a change, flavor the sauce with a touch of curry powder or mix in the seasonings and chopped vegetables of your choice, as we have done with our Southwest-Style variation, above. Do the same if making the dish with cooked scallops, crabmeat, hard-cooked eggs, or meat instead of turkey.

SERVED IN STYLE

We've included directions for serving creamed turkey in toast cups or puff pastry shells. Vary the dish by serving it on top of waffles or wrapped in crêpes (see page 104 for crêpe how-to) or spoon it into crisp baked potato shells.

Cut baked potatoes in half and scoop out the flesh, leaving a shell 1/4-inch thick. Fill the shells with creamed turkey

SOUTHWEST-STYLE CREAMY TURKEY OR CHICKEN

Prepare as directed at right, **substituting** 3/4 cup each chopped sweet green and red pepper and 1/2 cup coarsely chopped scallions for mushrooms, 2 teaspoons chili powder and 1/2 teaspoon ground cumin for thyme, chicken stock for mushroom liquid, and frozen corn kernels for green peas. Makes 4 servings.

TO PREPARE PUFF PASTRY SHELLS

1 Use individual frozen puff pastry shells. Bake as directed. When shells are browned, gently remove the center top of each with a knife or fork. Reserve top.

2 Remove and discard the inside of the shell. Fill as directed. Use reserved top as lid.

and sprinkle with 1 1/2 teaspoons of grated Parmesan cheese. Bake in a preheated 350°F oven until the cheese is lightly golden.

TO MAKE TOAST CUPS

1 Cut a circle from a slice of bread using a round cutter.

2 Gently press the circle of bread into a standard-size muffin-pan cup that has been sprayed with nonstick vegetable cooking spray.

3 Bake at 350°F until nicely browned—15 to 20 minutes. Remove to a rack to cool.

Creamy Turkey or Chicken

- ½ cup warm water
- ½ ounce dried porcini mushrooms
- 4 tablespoons (½ stick) butter or margarine
- 2 ounces small button mushrooms, sliced
- ¼ cup unsifted all-purpose flour
- 1 tablespoon chopped fresh thyme or 1 teaspoon dried thyme, crumbled
- 1¼ cups milk (about)
- 2 cups diced cooked turkey or chicken
- ½ cup frozen green peas, thawed and drained
- ¾ cup sour cream
- 1 teaspoon salt
- ¼ teaspoon black pepper

1 In a small bowl, pour water over the dried mushrooms and set aside for 20 minutes. Drain, reserving liquid. Rinse mushrooms twice under cold running water, drain on paper toweling, and coarsely chop. Strain reserved liquid through a coffee filter.

2 In a medium-size saucepan over moderate heat, melt 1 tablespoon of the butter. Add button and porcini mushrooms and cook, stirring occasionally, until button mushrooms are limp—3 to 5 minutes. Using a slotted spoon, lift mushrooms to a small bowl.

3 Melt the remaining 3 tablespoons butter in the same saucepan over moderate heat. Blend in flour and thyme and cook for 5 minutes, stirring occasionally, until bubbly. Add enough milk to reserved mushroom liquid to total 1½ cups, pour into pan, and cook, whisking constantly, until thickened and smooth—3 to 5 minutes.

4 Mix in turkey, peas, and reserved mushrooms and cook 5 minutes more.

5 Stir in sour cream and cook just until heated through. Do not boil. Stir in salt and pepper. Serve in toast cups, puff pastry shells, or baked potato shells. Makes 4 servings.

1 Serving: Calories 414; Total Fat 26 g; Saturated Fat 16 g; Protein 28 g; Carbohydrates 16 g; Fiber 2 g; Sodium 772 mg; Cholesterol 112 mg

prep time-30 minutes
cooking time-30 minutes

ROAST TURKEY

*O*ur tips show you how to make a classic gravy step by step and how to truss your Thanksgiving bird the quick and easy way.

TALKING TURKEY

We cover the basics on how to roast a turkey here. We also devote four pages to Thanksgiving, beginning on page 336. On those pages, we include festive holiday stuffings.

AT THE MARKET

Figure on about a pound per person when you buy a turkey. If you want plenty of leftovers, plan on a pound and a half.

Both fresh and frozen turkeys are fine. One benefit of a fresh turkey is that it doesn't have to take up space in your refrigerator for days, losing moisture while it thaws.

Frozen turkey must be completely thawed before it's roasted. Thawing should be done in the refrigerator. Allow 24 hours for every 5 pounds.

QUICK THAW

Don't be tempted to thaw the turkey at room temperature. Hasten thawing by placing the turkey in its unopened wrapper or a sealed plastic bag in a sinkful of cold (not warm) water. Change the water every 30 minutes until the meat feels soft. Allow 30 minutes per pound for this method.

TO STUFF OR NOT TO STUFF

A well-seasoned stuffing adds flavor to a turkey as it roasts, but it can also be problematic. A stuffed turkey takes longer to roast than one that isn't. More important, stuffing develops bacteria that can cause food poisoning if it's allowed to sit inside the bird too long.

Flavor an unstuffed bird by placing onions, celery, apples, or other aromatics in the body cavity before roasting and/or rub the skin with sage and salt and pepper. Prepare and bake dressing separately in a well-greased baking dish, drizzling it with pan juices, during the last 1/2 hour of roasting.

STUFFING NOTES

If you want to stuff the turkey, fill the cavity loosely since the stuffing will expand as the turkey roasts. Figure on at least 1/2 cup of stuffing per serving, baking any extra in a separate baking dish. Make the stuffing the day you intend to cook it and keep it refrigerated until ready to use. Wait to stuff the bird until you are about to put it in the oven. The stuffing is

(continued on page 282)

HOW TO MAKE GIBLET GRAVY

- **1 whole bay leaf**
- **4 cups cold water (about)**
- **1 cup Rich Chicken Stock or canned reduced-sodium chicken broth (about)**
- **1/3 cup unsifted all-purpose flour**
- **Salt and black pepper to taste**

1 While turkey is roasting, place neck, all giblets except liver, and bay leaf in a medium-size saucepan, add water to cover, set over high heat, and bring to a boil. Reduce the heat to low and simmer, covered, until giblets are nearly tender—about 45 minutes. Add liver and simmer, covered, 15 minutes more. Drain, reserving broth. Chop neck meat and giblets. Wrap and refrigerate until ready to proceed.

2 Skim 1/3 cup fat from pan; set aside. Pour remaining pan drippings into a 4-cup measure; add to it the reserved giblet broth and enough stock to total 4 cups.

3 Set roasting pan over moderate heat, and add 1 cup of the giblet broth-stock mixture. Simmer and stir to loosen browned bits—2 minutes. Pour back into 4-cup measure.

4 In a medium-size saucepan, heat reserved fat. Stir in flour and cook, stirring, until thick, smooth, and slightly browned—2 to 3 minutes.

5 Gradually stir in stock mixture. Cook, stirring, until smooth. Add reserved giblets and neck; heat through. Season with salt and pepper.

1. Preheat the oven to 325°F. Remove giblets and neck from turkey and reserve for gravy. Rinse turkey inside and out under cold running water; drain well and pat dry with paper toweling.

2. Rub neck and body cavities with salt and pepper. If using stuffing, spoon loosely into cavities and truss. If not using stuffing, place whole onion in neck cavity. Place carrots, celery, quartered onion, parsley, and bay leaves inside body cavity, then truss.

3. Place turkey, breast side up, on a rack in a large roasting pan, brush with butter, and tent loosely with foil. Roast until an instant-read thermometer inserted in the meatiest part of the thigh but not touching bone registers 180°F to 185°F—about 4 hours. Meanwhile, begin the Giblet Gravy as shown in box at left.

4. About 30 minutes before turkey is done, remove foil and brush skin generously with pan drippings. When turkey tests done, transfer to a heated platter and let stand while you finish the gravy. Remove vegetables and bay leaves, if used. Makes 12 servings.

1 Serving: Calories 565; Total Fat 27 g;
Saturated Fat 9 g; Protein 73 g;
Carbohydrates 2 g; Fiber 1 g;
Sodium 561 mg; Cholesterol 217 mg

prep time-2 hours
cooking time-about 4 hours

Roast Turkey with Giblet Gravy

Turkey:
- 1 fresh or thawed frozen turkey (about 12 pounds)
- 2 teaspoons salt
- 1/2 teaspoon black pepper
- 2 tablespoons butter or margarine, melted

Stuffing:
- 1 recipe your favorite stuffing or the stuffings on page 338

Or instead of stuffing:
- 2 medium-size yellow onions, 1 peeled whole, 1 peeled and quartered
- 2 medium-size carrots, peeled and quartered
- 2 medium-size stalks celery, cut into chunks
- 4 sprigs parsley
- 2 whole bay leaves

Giblet Gravy: (recipe and directions at left)

(continued from page 280)

done when an instant-read thermometer registers between 160°F and 165°F.

Scoop out the stuffing and place it in a serving dish before carving the bird or before the bird cools. Wrap and refrigerate the stuffing separately from the turkey.

ROASTING TIMES

There are two rules for roasting turkey. The first is that turkey must be roasted until a meat thermometer inserted in the deepest part of the thigh but not touching bone reaches 180°F. The second rule is that a turkey must never be roasted at very low temperature overnight. The low heat fosters bacterial growth.

Cooks disagree over whether to roast at moderate temperatures, as in our recipe, or by the high temperature method. Roasting at high temperatures—500°F for the first 1/2 hour and then 450°F—takes far less time, and is for unstuffed birds only.

Devotees believe this method produces the juiciest meat and crispiest skin since the high heat seals in the juices. However, it is apt to make your kitchen smoky. To avoid smoke,

it's important to remove fatty drippings as they collect, which means that you will not be left with any pan drippings. To keep the bird moist, water must regularly be added to the roasting pan.

TESTS OF TIME

Test a turkey for doneness by wiggling one of the legs. If it moves easily in its socket, the bird is done. Or make a tiny slit on the inside of the thigh. If the juices run clear and the meat shows no tinge of pink, the bird is done.

BROWNING

Basting promotes even browning. It can be done with a bulb baster or a spoon, but it's even easier with a pastry brush. Baste every 1/2 hour or so.

Tenting the top (breast) portion of the bird with foil helps to keep it from drying out. Don't wrap the entire bird or it will steam. Remove the foil for the last 1/2 hour of roasting to allow the skin to brown fully.

Alternatively, many cooks prefer oiled cheesecloth to foil. Cut cheesecloth long enough to fold in half and cover the bird. Soak the cloth in cooking oil or melted butter and wrap the bird. Basting can be done over the cheesecloth.

TIMETABLE FOR TRADITIONAL ROASTING OF A WHOLE TURKEY AT 325°F

Weight (pounds)	Unstuffed (hours)	Stuffed (hours)
8 to 12	2½ to 3	3 to 3½
12 to 14	3 to 3¼	3½ to 4
14 to 18	3¼ to 4¼	4 to 4¼
18 to 20	4¼ to 4½	4¼ to 4¾
20 to 24	4½ to 5	4¾ to 5¼

QUICK WAY TO TRUSS A TURKEY

1 Stuff neck and body cavities. Secure the neck skin to the back with round toothpicks or trussing pins.

2 Close vent (the opening of the body cavity) with toothpicks, a skewer, or trussing pins.

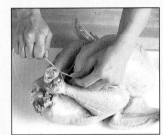

3 Tie the legs together securely over the vent with string. Insert meat thermometer.

4 To protect the wing tips from burning, tuck them securely behind the shoulders.

HOW TO CARVE A TURKEY

1. Using a knife and your fingers, cut and remove drumsticks, thighs, and wings at their joints. Hold the breast firmly with a fork. Using a long thin knife, make a deep cut—parallel to the platter—at about the height of the wing joint. **2.** Then carve the breast downward in thin slices.

EGG AND CHEESE DISHES

OMELETS

Fresh ingredients prepared before the cooking begins, moderate heat, and good timing are the key factors to the perfect omelet, whether plain or puffy.

OMELET BASICS

An omelet can be as simple or as original a creation as you like—the dish knows no bounds. In the 1950s, one New York restaurant became famous for serving only omelets, but offering 500 varieties.

Basically, however, there are two kinds of omelets: the French omelet, which can be filled or plain, and the puffy omelet, which is started on the stove but finished in the oven.

RULES OF THE GAME

The ingredients for omelets should be top quality. Use fresh eggs only and bring them to room temperature before beating so the omelet will turn out light and fluffy.

It's important that the eggs be well beaten. Beat the eggs vigorously with a whisk or use an egg beater. If possible, beat the eggs just before you're ready to pour them into the pan.

A spoonful of butter or margarine in the pan is essential. It keeps the outer surface of the omelet soft.

Depending on your taste, an omelet can be well done or soft, but it must never be cooked over high heat or it will toughen and burn. If it's cooked over too low a heat, it will remain on the burner too long and will toughen.

To avoid overcooking a filled omelet, make sure the filling is prepared. Grate the cheese, sauté the mushrooms, slice the ham, or mince the herbs for the filling ahead of time so that it only has to be sprinkled on and warmed lightly.

Fillings are normally added only to plain omelets. It is cumbersome to try to fold a filling into a puffy omelet.

THE RIGHT PAN

A 3-egg omelet is the maximum size that should be made. With a larger omelet, you'll risk having an overcooked outside and an undercooked inside. The perfect size pan for a 2- or 3-egg omelet is a 7- or 8-inch skillet. It should be light enough to lift and shake frequently with one hand.

If you make omelets frequently, it's worth investing in a pan just for that purpose so that the surface can remain smooth. Omelet pans have curved sides that make it easy to swirl and shake the egg mixture. They are available in a variety of materials.

HOW TO MAKE A ROLLED OR FILLED OMELET

1 As the omelet begins to set, tilt the pan and draw the edges to the center, allowing the liquid egg to run underneath.

2 To roll an unfilled omelet: When the eggs are set but still soft, tilt the pan and fold the eggs in thirds toward the middle. Seal the seam with a fork and slide the omelet onto a plate.

3 To fill an omelet: When the eggs are just set, sprinkle with cheese or other filling. Lift the edge with a spatula and fold in half. Slide onto a plate.

HOW TO MAKE AND BAKE A PUFFY OMELET

1 Separate the eggs. Whisk the yolks with milk. Beat the egg whites until stiff. Then fold them into the yolk mixture.

2 Melt butter in a 10-inch ovenproof pan. Carefully pour in the egg mixture and spread evenly with a rubber spatula. Cook over moderate heat until eggs are lightly browned on the bottom.

3 Transfer the pan to a preheated 350°F oven and bake about 15 minutes or until the eggs are set and lightly browned.

Perfect Cheese Omelet

- 3 eggs, at room temperature
- 1 tablespoon milk
- 1/4 teaspoon salt
- 1/4 teaspoon black pepper
- 1 tablespoon butter or margarine
- 1/4 cup finely shredded Cheddar cheese

1 In a medium-size bowl, whisk together eggs, milk, salt, and pepper.

2 In an 8-inch skillet or omelet pan, melt butter over low heat until foamy but not browned. Increase the heat to moderately high and tip the pan to coat with butter. Pour in egg mixture. As the omelet cooks, tilt the pan and draw the edges in toward the center with a fork. Shake pan gently to distribute the uncooked portion.

3 When the omelet is just set—after about 2 minutes—remove from the heat and sprinkle with cheese.

4 Loosen the edges of the omelet with a fork and as you tip the pan forward to fold the omelet in half. Slide the omelet onto a warmed serving plate. Makes 1 serving.

1 Serving: Calories 450; Total Fat 36 g; Saturated Fat 18 g; Protein 27 g; Carbohydrates 3 g; Fiber 0 g; Sodium 1440 mg; Cholesterol 702 mg

prep time-6 minutes
cooking time-2 minutes

MEXICAN CHEESE OMELET

Prepare as directed at left, **substituting** Monterey Jack or pepper Jack for Cheddar cheese and **adding** 2 tablespoons bottled salsa. Makes 1 serving.

MUSHROOM OMELET

Prepare as directed at left, **substituting** 1 cup butter-sautéed sliced mushrooms and 1 tablespoon minced chives for cheese. Makes 1 serving.

FRITTATAS

A frittata is an Italian dish combining eggs with vegetables and cheese—a delicious way to use leftovers for lunch or a light supper. Our notes cover frittatas as well as scrambled eggs.

FRITTATA NOTES

When it's turned out from the pan, a frittata is sort of an egg cake—relatively thick and cooked until firm but not dry.

To ensure that a frittata doesn't overbrown on the bottom before it has chance to cook through, the dish is started over low heat on top of the stove and then is finished under the broiler. Be sure to use a heavy skillet with an ovenproof handle. An old-fashioned cast-iron skillet works perfectly.

Another option is to flip the frittata and finish cooking it over burner heat. Place a large greased plate over the skillet, invert the half-cooked eggs on the plate, then slide it into the skillet and cook until browned. If the heat is kept low and the pan is well greased, there should be no sticking problem.

SERVED WITH STYLE

A frittata is always served flat, rather than folded like an omelet. Cut into large wedges, it's a lunch dish. Cut into small pieces, it's an hors d'oeuvre and is delicious either hot or at room temperature.

Because a frittata is full of vegetables and perhaps other ingredients as well, you get more servings per egg than with an omelet. A 6-egg frittata can easily serve 4.

MIX AND MATCH

In Italy, a frittata usually begins with chopped and browned onions. If you like, the onions can be the sole addition to the eggs and cheese. However, it's hard to resist adding more.

Favorite ingredients for frittatas include tomatoes and basil, fried green tomatoes, sliced zucchini or asparagus, home-fried potatoes, or leftover pasta—any and all of which are usually mixed with grated Parmesan cheese.

These suggestions are just the beginning. Use whatever fresh cooked or leftover vegetables and chopped cooked meat, poultry, or even shellfish you like. The ingredients can be stirred into the eggs or sprinkled on top.

The slightest trace of moisture keeps a frittata from setting properly. Squeeze as much liquid as possible from the spin-ach in our recipe, and cook zucchini or other vegetables until all the juices evaporate.

SCRAMBLED EGGS

This is the easiest skillet dish of all, although making it perfectly takes a little care.

For the basics, beat 2 eggs or more with salt and pepper just until the yolks and whites are blended. A tablespoon of water, milk, or cream can be added. Melt a little butter, margarine, or bacon drippings in a skillet and tilt the pan to coat the bottom well.

For creamy smooth eggs, cook the eggs over low heat, stirring constantly with a spatula, fork, or wooden spoon. The eggs are done when they're moist but firm, with no uncooked liquid remaining. Allow 3 to 3 1/2 minutes' cooking time for 2 to 4 eggs.

For large creamy curds, cook the eggs over low heat, occasionally pulling the cooked portions to the center, letting the uncooked portions run to the edges, until all the eggs are cooked to large moist curds.

For dry scrambled eggs, cook the eggs a minute or two past the moist-firm stage by either method above, until they look crumbly and dry.

For fluffy semidry eggs, beat the eggs until fluffy or process in a blender. Cook by either of the methods above.

DENVER SANDWICH

Sauté 1/3 cup each of finely chopped onion and green pepper and 2/3 cup of chopped cooked ham in 1 tablespoon of butter in a large skillet over moderate heat until the onion is tender—about 5 minutes.

Add 6 eggs prepared for scrambling and cook and stir until firm and creamy—about 4 minutes. Pile on 4 slices of buttered toast and serve immediately.

HOW TO MAKE A FRITTATA

1 Melt butter in an ovenproof skillet. Pour in the egg mixture and cook over lowest heat. As the eggs set, lift the edges and let the liquid egg run underneath.

2 When the eggs set, place skillet in a preheated broiler, 6 inches from the heat. Broil 2 minutes until browned.

Zucchini and Spinach Frittata

- 2 tablespoons olive oil
- 1 small red onion, finely chopped
- 2 cloves garlic, finely chopped
- 2 medium-size zucchini, halved lengthwise and thinly sliced
- 1 package (10 ounces) frozen spinach, thawed and squeezed dry
- ¼ cup chopped fresh basil
- ½ teaspoon salt
- ¼ teaspoon black pepper
- 6 eggs, lightly beaten
- ⅔ cup grated Parmesan cheese
- 1 tablespoon butter or margarine

1 In a large nonstick ovenproof skillet over moderate heat, heat oil 1 minute. Add onion and garlic and cook, stirring occasionally, until soft—about 5 minutes.

2 Add zucchini and cook, stirring frequently, until crisp-tender—about 3 minutes. Add spinach, basil, salt, and pepper and cook until spinach is tender and dry—about 5 minutes.

3 In a large bowl, whisk together eggs and Parmesan. Add vegetable mixture and stir until well combined.

4 Preheat the broiler. Wipe the skillet clean, set over moderate heat, add butter, and heat until bubbly. Pour in egg mixture and immediately reduce the heat to as low as possible. Cook without stirring until the bottom and sides are set, but the top is runny—about 12 minutes.

5 Transfer to the broiler, set 6 inches from the heat, and broil until the top is just set—about 2 minutes. Loosen the frittata with a small metal spatula and slide it onto a large platter. Cut into 4 wedges and serve either hot or at room temperature. Makes 4 servings.

1 Serving: Calories 309; Total Fat 23 g; Saturated Fat 8 g; Protein 20 g; Carbohydrates 9 g; Fiber 3 g; Sodium 757 mg; Cholesterol 340 mg

prep time-15 minutes • cooking time-28 minutes

BROCCOLI FRITTATA

Prepare as directed at left, **substituting** 4 cups broccoli florets for zucchini and spinach. **Blanch** broccoli for 2 minutes before coarsely **chopping** and **sautéing** in olive oil. Makes 4 servings.

PEPPER FRITTATA

Prepare as directed at left, **substituting** 2 cored, seeded, and diced medium-size sweet peppers (1 red, 1 green) for zucchini and spinach. Makes 4 servings.

SAVORY SOUFFLÉS

A white sauce enriched with egg yolks forms the base of a soufflé. Egg whites beaten stiff make it airy.

LIGHT AND EASY

Soufflés are easier to make than you may think, but be sure to bring the dish from the oven to the table as soon as it's done or your masterpiece will collapse. Our savory soufflés appear here, our dessert soufflés on page 320.

SEPARATING AND BEATING EGGS

Eggs are easiest to separate when cold. Be sure that no egg yolk is mixed into the whites: The presence of any yolk or other fat will prevent the whites from whipping properly. You'll get better volume if the bowl and whisk or beaters are bone dry.

Choose a large bowl with a rounded bottom for the egg whites: Unlined copper, stainless-steel, glass, or ceramic bowls are fine.

For better volume, let the egg whites stand 45 minutes before beating. The whites should be beaten until they form stiff glossy peaks. Dry peaks, caused by overwhipping, indicate that the protein in the egg white has begun to break down and is a sign that the foam will start to collapse. More soufflés fail due to overbeating than underbeating.

PREPARING THE DISH

A straight-sided baking dish allows a soufflé to rise perfectly. Cooks are divided over whether it's better to butter the dish or not. Those against argue that an unbuttered dish allows the soufflé mixture to cling to the sides and rise to its highest. But if your soufflés tend to stick, by all means grease the dish with butter, then coat it with fine dry bread crumbs or finely grated Parmesan cheese. Shake the dish to remove any excess.

Refrigerate the dish until ready to add the egg mixture. This step helps the soufflé to rise.

FOR EXTRA HEIGHT

For a tall soufflé, choose a dish slightly smaller than that called for in a recipe and make it taller with a collar.

Fold a piece of foil in half and trim it so that it is about 3 inches deep and long enough to go around the top of the dish. When you've mixed the soufflé, pour it into the dish, filling it to the top. Then tuck the collar inside the rim of the mold to a depth of about 1/2 inch, securing it with a paper clip. Then add the rest of the egg mixture. Remove the collar before serving.

HOW TO MAKE A SOUFFLÉ

1 Separate eggs, placing whites in a dry bowl.

2 Prepare the white sauce with cheese and cool.

3 With a whisk, beat yolks until frothy, then combine with sauce. Cook over low heat for 2 minutes. Cool, covered with wax paper.

4 Beat egg whites until they form glossy peaks, adding 1 or 2 extra whites if desired. Whisk about 1/4 of the whites into sauce.

5 Fold in the remaining whites with a rubber spatula and pour into prepared baking dish. Smooth top.

6 Make a circle in the center of the batter. During baking, the center will puff to form a "top hat."

WORK SAVER
Balloon Whip

For the loftiest beaten egg whites, use a balloon whip. This oversized whisk, used in tandem with a round-bottomed bowl, allows you to keep all the egg whites in motion simultaneously as they form tiny bubbles and mount in volume.

Double Cheese Soufflé

- 3 **tablespoons butter or margarine**
- 3 **tablespoons all-purpose flour**
- 1 **cup milk**
- 3/4 **cup coarsely grated Gruyère cheese**
- 1/4 **cup grated Parmesan cheese**
- 1/2 **teaspoon salt**
- 1/8 **to 1/4 teaspoon cayenne**
- 3 **eggs, separated**

1 In a medium-size saucepan over moderate heat, melt butter. Blend in flour, then gradually add milk, whisking until thickened and smooth—3 to 5 minutes. Add the cheeses, salt, and cayenne and cook, stirring, until cheeses melt.

2 In a small bowl, whisk egg yolks well. Mix in a little of the hot cheese mixture, then stir back into pan. Cook and stir over low heat for 2 minutes. Remove from the heat, smooth wax paper flat on the surface of the sauce, and cool to room temperature.

3 Preheat the oven to 350°F. With a balloon whip or in an electric mixer, beat egg whites until stiff but not dry. Stir about 1/4 cup of the beaten egg whites into cheese mixture, then gently fold in the remaining whites.

4 Spoon into an ungreased 5-cup soufflé dish, place on a baking sheet, and bake until puffy and browned—about 45 minutes. Serve immediately. Makes 4 servings.

1 Serving: Calories 303; Total Fat 23 g; Saturated Fat 13 g; Protein 16 g; Carbohydrates 8 g; Fiber 0 g; Sodium 616 mg; Cholesterol 219 mg

prep time-8 minutes
cooking time-52 minutes

CHEDDAR-SUN-DRIED TOMATO SOUFFLÉ

Prepare as directed at left, **substituting** 1 1/4 cups shredded medium to sharp Cheddar for Gruyère and Parmesan and **adding** 1/2 teaspoon dry mustard along with the cayenne. **Cook** 1/4 cup sun-dried tomatoes (not oil packed) in boiling water until tender—about 4 minutes (timing will vary according to the toughness of the tomatoes). **Squeeze** dry, **chop** fine, and **stir** into sauce along with the Cheddar. Makes 4 servings.

HARD-COOKED AND STUFFED EGGS

For perfect eggs, all you need to do is take them from the heat and wait. Our recipes provide five tasty stuffings.

PERFECT EGGS

Although they are called "hard-boiled" more often than not, hard-cooked eggs should never actually be boiled. The high heat of boiling water makes egg whites tough and rubbery. It's also apt to make the shells burst and to cause the iron in the yolk to bond with the sulfur in the white, forming a gray-green layer where they meet.

These problems can be avoided by following the steps in our recipe. The covered pan is removed from the heat the second the water comes to a boil and is set aside. In 15 minutes, the eggs are done. If the eggs are refrigerator cold when you put them in the water, they may need to sit for closer to 20 minutes after they are removed from the heat.

EASY SHELLING

You'll have the easiest time shelling eggs if you crack the wide end of the shells and plunge the eggs into ice water the moment they are drained from the cooking water.

A quick chill in ice water also helps to keep the gray-green ring from forming between the yolk and white.

When the eggs are cool, craze the shell by tapping it gently. This allows you to pull away the thin membrane that surrounds the egg when you peel off the shell. If the membrane sticks to the egg white, it will not peel neatly.

FRESH FLAVOR

Hard-cooked eggs can be prepared and refrigerated a day ahead, but should not be stuffed until shortly before serving. Stuffing eggs is easiest with a pastry bag. If you don't have one, improvise using a plastic bag with a tiny hole cut in one corner.

HOW TO STUFF A HARD-COOKED EGG

1 Peel eggs and cut in half lengthwise. Remove yolks, push through a sieve, and mix with stuffing ingredients.

2 Pipe filling through a pastry bag fitted with a number 6 star tip.

DEVILED EGGS

Prepare as directed at right, **substituting** 4 teaspoons each yellow mustard and white wine vinegar for capers and dill. **Add** 1 teaspoon each salt and sugar and **increase** white pepper to 1 teaspoon. **Add** 1/2 cup finely chopped celery. Makes 12 servings.

CURRIED EGGS

Prepare as directed at right, **substituting** 4 teaspoons curry powder and 3 tablespoons chopped chutney for capers and dill. Makes 12 servings.

CHILI EGGS

Prepare as directed at right, **substituting** 4 teaspoons chili powder and 1 teaspoon ground cumin for capers and dill. Makes 12 servings.

SPICY EGGS

Prepare as directed at right, **substituting** 1/4 cup prepared horseradish and 2 tablespoons chopped parsley for capers and dill. Makes 12 servings.

TEA-STAINED EGGS

Prepare eggs as directed in Step 1 at right, **drain**, and **crackle** shells all over. **Plunge** into strong iced tea and **refrigerate** several hours before peeling. Eat as is or stuff. Makes 12 servings.

The intriguing crackled Tea-Stained Eggs, above, are one of our recipe variations. Our Stuffed Hard-Cooked Eggs, right, are flavored with capers and dill.

1 Place eggs in a single layer in a large saucepan. Add enough water to cover by 1 inch. Set over high heat and bring to a full boil. Immediately remove the pan from the heat, cover, and set aside for 15 minutes.

2 Drain eggs and crack the wide end of each. Chill in a bowl of ice water. To peel, crack each shell all over by tapping it on a countertop. To make peeling easier, remove shell under cold running water.

3 Using a small sharp knife, halve eggs lengthwise. Scoop yolks into a sieve set over a medium-size bowl, then press yolks through the sieve with the back of a spoon.

4 Mix in mayonnaise, capers, dill, pepper, and salt to taste, using a fork to combine well. Spoon about 1 tablespoon of the yolk mixture into each egg white or pipe it with a pastry bag as directed at left. If desired, garnish each egg with additional capers and dill sprigs. Makes 12 servings.

1 Serving: Calories 147; Total Fat 13 g; Saturated Fat 3 g; Protein 7 g; Carbohydrates 1 g; Fiber 0 g; Sodium 117 mg; Cholesterol 227 mg

prep time-40 minutes • cooking time-20 minutes
chilling time-30 minutes

Stuffed Hard-Cooked Eggs

12 eggs

1/2 cup regular or reduced-fat mayonnaise

3 tablespoons capers, drained well and chopped

3 tablespoons snipped fresh dill or 1 1/2 teaspoons dried dill, crumbled

1/2 teaspoon ground white pepper

Salt to taste

CHEESE MOLDS

A molded appetizer is a hostess's best friend. It's showy, can be made ahead of time and, if you follow our simple instructions, easy to make.

JUST RIGHT

Too little gelatin makes a salad "weep" or melt; too much and it takes on a rubbery texture. It's worthwhile paying close attention to the recipe and measurements. See page 164 for more details about preparing molds and a how-to for unmolding gelatin dishes.

CHOOSING A CHEESE

The best cheeses to use in molds are soft or crumbly varieties that can be blended with other ingredients until smooth. Harder cheese that melts smoothly—Cheddar, for example—also works. Parmesan is a poor choice because it remains fairly gritty.

OUT OF THE BLUE

Roquefort is the most famous of the many blue cheeses. They include Danish blue, Gorgonzola, Stilton, Cheshire, blue Brie, among many others. The cheese maker sprinkles penicillin-mold spores into the cheese to give it its distinctive blue veining and flavor.

Most blue cheeses are made from cow's milk. Roquefort is made from sheep's milk and has a particularly creamy quality. To maintain its flavor, don't peel off its foil wrapper until you're ready to use it. You can substitute a less expensive blue cheese for Roquefort but be sure to select one that has not been made with artificial preservatives—they ruin the flavor and the texture.

CRUMBLY BUSINESS

It's easiest to work with crumbly blue cheese when it's refrigerator cold. Cut the cheese into 1/2-inch slices and stack. Using a sharp knife, slice through the stack in a crisscross fashion. Let the cheese come to room temperature before combining it with other ingredients.

THE RIGHT MOLD

Choose a mold with a plain design; corners, fluted edges, and raised designs make it difficult to turn out a creamy mold such as this with the design intact. If you don't wish to use a ring mold, the Roquefort mixture will set nicely in a straight-sided charlotte mold or 1-quart saucepan.

Creamy gelatins such as this one will unmold more easily if the mold is lightly oiled or sprayed with nonstick vegetable spray before the gelatin mixture is poured in. Oil should not be used on molds for clear gelled salads because it will cloud them.

Chill the mixture thoroughly, following the recipe instructions. Shake the mold and if the center wiggles, chill an hour or so longer.

Keep the mold refrigerated until it's time to unmold.

PRESENTATION

A Roquefort ring makes an elegant presentation on a buffet table. Set it out along with a basket of crackers, French bread rounds, or melba toast.

For a large party, make 2 or 3 recipes instead of a huge one. Double recipes of gelled salads take longer to chill and can be difficult to unmold. The dish can be unmolded 2 or 3 hours ahead of time, covered with plastic wrap, and refrigerated until needed.

LOW-CAL ROQUEFORT RING

Prepare as directed at right, **substituting** Vegetable Broth (page 45) for wine and skim milk for half-and-half.
Increase cream cheese to 12 ounces but use the reduced-fat variety. Also **reduce** Roquefort to 4 ounces. Makes 6 servings.

PIMIENTO RING

Prepare as directed at right, **substituting** 1/2 cup Vegetable Broth (page 45) for wine, 1/2 cup milk for half-and-half, and 12 ounces finely diced sharp Cheddar for Roquefort. **Reduce** cream cheese to 3 ounces. **Add** cheeses to the blender, a cube at a time, then **add** 1/4 cup mayonnaise and 1/8 teaspoon freshly grated nutmeg. **Blend** until smooth. **Pour** into a medium-size bowl and **fold** in 2 well-drained 4-ounce jars chopped pimientos. Makes 6 servings.

WORK SAVER
Ring Mold

A simple, inexpensive aluminum ring mold is handy to have in the kitchen. Easy to work with and to unmold, it can be used for chilled dishes such as a Roquefort ring and for cooked mousses, meat loaves, and custards. Best of all, when an otherwise ordinary salad, rice dish, or dessert is turned out of a ring mold and garnished, it suddenly becomes company best.

Roquefort Ring

1. Pour wine into a blender container; sprinkle in gelatin and let stand 3 to 4 minutes.

2. In a small saucepan over low heat, bring half-and-half to a simmer. Pour over softened gelatin and blend at low speed until gelatin dissolves completely—about 2 minutes. Gradually add cheeses and blend in at high speed. Add onion, garlic, and cayenne and blend until smooth and creamy. Taste and adjust seasonings, if desired.

3. Pour into a lightly oiled 4-cup ring mold and chill several hours or until firm.

4. Unmold on a bed of lettuce. Serve with crackers and apple or pear slices. Makes 6 servings.

1 Serving: Calories 317;
Total Fat 27 g;
Saturated Fat 17 g;
Protein 13 g;
Carbohydrates 3 g;
Fiber 0 g;
Sodium 807 mg;
Cholesterol 83 mg

prep time-5 minutes
chilling time-4 hours

1/2 cup dry white wine or reduced-sodium vegetable broth

1 envelope (1/4 ounce) unflavored gelatin

1/2 cup half-and-half

1 package (8 ounces) cream cheese, softened and cut up

8 ounces Roquefort cheese or other blue cheese, coarsely crumbled

2 tablespoons grated yellow onion

1 garlic clove, minced

1/8 to 1/4 teaspoon cayenne

RAREBITS

Welsh rarebit is one of the oldest recorded recipes but fits today's life perfectly—it's substantial but takes only minutes to make from start to finish.

WHAT'S IN A NAME?

The name Welsh rarebit, aka rabbit, is given two derivations. Some say that in days of old when Welsh hunters came home without bagging any game, they had toasted cheese for supper instead.

Others suggest that the word "rarebit" comes from "rearbit," the name for savories (such as toasted cheese) that used to be served at the end of a meal. In this case, the toasted cheese might have been Caerphilly, a famous mild white Cheddarlike Welsh cheese.

SERVING TIPS

Serve Welsh rarebit over any kind of toast you like. A toasted slice of a crusty French or Italian bread with chewy texture gives the dish an extra boost. Some rarebit lovers like to pass the dish under the broiler for a few seconds to brown the cheese lightly just before serving.

THE CHEESE

A well-aged Cheddar provides the smoothest melted texture for a rarebit—not to mention the finest flavor. If you want to make an English, Swiss, Cali-

fornia, Vermont, or Wisconsin rarebit, firm cheeses such as Cheshire, Gloucester, Swiss, Jarlsberg, Monterey Jack, and Colby can be substituted for the Cheddar.

LOW-FAT PERILS

Low-fat cheeses are not good candidates for rarebit because they do not melt well. But if you want to try a low-fat cheese, mix 1 tablespoon of cornstarch with the grated cheese to help keep it from separating and stringing as it melts.

TEMPERATURE AND TIMING

The two important things to remember when preparing a dish that calls for melted cheese are to cook it over low heat and for as short a time as possible. High heat causes the fat and protein in cheese to

separate. Prolonged cooking makes the cheese stringy and rubbery and creates lumps that no amount of heating or stirring will dissolve. Note: Never let melted cheese come to a boil.

To make sure that cheese melts quickly, heat the milk, beer, or other liquids first, then add the cheese.

Grate or shave the cheese and let it come to room temperature before adding it to the hot liquid. Once the cheese has been added, stir it constantly until it's melted and smooth. Then serve immediately.

ON THE STOVE

You'll have the best luck keeping cheese smooth if you melt it in a double boiler. The top part of the pot should be close to but must not touch the boiling water below.

If you don't have a double boiler, improvise by setting a stainless-steel or fireproof glass bowl over a saucepan of boiling water. Or use a flame moderator—an inexpensive insulating pad that is put on top of an electric or gas burner to separate the pan from direct heat.

MORE CHEESY TRICKS

Sprinkle shredded cheese on a casserole 5 to 10 minutes

HOW TO PREPARE A RAREBIT

1 Heat the milk and butter in the top of a double boiler until hot enough to melt the cheese.

2 Add shredded cheese gradually and stir until thick. Add seasoning.

before it is done so the cheese will not cook into a tough crust. Bread crumbs mixed with the cheese also help insulate it from too much heat.

Casseroles containing cheese are best cooked in an oven no hotter than 350°F.

WORK SAVER
Double Boiler

Delicate sauces are best cooked away from direct heat. A double boiler is the right pot for the job: Hot water in the lower section cooks the sauce in the section above. A glass double boiler insulates well and makes it easy to keep an eye on the cooking process.

Welsh Rarebit

½ **cup milk**

1 **tablespoon butter or margarine**

3 **cups shredded sharp Cheddar cheese**

1½ **teaspoons Worcestershire sauce**

½ **teaspoon dry mustard**

Pinch cayenne

1 In the top of a double boiler over simmering water, heat milk and butter until steaming—8 to 10 minutes.

2 Add cheese, a little at a time, and cook, stirring constantly, until smooth and quite thick.

3 Remove from the heat immediately. Stir in Worcestershire sauce, mustard, and cayenne and serve over hot buttered toast. Makes 4 servings.

1 Serving: Calories 392; Total Fat 32 g; Saturated Fat 20 g; Protein 22 g; Carbohydrates 3 g; Fiber 0 g; Sodium 614 mg; Cholesterol 101 mg

prep time-5 minutes • cooking time-15 minutes

MAIN DISH CUSTARDS

S avory custards are baked slowly in a pan of steaming water. The creamy combination of milk, eggs, cheese, and vegetables is meltingly delicious.

THE BAKING DISH

Savory custards are usually prepared as individual servings and are unmolded before they are brought to the table. Use custard cups, ramekins, or individual soufflé dishes. If you want to use a single baking dish, choose a ring mold so the custard will cook evenly.

Individual custards, called timbales, can be served by themselves as an appetizer or as a side dish with roasted meat or poultry or baked fish. They can also be the main event for lunch or supper with vegetables or a salad on the side.

If you are serving the timbales as the main dish, you might want to top them with parsley or mushroom sauce (see page 364) and a sprinkling of toasted bread crumbs.

SAVORY FLAVORINGS

Although delicious flavored simply with cheese, the ingredients in a custard pick up the flavors of cooked vegetables and meats beautifully and give

them a delicate richness.

Flavor timbales as you do your favorite quiches. Our Vegetable-Cheese recipe variation gives the basic proportions of vegetables to milk and eggs. Broccoli, spinach, asparagus, mushrooms, and corn are all good. You might also use cooked chicken, chicken livers, bacon, or ham.

Drain vegetables very dry after cooking to make sure they don't dilute the custard. Chop the meats fine or coarsely grind them to make sure they are distributed evenly in the custard mixture.

Depending on the ingredients you choose, you might substitute a half-and-half mix of

chicken broth and cream for the milk in the recipe.

A light sprinkling of nutmeg is the traditional seasoning for custards—both savory and sweet—but if it doesn't suit the ingredients in your custard, simply leave it out.

SERVED IN STYLE

Cool the timbales for 10 minutes before unmolding them. To unmold, run the blade of a knife around each and invert it on a plate. If it does not come out easily, give the bottom of the mold a sturdy slap.

Timbales can be served warm or chilled. Cold timbales are best accompanied by mayonnaise or a mayonnaise sauce.

LIGHT CHEESE TIMBALES

Prepare as directed at right, **substituting** evaporated skim milk for milk, 1 cup fat-free egg substitute for eggs, and 3/4 cup finely shredded reduced-fat Cheddar cheese for regular. **Add** 1/2 teaspoon Dijon mustard. Makes 6 timbales.

VEGETABLE-CHEESE TIMBALES

Prepare as directed at right, but **reduce** Cheddar cheese to 1/2 cup. **Fold** 1 cup puréed, well-drained, cooked broccoli, spinach, or zucchini into cheese mixture. **Reduce** baking time to 40 to 45 minutes. Makes 8 timbales.

HOW TO MAKE A TIMBALE

Because timbales are made in fairly deep molds, they require a long time in the oven in order to cook through. To prevent the custard from curdling, the molds are baked in a hot water bath from start to finish.

1 To prevent the filled molds from sliding on their way to the oven, set them on a folded kitchen towel in a roasting pan. Pour hot water into the pan to about 3/4 the height of the molds. Cover the pan loosely with foil and bake.

2 When the cooked timbales have cooled slightly, run a knife around the edge of the molds and invert on plates. Serve with sauce.

Cheese Timbales

- **1¹/₂ cups** milk or light or heavy cream
- **4 eggs**
- **1 teaspoon** finely grated yellow onion
- **¹/₂ teaspoon** salt
- **¹/₈ teaspoon** white pepper
- **¹/₈ teaspoon** ground nutmeg
- **Pinch cayenne**
- **³/₄ cup** finely shredded sharp Cheddar or Gruyère cheese
- **¹/₂ cup** grated Parmesan cheese

1 Preheat the oven to 325°F. Butter six 6-ounce ramekins or custard cups and set aside.

2 In a medium-size saucepan over low heat, heat milk until just warm. Remove from the heat and set aside.

3 In a medium-size bowl, lightly beat eggs. Gradually whisk in warm milk, onion, salt, pepper, nutmeg, and cayenne. Stir in cheeses.

4 Set a folded tea towel in a shallow roasting pan. Arrange prepared ramekins on the towel,

not touching, and spoon in cheese mixture. Ladle enough hot, but not boiling, water into the roasting pan to come ³/₄ of the way up the sides of the ramekins.

5 Cover the pan loosely with aluminum foil and bake until a knife inserted in the center of a timbale comes out clean—45 to 50 minutes. Makes 6 servings.

1 Serving: Calories 183; Total Fat 13 g; Saturated Fat 7 g; Protein 13 g; Carbohydrates 4 g; Fiber 0 g; Sodium 492 mg; Cholesterol 172 mg

*prep time-10 minutes
cooking time-about 55 minutes*

CHEESE TORTE

This unsweetened cheesecake makes a delicious appetizer or hors d'oeuvre. It can be baked the night before a party, chilled, and served cold.

FOR STARTERS

Tortes and cheesecakes are generally thought of as sweets but this one is not. Although made very much like the classic creamy Italian dessert cheesecake, ours is gently flavored with garlic. Our goat cheese variation gets its flavor from fresh herbs and pimiento.

SWEET OR SAVORY

Ricotta is a fresh cheese similar to cottage cheese but with silkier texture. Mixed with cream cheese, ricotta makes a smooth dense cake. For more about cheesecakes, see page 326 in our dessert chapter.

CRACKER CRUST

A crust made with ground crackers is perfect for a savory torte. Our recipe calls for butter-flavored crackers but you can vary your choices. If you do not want to make the crust in a food processor, simply spread the crackers on a piece of wax paper, roll them fine with a rolling pin, then mix them with butter in a bowl.

PERFECT TIMING

When the torte is done, it will shiver near the center when the pan is shaken. A toothpick plunged into the center should come out clean but moist. Keep the oven temperature low to moderate to prevent shrinkage and curdling.

SPLIT TOP?

The density of cheesecake makes it crack on top while it bakes. There is no way to prevent it. If presentation is important, add a topping. For a savory torte, it might be chopped fresh herbs, sautéed mushrooms, sliced grilled cherry tomatoes, or asparagus spears arranged as spokes.

To remove from a springform pan, run a narrow spatula around the edge of the cheesecake and release the spring clamp. Carefully lift off the sides. If a bit of cake clings to the side, remove it and push it back in place in the cake.

GOAT CHEESE TORTE

Prepare as directed at right, **adding** 1/4 teaspoon chopped fresh thyme or 1/8 teaspoon crumbled dried thyme and 1 tablespoon each chopped parsley and chives to the crust mixture. **Increase** cream cheese in filling to 16 ounces and **substitute** 1 cup crumbled chèvre or other soft white goat cheese for ricotta. **Omit** garlic. **Pour** 1/2 of the filling into crust, **sprinkle** with 1 cup diced red pimiento, and **top** with remaining filling. **Bake** for 1 hour. **Cool** to room temperature, and **release** from pan as directed. **Serve** chilled or at room temperature. Makes 8 servings.

HOW TO MAKE AND GARNISH A TORTE

1 Press cracker crust into the bottom of a greased springform pan.

2 Carefully pour in the filling and smooth with a rubber spatula. Bake.

3 When cooled, loosen the edges with a knife and release springform sides.

4 Garnish the top of the torte with minced herbs or colorful vegetables.

WORK SAVER
Springform Pan

This clever pan has removable sides. A torte or cake can be unmolded without sticking and falling apart. You can leave the torte on the base for serving or remove it by sliding a long-bladed spatula between the two.

Ricotta Torte

1. Preheat the oven to 325°F. For the Crust: Place crackers in a food processor and pulse to make coarse crumbs. Add butter and pulse until well combined.

2. Spray sides of a 9-inch springform pan with nonstick vegetable spray. Press crumbs onto bottom of pan.

3. For the Filling: Pulse filling ingredients in a food processor until well mixed. Pour filling into crust and bake until just set—50 to 60 minutes.

4. Cool to room temperature on a rack. Run a knife around the edge of the pan to loosen torte, remove to a serving platter, and cut into 8 wedges. Makes 8 servings.

1 Serving: Calories 468; Total Fat 41 g; Saturated Fat 23 g; Protein 13 g; Carbohydrates 14 g; Fiber 0 g; Sodium 629 mg; Cholesterol 198 mg

prep time-15 minutes
cooking time-1 hour

Crust:
- 42 butter-flavored round crackers
- 4 tablespoons butter, melted

Filling:
- 8 ounces cream cheese, softened and cut up
- 1 teaspoon salt
- 3 eggs
- 1 cup heavy cream
- 2 cups ricotta cheese
- 1 tablespoon minced garlic

SAVORY CUSTARDS

A wedge of oven-fresh quiche makes a delicious lunch. Cold, it's a great picnic dish and, baked in tart shells, it's the perfect hors d'oeuvre.

QUICHE NOTES

Quiche and timbales are first cousins. You can use a timbale recipe for a quiche filling and vice versa. But where deep-molded timbales require slow cooking, the custard in quiche—poured into a shallow pie shell—is cooked quickly, about 1/2 hour, at a moderate temperature.

MILK AND CHEESE CHOICES

Originally, quiches were made with heavy cream and no cheese. As the dish has evolved, however, cheese has become a near standard ingredient. It's cook's choice whether to make the custard with milk, light or heavy cream, or a mixture of milk and cream. You can also make a low-fat quiche with evaporated skim milk if there are not a lot of acidic ingredients.

PICK A CHEESE

Favorite cheeses for quiche include shredded Gruyère, Swiss, or Emmentaler, which are often mixed with grated Parmesan or Asiago for bite. For a change, stir in shredded Cheddar or crumble 2 to 4

ounces of blue cheese, chèvre, or another goat cheese into the pie shell before pouring in the custard. If you use blue or feta cheese, omit salt from the recipe.

CRISP CRUST

Quiches are generally made with simple short pastry as described in our recipe. For quiches and dessert tarts and pies with liquid fillings, the crust must be partially (or blind) baked before the filling is poured in. Without partial baking, the filling will make the dough soggy. For tarts with fillings that do not have to be baked, the crust must be fully baked to start.

NO SHRINKING

To prevent the pastry from bubbling or pulling away from

(continued on page 302)

HOW TO MAKE A QUICHE

Test the quiche after 25 minutes, sticking a clean knife into the center. If it comes out damp but with no filling clinging to it, the quiche is done. Overcooking causes curdling or a dry quiche.

1 Wrap dough over rolling pin and ease into a 10-inch pan. Press into pan. Trim, leaving a 1-inch overhang. Fold under for sides.

2 Roll the top edge with rolling pin to make it level with the side of the pan. Prick with a fork and set in freezer 15 minutes.

3 Loosely cover the crust with foil and fill with dried beans or baking weights. Bake for 25 minutes.

4 Remove foil and beans and continue baking until crust is light brown—10 to 15 minutes more.

5 Set pan on a baking sheet. Pour in filling to no more than 3/4 full. Place in a preheated oven.

6 Quiche will be delicately set and golden in about 1/2 hour. If top browns too fast, cover with foil.

Tomato Quiche

Crust:

- 1 cup unsifted all-purpose flour
- 1/8 teaspoon salt
- 1/2 cup (1 stick) cold butter, cut up
- 1/4 cup ice water

Filling:

- 1/2 cup sun-dried tomatoes (not oil packed)
- 3 eggs
- 1 cup milk or light or heavy cream
- 1/4 cup grated Parmesan cheese
- 1/2 cup shredded Gruyère cheese
- 1/2 teaspoon salt
- 1/8 teaspoon black pepper
- 1 firm-ripe medium-size tomato, sliced but not peeled

1 For the Crust: Pulse flour, salt, and butter in a food processor until mixture resembles coarse meal. Add water slowly through the feed tube and pulse just until pastry holds together. Remove and shape into a ball. Flatten the ball slightly, wrap in plastic wrap, and refrigerate 15 minutes.

2 Preheat the oven to 350°F. On a lightly floured work surface using a floured rolling pin, roll pastry from the center out to form a 12-inch circle ⅛-inch thick. Prepare piecrust in a 10-inch pan as shown at left.

3 For the Filling: Soak sun-dried tomatoes in boiling water to cover for 5 minutes. Drain well and chop fine; set aside.

4 In a medium-size bowl, whisk together eggs and milk. Add

reserved tomatoes, cheeses, salt, and pepper. Pour filling into crust, arrange tomato slices on top, and bake until custard is set—about 30 minutes. Cool 15 to 20 minutes before serving. Makes 6 servings.

1 Serving: Calories 347; Total Fat 24 g; Saturated Fat 14 g; Protein 12 g; Carbohydrates 22 g; Fiber 2 g; Sodium 590 mg; Cholesterol 167 mg

prep time-10 minutes
resting time-30 minutes
cooking time-30 minutes

(continued from page 300)

the sides of the pan during the first baking, be sure to prick and chill the pie shell and then line it with weighted aluminum foil before putting it in the oven.

For best results with a frozen unbaked pie shell, thaw the shell, then proceed as above.

MOISTURE PROOFING

If you know a quiche will have to sit for a while before it's served, you might want to moisture proof the pie shell before adding the filling.

Remove the weighted foil after partially baking the shell. Then while it is still warm, brush the bottom of the shell with beaten egg white.

Sprinkle the shell with a little grated cheese and return it to the oven for about 3 minutes. Let the shell cool. Wait until you're ready to put the quiche in the oven before pouring in the custard.

EASY BAKING

To make it easy to get the quiche in and out of the oven, place the cooled partially baked pie shell on a heavy-duty baking sheet. Use a ladle or measuring cup to pour in just enough filling. Then place the baking sheet and quiche in the preheated oven.

SERVED IN STYLE

Quiches and other French tarts are traditionally made in straight-sided pans. They are removed from the pans before serving, both for an attractive presentation and to make them easier to slice and serve.

The simplest pan to use is a classic metal tart pan with

fluted sides and a removable bottom. When the quiche is done and has cooled slightly, simply place the pan on top of a wide-mouthed bowl or jar and the rim will fall away.

You can put the quiche directly on a serving plate or remove the thin pan bottom before doing so. To remove the bottom, carefully slide a long-bladed spatula between crust and pan, then gently ease the quiche onto a plate.

OTHER CHOICES FOR PANS

The fluted quiche or tart pan is traditional but is by no means the only choice. Use a regular pie pan if you like. However, do not attempt to remove the quiche from the pan before serving: The slanted sides of the pastry may not hold up against the custard filling.

If you are cooking for a crowd, inexpensive aluminum pie pans are fine, though they will not hold the same volume of filling. Double the pans to prevent them from buckling under the weight of the filling.

PERFECT FILLING

Quiche puffs while it bakes, so when pouring in the custard, be sure you do not fill the pie shell more than ¾ full. When the quiche is removed from the oven, it will remain puffed for about 10 minutes.

The quiche should be golden when it's done. If it starts to color too fast, cover the top loosely with aluminum foil.

The custard filling will curdle if baked too long or at too high a temperature. Be sure to remove the quiche from the

oven when it is just done: It will continue to cook for a few minutes out of the oven. A knife inserted in the center should emerge clean but moist.

GOOD SNACKING

Quiche is delicious served at room temperature and it can also be reheated. To reheat, cover loosely with foil and place in a 350°F oven for 10 to 15 minutes: The filling will not puff the second time. Reheating more than once will dry out the custard.

FLAVOR VARIATIONS

One of the best things about quiche is that the custard filling blends with so many flavors. If sun-dried tomatoes or bacon are not to your taste, sprinkle in about ¾ cup of whatever additions suit your fancy. Meats, seafood, and vegetables that are not usually eaten raw should be cooked and drained.

Try crabmeat and scallions; spinach and goat cheese; eggplant, tomato, and Parmesan; red onion, basil, and provolone; shrimp or salmon and dill; ham

QUICHE LORRAINE

Prepare as directed on page 301, **substituting** ⅓ cup crumbled cooked bacon for sun-dried tomatoes. **Increase** Gruyère to 1 cup and **omit** Parmesan. Also **omit** tomato slices. Makes 6 servings.

and cheese; or mushrooms, Swiss cheese, and scallions.

MINI QUICHES

Quiches cooked in tiny tart pans are a great dish for parties. Depending on the size of the pans—usually 2 or 3 inches—you'll get 14 to 18 tarts per quiche recipe. Partially bake the mini crusts for 10 minutes at 375°F, fill, and bake for 10 to 15 minutes. Plan on about 3 mini quiches per person.

COOKING AHEAD

Unbaked pastry shells wrapped in foil can be refrigerated for 3 or 4 days or frozen for up to 4 weeks.

KITCHEN MATH

One 8-inch shell = 2½ cups filling = 4 to 6 servings
One 10-inch shell = 3¾ cups filling = 6 to 8 servings

WORK SAVER

Two-Part Pan

A pan with removable sides makes it easier to showcase a quiche or tart on a serving plate and makes it easier to cut and serve. The pan bottom, left in place, supports the fragile pastry.

A SWEET FINISH

FRUIT TARTS

A fruit tart is made of four delicious parts: sweet crust, custardy filling, fruit topping, and shiny glaze.

ABOUT CRUSTS

Tarts are generally made in a fluted pan with a removable bottom, which makes serving easy. Dessert tarts are usually given a fancier crust than fruit pies. Sugar crusts, like the one in our Summer Tart, are traditional. The buttery dough is enriched with egg yolk and sugar, like a sugar cookie.

Since the fruit on our fruit tarts does not require cooking, the crust must be fully baked before the toppings are added. Be sure to keep the crust covered with foil and weighted while it bakes. Without these precautions, a buttery sugar crust will brown too quickly, buckle, and shrink as it bakes.

If you prefer a simple short crust, use our piecrust recipe on page 307 or your own favorite, either plain or with a little sugar mixed in. Otherwise, try a crust of frozen puff pastry or the modified puff pastry explained in our Winter Fruit Tart variation at right.

SUGAR CRUST

Sugar in a pastry guarantees that it will be stickier to work with than plain pie dough, and any pastry made with butter becomes soft very quickly. Don't let either warning deter

you. Simply place the pastry in the refrigerator or freezer to firm up between each stage of preparation and work quickly when rolling and pressing it into the pan.

PASTRY CREAM

We've kept our pastry cream custard unflavored to let the fruit flavors dominate. If you want extra flavor, add 1/2 teaspoon of vanilla or almond extract, a bit of grated lemon or orange zest, or 1 teaspoon of Grand Marnier or other fruit liqueur. If the chilled pastry cream is too thick to spread smoothly, whisk hard to make it manageable.

GLAZED OVER

The glaze on most fruit tarts is simply jelly that is melted and allowed to set up once it has been brushed on. Strawberry or currant jelly gives fruit toppings a rosy blush as well as a sparkling finish. If you don't want the rosy tone, use a peach or apricot jelly.

If you do not plan to serve a tart as soon as it's done, brush the baked crust with a thin coating of glaze and let it gel before filling with pastry cream. It will help keep the crust from becoming soggy.

HOW TO ASSEMBLE A FRUIT TART

Prepare and bake the tart shell until golden. Keep the cooled shell in the pan while you fill and decorate it.

1 Pour cooled pastry cream into a tart shell and smooth to edges with a spatula.

2 Beginning at outer edge, arrange overlapping slices of fruit in concentric circles.

3 Using a pastry brush, brush glaze over fruit to edge of pastry.

WINTER FRUIT TART WITH RAISED CRUST

Prepare sugar crust as directed at right, **using** 1/2 cup (1 stick) butter and **omitting** sugar and egg. On a lightly floured work surface with a floured rolling pin, **roll** pastry into a 10- by 15-inch rectangle. **Fold** in thirds and **refrigerate** 20 minutes.

Roll the folded pastry into a rectangle as before. **Fold** the ends into the center, then **fold** in half crosswise. **Refrigerate** 20 minutes. Again **roll** pastry into a rectangle, **repeat** the double fold, and **refrigerate** 20 minutes. **Repeat** rolling, folding, and refrigerating one more time. Finally, **roll** pastry into a 71/2- by 10-inch rectangle.

Cut a 1/2-inch strip from each long side and **ease** remaining pastry onto a baking sheet. **Brush** long edges of rectangle with water and **press** strips on top to form a raised edge. **Prick** bottom of the pastry with a fork and **bake** at 350°F for 45 to 50 minutes. **Set** aside to cool completely.

Meanwhile, **prepare** pastry cream as directed. **Omit** fresh fruit and **prepare** a dried fruit topping: **Bring** 1 cup each sugar and water to a boil. **Place** 1 cup each dried apricots, pitted prunes, and seedless light raisins in separate small bowls. **Pour** sugar syrup equally into each and **let stand** at room temperature for 1 hour. **Spread** crust with pastry cream. **Drain** fruit and **pat** dry on paper toweling. **Arrange** fruit on pastry cream. **Omit** glaze. **Serve** immediately. Makes 6 to 8 servings.

Summer Tart

Sugar Crust:
- 1 cup unsifted all-purpose flour
- 1½ tablespoons sugar
- ¼ cup (½ stick) cold butter, cut up
- 1 egg yolk, lightly beaten
- 2 tablespoons ice water

Pastry Cream:
- 1½ cups milk
- ½ cup sugar
- 3 egg yolks
- 3 tablespoons all-purpose flour

Topping:
- 4 kiwifruits, peeled and thinly sliced
- 2 purple plums, halved, pitted, and thinly sliced
- 1 can (11 ounces) mandarin oranges, drained and patted very dry
- 15 raspberries

Glaze:
- ¼ cup strawberry jelly
- 1 tablespoon water

1 For the Crust: Pulse flour and sugar in a food processor to combine. Add butter and pulse until mixture resembles coarse meal. With the blade spinning, add egg yolk, then the water, 1 tablespoon at a time, until mixture forms a ball. Flatten ball slightly. Wrap in plastic wrap and refrigerate 1 hour.

2 On a lightly floured work surface using a floured rolling pin, roll pastry from the center out to form a 12-inch circle about ⅛-inch thick. Wrap pastry around a rolling pin and ease into a 10-inch tart pan with a removable bottom. Trim overhang to 1 inch higher than the pan edge, roll under to form edge, and press into rim of pan. Prick bottom and sides of pastry with a fork. Set in the freezer for 20 minutes.

3 For the Pastry Cream: In a medium-size saucepan over high heat, bring milk and ¼ cup of the sugar to a boil. Meanwhile, in a medium-size bowl, combine egg yolks with the remaining ¼ cup sugar and flour and whisk until smooth. Slowly whisk boiling milk mixture into yolk mixture. Return to saucepan, set over moderate heat, and whisk constantly until mixture comes to a boil. Continue to cook, whisking, for 1 minute. Strain through a sieve into a medium-size bowl. Smooth plastic wrap on the surface of the pastry cream and set aside to cool.

4 Preheat the oven to 350°F. Cover crust loosely with foil and weight with dried beans or baking weights. Bake until crust begins to brown—20 to 25 minutes; remove foil and beans and continue baking until crust is golden. Cool on a rack.

5 Assemble tart as directed at left. For the Glaze: In a small saucepan over moderately high heat, combine strawberry jelly and water and bring to a boil, whisking until smooth. Cool slightly and brush over fruit. Makes 6 servings.

1 Serving: Calories 404; Total Fat 13 g; Saturated Fat 7 g; Protein 8 g; Carbohydrates 66 g; Fiber 4 g; Sodium 127 mg; Cholesterol 153 mg

prep time-45 minutes • cooking time-50 minutes • resting time-1 hour 20 minutes

FRUIT PIES

The perfect fruit pie has a flaky crust and tastes of ripe fruit with a hint of spice. Follow these hints for great results.

FOR A CRISP CRUST

Most double-crust fruit pies are made with a plain short pastry. To prevent a soggy bottom crust, brush its interior with beaten egg white and allow it to air dry. Or sprinkle it with 2 tablespoons of dry bread crumbs before filling.

When ready to bake, set the pie on a preheated heavy-duty baking sheet in the oven. Start the pie at 425°F. After 15 minutes reduce the heat to 375°F.

A FINE FINISH

For a high-gloss top crust, before baking, brush the top with 1 egg beaten smooth with 1 teaspoon of sugar.

For a shiny crust, brush with 1 egg yolk beaten with 1 tablespoon of cold water.

For a satin-finish crust, brush with a little milk or cream.

For added crunch, sprinkle the glazed top crust with 1 teaspoon of sugar.

TO PATCH CRUST

Torn pie dough is easily mended. Moisten the dough around the torn area with cold water. Cut a piece of dough scrap slightly larger than the tear. Put the patch in place and press down firmly.

FOR PLUMP PIES

There is only one sure way to guarantee plump fruit pies. To a recipe of fruit filling add an extra 2 cups of prepared fruit. Place the fruit, sugar, butter, and seasonings in a skillet and cook, uncovered, over medium heat just until the fruit releases most of its juice. Drain the fruit, then boil the juice until reduced by half. Add the juice to the fruit and toss gently. Fill the pie shell, mounding fruit in the center so that it is about 2 inches higher than at the rim.

TO REDUCE FAT

As a butter substitute in the filling, use 2 tablespoons of marzipan (freeze the excess) blended with 2 tablespoons of skim milk. Or substitute 3 tablespoons of fruit butter.

Alternatively, bake open-face pies instead of double-crust pies. Or choose crumb crusts over conventional pastry.

TO AVOID BOILOVERS

Choose a pie pan with a channel or trough around the rim.

Add 1 to 1½ tablespoons of flour for each cup of fruit. Don't add extra liquid to the fruit.

Seal the pie by folding the top pastry under the bottom pastry at the pan rim, then crimp. Cut steam vents in the top crust.

BIGGER FRUIT FLAVOR

To boost the flavor of a pie, substitute light brown sugar or maple sugar for granulated.

Add 1 teaspoon of finely grated orange or lemon zest to the filling. Or dot the fruit with 2 tablespoons of marmalade. Orange or ginger marmalade is especially good in apple, peach, and pear pies.

APPLE CHOICES

Golden Delicious apples are a good choice because they hold their shape. Granny Smiths should not be used alone since they cook down to mush.

STREUSEL TOPPING

This quick and delicious topping can be used instead of a top crust.

In a bowl, **mix** ½ cup firmly packed light brown sugar, ½ cup sifted all-purpose flour, and ½ teaspoon ground cinnamon. **Using** a pastry blender, **cut in** ⅓ cup cold unsalted butter until mixture is crumbly. **Sprinkle** mixture evenly over any fruit pie. **Bake** as directed at right.

MIXING AND MATCHING APPLES

Apples vary in texture and flavor and are enjoyed for different purposes. Many sweet munching apples should not be used for pies since they become too soft when cooked. The apples listed below are choice pie apples. For the best results, use equal parts of two or three types, some sweet, some tart.

Tart	Flavor and Texture
Granny Smith	Moderately tart, firm, juicy
Jonathan	Mildly tart, crisp, juicy
Newtown Pippin	Piney tartness, crisp, coarse textured
Northern Spy	Tart, fine grained, tender, juicy
Rhode Island Greening	Pleasantly acidic, crisp, juicy
Winesap	Highly tart, spicy, crisp
Sweet	
Golden Delicious	Sweet, mild flavored, juicy
Gravenstein	Sweet/tart, crisp, juicy
McIntosh	Sweet/tart, aromatic, crisp, juicy
York Imperial	Slightly sweet, tender, juicy

Blue-Ribbon Apple Pie

- 1 recipe Double-Crust Pie Pastry (in box at right)
- 1/3 cup shredded Cheddar cheese (optional)
- 1 large egg, separated
- 4 tart apples
- 4 sweet apples
- 2 tablespoons lemon juice
- 1/2 cup firmly packed light brown sugar
- 1/2 cup granulated sugar
- 1/3 cup sifted all-purpose flour
- 1/4 teaspoon ground cinnamon
- 1/8 teaspoon ground allspice
- 1/8 teaspoon grated nutmeg
- 2 tablespoons butter
- 1 tablespoon cold water (optional)

1 Preheat the oven to 425°F. Make pastry, adding cheese to dry mixture if you wish. Fit ½ the pastry into a 9-inch pie pan, letting the edges hang over about 1 inch. In a cup, whisk egg white until frothy and brush on crust. Reserve yolk for top crust glaze. Roll top pastry and cut several slits for steam vents. Cover with plastic wrap until ready to use.

2 Peel, core, and slice apples ¼-inch thick, placing them in a bowl. Sprinkle with lemon juice as you go. Add sugars, flour, cinnamon, allspice, and nutmeg and toss lightly. Mound mixture in the piecrust; dot with butter.

3 Moisten rim of bottom pastry with a little water and place top pastry on pie. Seal the pie by folding top pastry under bottom pastry at the pan rim, then crimp. In a small bowl, make glaze for top (optional) by whisking together reserved egg yolk and cold water. Brush over top, carefully avoiding slits.

4 Bake at 425°F for 15 minutes; lower temperature to 375°F and bake 35 minutes more or until filling is bubbly and pastry nicely browned. If crimped edge browns too fast, cover with foil. Let pie cool on a rack for 20 minutes. Serve with ice cream or whipped cream. Makes 8 servings.

1 Serving: Calories 429; Total Fat 21 g; Saturated Fat 6 g; Protein 4 g; Carbohydrates 57 g; Fiber 2 g; Sodium 308 mg; Cholesterol 34 mg

prep time-1 hour • cooking time-50 minutes cooling time-20 minutes

DOUBLE-CRUST PIE PASTRY

For an 8- or 9-inch pie.

- 2 cups all-purpose flour
- 1 teaspoon salt
- 2/3 cup chilled vegetable shortening or lard
- 4-6 tablespoons ice water

1 In a mixing bowl, stir together flour and salt. Using a pastry blender, cut in shortening until mixture resembles coarse meal.

2 Sprinkle water over flour mixture 1 tablespoon at a time, mixing lightly with a fork, just until pastry holds together.

3 Divide pastry in half and shape into 2 balls. Flatten 1 ball slightly on a lightly floured work surface.

4 Using a floured rolling pin, roll pastry from center out to form a 12-inch circle about 1/8-inch thick.

5 Wrap pastry around rolling pin. Unroll into a pie pan. Repeat for top.

307

CHIFFON PIE

The filling in chiffon pie has a special quality. Egg yolks prepared with gelatin give it a custardy richness. Whipped egg whites make it light as air.

EGG WHITE UPDATE

Occasionally, an egg may be found to harbor the salmonella bacteria, which can be passed on by the hen or enter through a crack in the egg. Recipes that call for raw or partly cooked eggs, such as chiffon pie filling, carry a small risk of contamination.

To avoid the problem, we have used pasteurized dried egg whites, which are easily reconstituted and whipped to frothy heights. You may find dried egg whites in the baking section in supermarkets, or you can order it by calling 1-800-421-3447 or by writing to Deb El Foods, P.O. Box 876, Elizabeth, NJ 07206, U.S.A.

A SMOOTH FILLING

The custardy pie filling is thickened with a combination of gelatin and egg yolks. To ensure smoothness, cook the egg and gelatin mixture slowly, never letting it come to a boil. Whisk until thickened and heated to 160°F. This takes 5 to 8 minutes.

While the egg and gelatin mixture cools in the refrigerator, stir it occasionally to keep it from forming lumps.

When the custard mixture is sufficiently set, combine it with the egg whites. For maximum volume, add the egg whites by the spoonful, folding them in gradually so as not to lose the airiness of the whites.

CRUMB PIE SHELLS

Chiffon pie is traditionally made with a cookie crumb crust. Make the crumbs in a food processor or by sealing cookies in a heavy plastic bag and rolling with a rolling pin. To be sure the crumbs are evenly sized, grind only a few cookies at a time.

Crumb crusts can be used baked or unbaked. Baking the shell helps to hold it together. Tip: Unbaked shells will not crumble into the filling if frozen for 15 minutes first.

Purchased crumb shells may be too small for the amount of filling in our recipe. Extra filling can be eaten as pudding.

CHOCOLATE CHIFFON PIE

Prepare filling as directed at right, **substituting** 2 ounces finely chopped semisweet chocolate for lime zest and juice. Makes 8 servings.

PUMPKIN CHIFFON PIE

Prepare filling as directed at right, **substituting** 1/2 cup firmly packed light brown sugar for 1/2 cup granulated sugar and 3/4 cup milk for 1 cup water in Step 2. **Add** 1/2 teaspoon salt along with the gelatin. In Step 3, **reduce** number of egg yolks to 3. **Omit** lime zest and juice. In a large bowl, **combine** one 15-ounce can solid-pack pumpkin, 1 teaspoon ground cinnamon, 1/2 teaspoon ground ginger, and 1/4 teaspoon ground cloves. Gradually **stir** gelatin mixture into pumpkin mixture until well mixed. **Refrigerate**, covered, just until cool. **Proceed** with Steps 5 and 6 as directed. Makes 8 servings.

EGGNOG CHIFFON PIE

Prepare filling as directed at right, **adding** 1/2 teaspoon salt along with gelatin and **substituting** 1 cup milk for 1 cup water. **Omit** lime zest and juice and flavor with 1/3 cup dry sherry, 3/4 teaspoon ground nutmeg, and 1 teaspoon vanilla. Also, in Step 5, **reduce** sugar to 1/4 cup. Makes 8 servings.

TOP IT OFF

A piped ruffle of whipped cream around the edge of the crust gives chiffon pie a festive look. Garnish a citrus-flavored chiffon pie with a sprig of mint or a curl of zest. Glamorize an eggnog or chocolate chiffon pie with grated nutmeg or chocolate shavings or curls (see page 326).

FILL 'ER UP

1 Prepare the custard and let it set in the refrigerator until thick enough to form mounds when dropped from a spoon.

2 Fold egg whites into the custard, scooping custard from the bottom of the bowl over the top of the mound of egg whites.

Lime Chiffon Pie

Crumb Crust:

1¼ cups graham cracker or vanilla or chocolate wafer crumbs

5 tablespoons butter or margarine, melted

¼ cup sugar

1 teaspoon ground cinnamon, nutmeg, ginger, or other desired spice (optional)

Filling:

¾ cup sugar

1 envelope (¼ ounce) unflavored gelatin

1½ cups warm water

4 egg yolks, lightly beaten

1 to 2 tablespoons grated lime zest

⅓ to ½ cup lime juice

3 tablespoons pasteurized dried egg whites

1 For the Crust: In a medium-size bowl, toss crumbs, butter, sugar, and, if desired, cinnamon, with a fork until well mixed. Press mixture firmly into a 9-inch pie pan and refrigerate while preparing filling. (For a crisper crust, bake in a preheated 375°F oven for 6 to 8 minutes.)

2 For the Filling: In a small saucepan over low heat, combine ¼ cup of the sugar and gelatin. Gradually pour in 1 cup of the water and cook until sugar and gelatin are completely dissolved, occasionally scraping down sides of the pan with a rubber spatula.

3 Stirring constantly, pour gelatin mixture into egg yolks. Return to the pan and cook, stirring constantly, until an instant-read thermometer registers 160°F and mixture thickens—5 to 8 minutes.

4 Remove saucepan to a rack and stir in lime zest and juice. Smooth plastic wrap on the surface of the mixture and refrigerate, stirring occasionally, until mixture thickens and mounds when dropped from a spoon—about 45 minutes.

5 In the bowl of an electric mixer, sprinkle egg whites over the remaining ½ cup water and beat until dissolved. Continue beating until foamy, gradually adding the remaining ½ cup sugar. Beat until soft peaks form.

6 Gradually fold egg whites into thickened gelatin mixture until no streaks of white remain. Pour into prepared crust and refrigerate until set—3 to 4 hours. Makes 8 servings.

1 Serving: Calories 279; Total Fat 12 g; Saturated Fat 6 g; Protein 4 g; Carbohydrates 41 g; Fiber 1 g; Sodium 221 mg; Cholesterol 126 mg

prep time-45 minutes • cooking time-15 minutes • chilling time-4 to 5 hours

MERINGUE PIES

For a delicious finale to a summer meal, serve a light and refreshing meringue pie. Our meringue whips up high, wide, and handsome.

NEW MERINGUE

Traditionally, the meringue on pies is made with the whites of separated eggs beaten stiff with about 1/3 cup of sugar and 1/4 teaspoon of cream of tartar. Then they are piled onto the pie while the filling is still hot.

As an alternative, we have made the meringue on our pie with pasteurized dried egg whites because of concerns about the safety of raw eggs. The meringue topping does not remain in the oven long enough to actually cook through. See page 308 for more information about eggs.

PERFECT FILLING

The finest flavored lemon curd filling for pies starts with freshly squeezed lemon juice and grated lemon zest. Lemon curd can be made with or without cornstarch. Our version contains cornstarch to help it thicken smoothly.

Lemon curd can be prepared in a heavy saucepan over moderate heat. But if you've had trouble with lumps forming because the curd thickens too quickly on the pan bottom, use a double boiler and be sure to stir the mixture continuously. Wait until the filling is cooked before stirring in the lemon juice and zest. Citric acid slows the thickening process.

PIE SHELLS

Lemon meringue pies are usually made with a conventional pie shell. If you prefer, use a crumb crust. For further information about crumb crusts, see page 308. Our fancy edges, at right, are made with traditional piecrust and can be used with any pie.

MERINGUE TIPS

Spoon the meringue onto the pie, mounding it in the center and pushing it to the edge. Be sure the meringue touches the pastry all the way around. This keeps it from shrinking as it bakes. Use a small spatula to swirl the meringue.

Keep an eye on the meringue in the oven; it can darken very quickly. To prevent the meringue from beading or "weeping," make sure the oven temperature is not too high.

Let the pie cool before serving. To make it easier to cut through the meringue topping, use a wet knife.

TWO PRETTY EDGES FOR PIES

For a Scalloped Edge

1 Scallop the edge using a teaspoon and your fingers to form curves.

2 Press the tines of the fork in the center of each scallop for added decoration.

For a Twisted Edge

1 Cut and twist 2 strips of pastry about 1/2-inch wide. Dampen the pie rim.

2 Attach the braid to the rim, pressing it lightly to secure.

LIME MERINGUE PIE

Prepare crust as directed at right. For the Filling: In a medium-size saucepan, **beat** 3 egg yolks with one 14-ounce can sweetened condensed milk and 1/4 teaspoon salt until smooth. **Stir** in 2 teaspoons grated lime zest and 1/3 cup lime juice. **Set** over moderately low heat and **cook, stirring**, just until mixture registers 160°F on a candy thermometer. **Pour** hot filling into crust; **top** with meringue. **Bake** as directed. Makes 8 servings.

WORK SAVER

Pastry Mat and Rolling Pin Sleeve

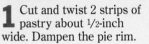

These accessories eliminate problems with sticking piecrust. The knitted-cotton rolling pin sleeve easily pulls off for washing. Many plastic pastry mats indicate what size to roll the dough for different pans. Mats make it easy to lift the dough and to clean up.

Lemon Meringue Pie

Crust:
- 1⅓ cups unsifted all-purpose flour
- ¼ teaspoon salt
- ½ cup chilled vegetable shortening
- 2 to 3 tablespoons cold water

Filling:
- 1 cup sugar
- ¼ cup cornstarch
- ¼ teaspoon salt
- 1½ cups cold water
- 3 egg yolks, lightly beaten
- 2 teaspoons grated lemon zest
- ⅓ cup lemon juice
- 1 tablespoon butter or margarine

Meringue:
- 3 tablespoons pasteurized dried egg whites
- 6 tablespoons warm water
- ⅓ cup sugar

1 For the Crust: In a large bowl, combine flour and salt. Using a pastry blender, cut in shortening until mixture resembles coarse meal. Sprinkle in water, 1 tablespoon at a time, forking until dough holds together. Shape into a ball, flatten slightly, wrap in plastic wrap, and refrigerate 15 to 30 minutes.

2 Preheat the oven to 475°F. On a lightly floured work surface, roll pastry from the center out to form an 11-inch circle about ⅛-inch thick. Wrap pastry around rolling pin and ease into a 9-inch pie plate. Trim overhang to 1 inch, roll under, and crimp, making a high fluted edge. Prick bottom and sides with a fork.

3 Cover crust loosely with foil. Weight with dried beans or baking weights and bake 8 to 10 minutes; remove foil and beans and bake until crust is golden—5 minutes more. Reduce the heat to 350°F. Remove to a rack and cool to room temperature.

4 For the Filling: In a medium-size saucepan, combine sugar, cornstarch, and salt. Gradually blend in water, set over moderate heat, and cook, stirring constantly, until mixture boils and thickens—about 3 minutes. Remove from the heat, blend a little of the hot mixture into beaten egg yolks, then stir back into the pan. Stir in lemon zest and juice and butter. Pour hot filling into the pie shell.

5 For the Meringue: In the bowl of an electric mixer, sprinkle egg whites over water and beat until foamy. With the mixer running, add sugar, 1 tablespoon at a time, then continue beating until soft peaks form.

6 Spoon meringue onto hot filling, swirling it into peaks and making sure it touches the crust all around. Bake until meringue is lightly tipped with brown—10 to 15 minutes. Remove to a rack; cool to room temperature. Makes 8 servings.

1 Serving: Calories 377; Total Fat 16 g; Saturated Fat 5 g; Protein 5 g; Carbohydrates 54 g; Fiber 1 g; Sodium 172 mg; Cholesterol 84 mg

prep time–45 minutes • chilling time–15 minutes cooking time–35 minutes

HARD MERINGUES

Meringue shells are a delight to eat. They're crunchy, sweet, and light without a speck of fat. Fill them with fruit or creamy toppings.

EGG WHITE TIPS

Meringue shells are baked long enough to cook through, so it's perfectly safe to use fresh egg whites in making them. When baked, meringues should be crisp and dry but not brown.

Eggs are easiest to separate when they are refrigerator cold, but the whites whip into peaks best when they've been brought to room temperature.

For the best results, use a round-bottomed bowl so that all of the egg whites are beaten evenly.

TINY BUBBLES

Tiny bubbles make the loftiest egg whites. To be sure that large bubbles are not formed at the start, begin whipping the whites slowly and gradually build up speed.

For egg whites of maximum height that are perfectly blended with the sugar, begin adding the granulated sugar about halfway through the whipping process.

To tell if the beaten egg whites and sugar have been fully blended, rub a dab of the mixture between your fingers. It should feel smooth; if grainy, beat 1/2 minute longer.

Perfectly beaten egg whites should stand in glossy peaks. If overbeaten, egg whites become dry and limp. Rescue overbeaten egg whites by beating in an extra egg white separately until glossy, then mixing it in with the others.

NO MOISTURE ALLOWED

Don't try to make meringue shells on a wet day. Humidity causes meringues to lose their crispness and to become gummy on the inside.

COOKING AHEAD

Meringue shells can be made several days before serving. Wrap in plastic wrap or foil and store in a cool, dry spot but not in the refrigerator.

MORE GOOD THINGS

Individual meringues and angel pies can be filled with any of the chiffon fillings on page 308.

You can also serve meringue shells filled with melon balls for a fat-free dessert. Or serve them filled with pastry cream, ice cream, or sherbet topped with fruit. Try them with lightly sweetened fresh strawberries or sliced peaches.

HOW TO MAKE MERINGUE SHELLS

Meringues can be formed with or without a pastry bag. Bake on a parchment-lined baking sheet. To make the parchment lie flat, put a few small dabs of meringue on the baking sheet, then put the parchment on top.

To Make Shells with a Pastry Tube

1 Fit pastry bag with a size 6 star tip. Pipe 6 coiled circles of meringue.

2 Pipe a second-tier ring of meringue along the outer edge of each circle.

To Make Shells with a Spoon

1 Make 6 equal-size mounds of meringue on a parchment-lined baking sheet.

2 Use the back of a tablespoon to make a hollow in the center of each mound.

To Make an Angel Piecrust

1 Spray a pie plate with nonstick vegetable spray or oil lightly. Fill with meringue.

2 Using the back of a spoon, spread meringue evenly from the center out.

Chocolate Angel Pie

Prepare meringue as in Step 1 at right, **halving** ingredients. **Spray** an 8-inch pie pan with non-stick vegetable spray and **spoon** in meringue. Starting from the center, **smooth** meringue evenly with a large spoon to form a pie shell. **Bake** as directed in Step 3. **Prepare** Chocolate Chiffon Pie filling as directed on page 308. **Spoon** into meringue shell and **chill** until set. Makes 6 servings.

Meringue Shells with Raspberry Sauce

Meringues:
- **1 cup egg whites (10 large eggs)**
- **3/4 cup granulated sugar**
- **1/2 cup sifted confectioners' sugar**

Sauce:
- **1/2 cup sugar**
- **1/2 cup water**
- **2 tablespoons Grand Marnier**
- **2 cups fresh raspberries**

1 For the Meringues: Preheat the oven to 250°F. In the large bowl of an electric mixer, slowly beat egg whites until frothy. With the mixer on low, gradually add ½ cup of the granulated sugar and continue beating until silvery. Raise mixer speed to moderate and slowly add the remaining ¼ cup of sugar, beating just until stiff peaks form. Fold in confectioners' sugar.

2 Pipe meringues into shapes with a pastry bag as shown at left or mound 1 cup of meringue at a time on a parchment-lined baking sheet. With a large spoon, make a well in the meringue. Repeat to make 5 more.

3 Bake 1 hour. Turn off oven (do not open door) and let meringues stand for 1 hour. Remove to a rack to cool.

4 For the Sauce: In a small saucepan over high heat, bring sugar and water to a boil; cool. Add Grand Marnier and raspberries and let stand for 2 minutes. Drain raspberries and spoon ⅓ cup into each meringue shell. Makes 6 servings.

1 Serving: Calories 251; Total Fat 0 g; Saturated Fat 0 g; Protein 5 g; Carbohydrates 57 g; Fiber 2 g; Sodium 67 mg; Cholesterol 0 mg

prep time-1 hour • cooking time-1 hour standing time-1 hour

FRESH ICE CREAM

Homemade ice cream is hard to beat. Best of all, it can be made richer or lighter, tarter or sweeter to suit your taste.

COLD COMFORT

To make true ice cream, you need an ice cream maker, which freezes the milk and cream slowly while in motion, so that large ice crystals do not have the chance to form.

Fortunately, there are electric ice cream makers (and hand-cranked models too) available today in every price range. The quality of the products varies, of course, but even inexpensive ice cream makers do a good job quickly. If they are cleaned, dried, and stored properly after each use, they will last a long time.

Making ice cream is great fun for parties and family get-togethers. Follow the manufacturer's directions to use your ice cream maker for mixing up ice milk, frozen yogurt, and sherbet as well.

ICE CREAM BASICS

Ice cream recipes always begin with a base in which some of the liquid ingredients are heated along with sugar and flavorings. This step ensures that the sugar dissolves properly and that the vanilla, chocolate, fruit, or other flavorings develop fully.

The base for our recipe is a super-rich French vanilla. It's a classic custard ice cream base made with egg yolks as well as milk and cream—meant to be eaten in small servings!

FLAVORFUL BEANS

We use a vanilla bean to flavor our ice cream base as it heats. Be sure to split the bean to release its essence. If you prefer to use vanilla extract instead, do not add it until after the base has been taken from the heat and cooled.

EGGLESS CREAM

You can also make a delicious—and less rich—ice cream without the eggs. For 2 quarts of vanilla ice cream, you'll need 1 quart of light cream, 1½ cups of sugar, 2 tablespoons of vanilla extract, and a pint of heavy cream.

Heat the light cream and sugar until the sugar dissolves fully. When the mixture has cooled, stir in the vanilla extract and

DOUBLE CHOCOLATE ICE CREAM

Prepare as directed at right, **substituting** firmly packed light brown sugar for granulated sugar. Also, **whisk** ¼ cup unsweetened Dutch-process cocoa powder into yolk-sugar mixture. Finally, **add** ½ cup mini chocolate chips to cold custard. Makes 1 quart, 8 servings.

MINT CHOCOLATE CHIP ICE CREAM

Prepare as directed at right, **adding** 1 cup puréed fresh mint leaves to milk in Step 1. **Add** ½ cup mini chocolate chips to cold custard. Makes 1 quart, 8 servings.

STRAWBERRY ICE CREAM

Prepare as directed at right, **adding** four 3- by ½-inch strips orange zest to custard while cooking, then **remove** along with the vanilla bean. In a food processor, **purée** 2 cups rinsed, hulled strawberries with ⅓ cup sugar and **stir** into cold custard. Makes 1 quart, 8 servings.

BLUEBERRY ICE CREAM

In a medium-size saucepan over moderate heat, **cook** 2 cups stemmed blueberries with ⅓ cup sugar and four 2- by ½-inch strips lemon zest, **stirring** frequently, until very soft—4 to 5 minutes. **Push** mixture through a fine sieve. **Stir** in ½ teaspoon ground white pepper and ½ teaspoon ground ginger. **Proceed** as directed, **stirring** blueberry purée into cold custard. Makes 1 quart, 8 servings.

PEACH ICE CREAM

Blanch, **peel**, and **pit** 2 large ripe peaches. Finely **chop** and **toss** with ⅓ cup firmly packed light brown sugar, 1 tablespoon lemon juice, and ¼ teaspoon ground ginger. **Prepare** as directed, **stirring** purée into cold custard. Makes 1 quart, 8 servings.

heavy cream. Chill and proceed as directed in the recipe.

FRUIT IN CREAM

Chopped and crushed fruit must be mixed or cooked with sugar before it's blended into ice cream. Without this step, the fruit will freeze into rock-hard tooth-cracking lumps.

PACK IT IN

Ice cream is very soft when it has finished turning in an ice cream maker. Pack it down well in its container, cover, and set it in the refrigerator freezer for several hours to mellow the flavor and firm up the texture.

French Vanilla Ice Cream

1³/₄ **cups milk**
2¹/₄ **cups heavy cream**
  1 **cup sugar**
  1 **vanilla bean, split lengthwise**
¹/₄ **teaspoon salt**
  6 **egg yolks**

1 In a large saucepan over moderate heat, scald milk and cream with ½ cup of the sugar, the vanilla bean, and salt just until small bubbles appear.

2 In a medium-size bowl, whisk egg yolks and the remaining ½ cup sugar. Gradually whisk a little milk mixture into yolk mixture, then pour back into pan. Cook over low heat, whisking constantly, until mixture coats a spoon—about 15 minutes.

3 Remove from the heat and cool to room temperature. Scrape seeds from vanilla bean into custard; discard the pod. Refrigerate custard, covered, until cold—1 to 2 hours.

4 Transfer to an ice cream maker and freeze according to manufacturer's directions. Makes 1 quart, 8 servings.

One ½-Cup Serving: Calories 405; Total Fat 30 g; Saturated Fat 18 g; Protein 5 g; Carbohydrates 30 g; Fiber 0 g; Sodium 124 mg; Cholesterol 259 mg

prep time-10 minutes • cooking time-15 minutes

LOW-FAT ICE CREAM

Prepare any of the ice creams on these pages as directed, **substituting** evaporated skim milk for whole milk and ³/₄ cup egg substitute for egg yolks. Makes 1 quart, 8 servings.

HOMEMADE ICES

I f it's refreshment you're after, nothing will cool you down or tingle your palate quite like a freshly frozen ice.

ICE PICKS

There are three kinds of ices popular today; our recipes include examples of each.

Sherbet is as smooth as ice cream but contains no cream. It can be made with milk, sugar, and flavorings or with fruit juices and water thickened with gelatin. Milk sherbet may be flavored with vanilla or chocolate, though fruit flavors are more typical.

Formerly, a third option for sherbet was to make it with egg whites. However, that method is no longer recommended because the egg whites in sherbet are not cooked and carry the risk of salmonella poisoning.

Sorbet is the French word for sherbet. It refers to ices made simply with fruit purées, sugar, and water.

Granitas are refreshing Italian-style ices, which are coarse textured and flavored with coffee, tea, fruit juices, or even wines.

FREEZING NOTES

Sherbets and sorbets are best made in an ice cream maker because the churning action allows the mixture to freeze slowly and smoothly with no large crunchy ice crystals.

There are many fine inexpensive and easy-to-use ice cream makers available today. They can be used for all kinds of fruit ices and ice creams.

EASY GRANITA

Granita should be made in the freezer rather than in an ice cream maker since coarse-textured crystals are important to its refreshing iciness. The process for making it is shown in the box at right.

FREEZER-MADE SHERBET

If you want to make sherbet or sorbet in the freezer without an ice cream maker, pour the mixture into pans as directed for granita. When the mixture begins to freeze, turn it out into a bowl and beat it with an electric mixer until fluffy.

Return the mixture to the tray or pan and freeze until firm. For finer textured sherbet, repeat the beating and refreezing 2 or 3 times.

JUICY FRUIT

If you're making milk sherbet, stir fruit juices into the milk mixture only after it's cooled; otherwise, it may curdle.

Using partially thawed frozen fruit juices and lemon- and limeade mixes to flavor an ice gives the mixture a head start in chilling.

When using fresh apples, pears, apricots, peaches, and nectarines, peel, core, and seed the fruits. Purée the fruit in a food processor or by pressing through a food mill. Add a little lemon or lime juice while puréeing to spark up the flavor and prevent the fruit from darkening.

For an unusual brilliant red-colored sherbet, sorbet, or granita, try pomegranate juice. To extract the juice, cut the pomegranates in half crosswise. Pull out the white membranes separating the seeds and ream each half on a juicer or reamer.

BERRY GOOD

The seeds in raspberries and blackberries should be strained out before they are frozen into sherbets or ices.

Purée fresh ripe or thawed frozen berries by pressing them through a fine sieve with the back of a spoon.

HOW TO MAKE FREEZER GRANITA

Granita is easily made in freezer trays. It needs to be stirred—but not too often—while it freezes.

1 Pour the granita mixture into an 8- by 8-inch pan or 2 ice-cube trays and freeze. When the mixture begins to form ice crystals, stir with a fork. Repeat 2 or 3 times during freezing process.

2 To serve, scrape across the surface with a spoon so that the frozen mixture comes up in thin shavings.

WORK SAVER
Ice Cream Maker

Today's ice cream makers run the gamut from inexpensive to costly. There is one for every pocketbook. Some use ice; some chill without it. All can be used for sherbets and sorbets as well as for ice cream.

Raspberry Sorbet

Prepare as directed at right, **substituting** one 10-ounce package thawed frozen raspberries for strawberries and 1 cup water for milk. Also, **add** 1 tablespoon lemon juice in Step 3. Makes 4 servings.

Cassis Sorbet

Prepare as directed at right, **substituting** 1½ cups water for milk and **reducing** sugar to ½ cup. **Omit** strawberries; instead, **add** 1 cup cassis (black currant liqueur) to syrup mixture. Makes 4 servings.

Citrus Sorbet

Prepare as directed at right, **substituting** 1 cup water for milk. **Omit** strawberries; instead, **add** 1¼ cups orange juice, ¼ cup lemon juice, and 3 tablespoons lime juice in Step 3. Makes 4 servings.

Orange-Espresso Granita

Prepare as directed at right, **substituting** 1½ cups water for milk. **Omit** strawberries; instead, **add** 2 tablespoons instant espresso powder and 2 tablespoons orange juice in Step 3. **Omit** Step 4. Instead, **pour** mixture into an 8" x 8" x 2" pan and **set** in the freezer. When small crystals begin to form, **stir** mixture with a fork; **stir** again 10 minutes later. **Continue** to freeze until large crystals form. To serve, **scrape** with a large spoon so that the ice breaks into shavings. Makes 4 servings.

Strawberry Milk Sherbet

1 **pint strawberries, rinsed and hulled**
1 **cup milk**
1 **cup sugar**

1 In a food processor, purée strawberries until smooth.

2 In a medium-size saucepan over high heat, bring milk and sugar to a rolling boil. Remove from the heat and cool until just warm.

3 In a medium-size bowl, whisk together milk mixture and strawberries.

4 Transfer to an ice cream maker and freeze according to manufacturer's directions. Makes 1 pint, 4 servings.

One ½-Cup Serving: Calories 253; Total Fat 2 g; Saturated Fat 1 g; Protein 2 g; Carbohydrates 58 g; Fiber 1 g; Sodium 31 mg; Cholesterol 8 mg

prep time-10 minutes

CREAMY MOUSSE

An airy mousse, so delicious to eat and impressive to serve, is really just a soft meringue and whipped cream flavored and folded together.

MERINGUE TO START

Swiss, or cooked, meringue (egg whites whipped with boiling sugar syrup over boiling water) is the base of our Chocolate Mousse. This is the safe alternative to making mousse the traditional way with whipped raw eggs.

Our cooking process brings the egg whites up to 160°F, thus destroying any salmonella bacteria—and eliminating the risk of food poisoning—that can be present in raw eggs. The process also stabilizes the airy beaten whites so they won't collapse. Seven minute icing is made the same way.

Note: You can also make mousse by using pasteurized dried egg whites instead of a cooked meringue.

LIGHT AND CREAMY

For whipped cream that stands tall, use heavy cream. Ultrapasteurized heavy cream does not whip as fast or as dramatically as regular heavy cream.

For cream to whip properly, it must be ice cold. It whips more quickly and stiffly if the bowl and beaters are cold too. If you use a portable beater, anchor the bowl on a kitchen

towel to help keep it from moving along the counter as the cream is whipped.

Cream for mousse should be whipped just before it is folded into the egg base. For stable whipped cream, dissolve 1/2 teaspoon of gelatin in 1 tablespoon of water by warming it in a ramekin in a small pan of water over moderate heat; cool

WORK SAVER
Candy Thermometer

A reliable candy thermometer is essential to a good sugar syrup. Test a thermometer's accuracy by placing it in a pan of cold water and bringing the water to a boil. Let it boil 10 minutes. If the thermometer registers higher or lower than 212°F, compensate accordingly when cooking candy or sugar syrups.

CAPPUCCINO MOUSSE

Prepare as directed at right, **adding** 1/2 teaspoon ground cinnamon to melting chocolate and **substituting** 1/4 cup freshly brewed espresso for water in the sugar syrup. If you like, **whip** an additional 1/2 cup cream and spoon on top before serving. Makes 8 servings.

and combine with 1 cup of cold heavy cream, then whip.

CHOCOLATE NOTES

The finer the quality of the chocolate you use, the finer the flavor of your dessert. For a grand finale, it may be worth a splurge on an especially good semisweet chocolate.

Chocolate scorches easily. For the best results, melt it in a double boiler or slip a flame moderator under the saucepan.

TABLE READY

Mousse makes a delicious filling for layer cakes, angel pies, tarts, and éclairs. If thinned with a little extra cream, it can also be ladled over angel cake.

WHIP AND FOLD

1 Beat egg whites in a heatproof bowl until frothy. Set the bowl, double-boiler style, in a saucepan over boiling water and continue beating on low while drizzling in boiling sugar syrup.

2 Whisk 1/3 of the hot meringue into the chocolate mixture. Gradually fold in balance.

3 With a rubber spatula, gently fold whipped cream into the chocolate mixture.

Chocolate Mousse

- 8 ounces semisweet chocolate, coarsely chopped
- 3 eggs, separated
- ¾ cup heavy cream
- ½ cup sugar
- ¼ cup water
- 1 teaspoon vanilla extract

1 In a double boiler, melt chocolate over simmering water. Meanwhile, beat egg yolks until thick. Whisk some of the melted chocolate into the egg yolks, then whisk egg yolk mixture back into the double boiler. Whisk in ¼ cup of the cream. Cook and stir until mixture thickens and reaches 160°F—about 4 minutes. Cool to room temperature, whisking often.

2 In a small saucepan over moderate heat, bring sugar and water to a boil. Brush the sides of the pan down with a pastry brush dipped in water, then cook without stirring until a candy thermometer inserted into the mixture registers 238°F—about 5 minutes.

3 In a medium-size heatproof bowl, with an electric mixer at medium speed, beat egg whites until frothy. Set bowl, double-boiler style, in saucepan over boiling water. At low speed, gradually beat in boiling sugar syrup until meringue peaks stiffly and a candy thermometer inserted at the center reaches 160°F. Whisk ⅓ cup of the hot meringue into the chocolate mixture, then fold in balance.

4 Beat the remaining ½ cup of the cream until soft peaks form; beat in vanilla. Fold into the chocolate mixture, transfer to serving dishes, and refrigerate, covered, at least 1 hour or until ready to serve. Makes 8 servings.

1 Serving: Calories 278; Total Fat 16 g; Saturated Fat 3 g; Protein 5 g; Carbohydrates 30 g; Fiber 0 g; Sodium 33 mg; Cholesterol 95 mg

prep time-9 minutes
cooking time-12 minutes
chilling time-1 hour

DESSERT SOUFFLÉS

Dessert soufflés are often served with a sweetened sauce. We've flavored our soufflé with an apricot purée and topped it with a vanilla custard.

THE RIGHT START

The most important elements of a soufflé are the perfectly whipped egg whites that form glossy, not dry, peaks. For the best results, be sure the eggs are fresh and let them come to room temperature before whipping.

Never use a plastic bowl for whipping egg whites: Traces of oil cling to plastic and will prevent egg whites from whipping properly. For more soufflé basics, see page 288.

SWEET AND SMOOTH

Like their savory cousins, dessert soufflés start with a base of white sauce. However, for the dessert version, the sauce is sweetened with sugar while it thickens. Ours is also enriched with a fruit purée.

When making any kind of sweet soufflé—fruit, chocolate, vanilla, or another—wait until the hot egg and white sauce mixture has been taken off the heat for a few minutes before mixing in the flavoring.

There are two ways to avoid curdling the egg yolks when they are mixed with the white sauce. The easiest is to let the white sauce cool to lukewarm before blending the two. But a quicker method is to mix a very small amount of the hot white sauce into the egg yolks to gently warm them through before stirring them into the remaining white sauce.

A soufflé can be prepared ahead to the point when the yolks and white sauce are blended. To prevent a skin from forming, smooth plastic wrap flat on the surface and chill until ready to proceed.

PERFECT FOLDING

The second most important element of a soufflé is proper folding—incorporating the whipped egg whites into the heavier yolk mixture. The trick is to fold in the whites without losing their frothiness.

The best way to fold soufflé ingredients is to add the whites in stages. First, blend 1/4 to 1/3 of the whites into the yolk mixture, beating them vigorously with a balloon whip or a whisk. This aerates and lightens the mixture and makes the folding process easier.

Scoop the rest of the whites into a mound on top of the yolk mixture. With a rubber spatula, cut down through the center, then along the bottom and

JAB AND SERVE

To prevent a soufflé from collapsing completely after the first cut, hold the serving fork and spoon perpendicular to the top and plunge them into the center. Scoop out individual servings.

FRUIT SOUFFLÉS

Prepare as directed at right, **substituting** 1 cup of any fruit purée—peach, raspberry, or strawberry, for example—for apricot purée. Makes 4 servings

up one side of the bowl. Bring the yolk mixture up and over the whites. Repeat, turning the bowl as you go, until the whites have been incorporated.

VOLUME BAKING

To make a soufflé rise extra tall, pour the batter into the

CUSTARD SAUCE

1½ cups milk
¼ cup sugar
⅛ teaspoon salt
3 egg yolks, lightly beaten
¾ teaspoon vanilla

1 In a medium-size saucepan over low heat, heat milk, sugar, and salt just until small bubbles appear on the surface. In a medium-size bowl, whisk ¼ cup of the milk mixture into egg yolks, then stir back into the pan. Cook over low heat, whisking constantly, until mixture coats the back of a spoon—about 10 minutes.

2 Remove from the heat and strain through a fine sieve into a bowl. Stir in vanilla. Cool to room temperature and refrigerate, covered, until ready to serve.

Note: This sauce can be made as much as a day ahead and refrigerated.

baking dish. Using a thin spatula, draw a circle in the batter 1 inch from the rim of the dish. During baking, the center will puff 1½ to 2 inches higher into a "top hat."

KITCHEN CHEMISTRY

Why do soufflés rise? When egg whites are beaten stiff, they're made up of countless minute air bubbles. When placed in a hot oven, every bubble expands, causing the soufflé to rise. The moment a soufflé is taken from the oven, the bubbles begin to contract, and the soufflé begins its descent. That's why it is necessary to get it to the table and serve it within 5 minutes.

Apricot Soufflé with Custard Sauce

- **3** tablespoons plus 1 teaspoon butter or margarine
- **1/2** cup plus 1 tablespoon sugar
- **1** can (17 ounces) pitted apricots in syrup, drained
- **3** tablespoons all-purpose flour
- **1** cup milk
- **1/2** teaspoon grated lemon zest
- **1/8** teaspoon salt
- **3** whole eggs, separated, plus 1 egg white
- **2** tablespoons lemon juice
- **2** tablespoons Grand Marnier

1 Prepare the custard sauce as described at left. For the Soufflé: Preheat the oven to 375°F. Butter a 6-cup soufflé dish using the 1 teaspoon butter. Sprinkle in the 1 tablespoon sugar and tilt the dish to coat evenly. Tap out excess sugar.

2 In a food processor, purée apricots and set aside.

3 In a medium-size saucepan over moderate heat, melt the remaining 3 tablespoons butter. Blend in flour and cook, stirring constantly, until smooth—about 2 minutes. Gradually add milk, lemon zest, salt, and the remaining 1/2 cup sugar and cook, stirring frequently, until thickened—about 4 minutes.

4 In a medium-size bowl, beat egg yolks until just combined. Whisk 1/2 cup of the hot milk mixture into yolks, then stir back into the pan. Cook over low heat, whisking constantly, until smooth and thick—about 3 minutes. Remove from the heat and stir in lemon juice, Grand Marnier, and apricot purée.

5 In an electric mixer, beat egg whites just until stiff peaks form. Do not overbeat. Mix about 1/4 of the egg whites into yolk mixture to lighten it, then gently fold in the remaining egg whites until no streaks remain.

6 Pour mixture into the prepared dish, place on a baking sheet, and bake, uncovered, in the lower third of the oven until puffed, golden brown, and the center jiggles only slightly when the dish is nudged—about 35 to 40 minutes. Serve immediately with the chilled custard sauce. Makes 4 servings.

1 Serving: Calories 538; Total Fat 22 g; Saturated Fat 12 g; Protein 14 g; Carbohydrates 69 g; Fiber 1 g; Sodium 279 mg; Cholesterol 366 mg

prep time-9 minutes • cooking time-57 minutes

CUSTARDS

Crème caramel and crème brûlée may be the most popular of all dessert custards. Our notes tell you how to make them without a chance of curdling.

CUSTARD TLC

Custard is easy to make, but certain rules must be followed in mixing, baking, and cooling.

When preparing the eggs, whisk them until combined, but don't overdo it. If bubbles form, they can bake right into the custard.

EGG EXCHANGE

Keep in mind that the greater the proportion of egg yolks in the custard mix, the smoother the texture will be, but the slower the custard will set. (Egg whites cook faster than yolks.) If you want to substitute whole eggs for yolks to save on fat and calories, the custard will set just fine, but you must keep an eye on the clock. Figure on 1 whole egg for each 2 yolks.

GOOD TIMING

Custard is usually baked in a somewhat thick-walled glass or ceramic dish or mold. There is a wide range of sizes and shapes to choose from, but if you select a dish or mold other than the one directed in a recipe, remember that the baking time will change.

Custard cooked in individual ramekins bakes at 325°F for about 45 minutes; in an 8-inch-wide flan mold at 325°F for 50 to 55 minutes; or in a 6-cup baking dish at 325°F for about 70 minutes.

READY, SET, COOL

It's important not to overcook custard. As soon as the eggs are set, it must be taken from the oven or it will separate into water and curds.

A custard should still be quivery when you take it from the oven: It will set up as it cools. You'll know that a custard is done if a knife stuck into the center about 1/2 inch comes out clean but moist.

NO CURDLING ALLOWED

Custards will curdle unless baked at a moderately low temperature, 325°F. Even then they may break and "weep" if left too long in the oven.

To ensure that custards cook evenly, bake them in a water bath. Choose a baking pan large enough to hold 8 ramekins without touching. Lay a folded kitchen towel in the pan, place the ramekins on top—the towel will prevent the ramekins from shifting or col-

CARAMELIZING

As the sugar syrup begins to brown, stir it or swirl the pan slowly and continuously so that the color develops evenly.

liding. Fill the ramekins with custard. Then set the pan on the oven shelf and pour in enough boiling water to come halfway up the sides of the ramekins.

As soon as the custards are done, remove them from the water bath so they stop cooking; then cool and refrigerate.

CARAMEL WATCH

Keep an eye on the sugar as it caramelizes. It can go from amber to dark brown very quickly. Adding a small amount of water to the sugar helps to slow down the process and prevent the sugar from scorching.

BOTTOMS UP

If made in ramekins or a flan mold, a custard should be unmolded when served. Run a knife around the edge to let in some air. Place the serving plate on top and quickly invert the mold and plate together. Lift off the mold and serve.

If you have made a crème caramel, be sure to use a serving plate—or individual dessert plates—with a rim to hold the caramel sauce.

VARIATION NOTE

To prepare the recipes at right and below in a single dish, **use** a 6-cup soufflé dish. **Bake** in a water bath in a 325°F oven about 70 minutes.

CRÈME BRÛLÉE

Prepare as directed at right, but **use** flameproof ramekins and **omit** caramel in Step 1. **Sprinkle** each baked custard with 1 1/2 teaspoons firmly packed light or dark brown sugar. **Place** in a preheated broiler 6 to 8 inches from the heat and **broil** until sugar melts—about 45 seconds. **Cool** to room temperature; **serve** at room temperature or chilled. Do not refrigerate too long or the crust will soften. Makes 8 servings.

DOUBLE CARAMEL

Prepare as directed at right, **substituting** firmly packed light or dark brown sugar for granulated sugar in the custard. Makes 8 servings.

LOW-FAT CRÈME CARAMEL

Prepare as directed at right, **substituting** 3 cups evaporated skim milk for whole milk and 1 1/2 cups egg substitute for whole eggs and yolks. **Reduce** sugar to 2/3 cup. Makes 8 servings.

Crème Caramel

Caramel:
- 1/2 cup sugar
- 1/3 cup water

Custard:
- 3 cups milk
- 3/4 cup sugar
- 1 vanilla bean, split lengthwise
- 4 strips orange zest (3 by 1/2 inch each)
- 3 strips lemon zest (2 by 1/2 inch each)
- 3 strips lime zest (2 by 1/2 inch each)
- 1/4 teaspoon salt
- 3 eggs plus 3 egg yolks

1 For the Caramel: In a small saucepan over moderately high heat, bring sugar and water to a boil. Continue boiling until sugar turns amber—about 5 minutes. Pour caramel into the bottoms of 8 ungreased 6-ounce ramekins. Tilt to coat the bottom and about 1 inch of the sides. Arrange ramekins on a folded kitchen towel in a baking pan large enough to hold them without touching.

2 For the Custard: In a medium-size nonreactive saucepan over moderate heat, bring milk, 1/4 cup of the sugar, vanilla bean, orange, lemon, and lime zests, and salt to a simmer. Remove from the heat and let stand, covered, 30 minutes.

3 Preheat the oven to 325°F. In a large bowl, whisk eggs and yolks with the remaining 1/2 cup sugar until blended. Strain in milk mixture and whisk to combine. Ladle custard into prepared ramekins.

4 Pour enough boiling water into the baking pan to come halfway up the sides of the ramekins. Bake, uncovered, until a knife inserted in the center of a custard comes out clean—about 45 minutes.

5 Remove ramekins from the water bath and cool to room temperature on a rack. Refrigerate until ready to serve.

6 To serve, run a knife around the edge of the custards, then invert onto rimmed plates. Makes 8 servings.

1 Serving: Calories 209; Total Fat 7 g; Saturated Fat 3 g; Protein 6 g; Carbohydrates 31 g; Fiber 0 g; Sodium 138 mg; Cholesterol 172 mg

prep time-20 minutes
cooking time-45 minutes
standing time-1 hour 30 minutes

SUMMER PUDDING

This old-fashioned English dessert is aptly named because it is chock-full of juicy fruit. But you can make it any time of year you like with frozen fruit.

NO BAKING

Dome-shaped summer pudding tastes something like a sponge cake laden with fruit. It's colorful, cool, and refreshing, but best of all the only cooking required is for softening and sweetening the fruit.

The pudding is made simply by lining a mold with sliced bread or pound cake, then filling it up with juicy fruit. It gets pressed into shape while it chills and then is ready to unmold and serve with a creamy or custardy sauce.

Keep in mind that some advance planning is necessary, because the pudding must chill at least 8 hours.

BREAD NOTES

Choose firm-textured white bread or homemade loaves for a summer pudding. Soft bread soaks up too much of the fruit mixture and becomes soggy.

To remove bread crusts quickly, stack 3 to 4 slices on a board and cut straight through the stack with a bread knife. Some summer pudding devotees do not remove the crusts, but if they're not totally saturated with fruit juice, the crusts create hard spots.

Some deep-sided molds are easier to line if the bread is first cut diagonally in half into triangles. Reserve several slices to top the mold once it has been filled with berries.

THE PUDDING MOLD

Choose a smooth-sided bowl or baking dish. A 5- to 6-cup charlotte mold, loaf pan, or soufflé dish is ideal.

PUDDING TIPS

You'll need about 3 pounds of fruit for a summer pudding. If you are using thawed frozen berries, you may want to stir in some of the bread trimmings to sop up some of the excess juice.

Reserve any extra fruit and juice to pour over the pudding when it is unmolded.

When ready to unmold the pudding, dip the mold in hot water for 30 to 45 seconds to soften the butter.

TOP OF THE HEAP

Use our cream toppings at right or use ice cream or fruit sherbet of a complementary flavor. Our custard sauce on page 320 is another good pudding topper.

PEACHY PUDDING

Prepare as directed at right, **substituting** 6 cups peeled, pitted, and thinly sliced ripe peaches or mixed fruits for berries and **increasing** the water to 1/2 cup. **Add** 3 tablespoons lemon juice and 1 teaspoon grated lemon zest along with the water. **Increase** cooking time to 10 to 12 minutes. **Remove** from the heat and **stir in** 1 cup raspberries. **Omit** bread and **line** dish with pound cake. You'll need one 12-ounce pound cake. **Trim** off the ends and **cut** the cake into 14 slices. Makes 8 servings.

RASPBERRY-WHIPPED CREAM SAUCE

In a medium-size chilled bowl, **beat** 1 cup chilled heavy cream until frothy. **Add** 2 tablespoons sugar, 1 teaspoon vanilla, and 2 tablespoons raspberry liqueur and **continue beating** to soft peaks. Makes 2 cups.

MOCK CRÈME FRAÎCHE

In a medium-size chilled bowl, **beat** 1/2 cup chilled heavy cream until frothy. **Add** 2 tablespoons sugar and 1/2 teaspoon vanilla. **Fold** 1/2 cup sour cream into whipped cream. Makes 1 1/3 cups.

HOW TO MAKE AND MOLD A SUMMER PUDDING

1 Line the mold with buttered bread. The slices should fit tightly, no gaps.

2 Lift the cooked fruit with a slotted spoon. Spoon the fruit into the mold to fill.

3 Arrange remaining bread slices on top to form a lid.

4 Place a plate that fits the mold on top. Weight down with a heavy can and refrigerate. Reserve excess juice.

Summer Berry Pudding

- **9 cups mixed strawberries, raspberries, blackberries, blueberries, red currants**
- **1/2 to 3/4 cup sugar**
- **2 tablespoons water**
- **3 tablespoons butter or margarine, melted**
- **1 loaf (16 ounces) sliced firm-textured white bread, crusts removed**

1 Rinse and hull berries if necessary. Quarter strawberries; leave other berries whole.

2 Place fruit in a 3-quart nonreactive saucepan over moderately high heat, add 1/2 cup sugar and the water and bring to a boil, stirring occasionally. Reduce the heat to low and cook until sugar dissolves and fruit juices begin to run—about 3 minutes. Cool for 10 minutes; taste and add more sugar if desired.

3 Butter bread on one side. Line the bottom and sides of a 6-cup bowl or soufflé dish with bread, buttered sides next to dish. Trim bread as needed for a close fit.

4 Using a slotted spoon, spoon fruit into the prepared dish, reserving about 1 cup of juice. Fit the remaining bread slices on the top, again trimming as needed. Fit a plate inside the top of the dish on top of the bread and weight down with a heavy can or jar. Refrigerate 8 hours or overnight.

5 Remove the weight and plate. Dip the dish in hot water for about 30 seconds. Run a thin-bladed knife around the edge of the pudding and gently ease bread away from dish. Place a serving plate on top of the dish and invert to unmold the pudding. Spoon reserved juice over any parts of the bread that have not been saturated. Makes 8 servings.

1 Serving: Calories 252; Total Fat 7 g; Saturated Fat 3 g; Protein 5 g; Carbohydrates 45 g; Fiber 3 g; Sodium 256 mg; Cholesterol 13 mg

prep time-45 minutes
cooking time-10 minutes
chilling time-8 hours or overnight

CHEESECAKE

Whether you like the unadorned classic or a more richly flavored variety, nothing beats a slice of fresh cheesecake with a hot cup of coffee.

CHEESECAKE NOTES

Our notes about dessert cheesecake are here. More cheesecake notes and information about springform pans appear with our savory version on page 298.

CHEESE CHOICES

Packaged cream cheese is universally available. If your cheese shop offers fresh cream cheese, by all means try it. Small-curd farmer's cheese, pot cheese, and Neufchâtel are good lower fat substitutes.

IN THE MIX

Our recipe calls for blending the ingredients in a food processor. If you prefer, use an electric mixer at low speed.

Mixing will be easier if you soften the cream cheese beforehand. Let it stand at room temperature for 1 or 2 hours or soften it in the microwave, unwrapped on a plate, at 100 percent power, allowing 1 to 1½ minutes for each 8 ounces.

Before the cheesecake goes into the oven, get rid of any air bubbles by lifting the pan a few inches and letting it drop onto the counter.

CRUMBLY CRUST

Cookie crumb crusts are traditional for cheesecake. For more details about making crumb crusts, see page 308.

Pour the buttery crumbs into the pan and press them into a smooth layer with your fingers or a spoon. Put the finished crust in the freezer for a few minutes before pouring in the cheesecake mixture.

SURFACE CRACKS

Bake cheesecake at the specified oven temperature. Too high a heat and the cheesecake is sure to crack. Even at a moderate temperature, the top may crack because of the weight of the filling. If so, simply cover it with a topping.

COOL IT

Cheesecake should never be served hot. Only when it cools—or better yet, chills—does it firm up properly. Set it on a rack for an hour or more until it reaches room temperature. Cover with foil or plastic wrap and refrigerate overnight or for up to 2 or 3 days.

To slice cheesecake cleanly, dip the knife into hot water between cuts and don't dry it.

HOW TO TOP A STRAWBERRY CHEESECAKE

1 Let glaze cool slightly; then, using a pastry brush, brush lightly over the top of the cheesecake.

2 Arrange hulled and sliced strawberries overlapping in concentric circles beginning at outside edge. Brush glaze lightly over berries.

CHOCOLATE GARNISHES

For curls: Let a thick bar of chocolate come to room temperature. Use a swivel-bladed vegetable parer to shave off curls.

For chocolate-dipped nuts: Melt milk chocolate over lowest heat or in the microwave. Dip walnut or pecan halves or whole macadamia nuts halfway into chocolate. Let cool.

CHOCOLATE CHEESECAKE

Prepare as directed at right, **adding** ¼ cup unsweetened Dutch-process cocoa powder blended with ¼ cup boiling water along with the sour cream in Step 1. For the crust, **substitute** chocolate wafers for graham crackers. Garnish with chocolate curls or chocolate-dipped nuts if desired. Makes 6 servings.

PUMPKIN CHEESECAKE

Prepare as directed, **substituting** 1½ cups firmly packed light brown sugar for granulated sugar and one 29-ounce can unsweetened pumpkin purée for sour cream. **Flavor** with ¼ teaspoon each ground cinnamon, cloves, and nutmeg. For the crust, **substitute** gingersnaps for graham crackers. Makes 6 servings.

Cheesecake with Strawberry Glaze

Filling:
- 3 packages (8 ounces each) cream cheese
- 1 cup sugar
- 3 eggs
- 1 cup sour cream

Crumb Crust:
- 1¼ cups graham cracker crumbs
- 5 tablespoons butter or margarine, melted
- ¼ cup sugar

Glaze:
- ¼ cup strawberry jelly
- 1 tablespoon water
- 1 pint strawberries, hulled and thinly sliced

1 For the Filling: Preheat the oven to 325°F. In a food processor, pulse cream cheese and sugar until smooth. With the motor running, add eggs 1 at a time. Scrape down work bowl sides, add sour cream, and pulse until smooth.

2 For the Crust: In a medium-size bowl, toss crumbs, butter, and sugar with a fork until well mixed. Press mixture firmly over the bottom of a 9-inch springform pan.

3 Pour filling into crumb crust and bake until filling shimmies only slightly in the center—about 50 minutes. Transfer to a rack and cool in pan to room temperature.

4 For the Glaze: In a small saucepan over moderately high heat, bring jelly and water to a boil. Remove from the heat and cool slightly. Brush cheesecake with about ⅓ of the glaze, arrange sliced strawberries decoratively on top, and brush with remaining glaze. Makes 6 servings.

1 Serving: Calories 911; Total Fat 68 g; Saturated Fat 41 g; Protein 15 g; Carbohydrates 66 g; Fiber 1 g; Sodium 670 mg; Cholesterol 290 mg

prep time-20 minutes • cooking time-50 minutes

BROWNIES

Few things smell better than brownies in the oven. They're the perfect first recipe for children to try their hands at. We offer them four ways.

CHOCOLATE CHOICE

To suit your taste, vary the flavor of brownies by replacing some of the unsweetened baking chocolate with bittersweet chocolate or with chocolate morsels.

BROWNIE TIPS

Fudgy brownies have more butter and chocolate, less flour, and no leavening. Usually, the butter and chocolate are melted together, then mixed with sugar, eggs, flavoring, and dry ingredients. Mixing is done by hand.

For cake-style brownies, the sugar and butter are creamed together, and leavening is added to the batter.

PAN PREP

Be sure to use the right size pan. If the size is off, the depth of the batter will change and the brownies will require a different cooking time.

When making brownies and other rich bar cookies containing fruits and nuts, it's important to both grease and flour the pan or the brownies are apt to stick.

For a rich brown finish, dust the pan with unsweetened cocoa powder instead of flour.

Lining the pan with foil makes it easy to get brownies out. For best results, smooth the foil over the bottom and then up and over the sides.

You can use the sides of the foil as handles to lift the entire sheet of brownies out. Grease the foil so that it's easy to peel it away from the brownies.

MELT DOWN

When melting chocolate, always begin by chopping the chocolate into small pieces or shaving the squares with a swivel-bladed vegetable parer.

Melt chocolate over the lowest heat possible. High heat brings the risk of scorching and causes chocolate to "seize," or form insoluble lumps.

Condensed steam can also make chocolate seize, so do not cover the pan during the melting process.

If, despite your precautions, your chocolate should seize, restore it to smoothness by stirring in 1 teaspoon of vegetable oil for every ounce of chocolate.

To be extra cautious when melting chocolate, use a double boiler or improvise one by putting a small saucepan or bowl inside a larger one containing simmering water.

BEAT THE CLOCK

To retain the rich moist texture of fudgy brownies, underbake them ever so slightly—the center will be somewhat soft, but the edges firm. A toothpick jabbed in the center should emerge with a moist crumb or two clinging to it. Brownies continue to cook for a few minutes after coming out of the oven.

COOL AND CUT

When the brownies are done, place the pan on a rack to cool. If baked with a foil liner, lift out the whole sheet of brownies when they have cooled. If you want to serve them hot with ice cream, lift out the sheet of brownies and cut into squares while still warm.

For 24 squares, make 3 evenly spaced parallel cuts lengthwise and 5 crosswise. Cut with a pizza wheel or a sharp knife with a serrated blade. Wipe the blade clean between cuts.

If the brownies are baked without a foil liner, loosen and lift out a corner square first.

Cooled brownies can be wrapped in foil and stored 2 or 3 months in the freezer, a week or 10 days in the refrigerator. Frozen brownies need about 15 minutes to thaw.

FUDGY FROSTED BROWNIES

Prepare as directed at right, **omitting** Step 3. In Step 4, **reduce** eggs to 3 and **beat** in all at once. Gradually **stir** in 1¼ cups unsifted all-purpose flour and ½ teaspoon salt; **omit** baking powder. **Stir** in nuts and bake 25 to 30 minutes. As soon as brownies are done, **sprinkle** with one 12-ounce package of mini chocolate chips. (If less is desired, **use** ½ package.) **Let stand** 5 minutes, then **spread** with a spatula. **Cool** before cutting. Makes twenty-four 2¼-inch squares.

BLONDIES

Prepare Fudgy Frosted Brownies, but **omit** chocolate. **Increase** flour to 1¾ cups and **mix** with 1 teaspoon baking powder. **Bake** 35 minutes. Do not frost. Makes twenty-four 2¼-inch squares.

TWO-TONE BROWNIES

Prepare Blondies, but **mix** 2 melted, cooled 1-ounce squares unsweetened chocolate into ½ the batter. **Spread** chocolate batter in prepared pan and **spread** plain batter on top; do not marbleize. **Bake** as directed. Makes twenty-four 2¼-inch squares.

1. Preheat the oven to 350°F. Line a 13" x 9" x 2" baking pan with foil. Lightly grease and flour and set aside.

2. In a small heavy saucepan over lowest heat, melt chocolate, stirring occasionally. Set aside to cool.

3. On a sheet of wax paper, combine flour, baking powder, and salt.

4. In the large bowl of an electric mixer, cream the butter at medium speed for 2 minutes. Add sugar and continue to cream for 2 minutes. Beat in eggs 1 at a time, beating well after each addition. Add vanilla and cooled chocolate. By hand, mix in dry ingredients, then stir in nuts.

5. Pour the batter into the prepared pan and bake until a wooden toothpick inserted in the center comes out clean—about 35 minutes. Transfer to a rack to cool before cutting. Makes twenty-four 2¼-inch squares.

Classic Brownies

5	squares (1 ounce each) unsweetened chocolate, coarsely chopped
1⅓	cups unsifted all-purpose flour
1	teaspoon baking powder
½	teaspoon salt
¾	cup (1½ sticks) butter or margarine, softened
1½	cups sugar
4	eggs
2	teaspoons vanilla extract
2	cups coarsely chopped walnuts or pecans

1 Square: Calories 244;
Total Fat 16 g;
Saturated Fat 6 g;
Protein 4 g;
Carbohydrates 23 g;
Fiber 2 g; Sodium 81 mg;
Cholesterol 60 mg

prep time-30 minutes
cooking time-35 minutes

One-Bowl Butter Cakes

Mixing up a one-bowl butter cake is a cinch—all the ingredients are blended together at the same time.

PIECE OF CAKE

One-bowl cakes bake into delicious layer or sheet cakes. Better yet, they are far quicker to make than traditional butter cakes, which call for preparing wet and dry ingredients separately and then combining them alternately. The one-bowl cake was developed for the electric mixer. All ingredients go into a large mixer bowl together—in an order that ensures thorough mixing without overbeating. Then they're beaten for several minutes, and that's all there is to it.

SUBSTITUTIONS

Our recipe calls for cake flour. You can also use all-purpose flour but the texture will not be quite as delicate. If you use all-purpose flour, reduce the measure by 2 tablespoons per cup.

The recipe calls for buttermilk, which is more acidic than regular milk. The acid activates the baking soda, creating a lighter cake. For a homemade replacement, mix 1 tablespoon of lemon juice or vinegar into 1 cup of milk. Let it stand until thickened—10 to 15 minutes.

QUICK ESCAPE

You'll know a butter cake is done when it pulls away from the sides of the pan and is springy to the touch.

To make it easy to remove the cake layers from the pans, line the bottoms with wax paper. Fold a square of wax paper diagonally 4 or 5 times to make a triangle. Lay the point at the center of the pan, then trim the opposite edge to follow the contour of the pan. Unfold and place in the pan.

BAKING CHECKLIST

Small things can make problems for layer cakes. If layers rise lopsidedly, the oven temperature might be inconsistent or the stove itself might not be level. If there are tunnels through the cake, you overmixed the batter or added too much flour. If the center falls, you used too much sugar; if the surface cracks, too much flour; if the texture is rubbery, too many eggs.

HOW TO FROST A CAKE

1 Place slips of wax paper around edge of a serving plate. Place cake layer on the plate; spread with 1/4 of frosting.

2 Spread a little frosting on the underside of top layer so that the 2 layers will stick together. Center the 2 layers.

3 Spread remaining frosting over top and sides of cake, covering sides from the bottom up. Remove wax paper.

CHOCOLATE PRALINE CAKE

Prepare as directed at right, **dusting** pans with flour instead of cocoa. **Substitute** firmly packed light brown sugar for granulated sugar and **fold** 1/2 cup toasted, chopped pecans into batter. Makes 12 servings.

SPICE CAKE

Prepare as directed at right, **dusting** pans with flour instead of cocoa. **Substitute** firmly packed light brown sugar for granulated sugar, **omit** chocolate, and **add** 1 teaspoon ground cinnamon, 1/2 teaspoon each ground nutmeg and ginger, and 1/4 teaspoon each ground allspice and cloves. Makes 12 servings.

CHOCOLATE BUTTER CREAM FROSTING

Prepare frosting as directed at right, **adding** 3 ounces melted semisweet chocolate or 1/2 cup sifted unsweetened cocoa. Makes enough to fill and frost one 9-inch layer cake or to frost one 13" x 9" x 2" sheet cake or 24 cupcakes.

ORANGE BUTTER CREAM FROSTING

Prepare frosting as directed at right, **substituting** 1/4 cup orange juice for cream and **adding** 1 tablespoon grated orange zest. Makes enough to fill and frost one 9-inch layer cake or to frost one 13" x 9" x 2" sheet cake or 24 cupcakes.

Devil's Food Cake

- 1 **tablespoon unsweetened cocoa powder (for dusting pan)**
- 2 **cups sifted cake flour**
- 1½ **teaspoons baking soda**
- 1 **teaspoon salt**
- ½ **teaspoon baking powder**
- 1½ **cups sugar**
- 1 **cup buttermilk, at room temperature**
- ½ **cup (1 stick) butter or margarine, softened**
- 1 **teaspoon vanilla extract**
- 3 **eggs, at room temperature**
- 3 **ounces semisweet chocolate, melted**

1 Preheat the oven to 350°F. Grease two 9-inch round cake pans, dust with cocoa, and tap out excess.

2 With an electric mixer at low speed, beat all remaining ingredients for 1 minute, scraping sides of bowl occasionally. Increase speed to medium-high and beat 2 minutes longer, scraping sides of bowl twice.

3 Pour batter into prepared pans and bake until a toothpick inserted in the center comes out clean—about 30 minutes. Cool cakes in pans on racks 10 minutes, then turn out of pans and cool to room temperature. Fill and frost with Butter Cream or Chocolate Butter Cream Frosting. Makes 12 servings.

1 Serving (Including Frosting): Calories 477; Total Fat 16 g; Saturated Fat 10 g; Protein 5 g; Carbohydrates 73 g; Fiber 0 g; Sodium 513 mg; Cholesterol 91 mg

prep time-25 minutes • cooking time-30 minutes

For the pale pink color of our Butter Cream Frosting, we used 2 drops of red food coloring and 1 drop of yellow. After icing the cake, we used a pastry tube to add ruffled borders of frosting.

Butter Cream Frosting

- ⅓ **cup butter or margarine, softened**
- 1 **box (16 ounces) confectioners' sugar, sifted**
- ¼ **cup light cream**
- 2 **teaspoons vanilla extract**
- 1 **or 2 drops of food coloring, optional**

1 In the bowl of an electric mixer, cream butter at medium-high speed until light and fluffy.

2 Reduce mixer speed to medium and alternately beat in sugar and cream, a little at a time. Add vanilla and beat until creamy. Makes enough to fill and frost one 9-inch layer cake or to frost one 10-inch tube cake, one 13" x 9" x 2" sheet cake, or 24 cupcakes.

2 Tablespoons: Calories 160; Total Fat 6 g; Saturated Fat 4 g; Protein 0 g; Carbohydrates 28 g; Fiber 0 g; Sodium 21 mg; Cholesterol 8 mg

prep time-8 minutes

ANGEL CAKE

*A*ngel cake owes its loftiness to egg whites alone. It's made without leavening and has won new favor as a fat-free alternative to rich desserts.

ANGEL BASICS

For angel cake, the volume of egg whites is critical, so the basic rules for whipping eggs must be followed to the letter.

Separate the eggs while they are refrigerator cold. If any yolk gets into the whites, remove it with paper toweling or the tip of a spoon: Any yolk or other fat present in the whites will prevent them from whipping properly.

Let the whites come to room temperature before beating. Use a clean, dry, large round-bottomed glass or metal bowl, not plastic. Use a clean, dry utensil for whipping; either an electric mixer or a balloon whip is fine.

Beat the egg whites at first only until billowing.

While you add the sugar, whip the whites again, this time until soft peaks form. The peaks should fall to one side when you withdraw the beater.

GENTLE BLENDING

We've used granulated sugar for our recipe. You can also use half confectioners' sugar if you prefer. However, if you do, sift it 2 or 3 times before beating it into the egg whites. This ensures that there are no lumps and that the sugar will blend easily with the whites. Whether granulated or confectioners', add the sugar to the cake batter only a few spoonfuls at a time.

(continued on page 334)

ANGEL CAKE

This version of the cake is baked the classic way, in a tube pan. Serve it with crushed berries and/or sweetened whipped cream.

- 1½ cups egg whites (about 15 eggs)
- 1½ teaspoons cream of tartar
- ¼ teaspoon salt
- 1½ cups sugar
- 1 cup sifted cake flour
- 2 teaspoons vanilla extract
- ¼ teaspoon almond extract

1 Place the oven rack at its lowest position. Preheat the oven to 325°F. In the large bowl of an electric mixer, beat egg whites, cream of tartar, and salt at medium speed until frothy. Then with the motor running, add sugar, 2 tablespoons at a time. Increase speed to high and continue beating until very soft peaks form.

2 Fold flour, ¼ at a time, into whites, then fold in vanilla and almond extracts.

3 Spoon batter into an ungreased 10-inch tube pan and gently smooth the surface with a spatula. Cut the spatula through the batter once to break and release any large air bubbles.

4 Bake the cake until the top springs back when lightly pressed—50 to 60 minutes. Invert the cake pan, inserting the central tube over the neck of a large bottle. When the cake is completely cool, loosen from the pan and turn out onto a cake plate. Makes 12 servings.

HOW TO ROLL AN ANGEL

1 While cake is still hot, roll it up with a clean, prepared kitchen towel, jelly-roll fashion. Let it cool, rolled, on a rack.

2 When cooled, carefully unroll the cake. Spread with filling, leaving a ½-inch margin all around.

3 Gently reroll the cake and dust with confectioners' sugar. Slice into rounds with a serrated knife.

Angel Roll with Lemon Filling

Filling:

- ½ **cup sugar**
- 2 **tablespoons cornstarch**

Pinch salt

- ¾ **cup cold water**
- 2 **egg yolks, lightly beaten**
- 1 **teaspoon grated lemon zest**
- 2½ **tablespoons lemon juice**
- 1½ **teaspoons butter or margarine**

Roll:

- ½ **recipe for Angel Cake (opposite)**

Confectioners' sugar

1 For the Filling: In a small saucepan, combine sugar, cornstarch, and salt. Gradually blend in water, set over moderate heat, and cook, stirring, until mixture boils and thickens—about 3 minutes.

2 Remove from heat, blend a little of the hot mixture into egg yolks, then stir back into the pan. Stir in lemon zest and juice, and butter. Transfer to a small bowl and cool 30 minutes. Cover and refrigerate while preparing cake.

3 For the Roll: Preheat the oven to 325°F. Prepare ½ recipe for Angel Cake through Step 2.

4 Spread batter in a greased wax-paper-lined 15½- by 10½-inch jelly-roll pan. Bake until top springs back when pressed—20 to 25 minutes. Sift confectioners' sugar over a kitchen towel.

5 As soon as the cake is done, loosen around the edges and invert at once on sugared towel.

Peel away wax paper. Trim off edges of the cake using a serrated knife. Sift confectioners' sugar over the cake and, while it is hot, roll it up in the towel so you have a roll 10½ inches long.

6 Transfer to a rack and cool for at least 30 minutes. Unroll the cake and remove towel. Spread filling over the cake, leaving ½-inch margins all around. Reroll the cake and dust with more confectioners' sugar. Makes 12 servings.

1 Serving: Calories 135; Total Fat 1 g; Saturated Fat 1 g; Protein 3 g; Carbohydrates 28 g; Fiber 0 g; Sodium 85 mg; Cholesterol 37 mg

prep time-45 minutes
cooking time-25 minutes
cooling and assembly-40 minutes

(continued from page 332)

FLOUR NOTES

You'll be best off using sifted cake flour for an angel cake; it gives the lightest and softest texture. If necessary, however, sifted all-purpose flour can also be used.

It's worthwhile being precise: Sift the flour before measuring it. Then add it to the whites 1/4 at a time by sifting it over the whites and folding it in.

FOLDING LESSONS

Fold the batter gently in a circular motion using a rubber spatula or a flat whisk and rotating the bowl as you go. Run the spatula down the side and along the bottom of the bowl, scooping the whites from the bottom to the top of the mound, incorporating the flour as you do so.

Be careful not to overdo it. The flour needs to be evenly mixed with the egg whites, but overmixing will deflate them and toughen the cake.

CAKE PAN

Angel cakes are traditionally baked in tube pans, see below. However, our Angel Roll box on page 332 shows how to adapt the recipe for a flat cake.

Do not grease the tube pan for a traditional angel cake. The batter must be able to cling to the sides of the pan and climb high while it bakes.

Make sure there are no large air bubbles in the batter once it has been poured into the cake pan. Smooth the top with a metal spatula, then draw the spatula through the batter in a slow circle around the center tube to release air bubbles.

BAKE IT RIGHT

To rise to their fullest, angel cakes must be baked gently in the lower part of the oven and just until lightly browned.

The moment the cake emerges from the oven, it must be turned upside down so that it hangs in the pan, see below. If your tube pan doesn't have supports along the top rim, place the pan upside down over the neck of a bottle while it cools.

SERVED IN STYLE

Run a thin spatula around the edge of the pan and center tube to loosen the cake before gently shaking it from the pan.

Angel cakes are rarely frosted. Rather, they are served dusted with confectioners' sugar or topped with sliced or crushed fruit with its juice, whipped cream, or another light sauce.

To serve angel cake, cut it with a sharp serrated knife, using a light sawing motion. Or use two forks—tines facing outward—pushing them in opposite directions to break pieces of cake apart.

COOKING AHEAD

Angel cake freezes beautifully. Simply put it in a plastic bag. Squeeze out as much air as possible, seal, and freeze for up to 3 months.

WHAT ABOUT THE EGG YOLKS?

There are a lot of leftover egg yolks with an angel cake and a number of ways to use them.

Mix beaten egg yolks with milk and grated cheese for a gratin topping or as a binder for ingredients in a casserole.

Beat yolks with a little water

for coating pounded veal or chicken cutlets before coating them with bread crumbs.

Stir up a fragrant pot of Greek Egg and Lemon Soup (see page 38).

Stir some extra yolks into a frittata (see page 286).

Use the occasion to make fresh mayonnaise (see page 366).

ANGEL ROLL WITH RASPBERRY CREAM

Prepare Angel Roll as directed on page 333, but **omit** lemon filling. Instead, **whip** 1/2 cup heavy cream with 1 tablespoon confectioners' sugar and 1/4 teaspoon vanilla extract until stiff. **Fold** in 1/4 cup seedless raspberry or strawberry jam and **fill** and **roll** the cake as directed. Makes 12 servings.

BROWN SUGAR ANGEL CAKE

Prepare Angel Cake as directed on page 332, **substituting** 1/2 cup firmly packed dark brown sugar for 1/2 cup of the granulated sugar and 2 teaspoons of maple extract for vanilla extract. **Omit** almond extract. Makes 12 servings.

CHOCOLATE ANGEL CAKE

Prepare Angel Cake as directed on page 332, **sifting** 1/2 cup unsweetened cocoa powder along with cake flour and **folding** in 1 tablespoon instant espresso powder along with vanilla extract. **Omit** almond extract. Makes 12 servings.

Or make your favorite custard, substituting 2 egg yolks for each whole egg.

WORK SAVER
Angel Cake Pan

Tube pans are specially made for high-rise cakes. The tall sides and central tube support the cake as it ascends. The tube also allows the cake to bake from the inside out while it bakes from the outside in, so that it doesn't have to stay in the oven too long. Supports, or "legs," along the rim allow the cake to cool hanging upside down so that it doesn't collapse or lose airiness.

A SWEET FINISH

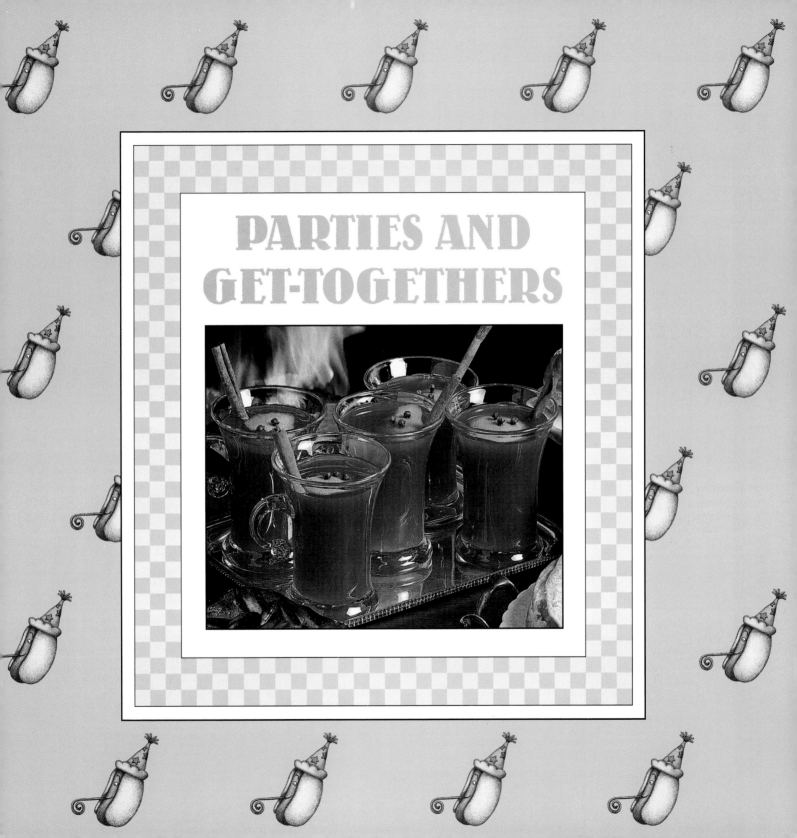

PARTIES AND GET-TOGETHERS

THANKSGIVING DINNER

*P*utting together a classic Thanksgiving feast with all the trimmings is not so difficult if you plan ahead.

GETTING STARTED

We've made a sumptuous Thanksgiving menu based on recipes from this book, including several new ones on the following spread—festive drinks and stellar stuffings. Complete information about stuffing and roasting turkey appears on pages 280 to 282.

We selected the recipes on our menu as much for their versatility as for their great taste. Each of our stuffings can be baked in a casserole to save on the time that the turkey stays in the oven. Our soup is prepared ahead and served chilled. Many of our recipes can be frozen and require only thawing, assembly, or warming on Thanksgiving Day.

We've also provided a list of the recipes on our menu that are good traveling dishes in case you are bringing part

(continued on page 338)

A THANKSGIVING MENU

Cranberry Drinks
(page 339)

Parmesan Twists
(page 29)

Sweet Potato and Carrot Vichyssoise (page 53)

Roast Turkey with Giblet Gravy (page 280)

A Selection of Stuffings
(page 338)

Gratin of Green Beans
(page 153)

Glazed Onions (page 141)

Corn Pudding
(page 154)

Parker House Rolls
(page 75)

Cranberry-Orange Relish (page 372)

Pumpkin Chiffon Pie
(page 308)

Blue-Ribbon Apple Pie
(page 306)

Selections from our menu include: Roast Turkey with Giblet Gravy; Minnesota Wild Rice, Bacon, and Onion Stuffing; Gratin of Green Beans; Cranberry-Orange Relish; Parker House Rolls; and Cran-Raspberry Spritzers.

MINNESOTA WILD RICE, BACON, AND ONION STUFFING

1/4 **pound lean sliced bacon, coarsely chopped**	1 **tablespoon dried sage, crumbled**
2 **large yellow onions, chopped**	2 **teaspoons dried thyme, crumbled**
2 **large stalks celery with leaves, chopped**	1 **teaspoon dried marjoram, crumbled**
2 **cups wild rice, washed**	1 **teaspoon salt**
4 1/2 **cups water**	1/2 **teaspoon black pepper**
	1/2 **cup chopped parsley**

1 In a 4-quart saucepan over moderately high heat, sauté bacon until crisp—about 5 minutes. Transfer to paper toweling; pour drippings into a 1-cup glass measure.

2 Pour 1/4 cup drippings back into pan. Add onions and celery and cook over moderate heat, stirring occasionally, just until tender—8 to 10 minutes.

3 Add wild rice, water, sage, thyme, marjoram, salt, and pepper and bring to a boil over high heat. Reduce the heat to low and simmer, covered, until all liquid is absorbed and rice is tender—50 to 60 minutes. Stir in reserved bacon and parsley. If baking the stuffing separately, preheat the oven to 325°F.

4 Stuff and truss the turkey or spoon the stuffing into a lightly greased 2-quart baking dish. Cover tightly with foil and bake about 45 minutes. Makes 14 servings.

One 1/2-Cup Serving: Calories 155; Total Fat 6 g; Saturated Fat 2 g; Protein 5 g; Carbohydrates 22 g; Fiber 2 g; Sodium 232 mg; Cholesterol 6 mg

prep time-40 minutes • cooking time-1 hour 50 minutes

OLD VIRGINIA CORNBREAD AND OYSTER STUFFING

1/4 **cup (1/2 stick) butter or margarine**	1/2 **cup Rich Chicken Stock or reduced-sodium canned chicken broth**
2 **large stalks celery with leaves, chopped**	1/2 **cup chopped parsley**
1 **large yellow onion, chopped**	1 **tablespoon dried sage, crumbled**
1 **package (7 ounces) cornbread stuffing mix**	2 **teaspoons dried thyme, crumbled**
4 **slices whole-wheat bread, cut into 1/2-inch cubes**	1 **teaspoon dried marjoram, crumbled**
1 **pint oysters, drained and liquid reserved, coarsely chopped**	1/2 **teaspoon salt**
	1/2 **teaspoon black pepper**

1 Preheat the oven to 325°F. In a 5- to 6-quart Dutch oven over moderate heat, melt butter. Add celery and onion and cook, stirring occasionally, just until tender—8 to 10 minutes. Remove from the heat.

2 Add cornbread stuffing mix, bread cubes, oysters, 1/2 cup of the reserved oyster liquid, stock, parsley, sage, thyme, marjoram, salt, and pepper and toss well.

3 Spoon stuffing into a lightly greased 2- to 2 1/2-quart baking dish. Cover tightly with foil and bake 45 minutes. Makes 12 servings.

One 1/2-Cup Serving: Calories 165; Total Fat 6 g; Saturated Fat 3 g; Protein 6 g; Carbohydrates 22 g; Fiber 1 g; Sodium 504 mg; Cholesterol 32 mg

prep time-40 minutes • cooking time-55 minutes

(continued from page 336)
of the feast to someone else's house this year.

There are many other recipes throughout the book that would also be good Thanksgiving choices. So browse through, plan ahead, and enjoy the holiday.

THE WEEKS BEFORE THANKSGIVING

Work out your menu down to the last detail and order any special foods. Mark your calendar for pickup dates.

Make any freeze-ahead recipes; these usually include soup, bread, rolls, and desserts. On our menu, freeze-ahead recipes include Parmesan Twists, Parker House Rolls, and piecrust dough.

Count noses and compare with the number of table settings you own. Review your menu, making sure you have all of the necessary cooking equipment. Buy or arrange to borrow or rent the extra pieces you need.

Decide on a centerpiece for the table. Make sure that all linen and tableware are on hand—washed, pressed, or polished—and ready to go.

HELPING HAND

If your task is to bring a dish to someone else's house, the following recipes from our menu are good bets for safe transport: Cranberry Drinks, Parmesan Twists, Sweet Potato and Carrot Vichyssoise, Min-nesota Wild Rice, Bacon, and Onion Stuffing, Gratin of Green Beans, Corn Pudding, Parker House Rolls, Cranberry-Orange Relish, Pumpkin Chiffon Pie, Blue-Ribbon Apple Pie.

THE WEEK BEFORE

Do the final grocery shopping, except for perishables. Start preparing the food and beverages that will keep well at room temperature or under refrigeration. From our menu, make the Cranberry-Orange Relish.

CRAN-RASPBERRY SPRITZERS

3 cups chilled dry white wine or cran-raspberry juice

1½ cups chilled cran-raspberry juice

1½ cups chilled carbonated raspberry beverage

Optional garnishes: fresh mint leaves fresh or frozen raspberries

1 Combine wine, cran-raspberry juice, and raspberry beverage in a 2-quart glass pitcher.

2 Serve as is or over ice. Garnish with mint leaves and raspberries if desired. Makes 8 servings.

One 6-Ounce Serving:
Calories 106;
Total Fat 0 g;
Saturated Fat 0 g;
Protein 0 g;
Carbohydrates 12 g;
Fiber 0 g; Sodium 6 mg;
Cholesterol 0 mg

prep time-10 minutes

Make or buy ice cubes.

Write a note to remind yourself to start thawing the turkey. Allow 24 hours for every 5 pounds of frozen turkey.

THE DAY BEFORE

Run errands and pick up last-minute items.

Arrange the centerpiece.

Assemble the table, if necessary, and set it as completely as possible. Arrange the chairs.

CRAN-RASPBERRY-ORANGE SHRUBS

Combine 1 quart cran-raspberry juice, ½ cup sugar, and zest of 1 orange cut into strips in a medium-size nonreactive saucepan. **Bring** to a boil over low heat and **simmer**, uncovered, **stirring** occasionally, for 10 minutes. **Remove** from the heat, **stir in** ⅔ cup orange juice, and **cool**. **Pour** into pitcher and **refrigerate**, covered, until chilled. **Remove** orange zest, **pour** ½ cup into punch cups or glasses, **add** club soda, and **top** with a scoop of sherbet. Makes 8 servings.

Set out all the serving dishes and utensils.

Remove the thawed turkey from its original bag; rinse and pat dry. Cover and refrigerate.

Thaw frozen dough. Make and refrigerate piecrusts. Make the crumb crust for the Pumpkin Chiffon Pie and refrigerate it.

Trim vegetables for a relish tray; refrigerate in plastic bags.

Prepare and refrigerate Sweet Potato and Carrot Vichyssoise.

Trim the green beans and onions. After cooking, draining, and cooling, seal them in plastic bags and refrigerate.

Prepare Corn Pudding to the point of topping with crumbs; cover and refrigerate.

Prepare the mix for the Cran-Raspberry-Orange Shrubs; cover and refrigerate.

THANKSGIVING DAY

Finish setting the table.

Prepare the stuffing; stuff the turkey and begin roasting.

When the turkey is cooked and resting before carving, prepare the gravy. See How to Make Giblet Gravy, page 280.

Fill and bake the apple pie.

Remove the Parmesan Twists and Parker House Rolls from the freezer bags; thaw at room temperature. At serving time, wrap the rolls loosely in aluminum foil. Heat in a 325°F oven for 5 to 8 minutes or until hot. Or bundle in paper toweling and microwave at 50 percent power for about 5 minutes.

Prepare the Gratin of Green Beans and Corn Pudding; glaze the onions.

WHAT TO DRINK WITH DINNER

Cider was a favorite festive drink of early settlers. It often was served mulled, meaning it was heated with sugar and spices. Children enjoyed their cider fresh, while adults drank theirs "hard" or fermented.

Sparkling mineral waters are a good choice for a festive meal. Sparkling apple juice or cranberry juice lightened with sparkling water as well as Cranberry Iced Tea (page 13) also pair nicely with Thanksgiving fare.

Serving wine with Thanksgiving dinner is a long-standing tradition in many homes. Good choices for white wines include Sauvignon Blanc and chardonnay, and for reds Pinot Noir and Merlot.

White wines are generally served chilled and red wines at a little under room temperature (60°F to 65°F). Open red wine about an hour before serving it to let it breathe.

THANKSGIVING FOR TWO

If there are only two for dinner—unless you're crazy for leftovers—you should probably opt for a roast turkey breast half or a tiny turkey. They come as small as 6 pounds. See page 276 for turkey breast roasting details.

Either selection will provide you with enough for another meal or two and some sandwiches as well. Serve either selection with stuffing, mashed potatoes, gravy, cranberry sauce, and all the other festive trimmings.

WINTER HOLIDAY BUFFET

*T*wo things that are sure to keep your guests happy at a holiday party— festive food and plenty of it.

A FESTIVE MIX

Parties during the winter holidays tend to be mixed gatherings: friends, family, business associates, young people and old. The best way to be sure your menu pleases everyone and is flexible enough to accommodate last-minute guests is to plan a buffet. Let everyone help themself to their favorite dishes and sample some festive new ones.

Our menu is made up of recipes from this book. All of them are good buffet selections that can be eaten with the fingers or at least require no more than a fork.

KEEP THE PARTY MOVING

One of the most important secrets for staging a successful party is to keep the guests circulating. Set up the bar and

(continued on page 342)

BUFFET MENU

Hot Mulled Cider Sparkling Fruit Bowl (page 342)

Viennese Hot Chocolate (page 11)

Goat Cheese Torte (page 298)

Country Pâté (page 346)

Spinach-Feta Triangles (page 25)

Pastry Puffs with Curried Chicken (page 343)

Tomato-Onion-Parmesan Tart (page 157)

Boiled Shrimp with Five Sauces (page 219)

Cilantro-Marinated Grilled Vegetables (page 201)

Winter Fruit Tart (page 304)

Pumpkin Cheesecake (page 326)

Our holiday crowd pleasers include: Hot Mulled Cider; Goat Cheese Torte; Pastry Puffs with Curried Chicken; and Cilantro-Marinated Grilled Vegetables.

HOT MULLED CIDER

4 cups apple cider	orange zest
10 whole cloves	1 cinnamon stick, cracked
10 black peppercorns	
Four 3- by ½-inch strips	1 vanilla bean, split

1 In a medium-size saucepan over moderate heat, bring all ingredients to a boil. Remove from the heat and set aside to steep for 30 minutes. Discard spices. Reheat until mixture begins to steam, ladle into mugs, wait 3 to 5 minutes, then serve. Makes 4 servings.

One 1-Cup Serving: Calories 112; Total Fat 0 g; Saturated Fat 0 g; Protein 0 g; Carbohydrates 28 g; Fiber 0 g; Sodium 17 mg; Cholesterol 0 mg

prep time-6 minutes • steeping time-30 minutes cooking time-5 minutes

SPARKLING FRUIT BOWL

2 packages (10 ounces each) frozen raspberries and strawberries	cardamom
	Six 3- by ½-inch strips orange zest
6 cups water	1 vanilla bean, split
1½ cups sugar	2 cups orange juice
10 whole cloves	2 cups club soda
½ teaspoon ground	

1 In a large nonreactive saucepan or Dutch oven, bring berries, water, sugar, cloves, cardamom, zest, and vanilla bean to a boil. Reduce the heat to moderately low and simmer, uncovered, stirring occasionally, about 10 minutes.

2 Strain through a fine sieve (do not press solids) and cool to room temperature. Stir in orange juice. When ready to serve, stir in club soda. Serve over ice. Makes 10 servings.

One 1-Cup Serving: Calories 167; Total Fat 0 g; Saturated Fat 0 g; Protein 1 g; Carbohydrates 42 g; Fiber 2 g; Sodium 11 mg; Cholesterol 0 mg

prep time-10 minutes • cooking time-10 minutes

(continued from page 340)
buffet as far away from each other as possible in the room and keep new dishes arriving. That way, guests are encouraged to get up, move around, munch, and socialize throughout the evening.

SOFT CHOUX

We've made pastry puffs with a creamy curried chicken filling as one of the main dishes for our buffet. The puffs are made with choux (pronounced shoe) pastry. The name means "cabbages," and refers to the

HOW TO MAKE PASTRY PUFFS

1 Make pastry as directed in Steps 2 and 3 at right. Beat mixture until smooth after each addition of egg. When done, the dough should just hold its shape, with no sign of runniness.

2 Using a pastry bag with a plain ¾-inch tip, pipe dough onto baking sheets, making 1-inch-wide mounds 2 inches apart. Smooth tops and brush with egg wash, making sure it does not drip.

3 Bake for 10 minutes at 450°F, reduce heat to 350°F, and bake 10 minutes. Reduce heat to 325°F and bake until puffs are lightly browned—about 15 minutes.

4 Turn off the oven. Pierce the sides of the puffs once with a knife to let the steam escape. Cool in the turned-off oven for 10 minutes. Transfer to racks to cool.

dough's usual appearance as little round pastry puffs.

Choux pastry is easy to make and to form into shapes with a pastry tube. When the puffs emerge from the oven, they are lightly browned on the outside and soft and airy inside. The airy interior makes them ideal for stuffing or filling. Tiny puffs filled with pastry cream are called cream puffs. Filled with ice cream or whipped cream, they're profiteroles; with crab-

meat or Niçoise salad, they're cocktail puffs. The pastry can also be used to form large shells that are split and topped with sweet or savory fillings.

CHOUX NOTES

For our curry-filled puffs, we've added 1 teaspoon of salt and ¼ teaspoon of cayenne to the choux pastry recipe. If you are making the pastry for a dessert, use only ⅛ teaspoon of salt and replace the cayenne with 1 tablespoon of sugar.

When making the dough, keep the heat moderate so that the butter and flour do not brown.

A wooden spoon is the best tool for beating the butter and flour and for mixing the eggs into the dough.

Make sure the eggs are at room temperature and that the dough has cooled slightly when the eggs are added to it.

Pipe the dough into shapes and bake as soon as possible: The raw dough becomes solid as it cools and will not puff properly.

PARTY PLANNING HELP AT HAND

If you're planning to entertain a large number of people—more than 12 to 15—you will probably need some help in the kitchen serving food and drinks and tidying up. Figure on 1 person as bartender plus 1 other helper for each 15 guests.

A PARTY BAR FOR 20 GUESTS

If you'd prefer to serve mixed drinks instead of mulled cider or punch, the following list provides some guidelines. To keep costs down for parties of 10 or more, serve both alcoholic and nonalcoholic punches but also have a limited selection of liquors and mixers on hand.

For 20 people figure on: 1 bottle of bourbon, 1 bottle of blended whiskey, 1 bottle of blended scotch, 2 bottles of gin, 2 bottles of vodka, 1 bottle of dry vermouth, 4 to 6 bottles of chardonnay or Sauvignon Blanc white wines, 3 bottles of Merlot or Côtes du Rhone red wines, 24 bottles of beer, 2 liters of cola, 2 liters of diet cola, 6 small bottles of ginger

ale, 12 small bottles of tonic water, 4 liters of club soda, 20 to 30 pounds of ice (to keep beer and white wine cold).

It's handy to have the following: 1 bottle of coffee or almond liqueur, 1 bottle of cognac or brandy, 1 bottle of sweet vermouth, 1 liter of lemon/lime soda, 1 quart of orange juice, 1 quart of cranberry juice, 1 quart of tomato juice.

PASTRY PUFFS WITH CURRIED CHICKEN

Choux Pastry for Puffs:
- 1/2 cup (1 stick) unsalted butter, cut up
- 1 cup water
- 1 cup unsifted all-purpose flour
- 4 large eggs
- 1 teaspoon salt
- 3/4 teaspoon dry mustard
- 1/4 teaspoon cayenne
- 1 cup shredded Gruyère cheese
- 1/2 cup grated Parmesan cheese
- 1 egg yolk mixed with 1 tablespoon heavy cream (egg wash)

Curried Chicken Filling:
- 1 tablespoon peanut or vegetable oil
- 1 large yellow onion, finely chopped
- 3 cloves garlic, finely chopped
- 1 teaspoon curry powder
- 1/4 teaspoon ground ginger
- 1/4 teaspoon sweet Hungarian paprika
- 1 large Granny Smith apple, peeled, cored, and finely chopped
- 10 ounces skinless, boneless chicken breasts, cut into 1/2-inch cubes
- 3/4 cup heavy cream
- 2 tablespoons mango chutney, finely chopped
- 1/2 teaspoon salt
- 1/2 teaspoon black pepper

1 For the Puffs: Preheat the oven to 450°F. Grease and flour a large baking sheet or cover with baking parchment; set aside.

2 In a medium-size heavy saucepan over moderate heat, bring butter and water to a boil. Remove from the heat, add flour, and mix with a wooden spoon until mixture resembles mashed potatoes. Return to the heat and stir until mixture is smooth and leaves sides of pan. Remove from the heat.

3 Make an indentation in the center of the warm dough. Drop in 1 egg and beat hard to combine until smooth. Repeat with remaining 3 eggs. Mix in salt, mustard, cayenne, Gruyère, and all but 2 tablespoons of Parmesan. Make puffs as shown in box at left.

4 For the Curried Chicken: In a large nonstick skillet over moderate heat, heat oil until hot—1½ to 2 minutes. Add onion and garlic and cook, stirring, until soft—about 5 minutes. Blend in curry, ginger, and paprika and cook 1 minute. Stir in apple and cook until soft—about 4 minutes. Add chicken and cook until no longer pink—about 2 minutes. Add remaining ingredients and bring to a boil. Reduce the heat to moderately low and simmer, uncovered, stirring, until sauce thickens—5 to 7 minutes more. Cool to room temperature.

5 Cut each puff in half crosswise. Spoon a teaspoonful of curry mixture into each, set top in place, and serve. Makes about 40 puffs.

1 Serving: Calories 83; Total Fat 6 g; Saturated Fat 3 g; Protein 3 g; Carbohydrates 5 g; Fiber 0 g; Sodium 60 mg; Cholesterol 47 mg

prep time-45 minutes
cooking time-45 minutes

BAR MATH

One 750-ml bottle of wine = just over five 5-ounce glasses of wine

One 750-ml bottle of liquor = 17 shots (each 1½ ounces)

One liter of liquor = 22½ shots (each 1½ ounces)

One liter of soda = seven 12-ounce highball glasses filled with ice and 1 shot of liquor

5 pounds of ice = twenty 12-ounce highball glasses

SUMMER PICNIC

*E*ating outdoors is one of summer's greatest pleasures, but there are a few things to consider before you pack up the picnic basket and hit the road.

A PORTABLE PARTY

It's possible to tote just about any food almost any distance as long as it's properly packed. Vacuum and insulated containers make it easy to keep foods chilled and fresh tasting. However, the fewer highly perishable or fragile foods you have to worry about, the more you will enjoy your picnic.

GOOD TRAVELERS

There are certain foods that are always dependable picnic fare. Choose from: firm cheeses; ham and other smoked or cured meat; cold cooked chicken and turkey; meat loaf and pâté; hard-cooked eggs; raw, roasted, or steamed vegetables; slaws and bean salads; vinegar dressings and marinades; breads, rolls, and crackers.

From the dessert list there are: fruit cobblers and crisps; brownies and other bars, cookies; sheet cakes with sturdy

(continued on page 346)

PICNIC MENU

Crudités
(pages 16-17)

Cold Zucchini Soup
(page 51)

Country Pâté
(page 346)

Baked Ham with
Peppery Bourbon-Brown
Sugar Glaze
(page 253)

Maryland Fried Chicken
(page 261)

Deviled Eggs
(page 290)

Hot German Potato
Salad (page 171)

Sweet and Sour
Cabbage and Carrot
Slaw (page 169)

White Sheet Cake with
Broiled Brown Sugar-
Coconut Icing
(page 347)

Brownies
(page 328)

Perfect Iced Tea
(page 13)

Lemon Squash
(page 13)

Our summer picnic take-alongs include: a choice of Crudités; Country Pâté with sweet pickles; Maryland Fried Chicken; Deviled Eggs; Hot German Potato Salad; and White Sheet Cake with Broiled Brown Sugar-Coconut Icing.

WORK SAVER

Insulated Totes

There are many insulated plastic and metal chests, fiberglass-lined zip bags, and polystyrene coolers that keep foods chilled. For frequent picnicking, choose totes with strong handles and lids that seal tightly. Be sure they're lightweight, well insulated, and waterproof.

(continued from page 344)
frostings; and unfrosted angel, sponge, and pound cakes.

SALADS AND SLAWS

To be on the safe side, avoid toting salads made with mayonnaise to picnics, especially in warm weather. The Hot German Potato Salad and Sweet and Sour Cabbage and Carrot Slaw on our menu are good choices. There are also other mayonnaise-free potato salad ideas on pages 170 to 171.

MEAT TREAT

Our Country Pâté turns a picnic into a memorable feast. It's simple enough to make for a casual summer outing but delicious enough to take center stage at any party buffet.

Pâté makes a wonderful picnic food since it is served cold and is not the least bit fragile. It's also the perfect accompaniment for other picnic greats such as crusty bread, cheese, mustard, and pickles.

PÂTÉ POINTERS

The best pâtés are allowed to age a bit. Plan to make it 2 or 3 days ahead of time.

Weighting the pâté while it cools and chills after baking gives it a desirable firm texture and makes it easy to slice.

SHEET CAKE

The frosting on our sheet cake is broiled onto it, so there's no danger of its sliding off and staying behind. Sheet cakes in general are fine for picnic fare since they can travel in their baking pans.

There are sheet cake pans made especially for traveling: They come with covers that slide on. Otherwise, simply cover the top of the pan with plastic wrap or aluminum foil—and be sure not to pack anything on top of it.

MAKE A LIST AND CHECK IT TWICE

Many a picnic has been less than perfect because some essential item was left behind.

COUNTRY PÂTÉ

- 3 whole bay leaves
- 1 pound thinly sliced bacon
- 1 tablespoon olive oil
- 1 large yellow onion, finely chopped
- 2 cloves garlic, finely chopped
- 1½ pounds ground pork shoulder
- 1 pound ground veal shoulder
- 3 eggs
- ⅓ cup dry port wine
- 2 teaspoons dried sage, crumbled
- 1 teaspoon dried thyme, crumbled
- 2 teaspoons salt
- 1 teaspoon black pepper

1 Preheat the oven to 350°F. Place bay leaves end to end down the center of an ungreased 9" x 5" x 3" loaf pan. Line pan with bacon, arranging slices crosswise so they overhang the sides. Cut 3 additional slices in half and line the short ends of the pan; set aside.

2 In a large skillet over moderate heat, heat oil until hot—1½ to 2 minutes. Add onion and garlic and cook, stirring frequently, until soft—about 5 minutes. Transfer to a large bowl and cool to room temperature. Mix in remaining ingredients. Spoon mixture into the prepared pan and pack down by rapping the pan on the work surface. Smooth the top and pull bacon up and over to cover. Use remaining bacon slices to cover the pâté. Cover with a double layer of aluminum foil.

3 Bake until an instant-read thermometer inserted into the center of the pâté registers 160°F—about 1½ hours. Remove the pan to a rack and cool to room temperature.

4 Fit a same-size loaf pan on top of the pâté and weight down with a heavy can or jar. Refrigerate at least 8 hours or overnight. Remove the pan and weight and unwrap the pâté; run a spatula around the edges to loosen and invert the pâté on a serving platter. Discard bay leaves. Cut into thin slices. Makes 12 servings.

1 Serving: Calories 274; Total Fat 19 g; Saturated Fat 7 g; Protein 21 g; Carbohydrates 2 g; Fiber 0 g; Sodium 530 mg; Cholesterol 125 mg

prep time-16 minutes • cooking time-1 hour 37 minutes

Make a checklist of foods and all the equipment that you need to transport and serve it.

If picnics are events that you enjoy often, it's worthwhile putting together a special picnic box or basket that contains all of the basics. Leave it packed from picnic to picnic.

Be sure to include such indispensables as a corkscrew, bottle opener, clips for closing bags of chips, bug repellent, adhesive strips, and antiseptic.

Don't forget to pack several medium-size garbage bags for disposing trash and recyclables when you get home.

White Sheet Cake with Broiled Brown Sugar-Coconut Icing

Cake:

2½ cups sifted cake flour

3 teaspoons baking powder

½ teaspoon salt

⅔ cup butter or margarine, at room temperature

1½ cups granulated sugar

1 teaspoon vanilla extract

½ teaspoon almond extract

¾ cup milk

4 egg whites, at room temperature

Icing:

⅔ cup firmly packed light or dark brown sugar

¼ cup (½ stick) butter or margarine, softened

¼ cup heavy cream

½ cup flaked coconut

1 For the Cake: Preheat the oven to 375°F. Grease and flour a 13" x 9" x 2" pan and set aside.

2 Sift flour, baking powder, and salt together onto a piece of wax paper and set aside. With an electric mixer at moderate speed, cream butter until light; gradually add 1¼ cups of the granulated sugar and continue to cream until fluffy. Reduce mixer speed to low and beat in vanilla and almond extract. Add sifted dry ingredients alternately with milk, beginning and ending with the dry, and adding about ⅓ of the total amount at a time.

3 In a separate bowl, beat egg whites until frothy. Slowly add remaining ¼ cup granulated sugar and beat to very soft peaks. Fold into batter just until blended. Spoon into the prepared pan and smooth the top with a spatula.

4 Bake until lightly browned and springy to the touch—25 to 30 minutes. Transfer to a rack and cool 5 minutes.

5 For the Icing: Preheat the broiler. In a large bowl with a wooden spoon, beat together all ingredients and spread evenly on the warm cake. Broil 5 inches from the heat until icing bubbles and browns slightly—3 to 4 minutes. Transfer to a rack to cool slightly before cutting. Makes 20 servings.

1 Serving: Calories 240; Total Fat 12 g; Saturated Fat 6 g; Protein 2 g; Carbohydrates 33 g; Fiber 0 g; Sodium 243 mg; Cholesterol 23 mg

prep time-40 minutes • cooking time-34 minutes

STAY COOL

The most important part of packing for a picnic is to keep cold foods cold. Chill food completely before packing it. Vacuum and insulated containers should also be chilled before they're filled. Keep the containers cold by packing them along with frozen chemical gels in an insulated hamper.

Well-chilled soft drinks and other beverages can be placed in an ice-filled insulated chest. As long as the lid is kept closed, it will take hours for the ice to melt. Larger chunks of ice melt more slowly than little cubes.

SERVING AND SAVING

Allow perishable foods to remain chilled until you're ready to serve them. When putting them out, keep them out of the sun.

The hotter the weather, the more careful you must be. If it is very hot, set out only enough for first servings and leave extras chill-packed in the cooler until wanted.

Plan to discard leftover perishables. Food deterioration is not always signaled by changes in color, taste, or odor.

KEEPING BUGS AT BAY

Spreading a picnic on the ground is like issuing an engraved invitation to ants and other crawlers that were there first. If possible, bring along a folding table so that the food can be elevated.

Keep dishes covered to discourage insects from settling in. Citronella candles and bug sprays can be helpful, but follow directions carefully when using around food.

How to Broil Icing

1 Spread icing evenly on the top of the cake while it is still warm.

2 Place 5 inches under preheated broiler and broil until bubbly.

WORK SAVER

Thermos Jugs

Bottle-top or wide-mouth vacuum containers in large sizes are just right for toting soups, drinks, and even salads. Chill or heat thermoses before using by filling the container with ice or hot water and setting it aside for about 15 minutes.

EASY BRUNCH

*T*he way to enjoy your own brunch party is to stick to a menu of make-ahead dishes. We've planned one for you.

BRUNCH NOTES

Everything on our brunch menu can be prepared before your guests arrive. Most of the dishes need only to be taken from the refrigerator and/or warmed through when you're ready for your guests to come to the table.

The recipes work well both for help-yourself buffet-style serving or dining at the table. They are also good choices for a brunch on the deck or patio.

All of the recipes are flavorful, but not too strong flavored to enjoy at a morning meal—something always to keep in mind when planning a brunch.

FOR STARTERS

If you've got a crowd coming, it's a good idea to have some savory finger foods to set out for munching while guests arrive and last-minute touches are being made on the main dishes and table.

Our Niçoise-Stuffed Patty Shells and a Roquefort Ring

(continued on page 350)

MENU FOR A SIT-DOWN BRUNCH FOR EIGHT

Brunch Drinks
(page 350)

Niçoise-Stuffed
Patty Shells
(page 30)

Roquefort Ring with
melba rounds
(page 293)

Cheese Strata
(page 351)

Gratin of Mushrooms
(page 153)

Red and White
Ribbon Mold
(page 165)

Wilted Spinach Salad
with Sesame Dressing
(page 167)

Santa Fe Cornbread
(page 73)

Strawberry Shortcake
made with
Cream Scones
(page 65)

Caffè Latte
(pages 10-11)
or coffee or tea

The perfect combination for a leisurely brunch: Cheese Strata; Wilted Spinach Salad; Strawberry Shortcake made with Cream Scones; juice and hot coffee.

BRUNCH DRINKS

Bloody Mary Mix: Pour 2¼ cups tomato juice, ¼ cup lemon juice, ½ teaspoon black pepper, ½ teaspoon salt, ½ teaspoon celery seeds, 1 teaspoon Worcestershire sauce, and ½ teaspoon hot red pepper sauce into a 1-quart jar, **cover** tightly, and **shake** well. **Refrigerate** for up to 1 week. **Shake** before using. Makes 4 servings.

Bloody Mary: Pour 2½ ounces vodka and 5 ounces bloody Mary mix over ½ cup cracked ice in a cocktail shaker and **shake** well. **Strain** into a 10-ounce chilled glass and **garnish** with celery stalk. Makes 1 serving.

Nonalcoholic Bloody Mary: Prepare as directed above, **omitting** vodka.

Nonalcoholic Minty Grapefruit Fizz: Place 4 ice cubes in a 12-ounce glass. **Add** 1 sprig mint and **pour** in 4 ounces grapefruit juice and 4 ounces ginger ale or club soda. **Garnish** with mint sprig and lemon zest. Makes 1 serving.

Screwdriver: Pour 2 ounces vodka and 5 ounces orange juice over ½ cup crushed ice in a blender and **blend** for 5 seconds. **Strain** into a 10-ounce glass. **Garnish** with orange zest. Makes 1 serving.

Orange Blossom: Rub orange zest around the rim of a chilled martini glass. **Dip** rim into sugar to coat lightly. **Pour** 2 ounces gin, 1 ounce orange juice, and 1 teaspoon superfine sugar into a cocktail shaker and **shake** well. **Strain** into glass and **garnish** with orange slice. Makes 1 serving.

WHAT'S FOR DESSERT?

Fruit desserts such as shortcake are a welcome finish for brunches. Use our recipe for Cream Scones on page 65 to make 8 individual shortcakes. They can be made in advance and frozen in an airtight plastic bag. Thaw in the bag at room temperature for an hour or so.

1 Combine 3 pints hulled and halved strawberries or 1 pint strawberries and 3 cups raspberries and/or blueberries with ½ cup of superfine sugar and let stand ½ hour or more.

2 Mash fruit lightly with a fork. Split each scone; fill and top with crushed berries and whipped cream. Serve on dessert plates with either a fork or spoon.

(continued from page 348)

served with melba toast fill the bill well since they're satisfying without being too filling. Moreover, they can be eaten easily as guests mingle.

STRATA STRATEGY

The centerpiece of our menu is a baked Cheese Strata, an English luncheon dish that's delicious enough for a party but so simple you barely have to think about it. It lets you serve the breakfast favorite of toast and eggs without having to make them to order.

Not only can strata be made in advance; it must be. If baked immediately after the ingredients are mixed together, the dish turns out watery and flat. Instead, the eggs, cheese, and bread are mixed together and allowed to rest in the refrigerator overnight.

The refrigeration allows time for the egg mixture to be completely absorbed by the bread. That way, when the mixture is put in the oven, the strata bakes up light, puffy, and brown, as it should be.

AN OMELET BRUNCH

An alternative brunch party can be planned around omelet making. Omelets must be cooked to order, but if everything else on the menu is made ahead, the shared task of cooking omelets can be fun. If you have a big eat-in kitchen, some guests can chat at the table while others do the cooking.

OMELET PLAN

Put out baskets of fresh rolls, muffins, bagels, and crusty breads along with a full array of preserves, butter, and cream cheese. Have a big bowl of cut-

up fresh fruit and pitchers of juices ready so that guests can help themselves for starters. To complement the omelet, set out a tossed salad of baby lettuces with a selection of dressings.

Set up an omelet-making station with a variety of fillings prepared ahead for special requests. The list might include shredded Swiss, Cheddar, and crumbled goat cheese; sautéed mushrooms, onions, and sweet peppers; salsa; fresh chopped herbs; cooked, drained, and chopped spinach; crumbled cooked bacon; slivered country ham or prosciutto. Or any other ingredients that suit your and your guests' fancies.

Have the eggs at room temperature. If you have two skillets and there are two omelet chefs on your guest list, they can work in tandem, with a third cook whisking up the eggs.

WAFFLE BRUNCH

A similar sort of brunch party can be planned around making fresh waffles. Notes on page 66 tell you how to adapt our Silver Dollar Griddle Cakes recipe for waffles by adding a little extra oil.

Have the waffle batter prepared before your guests arrive. It actually benefits from being mixed up an hour or more before cooking so that the flour has plenty of time to

absorb liquid and reach the perfect consistency.

If the batter thickens too much while resting, simply whisk in a little water or milk. Keep in mind that it's better to have waffle batter a shade too thick than too runny.

If possible, set up the waffle iron right next to the dining table. That way the waffle baking won't interrupt the party.

Set out a choice of toppings, such as plain and fruit butters, syrups, honey, preserves, chopped or puréed fruits, and powdered sugar.

Good accompaniments for waffles include baked ham, bacon, and sausage, which can be prepared ahead and kept warm in the oven until serving time.

PARTY DRINKS

Our mixed drink recipes at left, which include two non-alcoholic mixes, are all brunch classics that have tomato, grapefruit, or orange juice as their base.

At any brunch it's good to have a supply of chilled fruit juices on hand. Iced coffee and both regular and herbal iced teas are refreshing alternatives to hot coffee and tea and can be made ahead.

Sparkling white wine (or Champagne if it's in the budget) requires no more effort than chilling and opening a bottle and brings a festive note to the party.

Mix individual drinks just before serving; don't make them ahead of time.

To crush ice for drinks in a pinch, wrap ice cubes in a clean kitchen towel and pound them with a hammer.

HOW TO LAYER A STRATA

1 Line a greased baking dish with ½ of the quartered bread slices. Top with ½ of the bacon and vegetable mixture.

2 Sprinkle with ½ the grated cheese and top with a layer of bread.

3 Sprinkle with remaining bacon mixture and cheese. Mix together cream, milk, eggs, and seasonings. Pour over the strata, cover, refrigerate, and bake as directed.

CHEESE STRATA

This tasty brunch dish is as easy as can be, but it does require a little advance planning. The dish is prepped and assembled one day, refrigerated overnight, and baked and eaten the following day.

8 slices bacon	**trimmed of crusts and quartered**
1 cup chopped yellow onion	**2 cups shredded sharp Cheddar cheese**
1 cup chopped sweet green pepper	**1 cup light cream**
2 cloves garlic, minced	**½ cup milk**
½ teaspoon dried thyme, crumbled	**6 eggs**
3 small plum tomatoes, cored and diced	**2 teaspoons Dijon mustard**
8 slices day-old firm-textured white bread,	**½ teaspoon salt**
	¼ teaspoon black pepper

1 In a 12-inch nonstick skillet over moderate heat, cook bacon until crisp—8 to 10 minutes. Crumble onto paper toweling and reserve.

2 Discard all but 2 tablespoons of the drippings in skillet. Add onion, green pepper, garlic, and thyme and sauté, stirring frequently, until soft—about 5 minutes. Remove from the heat and stir in tomatoes and reserved bacon.

3 Grease a shallow 2-quart flameproof baking dish and line the bottom with ½ the bread. Spoon in ½ the bacon mixture and top with ¾ cup of the cheese. Layer remaining bread on top, cover with remaining bacon mixture, and top with another ¾ cup cheese.

4 In a large bowl, whisk together cream, milk, eggs, mustard, salt, and black pepper. Pour over the strata and cover tightly with lightly greased foil. Refrigerate overnight.

5 Remove the strata from the refrigerator 30 minutes before baking. Preheat the oven to 350°F. Bake, covered with foil, for 1 hour.

6 Preheat the broiler, remove foil, and sprinkle remaining ½ cup cheese over the strata. Broil 4 inches from the heat until cheese melts and is tipped with brown—about 2 minutes. Makes 8 servings.

1 Serving: Calories 448; Total Fat 33 g; Saturated Fat 16 g; Protein 21 g; Carbohydrates 16 g; Fiber 1 g; Sodium 836 mg; Cholesterol 231 mg

prep time-30 minutes • chilling time-overnight cooking time-1 hour 15 minutes

SUPER BOWL PARTY

A television or video party is the most informal of all gatherings. Snacks are all you need to prepare.

MAKE IT EASY

Plan a menu that can be prepared ahead. Our menu combines both hot and cold foods.

Set up the room with small tables or trays so the food will be within everyone's reach. Have an ice-filled cooler handy and keep it well supplied with drinks. You may also want to set up a party-size coffeemaker.

BOWLS OF POPCORN

To make 16 cups of popcorn, you will need ½ cup of popping corn. The corn can be popped a day or two in advance and stored in tightly closed plastic bags, but season it on serving day.

Sonoma Pop: Drizzle ¼ cup of extra-virgin olive oil over 8 cups of plain popcorn. Sprinkle with ½ cup of dried tomato bits and toss until well blended.

Parmesan Pop: Drizzle ¼ cup of melted butter over 8 cups of plain popcorn. Immedi-

ately sprinkle with ½ cup of grated Parmesan cheese and toss until well blended.

Herb Blend: Mix ¼ cup of melted butter with 1 teaspoon of dried thyme and ½ teaspoon each of crumbled dried basil, oregano, and rosemary. Drizzle over 8 cups of plain popcorn and toss until blended.

Great munchies include: Crudités; Buffalo Chicken Wings; Guacamole; Garlic Potato Chips; Popcorn; and Blondies.

PARTY MENU

Crudités
(pages 16-17)

Buffalo Chicken Wings
(page 353)

Red Pepper and Cheese Quesadillas (page 15)

World's Best Guacamole and tortilla chips (page 353)

Garlic Potato Chips
(page 150)

Strawberry Milk Sherbet
(page 317)

Blondies
(page 328)

Buffalo Chicken Wings

Chicken Wings:
- 2 1/4 pounds chicken wings, wing tips removed
- 1/2 teaspoon salt
- 1/2 teaspoon black pepper
- 1/4 teaspoon cayenne
- 1/4 cup hot red or green pepper sauce
- 2 tablespoons olive oil

Blue Cheese Sauce:
- 2 ounces blue cheese, crumbled
- 2/3 cup reduced-fat sour cream
- 1/2 teaspoon Worcestershire sauce

Optional accompaniments:
- celery stalks
- carrot sticks

1 For the Chicken Wings: Preheat the oven to 450°F. Sprinkle wings with salt, pepper, and cayenne. Arrange 1 layer deep, not touching, on a lightly greased baking sheet and bake until crisp and brown—about 30 minutes.

2 For the Sauce: In a food processor, pulse all ingredients until smooth.

3 In a large bowl, combine pepper sauce and oil. Add hot wings and toss to coat. Serve hot wings with cheese sauce and, if desired, carrot and celery sticks. Makes 4 servings.

1 Serving: Calories 564; Total Fat 44 g; Saturated Fat 16 g; Protein 40 g; Carbohydrates 1 g; Fiber 0 g; Sodium 173 mg; Cholesterol 35 mg

prep time-7 minutes • cooking time-30 minutes

World's Best Guacamole

- 2 ripe Haas avocados, halved and pitted (1 pit reserved)
- 1 medium-size tomato, cored, peeled, seeded, and coarsely chopped
- 1/2 cup finely chopped red onion
- 1/3 cup chopped fresh coriander (cilantro)
- 2 tablespoons lime juice
- 3/4 teaspoon ground cumin
- 3/4 teaspoon salt
- 3/4 teaspoon jalapeño pepper sauce

1 Scoop avocado flesh into a medium-size bowl and mash with a fork until not quite smooth. Add remaining ingredients and mix well. Place reserved pit in the center of bowl (to keep sauce from turning brown), cover with plastic wrap, and refrigerate until ready to use. Before serving, discard pit. Makes 2 1/2 cups.

1 Tablespoon: Calories 18; Total Fat 2 g; Saturated Fat 0 g; Protein 0 g; Carbohydrates 1 g; Fiber 0 g; Sodium 42 mg; Cholesterol 0 mg

prep time-12 minutes

PIZZA PARTY

*I*nstead of ordering pizza for this party, guests make and roll out the dough, then choose the toppings or fillings for their own pizza, calzone, or frico.

PARTIES AND GET-TOGETHERS

PIZZA NIGHT

Making pizza is as much fun for adults as it is for the younger set and a pizza party makes a great family get-together. Use the same dough to make calzone and frico.

ALL IN THE FAMILY

Pizza is made with a yeast dough, actually a type of plain bread dough. In most recipes, it rises once before it is rolled out, topped, and baked.

A calzone is a turnover made with pizza dough and filled with some of the same ingredients that are used to top pizza. The fillings for calzones tend to include more mozzarella and ricotta and less tomato sauce than pizza toppings.

A calzone can be enjoyed as a hot sandwich or sliced and eaten at room temperature. When you bite into a hot calzone, beware—the melted cheese in the stuffing can be a real tongue scorcher.

Frico is pizza dough that has been formed into round filled pies that are baked on a hot skillet instead of in the oven.

PIZZA PARTY MENU

Crudités (pages 16-17)

Pizza with Pepperoni and Mushrooms (page 356)

Frico and Calzone (page 357)

Orange-Espresso Granita (page 317)

Cheesecake with Strawberry Glaze (page 327)

Perfect Iced Tea (page 13)

Lemon Squash (page 13)

PARTY PLANNING

To streamline the process, prepare the dough in advance and refrigerate until friends and family are ready to roll.

Prepare the toppings or fillings and place them in separate bowls. Cover and refrigerate if necessary. Let

(continued on page 356)

Our pizza party menu includes: Pizza with Pepperoni and Mushrooms; turnover-shaped Calzones; and Frico.

PIZZA WITH PEPPERONI AND MUSHROOMS

Dough:
- ¼ cup warm water (110°F to 115°F)
- 1 packet (¼ ounce) active dry yeast
- 1½ cups unsifted all-purpose flour
- ¼ cup water, at room temperature
- 3 tablespoons olive oil
- ½ teaspoon salt

Topping:
- ½ cup tomato pizza sauce
- 6 ounces mozzarella cheese, shredded
- 2 ounces sliced pepperoni
- ⅔ cup sliced mushrooms

1 For the Dough: In a large bowl, combine warm water, yeast, and ¼ cup of the flour to make a sponge. Let rise, covered, for 30 minutes.

2 Stir sponge down, add water, remaining 1¼ cups flour, oil, and salt. Knead for 10 minutes (or use the dough hook of an electric mixer and knead for 5 minutes).

3 Remove the oven racks. Place a baking stone on the oven floor. Preheat the oven to 450°F. Dust a heavy upside-down baking sheet or a wooden baker's peel with cornmeal. On a lightly floured work surface using a lightly floured rolling pin, roll dough into a 12-inch circle. Flop dough over rolling pin and unroll onto cornmeal.

4 For the Topping: Spread sauce on dough, leaving a 1-inch margin. Scatter cheese, pepperoni, and mushrooms on top.

5 Gently shake pizza off the pan or peel onto the baking stone. Bake until crust is golden brown—20 minutes. Serve immediately. Makes 6 slices.

1 Slice: Calories 304; Total Fat 16 g; Saturated Fat 5 g; Protein 13 g; Carbohydrates 27 g; Fiber 2 g; Sodium 628 mg; Cholesterol 24 mg

prep time-60 minutes • cooking time-20 minutes

WORK SAVER

Paddle or Baker's Peel

If you want to bake pizza on a pizza stone or quarry tile, this tool is handy to have on hand. It's used for transferring the pizza to and removing it from the hot stone surface. Paddles come in several styles and sizes. The one you buy depends on the size pizza you like to make and, of course, on the size of your oven.

ROLL AND TOP

1 Roll dough into a 12-inch circle. With your fingers, gently push dough outward to form a shallow ½-inch-wide rim.

2 Using a large spoon, spread sauce lightly on dough, staying clear of rim. Arrange toppings of your choice on top. Sprinkle with cheese.

3 To slide the pizza onto a hot baking stone: Set the edge of the paddle on the stone. Tilt and shake the paddle. If it is properly dusted with cornmeal, the pizza will slide onto the stone. Bake about 20 minutes.

(continued from page 354)
them come to room temperature before using.

TASK FORCES

When it's time to get down to work, guests can divide the tasks. Someone will be needed to roll the dough into 12-inch circles. Someone else can spoon on and spread the sauce. And everyone can join in choosing their favorite topping.

WRAP, CHILL, OR FREEZE

If you want to make the dough ahead of time so it's ready when your guests arrive, it's easily done. Yeast dough can be made as much as a day ahead. Wrap it tightly in plastic wrap and refrigerate until you're ready to work with it. Allow an hour or so for it to reach room temperature.

The dough can also be frozen for up to 3 months. Thaw it in its wrappings in the refrigerator for several hours, then bring it to room temperature.

Commercial bread dough, available frozen at the supermarket, also can be thawed and used for pizza.

STEPS FOR BAKING

Preheat the oven for at least 20 minutes. It needs to be really hot when the pizza goes in.

Keep your hands lightly floured while working with the dough so that it doesn't stick.

If pizza dough becomes springy while you roll it, give it a rest for about 5 minutes.

If using frozen commercial bread dough, prick the rolled dough all over with a fork to keep it from puffing too much.

CALZONE

Prepare as directed through Step 3 at left. **Divide** dough into 4 pieces and **roll** each into a 6-inch circle. **Omit** pizza sauce, pepperoni, and mushrooms. **Sprinkle** mozzarella, 1½ cups ricotta cheese, and 1 pound crumbled cooked sweet Italian sausage on half of each circle, **leaving** a 1-inch margin. **Fold** in half and **pinch** edge to seal. **Bake** 25 minutes and **serve** immediately. Makes 4 servings.

FRICO

Prepare dough as directed through Step 3 at left. **Omit** pizza sauce, pepperoni, and mushrooms. **Divide** dough into 8 pieces and **roll** each into a thin circle 3 inches across. **Sprinkle** 4 circles with 2 tablespoons grated Parmesan cheese and 2 tablespoons finely chopped prosciutto ham. **Top** with remaining dough circles and **pinch** edges firmly to seal. In a cast-iron skillet over moderate heat, **brown** 7 minutes on each side. **Cut** each circle into 4 wedges and **serve** immediately. Makes 4 servings.

FOR A CRISPER CRUST

You can use ordinary baking sheets or round pizza pans dusted with cornmeal for your pizza. However, keep in mind

PIZZA POCKETS

To make calzone: 1. Roll dough into 6-inch circles. Top with cheeses and fillings of your choice. **2.** Fold dough in half. Pinch edge to seal. Bake on an ungreased baking sheet.

To make frico: 1. Roll dough into eight 3-inch circles. Top 4 with fillings. Cover with remaining circles. Pinch edges to seal. **2.** In a skillet over moderate heat, cook circles about 7 minutes on each side until browned.

that as the pizza bakes, the dough releases steam, which can make the crust soggy.

There are several ways to avoid the problem and ensure that your pizza has a crisp-bottomed crust.

If you enjoy making pizza or other flat breads such as focaccia often, it's worth buying a baking stone. Follow the manufacturer's directions or our how-to instructions at left. Preheat the stone along with the oven.

Because the stone is already very hot when the pizza makes contact with it, the dough crisps and starts to brown immediately.

OTHER CHOICES

Alternatively, use a perforated pizza pan. Tiny holes in the pan allow the steam to escape. Perforated pans are available in 13-, 14-, and 15-inch rounds.

If using a standard pan, slide the pizza onto the oven rack for the last 10 minutes of baking.

THICK AND JUICY

You can use a homemade sauce or a commercial puréed tomato sauce on your pizza. Tomato sauce for pizza should be a little thicker than for pasta so that it doesn't make the dough soggy. Cook the sauce down a little to thicken.

Some pizza makers spread sauce directly on the prepared dough. Others prefer to brush the dough with a little olive oil and sprinkle it with grated Parmesan or another hard cheese before spooning on the sauce.

FOCACCIA—ANOTHER TRICK WITH PIZZA DOUGH

Focaccia, a traditional Italian flat bread, has become very popular in Canada. Focaccia is moister and thicker than a pizza crust but can be made with the same dough.

Roll and push the dough into a rectangular or round shape about ¾ to 1 inch thick. Make shallow indentations in the rolled dough with your fingertips. Then brush the dough with plain or garlic-infused olive oil and sprinkle it with coarse salt and dried herbs such as rosemary or basil.

Bake in a preheated 450°F oven until golden—about 20 to 25 minutes. It should come out slightly moist and chewy. Serve plain as a splendid accompaniment for a salad. Or split the hot or cooled bread and tuck in sliced tomatoes, cheese, Italian ham, basil, or other favorite fillings.

AFTERNOON TEA

I t's wise to keep the refreshments for an afternoon tea or shower on the light side with deliberately small servings.

FANCY BITES

An afternoon gathering is the perfect occasion to try your hand at making fancy sandwiches. Our sandwich fillings can also be used in tea sandwiches that are cut into shapes with cookie cutters. For the best results, use thin-sliced fine-textured bread and combinations of white and whole-wheat breads for color. Be sparing with the fillings so that they don't ooze out. As a special touch, coat the sides of sandwiches with butter, then dip into minced parsley.

DO-AHEAD TIPS

Sandwich spreads can be made a day or two in advance and refrigerated. Sandwiches can be made a few hours ahead and arranged on the serving platter. Cover tightly with plastic wrap and refrigerate. Tea sandwiches are best when slightly chilled.

TEA FOR A CROWD

It's possible to make very good tea for a crowd. The most

TEA MENU

Watercress Pinwheel and Anchovy Ribbon Sandwiches (pages 359-360)

Pastry Puffs with Curried Chicken (page 343)

Sticky Buns (page 76)

Zucchini Bread (page 71)

Angel Roll with Lemon Filling (page 332)

Devil's Food Cake with Butter Cream Frosting (page 331)

Tea

---

dependable way is to prepare a strong infusion using 20 tea bags and 3 cups of boiling water for every 20 cups of tea. Let the tea bags steep for 5 minutes only and remove. Heat a teapot by rinsing it with scalding water. Add the tea. Fill another teapot with boiling water. To serve, pour about 2 tablespoons of the strong tea infusion into each cup, then top with hot water.

Our afternoon tea menu includes: Watercress Pinwheel Sandwiches; Anchovy Ribbon Sandwiches; and Devil's Food Cake baked as a sheet cake and iced and decorated with Butter Cream Frosting.

PARTIES AND GET-TOGETHERS

WATERCRESS PINWHEEL SANDWICHES

- 4 cloves garlic
- 1 large bunch watercress, stemmed and finely chopped
- 1/4 cup (1/2 stick) unsalted butter, softened
- 1/4 teaspoon salt
- 1/8 teaspoon black pepper
- 7 slices firm-textured white bread, crusts removed

1 Preheat the oven to 350°F. Spray a small sheet of aluminum foil with vegetable cooking spray, wrap garlic, and roast until tender—about 30 minutes. Pop garlic out of skins into a medium-size bowl.

2 Add watercress, butter, salt, and pepper and mix well. Set aside, covered, for 30 minutes.

3 Using a rolling pin, roll each slice of bread into a 4¹/₂-inch square. Drain excess liquid from watercress butter, then spread each slice with butter and roll up jelly-roll style. Slice each roll into ¹/₂-inch-thick slices. Makes 28 sandwiches.

One 2-Sandwich Serving: Calories 35; Total Fat 2 g; Saturated Fat 1 g; Protein 1 g; Carbohydrates 4 g; Fiber 0 g; Sodium 55 mg; Cholesterol 5 mg

prep time-50 minutes • baking time-30 minutes

PARTY SANDWICH SPREADS

Caviar Spread: In a medium-size bowl, **beat** together ¹/₂ cup whipped cream cheese and 1¹/₂ tablespoons black lumpfish caviar. Makes ¹/₂ to ³/₄ cup.

Toasted Pine Nut Spread: Prepare as directed for Caviar Spread, above, **substituting** ¹/₂ cup finely chopped toasted pine nuts for caviar. Makes ¹/₂ to ³/₄ cup.

Roasted Pepper-Shallot Spread: Prepare as directed for Caviar Spread, above, **substituting** ¹/₄ cup finely chopped, drained, and patted-dry roasted peppers for caviar. **Add** 1 finely chopped shallot, ¹/₄ teaspoon black pepper, and ¹/₈ teaspoon salt. Makes about ³/₄ cup.

Shrimp and Chive Spread: In a medium-size bowl, **beat** together ¹/₂ cup whipped cream cheese and ¹/₂ cup finely chopped cooked shrimp. **Add** 2 tablespoons finely snipped chives and ¹/₄ teaspoon black pepper. Makes about ³/₄ cup.

Ginger-Apricot Butter: In a medium-size bowl, **beat** together ¹/₂ cup softened unsalted butter, 2 tablespoons grated fresh ginger, and 2 tablespoons apricot jam. Makes ¹/₂ to ³/₄ cup.

ANCHOVY RIBBON SANDWICHES

- ¹/₂ cup whipped cream cheese
- 3 tablespoons finely chopped parsley
- ¹/₃ cup sour cream
- ¹/₄ cup finely chopped red onion
- 1 can (2 ounces) flat or rolled anchovies, drained well and chopped
- ¹/₈ teaspoon black pepper
- 1 loaf (16 ounces) unsliced firm-textured white bread, crusts removed

1 In a small bowl, combine cream cheese and parsley; set aside. In a second small bowl, mix sour cream, onion, anchovies, and pepper.

2 Using a serrated knife, cut the loaf of bread lengthwise into six ¹/₂-inch-thick slices. Spread 1 slice with 2 tablespoons parsley cream cheese. Top with a second slice and spread with ¹/₂ the anchovy mixture. Spread a third slice with 2 tablespoons parsley cream cheese; place, cream cheese side down, on top of the other 2 slices. Make a second ribbon loaf with remaining ingredients.

3 Wrap loaves tightly in plastic wrap and refrigerate until well chilled—about 3 hours. To serve, cut each loaf into ¹/₂-inch-thick slices, then cut each slice crosswise in half. Makes 30 sandwiches.

1 Sandwich: Calories 55; Total Fat 3 g; Saturated Fat 1 g; Protein 2 g; Carbohydrates 6 g; Fiber 0 g; Sodium 140 mg; Cholesterol 7 mg

prep time-1 hour • chilling time-3 hours

HOW TO MAKE PINWHEEL, RIBBON, AND CUTOUT SANDWICHES

1 For Pinwheels: Trim bread crusts and flatten slices with a rolling pin.

1 For Ribbons: Trim crusts and cut loaf into six ¹/₂-inch-thick slices.

1 For Cutouts: Trim crusts and flatten slices with a rolling pin.

2 Spread filling and roll jelly-roll style. Cut into ¹/₂-inch-thick slices.

2 Make two 3-slice loaves with alternating fillings.

2 Fill sandwiches and cut into shapes with cookie cutters.

SAUCES AND TRIMMINGS

Brown Sauces

These classic sauces are rich blends of broths and aromatics. Some are smooth, some are not; all are fine enhancers of meat, poultry, and other dishes.

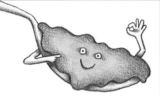

BASIC BROWN

The base for many brown sauces is Espagnole, "Spanish," Sauce, which is a good choice for any meat dish.

Learn the steps for making this simple but rich sauce and you can make as many variations as your imagination allows. Some variations follow:

Bigarade Sauce is slightly sweet. It's made for roast duck, but is also good with other poultry or pork.

Demiglaze Sauce is enriched with wine and thickened and strengthened by cooking down. It goes with beef or game.

Mushroom-Wine Sauce, also known as Marchands de Vin, is traditional with grilled steak.

Black Pepper Sauce, or Poivrade, is particularly good with grilled steak and burgers.

THE BROTH

The best sauces are made with full-flavored homemade broth.

If you use canned broth, choose a reduced-sodium variety and taste the sauce before salting it. It may not need additional salt.

THE ROUX

Many sauces, both brown and white, begin with a roux, a blend of butter and flour. The roux is the thickening agent for a sauce and it is where the sauce's flavor begins. It also prepares the flour for blending smoothly with liquids.

The roux for brown sauces is usually cooked over moderate heat until it reaches a nutty brown color and flavor. The roux for white sauces is not allowed to brown.

For our Espagnole Sauce, the flour is blended into butter-sautéed bits of ham, carrots, and onion, which are strained out when the sauce is done.

You'll know the sauce is done when it's thick enough to coat a spoon. Taste the sauce for flavor and adjust the seasoning as needed.

FOR STARTERS

Cook the sauce, uncovered, over moderate heat so that it reduces, concentrating the fla-

To the Rescue

If the sauce is too thin, a paste made of butter and flour will thicken it. Work together a tablespoon each of butter and flour with your fingers or a fork. Roll the mixture into small balls. Drop one at a time into the simmering sauce and stir. Continue adding until the sauce is as thick as desired.

vors. Lower the heat if the sauce threatens to come to a rolling boil; raise it a little if the sauce doesn't bubble gently.

REDUCED FAT

To prevent the sauce from becoming greasy, remove the fat with a bulb baster or a ladle. Better yet, refrigerate the sauce and lift off the layer of fat that solidifies on top. Reheat the sauce before serving or use it as a base for one of our brown sauce variations.

COOKING AHEAD

Espagnole Sauce keeps well for 2 or 3 days in a tightly sealed jar in the refrigerator. It also freezes well and is good to have on hand in the freezer.

Prepare and cool the sauce, pour it into small freezer containers, seal, date, and label. The sauce will hold its fresh flavor for about 3 months.

Or freeze the sauce in an ice-cube tray, later transferring the cubes to a freezer container. When you need a little Espagnole Sauce, remove a

MUSHROOM-WINE SAUCE

Prepare Espagnole Sauce as directed at right. In a large skillet over moderate heat, **sauté** 2 finely chopped shallots in 3 tablespoons butter until soft. **Stir** in 8 ounces thinly sliced button, shiitake, or portobello mushrooms and **cook** until tender. **Add** 2/3 cup dry red wine and **boil,** uncovered, until reduced by half. **Stir** into strained Espagnole Sauce. Makes 3 1/2 cups.

DEMIGLAZE SAUCE

Prepare Espagnole Sauce as directed at right, **adding** 1 additional cup Browned Beef Stock (page 32) and 1/2 cup dry red wine to the strained sauce. **Cook,** uncovered, until sauce reduces to 3 1/2 cups.

cube or two. The sauce thaws and melts quickly.

MANY USES

Add a cube of sauce to sautéed mushrooms, to meat juices from grilled steak, roast beef, or lamb, and stir it into gravy as a flavor booster.

Heat the cube of sauce with 1/4 cup of red wine or dry Madeira for a fast topper for steaks and chops.

Stir a cube into a pot of homemade soup, a classic tomato sauce for pasta, or into a meat stew to enrich the flavor.

Espagnole Sauce

- ¹/₄ **cup (¹/₂ stick) unsalted butter or margarine**
- 2 **ounces Black Forest or Virginia ham, finely chopped**
- 1 **medium-size yellow onion, finely chopped**
- 1 **carrot, peeled, halved lengthwise, and thinly sliced**
- ¹/₄ **cup unsifted all-purpose flour**
- 3 **cups Browned Beef Stock**
- 1¹/₂ **cups Rich Chicken Stock**
- 2 **tablespoons tomato paste**
- ¹/₂ **teaspoon salt**
- ¹/₄ **teaspoon dried thyme, crumbled**
- ¹/₄ **teaspoon black pepper**

1 In a large heavy saucepan over moderate heat, melt butter. Add ham and cook, stirring frequently, until lightly golden—about 8 minutes. Add onion and cook, stirring frequently, until soft—about 5 minutes. Add carrot and cook until tender—about 5 minutes.

2 Blend in flour, then gradually add beef and chicken stocks, tomato paste, salt, thyme, and pepper. Cook, stirring frequently and skimming any scum that rises to the surface, until sauce thickens and thickly coats the back of a spoon—about 30 minutes. Pour through a sieve to strain out vegetables. Makes 3 cups.

1 Tablespoon: Calories 18; Total Fat 1 g; Saturated Fat 1 g; Protein 0 g; Carbohydrates 2 g; Fiber 0 g; Sodium 51 mg; Cholesterol 5 mg

prep time-10 minutes
cooking time-55 minutes

Black Pepper Sauce

Prepare as directed at right, **increasing** black pepper to 1¹/₄ teaspoons. In a small saucepan, **boil** ¹/₄ cup dry white wine and 2 tablespoons white wine vinegar over moderate heat until reduced to 3 tablespoons. **Stir** into strained sauce. Makes 3 cups.

Bigarade Sauce

Prepare as directed at right. In a small saucepan over moderate heat, **boil** ¹/₃ cup sugar and ¹/₄ cup water, without stirring, until amber. Immediately **add** ¹/₂ cup dry white wine and ¹/₂ cup orange juice and **cook, stirring,** until sugar dissolves. **Stir** into the Espagnole Sauce along with 1 tablespoon lemon juice. (If you have poultry pan drippings, **pour** in ¹/₂ cup wine, **heat, scraping** up browned bits. **Add** to the sugar mixture.) Just before serving, **stir** in 2 tablespoons blanched, julienned orange zest. Makes 4 cups.

WHITE SAUCE

This simply made sauce—also known as béchamel or cream sauce, though it contains no cream—is basic to so many dishes that it's a cooking staple.

THIN, MEDIUM, THICK

White sauce is the most versatile of sauces. Its subtle flavor blends with its great range of foods and it can be made in thicknesses to suit a variety of dishes. The chart below right shows how to vary it.

Thin white sauce is used as a base for soups and for dishes such as creamed chipped beef.

Medium white sauce is good for casseroles and creamed vegetables and as a base for other sauces.

Thick white sauce is used as the base for soufflés and as a binder for croquettes.

FOR STARTERS

When preparing the roux—or butter and flour starter—for a white sauce, keep an eye on the mixture. It should never be allowed to brown. If it does, it will taste all right but you will not end up with a white sauce.

Prepare the roux in a heavy pan over low heat. It needs to cook gently for 2 to 3 minutes to get rid of the raw flour taste. Stir the butter and flour continually with a wooden spoon.

Pull the pan off the stove if the mixture begins to darken.

Lower the heat before the pan goes back on the burner.

SEASONINGS

Use ground white pepper instead of black as a seasoning for white sauce, unless you want the contrasting specks. Grated nutmeg is another traditional seasoning for the sauce—only a little is needed.

WITH VEGETABLES

If you are using white sauce to make creamed vegetables, begin by cooking the vegetables until crisp-tender and draining them well before mixing them with the sauce. For spinach and other leafy vegetables, squeeze out as much liquid as possible.

Liquid drained from onions, cauliflower, and other light color vegetables may be used for 1/2 the milk in the sauce. Use medium to thin white sauce, about a cupful to each 1 1/2 cups cooked vegetables.

COOK'S SECRETS

Sara Moulton
Executive Chef
Gourmet
Magazine

"One good way to keep sauce from lumping is to have the liquid the same temperature as the roux. Heat the milk or broth separately and add it to the roux gradually, whisking all the while."

FOR CASSEROLES

Mix a medium white sauce with an equal amount of chopped cooked chicken, turkey, tuna, salmon, or other seafood. Pour the mixture into a shallow baking dish, top with buttered bread crumbs or grated cheese, and bake, uncovered, in a preheated 425°F oven 15 to 18 minutes. Serve on toast or rice for a quick supper or lunch.

WHITE SAUCE MATH FOR 1 CUP OF SAUCE

	Butter	Flour	Milk
Thin	1 Tablespoon	1 Tablespoon	1 cup
Medium	2 Tablespoons	2 Tablespoons	1 cup
Thick	3 Tablespoons	3 Tablespoons	1 cup

CHEESE SAUCE

Prepare as directed at right, **adding** 1/2 teaspoon dry mustard along with flour and 1/2 to 3/4 cup shredded sharp Cheddar cheese along with salt and pepper and **stir** constantly until cheese melts. **Serve** with potatoes and vegetables. Makes 1 1/4 cups.

PARSLEY SAUCE

Prepare as directed at right, **adding** 1 tablespoon finely chopped parsley along with salt and pepper. **Serve** with fish fillets, carrots, and beets. Makes 1 cup.

MUSHROOM SAUCE

Prepare as directed at right, **sautéing** 1/2 cup finely chopped mushrooms in butter for 3 minutes at the end of Step 1. **Substitute** Browned Beef Stock (page 32) for milk, if desired. **Serve** with roast meat or chicken and use in casseroles. Makes 1 cup.

SPICY MUSTARD SAUCE

Prepare as directed at right, **adding** 2 tablespoons Dijon mustard and 1 teaspoon white wine vinegar along with salt and pepper. **Serve** with ham or poached or broiled fish. Makes 1 cup.

White Sauce

1 tablespoon
  butter or
  margarine
1 tablespoon all-
  purpose flour
1 cup hot milk
$1/4$ teaspoon salt
$1/8$ teaspoon white
  or black pepper

1 In a small heavy saucepan over low heat, melt butter. Blend in flour and whisk, stirring constantly, until smooth—2 to 3 minutes. Gradually stir in milk.

2 Increase the heat to moderate and cook, stirring constantly, until sauce is thickened and smooth, and no raw flour taste remains—3 to 5 minutes. Remove from the heat and stir in salt and pepper.

3 If not using the sauce immediately, place a single layer of plastic wrap flat on the surface to keep a skin from forming. Cool to room temperature and refrigerate until needed. Reheat in the top of a double boiler. Use as a base for other sauces, for thickening soups, or for preparing creamed vegetables, fish, or poultry. Makes 1 cup.

1 Tablespoon: Calories 18; Total Fat 1 g; Saturated Fat 1 g; Protein 1 g; Carbohydrates 1 g; Fiber 0 g; Sodium 48 mg; Cholesterol 4 mg

prep time-5 minutes • cooking time-8 minutes

HOLLANDAISE AND MAYONNAISE

*H*ollandaise and a homemade chilled mayonnaise are two simple sauces that will win a cook praise.

SLOW AND STEADY

The trick to hollandaise is to cook it through without curdling the eggs. We've used clarified butter in our recipe (see page 128 for how to clarify) so that the butter blends smoothly with the eggs. The clarified butter should be liquid but not hot when it's added to the eggs.

THE YOLKS

Traditionally, hollandaise sauce has been made in a double boiler to prevent curdling. But cooking eggs over low heat is no longer a good idea, since there is a small risk of salmonella poisoning. To eliminate the risk, eggs must be cooked to 160°F. In our new safe method, the yolk mixture is brought to a boil over direct heat, then the butter is added off heat. For smoothness, whisk nonstop.

To the Rescue

If your hollandaise sauce starts to curdle, remove it from the heat and whisk in a tablespoon of hot water and continue whisking until smooth. Or pour the sauce into a blender or a food processor and churn until velvety.

KEEP IT WARM

Hollandaise is served warm, not hot. To keep it warm, pour the freshly made sauce into a heavy bowl and cover tightly with plastic wrap. Place the bowl in a pan of warm (not hot) water. Serve within 20 minutes. If the sauce cools, reheat quickly by whisking over simmering water.

Leftover hollandaise cannot be reheated successfully but it can be reused. Stir it into eggs before scrambling them or into hot rice, polenta, or grits.

DIJON HOLLANDAISE

Prepare as directed at right, **adding** 2 tablespoons Dijon mustard along with salt and pepper. Makes 3 1/3 cups.

BÉARNAISE SAUCE

Simmer 1/3 cup chopped tarragon, 2 tablespoons white wine vinegar, and 1 tablespoon minced shallot 1 to 2 minutes over moderately low heat; **cool**. **Prepare** Hollandaise Sauce as directed at right, **substituting** tarragon mixture for lemon juice. Makes 3 1/2 cups.

BOILED MAYONNAISE

Pulse 4 egg yolks, 2 tablespoons water, and 1 tablespoon white wine vinegar in a food processor to combine. With the motor running, **drizzle** in 1 1/2 cups vegetable oil (or a combination of vegetable and olive oil). **Transfer** to the top of a double boiler and **cook** until a thermometer placed in sauce registers 160°F. **Stir** in a pinch of white pepper. Makes 2 1/3 cups.

AIOLI (GARLIC MAYONNAISE)

Prepare Boiled Mayonnaise as directed above, **adding** 1 clove minced garlic and 1/2 cup fresh white bread crumbs to the food processor. **Substitute** extra-virgin olive oil for vegetable oil and cayenne for white pepper. Makes 3 cups.

SERVED IN STYLE

Spoon 2 tablespoons of hollandaise over steamed asparagus, broccoli, or cauliflower. Or serve 2 or 3 tablespoons of the sauce over poached fish fillets.

EGGS BENEDICT

Split, toast, and butter English muffins, then top with ham, egg, and a generous spoonful of sauce. Make hollandaise and keep it warm while you prepare the ham and eggs.

MAYONNAISE NOTES

Mayonnaise is usually made with raw egg yolk. We've cooked our two mayonnaises to eliminate any possibility of salmonella bacteria in the eggs.

Boiled Mayonnaise is used like any salad dressing. Aioli (pronounced eye-o-lee) is a garlic-laced French mayonnaise that can be used either as a dressing or as a dipping sauce for steamed vegetables or seafood.

Mayonnaise is made in the food processor. Once the eggs and vinegar are well mixed, the oil is added at the slowest possible drizzle while the mixture spins. The drizzle allows the mixture to emulsify to a creamy richness; see page 176 for more about emulsifying. Pour the oil in too fast and you'll have a liquid dressing.

HOW TO PREPARE AN ARTICHOKE

The leaves of a steamed artichoke are perfect with hollandaise or aioli.

1 Cut off the stem and 1 inch of top. Remove bottom row of leaves. Steam, upright, in 1 inch of water with 1 to 2 tablespoons lemon juice added—30 to 40 minutes.

2 Serve with sauce. Pull off the leaves one by one. Dip the fleshy part of a leaf into sauce, then pull through the front teeth to extract the flesh.

3 When the leaves have been plucked, pull out the prickly choke and discard. Cut bottom, or "heart," into chunks, dip in sauce, and eat.

Hollandaise Sauce

2 egg yolks
2 tablespoons water
1/4 teaspoon salt
1 tablespoon lemon juice

6 tablespoons clarified unsalted butter
1/8 teaspoon white pepper

1 In a 1-quart saucepan over moderately high heat, bring yolks, water, salt, and lemon juice to a boil, whisking constantly.

2 Remove from the heat. Mixture will begin to curdle, but continue whisking until smooth. Stir in butter, 1 tablespoon at a time. Add pepper, stir to mix. Serve with steamed artichokes or asparagus, Eggs Benedict, or poached fish. Makes 1 cup.

1 Tablespoon: Calories 134; Total Fat 15 g; Saturated Fat 9 g; Protein 1 g; Carbohydrates 0 g; Fiber 0 g; Sodium 46 mg; Cholesterol 72 mg

prep time-5 minutes • cooking time-10 minutes

FRUIT COMPOTE

*S*erved warm or at room temperature, fruit compotes make an elegant dessert. They also can be an accompaniment to roasted or grilled meat.

BE CHOOSY

Select fruits that complement each other's color and flavor and that are ripe but firm. Soft fruits cook down to mush or emerge from the poaching syrup looking ragged.

If some of the fruits you choose are softer than the rest, lift them from the poaching syrup with a slotted spoon as soon as they are done and continue cooking the others.

QUICK PEEL

Use a swivel-bladed vegetable parer to strip the skin off pears. To remove the thin skins of peaches or apricots, blanch them in boiling water for 1 to 2 minutes. Lift out with a slotted spoon and plunge into ice water. The skins will split and peel off easily. The same technique is used for peeling tomatoes; see page 94 for how to.

For information about peeling tropical fruits, see page 162.

DRIED FRUITS

The flavor of dried prunes, apricots, and raisins enriches a fruit compote. Also try 2 cups of dried mango, papaya, and pineapple.

Poach dried fruits until they plump up and are tender when pierced with the tip of a knife. They may need more time in the poaching syrup than the fresh fruits.

SPICE IS NICE

Use a cinnamon stick and whole cloves rather than ground spices. Ground and grated spices will muddy the syrup, obscuring the bright, fresh color of the fruits.

Tip: Break the cinnamon into pieces and place them in a large tea ball along with the cloves; close it securely and drop it into the poaching syrup with the fruits. Or tie the spices in a square of cheesecloth and add to the sauce.

Either way, the spices can easily be removed and discarded after poaching.

JUST DESSERT

Many compotes—such as our main recipe—are delicious served hot over a scoop of vanilla ice cream. Alternatively, serve them with plain or vanilla yogurt, a scoop of cottage or ricotta cheese, or a dish of custard (page 322).

Poached whole fruits, such as our Seckel pears, are ideally served individually, standing upright on a dessert plate with a drizzle of custard sauce (page 320).

GOOD CHOICE

When poaching fruits, use a saucepan or kettle made of a nonreactive material; stainless steel and enameled steel or iron are good choices. The acid in fruits will react with metals such as aluminum or uncoated iron, and the compote will take on a metallic flavor and dark color.

WORK SAVER
Footed Compote

Fruit compotes are such elegant desserts that a bowl was named after them. The prettiest way to serve the dish is in a glass footed compote, which raises the fruit up and shows it off. Footed compotes can be found both new and old and in both plain and cut glass.

A GIFT OF FRUIT

To share your compote with friends, spoon it into pretty jars. Tie with ribbon and attach customized gift tags. Note: Compote must be kept refrigerated.

BRANDIED PEACHES

Prepare as directed at right, **substituting** 1 cup brandy for 1 cup water. Instead of the fruits called for in recipe, **use** 4 peeled, pitted, and halved peaches. **Prick** peaches several times with a fork and **poach** for 20 minutes. Makes 4 servings.

PICKLED PEACHES

Prepare Brandied Peaches as directed above, but for poaching liquid **use** 3 1/2 cups water and 1/2 cup white wine vinegar. **Add** 2 bay leaves and 1/2 tablespoon each black and white peppercorns. **Refrigerate**, covered, for 2 days; **discard** bay leaves before serving. Makes 4 servings.

Hot Curried Tropical Fruit

Prepare as directed at right, **adding** 1/4 cup thinly sliced fresh ginger and 1 tablespoon curry powder to poaching liquid. Instead of fruits called for in recipe, **use** 1 firm medium-size peeled and pitted sliced mango, 1 thinly sliced peeled and cored medium-size pineapple, and 1 sliced peeled and seeded papaya. **Reduce** poaching time to 15 minutes. Makes 4 servings.

Poached Seckel Pears with Strawberries

Prepare as directed at right, **substituting** 1/4 cup thinly sliced fresh ginger for cloves and red wine for water. **Reduce** sugar to 1 cup. For fruit, **use** 4 peeled and cored whole Seckel pears with stems (**core** from the bottom, **leaving** stems in place) and **poach** only 15 minutes. **Set aside** to cool for 5 minutes before stirring in 2 cups hulled strawberries. **Strain** poaching liquid into a saucepan, **boil** until reduced to about 1 1/2 cups, and **pour** over fruit. Makes 4 servings.

Hot Fruit Compote

Zest of 1 lemon, slivered
Zest of 1 orange, slivered
2 cinnamon sticks
1 tablespoon whole cloves
2 cups sugar
4 cups water

4 Bosc or Bartlett pears, peeled, cored, and halved
1 cup light seedless raisins
1 cup pitted prunes
1 cup peeled, pitted, and halved apricots

1 In a large heavy saucepan over high heat, bring lemon and orange zests, cinnamon, cloves, sugar, and water to a strong boil. Reduce the heat to moderate and add pears, raisins, prunes, and apricots.

2 Poach, covered, at the gentlest simmer until pears are just cooked but still firm—20 to 25 minutes. Serve warm or chill and serve cold. Makes 4 servings.

1 Serving: Calories 606; Total Fat 1 g; Saturated Fat 0 g; Protein 4 g; Carbohydrates 158 g; Fiber 12 g; Sodium 11 mg; Cholesterol 0 mg

*prep time-10 minutes
cooking time-
35 minutes*

MARMALADE

Homemade marmalade is well worth the effort. The process is much the same as for jams and jellies, but the rind, which is integral to marmalade's texture and flavor, takes a long time to soften.

PICK OF THE CROP

Choose fruit that is mature but not overripe. A medium-thick peel provides the necessary texture and a tangy bite.

Commercial pectins are not necessary for citrus marmalades. There is enough natural pectin in the rinds and pith to gel the marmalade. Pectin also is present in the seeds of citrus fruits. For added pectin strength, tie the excess pith and seeds in a small piece of cheesecloth and boil with the chopped rind. Remove before ladling the marmalade into jars.

SIMPLE STEPS

When combining the chopped fruit with other ingredients, follow the recipe measurements exactly. The correct proportions of sugar to fruit are crucial to proper gelling.

The best marmalades are cooked briefly, then set aside overnight to soften the peel and strengthen the flavor. They're finished with a slow simmer to the gelling stage.

For good, clear color, be sure to skim the marmalade at the

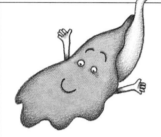

end of cooking.

To be sure the rind is distributed evenly, stir the marmalade occasionally while ladling it into jars.

HOW TO KNOW WHEN IT'S DONE

When the liquid reaches 218°F to 220°F on a candy thermometer, it's ready to gel.

Lacking a thermometer, there is another easy way to test whether marmalade is ready to gel. Take a spoonful of the hot liquid. Let it cool a moment and then tilt the spoon. If the liquid slides off in a jellylike sheet, it's ready. If the liquid slides off in individual drops or a thin thread, it's underdone.

CITRUS SYRUP

Too much sugar or undercooking makes runny marmalades or preserves. If the spread does not gel, it can be used as a pancake syrup or as dessert sauce.

TWO POTS

Choose a kettle made of a nonreactive material. It should be 3 times the volume of the ingredients and wide enough to allow fast evaporation while the fruit bubbles. You will also need a second large pot for processing the jars and lids.

CHOOSING AND TREATING JARS

Jars with rubber seals made for home canning are the safest. Canning jars can be reused if they're in perfect condition. Do not reuse 2-part metal vacuum lids; they will not seal airtight.

PUTTING UP

Before cooking the fruit, wash and rinse the jars, lids, and sealing rings. Place the jars in a large kettle, cover with water, bring to a boil, and boil 10 minutes. Remove the jars with tongs and keep them warm and dry by standing them on a baking sheet in a 250°F oven.

Sterilize the lids and sealing rings by dipping them in the boiling water or as the manufacturer directs. Do not put the lids in the oven because the sealing compound might melt.

A GOOD SEAL

Wipe the jar rims with a clean towel to remove drips; cap and seal the jars as directed and set aside to cool. After cooling, the sealed caps should be slightly concave.

If a lid fails to seal the jar properly, the marmalade can still be kept in the refrigerator and served within a week or two.

HOW TO MAKE MARMALADE

1 Wash the citrus fruits. Slice the rind into 3/4-inch-long slivers. Squeeze out the juice and chop the orange pulp.

2 Place the rind, juice, and pulp in a nonreactive kettle with water and simmer. Set aside overnight. Return to kettle, add sugar, and cook until mixture reaches 220°F. Remove from the heat and skim foam.

3 Ladle the mixture into sterilized jars, stirring it periodically to make sure the rind is evenly distributed.

Grapefruit Marmalade

2 large thick-skinned grapefruits
1 large thick-skinned lemon
2 cups water
4 cups sugar

1 Peel grapefruit and lemon; cut away inner white part leaving rind and white pith about ⅜-inch thick. Cut into slivers ¾-inch long and ⅛-inch wide. Discard excess pith, fiber, and seeds or tie in cheesecloth and use as directed at left in "Pick of the Crop." Chop fruit coarsely, reserving juice.

2 In an 8-quart nonreactive heavy kettle over moderately high heat, simmer rind, chopped fruit, reserved juice, and water, uncovered, for 10 minutes. Pour into a large heatproof glass bowl and let stand, covered, in a cool place overnight.

3 Return mixture to kettle, add sugar, and set over moderate heat. Insert a candy thermometer and bring to a boil, stirring until sugar dissolves. Continue boiling, stirring occasionally, until thermometer registers 218°F to 220°F.

4 Remove from the heat, skim off foam, and ladle into sterilized half-pint canning jars, leaving ¼-inch head space. Wipe rims and seal. Label and store in a cool, dark place. Makes 4 half-pints.

1 Tablespoon: Calories 52; Total Fat 0 g; Saturated Fat 0 g; Protein 0 g; Carbohydrates 14 g; Fiber 0 g; Sodium 0 mg; Cholesterol 0 mg

prep time-40 minutes plus overnight cooking time-50 minutes

Our Orange Marmalade, above, brimming with slivered zest, makes a tangy breakfast topper for English muffins or toast.

ORANGE MARMALADE

Prepare as directed at left, **substituting** 2 large navel or Valencia oranges for grapefruit. Do not discard seeds; instead, **tie** seeds in cheesecloth and **simmer** along with rind and chopped fruit. **Remove** bag of seeds before cooling overnight, then **proceed** as directed. Makes 4 half-pints.

GINGER-LIME MARMALADE

Prepare as directed, **substituting** 6 large limes for grapefruit and **using** 1½ cups sugar to each 1 cup fruit mixture. **Stir** in ⅓ cup finely chopped crystallized ginger after sugar dissolves in Step 3, then **proceed** as directed. Makes 4 half-pints.

Chutney and Fruit Relish

These delicious condiments are usually a little bit sweet and a little bit tart, balancing the flavors of ingredients as diverse as tomatoes and papayas.

VERSATILE CHUTNEY

Chutney comes to us from India. Many traditional chutney recipes feature the exotic fruits and spices used in other Indian dishes: mango, tamarind, papaya, ginger, and cinnamon. In Western kitchens, the ingredients list has expanded to include such standards as tomato, peach, gooseberry, apple, and cranberry.

SWEET-TART

Chutney gets its sweetness from fresh and/or dried fruit and sugar. It gets its spicy tartness from vinegar, onions, garlic, peppers, chiles and chili powder, grated fruit rinds, or tart berries.

A tart bright contrast of flavors makes chutney the perfect condiment to serve alongside curries, savory cheese dishes, or roasted and grilled meats and poultry. It can also be enjoyed in other ways.

Mix chutney with cream cheese to make a spread for cocktail crackers. Blend it into chicken salad or other sandwich salads. Or spread it on a slice of bread before making a ham or roast beef sandwich.

CHOOSING FRUIT

Firm-ripe fruit is the usual choice for chutney although tart green fruit is also used. There are as many chutney recipes calling for green tomatoes, for instance, as there are for ripe ones. If you substitute green fruit in a recipe, be sure to give it the taste test when all the ingredients are combined and adjust the sugar and vinegar to suit.

GINGER SNAPS

Fresh gingerroot, available in produce sections, is sold by the pound. In most stores, it's sold without any packaging so you can snap off whatever size piece you need. A little fresh ginger goes a long way.

If you have leftover ginger after making chutney, it can be frozen in a self-sealing bag for several weeks.

A TOUCH OF VINEGAR

Both cider and white vinegars are standard in chutneys. Cider vinegar gives the richer flavor; white vinegar preserves a lighter color. Wine and other balsamic vinegars are not recommended because their strong flavors interfere with the taste of the chutney.

STERILE JARS

It's important that the jars and caps used for canning chutneys and other preserves be scrupulously clean. Wash in soapy water, rinse, and sterilize for 10 minutes in enough boiling water to cover by 1 inch. Keep the jars immersed in the boiling water or set them in the oven as directed on page 370. If the jars are cold when they're filled, they will crack.

WORK SAVER

Canning Jars and Canning Funnel

The best canning jars are made of heavy glass and have replaceable 2-part lids or hinged glass lids with replaceable rubber gaskets. Canning funnels are available in both metal and plastic.

APPLE CHUTNEY

Prepare as directed at right, **substituting** 3 large sweet or tart apples for pears. Makes 3 half-pints.

PEAR-GINGER CHUTNEY

Prepare as directed at right, **adding** 1/4 cup finely chopped fresh ginger along with onion and pepper. Makes 3 half-pints.

PAPAYA-TOMATO CHUTNEY

Prepare as directed at right, **substituting** 3 cored and finely chopped large ripe tomatoes for pears. **Add** 1 cup diced, peeled, and seeded papaya during final 3 minutes of cooking. Makes 3 half-pints.

CRANBERRY-ORANGE RELISH

Prepare as directed at right, **substituting** 2 cups fresh or solidly frozen cranberries for pears. **Add** 1 finely chopped unpeeled large navel orange. **Reduce** cooking time to 8 to 10 minutes. No need to remove cranberries or to boil liquid until syrupy. Makes 2 half-pints.

Pear Chutney

- 1 tablespoon olive oil
- 1 medium-size red onion, finely chopped
- 1 small sweet red pepper, cored, seeded, and finely chopped
- 1 cup sugar
- 1 cup cider vinegar
- 3/4 teaspoon yellow mustard seeds
- 1/4 teaspoon salt
- 3 large ripe pears, peeled, cored, and cut into 1/2-inch dice

1 In a large heavy nonreactive saucepan over moderate heat, heat oil 1 minute. Add onion and pepper and cook, stirring frequently, until soft—about 5 minutes. Stir in sugar, vinegar, mustard seeds, and salt and bring to a boil. Add pears and cook until tender—about 5 minutes. Strain in a colander and return liquids to kettle.

2 Over high heat, bring liquids to a boil and cook, uncovered, until thick and syrupy—about 12 minutes. Return pears to kettle and stir to coat. Pour into sterilized half-pint canning jars, leaving 1/4-inch head space. Wipe rims and seal jars. Label and store in a cool, dark place. Makes 3 half-pints.

1 Tablespoon: Calories 30; Total Fat 0 g; Saturated Fat 0 g; Protein 0 g; Carbohydrates 7 g; Fiber 0 g; Sodium 11 mg; Cholesterol 0 mg

prep time-12 minutes
cooking time-20 minutes

Our fruit preserves above include, from left, Apple Chutney, Pear-Ginger Chutney, and Cranberry-Orange Relish.

HERBAL JELLIES

Jellies flavored with herbs complement meats, poultry, and other savory dishes. When combined with cheeses, they make fine hors d'oeuvre spreads.

NEW PRODUCTS

Commercial powdered pectin is needed for making herbal jellies. Newer light fruit pectins require less sugar than earlier products. Light fruit pectins are available mainly in late summer and fall but some stores carry them year-round. Check with your grocer.

Follow pectin measurements to the letter and use the recipes developed for the type you choose. Low-sugar pectin is used in all of our recipes.

FRESH HERBS

If you are using herbs from your garden, harvest the leaves early in the day when the dew is beginning to evaporate. Whether garden fresh or purchased, tender young leaves give the best color and flavor.

OTHER HERBS

Jellies can be flavored with almost any herb. Try basil, sage, rose or lemon geranium, lemon verbena, lemongrass, dill, or rosemary.

MINT CONDITION

Taste the mint infusion for our recipe after it has set for an hour. If it's weak, the mint flavor can be reinforced with dried spearmint flakes steeped in 1/2 cup of boiling water for 10 minutes. Strain and use the spearmint infusion in place of 1/2 cup of water.

Dried basil or other dried leaf herbs can boost the flavor of jelly bases but do not use ground herbs or spices; they will cloud and darken the jelly.

FOR BEAUTY'S SAKE

Skim herb jellies immediately after cooking to prevent cloudiness and bubbles.

For a special touch, add a sprig of the appropriate herb to the jelly before sealing the jar.

IMPROVING NATURE

Even the greenest herbs are drab when boiled. A couple of drops of green (and perhaps a single drop of yellow) will give mint jelly a garden-fresh look.

JAR TIPS

Jellies of all kinds are usually made in small—half-pint—jars. They must be sterilized in boiling water before use (pages 270 and 272) and kept hot until ready to fill. After sealing, the jars should be given a hot water bath as shown at right.

HOW TO MAKE AND VACUUM SEAL JELLIES

1 Prepare infusion of mint and water. Set aside to steep for 1 hour.

2 To strain, pour infusion through a sieve lined with cheesecloth.

3 Cook infusion along with sugar, pectin, and food coloring if desired. Skim.

4 Pour into sterilized jars using a canning funnel, leaving 1/2-inch space at top.

5 Top each jar of jelly with a sprig of mint—or match the appropriate herb sprig with other herbal jellies. Screw the lids on tight.

6 Use tongs to place jars on a rack in a kettle of simmering water. Water should cover the jars by an inch. Bring to a boil.

7 Boil jars for 15 minutes. Lift jars out with tongs. Set aside to cool and vacuum seal. To test seal after cooling, press in the center of each lid; there should be no give. If the lid presses down and springs back up, reprocess or simply refrigerate jelly and serve within a few days.

Mint Jelly

- 3 cups firmly packed young mint leaves, finely chopped
- 4½ cups water
- 3 cups sugar
- 1 package (1¾ ounces) powdered light fruit pectin
- ½ teaspoon butter
- 2 drops green food coloring (optional)

1 In a large saucepan over high heat, bring mint and water to a boil. Remove from the heat, stir well, and set aside, covered, for 1 hour.

2 Line a large sieve with 4 thicknesses of cheesecloth and set over a large bowl. Pour in mint mixture. When dripping has ceased, discard leaves (do not press solids in sieve). Measure mint infusion and add enough water to total 4½ cups. Pour back into saucepan.

3 In a small bowl, combine 1 cup of the sugar with the pectin. Slowly stir sugar-pectin mixture into mint infusion. Stir in butter to reduce foaming and add food coloring, if desired. Bring mixture to a full rolling boil over high heat, stirring constantly.

4 Quickly stir in remaining 2 cups sugar and return to a rolling boil, stirring constantly. Boil for 1 minute exactly, stirring constantly.

5 Remove from the heat, skim off foam, and ladle into sterilized half-pint canning jars, leaving ½-inch head space. Wipe rims, seal jars, and process for 15 minutes in a boiling water bath. Cool and test for airtight seals. Label and store in a cool, dark place. Makes 10 half-pints.

1 Tablespoon: Calories 27; Total Fat 0 g; Saturated Fat 0 g; Protein 0 g; Carbohydrates 7 g; Fiber 0 g; Sodium 2 mg; Cholesterol 0 mg

prep time-2 hours • cooking time-30 minutes standing time-1 hour 15 minutes

BASIL-CHILI JELLY

Prepare as directed at right, **substituting** basil for mint and **adding** 1 finely chopped jalapeño pepper in Step 1. Makes 10 half-pints.

ROSEMARY JELLY

Prepare as directed at right, **substituting** rosemary for mint. Makes 10 half-pints.

PICKLES AND RELISH

*H*omemade pickles and relishes breathe the flavors of summer into meals throughout the year.

RELISH INGREDIENTS

Small unwaxed cucumbers, or Kirbies, are best for relishes.

Use Kosher or canning salt. Iodized table salt has anticaking agents that create a film.

Granulated sugar is used for most relishes. Brown sugar is sometimes added for flavor.

White vinegar produces a bright relish, cider vinegar a more mellow flavor.

SOAK AND RINSE

Let the vegetables for relish soak in salted water to start. This step removes bitterness from cucumbers and starts the blending of flavors. Drain, then rinse in cold running water.

PICKLE TIPS

When making pickles, choose a reliable recipe. The ratio of vinegar, salt, and sugar to the pickles themselves is crucial to preventing spoilage.

Choose mature but not over-ripe unwaxed cucumbers and vegetables for pickles.

To ensure crisp pickles, pre-

TIED SPICES

Use whole spices tied in a cheesecloth bag for pickling. Ground spices muddy the liquid.

treat the sliced raw cucumbers and vegetables, covering them with ice for 3 or 4 hours, replenishing as necessary.

HEAD SPACE

When filling jars with pickles or relish, leave 1/2-inch head-room to allow for expansion when the jars are submerged in a hot water bath.

A HOT BATH

The hot water bath, shown in the how-to box on page 374, is necessary for safe and proper sealing of the jars. Screw-on caps will be slightly concave when correctly sealed.

BREAD AND BUTTER PICKLES

30	small to medium-size (4 to 5 inches long) pickling cucumbers, sliced 1/4-inch thick but unpeeled
8	large yellow onions, halved lengthwise and cut crosswise into thin slices
1	medium-size sweet red pepper, cored, seeded, and coarsely chopped
1/2	cup pickling or Kosher salt
4	cups crushed ice (about)
4	cups white vinegar
4 1/2	cups sugar
2	tablespoons mustard seeds
2	teaspoons celery seeds
1	tablespoon ground turmeric
1	teaspoon ground ginger
1	teaspoon black peppercorns

1 In a very large colander set over a larger bowl or kettle, combine cucumbers, onions, and red pepper. Sprinkle with salt and toss well. Cover vegetables with a 2-inch layer of crushed ice. Refrigerate for 3 to 4 hours, adding ice if needed.

2 In a large heavy nonreactive kettle over moderate heat, boil vinegar, sugar, mustard and celery seeds, turmeric, ginger, and peppercorns for 10 minutes. Add cucumber mixture and return just to a boil.

3 Ladle vegetables and liquid into sterilized 1-pint canning jars, leaving 1/2-inch head space. Run a long thin spatula around inside of jars to release trapped air bubbles. Wipe rims, seal jars, and process for 10 minutes in a boiling water bath. Cool and test for airtight seals. Label and store in a cool, dark place for 4 to 6 weeks. Makes 8 pints.

**1 Tablespoon: Calories 36; Total Fat 0 g;
Saturated Fat 0 g; Protein 0 g; Carbohydrates 9 g;
Fiber 0 g; Sodium 101 mg; Cholesterol 0 mg**

*prep time-2 hours • chilling time-3 hours
cooking time-20 minutes• standing time-4 to 6 weeks*

SWEET PEPPER RELISH

Prepare as directed at right, **omitting** cucumbers, **doubling** the amount of red and green peppers, and **adding** 2 cups finely diced celery. Makes 6 half-pints.

HOT PEPPER RELISH

Prepare Sweet Pepper Relish as directed above, **adding** 4 diced and seeded jalapeño peppers. Makes 6 half-pints.

1 In a large heavy non-reactive kettle, mix cucumbers, red and green peppers, and onion. Sprinkle with turmeric, pour in brine, and let stand, loosely covered, for 6 to 8 hours. Drain well, rinse several times, and return vegetables to the kettle.

2 Tie cinnamon, mustard seeds, allspice, and cloves in cheesecloth and add to the kettle along with sugar and vinegar. Bring to a rolling boil over high heat and cook until sugar dissolves completely. Reduce the heat to moderate and boil gently, uncovered, for 10 minutes. Discard spice bag.

3 Ladle relish into sterilized half-pint jars, leaving ½-inch head space. Wipe rims, seal jars, and process 10 minutes in a boiling water bath. Cool and test for airtight seal. Label and store in a cool, dark place. Makes 8 half-pints.

1 Tablespoon:
Calories 15;
Total Fat 0 g;
Saturated Fat 0 g;
Protein 0 g;
Carbohydrates 4 g;
Fiber 0 g;
Sodium 40 mg;
Cholesterol 0 mg

prep time-45 minutes
plus 8 hours or overnight
cooking time-15 minutes

Cucumber Relish

4 medium-size cucumbers, finely diced but not peeled
2 large sweet red peppers, cored, seeded, and coarsely chopped
2 large sweet green peppers, cored, seeded, and chopped
1 medium-size yellow onion, coarsely chopped
1 tablespoon ground turmeric

½ cup Kosher salt dissolved in 6 cups water (brine)
2 sticks cinnamon, broken in half
1 tablespoon mustard seeds
2 teaspoons whole allspice
1 teaspoon whole cloves
2 cups sugar
2 cups cider vinegar

A

Acidulated water: lemon juice, vinegar, or wine added to water to keep fruits and vegetables from darkening.

Al dente: Italian term meaning "firm to the bite." Usually used in reference to pasta or vegetables.

Antipasto: Italian term meaning "before the repast;" in other words, a first course.

Au jus: French term meaning "served in natural juices." Used in reference to meat.

B

Baste: to moisten with pan juices, marinade, or other liquid during roasting or broiling.

Batter: a flour-liquid mixture that is thin enough to pour.

Beat: to mix ingredients vigorously with a spoon, whisk, or electric mixer to combine and aerate.

Bind: to add eggs, cream, or other liquid fat to a dry mixture to hold it together.

Bisque: a thick cream soup usually containing seafood.

Blanch: to boil briefly to loosen skin from fruits and vegetables or to set their color.

Blend: to combine ingredients with a spoon, whisk, or blender until uniformly mixed.

Blind bake: to bake a pie shell or pastry before it's filled.

Boil (rolling or full, slow): to cook food in liquid that bubbles furiously or slowly.

Bouquet garni: herbs (usually parsley, bay leaf, and thyme) tied with string or wrapped in cheesecloth. Used for flavoring soups, stews, and sauces.

Braise: to prepare food by browning, then cooking slowly in a small amount of liquid in a covered pan on the stove or in the oven.

Brew: to steep in hot water.

Broth, stock: The two terms are often used interchangeably although stock refers to liquid in which the soluble parts of bones, meat, and vegetables have been cooked. A broth is a clear soup made from stock.

Brown: to sear the outer surface of meat, fish, poultry, or vegetables to seal in the juices.

C

Caramelize: to cook sugar until it liquefies and turns a golden brown.

Casserole: 1. an ovenproof baking dish. 2. a braised or baked dish of meats and/or vegetables.

Chop: to cut food into pieces with a knife or other cutter. Chopped pieces are larger than minced pieces.

Choux (pastry): French term meaning "cabbage." Refers to a pastry dough that when shaped and baked resembles little round cabbages. The pastries are filled after baking.

Chowder: a thick and chunky milk- or cream-based soup containing seafood or vegetables. Manhattan clam chowder, made with a tomato base, is the notable exception.

Chutney: a sweet and sour relish containing fruit, vinegar, sugar, and spices.

Clarified butter: melted butter from which the white milk solids have been removed. What remains is a clear golden liquid that is good for sautéing and other purposes because it can withstand a higher heat than butter.

Combine: to mix together two or more ingredients.

Compote: a dessert of fresh and/or dried fruit cooked in syrup, usually with citrus zest and whole spices.

Crab boil, shrimp boil: a spice mixture used in flavoring the cooking water for shellfish. Usually contains bay leaf, coriander and mustard seeds, allspice, cloves, and red pepper flakes.

Cream: to beat together until light and fluffy. Usually used in reference to butter or other shortening combined with sugar and eggs.

Crimp: to make a decorative edge on a pie shell.

Croutons: toasted or sautéed cubes of bread used as a garnish for salads or soups.

Crudités: raw vegetables served as hors d'oeuvres.

Crumble: 1. a fruit dessert topped with a crumbly sugar-butter-flour or crumb mixture. 2. to break food into small pieces with the fingers.

Cube: to cut with a knife into uniform squares.

Curdle: to cause milk, eggs, or sauces to separate, usually by overheating or by adding an acidic ingredient.

Cure: to preserve fish or meat by drying, salting, and/or smoking.

Cut in: to blend shortening with dry ingredients by cutting in with a pastry blender or two knives until it's the texture of coarse meal.

D

Dash, pinch: the smallest measure. A dash is one or two shakes of a liquid seasoning; a pinch the amount of a dry seasoning that can be picked up between thumb and forefinger.

Debeard: to clean mussels by pulling off the fibrous beard that protrudes from the shells.

Deep-fry: to cook in very hot fat deep enough to immerse food so that all sides brown and cook simultaneously.

Deglaze: to scrape up the browned bits in the pan in which meat, poultry, or fish has been cooked by adding a small amount of water, broth, wine, or other liquid and bringing to a boil.

Devil: to mix with hot or spicy seasonings.

Dice: to cut into small cubes usually no larger than ½ inch.

Dough: a mixture of flour, water, and/or milk, and often eggs, fat, and yeast or other leavening, that is firm enough to knead, roll, and shape.

Dredge: to prepare food for searing or sautéing by lightly coating with flour, cornmeal, or dry crumbs.

Dress: 1. to eviscerate fish or poultry. 2. to garnish a dish or to add dressing to a salad or a sauce to vegetables.

Drippings: meat or poultry fat and juices that drip into the pan during roasting.

Drizzle: to pour liquid slowly in a thin stream.

Dry rub: a mixture of dry seasonings rubbed onto food before it is cooked.

Dust: to sprinkle lightly with flour, confectioners' sugar, or other fine powdery ingredient.

Emulsify, emulsion: to bind oil, melted butter, or eggs with water or another nonoily liquid (often over heat) to create a smooth sauce.

En papillote: French for "in a paper casing." Refers to foods baked in a parchment or foil wrapper.

Flake: to separate into flaky pieces with fingers or a fork. Usually used in reference to cooked fish.

Flameproof: term for cookware that can be used directly on a burner or under a broiler without damage.

Flute: to seal and make an

attractive edge on a pie by pinching the dough all around the rim.

Fold: to incorporate a light mixture, such as whipped cream, into a heavier liquid mixture with a gentle scooping motion.

Fry: to cook in fat in a skillet. Food must be turned to brown and fry on all sides.

Giblets: edible internal organs of poultry and game including the liver, heart, and gizzard.

Glaze: the glossy finish given to food by brushing with beaten egg, milk, syrup, or melted preserves.

Gluten: a tough and elastic wheat protein that traps the gas bubbles created by leavening and enables batters and doughs to rise.

Grate, shred: to make small pieces by rubbing food against a grater or putting it through the shredding disk of a food processor. Grated food is finer textured than shredded.

Gratin (also *au gratin* or *gratiné*): French term meaning "crust." 1. a casserole browned under a broiler, usually sprinkled with crumbs or grated cheese and butter. 2. the shallow ceramic baking dish in which foods are gratinéd.

Grill: to cook over hot coals or other direct heat source.

Grill pan: a skillet with raised grids on the bottom, allowing food to be "grilled" on top of the stove with little or no fat over direct heat.

Grind: to cut or crush food into small particles by the use of a manual or electric grinder.

Hors d'oeuvre: a hot or cold appetizer served before the meal or as a first course.

Hot water bath: 1. a pan of hot water in which a dish is placed for gentle baking. 2. a large kettle of boiling water in which preserving jars are processed to destroy mold and bacteria that might spoil foods.

Hull: to remove the stem and/or calyx from fruits, vegetables, or berries.

Ice: to frost a pastry.

Infuse, infusion: 1. to brew in hot water, as with tea or coffee. 2. to steep herbs, spices, or other aromatics in oils, vinegars, and other liquids to extract flavor.

Jelly-roll style: refers to a thin sheet of sponge cake that is spread with filling and rolled up. Similar rolling is done with fish fillets, slices of meat, cookie doughs, and other types of cake.

Julienne: to cut into very thin strips. Cuts that are the size and shape of matchsticks are called matchstick strips.

Kabob: marinated meat cubes, seafood, or vegetables threaded on skewers and cooked over coals or under a broiler.

Knead: to work dough and develop its gluten by pressing, folding, and turning it with the hands until smooth and elastic.

Kosher salt: a coarse-crystal salt used in cooking.

Leaven: to cause dough or batter to rise by use of a leavening agent, such as baking powder, baking soda, or yeast, which releases gases during preparation and baking.

Marinade: a blend of oil, acidic ingredients such as wine or lemon juice, and herbs used to flavor or tenderize foods.

Marinate, macerate: to flavor and tenderize food by soaking in a marinade. Macerating usually refers to fruit.

Mash: to make food smooth and pulpy by crushing with a potato masher or the back of a spoon. Sometimes used interchangeably with purée.

Matchstick pieces: julienne cuts about ⅛ inch wide and 2 inches long.

Mince: to chop into fine pieces. Mincing produces a finer cut than chopping.

Muddle: a soup made out of a mixed selection of fish.

Niçoise: cooked in the style of Nice in southern France. Food prepared with tomatoes, onion, garlic, black olives, and sometimes anchovies.

Nonreactive: cookware made of glass, stainless steel, and other materials that do not react with acidic ingredients.

Nonstick: a special coating applied to cookware that keeps food from sticking.

Nonstick vegetable spray: an oil, alcohol, lecithin blend in a pressurized can. Used instead of pure fats to keep food from sticking to pans.

Osso buco: Italian for "hollow bone." An Italian dish of braised veal shanks, prized for the flavor imparted by the marrow bones.

Ovenproof: cookware that can withstand oven heat.

Pan-fry: to cook quickly in a skillet in which very little fat has been added.

Parboil: to boil food for a short time to cook it partially. Usually used in reference to vegetables that will be further cooked by another method.

Parchment: coated paper used for lining baking pans to prevent food from sticking.

Paupiette: thinly sliced meat or fish rolled around a filling.

Pectin: a substance extracted from fruit used to set jellies and jams.

Pinch: 1. to seal dough by pressing together. 2. a tiny amount of seasoning that can be picked up between thumb and forefinger.

Pipe: to force icings, butters, purées, or the like through a pastry bag fitted with a tip to decorate or stuff foods.

Pith: in citrus fruit, the white spongy lining of the rind that covers the flesh. It is bitter but edible.

Plump, rehydrate: to reintroduce moisture to dried food, usually by soaking briefly in

hot or cold liquid.

Poach: to cook in liquid at a slow simmer.

Preheat: to bring the oven or broiler up to desired temperature before baking or broiling.

Prick: to pierce with a fork. Pricking keeps pastry shells from buckling or shrinking as they bake, releases fat from ducks and geese as they roast, and prevents food from exploding in a microwave.

Pulp: the soft flesh of fruit or vegetables. The pulp of an orange is the part that you eat.

Pulse: to blend with very short bursts of power in a food processor or a blender.

Punch down: to release the air from risen yeast dough by punching it down in the center.

Purée: food reduced to a smooth mash by forcing it through a sieve, a food mill, or a blender.

Purge: to clean unshucked clams of impurities, usually by soaking in salt water mixed with a little cornmeal.

Ramekins: single-serving ovenware dishes.

Reduce: to concentrate the flavors in a liquid by boiling away some of the liquid rapidly in an uncovered pot. The result is called a reduction.

Refresh: to perk up freshness, usually by soaking or rinsing in cold water.

Rehydrate: See **Plump.**

Rice: to press food through the sievelike holes of a ricer.

Rind: the thick skin of fruits and vegetables; also the tough skin on bacon and ham.

Roast: to cook uncovered and without liquid in the oven or on a spit over an open fire.

Roux: a mixture of fat and flour that is sometimes browned over low heat and used as a thickener for sauces.

Sauté: French term meaning "to leap." To cook food rapidly in a small amount of hot fat, tossing and turning it until browned.

Scallop: 1. to bake in a casserole with a cream sauce under a bread crumb topping. 2. a slice of meat that is pounded thin. 3. a shellfish.

Score: to make shallow slashes on the surface of food. Scoring pastry adds texture; scoring meat helps to tenderize it.

Sear: to brown rapidly at high heat to seal in juices and develop flavor.

Set, set up: to congeal or solidify, as gelatin or custard.

Shred: See **Grate.**

Simmer: to cook in liquid that is just below the boiling point.

Skim: to remove floating matter, such as broth, fat, or scum, that floats on a liquid.

Sliver: to cut into fine, thin, splinterlike pieces.

Slurry: a thin mixture of flour and water used as a thickener, usually in stews and sauces.

Smoke point: the temperature at which fat or oil begins to smoke and break down.

Snip: to cut with scissors.

Steam: to cook on a rack over boiling water or broth.

Steep: to immerse dry ingredients in water or other liquid to extract flavor and color.

Stir-fry: to cook in fat over high heat while rapidly stirring and tossing food.

Stock: See **Broth.**

Strain, sieve: to separate solids from liquids by draining in a colander or mesh strainer.

Swirl: to stir gently with a circular motion, often to create a spiral design.

Toss: to mix by gently lifting the ingredients. Usually used in reference to mixing and dressing salads.

Truss: to secure poultry or a roast using skewers and/or string so that it keeps its shape during cooking.

Weeping: the beading or sweating seen on the surface of egg dishes such as meringue pie toppings or custards that are baked at too high a temperature.

Weight: to top prepared food with a heavy object to squeeze out liquid or to make it conform to the shape of a mold.

Whip: to beat air into a mixture, such as egg whites or cream, until it froths or stiffens and increases in volume.

Whisk: 1. a hand tool made with looped wires used for mixing foods. 2. to beat with a whisk.

Zest: the thin colored outer skin of citrus fruit. Grated or peeled, it is used to flavor foods and beverages.

INDEX

383

COOKWARE SIZES

METRIC VOLUME	CLOSEST SIZE IN CENTIMETERS	CLOSEST SIZE IN INCHES OR VOLUME	METRIC VOLUME	CLOSEST SIZE IN CENTIMETERS	CLOSEST SIZE IN INCHES OR VOLUME
CAKE PANS			**ROUND LAYER CAKE PANS**		
2 L	20 cm (square)	8 in. (square)	1.2 L	20 x 3.5 cm	8 x 1½ in.
2.5 L	22 cm (square)	9 in. (square)	1.5 L	22 x 3.5 cm	9 x 1½ in.
3 L	30.5 x 20 cm (rectangular)	12 x 8 in. (rectangular)	**PIE PLATE**		
3.5 L	32 x 21 cm (rectangular)	12½ x 8½ in. (rectangular)	1 L	22 x 3 cm	9 x 1¼ in.
4 L	33 x 22 cm (rectangular)	13 x 9 in. (rectangular)	**SKILLETS OR FRY PANS**		
5 L	35.5 x 25 cm (rectangular)	14 x 10 in. (rectangular)		30 x 30 x 5 cm	12 x 12 x 2 in.
				33 x 33 x 5 cm	13 x 13 x 2 in.
LOAF PANS			**CASSEROLES**		
1.5 L	20 x 12 cm	8 x 4 x 3 in.	500 mL		20 fl oz
2 L	22 x 12 cm	9 x 5 x 3 in.	750 mL		24 fl oz
3 L	25 x 12 cm	10 x 5 x 4 in.	1 L		1 qt
			1.5 L		1½ qt
			2 L		2 qt
			2.5 L		2½ qt

APPROXIMATE TEMPERATURES

REFRIGERATOR
1.8°C to 4°C   34°F to 40°F

FREEZER
–20°C to –17.8°C   –4°F to 0°F

OVEN

Celsius	80	100	110	120	140	150	160	180	190	200	220	230	240	260
Fahrenheit	170	200	225	250	275	300	325	350	375	400	425	450	475	500

METRIC EQUIVALENTS

One of the secrets of good cooking is to keep ingredients in their proportions. So whenever you use a recipe from this book, measure precisely if you want consistent success. Be aware, however, that U.S. liquid measures, used in these recipes, are not identical to their Canadian namesakes. For example, an American quart is about 8 (Canadian) ounces (1 cup) less than a Canadian quart.

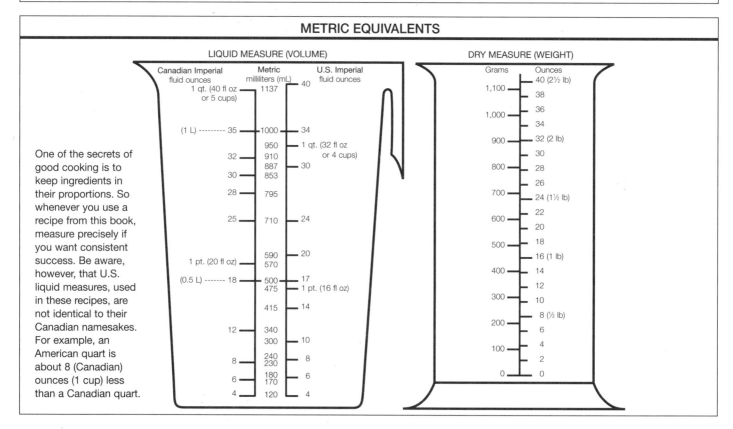